*Oracle Press*™

Oracle8*i* Java Component Programming with EJB, CORBA, and JSP

About the Authors

Nirva Morisseau-Leroy, MSCS, is an Oracle database administrator and application developer at the National Oceanic and Atmospheric Administration-University of Miami Cooperative Institute for Marine and Atmospheric Sciences assigned to the Hurricane Research Division (HRD) of AOML. She has more than 16 years of information systems experience as an Oracle DBA, application developer, and MIS director utilizing, Java, JDBC, SQLJ, SQL, Oracle PL/SQL, and UNIX C/C++. Her major areas of expertise are in user's requirement elicitation, object-oriented analysis and design, data modeling, relational and object-relational database analysis, design, implementation, and administration. Tri-lingual (French, Spanish, and English), Morisseau-Leroy is also one of the winners of the "Best Java Implementation" award presented by the NOAA's High Performance Computing and Communications (HPCC), at NOAATech2000, in Silver Spring, Maryland on October 21, 1999. Morisseau-Leroy can be reached via email at nmorisseauleroy@data-i.com.

Dr. Martin K. Solomon is a professor of computer science and engineering at Florida Atlantic University. His major areas of research include the design, implementation, and theory of database systems, computational complexity theory, and the philosophical aspects of computability. Dr. Solomon has published articles on these topics in such prestigious journals as *ACM Transactions on Database Systems*, *Communications of the ACM*, *Journal of Symbolic Logic*, and *British Journal for the Philosophy of Science*.

He has a strong professional interest in all aspects of the Oracle RDBMS, regularly teaches Oracle certification courses, and is a frequent contributor to the "South Florida Oracle Users Group Newsletter." Dr. Solomon can be reached by email at: marty@cse.fau.edu.

Julie Basu, Ph.D., is a development manager in the Java Platform Group at Oracle Corporation, and presently manages the OracleJSP project. She has more than 10 years of design and hands-on development experience at Oracle. She has worked on various projects relating to database programming interfaces, financial applications, and caching. Among her current interests are Web applications, XML, and electronic commerce.

Julie has published several papers in database conferences and journals—details are available on her home page at http://www.jbasu.com. She can be reached by email at julie@cs.stanford.edu.

Oracle Press™

Oracle8*i* Java Component Programming with EJB, CORBA, and JSP

Nirva Morriseau-Leroy
Martin K. Solomon
Julie Basu

Osborne/**McGraw-Hill**

Berkeley New York St. Louis San Francisco
Auckland Bogotá Hamburg London Madrid
Mexico City Milan Montreal New Delhi Panama City
Paris São Paulo Singapore Sydney Tokyo Toronto

Osborne/**McGraw-Hill**
2600 Tenth Street
Berkeley, California 94710
U.S.A.

For information on translations or book distributors outside the U.S.A., or to arrange bulk purchase discounts for sales promotions, premiums, or fund-raisers, please contact Osborne/**McGraw-Hill** at the above address.

Oracle8*i* Java Component Programming with EJB, CORBA, and JSP

Oracle is a registered trademark and Oracle8*i* is a trademark or registered trademark of Oracle Corporation.

1234567890 2CUF 2CUF 01987654321

Book P/N 0-07-212736-8 and CD P/N 0-07-212735-X
parts of

ISBN 0-07-212737-6

Publisher Brandon A. Nordin	**Copy Editor** Dennis Weaver
Vice President & Associate Publisher Scott Rogers	**Indexer** Karin Arrigoni
Acquisitions Editor Jeremy Judson	**Computer Designers** Jani Beckwith, Jim Kussow, Kelly Stanton-Scott
Project Editor Pamela Woolf	**Illustrators** Robert Hansen, Michael Mueller, Beth E. Young
Acquisitions Coordinator Ross Doll	**Series Design** Jani Beckwith
Technical Editors Jose Alberto Fernandez, Braden N. McDaniel	**Cover Design** Will Voss

This book was composed with Corel VENTURA ™ Publisher.

I dedicate this book to my eleven-year-old son,
Alain Morisseau-Leroy and all family members
who have encouraged me.

Nirva Morisseau-Leroy

To the memory of my parents, Bertha and Joseph Solomon,
to my wife Abby, to my two beautiful daughters,
Rachel Smith and Michelle "Daisy" Solomon,
and to my newly arrived grandson,
Garrett Alexander Smith.

Martin K. Solomon

To the memory of my inspiring grandparents, and to
my parents Smriti Kana and Sanjib Basu, who
have always encouraged me to follow my dreams.

Julie Basu

Contents at a Glance

PART IV

Building Web Applications with JavaServer Pages

PART V

Appendices

Contents

PART I
Overview

PART IV
Building Web Applications with JavaServer Pages

PART V

Appendices

Foreword

ur time is aptly called the Information Age. Today, we have easy access to vast amounts of information spread across the globe just by "pointing and clicking" in Web browsers. At the heart of the information revolution is the Internet. It connects diverse networks over widely distributed geographical areas, greatly expanding the scope of personal and commercial interactions. Internet-based e-commerce has experienced explosive growth over the past few years, with products being marketed over the Web and consumers being directly connected with suppliers. Business process efficiencies have been improved enormously through self-service applications such as home banking. An overwhelming majority of such e-business applications are powered by the Oracle database, which provides high scalability, demonstrated reliability and availability, and superior performance for SQL-based data storage and retrieval.

The boom in e-commerce has spurred the development of a new generation of enterprise applications that handle business-to-business and business-to-customer interactions. Java has emerged as the primary language for building such applications. Reasons for Java's popularity include its modern object-oriented programming model, portability across various platforms, and safety of memory operations. It also provides a rich framework of supporting libraries and tools. The Java 2 Enterprise Edition includes the Enterprise JavaBeans (EJBs) facility to build secure and scalable software components for business transactions and Java Servlets and JavaServer Pages (JSPs) to create dynamic Web pages. Previously popular distributed programming models, such as the Common Object Request Broker Architecture (CORBA), have also been mapped to Java, permitting CORBA components to be implemented using Java. Knowledge of these Java-based APIs and programming tools is essential for the Internet application developer.

From the start, Oracle realized the importance of the Internet Computing model and made strategic investments in Java. Oracle 8*i*, our Internet database, embeds a highly scalable Java Virtual Machine—Oracle 8*i* JServer—that is capable of executing Java programs directly within the database. JServer provides comprehensive support for the Java 2 Enterprise Edition. Secure execution of Enterprise JavaBeans and CORBA business components is supported within JServer, closest to the business data. The JDBC (Java Database Connectivity) API and the ANSI/ISO standard SQLJ (embedded SQL in Java) language are available not only on the client side but also within JServer to provide fast in-process access to SQL data. Oracle8*i* and Java together form the most powerful server platform for deploying secure e-commerce applications that can handle thousands of concurrent clients.

Oracle 8i Java Component Programming with EJB, CORBA, and JSP by Nirva Morisseau-Leroy, Martin K. Solomon, and Julie Basu, is precisely the book you need in order to quickly and efficiently build scalable Internet applications using Java and Oracle. The first part of the book reviews the component-based programming style, which is a very useful technique for writing modular and maintainable applications and gives an overview of application development with EJB, CORBA, and JSP components. The following three parts of the book deal with EJB, CORBA, and JSP in detail. Each part succinctly introduces the basic concepts, and then addresses advanced programming topics. The chapters are well written and easy to follow, and the concepts are explained clearly with numerous examples. The examples are drawn from real life and show you how to effectively use Java components to develop enterprise-level database applications step by step.

I was very impressed with the breadth and depth of topics covered by this book and with the excellent organization of material. I am really excited about the publication of this book. I know that it will serve as an effective and indispensable guide as you learn how to develop enterprise applications using Oracle8*i* and Java.

David A. Rosenberg
Vice President, Java Platform Group
Oracle Corporation

Acknowledgments

O ur book was made possible because of many people. I specially appreciate their support, advice, and feedback during the development of this project. Special thanks to Edward O. Griffin, technical director, Oracle Corporation to have assisted me with the new release of Oracle8i (versions 1.6 and 1.7). I would like to acknowledge the excellent technical suggestions of Jose Alberto Fernandez, Braden N. McDaniel, and my former co-author, Gerald P. Momplaisir. Many special thanks to my co-authors, Martin K. Solomon and Julie Basu. Thanks to Dr. Mark D. Powell, atmospheric scientist, and his H*WIND team at the NOAA's Hurricane Research Division, Dr. Joseph Prospero, director, CIMAS, University of Miami, Jeremy Judson, senior acquisitions editor, Monika Faltiss, Pamela Woolf, Dennis Weaver, and Ross Doll of the Osborne/McGraw-Hill editorial staff, and the Server Technologies Java/SQLJ Development Group, Oracle Corporation.

Nirva Morisseau-Leroy
Miami, Florida
July 2000

I appreciatively acknowledge the code testing assistance of Archana Dubey and Xiuqi Li and the useful suggestions of our technical editor, Jose Alberto Fernandez. I also greatly thank Jeremy Judson (for his usual invaluable encouragement), Pamela Woolf, Ross Doll, Monika Faltiss, and Dennis Weaver, all of whom are members of the Osborne/McGraw-Hill editorial staff. I express my appreciation to my wife, Abby, for her typing contributions, and my co-authors, Nirva Morisseau-Leroy and Julie Basu, for providing such a pleasant and helpful work team. Finally, I express thanks to the excellent system administrators in the CSE Department at FAU: Y. Serge Joseph, Mahesh Neelakanta, Arthur Souza, Marcelo Martins, and Nathan Carter.

Martin K. Solomon
Boca Raton, Florida
July 2000

I would like to acknowledge the help and encouragement provided by my family and friends. I am particularly grateful to Indrani and Subhendu Chaudhuri, who have so kindly shared many dinners and countless pots of tea with me. I thank my sister June Mukherjee and my friend Ena Singh for their gentle understanding and support. I am grateful to Jose Alberto Fernandez, Alex Yiu, and Brian Wright of Oracle Corporation for their thorough technical reviews and good suggestions. The editorial staff of Osborne/McGraw-Hill, Jeremy Judson, Pamela Woolf, Ross Doll, and Monika Faltiss, has been extremely helpful. My co-authors Nirva Morisseau-Leroy and Martin K. Solomon have been a pleasure to work with. I would like to specially thank Nirva for inviting me to participate in this project, and for her leadership and generous help throughout. Finally, I would like to express my thanks to Thomas Kurian and David Rosenberg of Oracle Corporation for backing this effort.

Julie Basu
San Mateo, California
July, 2000

Introduction

This book focuses on the development of Java component-based database applications with Enterprise JavaBeans (EJBs), CORBA, and Java Server Pages (JSPs). In particular, this book will teach you how to develop, deploy, and customize multi-tier database applications using JDBC and SQLJ implementations. Although the application programs presented in this book were designed to run against an Oracle database 8.xx and later, with minimum changes, they can also be used against any SQL-based, that is, "pure" relational or object-relational Database Management Systems (DBMS).

Database Schemas

Throughout this book you will learn how to develop database applications that manipulate a "pure" relational database schema and an object-relational database schema. The "Purchase Order," a financial relational database schema is part of a database design presented in the "Design of a Financial Administrative System Using the Semantic Binary Model." The "Scientific Observation," an object-relational database schema is part of the scientific database design presented in the "Atmospheric Observations, Analyses, and The World Wide Web Using a Semantic Database." Both schemas were presented in the *Oracle8i SQL Programming* book, OMH, November 1999.

The Purchase Order and the Observation schemas were designed for the Atlantic Oceanographic and Meteorological Laboratory (AOML), Miami, Florida, an Environmental Research Laboratories (ERL) of the National Oceanic and Atmospheric Administration (NOAA), part of the U.S. Department of Commerce (DOC). In particular, the Observation schema was designed for the Hurricane Research Division (HRD) at AOML and is currently being implemented by HRD as part of the H*WIND system that produces real-time surface wind analyses to National Hurricane Center's (NHC) forecasters and the FEMA Hurricane Liaison Team at NHC.

SQL Scripts to Create the Financial Purchase Order Schema

Use the following `createposchema.sql` SQL script to create the Purchase Order schema in the Oracle8*i* database:

```
--
-- File Name: poexample.sql
--
-- This scripts create all necessary tables, constraints and
-- sequences for the Purchase Order example.
--
-- This script assumes that you created a database
-- user and that an index called INDX.
-- Make sure that this user has a temp tablespace assigned.
--
-- Usage: sqlplus user/password
-- SQL> @poexample.sql
--
--
set termout on
set echo on
spool poexample.log
-- We need to drop these tables first because
-- of foreign key constraints

DROP TABLE DEPARTMENT_LIST CASCADE CONSTRAINTS;
CREATE TABLE DEPARTMENT_LIST(
departmentno            NUMBER(5),
shortname     VARCHAR2(6),
longname      VARCHAR2(20));

DROP TABLE ACCOUNT_LIST CASCADE CONSTRAINTS;
CREATE TABLE ACCOUNT_LIST (
accountno    NUMBER(5),
```

```
projectno    NUMBER(5),
departmentno              NUMBER(5),
PRIMARY KEY ( accountno ));

DROP TABLE EMPLOYEE_LIST CASCADE CONSTRAINTS;
CREATE TABLE EMPLOYEE_LIST(
employeeno  NUMBER(7),
departmentno              NUMBER(5),
type        VARCHAR2(30),
lastname    VARCHAR2(30),
firstname   VARCHAR2(30),
phone       VARCHAR2(10));

DROP TABLE CREDITCARD_LIST;
CREATE TABLE CREDITCARD_LIST (
cardno            VARCHAR2(15),
employeeno  NUMBER(7),
expirationdate   DATE);

DROP TABLE CHECKACCOUNT_LIST;
CREATE TABLE CHECKACCOUNT_LIST(
accountno   NUMBER(5),
employeeno  NUMBER(7));

DROP TABLE VENDOR_LIST;
CREATE TABLE VENDOR_LIST(
vendorno    NUMBER(6),
name        VARCHAR2(30),
address          VARCHAR2(20),
city        VARCHAR2(15),
state       VARCHAR2(15),
vzip        VARCHAR2(15),
country          VARCHAR2(15));

DROP TABLE PROJECT_LIST;
CREATE TABLE PROJECT_LIST (
projectno   NUMBER(5),
projectname      VARCHAR2(20),
start_date  DATE,
amt_of_funds     NUMBER,
PRIMARY KEY( projectno ));

DROP TABLE PURCHASE_LIST;
CREATE TABLE PURCHASE_LIST (
requestno   NUMBER(10),
employeeno  NUMBER(7),
vendorno    NUMBER(6),
purchasetype     VARCHAR2(20),
```

```
checkno        NUMBER(11),
whenpurchased    DATE);

DROP TABLE LINEITEM_LIST;
CREATE TABLE LINEITEM_LIST (
requestno    NUMBER(10),
lineno           NUMBER(5),
projectno    NUMBER(5),
quantity     NUMBER(5),
unit         VARCHAR2(2),
estimatedcost    NUMBER(8,2),
actualcost   NUMBER(8,2),
description VARCHAR2(30));

--
-- Add constraints to tables
--

ALTER TABLE DEPARTMENT_LIST
  ADD CONSTRAINT deptno_pk PRIMARY KEY(departmentno)
  USING INDEX TABLESPACE INDX;

ALTER TABLE ACCOUNT_LIST
  ADD CONSTRAINT acc_deptno_fk
  FOREIGN KEY(departmentno)
  REFERENCES DEPARTMENT_LIST(departmentno);

ALTER TABLE EMPLOYEE_LIST
  ADD CONSTRAINT employeeno_pk PRIMARY KEY(employeeno)
  USING INDEX TABLESPACE INDX;

ALTER TABLE EMPLOYEE_LIST
  ADD CONSTRAINT emp_deptno_fk
  FOREIGN KEY(departmentno)
  REFERENCES DEPARTMENT_LIST(departmentno);

ALTER TABLE CREDITCARD_LIST
  ADD CONSTRAINT cardno_pk PRIMARY KEY(cardno)
  USING INDEX TABLESPACE INDX;

ALTER TABLE CREDITCARD_LIST
  ADD CONSTRAINT credit_employeeno_fk
  FOREIGN KEY(employeeno)
  REFERENCES EMPLOYEE_LIST(employeeno);

ALTER TABLE CHECKACCOUNT_LIST
  ADD CONSTRAINT accountno_pk PRIMARY KEY(accountno)
```

```
    USING INDEX TABLESPACE INDX;


ALTER TABLE CHECKACCOUNT_LIST
   ADD CONSTRAINT check_employeeno_fk
   FOREIGN KEY(employeeno)
   REFERENCES EMPLOYEE_LIST(employeeno);

ALTER TABLE vendor_list
   ADD CONSTRAINT vendorno_pk PRIMARY KEY(vendorno)
   USING INDEX TABLESPACE INDX;

ALTER TABLE Purchase_list
   ADD CONSTRAINT requestno_pk PRIMARY KEY(requestno)
   USING INDEX TABLESPACE INDX;

ALTER TABLE LINEITEM_LIST
   ADD CONSTRAINT lineno_pk
   PRIMARY KEY(requestno,lineno,projectno)
   USING INDEX TABLESPACE INDX;

--
-- Create Sequences
--

DROP SEQUENCE deptno_SEQ;
CREATE SEQUENCE deptno_SEQ
   START WITH 200
   INCREMENT BY 1;

DROP SEQUENCE projectno_SEQ;
CREATE SEQUENCE projectno_SEQ
   START WITH 300
   INCREMENT BY 1;

DROP SEQUENCE employeeno_SEQ;
CREATE SEQUENCE employeeno_SEQ
   START WITH 100
   INCREMENT BY 1;

DROP SEQUENCE accountno_SEQ;
CREATE SEQUENCE accountno_SEQ
   START WITH 1000
   INCREMENT BY 1;

DROP SEQUENCE cardno_SEQ;
CREATE SEQUENCE cardno_SEQ
```

```
    START WITH 311200
    INCREMENT BY 1;

DROP SEQUENCE vendorno_SEQ;

CREATE SEQUENCE vendorno_SEQ
    START WITH 400
    INCREMENT BY 1;

DROP SEQUENCE requestno_SEQ;
CREATE SEQUENCE requestno_SEQ
    START WITH 500
    INCREMENT BY 1;

DROP SEQUENCE lineno_SEQ;
CREATE SEQUENCE lineno_SEQ
    START WITH 1
    INCREMENT BY 1;

spool off
```

SQL Scripts to Create the Scientific Observation Schema

Use the following `createobjschema.sql` SQL script to create the scientific Observation schema in the Oracle8*i* database:

```
--
-- File Name: obsexample.sql
--
-- This scripts create all necessary tables,
-- constraints and sequences for the Scientific
-- Observation example.


--
-- This script assumes that you created a database
-- user and an index INDX
--
-- Usage: sqlplus userpassword
-- SQL> @obsexample.sql
--
--
set termout on
set echo on
spool createobjschema.log

DROP TABLE PRODUCT_LIST;
```

```
DROP TYPE PRODUCT_TYPE;
DROP TABLE PASSED_OBSERVATION_LIST;
DROP TYPE PASSEDOBSARRAY;
DROP TYPE PASSEDOBS;
DROP TABLE OCEANIC_OBSERVATION_LIST;

DROP TYPE OCEANIC_OBSERVATION_TYPE;
DROP TYPE OCEANIC_OBSERVATION;
DROP TABLE QC_EVENT_LIST;
DROP TYPE QUALITY_CONTROL_EVENT;
DROP TABLE ATMOSEVENT_LIST;
DROP TYPE ATMOSEVENT;
DROP TABLE SCIENTIST_LISTDROP TYPE SCIENTIST;
DROP TABLE PLATFORM_TYPE_LIST;
DROP TYPE PLATFORM_TYPE;

CREATE TYPE PLATFORM_TYPE AS OBJECT(
key_id       NUMBER(8),
type         VARCHAR2(50),
description  VARCHAR2(50));

CREATE TABLE PLATFORM_TYPE_LIST OF PLATFORM_TYPE;

CREATE TYPE SCIENTIST AS OBJECT(
usr_id       NUMBER(6),
lastname     VARCHAR2(20),firstname    VARCHAR2(20),
platform_id  NUMBER,
for_platform REF PLATFORM_TYPE);

CREATE TABLE SCIENTIST_LIST OF SCIENTIST;

CREATE TYPE ATMOSEVENT AS OBJECT(
key_id          NUMBER(8),
when_t          DATE,
name         VARCHAR2(30),
type         VARCHAR2(20),
refkey          NUMBER(8),
transformed_to  REF atmosevent);

CREATE TABLE ATMOSEVENT_LIST OF ATMOSEVENT;

CREATE TYPE OCEANIC_OBSERVATION AS OBJECT(
latitude_deg      NUMBER(10,4),
longitude_deg     NUMBER(10,4),
windspeed_mps     NUMBER(10,4),
adj_windspeed_mps NUMBER(10,4),
wind_direction_deg NUMBER(6),
pressure_mb  NUMBER(6));
```

```
CREATE TYPE OCEANIC_OBSERVATION_TYPE AS OBJECT(
obs_id       NUMBER(8),
when_t       DATE,
at_time      CHAR(8),
station_id   NUMBER(6),

produced_id  NUMBER(8),
produced_by  REF PLATFORM_TYPE,
obsobj       OCEANIC_OBSERVATION);

-- List of all oceanic observations by date,
-- time, and platform type
CREATE TABLE OCEANIC_OBSERVATION_LIST
   OF OCEANIC_OBSERVATION_TYPE;

-- use qc_id_seq to update QUALITY_CONTROL_EVENT qc_id
CREATE TYPE QUALITY_CONTROL_EVENT AS OBJECT(
qc_id     NUMBER(8),
when_t    DATE,
at_time   CHAR(8),
event_id  NUMBER(8),
for_event  REF atmosevent,
whom_id NUMBER(6),
by_whom  REF scientist);

CREATE TABLE QC_EVENT_LIST OF QUALITY_CONTROL_EVENT;

CREATE OR REPLACE TYPE PASSEDOBS AS OBJECT(
obsid    NUMBER(8),
when_t   DATE);

CREATE TYPE PASSEDOBSARRAY AS TABLE OF PASSEDOBS;

CREATE TABLE PASSED_OBSERVATION_LIST(
qcid     NUMBER(8),
when_t   DATE,
at_time  CHAR(8),
idobj    passedObsArray)
NESTED TABLE idobj STORE AS pobsid_list;

ALTER TABLE POBSID_LIST
  STORAGE (MINEXTENTS 1 MAXEXTENTS 20);

--
-- Now create the constraints
--
```

```
ALTER TABLE PLATFORM_TYPE_LIST
  ADD CONSTRAINT PT_KEY_ID_PK PRIMARY KEY(KEY_ID)
  USING INDEX TABLESPACE INDX;

ALTER TABLE SCIENTIST_LIST
  ADD CONSTRAINT SL_USR_ID_PK PRIMARY KEY(USR_ID)
  USING INDEX TABLESPACE INDX;


ALTER TABLE ATMOSEVENT_LIST
  ADD CONSTRAINT AL_KEY_ID_PK PRIMARY KEY(KEY_ID)
  USING INDEX TABLESPACE INDX;

ALTER TABLE OCEANIC_OBSERVATION_LIST
  ADD CONSTRAINT O_OBS_ID_PK PRIMARY KEY(OBS_ID)
  USING INDEX TABLESPACE INDX;

ALTER TABLE QC_EVENT_LIST
  ADD CONSTRAINT QC_ID_PK PRIMARY KEY(QC_ID)
  USING INDEX TABLESPACE INDX;

ALTER TABLE QC_EVENT_LIST
  ADD CONSTRAINT qc_whom_id_fk
  FOREIGN KEY(whom_id)
  REFERENCES SCIENTIST_LIST(usr_id)
  ON DELETE CASCADE;

ALTER TABLE PASSED_OBSERVATION_LIST
  ADD CONSTRAINT passed_id_pk PRIMARY KEY (passed_id)
  USING INDEX TABLESPACE INDX;

ALTER TABLE PASSED_OBSERVATION_LIST
  ADD Constraint po_qc_id_fk
  FOREIGN KEY(qcid)
  REFERENCES QC_EVENT_LIST(qc_id)
  ON DELETE CASCADE;

ALTER TABLE PASSED_OBSERVATION_LIST
  ADD CONSTRAINT passed_qcid_ukey UNIQUE(qcid)
  USING INDEX TABLESPACE INDX;

ALTER TABLE PASSED_OBSERVATION_LIST
  MODIFY (qcid NOT NULL);

ALTER TABLE PRODUCT_LIST
  ADD CONSTRAINT pr_id_pk PRIMARY KEY (id)
  USING INDEX TABLESPACE INDX;
```

```
--
-- Now create the sequences
--
-- key_id sequence for PLATFORM_TYPE

DROP SEQUENCE PT_key_SEQ;

CREATE SEQUENCE PT_key_SEQ
  START WITH 1

  INCREMENT BY 1;

-- usr_id sequence for SCIENTIST
DROP SEQUENCE USERSEQ;

CREATE SEQUENCE USERSEQ
  START WITH 1
  INCREMENT BY 1;

-- key_id sequence for ATMOSEVENT
DROP SEQUENCE atm_key_seq;

CREATE SEQUENCE atm_key_seq
  START WITH 1
  INCREMENT BY 1;

DROP SEQUENCE OBSID_SEQ;
CREATE SEQUENCE OBSID_SEQ
  START WITH 1
  INCREMENT BY 1;

-- qc_id sequence for QUALITY_CONTROL_EVENT
DROP SEQUENCE qc_id_seq;
CREATE SEQUENCE qc_id_seq
  START WITH 1
  INCREMENT BY 1;

-- passed_id sequence for PASSED_OBSERVATION
DROP SEQUENCE passed_id_seq;
CREATE SEQUENCE passed_id_seq
  START WITH 1
  INCREMENT BY 1;

--
-- Now create the PL/SQL package
--
DROP PACKAGE OBSACTIONS;
CREATE OR REPLACE PACKAGE OBSACTIONS AS
```

```
--   Get a new Obs_id
     FUNCTION getObsId RETURN NUMBER;
     PRAGMA RESTRICT_REFERENCES(getObsId,WNDS,WNPS,RNPS);

--   Add a new Observation
     PROCEDURE insertObs(p_newobsid IN NUMBER,
                     p_whent          IN VARCHAR2,
                     p_attime         IN CHAR,
                     p_ptlid          IN NUMBER,
                     p_latdeg         IN NUMBER,

                     p_londeg         IN NUMBER,
                     p_wsmps          IN NUMBER,
                     p_adjwsmps  IN NUMBER,
                     p_wddeg          IN NUMBER,
                     p_pmb       IN NUMBER,
                     p_stlid          IN NUMBER);

END OBSACTIONS;
/
CREATE OR REPLACE PACKAGE BODY OBSACTIONS AS
--   Use the private FindCurrTime function to
--   find current time. This method is accessible
--   only to the functions and procedures specified
--   in the body section of the OBSACTIONS package.
--   It's analogous to a Java private method.
     FUNCTION FindCurrTime RETURN CHAR IS
     v_time  CHAR(8);
     BEGIN
         SELECT TO_CHAR(SYSDATE,'HH24MISS') INTO v_time FROM DUAL;
         RETURN v_time;
     EXCEPTION
        WHEN NO_DATA_FOUND THEN
             RETURN v_time;
     END FindCurrTime;


--   Get a new Obs_id
     FUNCTION getObsId RETURN NUMBER IS
       p_obsid NUMBER;
     BEGIN
         SELECT OBSID_SEQ.NEXTVAL INTO p_obsid FROM DUAL;
         RETURN p_obsid;
     EXCEPTION
         WHEN OTHERS THEN
             RETURN p_obsid;
     End getObsId;
```

```
--   Create an object of TYPE Oceanic_observation

--   This is a private method.
     FUNCTION OceanicObservation (p_latdeg  IN NUMBER,
                               p_londeg    IN NUMBER,
                               p_wsmps     IN NUMBER,
                               p_adjwsmps  IN NUMBER,
                               p_wddeg     IN NUMBER,
                               p_pmb       IN NUMBER)

                                  RETURN oceanic_observation IS
--      Create an oceanic_observation type.
        v_obs  oceanic_observation :=
           oceanic_observation(p_latdeg,p_londeg,
              p_wsmps,p_adjwsmps,p_wddeg,p_pmb);
     BEGIN
         RETURN v_obs;
     END OceanicObservation;

--   Add a new Observation
     PROCEDURE insertObs(p_newobsid IN NUMBER,
                         p_whent        IN VARCHAR2,
                         p_attime       IN CHAR,
                         p_ptlid        IN NUMBER,
                         p_latdeg       IN NUMBER,
                         p_londeg       IN NUMBER,
                         p_wsmps        IN NUMBER,
                         p_adjwsmps  IN NUMBER,
                         p_wddeg        IN NUMBER,
                         p_pmb       IN NUMBER,
                         p_stlid        IN NUMBER) IS

        v_date DATE := TO_DATE(p_whent,'DD-MON-YYYY');
        v_time  CHAR(8) := p_attime;
        v_newobsid  NUMBER := TO_NUMBER(p_newobsid);
        v_platformref  REF PLATFORM_TYPE;

        v_obs Oceanic_Observation :=
          Oceanic_Observation(p_latdeg,p_londeg,
            p_wsmps,p_adjwsmps,p_wddeg,p_pmb);
     BEGIN
--    Check input date p_whent
        IF  v_date IS NULL THEN
            SELECT SYSDATE INTO v_date FROM DUAL;
        END IF;

--      Check input time
        IF  v_time IS NULL THEN
```

```
                v_time := FindCurrTime;
          END IF;


--      Get platform_type REF
          SELECT REF(P) INTO v_platformref
              FROM platform_type_list P
              WHERE P.key_id = p_ptlid;


--      Insert new object
          INSERT INTO OCEANIC_OBSERVATION_LIST

            VALUES(
                    v_newobsid, v_date, v_time, p_stlid, p_ptlid,
                    v_platformref, v_obs
                  );
        -- commit;
      EXCEPTION
        WHEN NO_DATA_FOUND THEN
            NULL;
        WHEN OTHERS THEN
            NULL;
      END insertObs;


END OBSACTIONS;


DROP PACKAGE QCACTIONS;
CREATE OR REPLACE PACKAGE QCACTIONS AS
--  Get a new qc_id
      FUNCTION GETNEWQCID RETURN NUMBER;
      PRAGMA RESTRICT_REFERENCES(GETNEWQCID,WNDS,WNPS,RNPS);
--  Add a new QcSet
      PROCEDURE insertQcSet(p_newqcid IN NUMBER,
                            p_whent       IN VARCHAR2,
                            p_attime  IN CHAR,
                            p_evtid       IN NUMBER,
                            p_whom_id IN NUMBER);
--  Add a new row in the PASSED_OBSERVATION_LIST table
      PROCEDURE insertQcSetObs(p_qcid  IN NUMBER,
                               p_obsid      IN NUMBER);
END QCACTIONS;
CREATE OR REPLACE PACKAGE BODY QCACTIONS AS
--  Find current time
      FUNCTION FindCurrTime RETURN CHAR IS
        v_time  CHAR(8);
      BEGIN
          SELECT TO_CHAR(SYSDATE,'HH24MISS')
                    INTO v_time FROM DUAL;
          RETURN v_time;
```

```
            EXCEPTION
                WHEN NO_DATA_FOUND THEN
                    RETURN v_time;
            END FindCurrTime;

    FUNCTION GETNEWQCID RETURN NUMBER IS
            p_qcid NUMBER;
        BEGIN
                SELECT qc_id_seq.NEXTVAL INTO p_qcid FROM DUAL;

                RETURN p_qcid;
        EXCEPTION
            WHEN OTHERS THEN
                RETURN p_qcid;
        End GETNEWQCID;

    PROCEDURE insertQcSet(p_newqcid    IN NUMBER,
            p_whent    IN VARCHAR2, p_attime IN CHAR,
            p_evtid    IN NUMBER, p_whom_id IN NUMBER) IS

        v_date DATE := TO_DATE(p_whent,'DD-MON-YYYY');
        v_time  CHAR(8) := p_attime;
        v_newqcid  NUMBER := TO_NUMBER(p_newqcid);
        v_eventref  REF atmosevent;
        v_scientistref  REF scientist;

      BEGIN
    --    Check input date p_whent
            IF  v_date IS NULL THEN
                SELECT SYSDATE INTO v_date FROM DUAL;
            END IF;
    --    Check input time
            IF  v_time IS NULL THEN
                v_time := FindCurrTime;
            END IF;
    --    Get atmosevent REF
            SELECT REF(P) INTO v_eventref
                FROM ATMOSEVENT_LIST P
                WHERE P.key_id = p_evtid;
    --    Get scientist REF
            SELECT REF(P) INTO v_scientistref
                FROM SCIENTIST_LIST P
                WHERE P.usr_id = p_whom_id;
    --    Insert new row
            INSERT INTO QC_EVENT_LIST
                VALUES(p_newqcid,v_date,v_time,p_evtid,v_eventref,
                    p_whom_id,v_scientistref);
        EXCEPTION
```

```
          WHEN OTHERS THEN
              RAISE NO_DATA_FOUND;
       END insertQcSet;
   PROCEDURE insertQcSetObs(p_qcid IN NUMBER,p_obsid IN NUMBER) IS
       v_qcdate DATE;
       v_time  CHAR(8);
       v_qcid  NUMBER := TO_NUMBER(p_qcid);
       v_obsdate DATE;
       v_obsid  NUMBER := TO_NUMBER(p_obsid);

       v_cnt    NUMBER;
       BEGIN
--        Check p_qcid
          IF  v_qcid IS NULL THEN
              RAISE NO_DATA_FOUND;
          END IF;
--        Check v_obsid
          IF  v_obsid IS NULL THEN
              RAISE NO_DATA_FOUND;
          END IF;
--        Check QcSet exists
          SELECT Q.when_t, q.at_time INTO v_qcdate, v_time
            FROM QC_EVENT_LIST Q
            WHERE Q.qc_id = v_qcid;
--        Check Obsid exists
          SELECT O.when_t INTO v_obsdate
            FROM OCEANIC_OBSERVATION_LIST O
            WHERE O.obs_id = v_obsid;
          v_cnt := 0;
--        Check PASSED_OBSERVATION_LIST exists
          SELECT COUNT(1) INTO v_cnt
            FROM PASSED_OBSERVATION_LIST P
            WHERE P.qcid = v_qcid;
          IF  ( v_cnt = 0 ) THEN
              INSERT INTO PASSED_OBSERVATION_LIST
                VALUES(v_qcid,v_qcdate,v_time,PASSEDOBSARRAY());
          END IF;
          INSERT INTO TABLE
            (SELECT P.idobj FROM passed_observation_list P
                WHERE P.qcid = v_qcid)
            VALUES(PASSEDOBS(v_obsid,v_obsdate));
       EXCEPTION
          WHEN OTHERS THEN
              RAISE NO_DATA_FOUND;
       END insertQcSetObs;

   END QCACTIONS;
   /
```

Book Conventions

This book uses the following conventions:

- Classes are monofont: the standard Java class `Java.lang.*`

- Datatypes are monofont: the `REF CURSOR` datatype

- Filenames and extensions are lowercase monofont: `.class` files, the `.ser` extension

- Functions and procedures are monofont `insertQcSet()` and a function `GetObsId()`

- SQL keywords are Roman caps: CREATE TABLE, INSERT, DELETE

- Database table names are monofont caps: `PASSED_OBSERVATION`

- Java keywords in paragraphs are set in bold monofont: **`public`**

Providing Feedback to the Authors

The authors welcome your comments and suggestions on the quality and usefulness of this book. Your input is important to us. Please send comments to us via email:

Nirva Morisseau-Leroy   nmorisseauleroy@data-i.com
Martin K. Solomon   marty@cse.fau.edu
Julie Basu   jbasu@us.oracle.com

Retrieving Examples Online

Program source code and a glossary of terms can be found at http://www.data-i.com and http://www.osborne.com. Programs, whose source code appear at these sites, are listed in a file with the same name as the source name, for example, `ObsImp.sqlj`.

Disclaimer

The programs presented here are not intended for use in any inherently dangerous applications. It shall be the reader's responsibility to take all appropriate fail-safe, backup, redundancy, and other measures to ensure the safe use of such applications.

PART

I

Overview

CHAPTER

1

Introduction to Distributed Computing Systems

his book is about developing Java client-side and server-side software components using JDBC and SQLJ implementations. JDBC provides the capability of embedding dynamic SQL in Java programs, whereas SQLJ allows the embodiment of static SQL in Java programs. In static embedded SQL, all the SQL statements embedded in the program are known at compile time, while in dynamic (embedded) SQL at least some SQL statements are not completely known until runtime.

Throughout this book, you will learn how to develop, deploy, and customize multi-tier database software components that manipulate data residing in an Oracle8*i* data server, versions 8.1.5, 8.1.6, and the upcoming release 8.1.7. You will use these components as simple business objects; but more importantly, you will deploy them using component models such as Enterprise JavaBeans (EJBs), CORBA, Java servlets, JavaBeans, or JavaServer Pages (JSPs). These component models allow companies to deploy the same application into a variety of deployment servers and to distribute the same application to a variety of clients including Java standalone programs, EJB, CORBA, JSP, servlet, or Web browser clients.

Part I (Chapters 1 and 2) covers the most current trends in software component development, distributed computing systems concepts, and Web application development, including Java servlets.

Part II (Chapters 3–5) teaches you the fundamental concepts of the Enterprise JavaBeans (EJB) architecture (EJB 1.0 and 1.1). In these chapters, you will build and deploy simple and advanced database EJB components in the Oracle8*i* database.

In Part III (Chapters 6–9), you will develop and deploy Java CORBA components. Additionally, you will develop Java CORBA clients that use the EJB components that you will build in Part II.

In Part IV (Chapters 10–12), you will acquire the skills to develop JavaServer Pages and JavaBean components. In Chapter 12, you will build client applications using the Extensible Markup Language (XML), JSP, and servlets that will use the EJB and CORBA components that you build in Parts II and III.

In this chapter, you will learn the following:

- Concepts of components.

- Concepts of software components.

- Distributed computing systems.

- Basic building blocks of a component using Java. In that section, you will build a simple Java component using a JDBC and SQLJ implementation.

This chapter provides a broad overview on the most current trends in software component development and distributed computing systems concepts.

Components: Concepts

The days of large, monolithic systems are fast fading. The pace is aggressive, with development cycles shortened from months to weeks. The current trend favors a shorter-term development process where large and complex applications are being built using a series of smaller "parts," referred to as *components*, which can be developed in more realistic timeframes.

What Is a Component?

A component is an independent, application-level software unit that is developed for a specific purpose and not for a specific application. In a component-based approach, expertise in specific domains can be delegated among a team of developers, providing a compelling advantage in terms of development effort and time. For particularly large applications, the expertise required for development may even be distributed among several organizations.

A component approach to software development builds upon fundamental constructs of object-oriented paradigms. Although the terms "component" and "object" are often used interchangeably, a component is not an object. An object is an instance of a class that gets created at runtime. A component can be a class, but is usually a collection of classes and interfaces. At runtime, a component becomes "alive" when its classes get instantiated. Therefore, at runtime, a component becomes a web of objects.

Components are typically business objects that have predefined and reusable behaviors. Implementation detail is hidden in the interfaces, which isolate and encapsulate a set of functionality. Interfaces are the means by which components connect. An interface is a set of named operations that can be invoked by clients. More importantly, well-defined interfaces define the component's entry points, and a component's accessibility is done only via its interface. In a component-based approach, providers and clients communicate via the specification of the interface, which becomes the mediating middle that lets the two parties collaborate and work together. In the "Building a Component in Java" section of this chapter, you will use Java to build the `Observation` component. In Chapter 4, you will extend the functionality of the `Observation` component and deploy it as an enterprise Bean.

Figure 1-1 presents a high-level view of a component's composite.

Component-oriented programming addresses the aspects of programming components. Component construction itself can be performed using arbitrary programming languages, as long as the language supports the particular component standard's interface conventions. Many programming languages such as COBOL, Object COBOL, C, C++, Pascal, Object Pascal, Modula 2, Eiffel, or Smalltalk lack support for encapsulation, polymorphism, type safety, or a combination of these. The most prominent component-based programming language at this time is Java.

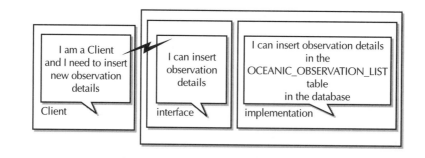

FIGURE 1-1. *Component's composite*

With the release of the Java 2 Enterprise Edition (J2EE) product (Sun Microsystems), the combination of EJB, servlets, and JSP offers a powerful platform on which to build component-based applications.

Software Components: Concepts

The basic motivation for using components is twofold: the "expectation" of code reusability by many applications and the concept of interfaces. Proper use of interfaces can bring many benefits, such as self-sufficient entities and concurrent and parallel application development. Components are best used in application assembly. In a component-based approach, evolution is favored over revolution. Component assembly enables developers to create new composites by assembling prefabricated components and connecting them together.

Composite systems consisting of components are called *software components*. "A software component is a unit of composition with contractually specified interfaces and explicit context dependencies only. A software component can be deployed independently and is subject to composition by third parties." [*European Conference on Object-Oriented Programming (ECOOP)*, 1996.]

Software components were initially considered to be analogous to hardware components and integrated circuits. A software component is self-contained—that is, environment and application independent. When assembled to form a functioning system, software components interact through the methods (operations) that they advertise in their interfaces. In Chapter 5, you will learn more about software components while building a component-based application consisting of three Enterprise JavaBeans.

Component and Software Component Benefits

The benefits of software components are manifold:

- **Independent**   A component is more generalized and is application independent.

- **Reusable**   Components are reusable assets. Compared to specific solutions to specific problems, components are more generalized to enable reuse in a variety of contexts.

- **Customization**   Individual components can be custom-made to suit specific requirements, whereas existing ones can be customized to meet those requirements.

- **Assembly**   Several components can be assembled to form a functioning system.

- **Easy to upgrade and maintain**   Upgrades of individual components end the problem of massive upgrades as done in monolithic systems.

- **Location transparent**   Components can live anywhere on a network—in computers best suited for running them—based on the functions the components provide.

- **Distributed**   Using distributed computing systems standards such as Enterprise JavaBeans, CORBA, or Microsoft's Distributed Component Object Model/Component Object Model (DCOM/COM), components and software components can be distributed throughout an enterprise network.

Distributed Computing Systems

A common characteristic of today's large corporate and government networks is heterogeneity. Heterogeneous systems consist of a combination of numerous operating systems spread across multiple hardware (mainframes, workstations, PCs, and so on) and software components. Distributed object computing supplies a paradigm for building the software infrastructure to unify components of the network and enable communication between them.

We focus here on the essential concepts of distributed computing systems and relate these concepts to information technology professionals responsible for constructing information systems and to database management systems—in particular the Oracle8*i* object-relational database (versions 8.1.5, 8.1.6, and 8.1.7)—that implement component-based model architectures inside the database server.

Underlying all distributed computing architectures is the notion of communication between computers. The most recent concept developed in distributed computing systems is distributed objects. Distributed object computing allows objects (business logic and data) to be distributed across a heterogeneous network; although these objects may reside at different address spaces or computers, they appear as parts of a unified whole.

The term *distributed object computing* refers to programs or applications that make remote invocation calls to other programs that reside at different address spaces, possibly on different computers and/or different networks. Distributed object computing is a framework for computing that has resulted from the convergence of object-oriented and client/server technologies. Importantly, this framework supports interoperability and reusability of distributed objects by allowing developers to build systems from assembling components from different vendors.

Distributed Object Architectures

Distributed object systems are the foundation for the three-tier architecture, in which the presentation logic or first tier resides on a client, the business logic resides on a middle tier, and the database (the back end) resides on the third tier. Distributed object technology extends the middle tier by allowing accessibility to multiple application objects rather than a single one. The result is a new architecture called *N-tier* or *multi-tier*. In the N-tier architecture, many application objects can coexist (that is, database servers, Java RMI, EJB, CORBA, DCOM objects, and so on) and communication between client-side and server-side objects is accomplished through some type of remote method invocation (RMI) protocol. An RMI protocol is used to communicate method invocations over long distances. For example, CORBA, Java RMI, and Microsoft DCOM all use their own RMI protocols. Each application object has an interface or some type of object wrapper that advertises the services that the object provides and, importantly, communication is done solely via that interface.

All distributed object protocols are built on the same basic architecture. Distributed object architectures are based on a network communication layer that comprises three parts: the *object server*, the *skeleton*, and the *stub*. The object server and the skeleton usually reside on the middle tier, although with Oracle8*i*, both reside in the third tier (that is, in the database server). The stub resides on the client machine and handles the cross-process communication between the client-side and the server-side object. The stub acts as proxy on the client and is responsible for communicating requests for the client to the object server through the skeleton. The stub and skeleton are responsible for making the object server (which may live on the middle tier or the third tier) look as if it is running locally on the client's machine.

In order to send data across different address spaces, the stub and skeleton use two processes called *marshaling* and *unmarshaling*. "Marshaling packs a method call's parameters (at a client's space) or return values (at a server's space) into a standard format for transmission. Unmarshaling, the reverse operation, unpacks the standard format to an appropriate data presentation in the address space of a receiving process" (*Oracle8i SQLJ Programming*, OMH, November 1999).

Distributed Computing Systems Standards

There exist several distributed object paradigms:

- The Object Management Group (OMG) developed the Common Object Request Broker Architecture (CORBA) in early 1990. CORBA, based on an abstract model called Object Management Architecture (OMA), employs an Object Request Broker (ORB) to create and manage communication between client-side and server-side objects. Remote access is done via the Internet Inter-ORB (IIOP) protocol. IIOP makes it possible for distributed programs written in different programming languages to communicate over the Internet. CORBA objects and interfaces are specified using the OMG Interface Definition Language (OMG IDL). OMG IDL allows client-side and server-side objects written in different programming languages to interoperate. Programming language mappings for OMG IDL (for Java, C, C++, Ada, and COBOL) include definitions of the language-specific data types and interfaces to access CORBA objects. CORBA objects can be distributed on many different hardware platforms (UNIX workstations, Windows NT, and so on). You will learn about CORBA in Chapters 6–9.

- The Distributed Component Object Model (DCOM), developed by Microsoft, is a component technology for distributing applications on the Windows architecture. DCOM is based on the Component Object Model (COM). COM allows clients to invoke services provided by COM-compliant components (COM objects). COM objects and interfaces are specified using the Microsoft Interface Definition Language (IDL), an extension of the DCE Interface Definition Language standard.

- The Java Remote Method Invocation (RMI) from Sun JavaSoft allows a Java object running in one Java Virtual Machine (JVM) to invoke methods on another Java object running in another JVM. RMI uses the Java Remote Method Protocol (JRMP) for remote invocation calls and was designed to operate only in the Java environment. In June 1999, Sun released the RMI over IIOP (RMI-IIOP) specification. RMI-IIOP, developed jointly by Sun and IBM, allows Java objects to communicate with CORBA objects. The RMI-IIOP specification supports both JDK 1.1.6 and higher and the Java 2 platforms.

■ The JavaBeans component architecture from Sun JavaSoft allows developers to create client-side components that can be assembled using visual application builders (for example, Oracle JDeveloper and Visual Café) and nonvisual widgets. See Chapter 11 to learn more about developing JavaBean components.

■ The Enterprise JavaBean (EJB) is a component model that allows developers to distribute components in the server (application servers and database servers). In EJB applications, remote invocation follows the RMI specification, but vendors are not limited to the RMI transport protocol. For example, the Oracle8*i* EJB server uses RMI over IIOP for its transport protocol. Server-side components are used on the middle tier application servers, which manage the components at runtime and make them available to remote clients. With the release of the Oracle8*i* database, developers can now store EJB and CORBA objects inside the database. EJB is used for the development and deployment of N-tier, distributed, and object-oriented Java applications. To learn more about EJB, see Chapters 3–5.

Advantages of Distributed Computing Systems

Some of the advantages are as follows:

■ **Decomposition of complex software applications into software components**   Consequently, software tasks can be delegated to developers concurrently and independently.

■ **Easier to upgrade and maintain**   Revamping and maintaining monolithic systems can be quite costly in terms of time and money. Software applications that model business objects are more flexible, extensible, and reusable.

■ **Distribution of software components to computers that best fit their task**   Moreover, software components can be used by multiple applications.

■ **Usage of *object wrappers* to access legacy systems**   Legacy systems are integral parts of today's enterprises' assets. Object wrappers, object-oriented interfaces that encapsulate legacy systems, allow legacy systems to fully participate in this new era of information systems by making them accessible to the enterprise and enabling communication between them. For example, Web browsers with CORBA or CORBA clients can directly invoke the object wrappers if they are wrapped using OMG IDL.

Building a Component in Java

In this section, you will learn the basic building blocks of a component using Java. More importantly, you will develop the `Observation` component—a simple business object—using a JDBC and SQLJ implementation. The `Observation` component allows a client to access an Oracle8*i* database and insert an array of oceanic atmospheric observations into the `OCEANIC_OBSERVATION_LIST` table. This table is part of the scientific observation schema presented in the "Introduction." In Chapter 4, you will extend the functionality of this component and deploy it into an Oracle8*i* database as an EJB component.

A component consists, at the very minimum, of an **interface** and an implementation class, which work together to provide a set of functionality. The `Observation` component consists of the following:

- `Observation` **interface**
- `ObsImp` implementation class
- `ObsHelper` class
- `ObsException` class
- `Client` class

Figure 1-2 presents the component's basic building blocks using Java. First, we present the definitions of the `ObsHelper` class and the `ObsException` class.

The `ObsHelper` Class

This class implements the `java.io.Serializable` **interface**. The `ObsHelper` class contains several constructors that allow you to create several `ObsHelper` objects according to your needs. You will use instances of this class to marshal and unmarshal data between the `Client` application and the `ObsImp`

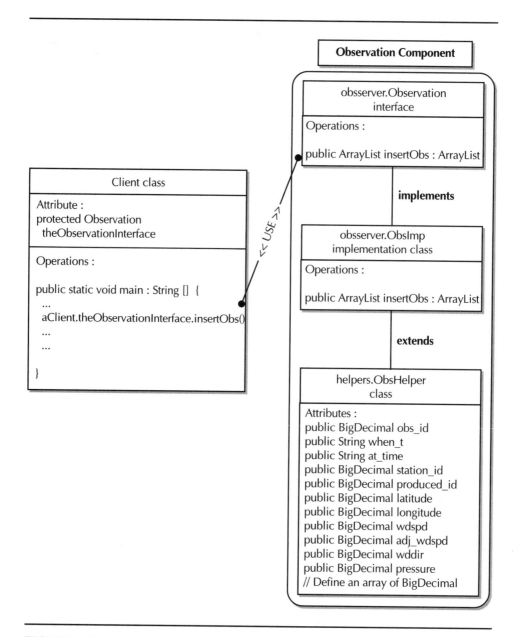

FIGURE 1-2. *High-level view of a component using Java*

class that you will develop in subsequent sections of this chapter. Here is the definition of the ObsHelper class:

```java
/*      Program Name:      ObsHelper.java
**
**      Purpose:           A Java serializable Helper class
**                         used for passing parameter objects
**                         (OCEANIC_OBSERVATION_TYPE)
**                         between clients, EJB and CORBA
**                         components.
*/

package helpers;

import java.io.Serializable;
import java.math.BigDecimal;

public class ObsHelper
    implements java.io.Serializable {

  // Member variables
    public BigDecimal obs_id = null;
    public String when_t = null;
    public String at_time = null;
    public BigDecimal station_id = null;
    public BigDecimal produced_id = null;
    public BigDecimal latitude = null;
    public BigDecimal longitude = null;
     public BigDecimal wdspd = null;
    public BigDecimal adj_wdspd = null;
    public BigDecimal wddir = null;
    public BigDecimal pressure = null;
    // Define an array of BigDecimal
    public BigDecimal[] idArray = null;

    // Default Constructor
     public ObsHelper () {
 }
    // Parameterized Constructor1
    public ObsHelper (
         BigDecimal obs_id, String when_t, String at_time,
         BigDecimal station_id, BigDecimal produced_id,
         BigDecimal latitude, BigDecimal longitude,
         BigDecimal wdspd, BigDecimal adj_wdspd,
         BigDecimal wddir, BigDecimal pressure) {
```

```
                        this.obs_id = obs_id;
                        this.when_t = when_t;
                        this.at_time = at_time;
                        this.station_id = station_id;
                        this.produced_id = produced_id:
                        this.latitude = latitude;
                        this.longitude = longitude;
                        this.wdspd = wdspd;
                        this.adj_wdspd = adj_wdspd;
                        this.wddir = wddir;
                        this.pressure = pressure;
            }
    }
```

The `ObsException` Class

Java contains the `Throwable` class that describes anything that can be thrown
as an exception. The `java.lang.Exception` class is the basic type that can
be thrown from any of the standard Java library class methods and from your
methods and runtime problems. More than likely, you will need to create your
own exceptions to denote a special error that your program is capable of creating.
To create your own exception class, you must inherit from an existing type of
exception. The `ObsException` class is a user-defined exception class that
extends the `java.lang.Exception` class. In Chapter 5, you will redefine the
`ObsException` class so that it inherits from the `java.rmi.RemoteException`
class. You will use this class in your EJB components to transport an exception from
your server objects to a client.

Here is the definition of the `ObsException` class:

```
/*     Program Name:    ObsException.java
**
**     Purpose:         An exception class to be
**                      transported from the component
**                      object to the clients.
**
**
*/

package helpers;

public class ObsException
      extends Exception {

   // Default Constructor
   public ObsException () {
   } // End of constructor
```

```
    // Parameterized constructor
    public ObsException (String msg ) {
        super(msg);
    } // End of parameterized constructor

}   // End of ObsException class
```

The `Observation` Interface

An *interface* is defined as a collection of named operations, each with a defined signature and possibly a return type. A Java **interface** defines a set of methods or constant declarations with no implementation of the method bodies. All the method declarations of a Java **interface** are automatically **abstract** and **public**. The `Observation` **interface** advertises one method, the `insertObs()` method. When invoked by the `Client` application, the `insertObs()` method returns an `ArrayList` object to the caller consisting of `Obshelper` objects.

Here is the definition of the `Observation` **interface**:

```
// Program Name: Observation.java
// Title:         Your Product Name
// Version:
// Copyright:     Copyright (c) 2000
// Author:        Your Name
// Description:   A Java interface that defines a
//                client's callable insertObs() method.
package obsserver;

// import helper classes
import helpers.ObsHelper;
import helpers.ObsException;

import java.util.ArrayList;
import java.sql.SQLException;

public interface Observation {

  //Insert an ArrayList of Observations
  // into the OCEANIC_OBSERVATION_LIST table
  // and return an ArrayList object
  // of Observation IDs
  public ArrayList insertObs()
        throws SQLException, ObsException;

} // End of Observation interface
```

The `ObsImp` Class: Implementation Using JDBC

In Java, you use the **implements** clause on a new class to implement a declared **interface**. Therefore, use the **implements** clause on the `ObsImp` class to implement the `Observation` **interface**. When you create a new class that implements a Java **interface**, the new class must implement every method of that **interface**. The `Observation` **interface** defines only one method, `insertObs()`, and it must be implemented in the `ObsImp` class. Here we provide an implementation using JDBC. In Chapters 4 and 5, this implementation will be revisited and extended.

The `ObsImp` class defines and implements several Java **private** methods (non-client callable) and one **public** method (client callable):

- The **private** `getNewObs()` method. This is a non-client callable method that invokes the overloaded `getNewObs(Connection conn)` method that in turn generates a new observation ID. This method returns to the caller an `ObsHelper` object consisting of an observation ID.

- The **private** `getNewObs(Connection conn)` method. This method calls the PL/SQL `ObsActions.getObsId()` function that generates a new observation ID. When invoked by the `getNewObs()` method, it returns an `ObsHelper` object to the caller. See the "Introduction" for a complete definition of the `ObsActions` PL/SQL package.

- The **private** `insertObs(ObsHelper obs)` method calls the PL/SQL `ObsActions.insertObs(…)` method that inserts an `OCEANIC_OBSERVATION_TYPE` into the `OCEANIC_OBSERVATION_LIST` table. It returns to the caller an `ObsHelper` object.

- The **public** `ArrayList insertObs(ArrayList inObs)` method is the only method callable by a client. Recall that this is the only method that is defined in the `Observation` **interface**. This method takes an `ArrayList` object of `ObsHelper` objects as an input parameter and returns an `ArrayList` object of observation IDs. It does so by calling successively the `insertObs(ObsHelper obs)` method.

- The **private static** `connectDb()` method connects to the database and returns a `java.sql.Connection` object to the caller.

Here is the definition of the `ObsImp` class:

```
// Program Name: ObsImp.java
// Title:        Your Product Name
// Version:
```

```
// Copyright:    Copyright (c) 2000
// Author:       Your Name
// Description:  A Java implementation class
//               that implements the client's callable
//               insertObs() method advertised in
//               the Observation interface.

package obsserver;

// import helper classes
import helpers.ObsHelper;
import helpers.ObsException;

// import application-specific exception
import java.sql.SQLException;

import java.sql.*;
import oracle.sql.*;

// Import supporting Java classes
import java.math.BigDecimal;
import java.util.ArrayList;

public class ObsImp implements Observation {

    // Default Constructor
    public ObsImp () {
    } // End of constructor

    // This method is NOT callable by clients.
    // Therefore, it is not listed in the
    // Observation interface.
    private ObsHelper getNewObs(Connection conn)
        throws SQLException, ObsException {

    // Create a CallableStatement object
    CallableStatement cstmt  = null;

    try {
            // Prepare a String for the call
            String sqlId = "{? = call OBSACTIONS.GETOBSID}";

            // Prepare the call using the conn object
            cstmt = conn.prepareCall(sqlId);

            // Declare that the ? is a return value of type Integer
            cstmt.registerOutParameter (1, Types.INTEGER);
```

```java
        // Get the new obsid by executing the query
        cstmt.execute ();

        // Store the result of the query
        // in the anObsId variable.
        BigDecimal anObsId = new BigDecimal(cstmt.getInt (1));

        // Return an ObsHelper object using the new id
        return new ObsHelper(anObsId);

    } // End try
    catch (SQLException e) {
        throw e;
    } // End catch

    // Clean up. This method guarantees that no matter what
    // happens in this method, the CallableStatement
    // object will always be closed after processing.
    //
    finally {
            if ( cstmt  != null ) cstmt.close();
    } // End finally()

} // End getNewObs(conn)

private ObsHelper insertObs(ObsHelper obs, Connection conn)
    throws SQLException, ObsException {

    // Create a CallableStatement object
    CallableStatement cstmt  = null;

    try {
        // Prepare the String to call the PL/SQL
        // OBSACTIONS.INSERTOBS() procedure.
        String sql =
           "{call OBSACTIONS.INSERTOBS(?,?,?,?,?,?,?,?,?,?,?)}";

        cstmt = conn.prepareCall(sql);

        // Set the input parameters for the
        // OBSACTIONS.INSERTOBS() PL/SQL procedure
        cstmt.setInt(1, obs.obs_id.intValue());
        cstmt.setString(2, obs.when_t);
        cstmt.setString(3, obs.at_time);
        cstmt.setInt(4, obs.produced_id.intValue());
        cstmt.setInt(5, obs.latitude.intValue());
        cstmt.setInt(6, obs.longitude.intValue());
        cstmt.setInt(7, obs.wdspd.intValue());
        cstmt.setInt(8, obs.adj_wdspd.intValue());
```

```java
        cstmt.setInt(9, obs.wddir.intValue());
        cstmt.setInt(10, obs.pressure.intValue());
        cstmt.setInt(11, obs.station_id.intValue());

        // You must call the execute() method of the
        // CallableStatement object. You'll get rather
        // weird errors when you forget to include it.
        cstmt.execute();

        // Return an ObsHelper object
        return new ObsHelper(obs.obs_id);
    }   // End try
    catch (SQLException e) {
        throw e;
    }   // End catch

    // Clean up
    finally {
            if  ( cstmt  != null ) cstmt.close();
    } // End finally()

} // End insertObs(obs,conn)

// Insert an ArrayList of OCEANIC_OBSERVATION_TYPE
public ArrayList insertObs(ArrayList inObs)
    throws SQLException, ObsException {

    int loopVar = 0;

    // Declare an array of ObsHelper objects
    ArrayList returnArrayList = inObs;

    int arrayListSize = inObs.size();

    Connection conn = null;

    try {
        // Use the Oracle thin JDBC driver
        // to connect to the database
        conn = connectDb();

        // Iterate and store an ArrayList of
        // obs_ids into returnArrayList
        while ( loopVar < arrayListSize ) {

            // get a new obs_id at each iteration
            ObsHelper anObsid = getNewObs(conn);
```

```java
          // Move an ObsHelper object into obs
          ObsHelper obs = (ObsHelper)inObs.get(loopVar);

          // Update the obs.obs_id with the new anObsid.obs_id
          obs.obs_id = anObsid.obs_id;

          // Call the insertObs(..) to add a
          // new row to the database and return
          // a new ObsHelper with the new obs_id.
          returnArrayList.add(insertObs ( obs, conn ));

          loopVar++;  // Increment the counter
      }  // End while
      // Reduce the size of the ArrayList Object to its
      // current size
      returnArrayList.trimToSize();

      // Return an ArrayList of ids
      return returnArrayList;
   }  // End try
   catch (SQLException e) {
       throw e;
   }  // End catch
   // Clean up
   finally {
                 if ( conn != null ) conn.close();
   } // End finally()
}  // End insertObs(ArrayList inObs)

// This method is called by all methods that need
// to connect to the database using the
// Oracle thin JDBC driver
private static Connection connectDb()
   throws SQLException {

   // Create a java.sql.Connection variable
   Connection conn = null;
       DriverManager.registerDriver
           (new oracle.jdbc.driver.OracleDriver());

     // connect to data-i.com database server
     conn = DriverManager.getConnection(
         "jdbc:oracle:thin:@data-i.com:1521:ORCL",
         "scott","tiger");
     // Return a java.sql.Connection object
     return conn;
   } // End connectDb()

} // End of ObsImp class
```

Now that you have built the `Observation` component, you need to compile the Java source files. Note that you used an `ArrayList` object as the input parameter and return type for some of the methods of the component. The Java `ArrayList` type is defined in JDK 1.2.x, so use a JDK 1.2.x-compliant compiler to compile the source code. If you do not want to use JDK 1.2.x, replace the `ArrayList` type with either a Java array or `Vector` type.

Use the `javac` command to compile your programs:

```
// Set your CLASSPATH, of course.
Javac -g helpers\*.java obsserver\*.java
```

Next, you will define an `ObsImp` class using a SQLJ implementation.

CAUTION
Make sure that the source code for the JDBC implementation and the SQLJ implementation do not reside in the same directory. When you compile a SQLJ program, the compiler generates a `.java` source file. If your JDBC implementation is in the same directory, it will be overridden. To avoid this problem, the source code for all the programs presented in the book are stored under a `JdbcImplementation` and `SqljImplementation` directory. You can download the files from www.data-i.com or www.osborne.com.

The `ObsImp` Class: Implementation Using SQLJ

This implementation, like the JDBC implementation, will be revisited and extended in Chapters 4 and 5. The implementation using SQLJ is very similar to the one using JDBC. There are, though, some subtle differences:

- In SQLJ, you use two types of connection objects to connect to the database: the `sqlj.runtime.ConnectionContext` **interface** and the `sqlj.runtime.ref.DefaultContext` class. An instance of either of them indicates the location of the data server where the SQL operation will execute. The following code fragment connects to the database:

```
// Declare a variable of DefaultContext type
protected static DefaultContext localHostCtx;

// Connect to the database. The Oracle.getConnection()
// method returns a DefaultContext object.
localHostCtx =
        Oracle.getConnection
            ("jdbc:oracle:thin:@data-i.com:1521:ORCL",
                "scott","tiger",true);
```

■ JDBC implementations that call stored functions or procedures require a particular environment setup in the program. If you forget any of the setup statements or try to execute them in an order different from the prescribed one, you'll get some weird Java errors. In SQLJ, you just call the function. For example

```
#sql [localHostCtx] returnId =
        {VALUES ObsActions.getObsId};
```

Note the simplicity of the statement and, more importantly, there is no environment to set up. Here, you associate the SQLJ `localHostCtx` `DefaultContext` object to the statement when you execute the SQL command in the database. To learn more about SQLJ connection objects, refer to Chapter 5 of *Oracle8i SQLJ Programming* (Osborne/McGraw-Hill, November 1999).

■ Making procedure calls in SQLJ is as easy as calling a function. For example

```
#sql [localHostCtx]
            { call ObsActions.insertObs(
            :IN obs_id, :IN when_t, :IN at_time, :IN produced_id,
            :IN latitude, :IN longitude, :IN wdspd, :IN adj_wdspd,
            :IN wddir, :IN pressure, :IN station_id)
        };
```

Here is the definition of the `ObsImp` class using an SQLJ implementation:

```
/* Program Name:  ObsImp.sqlj
// Program Name: ObsImp.java
// Title:        Your Product Name
// Version:
// Copyright:    Copyright (c) 2000
// Author:       Your Name
// Description:  A Java class using an SQLJ implementation
//               that implements the client's callable
//               insertObs() method advertised in
//               the Observation interface.

package obsserver;

// import helper classes
import helpers.ObsHelper;
import helpers.ObsException;

// import application-specific exception
import java.sql.SQLException;

import java.sql.*;
```

```
import oracle.sql.*;

// Import supporting Java classes
import java.math.BigDecimal;
import java.math.*;
import java.util.ArrayList;

// import SQLJ packages
import sqlj.runtime.*;
import sqlj.runtime.ref.*;
import oracle.sqlj.runtime.Oracle;
import oracle.jdbc.driver.*;

public class ObsImp implements Observation {
    // Create a global variable of type
    // sqlj.runtime.ref.DefaultContext.
    protected static DefaultContext localHostCtx;

    //Constructor
    public ObsImp() throws SQLException {
        // Connect to the database using
        // an SQLJ DefaultContext object
        connectDb();
        System.out.println("In ObsImp(), I got a connection");
    } // End of constructor

    // This method, not_callable by clients, connects to the database
    // And calls the overloaded getNewObs()
    // to get a new obs_id.
    private ObsHelper getNewObs()
        throws SQLException, ObsException {

      // Declare a variable.
      int returnId;

      // Call the getObsId() from the PL/SQL ObsActions package
      // to get a new obs_id
      try {
          // Use the localHostCtx DefaultContext object
          // to Call the PL/SQL function
          #sql [localHostCtx] returnId =
              {VALUES ObsActions.getObsId};

          BigDecimal anObsId = new BigDecimal(returnId);

          // Return an ObsHelper object using the new id
          return new ObsHelper(anObsId);
      }  // End try
      catch (SQLException e) {
          throw e;
```

```
        }   // End catch
    catch (java.lang.NullPointerException e) {
        throw e;
    }   // End catch
} // End getNewObs

// This method gets a new obs_id and adds a new
// OCEANIC_OBSERVATION_TYPE in the
// OCEANIC_OBSERVATION_LIST TABLE.
private ObsHelper insertObs(ObsHelper obs)
    throws SQLException, ObsException {
    try {
        BigDecimal obs_id = obs.obs_id;
        String when_t = obs.when_t;
        String at_time = obs.at_time;
        BigDecimal produced_id = obs.produced_id;
        BigDecimal latitude = obs.latitude;
        BigDecimal longitude = obs.longitude;
        BigDecimal wdspd = obs.wdspd;
        BigDecimal adj_wdspd = obs.adj_wdspd;
        BigDecimal wddir = obs.wddir;
        BigDecimal pressure = obs.pressure;
        BigDecimal station_id = obs.station_id;

        // call the PL/SQL
        // OBSACTIONS.INSERTOBS() procedure
        // using the localHostCtx DefaultContext object
        #sql [localHostCtx]
            { call ObsActions.insertObs(
             :IN obs_id, :IN when_t, :IN at_time, :IN produced_id,
             :IN latitude, :IN longitude, :IN wdspd, :IN adj_wdspd,
             :IN wddir, :IN pressure, :IN station_id)
            };
        // Return an ObsHelper object
        return new ObsHelper(obs.obs_id);
    }   // End try
    catch (SQLException e) {
        throw e;
    }   // End catch

} // End insertObs(obs)

public ArrayList insertObs(ArrayList inObs)
    throws SQLException, ObsException {

    int loopVar = 0;
    // Declare an array of ObsHelper objects
    ArrayList returnArrayList = inObs;

    int arrayListSize = inObs.size();
```

```
    try {
        // Iterate and store an ArrayList of
        // obs_ids into returnArrayList
        while ( loopVar < arrayListSize ) {
            // get a new obs_id at each iteration
            ObsHelper anObsid = getNewObs();

            // Move an ObsHelper object into obs
            ObsHelper obs = (ObsHelper)inObs.get(loopVar);

            // Update the obs.obs_id with the new anObsid.obs_id
            obs.obs_id = anObsid.obs_id;

            // Call the insertObs(..) to add a
            // new row to the database and return
            // a new ObsHelper with the new obs_id.
            returnArrayList.add(insertObs(obs));

            loopVar++;  // Increment the counter
        }  // End while
        returnArrayList.trimToSize();

        // Return an ArrayList of ids
        return returnArrayList;
    }  // End try
    catch (SQLException e) {
        throw e;
    }  // End catch
}  // End insertObs(ArrayList inObs)

// This method creates an instance of the
// SQLJ DefaultContext and stores the object
// into the localHostCtx variable.
// This method is called when a client creates an
// instance of the ObsImp class.
private static void connectDb()
    throws SQLException {

    // Instantiate Default Context for the specific host
    // and connect to the database
    localHostCtx =
      Oracle.getConnection
        ("jdbc:oracle:thin:@data-i.com:1521:ORCL",
            "scott","tiger",true);

  } // End connectDb()

} // End of ObsImp class
```

Next, compile the source code of the SQLJ implementation. To learn more about compiling and running SQLJ programs, refer to Appendix F and *Oracle8i SQLJ Programming* (Osborne/McGraw-Hill, November 1999).

Use the following command to compile the ObsImp class:

```
// Set your CLASSPATH
sqlj -status ObsImp.sqlj
```

The Client Class

This class uses the Observation component defined in the previous sections. It performs the following tasks:

■ Declare the global theObservationInterface variable of type Observation **interface**.

■ Define the Client() constructor. When the Client class is instantiated, its constructor creates an instance of the ObsImp class and stores the object in the theObservationInterface variable.

■ Create an ArrayList object consisting of a set of ObsHelper objects.

■ Invoke the insertObs() method advertised in the Observation **interface** and implemented in the ObsImp class. This method returns to the Client application an ArrayList object containing IDs.

■ Call the local printObsIds(obsids) method to display all the new observation IDs produced by the component.

Here is the definition of the Client class:

```
/* Program Name: Client.java
** Version:
** Description:  A client application: a JDBC implementation.
**               A Java standalone application that uses
**               the Observation Component.
*/

// Import the JDBC classes
import java.sql.*;

// import helper classes
import helpers.ObsHelper;
import helpers.ObsException;

// Make the obsserver.Observation Interface
// visible to the Client application
import obsserver.*;
```

```java
import java.sql.*;
import oracle.sql.*;

// Import supporting Java classes
import java.math.BigDecimal;
import java.util.ArrayList;

public class Client {

    // Declare a variable of Observation type
    protected Observation theObservationInterface = null;

    // Constructor
    public Client (){
      // Get an instance of the ObsImp class
      // and store it in the theObservationInterface variable,
      theObservationInterface = new ObsImp();
    } // End of constructor

    public static void main (String args [])
      throws Exception {

      // Get an instance of the ObsImp class
      Client aClientApp = new Client();
      System.out.println("I got an ObsImp instance");

      // Create an ArrayList object
      ArrayList obs = new ArrayList(2);
      System.out.println("I created an ArrayList object");

      // Store a set of ObsHelper objects
      // in the obs ArrayList object
      while (loopVar++ < 2) {
          BigDecimal obs_id = null;
          String when_t = "16-AUG-2000";
          String at_time = "085500";
          BigDecimal station_id = new BigDecimal(0);
          BigDecimal produced_id = new BigDecimal(1);
          BigDecimal latitude = new BigDecimal(0);
          BigDecimal longitude = new BigDecimal(0);
          BigDecimal wdspd = new BigDecimal(0);
          BigDecimal adj_wdspd = new BigDecimal(0);
          BigDecimal wddir = new BigDecimal(0);
          BigDecimal pressure = new BigDecimal(0);

          // Create an ObsHelper object
          ObsHelper obs1 =
              new ObsHelper(obs_id,when_t,at_time,station_id,
                            produced_id,latitude,longitude,
                            wdspd,adj_wdspd,wddir,pressure);
```

```
        // Insert an ObsHelper object into the ArrayList
        obs.add(obs1);

    } // End while

    System.out.println("I going to call the insertObs() method");
    // Invoke the insertObs() method of the ObsImp class
    // and get an ArrayList object consisting of a
    // of Obshelper objects representing a set of
    // observation Ids.
    ArrayList obsids =
        aClientApp.theObservationInterface.insertObs(obs);
    System.out.println("I called the insertObs() success!");

    System.out.println("I going to call the local "
                        +" printObsIds() method");
    // Display Observations
    printObsIds(obsids);

    System.out.println("I called printObsIds");

  } // End main()

  public static void printObsIds(ArrayList obs)
        throws Exception {

        int loopVar = 0;
        int arraySize = obs.size();

        System.out.println("I have Obsids, see size:"
                            +arraySize);

        while ( loopVar < arraySize ) {
            // Retrieve an ObsHelper object from
            // the ArrayList object.
            ObsHelper anObsid = (ObsHelper)obs.get(loopVar);
            System.out.println("id: " +anObsid.obs_id);

            loopVar++;
        } // End while
    } // // End printObsIds
} // End of Client class
```

Next, compile and run the `Client` application:

```
// Set your CLASSPATH
// First: compile the program
javac -g Client.java

// Second: run the program
java Client
```

Conclusion

In this chapter, you learned the essential concepts of components, software components, and distributed object computing systems. We introduced the major distributed object paradigms: CORBA, DCOM, Java RMI, and EJB. You developed a simple database application component that accesses an Oracle8*i* database and inserts an array of OCEANIC_OBSERVATION_TYPE type into the OCEANIC_OBSERVATION_LIST table. Finally, you wrote the Client application, a Java standalone program that uses the component.

In Chapter 2, you will learn about Web-based applications that generate dynamic content that can be customized to your needs. In particular, you will learn about Java Server Pages (JSPs) and servlets technologies that support dynamic content generation in a portable and cross-platform manner.

CHAPTER 2

Introduction to Web Applications

n the previous chapter, you learned about various programming models for distributed computing. In this chapter, you will be introduced to Web application concepts and architecture. The advent of the Internet has spawned a whole new generation of application programs that allow interaction over the World Wide Web. Starting with "toy" applications a few years ago, Web programming techniques have matured rapidly to provide enterprise-level functionality, reliability, and scalability in business applications. Business activity over the Internet, usually referred to as *e-business* or *e-commerce*, has expanded enormously over the last three years. Products are being advertised and marketed directly to consumers through Web-based "store fronts," business data is being interchanged electronically with partners, and business efficiency is being increased through self-service applications such as home banking. Literally a revolution has occurred in this area, which is still evolving rapidly. This chapter will give you an overview of some of the technology that is driving the e-business revolution.

The new e-business model has been made possible by sophisticated Web applications that can be invoked through simple mouse clicks from a remote computer across a network. These applications support interactive data entry and presentation through any standard Web browser. Behind the user-friendly screens, there are transactional business components that interact with databases such as Oracle8*i*. In this chapter, you will learn how such Web applications work. Specifically, you will learn about the following:

- The concept of a Web server, and how it works with the HTTP protocol

- The Servlet model for generating dynamic Web pages

- JavaServer Pages: their execution mechanism and advantages over servlets

- Component-based architecture for building elegant and powerful Web applications

What Is a Web Server?

At an abstract level, a Web server is a program that receives requests arriving over a network, executes some logic based on the parameters in the request, and returns the results back to the client application. Typically, these requests are submitted by a human user who clicks on the *hyperlinks* of a Web page displayed by a Web browser. The response generated by the Web server is handled and displayed by the browser. Figure 2-1 shows the general setup of a Web server and a Web browser communicating over a network.

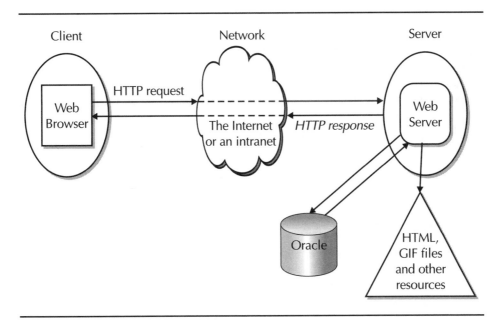

FIGURE 2-1.   *The basic setup of a Web server*

The Web server *listens* on a port on the machine where it is running. The standard mechanism for transporting client requests and server responses over the Internet or private intranets is the HTTP protocol. Incoming HTTP requests that are routed to the given machine and port are processed by that particular Web server. A machine may have more than one Web server running on it; as long as they are listening on different ports, there is no conflict.

Processing an HTTP request may involve a variety of functions by the Web server: it could read contents of files, execute programs that read from or write data to a database, and so on. In particular, it can execute a Java *servlet* using an embedded *servlet engine* and a Java Virtual Machine in order to generate dynamic content in Web pages. For example, an HTTP request may invoke a servlet that prints a greeting and the current time, which is dynamically computed based on the actual time of invocation. You will shortly see an example of such a servlet. Programs run by the Web server are known as *server-side* applications.

The most popular Web server today is the Apache Web server. It is "open source" software developed cooperatively by many programmers around the world, and is freely downloadable from `http://www.apache.org`. Reasons for its popularity include ease of use, flexibility, availability on multiple platforms (including the Linux operating system), and access to source code for debugging purposes. The Apache

Web server is written in C and has an extensible modular architecture that permits other functional modules to be plugged in.

Microsoft's Internet Information Server (IIS) is the next leading Web server in the market, and offers a powerful set of features. However, it runs mainly on Windows NT systems, and thus has limited scope. IIS supports Active Server Pages (ASPs) for generating dynamic Web pages. The JavaServer Pages technology is Sun Microsystem's Java-based counterpart to Microsoft's ASPs. Unlike the Java-based servlet and JSP technologies, the scripting language for ASPs is JScript or VBScript, and the component model is COM and DCOM. ASPs can use Microsoft's Active Data Objects (ADOs) to conveniently access databases, whereas JSP and servlets use the Java Database Connectivity (JDBC) API or SQLJ (embedded SQL in Java) for the same purpose.

The Web Browser

The Web server works in conjunction with the Web browser, which provides an intuitive user interface for Web-based interactions. A primary function of the browser is to display Web pages written in a "markup" language such as HTML (Hypertext Markup Language) or XML (Extensible Markup Language). Most Web pages contain hyperlinks, which are associated with Universal Resource Locators (URLs) that identify other Web resources. Clicking on a hyperlink causes the Web browser to generate a request for the underlying URL. The general format of a URL is as follows:

```
protocol servername[:portnumber] resourcename
```

For example, the URL could be specified as http://www.data-i.com, https://www.mybank.com:8080/accounts, mailto:user@earth.net, or ftp://www.myserver.com/aFile.txt. The first part of the URL is the protocol specification, such as http, https (secure HTTP), mailto (email protocol), and ftp (file transfer protocol). The name of the server machine could be represented in one of the following two ways:

- A numeric Internet address (IP address) such as 144:23:345:123, which represents the four bytes of the 32-bit address for the machine. The address 127.0.0.1 represents the local machine where the browser is running.

- A symbolic name such as www.data-i.com. The special symbolic name localhost usually indicates the local machine on which the browser is running.

The server name is optionally followed by a port number, such as 8080. The remainder of the URL string identifies a resource on the Web server. It can be designated using a hierarchical path structure separated by the **/** character. This hierarchical name is interpreted by the Web server.

The transport mechanism and destination of the generated request depends upon the protocol, the name of the server machine, and the port number designated in the URL. For example, the following request URL identifies a page named `examples/jsp/chapter2/WelcomeUser.jsp` that is to be obtained via HTTP from the local machine and port number 8080:

```
http://localhost:8080/examples/jsp/chapter2/WelcomeUser.jsp
```

The browser sends the HTTP request (typically a `GET` method) over a private intranet or the public Internet to the Web server that is presumably running on the host and port designated in the URL. The Web server interprets the incoming request and sends back a page corresponding to the request URL. The HTTP response is handled and displayed by the browser. Besides text contents, the returned page often contains URLs that reference other resources such as pictures or graphical images. The browser detects the presence of such URLs in the Web page, and then requests their contents in the same way as the main request. More complex audio or video data can also be downloaded from the Web server to the client machine where the browser is running, and presented via appropriate "plug-ins."

Apart from displaying text and image data, most Web browsers have the capability to execute application programs. For example, the Netscape Communicator Web browser embeds a Java Virtual Machine and can run small Java programs known as *applets* that are downloaded from the Web server. In contrast to applets that execute in the client browser, servlets (which you will learn about shortly) are Java programs that execute on the Java Virtual Machine in the Web server. Generally, browsers also implement a "document object model" to represent the pages being displayed. This object model allows client-side scripting languages, such as JavaScript or VBScript, to manipulate the document locally.

The leading Web browsers today are the Netscape Communicator and Microsoft Internet Explorer. These two browsers serve as the gateway to the World Wide Web and most intranets. Although the browsers differ in their exact capabilities, they all implement the standard HTTP protocol and the HTML markup language. As long as the browser conforms to these accepted standards, interaction with the Web server does not depend on which browser you use. In general, you can invoke servlets and JSP pages from either Netscape Communicator or from Internet Explorer without causing a difference in the generated Web page.

The HTTP Protocol

Central to communication over the Web is HTTP, which stands for *Hypertext Transfer Protocol*. It is the primary protocol on the Internet, superseding older protocols such as `ftp` and `gopher`. This simple, stateless protocol is based on a request/response paradigm—a request from an HTTP client generates a server response that is conveyed back to the HTTP client. The request/response message pair is sometimes called an HTTP *transaction*. The messages are transported over TCP/IP (*Transmission Control Protocol/Internet Protocol*), which is the underlying transport mechanism for the Internet and most intranets.

An HTTP message consists of headers and an optional body. The HTTP message headers provide various pieces of information about the data being transmitted in the body. For example, the `Content-type` header defines the "MIME" type of the data, such as whether it is HTML or XML, and the `Content-length` header specifies the number of bytes in the message body. The headers vary depending on whether the message is an HTTP request or an HTTP response.

HTTP Request

An HTTP request is normally submitted by typing in a request URL in the browser window, or by clicking on a hyperlink in the Web page currently being displayed by the browser. A request could also be generated programmatically. The request specifies a certain method that is to be executed by the Web server, such as `GET`, `POST`, `HEAD`, `PUT`, or `DELETE`. These methods are defined in the HTTP specification. The two most frequently used methods are `GET` and `POST`. The `GET` method is typically used to retrieve a page from the Web server. It can include request parameters in a *query string* as *parameter_name=parameter_value* pairs appended to the request URL. For example, typing in the following URL generates an HTTP `GET` request with a request parameter named `user` that has the value `Tara`:

```
http://www.data-i.com:8080/examples/jsp/WelcomeUser.jsp?user=Tara
```

In contrast, the `POST` method sends the parameters in the body of the HTTP request, and they do not appear in the request URL. The `POST` method is more suitable than `GET` for uploading large amounts of data such as the contents of a file or for sending private information such as a bank account number or password. This method is generally used when the request modifies data on the server. The `HEAD` method is less frequently used than `GET` or `POST`. It does not have a message body, and is generally used to communicate status information such as the page modification date (which is relevant for caching).

HTTP Response

An HTTP response is generated by the Web server as a result of processing an HTTP request. It consists of optional HTTP headers and a body. The headers are used by the Web browser to display the contents of the body. For example, if the `Content-type` header is specified as `text/html`, which is the most commonly used MIME type for Web pages, then the Web browser interprets the HTML tags in the message body for formatting the page contents. The response may consist of other types of data, such as plain text or binary. The Web browser uses the appropriate display mechanism depending on the `Content-type` of data received.

An·HTTP response always includes an HTTP status code in the header. HTTP defines standard status codes for different outcomes of request processing. For example, the status code 200 indicates that the request was serviced successfully, while the status code 500 indicates an internal server error. Another frequently encountered HTTP status code is 404, which means that the requested page could not be found by the Web server.

The HTML Markup Language

The HTTP protocol works hand in hand with the HTML markup language. HTML uses special markup tags for the contents to be displayed in a Web page. These tags are interpreted by a Web browser according to the semantics defined in the HTML specification. There are tags for different purposes—for example, to indicate how the text is to be formatted, to handle data entry by the user, and to navigate from one page to another. Tags are generally used in pairs—each "begin" tag has a matching "end" tag, and the text enclosed between the tags is subject to the effect of the tag. For example, text appearing between the `<B>` and `</B>` tags is displayed in bold font. Tags are typically nested in a hierarchical structure. As a complete example, consider the HTML page shown in Listing 2-1.

Listing 2-1   An HTML page

```
<HTML>
   <HEAD> <TITLE> The Welcome Page </TITLE> </HEAD>
   <BODY BGCOLOR="white">
      <H1> Welcome to Oracle 8<I>i</I> Java Components! </H1>
      <P><B><BIG> Hope you will enjoy reading the book! </BIG></B></P>
   </BODY>
</HTML>
```

The HTML code shown in Listing 2-1 specifies through the `<HEAD>` and `<TITLE>` tags that the title to be displayed in the browser window is "The Welcome Page." Then, the `<BODY>` tag denotes the start of the actual contents of the page. The `BGCOLOR` attribute of the `<BODY>` tag specifies that the background of the page is white. The block of text within the `<H1>` and `</H1>` tags is displayed as a first-level heading, with the "i" in the string Oracle8*i* shown in italics through the `<I>` and `</I>` tags. The `<P>` tag indicates the start of a new paragraph, and the `<B>` tag indicates that the text until the matching end tag is to be shown in bold font. The `<BIG>` tag specifies the font size to be used. The begin tags and end tags demarcate appropriate sections of the text. Figure 2-2 shows the Web page displayed by the browser for the `Welcome.html` file.

FIGURE 2-2. *Browser display of the Welcome.html page*

Likewise, there are tags to specify numbered and unnumbered lists, text colors, and fonts, as well as for displaying tables, frames, and forms. An HTML form is an important facility that is frequently used in building interactive Web applications. It provides a mechanism for accepting data from a user through "input boxes" in the Web page displayed by the browser. Data can be typed into these boxes by the user. A form also has one or more buttons for triggering some action after data entry. Clicking on an action button generates a new HTTP request to the server. This request can invoke a server-side program such as a servlet or a JSP. You will see how to use HTML forms in Part IV of this book.

Apart from data entry and presentation, HTML also supports navigation between pages. One of the most useful tags in HTML is the `<A>` tag, which defines a hyperlink to a URL for some Web resource. This simple but elegant tag provides the powerful "click and browse" capability in Web pages. When the `href` attribute has an HTTP link, the tag causes the browser to generate an HTTP request for the specified URL as a user clicks upon the link. The page returned as the HTTP response replaces the page that was originally being displayed in the browser window. This allows smooth "Web surfing" across various pages residing on different machines, often in totally different parts of the world. Working closely together, HTTP and HTML have truly revolutionized the way we use the Internet.

Generating Dynamic Content in Web Pages

Initially, Web servers handled pages with static content only, such as HTML files and images. However, this very soon proved inadequate. To be of practical use, a Web application needs to generate data that is user specific. For example, a home banking application needs to display the account balance for the particular account number provided in an HTTP request. Until a few years ago, the only mechanism for dynamically computing the contents of a Web page was the *Common Gateway Interface*, known as CGI. Vastly improved models of server-side programming are available now, but CGI is still supported by most Web servers. Using CGI, a Web server can execute a server-side application program. However, the drawback of CGI is that a new process is created to run each requested program, causing scalability problems. CGI was followed by more efficient but platform-specific technology such as ISAPI from Microsoft and NSAPI from Netscape. Other approaches include the Active Server Pages from Microsoft, but its use is limited to the Windows platform. Netscape also supports a server-side scripting technique called SSJS that uses JavaScript code snippets to generate dynamic Web pages.

The latest popular technology for dynamic content generation is that of Java servlets and JavaServer Pages (JSPs). Being Java-based, servlet and JSP programs can exploit the full power, portability, safety, modularity, and extensibility of the object-oriented Java platform. You will now learn about these two programming techniques, and understand the benefits they offer for server-side Web application development. The JSP framework is based on servlets, and hence understanding how servlets work is essential in learning about JSP.

The Servlet Model

This section gives you a quick tour of the servlet model.

A Java servlet is a server-side program that is invoked by the Web server to service HTTP requests. A servlet runs on a Java Virtual Machine in the Web server, and typically performs some computation to generate the contents of the HTTP response. In comparison to CGI and other techniques for server-side programming, servlets are a better alternative for a number of reasons:

- Unlike a CGI program, a new process is not created each time a servlet is invoked. Servlet invocation is usually based on threads that service individual HTTP requests. The number of threads that are spawned at a time can be restricted, preventing overloading of the server.

- Servlets are regular Java programs that are translated into platform-independent bytecode, and hence they are automatically portable to any machine where Java is available. They run within the secure boundaries of the Java Virtual Machine, and cannot cause memory access violations and server crashes.

- Servlets have full access to the rich APIs in the Java framework, such as Enterprise Java Beans, Java Mail, JNDI, and RMI.

The servlet technology is fairly new—the Servlet 2.0 specification was finalized in 1998. However, the servlet model and its implementations have matured rapidly, mainly due to their wide popularity among the Web developer community and strong support from the industry. The Servlet 2.2 API specification was published in December 1999. The next version (2.3) of the API is currently being defined through the Java Community Process (JCP) established by Sun Microsystems.

Writing a Simple Servlet

You will now see an example of a simple servlet, `HelloServlet`, that prints a greeting to the user along with the current time. This example illustrates the basic structure of a servlet and the general steps involved in servicing an HTTP request. Explanatory notes on the various steps are given here.

```
/** Program name: HelloServlet.java
 ** Purpose:       Print a greeting and the current time
 **/
package chapter2;

import javax.servlet.*;          // (See Note 1.)
import javax.servlet.http.*;
import java.io.PrintWriter;
import java.io.IOException;

public class HelloServlet extends HttpServlet { // (See Note 2.)
    public void doGet (HttpServletRequest request,
                   HttpServletResponse response) // (See Note 3.)
                throws ServletException, IOException {
        PrintWriter out= response.getWriter();   // (See Note 4.)
      response.setContentType("text/html");      // (See Note 5.)
      out.println("<HTML>");  // (See Note 6.)
      out.println("<HEAD><TITLE>The Hello Servlet</TITLE></HEAD>");
      out.println("<BODY BGCOLOR=\"white\">");
      out.println("<H2>Hello " + request.getParameter("user") +
              ", how are you?</H2>");  // (See Note 7.)
      out.println("<P><B>The current time is " + new java.util.Date());
                                       // (See Note 8.)
      out.println("<P>Hope you have a nice day! </B>");
      out.println("</BODY>");
      out.println("</HTML>");
      out.close();              // (See Note 9.)
    }
}
```

Notes on `HelloServlet.java`:

1. The first two **import** statements involve libraries from the servlet specification. These libraries are part of the `javax.servlet` package, and the `javax.servlet.http` package that deals with HTTP-based servlets in particular. Note the `javax` package prefix—it indicates that this package is part of the Java extension framework and not included in the core Java libraries (which have a `java` prefix). The set of classes and interfaces in the `javax.servlet` and `javax.servlet.http` packages for the Servlet 2.2 specification are listed in Appendix A.

2. This statement is the declaration of the `HelloServlet` class. Typically, a servlet extends the `javax.servlet.http.HttpServlet` abstract class, which defines methods such as `doGet()`, `doPost()`, and `service()`. The `doGet()`, `doPost()`, and other such `do…()` methods of the `HttpServlet` class provide default implementations of the corresponding methods in the HTTP request. One or more of these methods are generally overridden by the specific servlet class, such as `HelloServlet`. The `service()` method acts as the dispatcher to the appropriate request handlers, such as `doGet()` and `doPost()`. This method is rarely overridden by the servlet classes.

3. This statement defines a `doGet()` method. This method takes two arguments: an HTTP `request` object and an HTTP `response` object—of type `HttpServletRequest` and `HttpServletResponse`, respectively—which are both defined in the `javax.servlet.http` package. The execution of the method body may throw exceptions of type `javax.servlet.ServletException` or `java.io.IOException`.

4. This statement extracts the `PrintWriter` object, which is part of the HTTP `response` object. The `PrintWriter` object is used to write character data that is to be returned as output.

5. This statement sets the MIME type of the generated page. Typical values are `text/html` or `text/xml`, indicating HTML or XML content. The value may optionally include the character set encoding of the output, such as `text/html; charset=koi8-r`. The default character set encoding is ISO-8859-1, also known as Latin-1.

6. This statement is the `<HTML>` tag, which indicates the start of the generated page.

7. This statement extracts the value of the parameter named `user` from the HTTP `request` object through the method call `getParameter()`, and prints a welcome message.

8. This statement determines the current time by creating a new instance of the `java.util.Date()` class, and prints it to the response.

9. This statement closes the `PrintWriter` object, indicating the end of the response stream.

Running `HelloServlet.java`   Install the `HelloServlet` program on your Web server, following the instructions provided in Appendix E. Installation involves compiling the servlet code and placing the compiled Java class in an appropriate location that is accessible to the Web server in which the servlet will execute. For example, for the Tomcat server running on a UNIX machine, you can install the servlet under the `examples` application using the following shell command:

```
# UNIX script for compiling HelloServlet on Tomcat server
 javac -d ${TOMCAT_HOME}/webapps/examples/WEB-INF/classes \
     -g -classpath ${TOMCAT_HOME}/lib/servlet.jar \
     HelloServlet.java
```

This command assumes that the environment variable `TOMCAT_HOME` is set to the root directory of the Tomcat installation. Figure 2-3 shows the output generated when you invoke `HelloServlet` by typing in the appropriate URL, such as the following:

```
http://localhost:8080/examples/servlet/chapter2.HelloServlet?user=Tara
```

Notice that the fully qualified name `chapter2.HelloServlet` is used to denote the servlet class in the URL. The parameter `user` is set to the value `Tara` as a query string in the URL.

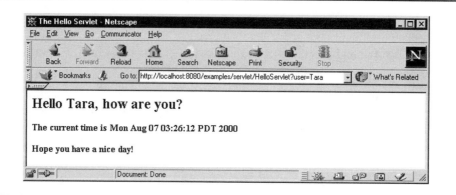

FIGURE 2-3.   *Output of HelloServlet*

The Servlet Execution Model

Now that you have seen how a servlet is written, the next question is how is it executed? Recall that a servlet is a regular Java class, which means that it can be compiled into bytecode using a standard Java compiler. The compilation step is generally manual; that is, the servlet developer compiles the class in a separate step (this compilation step is automatic for JSP pages, as you will shortly learn). In order to be executed, the generated class must be made available to the Java Virtual Machine. But there are additional actions to be taken before the servlet can run. For example, the servlet class needs to be instantiated. There are several questions: When exactly is the servlet instance created? Does the same servlet instance service all HTTP requests, or are there multiple instances of the servlet class? When is the servlet instance destroyed? In this section, you will learn the answers to these important questions.

The Servlet Engine   The servlet engine, also known as the servlet *container* or servlet *runner*, is the program that executes installed servlets. The servlet engine is responsible for the following tasks:

- Creating and initializing instances of the servlets

- Invoking the servlets based on HTTP requests, and forming HTTP responses from the generated output

- Destroying and garbage collecting servlet instances

The process of loading, creating, executing, and, finally, destroying a servlet instance constitutes the servlet *life cycle*. Figure 2-4 shows the different stages in the life cycle of a servlet.

The servlet engine typically creates a single instance of a servlet class, although a pool of servlet instances is sometimes used. Exactly when a servlet instance will be created depends on the configuration of the Web server. For example, it could be created when the Web server starts, or when the servlet is first invoked through an HTTP request. Irrespective of the creation time, the servlet's init() method is always called by the servlet engine before the servlet handles any request. The init() method performs any initialization logic needed by the servlet to service client requests. For example, a servlet could open a database connection in its init() method and use this connection to subsequently execute SQL queries. Likewise, the servlet's destroy() method will always be called before the instance is disposed of. The destroy() method can be used to perform any necessary cleanup operations, such as closing a database connection that was previously opened.

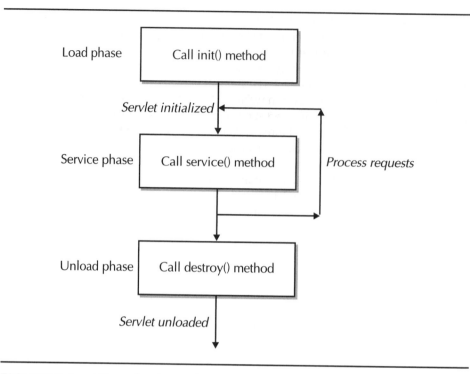

FIGURE 2-4. *Life cycle of a servlet*

After a servlet instance has been created and initialized, it is ready to service requests. When a request is received for that servlet, the servlet engine usually spawns a new thread to process it. This thread calls the `service()` method of the servlet class. Servlets typically extend the `javax.servlet.http.HttpServlet` class, and the implementation of the `service()` method is inherited from this superclass. The signature of the `service()` method is as follows:

```
protected void service(HttpServletRequest request,
                       HttpServletResponse response)
    throws ServletException, IOException
```

This method acts as the "dispatcher"—it determines the type of HTTP request (such as GET or POST) and simply invokes the appropriate method (`doGet()` or `doPost()`) for the servlet. The signature of these methods is the same as the `service()` method, as shown in the `doGet()` method of the `HelloServlet` example from earlier.

Now, consider what happens if multiple HTTP requests come in simultaneously, or a request arrives while the previous one is still being processed. In this case, the servlet engine generally uses another execution thread to call the `service()` method of the same instance of the servlet, even as the first request is being processed, as shown in Figure 2-5. This scheme implies that the request processing code in a servlet must be able to handle concurrent access by multiple threads (an exception to this rule is when the servlet class implements the `SingleThreadModel` **interface**, as discussed in the next paragraph). Therefore, when writing a servlet *you must ensure that the code is thread safe*. Use the **synchronized** statement in Java to appropriately guard code paths that would conflict on multithreaded execution. In particular, you should synchronize access to the instance variables of the servlet class, such as a variable that represents the database connection. Several database operations must often be grouped together as part of an atomic transaction corresponding to a single HTTP request. Therefore, access to the database connection needs to be coordinated among multiple threads that are servicing different HTTP requests.

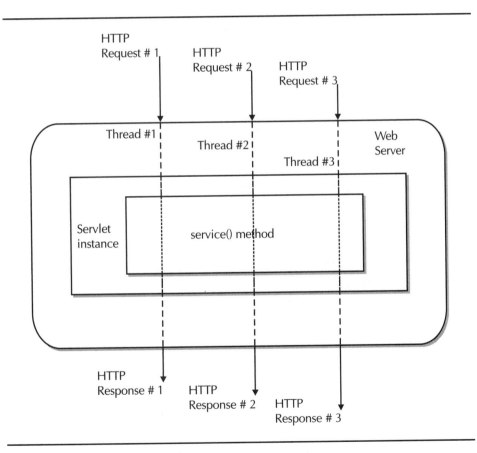

FIGURE 2-5. *Multithreaded access to a single servlet instance*

Protecting against multithreaded access can degrade the performance in some cases, and cause inefficient request processing. For example, to maintain separate database transactions for each request, all code in the `doGet()` or the `doPost()` method may need to be synchronized, which causes serial handling of simultaneous requests. In such cases, it is possible for the servlet to indicate that it wants an alternate execution scheme known as the "single-thread" model. In this scheme, shown in Figure 2-6, two requests are never dispatched simultaneously to the same servlet instance, eliminating synchronization issues. Instead, a pool of instances for this servlet is created by the servlet engine, and a free instance from this pool is used to service a new request. A servlet can elect this execution scheme by implementing the `javax.servlet.SingleThreadModel` **interface**. This is an empty

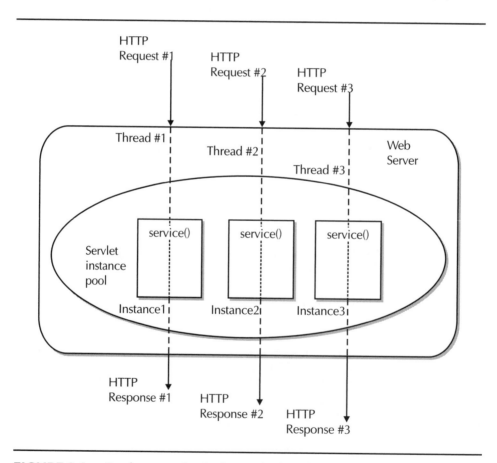

FIGURE 2-6.   *Servlet execution in the single-thread model*

interface with no methods, which simply acts as an indicator of the alternate execution mechanism. A servlet implementing this interface can effectively be considered thread safe.

Using Servlet Sessions

HTTP is fundamentally a stateless protocol. That is, each HTTP request is unrelated to any other request, even if these requests are from the same client. However, in the case of Web applications, interactions often need to be *stateful*. For example, a Web application for home banking may have a login page where the user provides an account number and password, and this information is needed for the next HTTP request where the user asks for the account balance. Another common example of stateful interaction is an online shopping service, where the user collects items in a virtual "shopping cart" that spans several requests (you will develop such an application in Chapter 11). Maintaining this information requires the concept of a *session*, which essentially groups together a series of requests from the same client.

Here is how HTTP session tracking works. Each session is identified by a unique key on the server. The HTTP response message can include the session key, which the client can save and attach to subsequent requests to that server in order to indicate the current session. There are three common techniques for session tracking in servlets:

- Through "cookies"

- By URL rewriting

- Via the built-in session tracking API for servlets

These techniques are discussed briefly below. Sessions can also be implemented in other less common ways that are not discussed here. Note that a session may be explicitly terminated by a servlet or be implicitly timed out by the server. Once a session expires, the session key is invalid even if an HTTP request with that key is later received.

Cookies   A *cookie* is simply some session identification data that can be sent to the client in a `Set-Cookie` HTTP header as part of the HTTP response message. A servlet can explicitly send a cookie by calling the `addCookie()` method of the `HttpServletResponse` object. The client can choose to retain this cookie and send it back to the server with all subsequent requests in order to identify the session. However, a Web browser may not support cookies, or the user may explicitly disable cookies in the browser. In these cases, the URL rewriting technique can be used.

URL Rewriting   In the URL rewriting technique, all URLs included in the server response are modified to carry the session-key information. For example, a user identifier could be appended to the URL as a query string, as follows:

```
http://localhost:8080/examples/servlet/shopOnline?userid=Pam
```

When the user subsequently clicks on an HTML hyperlink in the Web page displayed by the browser, this enhanced URL is used to reference the link. The servlet at the other end can extract the session identifier from the query string in the request URL. This technique has the disadvantage that all URLs in the response must be modified to include the session key, requiring additional work by the servlet. A more important issue is that of privacy, since the session identifier is exposed or implied in the generated page.

The Servlet Session API   The Java servlet API provides built-in support for session management. This API must be implemented by any Web server that supports servlets. By using this API, the servlet programmer is insulated from the details of exactly how the Web server tracks sessions—it may use cookies or URL rewriting behind the scenes.

Here is how the session API is used by the servlet programmer. The `HttpSession` object can be used to hold and retrieve session-related data. This object is an instance of the `javax.servlet.http.HttpSession` type, and can be obtained from the HTTP `request` object by calling its `getSession(boolean create)` method. If the `boolean` argument to the `getSession()` method is `true`, then a new session is started for this request if a session does not already exist. Otherwise, the object representing the existing HTTP session is returned. If `getSession(false)` is called instead, a `null` value is returned if a session does not exist. A servlet that creates a session is called a *stateful* servlet. *Stateless* servlets do not use sessions.

After the session object has been obtained through the `getSession()` call, a servlet can use it to store session-related data, such as a database connection or a shopping cart. This data is then accessible to all servlets subsequently invoked in the same HTTP session. Data is stored and retrieved from the `session` object using the `setAttribute()` and `getAttribute()` methods. For example, the following servlet code fragment first gets a `session` object, initializes a database connection object `conn`, and then associates a session attribute named `dbConnection` with the `conn` object:

```
public void doGet(HttpServletRequest request,
                  HttpServletResponse response)
        throws ServletException, IOException {
    ... ...
    // first, get the session object
```

```
javax.servlet.http.HttpSession session = request.getSession(true);
// initialize database connection
java.sql.Connection conn = … …;
// store database connection in the session object
session.setAttribute("dbConnection", conn);
… …
}
```

Subsequently, the database connection handle can be retrieved from the session object using the dbConnection key in the getAttribute() method, as follows:

```
java.sql.Connection conn = (java.sql.Connection)
                      session.getAttribute("dbConnection");
```

Notice that a cast is required to convert the retrieved object to the appropriate type. A method named removeAttribute(String name) is also available on the HttpSession type to delete a stored value.

The Servlet Context

In some cases, a Web application may need to maintain not just session-related state, but state that is associated with the entire application. For example, a pool of open database connections may need to be shared across all sessions in a Web application. Now, exactly what constitutes a Web application? It is a collection of programs and resources that perform a specific task, such as Web-based expense reporting. A Web application can consist of static HTML pages, logos and images, servlets and JSP pages, software components such as JavaBeans and Enterprise JavaBeans, supporting utility classes, and various other resources. Each Web application generally corresponds to a distinct path within the Web server. For example, an online expense reporting application could be located at http://www.data-i.com/webexpense. All URLs with this prefix refer to programs and resources within that application. This path is known as the *application root*, and is generally unique for each Web application.

For Servlet 2.2 implementations, each individual Web application corresponds to a distinct ServletContext instance. The ServletContext object is of type javax.servlet.ServletContext. A handle to this object can be retrieved by all servlets and JSP pages in the application by calling the getServletContext() method. The ServletContext object provides many useful methods. They can be used for several purposes, including the following:

■ To get information about the Web server. For example, the getServerInfo() and getMajorVersion() methods return information on the servlet engine and the supported version.

■ To get information about the Web application. For example, the
`getInitParameter()` and `getInitParameterNames()` return
information about the initialization parameters associated with the
`ServletContext` object. The `getRealPath()` method returns the
real path information for a given virtual path, such as `/welcome.html`.

■ To write messages to a log file through the `log()` method.

■ To share data across the entire application. Data representing the shared
state may be stored, retrieved, and deleted from the `ServletContext`
object using the methods `setAttribute()`, `getAttribute()`, and
`removeAttribute()`. These methods are similar to the corresponding
methods in the `HttpSession` object discussed previously.

■ To obtain a `RequestDispatcher` object for invoking other servlets and
JSP pages in the Web application. You will learn more about request
dispatching in Chapter 10.

The complete set of methods available for the `ServletContext` object appears
in Appendix A. The following code fragment shows an example of printing server
information, storing a variable named `connPool` in the context attribute named
`dbConnectionPool`, and making an entry in the log:

```
public void doGet(HttpServletRequest request,
                  HttpServletResponse response)
             throws ServletException, IOException {
 ... ... ...

ServletContext scontext = getServletContext();
PrintWriter out = response.getWriter();
out.println("Here is my server information:" +
             scontext.getServerInfo());
 ... ... ...
scontext.setAttribute("dbConnectionPool", connPool);
scontext.log("Database connection pool created.");
 ... ... ...
}
```

Servlet Implementations

For the Apache Web server, a popular servlet engine is Apache JServ. The Apache
Web server and JServ servlet engine are used in the Oracle Internet Application
Server (iAS) release 1.0. However, JServ implements the Servlet 2.0 interface only,
and is being superseded by engines like Tomcat that support the Servlet 2.2 API. It is
still useful to know about JServ, since it is being actively used in many environments.
Apache JServ consists of two separate components, one written in C and the other

written in Java. The C part is known as `mod_jserv`, and serves as a "connector" that links the Apache Web server to the Java part, which is the actual servlet engine.

The reference implementation for the Servlet 2.1 API is the Java Web Server from Sun Microsystems, which was released as part of the JavaServer Web Development Kit (JSWDK). This implementation is being superseded by the Tomcat project, which is a joint undertaking of Apache Software Foundation and Sun Microsystems. Tomcat serves as the reference implementation for the Servlet 2.2 specification. There are several other servlet engines available from different vendors, such as JRun from Allaire. Oracle8*i* release 8.1.7 provides a servlet engine, called the Oracle Servlet Engine, that runs within the database. This servlet engine implements the Servlet 2.2 API and executes on the Java Virtual Machine embedded in Oracle8*i*. The benefit of running servlet and JSP programs inside the database is that they can be executed closest to SQL data (using the server-side Oracle JDBC driver), in the secure environment of the database.

Introducing JavaServer Pages

The JavaServer Pages (JSP) technology is built on the servlet model described previously. The basic idea of JSP is to allow Java code to be mixed with static HTML or XML templates. The purpose of the Java logic is to generate dynamic content in the page, while the markup language handles structuring and presentation of data. A major design goal of JSP is to support clean separation of HTML or XML text from Java code so that the Web designers who handle presentation need not be expert Java programmers. To this end, the JSP specification provides built-in facilities for component-based programming through JavaBeans and tag libraries. You will get an overview of these techniques in the next section, and learn more about them in Part IV of this book.

The JSP technology is quite new, but it has gained wide support from Web application developers and the industry, and is evolving rapidly. The final version of the JSP 1.1 specification was published in November 1999, and the next version (1.2) is currently in progress.

At present, there are several vendors, including Oracle, that support JSP in their Web product offerings. The Oracle Internet Application Server (iAS) product released in June 2000 is based on the Apache Web server and the JServ servlet engine, and includes Oracle's own JSP implementation. Oracle release 8.1.7 has an integrated Servlet 2.2 and JSP 1.1 engine that can directly execute JSP and servlet programs within the database (using the embedded Java Virtual Machine). The reference implementations for the JSP 1.1 and Servlet 2.2 specifications are provided by the Tomcat server, which is being developed under the Apache Software Foundation (http://www.apache.org) with the close cooperation of Sun Microsystems and other industry partners. Earlier, the JSP 1.0 reference implementation was released by Sun Microsystems as part of the Java Web Server (JWS) and the JavaServer Web

Development Kit (JSWDK). Appendix E provides instructions on how to install the Oracle JSP engine with the JServ, JWS, and Tomcat servlet engines.

A Basic JSP Program

You saw an example of a simple servlet, the `HelloServlet`, in the preceding section. It reads the user's name supplied as an HTTP request parameter, and prints out a greeting and the current time. Rewriting this servlet as a JSP is a good exercise to understand the differences between the two programming models. The equivalent JSP code looks as follows:

```
<!-- Program name: WelcomeUser.jsp
  -- Purpose:       Greet the user and print the current time
  -->
<HTML>
  <HEAD><TITLE>The WelcomeUser JSP </TITLE><HEAD>
  <BODY>
    <H2> Hello <%= request.getParameter("user") %>, how are you?</H2>
    <P><B> The current time is <%= new java.util.Date() %>.
    <P>     Hope you have a nice day! </B></P>
  </BODY>
</HTML>
```

Notice that the Java code (shown in bold) in the JSP page is embedded in the HTML code through special `<% ... %>` notation. In particular, the `<%= ... %>` construct is used to embed Java expressions. These expressions are evaluated at runtime, their values converted to strings, and printed out as part of the response. You can also embed general Java statements, knows as *scriptlets*, to execute conditional and other dynamic logic in your JSP page.

In the `WelcomeUser.jsp` example, the method call `request.getParameter("user")` retrieves the parameter named `user` from the HTTP `request` object, just as in the `HelloServlet.java` code. However, no explicit declaration is necessary for the `request` object—it is implicitly available in a JSP. You will learn much more about the convenient shortcut JSP syntax and implicitly defined objects in Chapter 10.

It is immediately clear that the JSP program is much more compact and easier to write than the code for `HelloServlet`. As you can see in `WelcomeUser.jsp`, the static text or the dynamic expressions do not need to be printed out with explicit `println()` method calls as in the servlet. In this example, there are also no methods declared and no exceptions thrown in the JSP. Obviously, there is a lot of magic going on behind the scenes here. You will now learn how a JSP is compiled and executed.

JSP Execution Model

All JSP programs are executed by a JSP engine that runs within the Web server. The JSP engine generally runs as a servlet that is invoked whenever the request URL ends with a `.jsp` extension. This invocation scheme is known as *extension mapping*.

When the JSP engine is called, it first locates the JSP file referenced in the URL. If this file has not been previously translated, the JSP engine converts the "mixed" JSP source code into Java servlet code. The generated code conforms to the rules laid down by the JSP specification, and makes use of various JSP runtime classes (you will see a sample of generated code in Chapter 10). The details of the generated code are normally not of direct interest to a JSP programmer, but are relevant only for understanding the JSP execution mechanism. To give a brief overview, the generated servlet class implements the standard `javax.servlet.jsp.HttpJspPage` **interface**. This interface extends a supertype `javax.servlet.jsp.JspPage` that has two methods: `jspInit()` and `jspDestroy()`. These methods are invoked by the JSP engine to initialize and destroy the generated servlet. The `javax.servlet.jsp.HttpJspPage` **interface** additionally contains another method, `_jspService()`. This method is intended to generate the output page and is used to handle multithreaded processing of HTTP requests, just like the `service()` method in servlets. The `_jspService()` method contains the dynamic code such as JSP expressions and scriptlets that are embedded in the JSP page. The generated servlet code is compiled into Java bytecode using a standard Java compiler. Finally, the generated servlet class is loaded and executed on the servlet engine, and the results are returned to the client.

Subsequent or concurrently arriving requests invoke the same `_jspService()` method using a new thread spawned by the servlet engine. Therefore, care must generally be taken to ensure thread safety of the JSP code—for example, if there are class-level variable declarations. Alternatively, a JSP can choose the single-thread model of execution described earlier for servlets. It elects this option through a JSP *directive* in the page (JSP directives are described in Chapter 10). When the JSP class is finally unloaded (for example, when the Web server is shut down), its `jspDestroy()` method is called by the JSP engine. The JSP life cycle is thus very similar to the servlet life cycle discussed earlier, and is shown in Figure 2-7.

It is instructive to look more closely at what happens when you invoke a JSP by typing in a URL in your Web browser. Consider, for example, the following URL:

```
http://localhost:8080/examples/jsp/chapter2/WelcomeUser.jsp?user=Tara
```

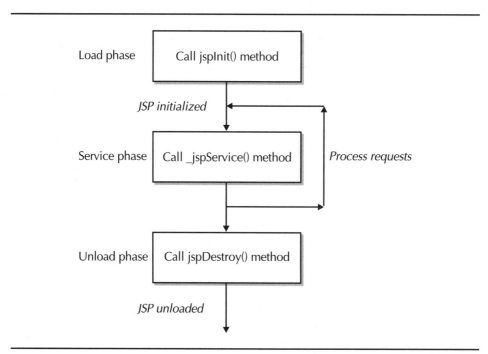

FIGURE 2-7. *Life cycle of a JSP*

Upon submission of this request, the following actions are typically carried out within the Web server:

1. The JSP engine is invoked because the request URL (without the query string user=Tara) ends in a .jsp extension.

2. The JSP engine locates the file WelcomeUser.jsp through the path hierarchy examples/jsp/chapter2 on the Web server. If the file cannot be found, a 404 HTTP status code is returned in the response.

3. After the JSP source file is found, the JSP engine determines if it needs to be translated—for example, if the class file is not present or the source has changed since the last translation. If translation is not required, execution control jumps to step 6.

4. The JSP engine translates the JSP file. This generates a servlet class definition in a Java source file, whose name is derived from the JSP filename (the exact name of the class is implementation dependent).

5. The generated Java code is compiled, producing bytecode for a servlet.

6. If the generated class has not been loaded previously, it is now loaded and its `jspInit()` method is called to initialize the class.

7. The `_jspService()` method in the generated class is invoked, producing the same output as shown in Figure 2-3.

The preceding sequence of steps is summarized in the flow chart of Figure 2-8.

JSP Versus Servlet

The JSP programming model is designed to provide a number of benefits over servlets, including the following:

- JSP provides shorthand syntax for mixing static code with dynamic logic, and JSP code is typically much more compact and easier to understand compared to a servlet.

- JSP supports clean separation of Java code in components such as JavaBeans and JSP tag libraries (discussed next). This permits JSP pages to be written primarily by Web designers who can focus on the presentation of data, and simply hook in the components developed by Java programmers. In contrast, servlets are pure Java classes, and are usually written by Java developers who are not HTML experts. These factors make it much harder to write and maintain servlet code that involves any nontrivial amount of presentation logic.

- JSP supports the "rapid application development" (RAD) model, in which JSP source file translation is automatically managed by the JSP engine. Another advantage of JSP is XML-compatible syntax, so that the JSP pages can be authored using XML-based authoring tools.

So, when and why would you ever need to use a servlet? As always, there are pros and cons to every approach. The choice depends on what task you are trying to accomplish. For example, if your program needs to dynamically generate binary data such as an image in the output page, or upload a file from the client machine, using a servlet is more appropriate. A JSP is primarily meant for writing character data like static HTML text. The built-in output mechanism in JSP is based on the `javax.servlet.jsp.JspWriter` object, which provides various methods for output of scalar data types, but does not include methods for writing raw bytes. The

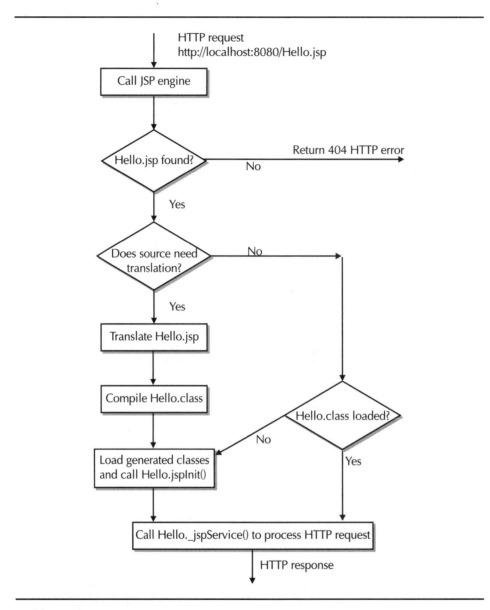

FIGURE 2-8. *Steps in compiling and running a JSP*

`JspWriter` object considers the character encoding of the generated output, which does not apply for unencoded byte streams. In contrast, a servlet provides two different mechanisms for writing data to the HTTP `response` object:

- The `response.getWriter()` method returns a `java.io.PrintWriter` object for writing character data. This data typically contains HTML tags and text in a local language that are interpreted appropriately by the browser using the character encoding of the HTTP response header.

- The `response.getOutputStream()` method returns a `javax.servlet.ServletOutputStream` object for writing binary data.

It is important to remember that both the JSP and servlet models are based on Java, and therefore both models inherit all the power and flexibility of the Java platform. The differences between the two models are solely in the level of abstraction and programming convenience that they provide. In particular, it is possible to call a servlet from a JSP, and vice versa. You see examples of this type of interoperation in Chapter 10.

Web Application Architecture

An essential design criterion of Web applications is ease of use. However, hidden behind the simple screens and attractive graphics are complex and powerful computational modules. For example, an online shopping facility provides user-friendly screens to browse around the product offerings and select items. At the "checkout" step, the business transaction typically involves making a payment through a credit card, storing the order in a database, and providing follow-up and tracking information to the purchaser. All of these tasks require secure, reliable, and scalable server-side application programs. You will now learn about architectures that support modular development and easy maintenance of such Web applications. These architectures make effective use of software *components*.

You learned about software components in the previous chapter. To review the concept, a software component is a program module with a well-defined interface and invocation semantics. For Web programming with servlets and JSP, such components can be used to generate dynamic content, which is then cleanly integrated with the static text and HTML presentation tags. The major benefit of using components is that they can be developed independently by Java programmers, while the presentation logic is written by HTML experts. Thus, a component-based JSP programming model effectively separates the roles and responsibilities of software developers from Web designers, whose skill sets generally do not overlap.

You will now explore different schemes for designing a Web application with JSP pages, starting with a very simple architecture and moving to progressively more sophisticated schemes. Which architecture you should choose depends on the needs of your application. However, keep in mind that the requirements of most applications evolve with time, and it is best to start with an architecture that will allow modular and scalable enhancement of functionality in the future, although it may seem overly complex for your initial needs.

The Java2 Enterprise Edition supports various types of components, including JavaBeans and Enterprise JavaBeans. Additionally, one can implement CORBA components in Java. The JSP 1.1 specification also introduced the notion of *tag libraries*, which are packaged utilities that can be easily invoked from a JSP through custom tags. In the discussion that follows, you will see how these different types of components can be used with JSP pages to design modular Web applications.

A Simple-Minded Application Architecture

First, consider what happens without a component-based programming style. This simple-minded architecture is shown in Figure 2-9. An example of this approach would be a JSP that opens and manages a database connection for an online shopping service in the page itself. Another example is a JSP that calls an EJB or CORBA component directly. This design scheme can be easy to program, but is adequate only for small applications. The disadvantage is that the JSP source can soon get unwieldy and cluttered up with excessive programming logic, such as JDBC calls and EJB lookup through JNDI routines. Ultimately this approach is likely to cause maintenance problems. Additionally, this simple page-based architecture may encounter scalability problems in handling simultaneous requests from a large number of clients, because of inadequate sharing of critical resources such as database connections.

Component-Based JSP Architecture

Using JavaBeans is one way to improve the simple architecture shown in Figure 2-9. JavaServer Pages have been specifically designed for use with JavaBeans. There are several standard JSP tags, such as `<jsp:useBean>` and `<jsp:setProperty>`, that support easy creation and manipulation of JavaBean components.

So, what is a JavaBean? In essence, a JavaBean is a standard Java class that follows certain design rules. It must be a **public** class, with a **public** constructor that has no arguments. Additionally, a typical characteristic of a JavaBean is that it has a set of attributes or *properties*, and it provides **public** accessor methods to read and write

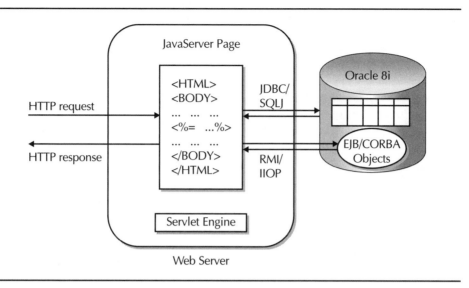

FIGURE 2-9.   *A simple-minded Web application architecture*

the property values. The JavaBean specification (which is part of the Java2 framework) defines default naming conventions for these accessor methods, so that they can be automatically inferred based on the property names. For example, the default names for the accessor methods of a property named X are getX() and setX(). A simple JavaBean class SimpleBean.java is shown in Listing 2-2.

Listing 2-2   A simple JavaBean

```
public class SimpleBean {
   public SimpleBean() {};
   private int X;  // a property of the bean
   public int getX() {  // getter method for property X
     return this.X;
   }
   public void setX(int newX) {  // setter method for property X
     this.X = newX;
   }
```

It is possible to use other names for the bean accessor methods, but in that case an accompanying "descriptor" class (of type java.beans.BeanInfo) must explicitly provide this information. These design rules followed by a JavaBean permit its properties to be dynamically examined and manipulated by the environment in which the bean is embedded.

A word of caution is necessary here—do not confuse a JavaBean with an Enterprise Java Bean! The names are similar, but their capabilities are very different. JavaBeans were originally designed for use in graphical user interfaces, but they also fit in well as easy-to-use components in a JSP. Typically, a JSP instantiates a JavaBean class through the `<jsp:useBean>` tag, sets its properties from the HTTP request parameters through the `<jsp:setProperty>` tag, and then calls the methods of the bean to generate dynamic content. In comparison, Enterprise JavaBeans are a much more heavyweight concept, with container-managed transactions and security. They are primarily designed to function as scalable and transactional business components in enterprise settings and distributed environments, as you will learn in Part II of this book.

Figure 2-10 shows an application architecture that uses JavaBeans, EJB components, and CORBA objects with JSP pages. One or more JavaBeans can be used in a JSP page to encapsulate the dynamic logic—for example, to execute SQL operations in the database, or call an EJB (which may itself access a database for transaction processing). This separation permits clean factoring of Java code from HTML, and makes maintenance easier. Note that you could directly call EJB and CORBA components in a JSP instead of going through a JavaBean. However, this approach has the previously noted problem of cluttering the JSP with Java code for JNDI lookup logic and exception handling. Therefore, it is often cleaner to use a JavaBean or a servlet as a "wrapper" for the EJB or CORBA object. You will see

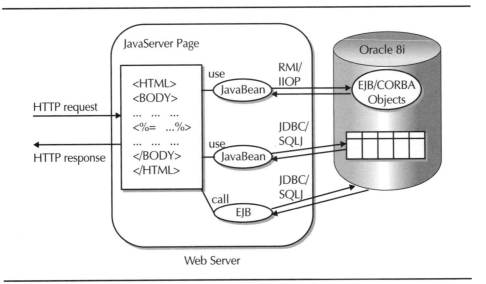

FIGURE 2-10.   *Component-based JSP architecture*

examples of this approach in Chapter 12. One obvious issue here is that the wrapper JavaBean or servlet must keep up with any changes made to the methods of the EJB or CORBA component.

The "Model-View-Controller" Architecture

The architecture shown in Figure 2-10 is doubtless an improvement over that of Figure 2-9. However, it may not be the best solution for more complex scenarios. For example, consider an application that requires the user to first authenticate. This is a very common requirement for Web applications. Validation of request parameters is also frequently necessary. It is advisable in these cases to factor out the "front-end" application logic into a separate servlet or JSP that does no presentation. This program intercepts client requests and typically initializes JavaBean, EJB, and other components before dispatching to other JSP pages that handle the presentation of computed data. The EJB and JavaBean components represent the "model," the presentation JSP pages define the "view," and the front-end JSP or servlet acts as the "controller" for request processing. Hence, the name "model-view-controller" (or MVC in short) is often used for this architecture. It is also known as the "Model 2" design pattern, based on terminology used in the early versions of the JSP specification. This architecture is illustrated in Figure 2-11.

Benefits of the MVC architecture include very clean separation of dynamic content and presentation. The controller JSP or servlet provides a single entry

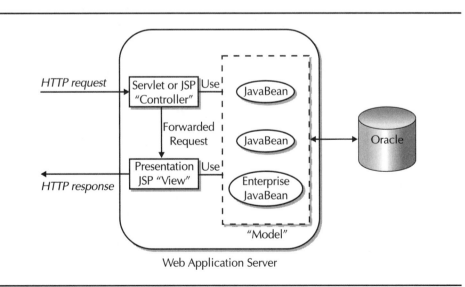

FIGURE 2-11. *The model-view-controller architecture*

point to the Web application, where the logic for user authentication, parameter validation, EJB lookups, and other such tasks can be conveniently centralized. The controller program can also dynamically select different presentation JSP pages, depending on the request parameters or the capabilities of the client— thus providing different views of the same data. The presentation JSP pages simply retrieve any JavaBean, EJB, or CORBA components that have been previously initialized by the controller program, and call the appropriate methods to cleanly extract and present the dynamic content.

Using JSP Tag Libraries

As you have learned, JSP is designed for use with JavaBean components. In addition to standard action tags such as `<jsp:include>` and `<jsp:forward>`, JSP provides several built-in tags to facilitate the use of JavaBeans. However, what if you wanted tags for plugging in other types of components that are more general than JavaBeans? A JavaBean must by definition have a no-argument constructor, so that it can be instantiated without any parameters from the embedding environment. This requirement is restrictive if initializing the component does involve passing some parameters. Also, the JavaBeans used in a JSP do not by default have access to the JSP context in which they are invoked, unless such logic is explicitly programmed. In short, under certain circumstances, more flexibility is necessary than what is provided by the set of built-in tags.

Rather than define additional tags, the JSP 1.1 specification introduces a portable tag extension mechanism for JSP pages. This scheme is based on *tag libraries*, which are pre-packaged utilities capable of being invoked through custom action tags in a JSP page. Briefly, here is how the scheme works. A custom action tag, or custom tag in short, has a specific name, zero or more attributes, and an optional body. Each custom tag corresponds to a *tag handler* class. The set of custom tags available in a tag library is described in a *tag library descriptor* file (which is written in XML). There is a special `taglib` directive that can be used to indicate which tag libraries are being used in a JSP page. Using this directive, you can specify the descriptor file associated to a tag library and the prefix that you will use for the custom tags in the tag library.

For example, the JSP page shown in Listing 2-3 uses SQL tags from the tag library named `sqltaglib.tld` that is located in the `WEB-INF` directory relative to the Web application root. These tags have a (local) prefix `ora`. The tags `<ora:dbOpen>`, `<ora:dbQuery>`, and `<ora:dbClose>` are used to open the database, execute a

SQL query and display the results as an HTML table, and close the database connection, respectively. You will learn more about using these tags in Chapter 12.

Listing 2-3   A JSP page with custom tags for SQL operations

```
<%@ taglib uri="/WEB-INF/sqltaglib.tld" prefix="ora" %>
 <HTML>
   <HEAD><TITLE> Example of a Tag Library </TITLE></HEAD>
    <BODY BGCOLOR="white">
       <ora:dbOpen URL="jdbc:oracle:oci8:@"
                    user="jspuser" password="jsp" connId="conn">
                    </ora:dbOpen>
       <ora:dbQuery connId="conn">
            select * from EMPLOYEE_LIST
       </ora:dbQuery>
       <ora:dbClose connId="conn" />
       <HR>
    </BODY>
 </HTML>
```

At runtime, the JSP engine invokes the appropriate tag handler class for each custom tag encountered in the page. This invocation is done through tag extension classes and interfaces defined by the JSP 1.1 specification. The properties of the tag handler class (which is implemented as a JavaBean class!) include the `PageContext` object for the JSP page and are set by the JSP engine during request processing. Thus, the tag library framework essentially provides a component model with convenient syntax.

The tag extension mechanism is very powerful, since it makes the JSP tag framework completely modular and extensible without sacrificing portability. Although this feature is quite new, several vendors already provide custom tag libraries (see http://jsptags.com for pointers to resources). You can easily design your own tag library with custom tags for your special component, and run it on different JSP engines. You will learn how to write your own custom tags in the "Using JSP Tag Libraries" section in Chapter 12.

Other Design Options

In addition to the architectures discussed, there are other choices in designing modular Web applications, depending on the specific requirements of your environment. For example, if the HTML template text is not static but must be determined at runtime depending on request parameters, then you can use the `<jsp:include>` and `<jsp:forward>` action tags to dynamically select the appropriate template text. You will see examples of this type of request processing in Chapter 10. In addition to dynamically choosing static HTML files, it is also possible to transfer request processing to general Web resources and in particular to other JSP pages and servlets, creating a "nested" workflow model. A detailed discussion of the various architectural choices for JSP applications and their comparative benefits appears in the book entitled *Professional JSP* by Karl Avedal et al, Wrox Press Inc.

Conclusion

This chapter introduces you to server-side Web programming with servlets and JSP. First, you learned about the basic concept of a Web server. The scope of the Internet has been tremendously expanded by browser-based easy access to files and programs hosted on a Web server running on a remote machine. E-business activities on the Internet have experienced a huge boom over the last two years, and the trend is here to stay. The HTTP protocol and the HTML markup language work hand in hand to provide simple but powerful frameworks for data transport and presentation across networks. They are the foundation of Web-based interactions. Java servlets and JavaServer Pages (JSP) are relatively new techniques for generating dynamic Web pages. They build on the HTTP and HTML technologies, and being Java-based, they have full access to the power, flexibility, and portability of the object-oriented Java platform.

In this chapter, you learned about some important features of the Servlet API, such as session tracking for "stateful" applications, and saw an example of a simple servlet. You understood the steps taken by the servlet container to run servlet programs, and the different stages in the servlet life cycle. Understanding servlets is key to understanding the JSP model, because it is based on the servlet framework. The JSP model has rapidly gained wide popularity among both Web designers and Java developers because of its convenient script-like tags and integrated support for component programming. Using the special `<% ... %>` notation in a JSP page, Java code can be embedded within HTML or XML text to generate dynamic content. JSP pages are therefore quicker and easier to write compared to servlets. Before execution, JSP sources are translated to Java servlets, and then run using the servlet engine. The JSP engine extends the functionality of the servlet engine with high-productivity features such as automatic retranslation of JSP files. This facility helps in the rapid development of your Web application. You also learned about the differences between the servlet and JSP models, and under what circumstances one approach is preferable over the other.

Last but not the least, you learned about designing modular and scalable Web applications. The JSP framework supports clean separation of the static content from the dynamic data through built-in support for JavaBean components. In addition, the JSP 1.1 specification defines a powerful tag extension framework for using third-party tag libraries and for building custom tags. JSP and servlet programs can also invoke Enterprise JavaBeans and CORBA objects; these components are typically used to encapsulate transactional business logic. You learned how these modular components can be used to build sophisticated Web applications that are easy to develop, understand, and maintain.

Part IV of this book, consisting of Chapters 10–12, deals with JSP programming. Basic programming techniques for JSP pages are covered in Chapter 10. Chapter 11 focuses on component-based development with JavaBeans and JSP, with emphasis on database applications. In Chapter 12, you will learn how to build Web applications with JSP and other types of components, such as Enterprise JavaBeans and CORBA objects deployed in Oracle8*i*. You will also learn how to use JSP tag libraries. As you will see, JSP and Java servlets are truly powerful tools for building sophisticated Web applications that manage their complexity through well-defined modular components.

PART II

Building Enterprise
JavaBean Components

CHAPTER 3

Introduction to Enterprise JavaBeans (EJBs)

nterprise JavaBeans (EJBs) is an architecture for component based distributed computing, *Enterprise JavaBeans Specification Version 1.0*, Sun Microsystems, Inc. EJB is a server-side component model that addresses issues that involve the management of distributed business objects in a multitier architecture. EJB components are Java components that run on a server (application or database server). They can run and execute anywhere, in any environment that has a Java interpreter (a Java Virtual Machine (JVM)) and an EJB container. Enterprise JavaBeans allows applications to communicate across multitier client and server environments, and across Internet and intranet structures. To effectively use Enterprise JavaBeans, you must understand the EJB technology. The book includes three chapters on the subject. In this chapter, you learn the overall architecture of EJB along with its major components, whereas in Chapters 4 and 5 you learn how to apply this knowledge while building EJB components that implement business rules. Although the material is quite theoretical, a good understanding of it is fundamental for any application developers who want to develop EJB applications.

In this chapter, you will consider

- The elements of the Enterprise JavaBeans Specification 1.0. An EJB 1.1 Specification was released on December 17, 1999. However, the major structures of the EJB framework are common to both releases and have not changed from one to the other. So, you will learn the major elements of the EJB 1.1 Specification while learning those of the EJB 1.0 release.

- The components of the EJB architecture.

- The components of an EJB application.

- Types of Enterprise JavaBeans: session Beans and entity Beans.

- The EJB deployment descriptor.

- The `ejb-jar` file.

- The transaction management and security for EJBs.

- The EJB exceptions.

- The benefits of Enterprise JavaBeans.

- The Oracle8*i* JServer architecture: JServer includes an EJB server and EJB container.

- How to write your first Enterprise JavaBean.

In Chapter 1, you learned the concept of components. Remember that *components* are predeveloped pieces of application code that can be assembled into working application systems. They provide robust and reusable business logic. A component can live anywhere on a network, in the same address space (computer) as a client, application server, or database server.

The EJB Specification (1.0 or 1.1) defines the basic architecture of an EJB component, specifying the structure of its interfaces and the mechanisms by which it interacts with its container and with other components. Moreover, it provides guidelines to create and implement EJB components that can work together to form a larger application. Application builders can combine EJB components from different developers or different vendors to construct an application.

The Enterprise JavaBeans initiative was announced at the JavaOne 97 Conference, and a draft was posted in December, 1997. The EJB 1.0 formal specification was released on March 21, 1998. The final release of the most recent EJB Specification, Enterprise JavaBeans 1.1, was posted on December 17, 1999. The EJB 1.1 Specification brought many changes that hinder the forward compatibility of Beans originally developed for EJB 1.0 containers. Depending on the vendor's implementation, the migration of 1.0-compatible enterprise Beans to 1.1 can be quite painful. EJB components developed with 1.0 will not work with 1.1.

The Oracle8*i* versions 8.1.5 and 8.1.6 implement the EJB version 1.0 Specification, thus providing a server and container that host 1.0-compatible enterprise Beans. Both database versions support session Beans only, as required by the specification. Entity beans will be supported in the 8.1.7 release, scheduled to be available sometime this year. Oracle8*i* version 8.1.7 will be 1.1 compliant. Note that session Bean codes developed to execute in the Oracle8*i* EJB container in versions 8.1.5 and 8.1.6 will also run in 8.1.7. The majority of enterprise Beans that you will develop in the book have been deployed (as is, code wise) in the Oracle8*i* database versions 8.1.5 and 8.1.6 and the 8.1.7 (beta version). However, note that Beans deployed in a specific release must be recompiled before redeployment in another release. For example, if you have deployed Enterprise JavaBeans in the Oracle8*i* database version 8.1.5 and want to deploy the same Beans in 8.1.6 or the upcoming 8.1.7 release, you must recompile all the components before deploying them. Additionally, for the 8.1.7 release only, you will need to change code if you are doing client-side transaction demarcation or if you are using the Java Transaction Service (JTS) directly. You will learn more about client-side transaction demarcation programs (EJB and CORBA client programs) and the use of JTS in Chapters 4 and 9, respectively.

In this chapter, you will learn about the major elements of the EJB 1.0. To learn more about the differences between EJB specifications, see *Enterprise JavaBeans 1.1 Documentation* and *Create Forward-Compatible Beans in EJB, Part 1,* http://java.sun.com/ products/ejb/docs.html and http://www.javaworld.com/javaworld/jw-12-1999/jw-12-ssj ejb1.html.

Enterprise JavaBeans Specification (1.0)

The Enterprise JavaBeans (Sun Microsystems) specification is a framework for Java server-side services that details services such as transactions, security, and naming. A framework is a set of classes that embodies an abstract design for solutions to a family of related problems. A *transaction* is an atomic unit of work consisting of one or more operations where all changes performed by these operations are executed as a whole and are either totally applied or totally undone. Operations that are applied as a whole are called *commit*, whereas undone operations are called *rollback*.

The EJB 1.0 Specification defines the major structures of the EJB framework. It defines the interfaces and general behavior of Enterprise JavaBeans components, including the two types of enterprise Beans such as session Beans, which contain business-process models, and entity Beans that can act as persistent data containers on the network. Moreover, EJB 1.0 defines the contract between the EJB components, which specifies their role, responsibility, and the services that they must provide.

Vendors that want to create EJB server implementations must provide the required services as stated in the EJB Specification (1.0 or 1.1). Today, many vendors such as BEA, GemStone, IBM, Persistence Software, Netscape/Sun, Oracle, Borland, Tandem, Symantec, Sybase, and Visigenic have adapted their solutions to support the EJB Specification.

Enterprise JavaBeans Design Goals

The EJB specification has several design goals:

- **Operating-system independent**   Enterprise JavaBeans can run on any platform, such as UNIX, Microsoft Windows, Hewlett-Packard, and Mac OS.

- **Middleware independent**   EJB components can run on any middleware solution that implements the EJB specification.

- **Interoperability between enterprise Beans with other Java programming language APIs, non-Java programming language applications, and CORBA**   CORBA and non-Java clients can use enterprise Beans and vice versa. However, this is not true in most implementations. At the present time, only primitive types and remote object references are interoperable.

- **Ease of development and deployment of distributed applications.**

- **Component reusability and portability**   Developers can reuse Enterprise JavaBeans, and they are portable from one EJB vendor to another.

Enterprise JavaBeans Roles

The EJB Specification establishes six roles in the application development and deployment of EJB components:

■ The *Bean provider* is responsible for writing the required interfaces and classes as defined in the Specification. If you are a Java developer, you can easily become a Bean provider; that is, you can develop your own EJB components. Remember that EJB components are Java components. Enterprise JavaBeans are simple, portable, reusable, and deployable components for implementing business logic. You can also purchase existing Enterprise JavaBeans and plug them into your application, or you can combine your own with those of other vendors to build your application. The interesting aspect of your job as a Bean provider is that you no longer have to worry about complex issues such as multi-threaded, transactional, and distributed process computing. Consequently, you can concentrate on writing applications that deal strictly with the business logic rather than communication and network issues.

■ The *application assembler* gathers one or more Beans developed by the Bean providers to produce larger application units (new enterprise Beans or non-EJB applications). This role is defined in both EJB 1.0 and 1.1. Additionally, the 1.1 version of the EJB Specification addresses the issue of the ability to specify external references that the Bean may make at runtime. External references come into play when a Bean wants to call another Bean. In this scenario, the Bean assembler must provide a linkage between the Beans when assembling the application unit.

■ The *deployer*, an expert at a specific operational environment, is responsible for correctly installing the EJB classes and interfaces in the EJB server. For example, if a Bean provider develops Enterprise JavaBeans and wants to deploy them in an Oracle8*i* database, the Oracle database administrator (DBA) will deploy your Beans in the database. In this book, you will acquire the skills to deploy your Beans. However, more than likely, your DBA will assume this role. At deployment time, a deployer will make the EJB home **interface** object available for clients to use enterprise Beans. To make the Bean available, EJB server vendors must provide a namespace and a Bean home reference name to clients that want to use the Bean. A *namespace* is a hierarchical collection of objects and is analogous to UNIX system files and directories. Oracle and other EJB server vendors provide a JNDI-accessible namespace to store the home object reference. Sun Microsystems supplies JNDI in the `javax.naming` package. The *Java Naming and Directory Interface* (JNDI) API (Sun

Microsystems, Inc.) is an API that provides directory and naming functionality to Java applications. It is defined to be independent of any specific directory service implementation. JNDI allows Java applications to access a variety of directories in a uniform way. To learn more about the JNDI API, see Chapter 5 of the book and *Java Naming and Directory Interface Application Programming (JNDI API)*, http://java.sun.com/products/jndi/.

■ The *server provider*, a vendor (operating system (OS), middleware, or database), provides an EJB server that can implement a session and entity Bean container. An EJB server is an application framework in which EJB containers run. The server provider can include containers and deployment tools for their specific server and can publish their low-level interfaces so other vendors can develop containers and deployment tools that interoperate with theirs.

■ The *container provider* is responsible for providing software tools to install EJB classes and interfaces into an EJB server; it also provides tools to monitor and manage the container that in turn monitors and manages the Beans at runtime. For example, Oracle provides the `deployejb` software tool that allows the deployer to generate the Java classes that clients use to access EJB home and remote objects. You will learn more about the Oracle `deployejb` tool in subsequent sections of this chapter. Additionally, the container providers supply installation of references in a JNDI-accessible namespace and versioning support for installed EJB components. The integration and accessibility of services in a server using JNDI is addressed partially in the EJB 1.1 Specification and in more detail in the Java 2 Enterprise Edition (J2EE) Specification.

■ The *system administrator* uses runtime monitoring and management tools to oversee the system. The EJB server and container providers usually provide these tools. Note that while an EJB server and container are two distinct components in an environment, the same vendor can provide both components. For example, Oracle Corporation has integrated an EJB server and EJB container inside the Oracle8*i* (versions 1.5 and 1.6) database.

Enterprise JavaBeans Architecture

Enterprise JavaBeans is an architecture for server-side components—in particular, components of distributed transaction applications. To understand how an EJB application works, you need to understand the basic parts of the EJB system.

The EJB architecture consists of several components:

■ The EJB server

■ The EJB container

- The EJB application

- The client application

Enterprise JavaBeans Server

The *EJB server* (see Figure 3-1) is the high-level application that manages the EJB *containers* and provides access to system services. It typically runs all the enterprise Beans within an `ejb-jar` file and provides service objects such as transaction and security services. Enterprise JavaBeans execute within an EJB container, which in turn executes within an EJB server. Any server that can host an EJB container and provides it with the necessary services can be an EJB server. Some examples of EJB servers are database, application, and middleware servers.

The EJB server implements system services outside the enterprise Beans, contains the EJB container, and provides the container with lower-level services such as network connectivity. In turn, the container provides services to the Bean. In the EJB 1.1 Specification, the EJB server is required to provide an object's availability and accessibility via JNDI and transaction services.

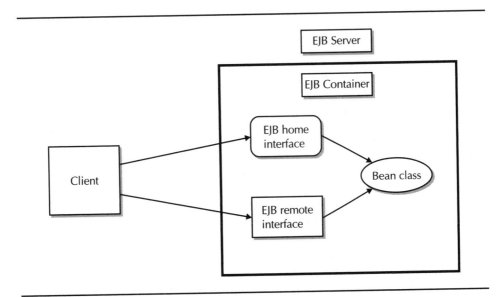

FIGURE 3-1. *Enterprise JavaBeans architecture*

Enterprise JavaBeans Container

Enterprise JavaBeans are components that live and operate in an EJB container. They do not operate in a vacuum. Container vendors are responsible for providing the necessary tools to install Enterprise JavaBeans in an EJB container.

An EJB container is an abstraction that separates the business logic from the underlying implementations. There are a lot of interactions between the Beans and the server. The container provides the appropriate services to the Bean so it can access its environment. It presents a uniform interface that manages the interactions between enterprise Beans and the server. It can manage many instances and many EJB components consisting of several EJB classes. The container resides in an EJB server that can reside anywhere on a network—for example, in application, database, or middleware servers. Consequently, the container can also exist anywhere its server resides. The EJB container provides a set of services, such as transaction and resource management (security, cache management, messaging management), versioning, scalability, mobility, persistence, and database connectivity, to the enterprise Bean it contains. Since the EJB container handles all these functions, the EJB component developer can concentrate on business rules—thus leaving service tasks to the container.

A container vendor will provide a set of tools or classes that run within the EJB server. For example, Oracle provides the `deployejb` and `session_sh` tools; the former allows you to deploy EJB components into the Oracle8*i* version 1.5 and higher, and the latter allows you to manipulate the namespace where the EJB object names reside. See the section of "The Oracle8*i* JServer Architecture" in this chapter and Appendix D, "SQLJ Quick Reference Guide" of the *Oracle8i SQLJ Programming* book to learn more about these tools.

Two of the major responsibilities of the container are to make the EJB objects accessible to the clients and respond to client lookups. It does so by creating and activating Enterprise JavaBeans as required. The container accomplishes the former by *publishing* the "names" of its contained Enterprise JavaBeans with some type of naming service (typically JNDI). The term "publish" refers to the act of storing in a namespace a reference to the EJB home and EJB objects. Remember that a namespace is analogous to a UNIX directory. Clients using EJB locate a home reference object via the `lookup()` method of the `javax.naming.Context` **interface**. The reference to the home object allows clients to create new Bean instances or use existing ones. Chapters 4 and 5 include more information regarding clients' lookup mechanisms.

An EJB user never interacts directly with the EJB container. An enterprise Bean's environment includes its context (`javax.ejb.SessionContext` or `javax.ejb.EntityContext`, depending on the type of EJB), a set of properties, and all the services that a Bean needs to perform the required business logic.

See Note 1 of "Note on Listing 3-6" in the "Enterprise Beans Class" section of this chapter for a detailed discussion on the `javax.ejb.Session Context` **interface**.

The EJB container does not implement or extend a specific interface or class from the EJB Specification. But it does have certain responsibilities (the "container contract" as defined by EJB 1.0 and 1.1) to which it must adhere. Remember that the container's first responsibility is to publish the "names" of the contained Enterprise JavaBeans with a naming service and must respond to JNDI lookups by creating and/or activating Enterprise JavaBeans when requested. Additionally, the container must give the Bean its `javax.naming.Context` object, through which all other environmental objects can be retrieved. The notion of context is defined in the `javax.naming.Context` **interface**. This interface represents a naming context, which consists of a set of name-to-object bindings and contains methods for examining and updating these bindings.

Components of an EJB Application

A component model defines a set of **interface**s and classes (for example, in the form
of Java packages) that must be used in a particular way. A component isolates and encapsulates a set of functionality. A component is developed for a specific purpose—not for a specific application—and once it is defined, it becomes an independent piece of software that can be distributed and used in other applications.

Enterprise JavaBeans are Java components that can be written in Java or SQLJ. SQLJ is an extension to Java that allows you to use static embedded SQL statements in your Java programs. Note that in static embedded SQL, all the SQL statements embedded in the program are known at compile time, while in dynamic (embedded) SQL at least some SQL statements are not completely known until runtime. JDBC allows Java developers to use dynamic embedded SQL in their Java programs, whereas SQLJ is used for embodiment of static SQL. To learn more about JDBC versus SQLJ, see the *Oracle8i SQLJ Programming* book.

Types of Enterprise JavaBeans

An enterprise Bean is a building block that can be used alone or with other enterprise Beans to build a larger application. There are two types of enterprise Beans: session Beans and entity Beans. Session Beans are an extension of the client application, and entity Beans are persistent objects (for example, rows of a database table). A nice feature of types of EJB containers (session or entity Bean containers) is that they manage the Bean's transaction and security environments for the Bean provider. Note that session Beans live in a session Bean container, whereas entity Beans live in an entity Bean container.

Session Beans

A session Bean is an object that is used by a single client and is not shared between several clients. The EJB 1.0 Specification refers to a session Bean as "a logical extension of the client program that runs on the server." Session Beans have the following characteristics:

- They represent a transient conversation with a single client and execute on behalf of this single client. Note that a client initiates a conversation with a session Bean when it invokes a method of a Bean class.

- They are relatively short-lived; that is, their life is associated with the life of the client that uses them. For example, a client database application establishes a database session when the client connects to the database. In Oracle8*i*, a client can use session Beans that are stored in the database. However, when the client disconnects or crashes, the Oracle8*i* EJB container will remove any session Bean that the client had requested.

- They can be transactional; thus they can be used to manipulate data in a database. For example, the Oracle8*i* EJB server allows you to write session Beans that can retrieve, insert, update, and remove data in relational tables as well as in tables of objects. Moreover, Beans' classes that implement business logic can call Java stored procedures, SQLJ stored procedures, and PL/SQL procedures and functions, and execute embedded dynamic (JDBC) and static SQL (SQLJ) statements.

Types of Session Beans: STATELESS and STATEFUL

At deployment time, a session Bean is specified as having either a STATELESS or a STATEFUL state management mode. A session Bean is said to be STATELESS when the Bean can be used by any client (moreover, its state is not retained across methods and transactions), or STATEFUL when the session Bean does retain its state. A STATELESS session Bean is referred to as a Bean that contains no conversational state, whereas a STATEFUL session Bean contains a conversational state. Note that the distinction between STATELESS and STATEFUL session Beans is not important to the Oracle8*i* EJB server. This is so because the Oracle8*i* ORB and Java VM run under the multi-threaded server (MTS).

Entity Beans

An entity Bean is a long-lived object that can be accessed from session to session and can be shared by multiple clients. Entity Beans have the following characteristics:

- They represent data from persistent storage devices, such as a database. Since data in databases are sharable (that is, accessible at the same time by multiple concurrent users), entity Beans therefore allow shared access from multiple users.

- They are transactional: Entity Beans allow developers to write applications that automatically update data that resides in databases. A nice feature of Enterprise JavaBeans (session or entity Beans) is that transaction management is no longer a developer's concern. Note that Enterprise JavaBeans live in an EJB container and a container runs in an EJB server. Transaction management is controlled by the EJB server and the EJB container.

- They are persistent and therefore survive crashes of the EJB server and do not die when clients die or disconnect from the database. As long as the data remains in the database, the entity Bean exists. The model can be used for relational, object-relational, or object-oriented databases.

The goal of this book is to teach you how to create session Beans for the Oracle8*i* database. The Oracle8*i* database (versions 1.5 and 1.6) implements only session Beans as required by the EJB 1.0 Specification. The upcoming Oracle8*i* 8.1.7 release will be 1.1-compliant, and thus will implement both session and entity Beans. Note that the definition of the components of an enterprise Bean have not changed from the EJB 1.0 Specification to the EJB 1.1 Specification, thus learning how to write 1.0-compatible session Beans is similar to learning how to write 1.1-compatible session Beans. However, if you want to learn more about entity Beans, see the Bibliography at the end of the book for a listing of material related to Enterprise JavaBeans, including entity Beans.

An enterprise Bean (session or entity) consists of the following components:

- The home **interface**.

- The remote **interface**.

- The Bean class. Note that you may create one or more Bean classes for your EJB application.

- The deployment descriptor.

Enterprise Home Interface

When a client needs to use an enterprise Bean, it does so via its home **interface**. An EJB server registers the EJBHome object with a specific name server so that clients can find a reference to it. Session or entity Beans must have their own EJB home **interface**. The Bean provider defines the home **interface**, and the EJB container creates (at deployment time) a class that implements it. The home **interface** lists methods for creating new Beans, removing Beans, and finding Beans. For example, a home **interface** includes one or more create() methods that clients can use to create a new Bean's instances. In this book, the concept of an instance refers to the concept of a Java instance, which is defined as an instance of Java class. A Java instance for a specific Java class is created at runtime via an instantiation of that class. Consequently, a Bean's instance gets created at runtime by the instantiation of a Bean class or enterprise Bean. You will learn more about a Bean class in subsequent sections of this chapter and in Chapter 4.

An enterprise Bean's home **interface** describes how a client program or another enterprise Bean creates, finds, and removes an enterprise Bean from its container. The EJB home **interface** is a Java RMI **interface**, and as such it must follow the rules of Java RMI interfaces. See the Remote Method Invocation Specification, http://java.sun.com./products/jdk/1.1/docs/guide/rmi/spec/rmiTOC.doc.html, to learn more about RMI.

The rules of Java RMI are as follows:

- Each method must declare java.rmi.RemoteException in its **throws** clause, in addition to any application-specific exceptions.

- A remote object of any Java *serializable* type can be used as an argument or a return value. This includes Java primitive types, remote Java objects, and non-remote Java objects that implement the java.io.Serializable **interface**. Remember that the java.io.Serializable **interface** is a very important **interface** for marshaling and unmarshaling Java objects. In the *Oracle8i SQLJ Programming* book, "Marshaling packs a method call's parameters (at a client's space) or return values (at a server's space) into a standard format for transmission. Unmarshaling, the reverse operation, unpacks the standard format to an appropriate data presentation in the address space of a receiving process." The contents of Java serializable objects are stored in Java streams (that is, a sequences of bytes) with sufficient information for the receiver process to restore the object to a compatible version of its class.

- A remote object passed as an argument or return value (either directly or embedded within a local object) must be declared as the remote **interface**.

The home **interface** is defined as extending the javax.ejb.EJBHome **interface** that in turn extends the java.rmi.Remote **interface**. Listing 3-1 presents the definition of the javax.ejb.EJBHome **interface**.

Listing 3-1: The `javax.ejb.EJBHome` **interface**

(**See Note 1.**)
```
public interface javax.ejb.EJBHome
extends java.rmi.Remote{
  public abstract EJBMetaData getEJBMetaData()
    throws RemoteException; // (See Note 2.)
public HomeHandle getHomeHandle()
    throws RemoteException; // (See Note 3.)
  public abstract void remove(Handle handle)
    throws RemoteException,RemoteException; // (See Note 4.)
public abstract void remove(Object primaryKey)
    throws RemoteException,RemoteException; // (See Note 5.)
}
```

Notes on Listing 3-1:

1. This statement defines the `javax.ejb.EJBHome` **interface** extending the `java.rmi.Remote` **interface**.

2. The `EJBMetaData` **interface** allows the client to obtain information about the enterprise Bean. The information obtainable via the `EJBMetaData` **interface** is used by vendors' tools and clients that need to perform dynamic invocation on enterprise Beans. All Java methods within a Java class that extend the `java.rmi.Remote` **interface** must use `RemoteException` in their **throws** clause. This exception is thrown when the method fails due to a system-level failure.

3. This method returns a `HomeHandle` object. The `RemoteException` exception is thrown when the method fails due to a system-level failure.

4. This method gets rid of an EJB object identified by its `handle`. The first `RemoteException` exception is thrown if the enterprise Bean or the container does not allow the client to delete the object. The second exception is triggered when the method fails due to a system-level failure.

5. This method deletes an EJB object identified by its primary key. The sequence of events to throw `RemoteException` is the same as in Note 3, except that the EJB object is a primary key in a table stored in a database. This method is used only for entity Beans.

An Enterprise JavaBean is retrieved through an object that inherits from the `EJBHome`. There is a one-to-one relationship between an Enterprise JavaBean class and an `EJBHome` object within a specific namespace. The `EJBHome` is used as a factory for its Enterprise JavaBean objects. The process for the client of locating a home object is called "object look up." At lookup time, an instantiation of the home object is initiated within the server; clients will first get a reference to the `EJBHome` subclass and use a `create()` method listed in the home **interface** to request a reference to the remote object and then request an instance of an Enterprise JavaBean. When the home **interface** is instantiated, the EJB home server object also creates the remote **interface** and enterprise Bean instances.

References to EJB home objects are usually placed in a naming service, and clients use JNDI to access them. Remember that the EJB server usually provides the namespace to store these object references. For instance, the Oracle8*i* EJB server provides a default namespace called `test` that a developer can use to store EJB objects. Oracle also provides the `session_sh` tool that allows you also to create a namespace of your choice.

All EJB home **interfaces** must extend `javax.ejb.EJBHome`. In the "Writing Your First Enterprise JavaBean" section of this chapter, the home **interface** of your Bean will also extend this **interface**. Note also that the container vendor must provide the home object that implements the home **interface**, since only the vendor can implement the code that can act as the factory to create the enterprise Beans.

The requirements for the enterprise Beans home **interface** signatures are as follows:

- The **interface** must extend the `javax.ejb.EJBHome` **interface**.

- The arguments and return values of the methods defined in this **interface** must be Java RMI valid types, and their exception specification or **throws** clause must include the `java.rmi.RemoteException` exception.

- A session Bean's home **interface** defines one or more `create(...)` methods.

- Each `create()` method must be named "create", and it must match one of the `ejbCreate()` methods defined in your Bean class. The matching `ejbCreate()` method must have the same number and types of its arguments.

- The return type for a `create` method must be the enterprise Bean's remote **interface** type.

- All the exceptions defined in the **throws** clause of an `ejbCreate()` method of the enterprise Bean class must be defined in the **throws** clause of the matching `create()` method of the remote **interface**.

- The **throws** clause of the `create()` method must also include the `javax.ejb.CreateException` exception.

The EJB home **interface**s that you define for your enterprise Beans must extend the `javax.ejb.EJBHome` **interface**. Listing 3-2 is an example of an EJB home **interface**.

Listing 3-2: The `My8iEJBHome` home **interface**

```
// (See Note 1.)
public interface My8iEJBHome extends javax.ejb.EJBHome {
  // (See Note 2.)
  My8iEJB create() throws CreateException, RemoteException;
}
```

Notes on Listing 3-2:

1. This statement declares the `My8iEJBHome` **interface** that extends the `javax.ejb.EJBHome` **interface**. Remember that all developers' EJB **interfaces** must extend the `EJBHome` **interface**.

2. This statement declares a `create()` method that clients use to create new Bean instances or to access existing ones. In particular, this method will create an instance of the `My8iEJB` remote **interface**.

Enterprise Bean's Home Interface Methods

The home **interface** of your enterprise Bean will contain one or more `create()` methods. When you write the Bean class, you need to define one or more `ejbCreate()` methods. You must declare corresponding `create()` methods with matching signatures to all `ejbCreate()` methods declared in the Bean class. `create()` methods allow you to create enterprise Bean instances. In addition to the `create()` methods, entity Beans can also have `finder` methods. Refer to the `My8iEJBHome` **interface** for a complete example demonstrating how to write a home **interface** for an enterprise Bean.

Remember, the EJB container implements the home **interface** of each enterprise Bean installed in the container, and the container makes the home **interfaces** available to the client through JNDI. Consequently, the Oracle8i EJB container will implement the home **interfaces** of all enterprise Beans that you wish to install in an Oracle8i database.

Enterprise Remote Interface

An EJB remote **interface** advertises the methods callable by clients. Like a Java **interface**, the EJB remote **interface** defines the behavior of the EJB component. The behavior is the contract that the object **interface** offers publicly. A client that wants to use an EJB object would do so via the EJB remote **interface**, which defines its access points. The Bean developer provides the remote **interface** definition and, at deployment time, the EJB container creates the class that implements it.

The requirements for the enterprise Bean's remote **interface** are as follows:

■ The **interface** must extend the `javax.ejb.EJBObject` **interface.**

■ The methods defined in this **interface** must follow the rules for Java RMI **interfaces.**

■ The **throws** clause must include the `java.rmi.RemoteException` exception.

■ There must be a matching method for each method defined in the remote **interface**. The matching method must have

　■ The same name.

　■ The same number and types of its arguments and the same return type.

　■ All the exceptions defined in the **throws** clause of the matching method of the enterprise Bean class must be defined in the **throws** clause of the same method listed in the remote **interface**.

EJB remote **interfaces** must extend the `javax.ejb.EJBObject` **interface**. The Bean's methods are called indirectly via the `EJBObject` that acts like a proxy. Each `EJBObject` lives in a home and has a unique identity within its home. For session Beans, the EJB container generates a unique identity number for each newly created session object. A session `EJBObject` supports the business logic of a session Bean object. At runtime, the `EJBObject` object delegates the invocation of a Bean method to the session Bean instance. For entity Beans, the Bean developer must provide a primary key for the newly created entity object or existing one, and the container uses the primary key to identify the entity object within its home. Note that all client invocations come through the `EJBObject` and it is the `EJBObject` object, not the home object, that really implements the EJB remote **interface**.

The `javax.ejb.EJBObject` Interface

The EJB Specification refers to services that may be provided by either the EJB container or the `EJBObject`. Note that the container vendor provides both the EJB container and `EJBObject`, and both have distinct entry points into the Bean. Also, note that the `EJBObject` object is created at deployment time. The container vendor must supply the tool to create this object. In step 9 of the "Writing Your First Enterprise JavaBean" section of this chapter, you will deploy a session Bean in an Oracle8*i* database. Oracle provides the `deployejb` tool that allows you do so.

When you deploy an enterprise Bean, the vendor's tool will generate the client and server *stub* classes (see Figure 3-2) for you. EJB clients use the client stub class to remotely invoke the EJB objects. The client stub acts as a proxy to the server stub, and the server stub is a proxy to the actual object's method. A client first does a

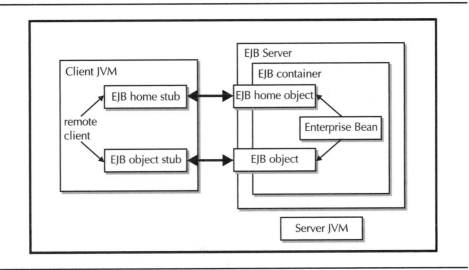

FIGURE 3-2. *Client's communication via client- and server-side stub and classes*

lookup for a home server object reference, gets a reference to the remote object, and then invokes methods on the Bean object as if the Bean object resided in the client's address space. At client lookup time, the client proxy packs the call parameters into a request message. The server proxy (server-side stub class) unpacks the message.

The Bean's remote **interface** extends the EJBObject **interface**, and the EJBObject class implements this remote **interface**—making the EJBObject class specific to the Bean class. For each Bean class, there will be a customized EJBObject class. The EJBObject **interface** is by definition a Java RMI **interface** and as such must follow RMI rules as defined by the Java RMI Specification. Listing 3.3 presents the definition of the EJBObject **interface**.

Listing 3-3: The `javax.ejb.EJBObject` **interface**

```
// (See Note 1.)
Public interface javax.ejb.EJBObject
  extends java.rmi.Remote {
    // (See Note 2.)
    public EJBHome getEJBHome() throws RemoteException;
    // (See Note 3.)
    public Object getHandle () throws RemoteException;
    // (See Note 4.)
    public void remove()() throws RemoteException;
}
```

Notes on Listing 3-3:

1. This statement defines the `javax.ejb.EJBObject` **interface** as extending the `java.rmi.Remote` **interface**. This is a very important **interface** in the EJB API. Remember that the `EJBObject` and the container work as a pair. Thankfully, the container vendor provides both the container and the `EJBObject` classes. At deployment time, the Oracle `deployejb` tool will automatically generate the container and the `EJBObject` classes for you.

2. This statement defines the `getEJBHome()` method that returns an `EJBHome` object to the caller. In the "Enterprise Home Interface" section of this chapter, you learned that clients needing the use of Enterprise JavaBeans create them through their home `interface`. More importantly, a reference to the home object must be placed in a naming service that is accessible from clients using JNDI. When you deploy an enterprise Bean in an Oracle8*i* database, the Oracle tool will store a reference to your Bean's home into the namespace that you designated in the deployment descriptor file that you will create for your Bean. In this book, we will use the default namespace called `test` that Oracle creates for you when you install the Oracle8*i* database.

3. This statement defines the `getHandle()` method and returns a Java `Object` object to the caller. A `Handle` is an object that identifies an EJB object. Clients that have a reference to an EJB object can obtain the object's handle by invoking the *getHandle()* method on the reference.

4. This statement defines a `remove()` method that clients and the EJB container use to remove an EJB object.

The container and `EJBObject` objects (see Figure 3-3) collaborate and work together to implement the services required by a container. For example, the container is responsible for transaction management and knows which transaction attributes to apply to Bean's methods, but it is through the `EJBObject` that these methods are invoked. In turn, the `EJBObject` must communicate with the container to determine in what transaction context to call the business method.

Client programs execute methods on remote EJBs by way of an EJB object. The EJB object implements the remote **interface** of the Bean class on the server. The remote **interface** advertises the business methods of the Bean class. The EJB container uses the remote **interface** of your Bean to generate both the client-side and the server-side stub classes, where the former passes client calls to an EJB object and the latter returns the resulting information back to the client.

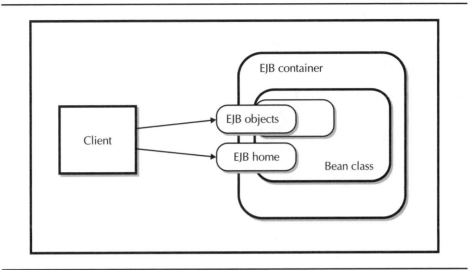

FIGURE 3-3.   *EJB container and EJBObject collaborate*

The EJBObject **interface** must be extended by all Enterprise JavaBeans remote **interfaces**. Consequently, remote **interfaces** that you develop also extend the EJBObject **interface**. Listing 3-4 is an example of an EJB remote **interface**.

Listing 3-4:   The My8iEJB interface

```
// (See Note 1.)
public interface My8iEJB extends javax.ejb.EJBObject {
  // (See Note 2.)
  public String getFirst8iEJB()
    throws RemoteException;
}
```

Notes on Listing 3-4:

1. This statement declares the **public** My8iEJB **interface** that extends the javax.ejb.EJBObject **interface**.

2. This statement declares a method that returns a Java String object to the caller. This method must match exactly the Bean class method.

Enterprise Bean's Remote Interface Methods

Methods signatures, whose implementations reside in an enterprise Bean class, must be listed in the EJB remote **interface**. These methods match exactly the methods implemented in the Bean class. Clients that use Enterprise JavaBeans do not have access directly to the Bean object. That is, the methods of your Bean will never be invoked directly from the client.

Enterprise Beans Class

A Bean class is a program written in Java or SQLJ. It is a body of code with fields and methods that implements some enterprise business logic. A Bean class lives in an EJB container and runs on the server (application or database server). It is a Java class that must follow certain rules:

- It must be defined as **public**.

- It must implement either the `javax.ejb.SessionBean` or `javax.ejb.EntityBean` **interface**. Session Beans implement the `javax.ejb.SessionBean` **interface**, whereas entity Beans implement the `javax.ejb.EntityBean` **interface**. Each **interface** has its specific semantics and methods.

- It may also implement the enterprise Bean's remote **interface**, but is not required to do so.

- It must implement one or more business methods and the `ejbCreate()` methods, and can optionally implement the `javax.ejb.SessionSynchronization` **interface**.

Here we present the definition of the `javax.ejb.SessionBean` **interface**. For a definition of the `javax.ejb.EntitySession` **interface**, see Appendix B of this book and Chapter 18 of the EJB 1.0 Specification.

The definition of the `javax.ejb.SessionBean` **interface** is shown in Listing 3-5.

Listing 3-5: The `javax.ejb.SessionBean` **interface**

```
// (See Note 1.)
public interface javax.ejb.SessionBean
  extends javax.ejb.EnterpriseBean {
    public abstract void ejbActivate(); // (See Note 2.)
    public abstract void ejbPassivate(); // (See Note 3.)
    public abstract void ejbRemove(); // (See Note 4.)
    // (See Note 5.)
    public abstract void setSessionContext(SessionContext ctx);
}
```

Notes on Listing 3-5:

1. This statement declares the Java **public** `javax.ejb.SessionBean`
   interface that extends the `javax.ejb.EnterpriseBean` **interface**.
   Every Bean class must implement the `EnterpriseBean` **interface**, which
   extends the `java.io.Serializable` **interface**, an important
   interface for transporting (marshaling and unmarshaling) Java objects over
   networks.

2. This statement declares the `ejbActivate()` method. This method is
   called when the instance is activated from its "passive" state. Note that the
   temporary transfer of the state of an idle session Bean to some form of
   secondary storage is called *passivation,* and the transfer back is called
   activation. At activation time, the EJB instance will acquire any resource
   that it had released earlier with the `ejbPassivate()` method. The
   Oracle8*i* EJB server does not use the `ejbActivate()` method nor the
   `ejbPassivate()` method.

3. This statement declares the `ejbPassivate()` method. This method is
   called before the instance enters the passive state. It will release any
   resource that it can reacquire later in the `ejbActivate()` method.

4. This statement declares the `ejbRemove()` method. A container invokes
   this method before it ends the life of a session object to release system
   resources and destroy a Bean instance at the client's request.

5. This statement declares the `setSessionContext(SessionContext ctx)` method. The container uses this method to store a reference to the
   context object into a variable. This method is called at the Bean's creation.

Listing 3-6 gives the definition of the `javax.ejb.SessionContext`
interface.

Listing 3-6: The `javax.ejb.SessionContext` **interface**

```
public interface javax.ejb.SessionContext
   extends javax.ejb.EJBContext {
      public abstract EJBObject getEJBObject();
}
```

Note on Listing 3-6:
    The EJB container provides the session Bean instances with a
`SessionContext` **interface** class that consists of several methods that allow a
client to manipulate an instance context that is maintained by the container. The
`SessionContext` **interface** provides access to the runtime session context that
the container supports for a session Bean. The session context provides the session

Bean instance with references to its remote **interface** and transaction and security services information. At runtime, after an instance has been created, the EJB container passes an EJBContext object to that instance and the context object remains associated with the instance for its lifetime. Similarly, for entity Beans, the javax.ejb.EntityContext **interface** provides access to the runtime entity context that the EJB container (entity Bean container) supports for an entity Bean instance. Both the SessionContext and EntityContext **interfaces** extend the EJBContext **interface** and provide additional methods specific to an enterprise Bean type. Listing 3-7 gives the definition of the EJBContext **interface**.

Listing 3-7: The javax.ejb.EJBContext **interface**

```
public interface javax.ejb.EJBContext {

    // Obtain the java.security.Identity of the caller
    public abstract Identity getCallerIdentity();

    // Obtain the enterprise bean's home interface
    public abstract EJBHome getEJBHome();

    // Obtain the enterprise bean's environment properties
    public abstract Properties getEnvironment();

    // Test if the transaction has been marked for rollback only
    public abstract boolean getRollbackOnly();

    // Obtain the transaction demarcation interface
    public abstract UserTransaction getUserTransaction();

    // Test if the caller has a given role
    public abstract boolean isCallerInRole(Identity role);

    // Mark the current transaction for rollback
    public abstract void setRollbackOnly();
}
```

All session Beans must implement the SessionBean **interface**. Note that the setSessionContext() method is called by the Bean's container to associate a session Bean instance with its context. The container maintains the session Bean's Context throughout the Bean's life. Listing 3-8 is an example of a session Bean class.

Listing 3-8:   The `My8iEJBClass` class

```
// (See Note 1.)
public class My8iEJBClass
  implements javax.ejb.SessionBean {
  // (See Note 2.)
  public String getFirst8iEJB()
     throws RemoteException {
     String aString =
           "First EJB application stored in the "
           + " Oracle8i database on data-i.com server "
           + " from the Oracle8i Java Component Programming "
           + " with EJB, CORBA, and JSP book.";
     return aString;
  }
  public My8iEJBClass() {
  }
  // (See Note 3.)
  public void ejbCreate()
     throws RemoteException, CreateException {
  }
  public void ejbActivate()
     throws RemoteException {
  }
  public void ejbPassivate()
      throws RemoteException {
  }
  public void ejbRemove()
      throws RemoteException {
  }
  // (See Note 4.)
  public void setSessionContext(SessionContext ctx)
      throws RemoteException {
  }
}
```

Notes on Listing 3-8:

1. This statement declares the Java **public** `My8iEJBClass` class that extends the `javax.ejb.SessionBean` **interface**. The `SessionBean` **interface** is implemented by every session Bean class. The container uses the `SessionBean` methods to notify the enterprise Bean instances of the instance's life cycle events.

2. This statement declares a method that returns a Java `String` to the caller. It is the matching method for the corresponding method listed in the remote **interface**. Remember that a method listed in an EJB remote **interface** must be an exact match of a method implemented in its Bean class. See Listing 3-4 for a partial listing of the remote **interface**.

3. This statement declares the `ejbCreate()` method. Remember that for each `create()` method listed in the home **interface**, there must be a corresponding `ejbCreate()` method in its Bean's class. All the exceptions defined in the **throws** clause of an `ejbCreate()` method must be defined in the **throws** clause of the corresponding `create()` method. The same number and types of arguments must be defined in both methods.

4. This statement sets the associated session context. This method is called after an instance of the Bean has been created. Remember that the `SessionContext` **interface** provides access to the runtime session context of Enterprise JavaBeans and that the session context remains associated with the instance for the lifetime of the instance.

Enterprise Bean Class Methods

The Bean class must define one or more methods that implement the enterprise business logic and the signatures must follow certain rules:

- The business method must be declared **public**.

- Methods arguments and return value types must be legal types for Java RMI.

- The **throws** clause may define arbitrary application-specific exceptions.

Additionally, the class must implement one or more `ejbCreate()` methods, and these methods must follow certain rules (EJB 1.0 Specification):

- The method name must be named `ejbCreate`.

- The method must be declared **public**.

- The return type must be **void**.

- Methods arguments must be legal types for Java RMI **interface**s.

- The **throws** clause may define arbitrary application-specific exceptions.

- The **throws** clause may include `java.rmi.RemoteException`.

- The **throws** clause may include `javax.ejb.CreateException`.

Enterprise JavaBeans Deployment Descriptor

In the "Enterprise JavaBeans Roles" section of this chapter, you learned about the deployer role. Remember that the deployer is responsible for taking the EJB interfaces, classes, and their supporting classes and installing them in the EJB server. A deployer addresses issues such as runtime linkage information (for example, the EJB server namespace and the name of your database server) that clients use to access the database. As a Bean developer, you may be required to deploy the Enterprise JavaBeans that you develop. In this book, you will acquire the skills to do so through a good understanding of Enterprise JavaBeans and the characteristics of their runtime environment.

Deployment descriptors are serialized classes that serve a function similar to property files. They allow you to describe and customize runtime attributes—runtime behaviors of server-side components (for example, security, transactional context, and so on) without having to change the Bean class or its interfaces. The `DeploymentDescriptor` class is the common base class for the `SessionDescriptor` (session Beans only) and `EntityDescriptor` (entity Beans only) deployment descriptor classes. A deployment descriptor can define one or multiple enterprise Beans. In Oracle8*i* versions 8.1.5 and 8.1.6, the deployment descriptor file is supported in text format, whereas in the 8.1.7 release the deployment descriptor file will be supported in both the Extended Markup Language (XML) and Oracle's text format.

After you create the **interface** classes and the Bean class for your enterprise Bean, you need to create a deployment descriptor file for it. The deployment descriptor acts as a property sheet (a file) in which you list the runtime and security requirements of the Bean as well as the transaction management associated with your Bean. Once the deployment descriptor is complete and saved to a file, the Bean can be packaged in a `jar` (Java archive) file for deployment.

At deployment time, additional classes are generated that are needed internally by the EJB container. The container vendor will provide you with the correct tool to deploy your Enterprise JavaBeans. Remember that Oracle provides the `deployejb` tool that you must use to deploy Enterprise JavaBeans in the Oracle8*i* database. The additional classes generated at deployment time allow the EJB container to manage enterprise Beans at runtime. In the "Transaction Management and Security for EJBs" section of this chapter, you will learn how an EJB container controls transaction management via transaction attributes specified in a deployment descriptor file. Deployment of a Bean consists of the installation of one or more EJB jar files as well as the assignment of properties, runtime parameters, and security constraints for the Beans. For a definition of the EJB 1.0 `javax.ejb.deployment.Deployment-Descriptor` class, see Appendix B.

The EJB container uses the
`javax.ejb.deployment.Deployment Descriptor` class to manage Enterprise
JavaBeans at runtime. Recall that the container is responsible for controlling the
Bean's transaction and security. When you create a deployment descriptor file for
your enterprise Beans, you list the transaction and security attribute values in this file
to instruct the container how to manage the Bean's runtime environment. The EJB
container reads this file to determine which transaction attributes apply to the entire
Bean or to some specific Bean's methods.

Listing 3-9 is an example of a simple deployment descriptor file. Use any ASCII
editor to create this file.

Listing 3-9:   An EJB Deployment Descriptor File

```
// (See Note 1.)
SessionBean server.My8iEJBClass {
    // (See Note 2.)
    BeanHomeName = "test/My8iEJB";
    // (See Note 3.)
    HomeInterfaceClassName = server.My8iEJBHome;

    RemoteInterfaceClassName = server.My8iEJB;
    // (See Note 4.)
    AllowedIdentities = {PUBLIC};
    // (See Note 5.)
    SessionTimeout = 0;
    // (See Note 6.)
    StateManagementType = STATEFUL_SESSION;
    // (See Note 7.)
    RunAsMode = CLIENT_IDENTITY;
    // (See Note 8.)
    EnvironmentProperties {
    }
}
```

Notes on Listing 3-9:

1. This statement declares the `server.My8iEJBClass` Bean as a session Bean.
    When you write a deployment descriptor file, remember to include the full
    path for the EJB **interfaces** and classes that you want to include in this file.

2. This statement stores the name of the EJB object and the namespace (the
    naming service) where the object is located. The `test` directory is a default
    namespace created when you install the Oracle8*i* database. When you
    deploy the `My8iEJB` Bean, Oracle will make the naming service accessible
    to clients that need to use the Beans.

3. This statement and the subsequent one store a Bean's home and remote
    reference, respectively.

4. This statement defines the security attribute to be associated with the runtime execution environment of the enterprise Bean's methods. The EJB Specification allows you to specify an identity value for a specific user, a *role* (database role), for an entire enterprise Bean, or specific methods of a Bean. For example, you can create database roles in an Oracle database. Creations of Oracle database `role` are beyond the scope of this book. To learn how to create a `role` for an Oracle database, see the *Oracle8i SQL Reference*, Volume 2. Remember that a deployment descriptor includes access control entries that allow the container to perform runtime security management on behalf of the enterprise Bean. In this example, we specify that users who have been granted the Oracle system `role` PUBLIC can use the Bean as a whole; that is, all users who have been assigned the PUBLIC `role` can access all the methods of the Bean.

5. This statement sets a session timeout value. You can use this object to set the session timeout value in seconds. A zero value means that the container should use a container default value.

6. This statement sets the session Bean's management type indicating that the session type is STATEFUL_SESSION. In the Oracle8*i* database, STATELESS and STATEFUL Beans are the same.

7. This statement sets the RunAsMode attribute to indicate to the container which security identity to associate with the execution of an enterprise Bean's method. For example, if you specify in the deployment descriptor a security identity for a specific method, this security identity is associated with the invocation call at invocation runtime. Use the RunAsMode attribute to specify the security identity of the client whose value is CLIENT_IDENTITY, privileged system account (SYSTEM_IDENTITY), or a specific user account (SPECIFIED_IDENTITY). Note that the value specified at the Bean level applies to all the methods that do not have a specific method-level security identity. For STATEFUL Beans, because the RunAs security identity associated with an instance is determined at instance creation time, the method level may be different for different methods of the same Bean. For STATELESS Beans, the specified RunAs identity must be the same for all the methods that are executed in the same transaction.

8. Here, the Bean developer will define the runtime environment property values for the Bean. The enterprise Bean provider must define the runtime environment properties—that is, the *key:value* pairs the enterprise Bean's instances will require at runtime. The values are typically edited at deployment time by the container provider tools. In subsequent chapters of this book, you will learn how to list these environment properties in the deployment descriptor file.

Throughout this book, as you develop more EJB components, you will learn how to list your Bean's transaction and security requirements in the deployment descriptor file. Your vendor may provide the tool to create this file or you may use another vendor's tool to do so. For example, the Oracle JDeveloper tool allows you to create Enterprise JavaBeans through its EJB Wizard. When you use the tool to create your EJB component, it will automatically create a deployment descriptor file for you.

`ejb-jar` File

The output of a Bean developer is a `jar` file, called `ejb-jar`, consisting of the EJB **interfaces** (home and remote), classes, their dependent classes, the environment properties, and the deployment descriptor for Enterprise JavaBeans. The EJB Specification defines the format of the `ejb-jar` file. The `ejb-jar` file is a standard format used by the EJB tool to "package" Enterprise JavaBeans. EJB files are packaged for deployment. When you deliver an enterprise Bean's package to a deployer, it should include two files:

- A `jar` file (the `ejb-jar` file) composed of all the Java **interface** and class files for the enterprise Beans.

- A `manifest` file whose entries describe the contents of the `ejb-jar` file. This is a text file and it must be named "`META-INF/MANIFEST.MF`". Application developers writing Enterprise JavaBeans do not have to create a `manifest` file. The `jar` command automatically creates this file for you and stores it in the Bean's `ejb-jar` file. Listing 3-10 is an example of a manifest file.

Listing 3-10: An EJB manifest file

```
META-INF/MANIFEST.MF
Server/My8iEJB.class
Server/My8iEJBHome.class
Server/My8iEJBClass.class
Server/My8iEJB.ejb
```

The Client Application

The EJB Specification define a contract between a client and a container. The contract provides a uniform model for clients using enterprise Beans that live in a client's address space, but more importantly, in different address spaces. In order for clients to use enterprise Beans, Bean and server providers must provide the following:

- An EJB object identity

- EJB methods

- An EJB home `interface`

Java and non-Java client applications using Enterprise JavaBeans do so via a Bean's home `interface` reference. Oracle and other vendors that implement EJB specifications allow clients to use JNDI to locate a reference to an enterprise Bean's home `interface`. At lookup time, clients must know the location of the namespace and the name of the reference to the Bean's home object. As a Bean developer, you must provide this information to the client.

Next, you will learn how to locate a Bean's home `interface` that resides in an Oracle8*i* database.

Locating an Enterprise Bean's Home Interface

For the Oracle8*i* EJB server, JNDI serves as an `interface` (SPI driver) to the OMG `CosNaming` class that provides a naming service for "published" EJB and CORBA objects. Right now, you do not need to know too much about either the OMG `CosNaming` class or JNDI for you to develop Enterprise JavaBeans and deploy them in the Oracle8*i* database. However, to use JNDI you need to know two things:

- How to use the JNDI methods that allow you to access a Bean's home `interface` object. Home `interface` objects are permanently stored in namespaces that are made accessible to JNDI. For example, EJB home `interfaces` are published in the Oracle8*i* database. When you deploy a Bean in an Oracle8*i* database, the Oracle8*i* EJB server stores the home object reference in the namespace that you define in the deployment descriptor file for your Bean. Use the deployment descriptor file to specify the name of the namespace where a Bean resides and the name of the Bean itself. For example:

  ```
  // The name of the namespace is called test.
  // The name of the Bean is called My8iEJB
  BeanHomeName =  "/test/My8iEJB";
  ```

- How to set up the environment for the JNDI `Context` object. Remember that a `Context` object is what binds (associates) a Bean's name to a Bean's object. More importantly, the `Context` object contains methods for examining and updating these bindings.

Retrieving a `Context` Object

Before retrieving a JNDI `Context` object, a client needs to set up the Bean's security environment properties. Remember that the EJB container uses these properties for security management. Six properties are passed to the `javax.naming.Context`. (See Appendix B and Chapter 5 for detailed explanations of these properties.) Use a Java `Hashtable` object to pass the properties to the `Context` object.

In the Oracle8*i* database environment, when you use JNDI to retrieve a `Context` object, the first `Context` object that you receive is bound to the root-naming context of the Oracle8*i* publishing context. You get the Oracle root-naming context via a JNDI `InitialContext` object:

```
// First, create a Hashtable to store the
// security environment properties needed by JNDI.
Hastable env = new Hashtable();

// Second, store the properties in the env object.
env.put(Context.URL_PKG_PREFIXES, "oracle.aurora.jndi");
..
..
// Third, create an initial context object
// by calling the InitialContext() constructor
Context anInitialContext = new InitialContext(env);
```

Once you have the `Context` object, you can invoke its `lookup()` method to get the reference to the home object. To do this, you must know the full path of the published object, the host system where the object is located, the IIOP port for the listener on that system, and the database system identifier (SID). In Listing 3-11, the `objectName` variable contains the namespace's name concatenated with the Bean's class name, and the `serviceURL` contains the IIOP connection set up to connect to an Oracle8*i* database.

Listing 3-11: Variable Declarations

```
// Declare a Java variable that contains
// the namespace and the name of the published object.
String objectName = "/test/My8iEJB";
// Use the host name where the Oracle8i database is located
// sess_iiop://localHost:2481:orcl. For example:
String serviceURL = sess_iiop://data-i.com:2481:orcl;
```

In Listing 3-12, you use the `lookup()` method of the `InitialContext` object to obtain the home object reference.

Listing 3-12:   Obtain a reference to an EJB home `interface`

```
// Create a home interface object
// to hold a reference to the home object.
My8iEJBHome my8iEJBHome =
    (My8iEJBHome)
        anInitialContext.lookup(serviceURL + objectName);
```

Creating a Bean's Remote Interface Instance

After you have the Bean's home reference, you can invoke one of the `create()` methods of the Bean's home **interface** object to get a Bean's remote **interface** instance. For example, use the following to get the `my8iEJB` remote instance:

```
// Create a remote interface object.
My8iEJB my8iEJBBean = null;

// Use the create() method of the home object
// to create an instance of the Bean's remote interface.
my8iEJBBean = my8iEJBHome.create();
```

Calling a Bean's Method

Now that you have the Bean's remote **interface** instance, use the instance to invoke the enterprise Bean's method defined in the Bean class:

```
...
// Invoke the Bean's method.
OutputFromBean = my8iEJBBean.getFirst8iEJB();
```

Transaction Management and Security for EJBs

One of the nice features of the EJB framework is that transaction management is no longer a developer's responsibility. The burden of managing transactions is shifted from the Bean's providers to the EJB server and container. Therefore, the EJB server and container vendors (vendors that implement the EJB specification) provide transaction management. When you develop enterprise Beans for an Oracle8*i* database, the Oracle8*i* EJB server and container will manage the Beans' transactions for you.

Support for Transaction

Enterprise JavaBeans allow Bean providers to develop applications that access and manipulate data in a single database and distributed databases (multiple databases that live anywhere on a network). More importantly, the site location may use EJB servers and containers from several different vendors implementing the same EJB specification. However, Enterprise JavaBeans and CORBA components that reside in an Oracle8*i* database can only use EJB and CORBA objects that reside in the same Oracle8*i* data server. In other words, these components cannot access EJB or CORBA objects that reside in distributed databases.

A container manages transactions via the declarative transaction management that is in turn controlled by a *transaction attribute*. When you write the deployment descriptor for an enterprise Bean, you can specify the transaction attribute value to instruct the container how to manage the Bean's transactions. The EJB Specification (versions 1.0 and 1.1) define the following transaction attribute values:

- TX_NOT_SUPPORTED

- TX_BEAN_MANAGED

- TX_REQUIRED

- TX_SUPPORTS

- TX_RQUIRES_NEW

- TX_MANDATORY

In Chapter 4, you will learn the semantics and the details concerning the EJB transaction attribute and their values as you develop more EJB applications that use them. For now, just remember that you can control how a Bean executes at runtime by listing transaction attribute values in your Bean's deployment descriptor. When you do so, you automatically delegate transaction management to the EJB container.

EJB container providers must implement the `javax.jts.UserTransaction` **interface** that is defined as part of the Java Transaction Service (JTS) API. JTS defines all the Java programming language **interfaces** related to transaction management on the Java platform. Appendix B of the EJB 1.0 Specification provides the documentation on the `javax.jts` package. See also "*Understanding Enterprise Java APIs Why corporate Java developers need to know about JNDI, JTS, and JMS,*" http://www.componentmag.com/html/from_pages/feature .shtml and "*Java Transaction Service (JTS),*" http://java.sun.com/products/jts.

Listing 3-13 lists the classes and **interfaces** that are part of the package `javax.jts` and that are relevant to Enterprise JavaBeans.

Listing 3-13:   JTS classes

```
interface UserTransaction
class HeuristicCommitException
class HeuristicException
class HeuristicMixedException
class HeuristicRollbackException
class TransactionRequiredException
class TransactionRolledbackException
class InvalidTransactionException
```

Note that although the Enterprise JavaBeans architecture focuses on the Java API and Java programming language, EJB can also communicate with non-Java clients and servers.

Support for Distribution

The EJB 1.0 Specification includes the CORBA mapping of the Enterprise JavaBeans architecture that allows any CORBA client to invoke any enterprise Bean object on a CORBA-enabled server using the industry standard Internet Inter-ORB Protocol (IIOP). Note that Oracle8*i* versions 8.1.5 and 8.1.6 support distribution only within the same database. Thus, EJB and CORBA clients living in an Oracle8*i* data server can use EJB and CORBA objects that reside in the same database. However, EJB and CORBA clients that reside anywhere on a network can access enterprise Beans and CORBA objects residing in any Oracle8*i* data server via RMI over IIOP and IIOP, respectively.

The Enterprise JavaBeans framework also shifts the implementation of security management from developers to the EJB server and container.

Support for Security

The EJB architecture uses the `java.security` package, which provides security-related **interfaces** for the Java programming language. For example, for security purposes, enterprise Beans use the `java.security.Identity` classes as the API to describe the client's identity, determining a specific user or security role. The EJB container will map the instances of the `java.security.Identity` class to user accounts and roles of the EJB server.

The `javax.ejb.EJBContext` **interface** contains two specific methods that allow a Bean instance to obtain a client identity that invokes a method:

- `GetCallerIdentity()`
- `IsCallerInRole(Identity clientIdentity)`

The EJB container uses both methods to identify clients that invoke enterprise Beans.

EJB Exceptions

Upon clients' requests, the EJB container handles all exceptions that are thrown by the enterprise Bean's methods. For system-level or communication failure, the Bean's methods are likely to throw `java.rmi.RemoteException`.

The EJB remote and home **interfaces** are both Java RMI **interfaces.** Methods in Java RMI **interfaces** must include the mandatory `java.rmi.RemoteException` exception in their signatures. Consequently, methods in EJB remote and home **interfaces** must also include the `java.rmi.Remote Exception` exception in their **throws** clauses.

Remember that clients access Enterprise JavaBeans via their remote and home **interfaces**. When an EJB client makes a request, the `java.rmi.Remote Exception` exception is thrown to the client when a system-level or a communication subsystem failure occurs between the client and the EJB components. Communication or system failure may occur between the client and the following components:

- **The EJB container** The container throws the `java.rmi.RemoteException` exception to the client when it cannot complete a client's request. Remember, a client initiates a request by invoking a method on a Bean's class.

- **The enterprise Bean class** The Bean throws the `java.rmi.RemoteException` exception to the client when a system-level error occurs—for example, a database error.

In addition to the mandatory `java.rmi.RemoteException` exception, the **throws** clause of the methods of EJB **interfaces** and classes may include any number of application-specific exceptions. For example, EJB classes that access relational and object-relational databases would include the `SQLException` exception from the `java.sql` package. In the EJB applications that you will develop in subsequent chapters of the book, the methods listed in the **interfaces** and classes will access an Oracle8*i* database. Consequently, in addition to the mandatory `java.rmi.RemoteException` exception, these methods will include the `SQLException` exception. Note that when enterprise Beans throw application-specific exceptions, they are passed unchanged by the container to the EJB clients; the container must not convert an application-level exception into the `java.rmi.RemoteException` exception.

In addition to the `java.rmi.RemoteException` and application-specific exceptions, the `create()`, `remove()`, and `finder()` methods (listed in EJB home **interfaces**) must include the `javax.ejb.CreateException`, `javax.ejb.RemoveException`, and `javax.ejb.FindException` exceptions in their **throws** clauses. Note that the `javax.ejb.FindException` is included in the `finder()` method, and this method is only applicable to entity Beans.

Exceptions other than the `java.rmi.RemoteException` exception may be thrown when clients are running transactions. Recall that one of the key features of Enterprise JavaBeans is support for distributed transactions. Clients initiating transactions may receive transaction-related exceptions. For example, the `javax.jts.TransactionRolledbackException` exception may be thrown when the transaction has been marked for rollback. A rollback occurs when the transaction cannot commit. Remember that a transaction is a unit of work that completes when a `commit` statement is issued or gets terminated with a `rollback` statement.

Benefits of Enterprise JavaBeans

In the *Enterprise JavaBeans Technology Server Component Model for the Java* (http://java.sun.com/products/ejb/white_paper.html#ejbcompmod), EJB benefits are summarized as follows:

- **Component portability, customization, and reusability**   EJB components are portable across any vendor's EJB-compliant application server and can run on any platform. The Enterprise JavaBeans architecture defines a standard model for Java application servers to support "write once, run anywhere" (WORA) portability. Remember that application behaviors and runtime settings are defined in an enterprise Bean's deployment descriptor file. EJB components can be customized to run in an enterprise's environment by just changing the set of attributes listed in the deployment descriptor file; therefore, there is no need to access the program source code. Once defined and packaged, EJB components can be reused.

- **Architecture robust and independent**   EJB Specifications (1.0 or 1.1) define a robust server-side component model, and applications that are developed for one platform can be redeployed to another platform.

- **Faster application development**   Complex issues such as component communication, transaction management, and thread management are no longer the developer's responsibility. Consequently, Bean providers can concentrate on developing EJB classes that implement business logic versus implementing complex infrastructure services in their program.

- **Component compatibility** Enterprise JavaBeans are compatible with popular distributed paradigms such as OMG CORBA and Microsoft DCOM.

- **Versatility and scalability** EJB model supports Web-based (Internet/intranet) applications. EJB architecture is appropriate for small-scale and large-scale applications.

The Oracle8*i* JServer Architecture

Oracle developers have been developing server-side applications for a long time. These applications were written in PL/SQL, an Oracle RDBMS procedural language extension to SQL that has tight integration with SQL data. The language integrates features such as exception handling, overloading, and a limited amount of information hiding (accomplished by declaring variables and types in a package body instead of a package specification). In addition to providing these capabilities, PL/SQL subprograms (procedures and functions) and triggers can be stored in the Oracle database server. A subprogram consists of a set of PL/SQL statements that are grouped together as a unit to perform a set of related tasks. They are created and stored in compiled form in the database. Additionally, application programmers can create PL/SQL packages. A PL/SQL package consists of a set of (usually related) PL/SQL functions and procedures. Instead of creating many individual PL/SQL functions and procedures whose functionality is related, developers can create a package that contains all related functions and procedures.

With the release of Oracle8*i* 1.5 and 1.6, Java developers can develop server-side applications in Java or SQLJ, in the form of Java or SQLJ stored procedures, Enterprise JavaBeans components, or CORBA components.

Prior to the release of the Oracle8*i* database, the data server consisted of the following:

- A SQL engine

- A PL/SQL engine

With Oracle8*i*, the Oracle database, in addition to the SQL and PL/SQL engines, includes the Oracle8*i* JServer, a Java server platform. Presently, customers who have migrated from previous Oracle database releases to Oracle8*i* can access SQL data with two different application programming **interfaces** (APIs): JDBC and SQLJ. To learn more about SQLJ, see the *Oracle8i SQLJ Programming* (Osborne/McGraw-Hill, ISBN 0072121602) book.

Oracle8*i* JServer Basics

The JServer (see Figure 3-4) environment consists of the following:

- The Oracle Aurora Java Virtual Machine (JVM) and Java class libraries

■ The Aurora/ORB, an Object Request Broker, and the Oracle8*i* EJB server and container

Both components, the JVM and the Aurora/ORB, are tightly integrated with PL/SQL and the Oracle relational database management systems (RDBMS) functionality.

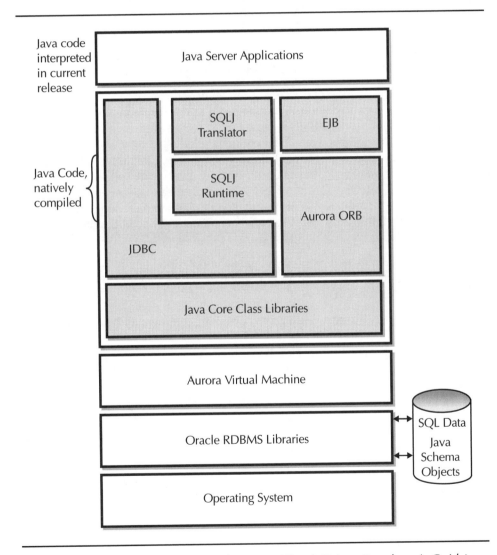

FIGURE 3-4. *Oracle8i JServer architecture (Oracle8i Java Developer's Guide)*

The JServer Java Virtual Machine (JVM) is a Java 1.1.*x*-compliant (Oracle8*i* version 8.1.5) and Java 1.2.1-compliant (Oracle8*i* version 8.1.6) Java execution environment.

Oracle8*i* EJB Server and Container

The Oracle8*i* JServer complies with the EJB 1.0 Specification. The Oracle*i* EJB implementation (see Figure 3-5) offers the following features:

- A JNDI **interface** to the OMG CosNaming class service to locate and activate Beans. EJB and CORBA clients use EJB and CORBA applications via this **interface**.

- Secure Socket Layer (SSL) connections for added security.

- An implementation of the Java Transaction Service (JTS) for client-side transaction demarcation. A transaction is said to be demarcated when a client specifically calls the begin() and the commit() methods of the JTS package, respectively. EJB vendors, including Oracle, provide their own **interface** implementations. For example, Oracle provides the oracle.aurora.jts.client.AuroraTransactionService and oracle.aurora.jts.util.TS **interfaces** that you must import in your client programs when you want your client to have some control over a Bean's transaction. See Chapters 4 and 5 to learn how to write EJB clients that use the begin() and the commit() methods.

- An implementation of the Java Transaction Architecture (JTA), Oracle8*i* 8.1.7 (beta version) or Java Transaction Service (JTS) for client-side transaction demarcation.

- The UserTransaction **interface** for Bean-managed transactions.

JServer comes with a built-in CORBA 2.0 (Inprise Visibroker for Java 3.2 for Oracle8*i* 1.5, and Visibroker 3.4 for Oracle8*i* 1.6) and support for Enterprise JavaBeans (EJB 1.0 Specification only). Visibroker 3.4 is compatible with both JDK 1.1 and Java 2. Oracle and Java developers can develop in any language to communicate directly with the Oracle8*i* data server through the industry standard IIOP protocol.

Oracle delivers JServer with many tools and utilities, all written in Java, that provide ease of development and deployment of Java and SQLJ components. Currently, users who want to manipulate SQL code that resides in the Oracle8*i* database can do so via SQLPLUS (Oracle tool) or a Java client. Java users can execute Java code by calling Java/SQLJ stored procedures, the session Beans' methods, or CORBA object methods that reside in the Oracle8*i* data server.

Whether you are using the Oracle SQLPLUS tool or your client program to access SQL data, you must establish a database session in the server. Oracle clients

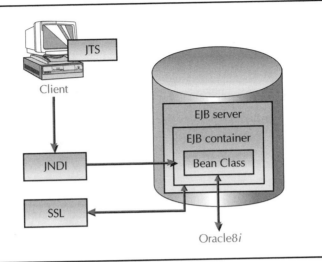

FIGURE 3-5. *Oracle8i EJB architecture*

do so by connecting to the database via Net8, JDBC, or IIOP (see Figure 3-6). Java clients can use the IIOP protocol to establish a JServer session. JServer sessions are analogous to database sessions, except that they scope Java's object memory. A JServer session encompasses the lifetime of all objects referenced by Java static variables. From a client's point of view, like in a database session, each JServer session has its own private object memory.

You will find that developing for either CORBA or EJB within the JServer framework offers a large degree of conceptual similarity. For example, access to both types of components is similar. Objects are published in the Oracle8i database using the OMG `CosNaming` class service and can be accessed using Oracle's JNDI **interface** to `CosNaming` or simply JNDI (see Figure 3-7). To learn more about CORBA and the OMG `CosNaming` service, see Part III (Chapters 6–9) of the book.

Oracle8i JServer comes with many tools that you can use to develop EJB and CORBA applications. These are command-line tools that you can run from a UNIX shell or at a Windows DOS prompt. The specific tools related to EJB are as follows:

- `deployejb`
- `ejbdescriptor`
- `dropjava`
- `sess-sh`
- `remove`

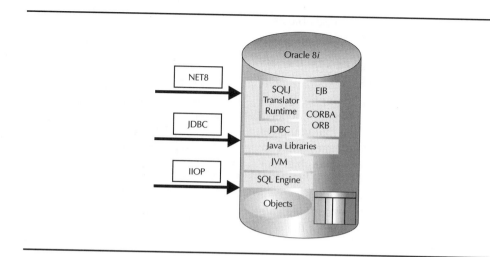

FIGURE 3-6. *Accessing the Oracle8*i database

These tools allow you to compile OMG IDL, load Java classes or source code files into the database, publish objects in the session namespace, and display and manipulate published object names that reside in the namespaces. For detailed explanations on the various options for the EJB tools, see Appendix F. Remember that when you want to make an EJB or a CORBA object available and accessible to

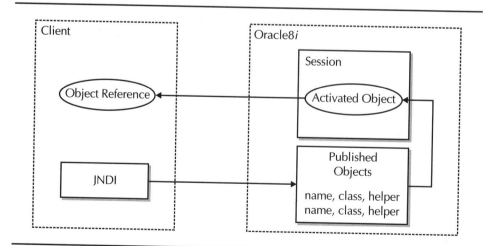

FIGURE 3-7. *Oracle8*i published objects

clients, you must publish these objects. Use the Oracle `publish` tool to publish CORBA objects and the `deployejb` tool for EJB objects.

Oracle `deployejb` Tool

The `deployejb` tool makes an EJB component ready for clients to use it. It uses the deployment descriptor for the Bean and the `jar` file that contains the EJB **interfaces**, classes, and their dependent classes. The tool converts the deployment descriptor file that you create for your enterprise Beans to a Java serialized object, and generates and compiles classes that enable communication between clients and published objects. Remember that you must have specific Oracle system privileges to publish objects in the database. More than likely, the Oracle DBA will perform this task. For an excellent example of how to use the tool, see step 9 of the "Writing Your First Enterprise JavaBean" section of this chapter. Listing 3-14 gives the syntax for the `deployejb` tool.

Listing 3-14: The Oracle `deployejb` Tool

```
deployejb -user <username> -password <password>
-service <serviceURL> -descriptor <file>
-temp <dir> <beanjar>
  [-addclasspath <dirlist>]
  [-describe]
  [-generated <clientjar>]
  [-help]
  [-iiop]
  [-keep]
  [-republish]
  [-role <role>]
  [-ssl]
  [-useServiceName]
  [-verbose]
  [-version]
```

Here is an example of the `deployejb` tool:

```
deployejb -temp temp -u scott -p tiger
-s %ORACLE_SERVICE%
-descriptor My8iEJB.ejb -generated My8iEJBClient.jar My8iEJB.jar
```

Oracle `ejbdescriptor` Tool

The `ejbdescriptor` tool allows a developer to convert a deployment descriptor file from ASCII readable (`.txt`) format to non-readable (`.ejb`) format. The syntax is as follows:

```
ejbdescriptor {-parse | -dump} <infile> <outfile>
```

Use the -parse option to create a serialized deployment descriptor
<outfile> from <infile>:

```
Ejbdescriptor -parse My8iEJB.txt My8iEJB.ejb
```

Use the -dump option to create text file <outfile> from serialized
deployment descriptor <infile>:

```
Ejbdescriptor -dump My8iEJB.ejb My8iEJB.txt
```

Oracle dropjava Tool

The dropjava tool transforms command-line filenames and uncompressed jar
or zip file contents to schema object names, then drops the schema objects and
deletes their corresponding digest table rows. You can enter .java, .class,
.sqlj, .zip, .jar, and resource filenames on the command line in any order.
Here is the syntax:

```
dropjava {-u | -user} <user>/<password>[@<database>]
[options] {<file>.java | <file>.class | file.sqlj |
<file>.jar | <file>.zip> | <resourcefile>} ...
   [{-o | -oci8}]
   [{-S | -schema} <schema>] [-stdout ]
   [-s | synonym] [{-t | -thin}]
   [{-v | -verbose}]
```

Here is an example of the dropjava tool:

```
dropjava -u scott/tiger -schema SCOTT My8iEBJ.jar
```

Oracle sess_sh Tool

The sess_sh (session shell) tool is an interactive **interface** tool that allows
you to manipulate a database instance's session namespace. You specify database
connection arguments when you start sess_sh. Use this tool to create, view, and
delete namespaces. In the Oracle database environment, the sys user only has the
privilege of manipulating namespaces. Therefore, if you want to have access to the
Oracle session namespaces, we suggest that you contact your database
administrator. Here is the syntax for the tool:

```
sess_sh [options] -user <user>
-password <password> -service <serviceURL>
[-d | -describe]
[-h | -help]
[-iiop] [-role <rolename>]
[-ssl] [-useServiceName] [-version]
```

Here is an example of the use of the `sess_sh` tool:

```
sess_sh -user scott -password tiger
  -service sess_iiop://data-i.com:2481:orcl
```

Oracle remove Tool

The `remove` tool removes a `PublishedObject` or `PublishingContext` from a session namespace. It does not remove the Java class schema object associated with a `PublishedObject`. Here is the syntax:

```
remove <name> -user <username>
-password <password> -service <serviceURL>
[options]
   [{-d | -describe}]   [{-h | -help}]
   [-iiop]   [{-r | -recurse}]
   [-role role]   [-ssl]
   [-useServiceName]   [-version]
```

Here is an example of the `remove` tool:

```
remove /test/My8iEJB -user scott -password tiger
  -service sess_iiop://data-i.com:2481:orcl
```

In Chapters 6 and 7, you will learn about Oracle tools to manipulate CORBA components, and in Chapters 10, 11, and 12 you will learn about other tools related to Java Server Pages (JSP) and Extended Markup Language (XML).

Writing Your First Enterprise JavaBean

With this basic understanding of the Enterprise JavaBeans framework, you are now ready to create EJB applications in Java and SQLJ. Next, you will use the skills that you have acquired to develop a simple session Bean in Java, deploy the Bean in an Oracle8*i* database, and write an EJB client that uses your enterprise Bean. Note that all program codes developed in the book have been deployed in the Oracle8*i* versions 8.1.5, 8.1.6, and 8.1.7 (beta version).

Writing an Enterprise JavaBean is fairly simple. EJB Specifications 1.0 and 1.1 both provide the same standard model for constructing Enterprise JavaBeans (session or entity Beans). When you follow the model, you can use the services provided by the EJB server and the EJB container. Remember that when you build your enterprise Beans, you no longer need to think about complex issues such as multi-threaded, transactional, and distributed process computing; the EJB server and the EJB container provide these services for your Beans.

In this section, you will assume the role of a Bean provider, and as such you will provide the following:

- The EJB remote **interface**.

- The EJB home **interface**.

- The Bean class or classes.

- The environment properties for the Bean, such as *key:value* pairs that the Bean requires at runtime. Environment properties are defined as a standard `java.util.Properties` object. The Java `Properties` class is a subclass of the Java `Hashtable` class that represents a set of properties and property values. See *Teach Yourself Java 2 in 21 Days* (Wrox Press, April 1999) or any other Java reference book to learn more about both the `Properties` and `Hashtable` classes. The environment properties are listed in the deployment descriptor file.

- The deployment descriptor.

- The `ejb-jar` file. Note that you can create one `ejb-jar` file for each of the Enterprise JavaBeans that you will develop, or you can create one file that includes all your enterprise Beans. The `ejb-jar` file includes all the EJB classes and their dependent classes, the deployment descriptor, the EJB remote and home **interfaces** and their dependent classes, the environment properties, and the `Manifest` file that identifies the deployment descriptor of one or more enterprise Beans.

Here, you will write a session Bean that illustrates the process of building an enterprise Bean. This section is designed to enhance your understanding of the Enterprise JavaBeans model by providing concrete step-by-step guidelines for building and using session Beans applications. Remember that Oracle8*i* EJB server implements only session Beans. Therefore, you will use the materials presented in Chapters 3, 4, and 5 to acquire the skills for building and deploying session Beans in the Oracle8*i* database, and developing EJB clients that use them.

The user requirements for your session Bean are straightforward:

- Build a session Bean whose method returns a Java `String`. The content of the string is as follows: "`First EJB application stored in the Oracle8i database on data-i.com server from the Oracle8i Java Component Programming with EJB, CORBA, and JSP book.`"

- Build a client that invokes the Bean's method, stores the value returned by the Bean's method into its local variable, and then displays the value.

A high-level view of the EJB application is shown in Figure 3-8. The client application is a Java program that invokes a method and interacts with a session Bean through its home and remote **interfaces**. EJB clients can be any Java/SQLJ programs such as applets, servlets, and applications. In the `My8iEjB` session Bean application, the client invokes the method published in the remote **interface** to access the business logic implemented by the Bean class. Remember that an enterprise Bean's remote **interface** describes *what* the Bean does and the Bean's class describes *how* the Bean does the work.

The steps to create a session Bean are as follows:

1. Set the system `CLASSPATH` and `PATH` environment variables.

2. Create one or more directories to store the Java source code that you want to develop. While doing so, think about the package names that you want to use for your EJB applications. In this section, you will create two directories called `client` and `server`, respectively. You will use a Java package named `client` to store the Java client application source code and the Java class file, and the package named `server` to store the Java source code and the Java class files for all EJB **interfaces** and classes related to the `My8iEJB` session Bean.

3. Write the remote **interface**.

4. Write the home **interface**.

5. Write the Bean's implementation class.

6. Compile the home and remote **interfaces** and the Bean's class.

7. Define a deployment descriptor for the enterprise Bean.

8. Create an `ejb-jar` file.

9. Deploy an Enterprise JavaBean.

10. Write the client.

11. Compile the client.

12. Run the client.

Step 1: Set the system `CLASSPATH` and `PATH` environment variables. See the `Makefile` and the `SetupEnvironment` files to learn how to set up the environment on the UNIX and Windows platforms, respectively. These files are part of the online code files that you can download from either the www.data-i.com or www.osborne.com site.

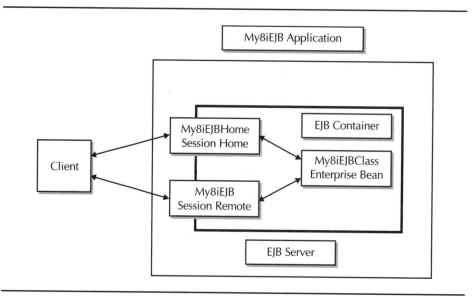

FIGURE 3-8. *High-level view of the* My8iEJB *session Bean application*

Step 2: Create the `client` and the `server` directories whose names correspond to the names of your Java packages.

Step 3: Write the EJB remote **interface**. A remote **interface** is a required component for all session Beans. Remember that the Bean's remote **interface** defines the access point to the Bean's class and advertises the methods callable by clients. The `My8iEJB` remote **interface** must extend the `javax.ejb.EJB Object` **interface**, and its `getFirst8iEJB()` business method must include the `java.rmi.RemoteException` exception in the method's **throws** clause. Here is the definition of the `My8iEJB` remote **interface**:

```
// Program Name: My8iEJB.java
// Version:
// Author:        Your Name
// Description:   An EJB remote interface that
//                advertises the method of the
//                the My8iEJBClass Bean class.
//
package server; // (See Note 1.)

// Mandatory Java and ejb packages
// for EJB remote interfaces
import java.rmi.*; // (See Note 2.)
```

```
import javax.ejb.*;

// Define a public interface that extends the
// javax.ejb.EJBObject interface
public interface My8iEJB extends EJBObject {

  // Define the public method that matches
  // exactly the method defined in the Bean class
  public String getFirst8iEJB()
     throws RemoteException;
}
```

Notes on the My8iEJB **interface**:

1. This statement defines this **interface** to be part of the server package.

2. This statement imports the java.rmi.* and the javax.ejb.* packages, respectively. Remember that an EJB remote **interface** is a Java RMI **interface**. So, your EJB remote needs to have access to the RemoteException exception.

Step 4: Write the EJB home **interface**. Clients locate an enterprise Bean via a reference to its home **interface**. The EJB home **interface** is a required component for building EJB applications. Consequently, the My8iEJBHome home **interface** must extend the javax.ejb.EJBHome **interface**. You must define at least one create() method, and the method must include the java.rmi.RemoteException and CreateException exceptions in its **throws** clause. You may define as many create() methods as you wish. However, each create() method defined in the home **interface** must have an exact corresponding ejbCreate() method defined in the Bean's class. More importantly, the create() method is responsible for creating new instances of an EJB remote **interface** or letting clients reuse existing remote instances. Consequently, the return type of the create() method must be of an EJB remote **interface** type. So, use the My8iEJB remote **interface** that you defined in step 3 as the return type of the create() method listed in the home **interface**. Here is the definition of the My8iEJBHome home **interface**:

```
// Program Name:   My8iEJBHome.java
// Version:
// Author:         Your Name
// Description:     An EJB home interface that is used
//                  to create instances of the
//                  My8iEJB EJB remote interface
//
```

```
package server;

import java.rmi.*;
import javax.ejb.*;

// This interface must be public and
// must extend the java.ejb.EJBHome interface
public interface My8iEJBHome extends EJBHome {

// The definition of the developer's home interface
// must include one or more create() methods.
// Each create() method listed here must have a
// matching ejbCreate() method listed in the Bean class.

  My8iEJB create() throws CreateException, RemoteException;

}
```

Step 5: Write the Bean class. The Bean class usually implements some business logic. This simple Bean has one business method that returns a Java `String` object to the client when invoked. All session Beans must extend the `javax.ejb.Session` Bean **interface**. All defined methods must include the `RemoteException` exception in their **throws** clause, where they also may include any application-specific exceptions. However, remember that application-specific exceptions listed here must also be listed in the **throws** clause of the remote **interface**. The Bean class must define an `ejbCreate()` method for each `create()` method listed in its home **interface**, and both method signatures must match exactly. Additionally, a Bean class must define the `ejbActivate()`, `ejbPassivate()`, and `ejbRemove()` methods. Although the Oracle8*i* (1.5 or 1.6) database does use these methods, you still need to list them in the Bean class. Here is the definition of the `My8iEJBClass` class:

```
// Program Name:  My8iEJBClass.java
// Version:
// Author:        Your Name
// Description:   An EJB Bean class consisting
//                of a method that returns when
//                invoked by a client returns a
//                Java String.
//

package server;

import java.rmi.RemoteException;
import javax.ejb.*;

// The Bean class must extend the
```

```
// javax.ejb.SessionBean interface
public class My8iEJBClass implements SessionBean {
  // (See Note 1.)
  public String getFirst8iEJB()
     throws RemoteException {
     String aString =
             "First EJB application stored in the "
             + " Oracle8i database on data-i.com server "
             + " from the Oracle8i Java Component Programming "
             + " with EJB, CORBA, and JSP book.";
     return aString;

  // Note the ejbCreate() method that
  // corresponds to the create() method in the
  // definition of the home interface.
  public void ejbCreate()
     throws RemoteException, CreateException {
  }
  // (See Note 2.)
  public void ejbActivate()
     throws RemoteException {
  }
  public void ejbPassivate()
      throws RemoteException {
  }
  public void ejbRemove()
      throws RemoteException {
  }
  // (See Note 3.)
  public void setSessionContext(SessionContext ctx)
      throws RemoteException {
  }
}
```

Notes on the `My8iEJBClass` class:

1. This statement declares a simple business implementation method. It is an exact match of the business method published in the remote **interface**.

2. This statement and the two others that follow it define the `ejbActivate()`, the `ejbPassivate()`, and the `ejbRemove()` methods. You must declare them in the Bean's class.

3. This method defines the `setSessionContext()` method that the container uses internally to attach a `java.naming.Context` object to the Bean object. The `SessionContext` object remains with the Bean for its entire life cycle until the client disconnects or dies.

Step 6: Compile the home and remote **interfaces** and the Bean's class. Set up one or more variables for your CLASSPATH and compile the remote and home **interfaces** and the Bean class:

```
// Assume that you created a variable
// named YOUR_CLASSPATH_VARIABLE in which
// you stored your CLASSPATH.
Javac -classpath %YOUR_CLASSPATH_VARIABLE% -g
My8iEJB.java My8iEJBHome.java My8iEJBClass.java
```

Step 7: Define a deployment descriptor for the enterprise Bean. If no errors arise from step 6, you may proceed (otherwise, correct your errors). Remember that you list in this file the transaction and security attribute values to instruct the EJB container how to manage the transaction and security environment of your Bean at runtime.

```
// File Name:    My8iEJB.ejb
// Version:
// Author:       Your Name
// Description:  A deployment descriptor for
//               the My8iEJB session Bean.
//
// Define the server.My8iEJBClass to be
// a session Bean.
SessionBean server.My8iEJBClass {

    // define the path for the namespace and
    // the name you wish to use to store
    // a reference to the home interface of the
    // session Bean.
    BeanHomeName = "test/My8iEJB";

    // Store the home interface name
    HomeInterfaceClassName = server.My8iEJBHome;

    // Store the remote interface name
    RemoteInterfaceClassName = server.My8iEJB;

    // Use the Oracle PUBLIC role
    // instructing the EJB container
    // to allow all users who have been
    // granted this system role to use
    // the My8iEJB session Bean.
    AllowedIdentities = {PUBLIC};

    // You can set this variable in seconds.
```

```
    // However, the value of 0 instructs
    // you to use the container's default.
    SessionTimeout = 0;

    // We must set the state management
    // variable. We can set it to be
    // STATEFUL_SESSION or STATELESS_SESSION
    // Oracle8i does not care. All session Beans
    // stored in the database are considered STATELESS.
    StateManagementType = STATEFUL_SESSION;

    // Instruct the container that it must
    // use the CLIENT_IDENTITY attribute
    // to request that the container
    // checks the security identity of the client.
    RunAsMode = CLIENT_IDENTITY;
}
```

Step 8: Create an `ejb-jar` file. The deployment of Enterprise JavaBeans is made easier through the use of a `.jar` file consisting of related **interfaces**, classes, and their dependent classes. Use the `jar` command with the zero (0) option so that you can generate an uncompressed `.jar` file as required by Oracle8*i* version 1.5. The new release of Oracle8*i* 1.6 supports both uncompressed and compressed JAR files. Note that other vendors may have different requirements. At a UNIX or DOS prompt, type the following:

```
// Use the following command if you are in the
// parent directory where the server directory
// is located.
jar cvf0 server/My8iEJB.jar server/*.class

// Use the following command if you are in the
// server directory.
jar cvf0 My8iEJB.jar *.class
```

Step 9: Deploy an Enterprise JavaBean. Enterprise Beans are usable only after they have been deployed. Note that, only at deployment time, the client-side and server-side stub classes and those used internally by the EJB server and container are generated. The Oracle `deployejb` tool accomplishes two tasks: It loads the **interfaces** and classes contained in the `ejb-jar` file into the Oracle8*i* database and generates the `EJBHome` and `EJBObject` classes on the database server and the appropriate classes needed by the EJB server and container and the client.

When you use the `deployejb` tool, it generates a `.jar` file consisting of the client-side stub classes that the client needs to use an enterprise Bean. You can specify a name for the .jar file or you can use the default name generated by the tool. When you deploy the My8iEJB session, you will use My8iEJBClient.jar for the name of the .jar file to instruct the deployejb tool where to store the client stub classes.

Set your CLASSPATH and deploy the My8iEJB session Bean. You may define the ORACLE_SERVICE variable in which you would store the Oracle8*i* service URL or you may use it without defining a variable. Here is an example of the declaration of the ORACLE_SERVICE variable (DOS prompt) followed by the deployejb command:

```
// First, set your CLASSPATH.
// Define a variable: Windows environment
SET ORACLE_SERVICE=sess_iiop://data-i.com:2481:orcl

// UNIX environment
setenv ORACLE_SERVICE sess_iiop://data-i.com:2481:orcl

deployejb -republish
-temp temp -u scott -p tiger
-s %ORACLE_SERVICE% -verbose
-descriptor My8iEJB.ejb -generated My8iEJBClient.jar My8iEJB.jar
```

Listing 3-15 is an example of the output generated by the deployejb tool.

Listing 3-15: Sample output from the deployejb tool

```
...

...
server/My8iEJBHelper already resolved
resolving: server/My8iEJBHolder
server/_st_My8iEJBHome already resolved
oraclex/java/lang/ObjectHelper already resolved
oraclex/java/lang/ObjectHolder already resolved
server/My8iEJBHomeOperations already resolved
done
Generating EJBHome and EJBObject on the server...done
Publishing EJBHome...done
```

Step 10: Write the client. EJB clients—that is, Java/SQLJ applet; servlet; applications; and Java Server Page (JSP), CORBA clients, and non-Java clients—can use Enterprise JavaBeans. The first step of the MyFirstEJBClient client (see Figure 3-9) is to locate a reference to the EJB home **interface**. You defined the My8iEJBHome home **interface** in step 4 of this section. You locate a Bean's home object reference via JNDI. Create the env Hashtable object, store the

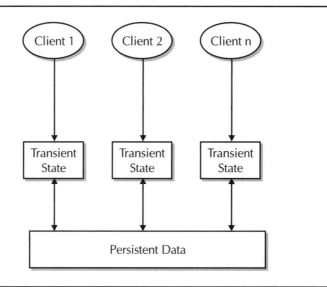

FIGURE 3-9.   *Clients accessing session Beans*

security environment properties of your Bean in the `env` object, and pass these properties to the `InitialContext ic` object.

Now that you have the `ic` Context object, use its `lookup()` method to locate the Bean's home reference. Use the home reference to create a Bean's remote **interface** instance (`my8iEJBBean`) and use `my8iEJBBean` to remotely invoke the Bean's `getFirst8iEJB()` method.

In this section, the `MyFirstEJBClient` client is a Java application and the source code resides in the package called `client`. In Part IV of the book, you will learn how to develop servlet and JSP clients that use EJB. Here is the listing of the `MyFirstEJBClient` client:

```
/*      Program Name: MyFirstEJBClient.java
**      Purpose:     A Java client that uses
**                   the My8iEJB session Bean
**                   stored in Oracle8i data server.
**      Client tasks:
**      1. Locates the remote home Bean interface.
**      2. Authenticates the client to the server.
**      3. Activates an instance of the My8iEJBClass Bean class.
**      4. Invokes the getFirst8iEJB() method of the Bean
*/
```

```
package client;  // (See Note 1.)

// Import the Bean's remote interface (See Note 2.)
import server.My8iEJB;

// Import the Bean's home interface
import server.My8iEJBHome;

// import the ServiceCtx class from the Oracle package
// (See Note 3.)
import oracle.aurora.jndi.sess_iiop.ServiceCtx;

// (See Note 4.)
// import the Java mandatory classes to use JNDI
import javax.naming.Context;
import javax.naming.InitialContext;

// (See Note 5.)
// import application-specific Java classes
import java.util.Hashtable;
import java.sql.*;

public class MyFirstEJBClient {

  // (See Note 6.)
  public static void main(String[] args)
       throws Exception  {
  // Check input parameter
  if (args.length != 4) {
      System.out.println("usage: Client "
           +"serviceURL objectName user password");
      System.exit(1);
   }  // End if

   // Create String objects to store input parameters
   // that contain:
   // args [0] = sess_sh://data-i.com:2481:orcl;
   // args [1] = /test/My8iEJB;
   // args [2] = scott;
   // args [3] = tiger;
   String serviceURL = args [0];
   String objectName = args [1];
   String user = args [2];
   String password = args [3];

   // Create a Hashtable object to store the
   // environment variables
   Hashtable env = new Hashtable();
```

```
    // Required Setup of JNDI security environment properties
    // to be passed to a Context object.

    // (See Note 7.)
    env.put(Context.URL_PKG_PREFIXES, "oracle.aurora.jndi");
    env.put(Context.SECURITY_PRINCIPAL, user);
    env.put(Context.SECURITY_CREDENTIALS, password);
    env.put(Context.SECURITY_AUTHENTICATION,
        ServiceCtx.NON_SSL_LOGIN);

    // Create an instance of the Context class
    Context ic = new InitialContext (env);

    // Create an instance of the EJB object home interface
    My8iEJBHome my8iEJBHome = null;

    // Create a remote object.
    My8iEJB my8iEJBBean = null;

    System.out.println("Variable Created Properly");
System.out.println("serviceURL : " + serviceURL);
System.out.println("objectName : " + objectName);

    try {
        // Use the home interface to
        // locate the EJB object (See Note 8.)
        my8iEJBHome =
            (My8iEJBHome)ic.lookup (serviceURL + objectName);
        System.out.println("Home Lookup Properly");

        // Create a Bean instance (See Note 9.)
        my8iEJBBean = my8iEJBHome.create();

        System.out.println("Bean Created Properly");

    }  // End of try
    catch ( Exception ex ) {
        System.out.println("Cannot locate"
            +" or create My8iEJB object");
        System.err.println("error : " + ex);
        System.exit(1);
    }  // End of catch

    // Create a Java String to store the result from
    // invoking the Bean's method
    String outputFromBean = null;
```

```
// Invoke the EJB Remote Method: getFirst8iEJB().
// Use the my8iEJBBean remote instance to
// invoke the Bean's method and store the result
// in the outputFromBean Java variable.

try {
    // (See Note 10.)
    outputFromBean = my8iEJBBean.getFirst8iEJB();
    System.out.println("Method Invocation went well: "
            + outputFromBean);
}  // End of try
 catch (Exception ex) {
        System.err.println(" Unable to invoke "
        + " the getFirst8iEJB() method : " + ex);
        System.exit(1);
}  // End of catch
}
}
```

Notes on the `MyFirstEJBClient` application:

1. This statement declares the `MyFirstEJBClient` class and specifies that the Java class file resides in a package named `client`.

2. This statement and the one that follows it import the `server.My8iEJB` remote and `server.My8iEJBHome` home **interfaces**, respectively. Clients who use enterprise Beans must import these **interfaces** in their programs. Note that you don't need to import the `server.My8iEJBClass` class in your client program. Why? Remember that the client does not have direct access to this class. The Bean's home and remote **interface** objects are the only required classes that clients need to use a Bean's methods.

3. This statement imports the Oracle `ServiceCtx` class that extends the JNDI `Context` class. Clients using Enterprise JavaBeans that reside in an Oracle8*i* database must set up the type of security for the database connection. There are three possible values (see Appendix A):

   ■ **NON_SSL_LOGIN** A client is authenticated at login time with the username and password.

   ■ **SSL_CREDENTIAL** A client authenticates itself to the server providing a username and password that are encrypted over a Secure Socket Layer (SSL) connection. The server authenticates itself to the client by providing credentials.

■ **SSL_LOGIN**   A client authenticates itself to the server with a username and password within the Login protocol, over an SSL connection. The server does not authenticate itself to the client.

4. This statement and the one that follows it import the `Context` and the `InitialContext` classes, respectively. A client needs an `InitialContext` object to look up a Bean's home **interface** reference.

5. This statement and the one that follows it import the `Hashtable` and any application-required specific Java packages. Remember that you need to create a `Hashtable` object in which to store the security environment properties of your Bean.

6. This statement defines a `main()` method. This client is a Java application; therefore, you need to define a `main()` method in the class.

7. This statement and the three following statements set up the security environment properties required by the JNDI `Context` object for authenticating clients that access the database. The Oracle data server is a secure server; therefore, a client application must authenticate itself before accessing the data server. The client authenticates itself when a CORBA or an EJB object starts a new session.

8. This statement gets the Bean's home **interface** reference via the `InitialContext lookup()` method.

9. This statement uses the `create()` method of the home **interface** object to create a Bean's remote **interface** instance.

10. This statement uses the Bean's remote instance to invoke the Bean's class method.

Step 11: Compile the client. Note that you need to include in your `CLASSPATH` the `My8iEJB.jar` `ejb-jar` file that you created in step 8 of this section and the `My8iEJBClient.jar` `jar` file that the Oracle `deployejb` tool generated for you in step 9.

```
// Set your CLASSPATH and compile the client.
javac -classpath %YOUR_CLASSPATH_VARIABLE% MyFirstEJBClient.java
```

Step 12: Run the client.

```
// If you did not set up your CLASSPATH
// do it now. Run the client.
// You may wish to create a variable to
// store the Oracle8i service URL. For example,
```

```
// the ORACLE_SERVICE variable content is:
// sess_sh://data-i.com:2481:orcl
// Run the client.

java -classpath %YOUR_CLASSPATH_VARIABLE%
client.MyFirstEJBClient %ORACLE_SERVICE% /test/My8iEJB scott tiger
```

Listing 3-16 is the resulting output that you should get after running the client.

Listing 3-16:   Client's output

```
Variable Created Properly
serviceURL : sess_iiop://data-i.com:2481:ORCL
objectName : /test/My8iEJB
Home Lookup Properly
Bean Created Properly
Method Invocation went well:
First EJB application stored in the Oracle8i database
on data-i.com server from the Oracle8i Java Component
Programming with EJB, CORBA, and JSP book.
```

Conclusion

In this chapter, you learned the fundamental characteristics of the Enterprise JavaBeans technology and the Oracle8*i* JServer architecture. In particular, you learned the following:

- The two different types of Beans: session and entity.

- How the Enterprise JavaBeans framework encapsulates transaction management so that Bean developers don't have to worry about it.

- How to build a session Bean and how to define EJB home and remote **interfaces** and Bean classes.

- How Beans are packaged for deployment in `ejb-jar` files.

- How to define a deployment descriptor file.

- How to deploy a session Bean in an Oracle8*i* database.

- How to write EJB clients that use session Beans that reside in an Oracle8*i* database.

In Chapter 4, you will learn how to create EJB components (in Java and SQLJ) that manipulate data stored in an Oracle8*i* database.

CHAPTER

4

Developing EJB Session Beans

n Chapter 3, you learned the basic concepts of the Enterprise JavaBeans (EJB) technology; you developed and deployed the `My8iEJB`, a simple session Bean whose method, when invoked by a client, returns a Java `String` to the caller. In this chapter, you will acquire the skills to develop session Beans that manipulate data stored in an Oracle8*i* database. More importantly here, you will learn how to write your Bean classes using JDBC and SQLJ.

In this chapter, you will learn the following:

■ How the Oracle8*i* JServer supports transactions for EJB and CORBA components

■ How to use EJB transaction attributes to define the transaction policy of Enterprise JavaBeans

■ How to develop session Bean database applications

Oracle8*i* JServer: Transactional Support

EJB and CORBA component models implement transaction context propagations and distributed transactions. However, it is up to the vendors to decide which technique to implement. For example, Oracle8*i* JServer (versions 8.1.5 and 8.1.6) implements transaction context propagation and does not implement distributed transactions. In 8.1.7, distributed transactions will be supported only in non-Bean clients.

Transactions are described in terms of the ACID properties. A transaction is

■ **Atomic**   A unit of work where all changes that take place during the transaction either all work or all fail.

■ **Consistent**   Changes made during a transaction must always leave the database in a consistent state.

■ **Isolated**   Changes made during a transaction are not visible outside of the transaction.

■ **Durable**   Changes made during a transaction are permanent (committed) or are all rolled back.

The Oracle8*i* JServer supports two transaction APIs for use in CORBA and EJB applications:

■ The *Java Transaction Service (JTS) API* specifies the implementation of a transaction manager, which supports a mapping of the Java Transaction API (JTA) 1.0 Specification, that implements a Java mapping of the OMG Object Transaction Service (OTS) 1.1 Specification. The Oracle8*i* database (versions 8.1.5, 8.1.6, and in the upcoming 8.1.7 release) supplies JTS in the Oracle8*i* JServer. In Oracle8*i* version 8.1.7, JTS is supported only for backward compatibility; Oracle 8.1.7 is EJB 1.1-compliant, which requires the use of JTA for uniform support in standalone Java clients and server-side objects. CORBA developers must use JTS for client-side demarcated transactions and server-side object transaction management. A transaction is said to be demarcated when it has a definite beginning and ending point. Developers can explicitly demarcate a transaction by executing a `begin()` method and explicitly ends the transaction by executing a `commit()` or a `rollback()` method. Note that non-Bean EJB client applications can also use JTS to manage transactions, whereas Bean clients cannot. In Oracle8*i*, a non-Bean client resides outside the Oracle database, whereas a Bean client resides only inside the database. See Chapter 8 to learn more about CORBA client-side and server-side objects using JTS.

■ The `javax.jts.UserTransaction` **interface** defines the methods that allow an application to explicitly manage transaction boundaries. The Enterprise JavaBeans architecture requires that EJB containers support transaction demarcation by providing an implementation of the `UserTransaction` **interface**. This interface is used by Bean clients for `TX_BEAN_MANAGED` Beans as well as by non-Bean clients. For example, Oracle provides the `oracle.aurora.jts.client.AuroraTransactionService`, an implementation of the `UserTransaction` **interface** that allows EJB developers to explicitly demarcate transactions in their programs. You explicitly demarcate your transactions by executing the appropriate `begin()` or `commit()` method of the `UserTransaction`. For example, a client starts a transaction by invoking explicitly the `UserTransaction.begin()` method; it explicitly ends the transaction by invoking either the `UserTransaction.commit()` or `UserTransaction.rollback()` method. For server-side transactions, you choose implicit demarcation by having the EJB container manage your transactions for you. `UserTransaction` is used in enterprise Beans, where a Bean is running using the `TX_BEAN_ MANAGED` transaction attribute.

Note that nested transactions are not supported in the Oracle8*i* JServer (Oracle8*i* versions 8.1.5, 8.1.6, and 8.1.7). Transactions are said to be *nested* when a program attempts to begin a new transaction before committing or rolling back any existing transaction. Attempts to use nested transactions cause the transaction service to throw a `SubTransactionUnavailable` exception. Also note that methods of the JTS that support transaction timeout, such as JTS `setTimeout()`, and transaction services supplied with Oracle8*i* (versions 8.1.5 and 8.1.6) do not interoperate with other OTS implementations, nor do they manage distributed transactions. In Oracle8*i* (version 8.1.7), transaction control distributed among multiple database servers will be available for standalone Java clients and not for server-side objects. Also notice that as part of EJB 1.1, `UserTransaction` has been moved from `javax.jts.UserTransaction` to `javax.jta.UserTransaction`.

EJB Declarative Transaction Attributes Revisited

In this section, you will learn the semantics of EJB transaction attributes and how to use them in order for the Oracle8*i* EJB container to properly manage the Bean's transaction environment. In subsequent sections of this chapter, you will develop EJB applications that use the transaction attributes so as to provide you a better understanding of how and when to list them in a Bean deployment descriptor file.

EJB servers are transactional servers. Bean providers can elect to have the EJB container manage all transactions. You do so via EJB transaction attributes. You define the transaction policy of Enterprise JavaBeans through transaction attributes listed in an EJB deployment descriptor file. The ability to specify how enterprise Beans participate in transactions through attribute-based programming is one of the most important features of the EJB component model.

A transaction attribute tells the EJB container how to manage transaction scopes before and after the execution of enterprise Bean methods. In EJB, a transaction scope includes those Beans (session or entity Beans) that are participating in a particular transaction. The scope of a transaction starts when a client invokes a Bean's method. Remember that a transaction is made up of one or more tasks and all the tasks that make up the unit of work must succeed for the entire transaction to succeed.

In situations where a client program is designed so that it can use several Beans during a specific transaction, once the transactional scope has started, it is propagated to all other newly created Beans. A transaction is propagated to another Bean when that other Bean method is invoked.

The EJB servers implement two-phase commits: transaction context propagation and distributed transaction. The Oracle8*i* EJB server (Oracle8*i* versions 1.5 and 1.6) implements only the transaction context propagation. Consequently, transaction contexts generated in the Oracle8*i* EJB server are never propagated outside of the

Oracle8*i* database. Note that transaction contexts cannot span multiple servers or multiple database sessions in a single service.

The `QualityControl` application that you will develop in Chapter 5 illustrates how a transaction scope is propagated from one Bean to another. In the `QcClient` client application, the scope of the transaction includes the `QcBean` and `ObservationBean` Beans. The transaction scope starts when `QcClient` creates an `observationRemote` instance and invokes the `getAllObs()` method of the `ObsImp` class. The transaction scope that got started is then propagated to the newly created `QcRemote` instance. See Chapter 5 for a complete definition of the `QcClient` application.

Transaction Control

Use the `TransactionAttribute` variable in an EJB deployment descriptor file to instruct the EJB container how to manage a Bean transaction environment. Transaction control can be done at two levels:

■ **Bean level**   When specified at the Bean level, the transactional attribute applies to all the methods of the Bean. Listing 4-1 is an example that illustrates a transaction control specified at the Bean level:

Listing 4-1   Bean-level transaction control

```
// File name: Obs.ejb
// Purpose  : Deployment descriptor file for the
//            Observation session Bean.

SessionBean obsserver.ObsImp {

    BeanHomeName = "test/ObservationBean";
    HomeInterfaceClassName = obsserver.ObsHome;
    RemoteInterfaceClassName = obsserver.ObsRemote;

    SessionTimeout = 0;
    AllowedIdentities = { SYSDBA };
    //
    TransactionAttribute = TX_REQUIRED;
    RunAsMode = CLIENT_IDENTITY;
}
```

■ **Method level**   At this level, the transactional attribute applies at the method level only and overrides the value specified at the Bean level. This is true for all transaction attribute values except the TX_BEAN_ MANAGED attribute. Recall that the TX_BEAN_MANAGED attribute cannot be mixed with other attributes, nor can it be overridden at a method level.

Listing 4-2 is an example that demonstrates a transaction control specified at a method level:

Listing 4-2   Method-level transaction control

```
// File name: Obs2.ejb
// Purpose  : Deployment descriptor file for the
//            Observation session Bean.

SessionBean obsserver.ObsImp {

   BeanHomeName = "test/ObservationBean";
   HomeInterfaceClassName = obsserver.ObsHome;
   RemoteInterfaceClassName = obsserver.ObsRemote;

   SessionTimeout = 0;
   AllowedIdentities = { SYSDBA };
   // Transaction control at the Bean-Level
   TransactionAttribute = TX_NOT_SUPPORTED;
   RunAsMode = CLIENT_IDENTITY;

   public ObsHelper insertObs(ObsHelper obs){
     // Transaction Control at method-level
     TransactionAttribute = TX_REQUIRED;
   }
}
```

The EJB Specification (1.0 and 1.1) defines six possible values for the transaction attribute:

- TX_NOT_SUPPORTED
- TX_REQUIRED
- TX_SUPPORTS
- TX_REQUIRES_NEW
- TX_MANDATORY
- TX_BEAN_MANAGED

TX_NOT_SUPPORTED   The TX_NOT_SUPPORTED attribute can be declared for the entire Bean or for specific methods on a Bean. When declared for the entire Bean, TX_NOT_SUPPORTED instructs the Oracle8*i* EJB container not to invoke transaction support for the Bean's methods. The TX_NOT_SUPPORTED can be declared at the Bean level (therefore, it applies to all the methods of the Bean) or at a method level. A transaction attribute value declared at a method level will explicitly override the transaction attribute value specified at the Bean level. This is true for all EJB transaction attributes except the TX_BEAN_MANAGED attribute value. Note that a Bean that is running under TX_NOT_SUPPORTED cannot perform any SQL operations. In fact, the Oracle8*i* EJB server will throw an exception if this is attempted. The My8iEJB application, which you developed in the "Writing Your First Enterprise JavaBean" section of Chapter 3, is a good example illustrating the use of the TX_NOT_SUPPORTED attribute value. Note that this EJB application does not perform any SQL operations. You could modify the My8iEJB.ejb deployment descriptor file by specifying the TX_NOT_SUPPORTED transaction attribute value:

```
// File Name:     My8iEJB.ejb
…

…

    // Instruct the container that it must
    // use the CLIENT_IDENTITY attribute
    // to request that the container
    // checks the security identity of the client.
    RunAsMode = CLIENT_IDENTITY;

    // Additional code to specify
    // A transaction attribute value
    TransactionAttribute = TX_NOT_SUPPORTED;
}
```

Note that if you modify a Bean deployment descriptor file, you must redeploy this Bean. Remember that the EJB container only looks at the descriptor file during deployment process, but it enforces the Bean transaction policy at runtime.

TX_REQUIRED   In the Oracle8*i* database, a transaction can involve many client-side and server-side objects and may encompass one or many methods of these objects. The TX_REQUIRED value tells the container that a Bean method must be invoked within a transaction scope. The scope of a transaction is defined by a transaction context (a pseudo-object) that carries the state of the transaction from one object to another. For example, when a client invokes a *begin transaction* method, the client transaction service implicitly creates a client transaction context. After the context is created, subsequent method calls will be made within the client transaction context.

When the TX_REQUIRED transaction attribute value is declared in the deployment descriptor, there are two possible scenarios:

■ **A client explicitly starts a transaction**   Non-Bean client applications can use the JTS or JTA
    oracle.aurora.jts.client.AuroraTransactionService
    and oracle.aurora.jts.util.TS **interfaces** to control

transaction environment, whereas Bean clients can do so via the
`javax.jts.UserTransaction` **interface** (8.1.5 and 8.1.6, but
`javax.jta.UserTransaction` for 8.1.7). Both sets of interfaces define
`begin()` and `commit()` methods that allow clients to control a Bean's
transaction environment. For example, a client starts a transaction by
invoking a `begin()` transaction method. When the client calls the
`begin()` method, the client transaction service implicitly creates a
transaction context object and then propagates the transaction context to
each object that the client calls. It appears as though the client transaction
service is using the transaction object when in fact this object is being used
by the EJB container to delegate calls to the Bean's methods. Listing 4-3
illustrates how a non-Bean client can explicitly start a transaction by
invoking the `begin()` method from the `oracle.aurora.jts.util.TS`
interface; Listing 4-4 is an example of how a Bean uses a
`SessionContext` instance to invoke the `begin()` and `commit()`
methods from the `UserTransaction` **interface**.

Listing 4-3   Non-Bean client-demarcated transaction

```
// Transaction control by a non-Bean client
// Import the interfaces
import oracle.aurora.jts.client.AuroraTransactionService;
import javax.jts.*;
import oracle.aurora.jts.util.TS;
..
..
public class ObsClientApp {
..
..


// A transaction service must
// be initialized before a client
// can start a transaction.
AuroraTransactionService.initialize (ic, serviceURL);

// A client takes control by
// starting a transaction explicitly.
TS.getTS ().getCurrent ().begin ();

// Call one or more server-side methods

// A client explicitly ends a transaction
// by committing.
```

```
TS.getTS ().getCurrent ().commit (false);

// or
TS.getTS ().getCurrent ().commit (true);
..
}
```

Listing 4-4   Bean client-demarcated transaction

```
// Transaction control by an enterprise Bean client
// Import the UserTransaction interface
import javax.jts.UserTransaction;
..
..
public class PassedObsImp implements SessionBean {
    SessionContext ctx;
..
..
public void setSessionContext (SessionContext ctx) {
    this.ctx = ctx;
}
..
// Start the transaction
ctx.getUserTransaction ().begin();
..
..
// Invoke some methods

// End the transaction
ctx.getUserTransaction ().commit();
}
```

■ **A client does not start a transaction**   Remember that as a Bean provider, you do not have to explicitly control transactions via a client. Based on the transactional attributes specified for a Bean in the deployment descriptor file, the EJB server will implicitly manage the Bean transactions for you. In the case where a client does not start a transaction, the container starts a new transaction for each method call and the transaction tries to commit after each call completes. The commit protocol is completed before the Bean's results are sent to the client. If there are other Beans that are participating in the current transaction (that is, if a transaction scope has started), the Oracle8*i* EJB server will send the transaction context to these server objects as well as to other requested resources.

TX_SUPPORTS   This attribute value instructs the container to include the entire Bean or a specific method within the transaction scope in which it is invoked. If the client has established a transaction context, then the Bean container uses that context. If the client has not established transaction context, then the EJB methods are invoked with no transaction support. More importantly, if a Bean method is part of a transactional scope and it invokes another Bean method, then the transaction is propagated from the former to the latter.

TX_REQUIRES_NEW   This attribute instructs the container to always invoke the Bean methods with a new transaction. The Bean container starts a transaction before each invocation of a Bean method and attempts to commit the transaction when the method completes. Note that any existing transaction will be suspended before the new transaction is created and will be resumed after the new transaction ends.

TX_MANDATORY   When specified at the method level, the `TX_MANDATORY` attribute value instructs the EJB container to use the client transaction context for transaction management. If the client has not created a transaction object, the container throws the `TransactionRequired` exception to the client. Note that in this scenario, the client transaction context is propagated to the resources or other enterprise Bean objects that are invoked from the enterprise Bean object.

TX_BEAN_MANAGED   As indicated by its name, the `TX_BEAN_MANAGED` value instructs the container to delegate transaction management to the Bean itself. A session Bean accesses the transaction service through a `SessionContext` object. The `SessionContext` object is a parameter in the `setSessionContext()` method. The container must give the Bean its `Context` object, through which all other environmental objects can be retrieved.

At initialization time (that is, when the Bean is instantiated), the Bean calls the `setSessionContext()` method to obtain its `SessionContext` object. The EJB container supplies this object to the `setSessionContext()` method.

When the `TX_BEAN_MANAGED` attribute value is specified in the deployment descriptor file, the Bean class must use the `javax.jts.UserTransaction` **interface** method to manage transactions on its own. More importantly, the `TX_BEAN_MANAGED` attribute value cannot be mixed with other transaction attribute values or cannot be overridden by method-level attribute declarations. When using Bean-managed transactions, the transaction boundaries span Bean methods: you can begin a transaction in one method, and the transaction can be rolled back or committed in a separate method called subsequently.

The container makes the `javax.jts.UserTransaction` interface available to the enterprise Bean through the `EJBContext.getUserTransaction()` method, as illustrated in the following example:

```
import javax.jts.UserTransaction;
... EJBContext ic = ...;
...
UserTransaction tx = ic.getUserTransaction();
tx.begin();
 ... // do work tx.commit();
```

The container must manage transactions on a `TX_BEAN_MANAGED` Bean as follows:

- When a client invokes a `STATEFUL TX_BEAN_MANAGED` session Bean, the container suspends any incoming transaction. In this scenario, the container allows the session instance to initiate a transaction using the `javax.jts.UserTransaction` interface. The instance becomes associated with the transaction and remains associated until the transaction terminates.

- When a Bean-initiated transaction is associated with the instance, methods on the instances run under that transaction.

A business method that initiated the transaction can complete without committing or rolling back the transaction. However, the container must retain the association between the transaction and the instance across multiple client calls until the transaction terminates. For example, in scenarios where a Bean client starts an inner transaction (by invoking a Bean's method) after it has started a transaction service, the outer transaction would be suspended and resumed after the container-managed transaction (inner transaction) has been started, used, ended, or suspended.

Transaction Attributes Guidelines

Here are some guidelines regarding the use of transaction attributes:

- The default choice for a transaction attribute should be `TX_REQUIRED`. Enterprise JavaBeans with the `TX_REQUIRED` attribute can be easily composed to perform work under the scope of a single transaction using a specific transaction API.

- The `TX_REQUIRED_NEW` transaction attribute is useful when your Bean's methods need to commit unconditionally, whether or not a transaction is already in progress. An example is a Bean method that performs logging. The `serversideLogging` session Bean (Appendix B of the *Oracle8i Enterprise JavaBeans and CORBA Developer's Guide*) is an example of a Bean that performs logging.

Access Control

Use the deployment descriptor file to define the access control policy of your Beans. You do so by assigning a value to the `AllowedIdentities` transaction attribute. The transaction attribute value can be a user name, an Oracle `ROLE`, or a mixture of the two. When you assign an attribute value to the `AllowedIdentities` (user name, `ROLE`, or a mixture) attribute, only users identified by the specific attribute value—that is, users having the `ROLE`—can use the Bean. Like transaction control, access control to a Bean can be specified at the Bean level or the method level.

Bean-Level Access Control

In the `Obs.ejb` deployment descriptor file that you will develop in the "Developing Session Bean Database Applications" section of this chapter, you will use the `AllowedIdentities` attribute to specify access control for the entire Bean. In this example, you will assign the Oracle `SYSDBA` role to this attribute so those Oracle users who have been granted this role can use this Bean. Recall that access control specified at the Bean provides access to all methods defined in the specific Bean. For example

```
// All users who have been granted the Oracle ROLE SYSDBA
// can use all the methods of the Bean.
AllowedIdentities = {SYSDBA};

// Or, allowed only user SCOTT to use the Bean
AllowedIdentities = {SCOTT};
```

Bean Method-Level Access Control

You can override a specific Bean-level access control by specifying access control at a method level. In the deployment descriptor file, you may list Bean method definitions that also include their specific access control. For example,

```
// ejb deployment descriptor file
...
...
// Declare at the Bean-level
AllowedIdentities = {SYSDBA};

// Override the Bean-level control
```

```
// with a method-level control
public void insertObs(ObsHelper obs)
        throws SQLException,RemoteException {
        TransactionAttribute = TX_REQUIRED;
        RunAsMode = CLIENT_IDENTITY;

        // Only Oracle User SCOTT can invoke this method
        AllowedIdentities = {SCOTT};
    }
```

Note that when you specify method access control, the method must be either a public business method or the `ejbCreate()` method of the Bean. Here, you use the `ejbCreate()` method to override the Bean-level control:

```
public void ejbCreate()
        throws RemoteException, CreateException {
        AllowedIdentities = {SCOTT};
    }
```

Session Synchronization

EJB developers that need the EJB container to notify them of the transactional state of their Bean can optionally implement the `SessionSynchronization` **interface** in their Bean class. When implemented, the container uses the `SessionSynchronization` **interface** to save the Bean's state in the database and use the state to notify the Bean of transaction boundaries. The EJB container uses the methods specified in the `SessionSynchronization` **interface** to do so. Listing 4-5 shows the definition of the javax.ejb.SessionSynchronization **interface**:

Listing 4-5   The javax.ejb.SessionSynchronization interface

```
public interface javax.ejb.SessionSynchronization {
    // (See Note 1.)
    public abstract void afterBegin()
        throws RemoteException;
    // (See Note 2.)
    public abstract void afterCompletion(boolean committed)
        throws RemoteException;
    // (See Note 3.)
    public abstract void beforeCompletion()
        throws RemoteException;
}
```

Notes on the `javax.ejb.SessionSynchronization` **interface**:

I. The `afterBegin()` method notifies a session Bean instance that a new transaction has started. Once the transaction has started, the transaction is propagated to the subsequent Bean's methods, whose invocation will be executed in the context of the specified transaction. For example, the `afterBegin()` method could be used to read data from a database and cache the data in the instance fields.

2. The `afterCompletion()` method, as its name suggests, tells the instance whether the transaction has been completed or not (committed or rolled back). Unlike the `afterBegin()` method, this method executes with no transaction context. The `committed` parameter is set to `true` if the transaction has been committed or `false` when rolled back.

3. The `beforeCompletion()` method notifies a session Bean when a transaction is about to be committed. For example, an instance can use this method to write any cached data to a database. Like the `afterBegin()` method, this method executes in the proper transaction context.

CAUTION
If you are using JDBC or SQLJ calls in your Bean to update a database, do not use JDBC or SQLJ to perform transaction services. You cannot use direct SQL commits or rollbacks in your programs through JDBC or SQLJ. Let the Bean itself manage the transactions by specifying the `TX_BEAN_MANAGED` *attribute in the deployment descriptor or via the* `javax.jts.UserTransactions` ***interface***.

For example, do not use explicitly the `commit()` method of the `Connection` **interface** of the `java.sql` package to commit changes to the database. Listing 4-6 illustrates how you would normally use the `commit()` method in an implementation using JDBC:

Listing 4-6   The use of the `commit()` method

```
Connection aConnection = …;
…
…
// When you use the commit() method,
// you are committing explicitly.
// DO NOT EXPLICITLY COMMIT IN YOUR BEAN
aConnection.commit();
```

Although the EJB component offers lots of flexibility to Bean providers, some restrictions are applied to business methods implemented by the Bean class.

Bean developers must follow these restrictions when implementing the methods of a Bean class.

Programming Restrictions

The EJB 1.0 specification contains the following programming restrictions:

- An EJB cannot start new threads nor terminate a running thread. In Oracle8*i* (versions 8.1.5 and 8.1.6), if an EJB starts a new thread, no exception is thrown but the application behavior becomes unpredictable due to interactions with local thread objects in the ORB.

- An EJB is not allowed to use thread synchronization primitives.

- An EJB is not allowed to use the calls to an underlying transaction manager directly. The only exception is employing enterprise Beans with the `TX_BEAN_MANAGED` transaction attribute. These beans can use the `javax.jts.UserTransaction` **interface** to demarcate transactions.

- An EJB is not allowed to change its `java.security.Identity`. Any attempt to do so results in the `java.security.SecurityException` being thrown.

- An EJB is not allowed to use JDBC or SQLJ `commit` and `rollback` methods or to issue direct SQL `commit` or `rollback` commands in the methods of a Bean class.

With the release of Oracle8*i* version 8.1.7, the Oracle database will support the EJB 1.1 Specification. Consequently, programming restrictions contained in EJB 1.1 would apply.

Developing Session Bean Database Applications

By definition, session Beans implement some business tasks. They are Java components that contain business-process models. Remember that a component is an independent piece of software (that is, application-independent) designed for a specific task. In this chapter, the first objective is to create the `ObservationBean` session Bean to manipulate atmospheric observation data stored in the Oracle8*i* data server at the Hurricane Research Division (HRD) of the National Oceanic and Atmospheric Administration (NOAA). More specifically, the `ObservationBean` will provide a set of business methods allowing clients (atmospheric scientists) to manipulate the OCEANIC_OBSERVATION_LIST table. This table is part of the *Scientific Observation Schema* presented in the "Introduction." For a complete listing of the PURCHASE_ORDER and OBSERVATION schemas, see the "Introduction" at the beginning of the book.

In this section, you will use Java to write all the components of the ObservationBean Bean. The Enterprise JavaBean will be loaded and published in an Oracle8*i* database (versions 8.1.5 and 8.1.6). Remember that the Oracle8*i* EJB server provides a JNDI-accessible namespace in which, at deployment time, it stores the name of the published Bean and the reference to the Bean home object. Access to an Oracle database can be accomplished by several means:

- **Java Database Connectivity (JDBC)**   Provides the capability of embedding dynamic SQL statements in Java programs to manipulate data stored in an Oracle8 or Oracle8*i* (versions 1.5 and 1.6) database. Use JDBC in a Java client (located anywhere on a network) to manipulate SQL code residing in an Oracle database. Also, use JDBC in Java source code that resides inside an Oracle8*i* (versions 1.5 and 1.6) database in the form of Java or SQLJ stored procedures, Enterprise JavaBeans, and CORBA (Java only) applications.

- **SQLJ**   Provides the capability of embedding static SQL statements in Java programs.

- **Internet Inter-ORB Protocol (IIOP)**   Provides access to EJB and CORBA components stored in an Oracle8*i* version 1.5 and higher.

Overview of Oracle JDBC Drivers

For Java or SQLJ clients accessing an Oracle database, Oracle Corporation provides four types of JDBC drivers:

- **thin driver**   A 100-percent Java driver for client-side use, specifically in cases where you cannot use JNDI code. This driver does not require an Oracle installation in the client address space. Use this driver for Web browser clients such as applets, servlets, and Java Server Pages (JSP). The following code fragment uses the Oracle thin driver to open a database connection:

    ...

```
// Create a Java String to hold your host name:
String myhost = "data-i.com";
```

```
// Most common syntax for the connection string is:
String connStr1 = "jdbc:oracle:thin:myhost:1521:orcl";

// OR
String connStr2 =
"jdbc:oracle:thin:@(description=(address=(host=myhost)
    (protocol=tcp)(port=1521))(connect_data=(sid=orcl)))";

// Opening a Connection for the JDBC Thin driver
// using connStr1.
Connection conn =
    DriverManager.getConnection(connStr1, "scott", "tiger");

// OR opening a Connection for the JDBC Thin driver
// using connStr2.
Connection conn =
DriverManager.getConnection(connStr2, "scott", "tiger");
```

■ **OCI drivers (OCI8 and OCI7)**   For client-side use with an Oracle client installation. Use this driver if your clients reside in the same server as your database server or for clients that reside anywhere on a network where Oracle client software has been installed on the client machine. Use the Oracle OCI7 or OCI8 driver to open a database connection:

```
// Opening a Connection for the JDBC OCI driver.
String myHostString = "data-i.com";
Connection conn =
    DriverManager.getConnection ("jdbc:oracle:oci8:@myHostString",
                                    "scott", "tiger");
...
...

...
```

■ **Server-side thin driver**   This is functionally the same as the client-side thin driver, but is used for code that runs inside an Oracle server. Use this driver for Java or SQLJ stored procedures, Enterprise JavaBeans, and CORBA applications that reside in an Oracle8*i* database or to access a remote Oracle server from an Oracle server acting as a middle tier. The syntax is the same as the thin driver for Java standalone client programs. For a code sample, see the *thin driver* bullet listing from earlier.

- **Server-side internal driver**   For code that runs inside the target server (that is, inside the Oracle server that it must access). Use this driver the same way you would use the server-side `thin` driver described earlier.

The server-side and client-side Oracle JDBC drivers provide the same basic functionality. They all support the following standards and features (see *Oracle8i JDBC Developer's Guide and Reference*):

- JDK 1.2.*x*/JDBC 2.0 or JDK 1.1.*x*/JDBC 1.22 (with Oracle extensions for JDBC 2.0 functionality). Note that these two implementations use different sets of class files.

- The same syntax and APIs.

- The same Oracle extensions.

- Full support for multithreaded applications.

Listing 4-7 illustrates how to code a Java program to access an Oracle data server:

Listing 4-7   Connecting via Oracle JDBC drivers

```
// Import the appropriate Java packages.
// The following packages are required for
// all Java/SQLJ client programs accessing
// an Oracle database.
import java.sql.*;
import oracle.jdbc.driver.*;

// You must register the OracleDriver for
// Java programs accessing the database.
  DriverManager.registerDriver
        (new oracle.jdbc.driver.OracleDriver());
String myhost = "data-i.com";
// Opening a Connection for the JDBC Thin driver.
Connection conn = DriverManager.getConnection
   ("jdbc:oracle:thin:@(description=(address=(host=myhost)
       (protocol=tcp)(port=1521))(connect_data=(sid=orcl)))",
      "scott", "tiger");

// Opening a Connection for the JDBC OCI driver.
String myHostString = "data-i.com";
Connection conn =
  DriverManager.getConnection ("jdbc:oracle:oci8:@myHostString",
           "scott", "tiger");
```

```
// Server-side internal driver
Connection conn =
  new oracle.jdbc.driver.OracleDriver ().defaultConnection ();

// Connecting with the OracleDriver class
// getConnection() method using the
// internal server-side driver.
Connection conn =
    DriverManager.getConnection("jdbc:default:connection:");
```

Connecting Using JNDI

Use the `lookup()` method of the JNDI `InitialContext` to create a new `ServiceCtx` object specifying the URL in the service identifier:

```
// Create a Hashtable object
Hashtable environment = new Hashtable();

// Set the environment properties using
// the Context URL_PKG_PREFIXES property
// javax.naming.Context.SECURITY_PRINCIPAL
// javax.naming.Context.SECURITY_CREDENTIALS
// javax.naming.Context.SECURITY_ROLE
// javax.naming.Context.SECURITY_AUTHENTICATION

ServiceCtx service = (ServiceCtx)
initContext.lookup("sess_iiop://localhost:2481:ORCL");
```

You are now ready to build the `ObservationBean` session Bean. The first step in a project development is to elicit users' requirements. So, assume that you consulted the users and the requirements of the `ObservationBean` session Bean are as follows.

Write a session Bean that allows users to manipulate `OCEANIC_OBSERVATION_TYPE` objects stored in the `OCEANIC_OBSERVATION_LIST` table. Specifically, clients should be able to

- Insert a new `OCEANIC_OBSERVATION_TYPE` object.

- Insert an array of new `OCEANIC_OBSERVATION_TYPE` objects.

- Get a list of all `OCEANIC_OBSERVATION_TYPE` objects.

- View all information regarding an `OCEANIC_OBSERVATION_TYPE` object based on a specific observation ID (`obs_id`).

The `OCEANIC_OBSERVATION_LIST` table is part of the Scientific Observation Schema. See the "Introduction" for a complete listing of the schema. Listing 4-8 presents the Oracle types and table that the `ObservationBean` uses:

Listing 4-8 OCEANIC_OBSERVATION and OCEANIC_OBSERVATION_TYPE types and OCEANIC_OBSERVATION_LIST table

```
CREATE TYPE OCEANIC_OBSERVATION AS OBJECT(
     latitude_deg          NUMBER(10,4),
     longitude_deg         NUMBER(10,4),
     windspeed_mps         NUMBER(10,4),
     adj_windspeed_mps     NUMBER(10,4),
     wind_direction_deg    NUMBER(6),
     pressure_mb           NUMBER(6))/
CREATE TYPE OCEANIC_OBSERVATION_TYPE AS OBJECT(
     obs_id        NUMBER(8),
     when_t        DATE,
     at_time       CHAR(8),
     station_id    NUMBER(6),
     produced_id   NUMBER(8),
     produced_by   REF PLATFORM_TYPE,
     obsobj        OCEANIC_OBSERVATION)
/
CREATE TABLE OCEANIC_OBSERVATION_LIST
     OF OCEANIC_OBSERVATION_TYPE
/
```

The `ObservationBean` also uses the `OBSACTIONS.GETOBSID()` PL/SQL function and the `OBSACTIONS.INSERTOBS()` PL/SQL procedure. The former generates a new observation ID, whereas the latter adds a new row of `OCEANIC_OBSERVATION_TYPE` into the `OCEANIC_OBSERVATION_LIST` table. Both `GETOBSID()` and `INSERTOBS()` are part of the `OBSACTIONS` PL/SQL package (see Listing 4-9). As a Java developer, you may elect not to write PL/SQL functions or procedures. The decision to use only Java or SQLJ or a combination of Java/SQLJ and PL/SQL depends on the application that you are developing. Oracle Corporation recommends the use of Java or PL/SQL in the following scenarios:

"PL/SQL is an extension of SQL; there is no data type conversions. In scenarios with lots of database read/writes and very little computation, code written in PL/SQL will always run significantly faster than similar code written in Java. However, in cases where lots of computation and few database read/writes are needed, use Java because code written in Java will always run significantly faster than similar code written in PL/SQL."

(See http://technet.oracle.com/products/oracle8i/htdocs/jserver_faq/815faq0005.html.)

In the `ObservationBean` application, the decision to use PL/SQL functions and procedures is twofold:

- **Better performance** The `ObservationBean` is a full-fledged database application. In this scenario, from a performance standpoint, PL/SQL is faster than similar Java code.

- **Use of PL/SQL procedures/functions** If you are a Java developer or Bean provider and developing Java applications that access an Oracle database, it's imperative that you know how to call PL/SQL procedures and functions. You may not be required to write PL/SQL code, but you may be forced to use it in your Java programs. In this chapter, you have the opportunity to learn how to do so.

Listing 4-9 The OBSACTIONS PL/SQL package

```
CREATE OR REPLACE PACKAGE OBSACTIONS AS
--   Get a new Obs_id
     FUNCTION getObsId RETURN NUMBER;
     PRAGMA RESTRICT_REFERENCES(getObsId,WNDS,WNPS,RNPS);

--   Add a new Observation
     PROCEDURE insertObs(p_newobsid  IN NUMBER,
                         p_whent        IN VARCHAR2,
                         p_attime       IN CHAR,
                         p_ptlid        IN NUMBER,
                         p_latdeg       IN NUMBER,
                         p_londeg       IN NUMBER,
                         p_wsmps        IN NUMBER,
                         p_adjwsmps     IN NUMBER,
                         p_wddeg        IN NUMBER,
                         p_pmb          IN NUMBER,
                         p_stlid        IN NUMBER);

END OBSACTIONS;
/
CREATE OR REPLACE PACKAGE BODY OBSACTIONS AS
--   Use the private FindCurrTime function to
--   find current time. This method is accessible
--   only to the functions and procedures specified
--   in the body section of the OBSACTIONS package.
```

```
--   It's analogous to a Java private method.
     FUNCTION FindCurrTime RETURN CHAR IS
     v_time  CHAR(8);
     BEGIN
          SELECT TO_CHAR(SYSDATE,'HH24MISS') INTO v_time FROM DUAL;
          RETURN v_time;
     EXCEPTION
       WHEN NO_DATA_FOUND THEN
            RETURN v_time;
     END FindCurrTime;

--   Get a new Obs_id
     FUNCTION getObsId RETURN NUMBER IS
       p_obsid NUMBER;
     BEGIN
          SELECT OBSID_SEQ.NEXTVAL INTO p_obsid FROM DUAL;
          RETURN p_obsid;
     EXCEPTION
          WHEN OTHERS THEN
               RETURN p_obsid;
     End getObsId;

--   Create an object of TYPE Oceanic_observation
--   This is a private function.
     FUNCTION OceanicObservation (p_latdeg  IN NUMBER,
                                  p_londeg   IN NUMBER,
                                  p_wsmps    IN NUMBER,
                                  p_adjwsmps IN NUMBER,
                                  p_wddeg    IN NUMBER,
                                  p_pmb      IN NUMBER)
                                        RETURN oceanic_observation IS

--     Create an oceanic_observation type.
       v_obs  oceanic_observation :=
          oceanic_observation(p_latdeg,p_londeg,
             p_wsmps,p_adjwsmps,p_wddeg,p_pmb);
     BEGIN
          RETURN v_obs;
     END OceanicObservation;

--   Add a new Observation
     PROCEDURE insertObs(p_newobsid IN NUMBER,
                     p_whent          IN VARCHAR2,
                     p_attime         IN CHAR,
                     p_ptlid          IN NUMBER,
                     p_latdeg         IN NUMBER,
                     p_londeg         IN NUMBER,
```

```
                        p_wsmps        IN NUMBER,
                        p_adjwsmps     IN NUMBER,
                        p_wddeg        IN NUMBER,
                        p_pmb          IN NUMBER,
                        p_stlid        IN NUMBER) IS

        v_date DATE := TO_DATE(p_whent,'DD-MON-YYYY');
        v_time  CHAR(8) := p_attime;
        v_newobsid  NUMBER := TO_NUMBER(p_newobsid);
        v_platformref  REF PLATFORM_TYPE;

        v_obs Oceanic_Observation :=
          Oceanic_Observation(p_latdeg,p_londeg,
            p_wsmps,p_adjwsmps,p_wddeg,p_pmb);
     BEGIN
--    Check input date p_whent
       IF  v_date IS NULL THEN
           SELECT SYSDATE INTO v_date FROM DUAL;
       END IF;

--    Check input time
      IF  v_time IS NULL THEN
          v_time := FindCurrTime;
      END IF;

--     Get platform_type REF
      SELECT REF(P) INTO v_platformref
          FROM platform_type_list P
          WHERE P.key_id = p_ptlid;

--    Insert new object
      INSERT INTO OCEANIC_OBSERVATION_LIST
        VALUES(
              v_newobsid, v_date, v_time, p_stlid, p_ptlid,
              v_platformref, v_obs
             );
      -- commit; (See Note 1.)
   EXCEPTION
     WHEN NO_DATA_FOUND THEN
           NULL;
     WHEN OTHERS THEN
           NULL;
   END insertObs;

END OBSACTIONS;
/
```

Note on the OBSACTIONS PL/SQL package:

1. Note that there is no need to commit explicitly in the PL/SQL package. The EJB container will do so for you according to the transaction attribute value that you will specify in the deployment descriptor file for the ObservationBean. In the "The obs.ejb Deployment Descriptor File" section of this chapter, you will use the TX_REQUIRED transaction attribute value to instruct the EJB container to start a new transaction for each method call. Recall that the transaction will try to commit before the call completes.

The second step in developing an application is to produce an analysis for the application. In this step, you provide a high-level view of the application. Here, you will use Java to write the source code. Consequently, the high-level view consists of Java interfaces and a Bean class and their supporting classes, including their relationships (if any) with each other. Figure 4-1 presents the high-level view of the Observation session Bean.

The components of the ObservationBean Enterprise JavaBean are as follows:

- The ObsHelper **class**, a Java serializable class that the Observation Bean uses for marshaling and unmarshaling ObsHelper objects between client-side and server-side objects

- The ObsRemote **interface** that **extends** the javax.ejb.EJBObject **interface**

- The ObsHome **interface** that **extends** the javax.ejb.EJBHome **interface**

- The ObsImp **class** that **implements** the javax.ejb.SessionBean

- The obs.ejb deployment descriptor file

Figure 4-1 does not include the deployment descriptor file and the client application that will use the ObservationBean enterprise Bean. Usually, the high level of an EJB component does not include these components. Remember, however, that an EJB deployment descriptor file is an important component in the EJB model; therefore, you will write a deployment descriptor file and also a client application that will use the ObservationBean session Bean. Note that the source code for all the programs presented in this chapter are included in the Ch4ReaderCode.zip file. This file contains two versions of the ObsRemote **interface**, ObsImp class, and Chapter4Client class. The first version is identical to the one that we present in this chapter. In the second version, we used a Java ArrayList object instead of a Java array. Notice that you will also use the latter in the application that you will develop in Chapter 5.

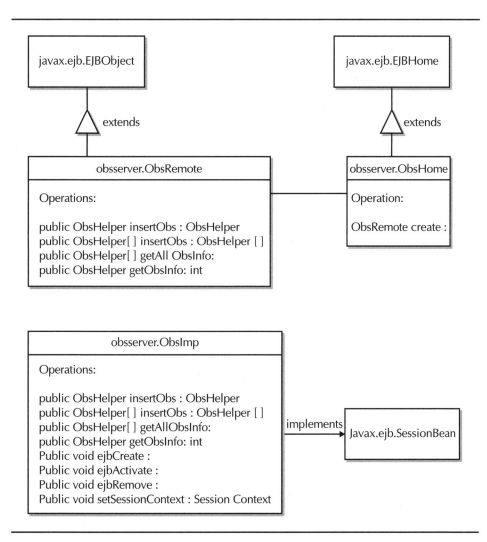

FIGURE 4-1. *High-level view of the **Observation** session Bean*

Note in Figure 4-1 that the ObservationBean session Bean consists of two Java packages: the helpers and obsserver packages. The ObsHelper class resides in the helpers package, whereas the ObsRemote remote **interface**, the ObsHome home **interface**, and the ObsImp Bean class reside in the obsserver package. The ObsRemote remote **interface** and the ObsImp Bean class use the ObsHelper class. Specifically, the ObsHelper class is used as an input parameter and/or a return type for the method advertised in the remote **interface** and implemented in the Bean class.

The `ObsHelper` Class

This class implements the `java.io.Serializable` **interface**. You will use instances of this class to marshal and unmarshal data that your Bean class needs to manipulate data stored in Oracle relational and object-relational tables. Here is the `ObsHelper` class:

```
/*      Program Name:      ObsHelper.java
**
**      Purpose:           A Java serializable Helper class
**                         used for passing parameter objects
**                         (OCEANIC_OBSERVATION_TYPE)
**                         between clients, EJB and CORBA
**                         components.
*/

package helpers;

import java.io.Serializable;
import java.math.BigDecimal;

public class ObsHelper
    implements java.io.Serializable {

    // Member variables
      public BigDecimal obs_id = null;
      public String when_t = null;
      public String at_time = null;
      public BigDecimal station_id = null;
      public BigDecimal produced_id = null;
      public BigDecimal latitude = null;
      public BigDecimal longitude = null;
      public BigDecimal wdspd = null;
      public BigDecimal adj_wdspd = null;
      public BigDecimal wddir = null;
      public BigDecimal pressure = null;
      // Define an array of BigDecimal
      public BigDecimal[] idArray = null;

    // (See Note 1.)
      // Default Constructor
      public ObsHelper () {

    }
```

```
  // Parameterized Constructor1
   public ObsHelper (
       BigDecimal obs_id, String when_t, String at_time,
       BigDecimal station_id, BigDecimal produced_id,
       BigDecimal latitude, BigDecimal longitude,
     BigDecimal wdspd,     BigDecimal adj_wdspd,
       BigDecimal wddir,      BigDecimal pressure) {

           this.obs_id = obs_id;
           this.when_t = when_t;
           this.at_time = at_time;
           this.station_id = station_id;
           this.latitude = latitude;
           this.longitude = longitude;
           this.wdspd = wdspd;
           this.adj_wdspd = adj_wdspd;
           this.wddir = wddir;
           this.pressure = pressure;
   }
 // Parameterized Constructor2
 // Use this constructor to initialize only obs_id
   public ObsHelper (BigDecimal obs_id) {
       this.obs_id = obs_id;
   }
// Parameterized Constructor3
// Use this constructor to initialize only idArray
   public ObsHelper (BigDecimal[] arrayOfId) {

       if ( arrayOfId.length > 0 ) {
           int loopVar = 0;
           idArray = new BigDecimal[arrayOfId.length];

           // iterate
           while ( loopVar < arrayOfId.length ) {
             idArray[loopVar++] = arrayOfId[loopVar++];
         }
       }
}
```

Note on the `ObsHelper` class:

1. This class contains several constructors that allow you to create several `ObsHelper` objects according to your needs.

The `ObsRemote` Remote Interface

The following EJB `ObsRemote` **interface** defines methods callable by clients using the `ObservationBean` session Bean. As described by the EJB Specification, EJB remote interfaces must extend the `java.ejb.EJBObject` **interface** and all method signatures must include `java.rmi.RemoteException` in their **throws** clauses. In addition to `RemoteException`, the method definitions can include any application-specific exception in their **throws** clauses. Note that all the business methods advertised in the `ObsRemote` **interface** are accessing an Oracle8*i* database. Recall that Java methods accessing a database need to include `java.sql.SQLException` in their **throws** clauses. Consequently, the `getNewObs()`, `insertObs()`, `getAllObs()`, and `getObsInfo()` methods include both `RemoteException` and `SQLException` in their **throws** clauses.

CAUTION
Business methods specified in the remote interface must match exactly their implementation body defined in the corresponding Bean class.

Note that the version of the `ObsRemote` **interface** presented here uses a Java array of **ObsHelper** types as input parameters and return types. In Chapter 5, we will present another version that uses a Java `ArrayList` of `ObsHelper` types. The Chapter 4 version of the *ObservationBean* runs in the Oracle8*i* database versions 8.1.5, 8.1.6, and the beta release of 8.1.7, whereas the Chapter 5 version of the Bean can only run in 8.1.6 and 8.1.7. This is so because the latter uses the Java `ArrayList` JDK1.2*x*-compliant. Here is the `ObsRemote` **interface**:

```
// Program Name: ObsRemote.java
// Title:        Your Product Name
// Version:
// Copyright:    Copyright (c) 2000
// Author:       Your Name
// Description:  EJB remote interface for
//               the Observation Bean.

package obsserver;

// import helper classes
import helpers.ObsHelper;
import java.util.Vector;
```

```
// Mandatory Java packages for all EJB.
import java.rmi.*;
import javax.ejb.*;

// Application-specific exception or
// SQLException for database applications.
import java.sql.SQLException;

public interface ObsRemote extends EJBObject {

  // This method gets a new obs_id from the database
  public ObsHelper getNewObs( )
     throws SQLException, RemoteException;

  // Use an ObsHelper object as a passing
  // parameter to transport data that you need
  // to insert in the database.
  // the ObsRemote and ObsHome interfaces and the
  // Bean class reside in an Oracle8i database.
  public ObsHelper insertObs(ObsHelper obs)
     throws SQLException, RemoteException;

  // Overload the insertObs method to pass
  // an array of ObsHelper objects to the Bean class.
  public ObsHelper[] insertObs(ObsHelper[] obs)
      throws SQLException, RemoteException;

  // Get all observation information and return
  // the info in an array of ObsHelper objects
  public ObsHelper[] getAllObs()
      throws SQLException, RemoteException;

    // Get observation information and return
  // an ObsHelper object based on observation id.
  public ObsHelper getObsInfo(int obsid)
      throws SQLException, RemoteException;
}
```

The ObsHome Home Interface

All EJB home interfaces must extend the java.ejb.EJBHome **interface**.
Consequently, the ObsHome **interface** also extends the EJBHome **interface**.
You must specify one or more create() methods in the home **interface**. Recall
that the create() method provides the capability of creating new Bean instances
or reusing existing ones depending on the type of Bean you define. The return type
of the create() method must be the EJB remote **interface** (in this case,

ObsRemote) and it must include both CreateException and
RemoteException in its **throws** clause. Here is the ObsHome **interface**:

```
// Program Name: ObsHome.java
// Version:
// Copyright:     Copyright (c) 2000
// Description:   EJB home interface for the
//                Observation session Bean.
//

package obsserver;

import java.rmi.*;
import javax.ejb.*;

public interface ObsHome extends EJBHome {

  // Create an instance of the ObsRemote interface
public ObsRemote create()
      throws CreateException, RemoteException;
}
```

The ObsImp Bean Class: Implementation Using JDBC

The ObsImp Bean class is the JDBC version of the implementation of the business
methods. A SQLJ implementation of this class is presented at the end of this chapter.
The ObsImp Bean class specifies the method bodies that match exactly those
defined in the ObsRemote **interface**. As required by the EJB Specification, a
Bean class must extend the SessionBean **interface**, and the ObsImp Bean
class does so. The ObsImp class illustrates a JDBC implementation and uses
explicitly the server-side internal JDBC driver to establish a database session. Here
is the ObsImp class:

```
/* Program Name:  ObsImp.java
** Version:
** Description:   An EJB Bean class that allows
**                client to insert a ObsHelper
**                object, an array of ObsHelper,
**                and retrieve an array of ObsHelper.
**                An implementation using JDBC.
*/

package obsserver;

// import helper classes
import helpers.ObsHelper;
```

```java
import java.rmi.RemoteException;
import javax.ejb.*;

// import application-specific exception
import java.sql.SQLException;

import java.sql.*;
import oracle.sql.*;

// Import supporting Java classes
import java.math.BigDecimal;
import java.util.Vector;

// This statement defines a Bean class that
// implements the javax.ejb.SessionBean interface
// as specified by EJB specifications.
public class ObsImp implements SessionBean {

    // This method, callable by clients, connects to
    // the database and calls the overloaded getNewObs(conn)
    // to get a new obs_id.
    // First, the method calls the connectDb() method to establish
    // a connection to the Oracle8i database.
    // Second, it calls the getNewObs(conn) overloaded
    // method using the conn (of java.sql.Connection type)
    // object as an input parameter to the method.
    // When invoked, the getNewObs(conn) generates
    // the new observation identification number (obs_id).
    public ObsHelper getNewObs()
        throws SQLException, RemoteException {

      Connection conn = null;
      try {
            // Use the internal JDBC driver
            // to connect to the database
      conn = connectDb();
            // get a new obs_id
         ObsHelper obs = getNewObs(conn);
            // Return an ObsHelper object
         return obs;

      } // End try
      catch(SQLException e) {
                // throw a new SQLException
                   throw e;
             }  // End catch()
```

```
} // End getNewObs()

// This method is NOT callable by clients.
// Therefore, it is not listed in the
// ObsRemote interface. It calls the PL/SQL
// OBSACTIONS.GETOBSID() function to generate the new obs_id.
// To do so, it needs the methods of a java.sql.Connection object
// (See Note 1.)
public ObsHelper getNewObs(Connection conn)
    throws SQLException, RemoteException {

  // Create a CallableStatement object
    CallableStatement cstmt  = null;
  try {
      // Prepare a String for the call
        String sqlId =
          "{? = call OBSACTIONS.GETOBSID}";

      // Prepare the call using the conn parameter
      cstmt = conn.prepareCall(sqlId);

      // Declare that the ? is a return value of type Integer
      cstmt.registerOutParameter (1, Types.INTEGER);

      // Get the new obsid by executing the query
      cstmt.execute ();

      // Store the result of the query
      // in the anObsId variable.
    BigDecimal anObsId = new BigDecimal(cstmt.getInt (1));

      // Return an ObsHelper object using the new id
      return new ObsHelper(anObsId);

    }  // End try
    catch (SQLException e) {
        throw e;
    }  // End catch

  // Clean up. This statement uses the finally()
  // method to clean up any loose ends and exit the method
  // gracefully. Note that you must always close
  // a CallableStatement object after using it.
  // This method guarantees that no matter what
  // happens in this method, the CallableStatement
  // object will always be closed after processing.
```

```
            finally {
                if ( cstmt != null ) cstmt.close();
        } // End finally()

} // End getNewObs(conn)

// This method, a client-callable method, gets a
// new obs_id number and adds a new OCEANIC_OBSERVATION_TYPE in the

// OCEANIC_OBSERVATION_LIST TABLE. It does so by calling the
// overloaded insertObs(obs,conn) method. Recall that its
// method definition is specified in the ObsRemote interface.

public ObsHelper insertObs(ObsHelper inObs)
    throws SQLException, RemoteException {

 ObsHelper obs = inObs;
 Connection conn = null;

    try {
        // Use the internal JDBC driver
        // to connect to the database
        conn = connectDb();

        // Get a new obs_id from the database
        ObsHelper anObsid = getNewObs(conn);

        // Update the input obs_id
        obs.obs_id = anObsid.obs_id;

        // call the insertObs(obs,conn) method to
        // insert a new OCEANIC_OBSERVATION_TYPE
        // into the OCEANIC_OBSERVATION_LIST
        anObsid = insertObs(obs,conn);

        // Return an ObsHelper object
        return new ObsHelper(anObsid.obs_id);

    }  // End try
    catch (SQLException e) {
        throw e;
    }  // End catch
 } // End insertObs(obs)

// This statement defines an auxiliary or non-client callable
// method that inserts the Oracle OCEANIC_OBSERVATION_TYPE
// type in the OCEANIC_OBSERVATION_LIST table. It does so
// by calling the PL/SQL OBSACTIONS.INSERTOBS(...) procedure.
```

```
public ObsHelper insertObs(ObsHelper obs, Connection conn)
   throws SQLException, RemoteException {

// Create a CallableStatement object
   CallableStatement cstmt  = null;

 try {
     // Prepare the String to call the PL/SQL
      // OBSACTIONS.INSERTOBS() procedure. (See Note 2.)
      String sql =
       "{call OBSACTIONS.INSERTOBS(?,?,?,?,?,?,?,?,?,?,?)}";

      cstmt = conn.prepareCall(sql);

      // Set the input parameters for the
      // OBSACTIONS.INSERTOBS() PL/SQL procedure
      // This statement and the ten that follow use a
      // combination of setInt() and setString() methods
      // of a CallableStatement object to set the input
      // parameters of the OBSACTIONS.INSERTOBS() procedure.
      cstmt.setInt(1, obs.obs_id.intValue());
      cstmt.setString(2, obs.when_t);
      cstmt.setString(3, obs.at_time);
      cstmt.setInt(4, obs.produced_id.intValue());
      cstmt.setInt(5, obs.latitude.intValue());
      cstmt.setInt(6, obs.longitude.intValue());
      cstmt.setInt(7, obs.wdspd.intValue());
      cstmt.setInt(8, obs.adj_wdspd.intValue());
      cstmt.setInt(9, obs.wddir.intValue());
      cstmt.setInt(10, obs.pressure.intValue());
      cstmt.setInt(11, obs.station_id.intValue());

      cstmt.execute();

      // Return an ObsHelper object
      return new ObsHelper(obs.obs_id);
   }  // End try
   catch (SQLException e) {
      throw e;
   }  // End catch
   // Clean up
   finally {
         if  ( cstmt  != null ) cstmt.close();
         // DO NOT CLOSE CONNECTION INSIDE THE DATABASE
         // if  ( conn  != null ) conn.close();
    } // End finally()
} // End insertObs(obs,conn)
```

```
// Insert an array of OCEANIC_OBSERVATION_TYPE

public ObsHelper[] insertObs(ObsHelper[] inObs)
    throws SQLException, RemoteException {

  int loopVar = 0;
  // Declare an array of ObsHelper objects
  ObsHelper[] returnArray = new ObsHelper[inObs.length];

  Connection conn = null;
  try {
      // Use the internal JDBC driver
      // to connect to the database
      conn = connectDb();

      // Iterate and store an array of
      // obs_ids into returnArray[]
      // This statement defines a while loop
      // that calls successively the getNewObs(conn)
      // and  insertObs(obs,conn) method respectively.
      while ( loopVar < inObs.length ) {
          // get a new obs_id at each iteration
          ObsHelper anObsid = getNewObs(conn);

          // Move an ObsHelper object into obs
          ObsHelper obs = inObs[loopVar];

          // Update the obs.obs_id with the new anObsid.obs_id
          obs.obs_id = anObsid.obs_id;

          // Call the insertObs(..) to add a
          // new row to the database and return
          // a new ObsHelper with the new obs_id.
          returnArray[loopVar] = insertObs ( obs, conn );

          loopVar++;  // Increment the counter
      }  // End while

      // Return an array of ids
      return returnArray;
  }  // End try
  catch (SQLException e) {
      throw e;
  }  // End catch
}  // End insertObs(ObsHelper[] inObs)

// This method uses dynamic SQL to get
// all data from the OCEANIC_OBSERVATION_LIST table
```

```
// The results of the query are stored in a Java array.
// In Chapter 5, you will replace the Java array
// with a Java ArrayList object.
public ObsHelper[] getAllObs()
      throws SQLException, RemoteException {

  Connection conn = null;

  // Need a Java Vector to store the
  // table rows since you do not know
  // how many rows are being retrieved.
  Vector obsList = null;

  // Declare a Java ResultSet object
  ResultSet rset = null;

  // Declare a PreparedStatement variable
  // Note here, specifically, you are using JDBC
  // (dynamic SQL in the Java program) to retrieve
  // a list of all observations stored in the
  // OCEANIC_OBSERVATION_LIST table.
  PreparedStatement pstmt = null;

  // Prepare the SQL SELECT statement
  String sql =
    "SELECT P.obs_id, TO_CHAR(P.when_t,'DD-MM-YYYY'),"
    + "P.at_time, P.station_id, P.produced_id, "
    + "P.obsobj.latitude_deg, P.obsobj.longitude_deg, "
    + "P.obsobj.windspeed_mps, P.obsobj.adj_windspeed_mps, "
    + "P.obsobj.wind_direction_deg, P.obsobj.pressure_mb "
    + "FROM OCEANIC_OBSERVATION_LIST P";

  try {
      // Use the internal JDBC driver to connect to the database
      conn = connectDb();

      pstmt = conn.prepareStatement(sql);

      // Execute the query and store
      // the result in a Java ResultSet.
      rset = pstmt.executeQuery();

      // Instantiate the obsList Vector
    obsList = new Vector();

      while (rset.next()) {
          ObsHelper oneObs = populateData(rset);
          // Insert oneObs object into the Java obsList Vector
```

```
                 obsList.addElement(oneObs);
        }  // End while

        // Get the size of the obsList Vector
        int arraySize = obsList.size();

        // Create an ObsHelper array using the size
        // of the obsList Vector
        ObsHelper anArrayOfObsHelper[] = new ObsHelper[arraySize];

        // Copy all info from the vector to the
        // anArrayOfObsHelper array
        obsList.copyInto(anArrayOfObsHelper);

        // Return an array of ObsHelper objects to the caller
        return anArrayOfObsHelper;
} // End try
catch (SQLException e) {
    throw e;
}  // End catch
catch (java.lang.Exception e) {
    throw new SQLException("ArrayList error in Select "
    + " Observations: " + e.getMessage());}  // End catch

// Clean up
finally {
  if ( rset  != null ) rset.close();
   if ( pstmt  != null ) pstmt.close();
  }
}  // End getAllObsInfo()

// Get observation info for a specific obs_id
// This statement defines a method that retrieves the
// information of a specific row from the table identified
// by an observation ID.
public ObsHelper getObsInfo(int obsid)
        throws SQLException, RemoteException {

    Connection conn = null;

    // Declare a Java ResulSet object
    ResultSet rset = null;

    // Declare a PreparedStatement variable
    PreparedStatement pstmt = null;

    // Prepare the SQL SELECT statement
    // Note the use of JDBC(dynamic SQL in the Java program)
```

```java
        // to perform the query.
        String sql =
          "SELECT P.obs_id, TO_CHAR(P.when_t,'DD-MM-YYYY'),"
          + "P.at_time, P.station_id, P.produced_id, "
          + "P.obsobj.latitude_deg, P.obsobj.longitude_deg, "
          + "P.obsobj.windspeed_mps, P.obsobj.adj_windspeed_mps, "
          + "P.obsobj.wind_direction_deg, P.obsobj.pressure_mb "
          + "FROM OCEANIC_OBSERVATION_LIST P "
          + "WHERE P.obs_id = ?";

        try {
            conn = connectDb();

            pstmt = conn.prepareStatement(sql);

            pstmt.setInt(1, obsid);
            rset = pstmt.executeQuery();

            ObsHelper oneObs = null;
            while (rset.next()) {
               oneObs = populateData (rset);
            }
            // Return an ObsHelper object
               return oneObs;

       }    // End try
       catch (SQLException e) {
            throw e;
      }   // End catch

       // Clean up
       finally {
            if ( rset  != null ) rset.close();
            if ( pstmt != null ) pstmt.close();
       } // End finally
  } // End getObsInfo()

// This method populates the result set data
// to an ObsHelper object.
public ObsHelper populateData (ResultSet rset)
   throws SQLException {

   try {
     // Declare an ObsHelper object
     // using the default constructor.
     ObsHelper oneObs = new ObsHelper();

     // Set the member variables of the ObsHelper object.
```

```
// Note that you could also use the parameterized
// contructor1 defined in the ObsHelper class.

oneObs.obs_id   = new BigDecimal(rset.getInt(1));
oneObs.when_t   = rset.getString(2);
oneObs.at_time  = rset.getString(3);

rset.getInt(4);
if  (rset.wasNull())
    oneObs.station_id = null;
else
    oneObs.station_id = new BigDecimal(rset.getInt(4));
rset.getInt(5);
if  (rset.wasNull())
    oneObs.produced_id = null;
else
    oneObs.produced_id = new BigDecimal(rset.getInt(5));
rset.getInt(6);
if  (rset.wasNull())
    oneObs.latitude = null;
else
    oneObs.latitude = new BigDecimal(rset.getInt(6));
rset.getInt(7);
if  (rset.wasNull())
    oneObs.longitude = null;
else
    oneObs.longitude = new BigDecimal(rset.getInt(7));
rset.getInt(8);
if  (rset.wasNull())
    oneObs.wdspd = null;
else
    oneObs.wdspd = new BigDecimal(rset.getInt(8));
rset.getInt(9);
if  (rset.wasNull())
    oneObs.adj_wdspd = null;
else
    oneObs.adj_wdspd = new BigDecimal(rset.getInt(9));
rset.getInt(10);
if  (rset.wasNull())
    oneObs.wddir = null;
else
    oneObs.wddir = new BigDecimal(rset.getInt(10));
rset.getInt(11);
if  (rset.wasNull())
    oneObs.pressure = null;
else
    oneObs.pressure = new BigDecimal(rset.getInt(11));
return oneObs;
```

```
    } // End try
    catch (SQLException e) {
        throw e;
    }   // End catch
    catch (java.lang.NullPointerException e) { -
        throw new java.lang.NullPointerException
            (e.getMessage());
    } // End catch
} // End populateData()

// This method is called by all methods that need
// to connect to the database using the
// internal JDBC driver
public static Connection connectDb()
    throws SQLException, RemoteException {

    // Note that this method is only accessible
    // to the Bean class methods and NOT to clients.
    // Create a java.sql.Connection variable
    Connection conn = null;

    // Instantiate using the Oracle8i internal JDBC driver
    conn =
     DriverManager.getConnection("jdbc:default:connection:");

    // Return a java.sql.Connection object
    return conn;

} // End connectDb()


// This statement and the five methods that follow define
// the mandatory enterprise Bean methods.
// Note that you can code the ejbCreate() method so that it
// obtains a java.sql.Connection object for you.
// Recall that the ejbCreate() method is automatically
// called when a client invokes the create() method on
// the EJB home interface. If you include the logic to
// establish a database connection, this
// connection will be live for the life time
// of the Bean. Also note that you can also perform here the
// prepare statements; that way statements are compiled once
// and not every time the methods are invoked.
public void ejbCreate()
    throws RemoteException, CreateException {
} // End ejbCreate()

public void ejbActivate()
```

```
      throws RemoteException {
   } // End ejbActivate()

   public void ejbPassivate()
       throws RemoteException {
   } // End ejbPassivate()
   public void ejbRemove()
       throws RemoteException {
   } // End ejbRemove()

    public void setSessionContext(SessionContext ctx)
       throws RemoteException {
   } // End setSessionContext()

} // End of ObsImp class
```

Notes on the ObsImp class:

1. This statement defines a non-client callable business method. Note that this method could have been declared **private** or **protected**. Before calling a PL/SQL procedure or function in a Java program, there is a particular setup that JDBC requires. (See the *Oracle8i JDBC Developer's Guide, Release 8.1.5 and higher*.) Briefly

    ■ Connect to the database and get a java.sql.Connection object. Note that this method does not connect to the database. Instead, it uses the conn parameter passed to it by a caller method.

    ■ Create a CallableStatement variable.

    ■ Use the prepareCall() method of the Connection object.

    ■ Use the setXXXX methods of the CallableStatement object to set input and/or output parameters for the PL/SQL function or procedure, if any.

    ■ Use the execute() method of the CallableStatement object to execute the query.

    ■ Use the getXXXX methods of the CallableStatement object to retrieve the query results.

2. This statement calls the OBSACTIONS.INSERTOBS() PL/SQL procedure to add a new row in the OCEANIC_OBSERVATION_LIST table. The OBSACTIONS.INSERTOBS() is a procedure that implements the insertion logic in the database. Note that the JDBC setup to call a PL/SQL procedure is analogous to the setup for PL/SQL function calls.

The `obs.ejb` Deployment Descriptor File

In this section, we use two deployment descriptor files to demonstrate how to declare Bean-level access and transaction control versus method-level declarations. If you wish to use both files, you will need to deploy the `ObservationBean` enterprise Bean twice. Note that there is no need to modify the individual components of the `ObservationBean` session Bean nor recompile them, just redeploy them. When you want to change the transaction or the access policy of your Beans, all you need to do is to change or update your deployment descriptor file and redeploy the Beans.

CAUTION

The format used to package Enterprise JavaBeans is defined by the EJB Specification. Note that between EJB 1.0 and EJB 1.1, the specification changed the way deployment descriptor files are written. Deployment descriptors for EJB 1.1-compliant servers must be defined in the Extensible Markup Language (XML). In the upcoming release of Oracle8i (version 8.1.7), the deployment descriptor file will be defined in XML as required by the EJB 1.1 Specification. In this book, you will use Oracle's proprietary representation of the descriptor because it supports both EJB 1.0 and EJB 1.1 containers.

Here is the `Obs.ejb` descriptor file:

```
// File name: Obs.ejb
// Purpose   : Deployment descriptor file for the
//             Observation session Bean.

SessionBean obsserver.ObsImp {

    // (See Note 1.)
    BeanHomeName = "test/ObservationBean";
    HomeInterfaceClassName = obsserver.ObsHome;
    RemoteInterfaceClassName = obsserver.ObsRemote;

    SessionTimeout = 0;
    // (See Note 2.)
    AllowedIdentities = { SYSDBA };
    TransactionAttribute = TX_REQUIRED;
    RunAsMode = CLIENT_IDENTITY;
```

Notes on the `obs.ejb` file:

1. This statement and the two that follow define the `test/ObservationBean` (the namespace and the name of the published object), the name of the home and remote interface.

2. This statement and the one that follows it declare a Bean-level access and transaction control, respectively. Recall that when specified at the Bean level, the identity and transaction attributes are applied to all the Bean methods.

The `obs.jar` File

Now that you have developed the `ObservationBean` session Bean, use the `SetupAndRun` file to compile all the components and create the `obs.jar` file. The `obs.jar` file must include the following class files:

- `helpers/ObsHelper.class`

- `obsserver/ObsRemote.class`

- `obsserver/ObsHome.class`

- `obsserver/ObsImp.class`

Deploying the `ObservationBean` Session Bean

At the prompt, set your `CLASSPATH` and deploy the enterprise Bean:

```
// NT prompt
deployejb -republish -keep -temp temp -u scott -p tiger
    -s %ORACLE_SERVICE% -verbose
    -descriptor Obs1.ejb -generated ObsClient.jar Obs.jar

// UNIX prompt
deployejb -republish -keep -temp temp -u scott -p tiger \
    -s $ORACLE_SERVICE -verbose \
    -descriptor Obs1.ejb -generated ObsClient.jar Obs.jar
```

Writing the Client Application

This simple client application will do the following:

- Set up the JNDI environment variables

- Locate a reference to the `ObsHome` **interface**

- Create an `ObsRemote` instance

- Use the `ObsRemote` instance to successively call all the methods defined in the `ObsRemote` interface and implemented in the `ObsImp` Bean class

In Chapters 8 and 12, you will learn how to write CORBA and Java Server Pages (JSPs) clients that use session Beans. Here is the `Chapter4Client` application:

```java
/* Program Name: Chapter4Client.java
** Version:
** Description:  An EJB client: a JDBC implementation.
**
*/
// Import the JDBC classes
import java.sql.*;

// import helper classes
import helpers.ObsHelper;

import obsserver.ObsRemote;
import obsserver.ObsHome;

// import the ServiceCtx class from the Oracle package
import oracle.aurora.jndi.sess_iiop.ServiceCtx;

// import the Java mandatory classes to use JNDI
import javax.naming.Context;
import javax.naming.InitialContext;

// import application-specific Java classes
import java.util.Hashtable;

import java.util.*;
import java.math.*;


public class Chapter4Client {    public static void main (String args
[])
      throws Exception {

      // Check input parameter
      if (args.length != 4) {
        System.out.println("usage: Client "
                  +"serviceURL objectName user password");
        System.exit(1);
      }  // End if

      String serviceURL = args [0];
      String objectName = args [1];
      String user = args [2];
      String password = args [3];
      Hashtable env = new Hashtable();
```

```java
    // Set the JNDI environment for the client
    // to locate the EJB object
    env.put(Context.URL_PKG_PREFIXES, "oracle.aurora.jndi");
    env.put(Context.SECURITY_PRINCIPAL, user);
    env.put(Context.SECURITY_CREDENTIALS, password);
    env.put(Context.SECURITY_AUTHENTICATION,
                    ServiceCtx.NON_SSL_LOGIN);

    // Create an instance of the Context class
    Context ic = new InitialContext (env);


    ObsHome myObsHome = null;


    ObsRemote myObservationBean = null;

    try {
        // Use the home interface to
        // locate the EJB object
        myObsHome =
          (ObsHome)ic.lookup (serviceURL + objectName);
        System.out.println("Home Lookup Properly");

        // Create a Bean instance
        myObservationBean = myObsHome.create();
        System.out.println("Bean Created Properly");

        getAllObsInfo (myObservationBean);
        System.out.println("getAllObsInfo done");

        getOneObsInfo (myObservationBean);
        System.out.println("getOneObsInfo done");

        insertAnArrayOfObs (myObservationBean);
        System.out.println("insertAnArrayOfObs done");
  }  // End of try
  catch ( Exception ex ) {
        System.out.println("Cannot locate"
                +" or create object");
        System.err.println("error : " + ex);
        System.exit(1);
  }  // End of catch
} // End main

public void getAllObsInfo (ObsRemote myObservationBean)
    throws Exception {
```

```java
        try {
            // Invoke the getAllObs() method implemented in the
            // ObsImp class.
            ObsHelper[] arrayOfObs = myObservationBean.getAllObs();

            int loopVar = 0;
            while ( loopVar < arrayOfObs.length ) {
                ObsHelper obs = arrayOfObs[loopVar];

                System.out.println ("Inside JdbcProcClient "
                  + "obs.obs_id:  " +obs.obs_id);

                loopVar++;
            }
        }  // End try
        catch (SQLException e) {
            System.err.println( e.getMessage() );
            System.exit(1);
        }  // End catch
    } // End getAllObsInfo ()

    /* Testing getObsInfo() */
    public static void getOneObsInfo (ObsRemote myObservationBean)
      throws Exception {
      try {
          int obs_id = 2;
          // Invoke the Bean class method
          ObsHelper obs = myObservationBean.getObsInfo(obs_id);

          System.out.println ("Inside JdbcProcClient obs.obs_id:  "
                          +obs.obs_id);
          System.out.println("when_t: " +obs.when_t);
      }  // End try
      catch (SQLException e) {
          System.err.println( e.getMessage() );
          System.exit(1);
      }  // End catch
    } // End getOneObsInfo ()

    /* Testing insertObs(ObsHerper[] obs) */
    public static void insertAnArrayOfObs (ObsRemote myObservationBean)
          throws Exception {
        try {
            int loopVar = 0;

            while (loopVar++ < 2) {
                BigDecimal obs_id = null;
                String when_t = "04-JUL-2000";
                String at_time = "085500";
```

```
          BigDecimal station_id = new BigDecimal(0);
          BigDecimal produced_id = new BigDecimal(1);
          BigDecimal latitude = new BigDecimal(0);
          BigDecimal longitude = new BigDecimal(0);
          BigDecimal wdspd = new BigDecimal(0);
          BigDecimal adj_wdspd = new BigDecimal(0);
          BigDecimal wddir = new BigDecimal(0);
          BigDecimal pressure = new BigDecimal(0);

          ObsHelper obs1 =
              new ObsHelper(obs_id,when_t,at_time,
                    station_id,produced_id,latitude,
                    longitude,wdspd,adj_wdspd,wddir,pressure);

          ObsHelper obs2 = myObservationBean.insertObs(obs1);
          System.out.println ("Inside JdbcProcClient " +
                  "obs2.obs_id:  " +obs2.obs_id);
      }
  }  // End try
  catch (SQLException e) {
        System.err.println( e.getMessage() );
        System.exit(1);
  }  // End catch
 } // End insertAnArrayOfObs ()
} // End of Chapter4Client class
```

The `ObsImp` Bean Class: Implementation Using SQLJ

Note that you can use either the `ObsImp.java` or the `ObsImp.sqlj` Bean class, but not both. More importantly, if you deploy either the `ObsImp.java` or the `ObsImp.sqlj` implementation, use the Oracle `dropjava` tool to drop a deployed enterprise Bean before deploying another one bearing the same name. The `-republish` option of the Oracle `deployejb` tool does not remove unwanted dependent classes.

The implementation using SQLJ is very similar to the implementation using JDBC. The former introduces very few new concepts that require detailed explanations, except the concept of the SQLJ `iterator`. We will present here a brief description of the SQLJ `iterator`. To learn more about this concept, see *Oracle8i SQLJ Programming*.

SQLJ Iterator

An SQLJ `iterator` is a strongly typed version of the embedded SQL cursor and is used to receive `SELECT` statement output. There are two categories of iterators: named iterators and positional iterators.

Iterator Class Declarations   The first step in iterator processing is to define the iterator class in a SQLJ declaration. An iterator class declaration specifies a Java class that SQLJ constructs for you. The SQLJ translator replaces a SQLJ iterator declaration with a Java declaration for a class with the same name as the iterator. For example, in the ObsImp SQLJ program, you will find a named iterator declaration:

```
#sql iterator ObsIter
            (java.lang.Integer obs_id,String whent,
             String attime,java.lang.Integer stat_id,
             java.lang.Integer prod_id,java.lang.Float lat_deg,
             java.lang.Float lon_deg,java.lang.Float wdspd_s,
             java.lang.Float adjwdspd,java.lang.Float wddir_s,
             java.lang.Integer pres);
```

An ObsIter iterator instance can be populated by any SELECT statement whose set of SELECT list elements (that is, the expressions that follow the keyword SELECT) is a subset of the set of ObsIter attributes. That is, an ObsIter instance can be populated by any SELECT statement whose SELECT list consists only of the columns obs_id, whent, attime, stat_id, prod_id, lat_deg, lon_deg, wdspd_s, adjwdspd, wddir_s, and pres.

The SQLJ translator will translate the SQLJ ObsIter iterator declaration into a Java declaration for a Java class ObsIter. This ObsIter Java class will contain the following:

- A next() method that retrieves data from the iterator row by row

- Accessor methods obs_id(), whent(), attime(), stat_id(), prod_id(), lat_deg(), lon_deg(), wdspd_s(), adjwdspd(), wddir_s(), and pres() that return the values of the columns of the OCEANIC_OBSERVATION_LIST table in the row currently being processed

- A close() method that deactivates the iterator instance

Named Iterator Processing   The following steps summarize named iterator processing:

- Use a SQLJ declaration to define the iterator class.

- Declare an instance of the iterator class.

- Populate the iterator instance with the output from a compatible SELECT statement in a SQLJ executable statement.

- Use the next() method of the iterator class to retrieve the next row from the iterator instance.

- Extract the column values from the current iterator row by using the iterator class accessor methods.

- Deactivate the iterator instance by invoking the close() iterator class method.

Here is the definition of the `ObsImp` SQLJ program:

```
/* Program Name:  ObsImp.sqlj
** Version:
** Author:       Your Name
** Description:  An EJB Bean class that allows
**               client to insert a ObsHelper
**               object, an array of ObsHelper,
**               and retrieve an array of ObsHelper.
**               An implementation using SQLJ.
**
*/
package obsserver;

// import helper classes
import helpers.ObsHelper;

import java.rmi.RemoteException;
import javax.ejb.*;

// import application-specific exception
import java.sql.SQLException;

import java.sql.*;
import oracle.sql.*;

// Import supporting Java classes
import java.math.BigDecimal;
import java.math.*;
import java.util.Vector;

public class ObsImp implements SessionBean {

// Define a SQLJ iterator
#sql iterator ObsIter
            (java.lang.Integer obs_id,String whent,
             String attime,java.lang.Integer stat_id,
             java.lang.Integer prod_id,java.lang.Float lat_deg,
             java.lang.Float lon_deg,java.lang.Float wdspd_s,
             java.lang.Float adjwdspd,java.lang.Float wddir_s,
             java.lang.Integer pres);

    // This method, callable by clients, connects
    // implicitly to the database and
    // Call the getObsId()PL/SQL ObsActions package
    // to get a new obs_id.
```

```java
public ObsHelper getNewObs()
    throws SQLException, RemoteException {

  int returnId;

  // Call the getObsId() from the PL/SQL ObsActions package
  // to get a new obs_id
  try {

    // This statement calls the ObsActions.getObsId method.
    // Note the simplicity of the SQLJ declaration and the
    // absence of explicit java.sql.Connection and
    // CallableStatement objects and the required setup
    // for JDBC programs calling PL/SQL procedures or functions.
    // Call the PL/SQL function
    #sql returnId = {VALUES ObsActions.getObsId};

    BigDecimal anObsId = new BigDecimal(returnId);

    // Return an ObsHelper object using the new id
    return new ObsHelper(anObsId);

  }  // End try
  catch (SQLException e) {
    throw e;
  }  // End catch
  catch (java.lang.NullPointerException e) {
    throw new SQLException("Cannot generate new   "
              +"Observation Id " + e.getMessage());
  }
} // End getNewObs()

// This statement declares the insertObs() methods.
// Note the absence of a Connection object in
// the definition of the method.
// This method gets a new obs_id and adds a new
// OCEANIC_OBSERVATION_TYPE in the
// OCEANIC_OBSERVATION_LIST table. Clients
// invoke this method.  nirvapublic ObsHelper insertObs
(ObsHelper obs)
    throws SQLException, RemoteException {
  try {
      // Get a new obs_id from the database
      ObsHelper anObsid = getNewObs();

      BigDecimal obs_id = anObsid.obs_id;
      String when_t = obs.when_t;
      String at_time = obs.at_time;
```

```
        BigDecimal produced_id = obs.produced_id;
        BigDecimal latitude = obs.latitude;
        BigDecimal longitude = obs.longitude;
        BigDecimal wdspd = obs.wdspd;
        BigDecimal adj_wdspd = obs.adj_wdspd;
        BigDecimal wddir = obs.wddir;
        BigDecimal pressure = obs.pressure;
        BigDecimal station_id = obs.station_id;

        // This statement uses the IN parameters
        // for Java host variables within the SQLJ declaration.
        // Java host variables can also have OUT parameters
        // that store data from PL/SQL functions and procedures
        // within a SQLJ declaration. This statement calls the
        // PL/SQL OBSACTIONS.INSERTOBS() procedure.
        #sql  { call ObsActions.insertObs(
                :IN obs_id, :IN when_t, :IN at_time, :IN produced_id,
                :IN latitude, :IN longitude, :IN wdspd, :IN adj_
                 wdspd,
                :IN wddir, :IN pressure, :IN station_id )
              };

        // Return an ObsHelper object
       return new ObsHelper(anObsid.obs_id);
   }  // End try
   catch (SQLException e) {
       throw e;
   }  // End catch
} // End insertObs(obs)


 // Insert an array of OCEANIC_OBSERVATION_TYPE
 public ObsHelper[] insertObs(ObsHelper[] inObs)
    throws SQLException, RemoteException {
   int loopVar = 0;

   // Declare an array of ObsHelper objects
   int arraySize = inObs.length;

   ObsHelper[] returnArray = new ObsHelper[arraySize];

   try {
       // Iterate and store an array of obs_ids into returnArray[]
       while ( loopVar < arraySize ) {

               ObsHelper obs = inObs[loopVar];

               // Call the insertObs(..) to add a new row
```

```
                    // to the database

                    returnArray[loopVar] = insertObs ( obs );
                    loopVar++;
            } // End while

            // Return an array of ids
            return returnArray;

        }   // End try
        catch (SQLException e) {
          throw e );
        }   // End catch

    } // End insertObs(ObsHelper[] inObs)

    // This method uses dynamic SQL to return
    // all data from the OCEANIC_OBSERVATION_LIST table
    public ObsHelper[] getAllObs()
            throws SQLException, RemoteException {

        // Need a Java Vector to store the
        // table rows since you do not know
        // how many rows are being retrieved.
        Vector obsList = null;

        // Declare a SQLJ iterator variable
        ObsIter anSqljRs = null;

        try {
                // This statement populates the query result
                // into the anSqljRs SQLJ iterator instance.
                #sql anSqljRs =
                    { SELECT P.obs_id AS obs_id,
                      TO_CHAR(P.when_t,'DD-MM-YYYY') AS whent,
                      P.at_time AS attime, P.station_id AS stat_id,
                      P.produced_id AS prod_id,
                      P.obsobj.latitude_deg AS lat_deg,
                      P.obsobj.longitude_deg AS lon_deg,
                      P.obsobj.windspeed_mps AS wdspd_s,
                      P.obsobj.adj_windspeed_mps AS adjwdspd,
                      P.obsobj.wind_direction_deg AS wddir_s,
                      P.obsobj.pressure_mb AS pres
                        FROM OCEANIC_OBSERVATION_LIST P
                    };

                while (anSqljRs.next()) {
                  // Declare an ObsHelper object
```

```
            ObsHelper oneObs = populateData (anSqljRs);

            // Insert oneObs object into the Java obsList Vector
            obsList.addElement(oneObs);

    }   // End while

    // Get the size of the obsList
    int arraySize = obsList.size();

    // Create an ObsHelper array using the obsList vector
    ObsHelper[] anArrayOfObsHelper = new ObsHelper[arraySize];

    // Copy all info from the vector to the anArrayOfObsHelper array
    obsList.copyInto(anArrayOfObsHelper);

    // Return the array to the caller
    return anArrayOfObsHelper;
} // End try
catch (SQLException e) {
    throw e;
}   // End catch
catch (java.lang.Exception e) {
  throw new SQLException("ArrayList error in Select "
      +" Observations:   " + e.getMessage());
}   // End catch

  // Clean up nirva
  finally {
        if ( anSqljRs != null ) anSqljRs.close();
  } // End finally()

}   // End getAllObs()

// Get observation info for a specific obs_id
public ObsHelper getObsInfo(int obsid)
    throws SQLException, RemoteException {

  int obs_id = obsid;

  ObsIter anSqljRs = null;

  try {
      #sql anSqljRs =
          { SELECT P.obs_id AS obs_id,
            TO_CHAR(P.when_t,'DD-MM-YYYY') AS whent,
            P.at_time AS attime, P.station_id AS stat_id,
            P.produced_id AS prod_id,
```

```
            P.obsobj.latitude_deg AS lat_deg,
            P.obsobj.longitude_deg AS lon_deg,
            P.obsobj.windspeed_mps AS wdspd_s,
            P.obsobj.adj_windspeed_mps AS adjwdspd,
            P.obsobj.wind_direction_deg AS wddir_s,
            P.obsobj.pressure_mb AS pres
          FROM OCEANIC_OBSERVATION_LIST P
          WHERE P.obs_id = :obsid
      };
      return populateData (anSqljRs);

  }   // End try
  catch (SQLException e) {
     throw e;
  }   // End catch
  catch (java.lang.NullPointerException e) {
      throw new SQLException("Observation does not exist "
          +"for obs_id: " +obsid +" " + e.getMessage());
  }

  // Clean up:
  // This statement closes the anSQLJRs SQLJ iterator instance.
  // Like a Java ResultSet instance, you must close the
  // anSQLJRs SQLJ iterator instance.
  finally {
          if ( anSqljRs  != null ) anSqljRs.close();
  }   // End finally()

}   // End getObsInfo()

// This method populates the result set data
// to an ObsHelper object.
Public ObsHelper populateData (ObsIter anSqljRs)
  throws SQLException {

  try {
    // Declare an ObsHelper object
    // using the default constructor.
    ObsHelper oneObs = new ObsHelper();

    // Use the accessor methods from the
    // anSqljRs SQLJ iterator instance.
    // Set the member variables of the ObsHelper object.
    //  This method uses the accessor methods
    // to set the data members of an ObsHelper object.
    oneObs.obs_id   =
            new BigDecimal(anSqljRs.obs_id().intValue());
    oneObs.when_t   = anSqljRs.whent();
```

```
    oneObs.at_time  = anSqljRs.attime();

    if  (anSqljRs.stat_id() == null)
        oneObs.station_id = null;
    else
        oneObs.station_id =
            new BigDecimal(anSqljRs.stat_id().intValue());
    if  (anSqljRs.prod_id() == null)
        oneObs.produced_id = null;
    else
        oneObs.produced_id =
            new BigDecimal(anSqljRs.prod_id().intValue());
    if  (anSqljRs.lat_deg() == null)
        oneObs.latitude = null;
    else
        oneObs.latitude =
            new BigDecimal(anSqljRs.lat_deg().intValue());
    if  (anSqljRs.lon_deg() == null)
        oneObs.longitude = null;
    else
        oneObs.longitude =
            new BigDecimal(anSqljRs.lon_deg().intValue());
    if  (anSqljRs.wdspd_s() == null)
        oneObs.wdspd = null;
    else
        oneObs.wdspd =
            new BigDecimal(anSqljRs.wdspd_s().intValue());
    if  (anSqljRs.adjwdspd() == null)
        oneObs.adj_wdspd = null;
    else
        oneObs.adj_wdspd =
            new BigDecimal(anSqljRs.adjwdspd().intValue());
    if  (anSqljRs.wddir_s() == null)
        oneObs.wddir =  null;
    else
        oneObs.wddir =
            new BigDecimal(anSqljRs.wddir_s().intValue());
    if  (anSqljRs.pres() == null)
        oneObs.pressure = null;
    else
        oneObs.pressure =
                new BigDecimal(anSqljRs.pres().intValue());
    return oneObs;
} // End try
catch (SQLException e) {
    throw e;
}  // End catch
catch (java.lang.NullPointerException e) {
```

```
        throw new java.lang.NullPointerException
          (e.getMessage());
   }

} // End populateData()

public void ejbCreate()
   throws RemoteException, CreateException {
} // End ejbCreate()

public void ejbActivate()
   throws RemoteException {
} // End ejbActivate()

public void ejbPassivate()
   throws RemoteException {
} // End ejbPassivate()

public void ejbRemove()
   throws RemoteException {
} // End ejbRemove()

public void setSessionContext(SessionContext ctx)
   throws RemoteException {
} // End setSessionContext()

}   // End of ObsImp class
```

Note on the `ObsImp` class (implementation using SQLJ):

1. Note the simplicity and the elegance of the implementation using SQLJ versus JDBC. Also note that when you use SQLJ in the server, you do not need to connect explicitly to the database—that is, the connection does not have to be explicitly initialized the way you did in the implementation using JDBC. In SQLJ server-side programs, the connection is implicit. To learn more about SQLJ, see *Oracle8i SQLJ Programming*.

Conclusion

In this chapter, you learned how to define the access and transaction policy of enterprise Beans. You developed the `ObservationBean` session Bean, a database component application that provides a set of business methods to manipulate the `OCEANIC_OBSERVATION_LIST` table. Additionally, you learned how to write the `ObsImp` Bean class using both JDBC and SQLJ.

In Chapter 5, you will learn more advanced EJB concepts while developing a session Bean that models the process of atmospheric observations that undergo quality control. At the Hurricane Research Division (HRD) of the National Oceanic and Atmospheric Administration (NOAA), the scientists use atmospheric observations that undergo quality control to produce a real-time analysis of tropical cyclone surface wind observations. These analyses are designed to help forecasters from the National Hurricane Center (NHC) determine the storm's current intensity and the extent of its damaging winds.

CHAPTER

5

Developing Session Beans: Advanced Topics

n Chapter 4, you learned that a transaction is described in terms of the ACID properties (atomic, consistent, isolated, and durable). Transactions that meet these criteria are considered reliable. Here, you will build a transactional application that meets these criteria.

In this chapter, you will learn the following:

- How to manage Enterprise JavaBeans in Oracle8*i* database sessions

- How to demarcate transactions explicitly in your programs

- How to build reliable transactional applications using client transaction demarcation

Managing Beans in Database Sessions

Enterprise JavaBeans running in the Oracle8*i* EJB container execute within a database session. A client starts a new server session implicitly when it activates an EJB or a CORBA server object. In this section, you will learn how to manage enterprise Beans in Oracle database sessions. See Chapter 7 to learn more about managing CORBA objects in database sessions.

The Oracle8*i* JServer creates a database session when a client invokes the JNDI `lookup()` method. Remember that a client invokes the `lookup()` method to retrieve a reference to an EJB's home **interface**. The Oracle8*i* database gives you the ability to control session startup explicitly, either from a Java program (a client object residing outside the database) or an EJB or a CORBA server object. Additionally, the Oracle database allows EJB objects to control the duration of a database session and also to terminate a session.

Client Object Starting a New Session

In client-side programs residing anywhere on a network, you start a new database session when the client invokes the JNDI `lookup()` method. The `lookup()` method requires an input parameter consisting of a URL concatenated with the name of the published object. To start a new session to the Oracle8*i* database, supply the `sess_iiop://localhost:port#:SID` URL concatenated with the desired object's published name. Note that the session is established while locating a reference to a Bean home object. However, you can start a session without accessing any object in particular. To do so, just use the `sess_iiop:// localhost:port#:SID` URL. For example, the Oracle `deployejb` and `sess_sh` tools start a new database session without accessing any object (see Appendix F to learn more about these tools).

Remember that you use the `deployejb` tool to deploy your enterprise Beans in the Oracle8*i* data server and the `sess_sh` tool to create, view, and delete namespaces. Here is the syntax for both tools:

```
// The Oracle deployejb tool starts a new database session
// to the Oracle8i database located at data-i.com.
deployejb-user scott/tiger -service sess_iiop://data-i.com:2481:ORCL

// The Oracle sess_sh tool starts a new database session
sess_sh -user sys -password syspassword
  -service sess_iiop://data-i.com:2481:ORCL
```

In Listing 5-1, use the following code fragment to start a new database session and retrieve a reference to the `ObservationBean` home **interface**:

Listing 5-1: Standalone client starting a new database session

```
// Set up environment variables
Hashtable env = new Hashtable ();
env.put (Context.URL_PKG_PREFIXES, "oracle.aurora.jndi");
env.put (Context.SECURITY_PRINCIPAL, user);
env.put (Context.SECURITY_CREDENTIALS, password);
env.put (Context.SECURITY_AUTHENTICATION,
                          ServiceCtx.NON_SSL_LOGIN);
// get a handle to the InitialContext
Context ic = new InitialContext (env);

// Start a new database session while retrieving
// a reference to the ObservationBean home interface
ObsHome observationHome =
    (ObsHome)ic.lookup ("sess_iiop://data-i.com:2481:ORCL"
                      + "/test/ObservationBean");
```

Server Object Starting a New Session

In enterprise Beans residing in the Oracle8*i* database, you also start a new database session when you invoke the JNDI `lookup()` method. To start a new session inside the database, supply the `sess_iiop://thisServer` URL concatenated with the object's published name. For example, in the `QcSetImp` implementation class of the `QcSetBean` session Bean, use the code fragment shown in Listing 5-2 to start a new database session while retrieving a reference to the QcObsBean home **interface**:

Listing 5-2: EJB Bean starting a new database session

```
// Set up the environment (See Note 1.)
Hashtable env = new Hashtable();
env.put (Context.URL_PKG_PREFIXES, "oracle.aurora.jndi");
// Create InitialContext
Context ic = new InitialContext(env);
// Store the object published name
String objectName = new String("/test/QcObsBean");
// Create a new database session while
// retrieving a reference to the home object
// (See Note 2.)
QcObsHome anQcObsHome =
  (QcObsHome)ic.lookup("sess_iiop://thisServer"
                       +objectName);
```

Note on Listing 5-2:

1. Note that server objects starting a new session within a previously established session are only required to set the URL_PKG_PREFIXES environment variable because the other environment variables, such as SECURITY_PRINCIPAL, SECURITY_CREDENTIALS, and SECURITY_AUTHENTICATION, would have been previously set up. You will develop both the QcSetBean and QcObsBean session Beans in the "Building a Transactional Application" section of this chapter.

2. Use this code only when you need a new database session. Enterprise JavaBeans executing in the Oracle8i database can invoke other Beans in the same database session in which they are executing. For better performance, avoid creating new database sessions. To learn more about activating server objects in the same session, see the "Server Object Accessing the Same Session" section of this chapter.

Once the Oracle8i JServer creates a database session, it can be accessed by several separate clients residing on a network or by an existing EJB object. While executing in a specific session, an existing EJB can invoke other Bean's methods within the same session.

Two Clients Accessing the Same Session

To allow two clients to access the same Oracle8*i* database session, do the following:

1. In the first client, save the Bean `Handle`.

2. In the second client, retrieve the `Handle` and use it to access the Bean instance.

Enterprise Bean `Handle`

The EJB Specification defines the `javax.ejb.Handle` **interface** (see Listing 5-3) that provides the capability for several clients to get a reference to an EJB object via a `Handle` object. A `Handle` is an object that identifies an EJB object. A client program can start a new database session, save a `Handle` for the EJB object in a file, and use it at a later time to re-obtain a reference to the EJB object. Several other clients that are executing in the same database session can use the same `Handle` to access the EJB object. The implementation class for the `Handle` **interface** is typically provided by the EJB container and is generated at deployment time. More importantly, the handle's class must implement the `java.io.Serializable` **interface**. Here is the definition of the `Handle` **interface**:

Listing 5-3:   The `javax.ejb.Handle` **interface**

```
public interface javax.ejb.Handle{
   public abstract EJBObject getEJBObject();
}
```

The `Handle` **interface** defines the `getEJBObject()` method that allows a client to retrieve a reference to the `EJBObject`. Recall that you learned about the `EJBObject` **interface** in Chapter 3. Listing 5-6 illustrates how you would use the `getEJBObject()` method to retrieve a reference to a Bean remote **interface**.

Recall that EJB remote interfaces must extend the `javax.ejb.EJBObject` **interface**. More importantly, all client invocations come through an `EJBObject` object. The implementation of the methods defined in the `javax.ejb.EJBObject` **interface** is provided by the EJB container as well and is also generated at deployment time. As a reminder, in Listing 5-4 we present again the definition of the `javax.ejb.EJBObject` **interface**.

Listing 5-4: The `javax.ejb.EJBObject` **interface**

```
Public interface javax.ejb.EJBObject
  extends java.rmi.Remote {
    public abstract EJBHome getEJBHome() throws RemoteException;
    public abstract Handle getHandle () throws RemoteException;
    public abstract Object getPrimaryKey()throws RemoteException;
    public abstract boolean isIdentical(EJBObject obj)
            throws RemoteException;
    public void remove()() throws RemoteException;
}
```

The `getHandle()` method (see Listing 5-4) returns a `Handle` for the EJB object. Consequently, a client that has a reference to an EJB object can obtain the object's `Handle` by invoking the `getHandle()` method on the reference. Listing 5-6 illustrates the use of the `getHandle()` method. Note that all EJB object handles implement the `Handle` **interface**.

Saving a Bean `Handle`
Use the code fragment in Listing 5-5 to save a Bean `Handle` in a file.

Listing 5-5: Saving a Bean `Handle`

```
// Get a reference to the ObsHome reference
ObsHome anObsHome =
  (ObsHome) ic.lookup("sess_iiop://data-i.com"+
          ":2481:ORCL/test/ObservationBean");
// Get a reference to the ObsRemote interface
ObsRemote anObsRemote = anObsHome.create();

// Assume that you saved the name of a file in the
// handlefile variable.
// create an object output stream from a file stream
FileOutputStream fostream = new FileOutputStream(handlefile);
ObjectOutputStream ostream = new ObjectOutputStream(fostream);

// Get the bean Handle using getHandle() and
// Save the Bean Handle by writing it in a file
ostream.writeObject(anObsRemote.getHandle());

// You must clean the streams. Use the
// following statements to do so:
ostream.flush ();
fostream.close ();
```

Retrieving a Bean `Handle`

In client programs that are executing in the same database session, use the code fragment shown in Listing 5-6 to retrieve the Bean `Handle` that another client had previously saved in a file; use the `getEJBObject()` method of the `javax.ejb.Handle` **interface** to get a reference to a Bean remote **interface**:

Listing 5-6:   Retrieving a `Handle` and getting a reference to a remote **interface**

```
// Assume that you pass to the second client
// the name of the file in which you saved the Bean Handle.
// Get a handle for the bean, by reading the file whose name
// is stored in the handlefile variable.
FileInputStream finstream = new FileInputStream (handlefile);
ObjectInputStream istream = new ObjectInputStream (finstream);
finstream.close ();

// Use the readObject() method of the istream class
// to handle a ObsRemote interface and create
// a javax.ejb.Handle object.
javax.ejb.Handle handle  = (javax.ejb.Handle)istream.readObject ();

// Use the getEJBObject() method of the Handle class
// to re-obtain a reference to the ObsRemote interface.
ObsRemote anObsRemote = (ObsRemote)handle.getEJBObject ();
...
...
// Use the remote reference to invoke Bean methods.
anObsRemote.insertObs(anObservation);
```

Server Object Accessing the Same Session

EJB Beans can look up other server objects in the database session in which they are executing. If you want a server object to look up and activate another published object in the same session in which it is running, use `sess_iiop:// thisServer/:thisSession` as a URL concatenated with the object's published name. For example,

```
// Create InitialContext
Hashtable env = new Hashtable();
env.put (Context.URL_PKG_PREFIXES, "oracle.aurora.jndi");
Context ic = new InitialContext(env);
SomeObjectHome anObjectHome =
   (SomeObjectHome)ic.lookup("sess_iiop://thisServer/:thisSession"
                        +"/test/SomeObject");
```

Server Object Controlling Session Duration

Standalone Java client programs cannot explicitly control the duration of an Oracle database session, whereas a server-side object can. Use the `oracle.aurora.net.Presentation.sessionTimeout(int x)` method to control the session duration of server-side objects. The `sessionTimeout()` method takes an `int` parameter and is part of the `aurora.zip` file. If you want to use the `session-Timeout()` method, you must add `(ORACLE_HOME)/javavm/lib/ aurora.zip` to your CLASSPATH. Note that the session timeout is set in seconds. The following code fragment sets the session duration:

```
// Create a variable
int aTimeValue = 30;
...
// Use the above variable to set the session duration
oracle.aurora.net.Presentation.sessionTimeout(aTimeValue);
```

Server Object Ending a Session

To terminate an Oracle8*i* database session explicitly, standalone Java client programs can use the `System.exit(int x)` method whose `int` input parameter is an exit value. However, in server-side programs residing in the Oracle8*i* database, the execution of the `System.exit()` method does not terminate a session. To terminate a database session explicitly, server-side programs must use the `oracle.aurora.vm.OracleRuntime.exitSession(int x)` method. Like the `System.exit()` method, the `exitSession()` method takes an `int` parameter as an exit value. For example

```
// End a database session inside the Oracle database
oracle.aurora.vm.OracleRuntime.exitSession(1);
```

Demarcating Transactions

Recall that Bean providers can elect to have the EJB container manage implicitly all transactions for them via a transaction policy defined in a deployment descriptor file. However, if you want to provide Java client programs (non-Bean–client programs) or EJB Beans (Bean-client programs) with the capability to explicitly control transaction boundaries programmatically, you can do so via the Java Transaction Service (JTS). JTS provides your applications with finer-grained control of the transactional properties than that offered by the declarative transaction attributes.

A transaction is said to be *client-side demarcated* or *server-side demarcated*. Recall that "demarcated transactions" means that a transaction has a definite starting point and ending point.

Client-Side Demarcated Transaction (Standalone Java Programs)

In Oracle8*i* versions 8.1.5 and 8.1.6, EJB clients can use the Java Transaction Service API (JTS) to demarcate transactions programmatically. In Oracle8*i* version 8.1.7, EJB clients must use the Java Transaction API (JTA) to demarcate transactions. In either case, developers can explicitly demarcate transactions in their programs by executing the appropriate `begin()` or `commit()` method provided by the transaction API implemented by the Oracle8*i* database. For client-side demarcated transactions using JTS (Oracle8*i* versions 8.1.5 and 8.1.6), include the `oracle.aurora.jts.client.AuroraTransactionService` package in your client source code with the following `import` statements:

```
import oracle.aurora.jts.client.AuroraTransactionService;
import oracle.aurora.jts.client.TS;
```

For example, in the `QcClient` program that you will develop later in this chapter, you will use JTS to explicitly demarcate the transaction:

```
// Demarcate and start the transaction
// (Oracle8i versions 8.1.5 and 8.1.6)
TS.getTS ().getCurrent ().begin ();
...
// Look up and instantiate one or more Beans.
// Invoke Bean methods.

// End the transaction with either of the following statements:
TS.getTS ().getCurrent ().commit (true/false);
TS.getTS ().getCurrent ().rollback ();
```

Note that the upcoming release of the Oracle8*i* database (version 8.1.7) will be EJB 1.1-compliant. The EJB 1.1 Specification requires that an EJB container support application-level transaction demarcation by implementing the `javax.transaction.UserTransaction` **interface**. This interface replaces the `javax.jts.UserTransaction` **interface** supported by EJB 1.0-compliant containers. The JTA API provides a uniform way for EJB Beans (TX_BEAN_MANAGED Beans) and standalone Java client programs to control transaction boundaries programmatically. To learn more about JTA, see "Java Transaction API (JTA)" at http://java.sun.com/products/jta/index.html.

The following code fragment demonstrates how to use JTA in an EJB client:

```
// Demarcate and start the transaction
// (Oracle8i version 8.1.7 beta)
// First, import the javax.transaction.* package in your program.
```

```
Import javax.transaction.*;
...

...
public class Client {
  public static void main ( String[] arg ) throws Exception {
      // 1. Authenticate to the database as you normally do
      // for any client and set up environment variables
      Hashtable env = new Hashtable ();
      env.put (Context.URL_PKG_PREFIXES, "oracle.aurora.jndi");
      env.put (Context.SECURITY_PRINCIPAL, user);
      env.put (Context.SECURITY_CREDENTIALS, password);
      env.put (Context.SECURITY_AUTHENTICATION,
                          ServiceCtx.NON_SSL_LOGIN);
      // get a handle to the InitialContext
      Context ic = new InitialContext (env);

      // 2. Retrieve the UserTransaction object from JNDI namespace
      UserTransaction ut;
      ut = (UserTransaction)ic.lookup(…);

      // 3. Use the begin() method of the UserTransaction
      // to start the transaction
      ut.begin();
      ...
      // Invoke your Bean's methods.
      ...
      // 4. Use the commit() method of the UserTransaction
      // to end the transaction
      ut.commit();
      ...
  } // End main()

} // End Client class
```

Also notice that Oracle8*i* version 8.1.7 will support JTS, but only for backward compatibility.

Server-Side Demarcated Transaction

Transactions are demarcated differently if the originator is a client-side or a server-side object. For EJB Beans, EJB providers can let the EJB container implicitly demarcate a transaction for them or they can use the `javax.jts` `.UserTransaction` **interface** (Oracle8*i* versions 8.1.5 and 8.1.6) to explicitly demarcate a transaction. Implicit transaction demarcation is the preferred way since it pushes the responsibility to the EJB container. More importantly, there is no need to start or stop any transaction in implicit declarative transactions. To explicitly demarcate transactions, Beans use the UserTransaction **interface**. The use of this interface requires the TX_BEAN_MANAGED transaction attribute value.

Oracle provides the oracle.aurora.jts.client.AuroraTransaction-Service class, an implementation of the UserTransaction **interface** that allows EJB developers to explicitly demarcate transactions in their programs. For TX_BEAN_MANAGED Beans (Oracle8*i* versions 8.1.5 and 8.1.6), use the following code fragment to explicitly demarcate transactions in EJB server objects:

```
// Include the following import statement
// Oracle8i versions 8.1.5 and 8.1.6.
import javax.jts.UserTransaction;

// Use a SessionContext object to start the transaction
ctx.getUserTransaction ().begin();
..
..
// Invoke some methods

// Use a SessionContext object to end the transaction
ctx.getUserTransaction ().commit();
```

In Oracle8*i* version 8.1.7, you would use the same code to explicitly demarcate transactions in EJB Beans. For TX_BEAN_MANAGED Beans (8.1.7), use the following code fragment to control transaction boundaries:

```
// Include the following import statement
// Oracle8i version 8.1.7
import javax.transaction.UserTransaction;
...
...
// Retrieve the UserTransaction from the session context
UserTransaction ut;
ut = (UserTransaction)ic.lookup(…);

// Use the begin() method of the UserTransaction
// to start the transaction
ut.begin();
...
// Invoke your Bean's methods.
...
// Use the commit() method of the UserTransaction
// to end the transaction
ut.commit();
```

Building a Transactional Application

In this section, you will develop a transactional application that encapsulates the process of atmospheric observations undergoing quality control. This application allows multiple EJB components to perform work that is part of a single atomic transaction. It uses JTS, which provides either standalone Java client programs or EJB Beans the capability to control their transaction boundaries. This application requires the use of three session Beans: the `ObservationBean`, `QcObsBean`, and `QcSetBean` Beans. You developed the `ObservationBean` Bean in Chapter 4. Here, you will build the `QcObsBean` and `QcSetBean` Beans. While developing this application, you will learn the concepts of client transaction demarcation and transaction context propagation.

Transactions in EJB: Revisited

The EJB model implements two-phase commits: transaction context propagation and distributed transactions. However, EJB vendors are not required to implement the two-phase commits. For example, the Oracle8*i* database (versions 8.1.5 and 8.1.6) implements only the transaction context propagation. The upcoming release, Oracle8*i* version 8.1.7, will support both transaction context propagation and distributed transactions.

Transaction Attribute	Client Transaction	Enterprise Bean Transaction
TX_NOT_SUPPORTED	None	None
TX_NOT_SUPPORTED	T1	None
TX_REQUIRED	None	T2
TX_REQUIRED	T1	T1
TX_SUPPORTS	None	None
TX_SUPPORTS	T1	T1
TX_NEW_REQUIRED	None	T2
TX_NEW_REQUIRED	T1	T2
TX_MANDATORY	None	Error
TX_MANDATORY	T1	T1

TABLE 5-1. *Transactions in EJB*

Transactional scope is an important concept in the EJB framework. In Enterprise JavaBeans, the scope of a transaction includes every Bean that participates in a unit of work. A transaction is propagated to a Bean when a client invokes the methods of that Bean. Consequently, at invocation time, the invoked Beans are included in the scope of that transaction. There are two important factors in transactional propagation: the thread of execution in which the Beans are running and the EJB transactional attributes.

In Chapter 4, you learned about the EJB transaction attribute values (see the "EJB Declarative Transaction Attribute Revisited" section). Tables 5-1 and 5-2 present the various transaction attributes and situations in which a transaction is in effect. The first row indicates what occurs when a client invokes a Bean's methods without a transaction context; the second row indicates what happens when a client invokes a Bean's methods with a transaction context. In Tables 5-1 and 5-2, T1 and T2 represent two different transactions.

Table 5-2 shows four possible scenarios:

1. In the first scenario, the client and the instance have not opened a transaction context. Consequently, the Bean's method is invoked without a transaction context.

2. In the second scenario, the client opens a transaction context but the instance does not. The client transaction is suspended and the Bean method is invoked with no transaction context.

3. In the third scenario, the client does not open a transaction context but the instance opens one. Therefore, the Bean method is invoked in its own transaction context.

4. In the fourth scenario, both the client and the instance open a transaction context. The client transaction is suspended, the method is invoked in the Bean's transaction context, and the client's transaction context is resumed after the method completes.

Client Transaction	Instance Current Transaction	Transaction Being Used
None	None	None
T1	None	None
None	T2	T2
T1	T2	T2

TABLE 5-2. *Transactions in TX_BEAN_MANAGED Beans*

Note that `TX_MANAGED_BEAN` transactions differ depending on whether the session Bean is `STATELESS` or `STATEFUL`. For example, a `STATEFUL` Bean can maintain an open transaction across method invocations, whereas a `STATELESS` Bean cannot. In an open transaction mode, the EJB container suspends the Bean's context after each invoked method completes, then resumes it when the next method is invoked.

Next, you will build a transactional application. Before delving into coding, let's first state the user requirements.

User Requirements

The user requirements are as follows:

- Retrieve a list of atmospheric observations from an Oracle database.

- Quality control atmospheric observations and select a set of valid ones.

- Create one new and unique entry in the `QC_EVENT_LIST` table where an entry is made of an Oracle `QUALITY_CONTROL_TYPE` type.

- Create one new and unique entry in the `PASSED_OBSERVATION_LIST` table where an entry consists of attributes associated to a specific `QC_ID` from the `QC_EVENT_LIST` table and a set of quality controlled atmospheric observations.

- Do not allow the application to insert data into the `QC_EVENT_LIST` table if the user has not selected a set of valid observations or there is no observation data.

- Do not allow the application to insert data into the `PASSED_OBSERVATION_LIST` table if the application was unable to insert data into the `QC_EVENT_LIST` table.

Based on the above requirements, you will build an application that manages data within a single Oracle database. More importantly, you will use client-side transaction demarcation to ensure that all database changes are managed within one transaction, and all are committed or all are rolled back.

The application will manipulate data from two Oracle tables: the `QC_EVENT_LIST` and `PASSED_OBSERVATION_LIST` tables. Both tables are part of the Scientific Observation Schema. See the "Introduction" for a complete listing of the schema. Listing 5-7 presents the Oracle types and tables that the `QcSetBean` and `QcObsBean` Beans use.

Listing 5-7: QUALITY_CONTROL_TYPE, PASSEDOBS, and PASSEDOBSARRAY
types and QC_EVENT_LIST and PASSED_OBSERVATION_LIST tables

```
CREATE TYPE QUALITY_CONTROL_EVENT AS OBJECT(
     qc_id        NUMBER(8),
     when_t       DATE,
     at_time      CHAR(8),
     event_id     NUMBER(8),
     for_event    REF atmosevent,
     whom_id      NUMBER(6),
     by_whom      REF scientist);

CREATE TABLE QC_EVENT_LIST OF QUALITY_CONTROL_EVENT;

CREATE OR REPLACE TYPE PASSEDOBS AS OBJECT(
     obsid        NUMBER(8),
     when_t          DATE);

CREATE TYPE PASSEDOBSARRAY AS TABLE OF PASSEDOBS;

CREATE TABLE PASSED_OBSERVATION_LIST(
     qcid         NUMBER(8),
     when_t       DATE,
     at_time      CHAR(8),
     idobj        passedObsArray)
NESTED TABLE idobj STORE AS pobsid_list;
```

The QcObsBean and QcSetBean Beans use procedures and functions that
reside in the QCACTIONS PL/SQL package. See the "Introduction" for a complete
listing of the QCACTIONS package.

The QcObsBean session Bean uses two PL/SQL procedures:

- The QCACTIONS.INSERTQCSETOBS(ArrayList qcObs) procedure
  allows a user to insert obs_ids of quality controlled observations. Its input
  parameter is an ArrayList object of QcObsHelper objects.

- The QCACTIONS.GETQCOBS(int qc_id, OracleTypes.Cursor)
  procedure retrieves all observation data associated to a specific qc_id ID.
  This procedure takes a qc_id and an OracleTypes.Cursor type as
  input parameters and returns a cursor consisting of a set of observation
  data. Use the OracleTypes.Cursor type for PL/SQL procedures or
  functions that return an Oracle REFCURSOR type. To populate the result,
  use an OracleResultSet. The OracleResultSet type is analogous to
  a java.sql.ResultSet; likewise, it provides a next() method that
  allows you to retrieve the data that you get from the database.

CAUTION
The `OracleTypes.CURSOR` *data type is specific to only the Oracle's JDBC drivers.*

The `QcSetBean` session Bean uses one PL/SQL function and one procedure:

■ The `QCACTIONS.GETNEWID()` function produces a new `QcSet` ID.

■ The `QCACTIONS.INSERTQCSET()` procedure inserts a new row into the `QC_EVENT_LIST` table.

Bean High-Level Views

Figures 5-1, 5-2, and 5-3 show the high-level view of the `QcObsBean` and `QcSetBean` session Beans and the `QcClient` application. Figure 4-1 (in Chapter 4) shows the high-level view of the `ObservationBean` session Bean.

Note that the source code for all the programs presented in this chapter is included in the Ch5ReaderCode.zip file. The file also includes implementations using SQLJ for all the Beans developed in this chapter and can be downloaded from the www.data-i.com or www.osborne.com Web site.

Common Classes: Java `Serializable` Classes

The `ObsHelper`, `QcObsHelper`, and `QcSetHelper` classes are used for marshaling and unmarshaling data from/to client objects and server objects. All three classes implement the `java.io.Serializable` interface. The concept of serialization is very important when you want to ship Java objects across a network, that is, across different address spaces.

■ The `ObsHelper` class is a wrapper class that maps the attributes of the `OCEANIC_OBSERVATION_LIST` table. Remember, you designed that class in Chapter 4. The `QcObsBean`, `QcSetBean`, and `ObservationBean` session Beans and the `QcClient` application that you will develop later in this section use this class.

■ The `QcObsHelper` class is a wrapper that maps some of the attributes of the `PASSED_OBSERVATION_LIST` table.

■ The `QcSetHelper` class is a wrapper for the `QC_EVENT_LIST` table.

■ The `ObsException` class is a user-defined Java exception class.

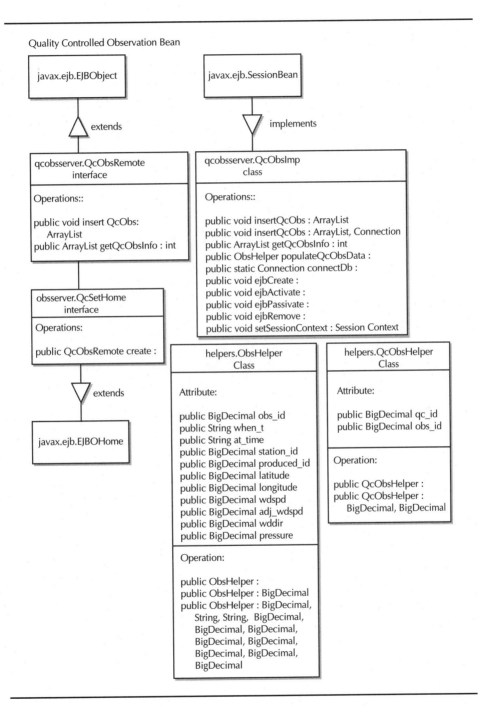

FIGURE 5-1.   *High-level view of the QcObsBean Bean*

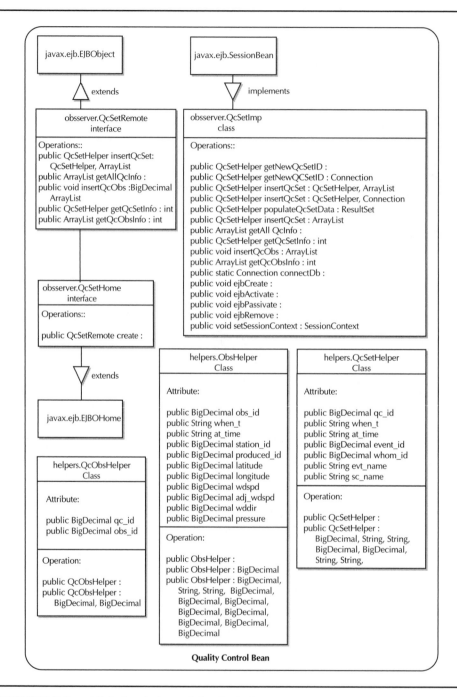

FIGURE 5-2. *High-level view of the QcSetBean Bean*

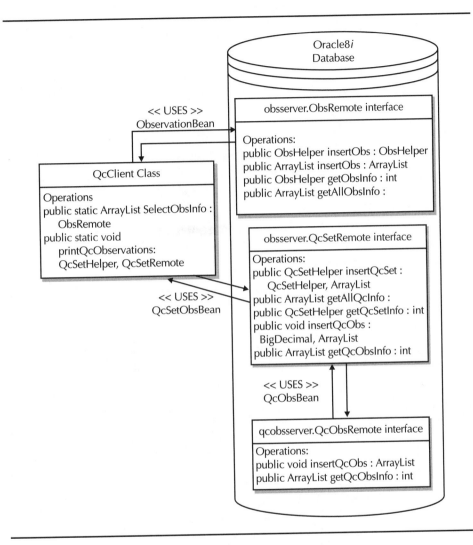

FIGURE 5-3. *QcClient and EJB Beans interactions*

Creating the `QcObsHelper` Class

The `QcObsHelper` class maps the attributes of the `PASSED_OBSERVATION_LIST` table and consists of default and parameterized constructors. Here is the definition of the class:

```
/*     Program Name:      QcObsHelper.java
**
**     Purpose:           A Java serializable Helper class
```

```
**                    used for passing parameter objects
**                    (PASSEDOBS) between clients,
**                    EJB and CORBA components.
**
*/
package helpers;

import java.io.Serializable;
import java.math.BigDecimal;

public class QcObsHelper
    implements java.io.Serializable {

    public BigDecimal qc_id = null;
    public BigDecimal obs_id = null;

    // Default Constructor
    public QcObsHelper ( ) {
    }

    // Parameterized Constructor1
    public QcObsHelper ( BigDecimal qc_id, BigDecimal obs_id ) {
        this.qc_id = qc_id;
        this.obs_id = obs_id;
    }
}
```

Creating the `QcSetHelper` Class

The `QcSetHelper` class maps the attributes of the `QC_EVENT_LIST` table. Here is the definition of the class:

```
/*    Program Name:    QcSetHelper.java
**
**    Purpose:         A Java serializable Helper class
**                     used for passing parameter
**                     (QUALITY_CONTROL_EVENT) objects
**                     between clients, EJB and CORBA
**                     components.
*/
package helpers;

import java.io.Serializable;
import java.math.BigDecimal;

public class QcSetHelper
    implements java.io.Serializable {

    public BigDecimal qc_id = null;
```

```
public String when_t = null;
public String at_time = null;
public BigDecimal event_id = null;
public BigDecimal whom_id = null;
public String evt_name = null;
public String sc_name = null;

// Default Constructor
public QcSetHelper () {
}

// Constructor1
public QcSetHelper (BigDecimal qc_id, String when_t,
                    String at_time,BigDecimal event_id,
                    BigDecimal whom_id) {
   this.qc_id = qc_id;
   this.when_t = when_t;
   this.at_time = at_time;
   this.event_id = event_id;
   this.whom_id = whom_id;
}
// Constructor2
public QcSetHelper (BigDecimal qc_id, String when_t,
     String at_time, BigDecimal event_id,BigDecimal whom_id,
     String evt_name,String sc_name) {

   this.qc_id = qc_id;
   this.when_t = when_t;
   this.at_time = at_time;
   this.event_id = event_id;
   this.whom_id = whom_id;
   this.evt_name = evt_name;
   this.sc_name = sc_name;
}
// Constructor3
public QcSetHelper ( BigDecimal qc_id ) {
   this.qc_id = qc_id;
}
}
```

Creating the `ObsException` Class

Some methods of the `QcSetBean` and `QcObsBean` session Beans can throw
`ObsException`. For an exception to be transported from server objects to a client,
you must define a class for the exception, as shown in the code here:

```
/*    Program Name:    ObsException.java
**
**    Purpose:         An exception class to be
```

```
**                  transported from the server
**                  objects to the clients.
**
**
*/
package helpers;

import java.rmi.*;

public class ObsException
   implements RemoteException {

   // Default Constructor
   public ObsException (String msg ) {

      super(msg);
   }
}
```

The QcObsBean Session Bean

The QcObsBean Bean allows a user to insert a new record into the PASSED_OBSERVATION_LIST table and retrieve all quality controlled atmospheric observations for a specific QcSet ID.

The components of the QcObsBean Bean are as follows:

- The ObsHelper class

- The QcObsHelper class

- The ObsException class

- The QcObsRemote **interface**

- The QcObsHome **interface**

- The QcObsImp class

- The QcObs.ejb deployment descriptor

Creating the QcObsRemote Interface

The QcObsRemote **interface** advertises the methods callable by clients. Here is the definition of the interface:

```
// Program Name: QcObsRemote.java
// Title:        Your Product Name
// Version:
```

```
// Copyright:     Copyright (c) 2000
// Author:        Your Name
// Company:       Your Company
// Description:
//
package qcobsserver;

// import helper classes
import helpers.QcObsHelper;
import helpers.ObsException;
import java.util.ArrayList;

import java.rmi.*;
import javax.ejb.*;
import java.sql.SQLException;

public interface QcObsRemote extends EJBObject {

    // Insert an QcObsHelper object in an Oracle8i
    // database
    public void insertQcObs(ArrayList qcObs)
        throws SQLException, RemoteException;

    // Get observation information and return
    // an ArrayList object of ObsHelper objects based on qc id.
    public ArrayList getQcObsInfo(int qcid)
        throws SQLException, ObsException, RemoteException;
    }
```

Creating the QcObsHome Interface

The QcObsHome **interface** consists of one create() method that is used by clients to create instances of the QcObsBean Bean. Here is the definition of the interface:

```
// Program Name: QcObsHome.java
// Title:        Your Product Name
// Version:
// Copyright:    Copyright (c) 2000
// Author:       Your Name
// Company:      Your Company
// Description:
//
package qcobsserver;

import java.rmi.*;
import javax.ejb.*;

public interface QcObsHome extends EJBHome {
```

```
    // Create an instance of the QcSetRemote interface
    public QcObsRemote create()
       throws CreateException, RemoteException;
}
```

Creating the `QcObsImp` Class

The `QcObsImp` class provides the method bodies for all the method signatures
defined in the `QcObsRemote` interface. Its `insertQcObs()` method calls the
PL/SQL `QCACTIONS.INSERTQCSETOBS()` procedure to insert data into the
`PASSED_OBSERVATION_LIST` table. Here is the definition of the `QcObsImp` class:

```
/* Program Name:   QcObsImp.java
** Version:
** Author:         Your Name
** Description:    An EJB Bean class that allows
**                 client to insert a QcObsHelper
**                 object, an ArrayList of QcObsHelper,
**                 and retrieve an ArrayList of ObsHelper
**
*/
package qcobsserver;

// import helper classes
import helpers.ObsHelper;
import helpers.QcObsHelper;
import helpers.ObsException;

import javax.ejb.SessionContext;
import javax.jts.UserTransaction;
import java.rmi.RemoteException;
import javax.ejb.*;

// import application-specific exception
import java.sql.SQLException;
import java.sql.*;
import oracle.sql.*;

// Import Oracle jdbc driver
import oracle.jdbc.driver.*;

// Import supporting Java classes
import java.math.BigDecimal;
import java.math.*;
import java.util.ArrayList;

public class QcObsImp implements SessionBean {
```

```java
SessionContext ctx;

// Insert new row of data into the
// PASSED_OBSERVATION_LIST table
// Client callable method.
public void insertQcObs (ArrayList qcObs)
    throws SQLException, RemoteException {

  Connection conn = null;
  int arraySize = qcObs.size();
  int loopVar = 0;

  try {
      // Use the internal JDBC driver
      // to connect to the database
      conn = connectDb();

      while  ( loopVar < arraySize ) {
          QcObsHelper anQcObs = (QcObsHelper)qcObs.get(loopVar);

          // Insert anQcObs into the NESTED
          // table of the PASSED_OBSERVATION_LIST table
          insertQcObs(anQcObs, conn);

          loopVar++;
        } // End while
    } // End try
    catch (SQLException e) {
       throw e;
    }  // End catch
    catch (java.lang.NullPointerException e) {
        throw e;
    } // End catch
} // End insertQcObs(ArrayList qcObs)

// Insert new row of data into
// the PASSED_OBSERVATION_LIST table
public void insertQcObs (QcObsHelper qcObs, Connection conn)
        throws SQLException, RemoteException {
  // Create a CallableStatement object
 CallableStatement cstmt  = null;
 try {
      // Prepare the String to call the PL/SQL
      // QCACTIONS.INSERTQCSETOBS() procedure.
      // This statement prepares a Java String consisting
      // of the appropriate statement to call the PL/SQL
      // QCACTIONS.INSERTQCSETOBS() procedure that will
      // insert a new record in the PASSED_OBSERVATION_LIST table
```

```java
        // stored in the database.
        String sql =
          "{call QCACTIONS.INSERTQCSETOBS(?,?)}";
        cstmt = conn.prepareCall(sql);
        cstmt.setInt(1, qcObs.qc_id.intValue());
        cstmt.setInt(2, qcObs.obs_id.intValue());
        cstmt.execute();
    } // End try
    catch (SQLException e) {
        throw e;
    } // End catch
    catch (java.lang.NullPointerException e) {
        throw e;
    } // End catch
    // Clean up
    finally {
            if ( cstmt  != null ) cstmt.close();
    } // End finally()
} // End insertQcObs(qcObs,conn)

// Get observation information and return
// an array of QcObsHelper objects based on qc id.
public ArrayList getQcObsInfo(int qcid)
    throws SQLException, ObsException, RemoteException {
  // Create a CallableStatement object
  CallableStatement cstmt  = null;

  Connection conn = null;
  OracleResultSet rset = null;
  ArrayList obsList = null;
  try {
      conn = connectDb();
      // Prepare the String to call the PL/SQL
      // QCACTIONS.GETQCOBS() procedure.
      // This statement prepares a Java String consisting
      // of the appropriate statement to call the
      // PL/SQL QCACTIONS.GETQCOBS() procedure that will
      // return all the elements of the NESTED TABLE,
      // an attribute of the PASSED_OBSERVATION_LIST
      // table in the database. String sql =
        "{call QCACTIONS.GETQCOBS(?,?)}";

      cstmt = conn.prepareCall(sql);
      // Declare that the ? is a return value of Integer
      cstmt.setInt(1, qcid);
      // Declare that the ? is a return value of
      // type OracleTypes.CURSOR
      // The QCACTIONS.GETQCOBS() procedure takes
```

```
        // two parameters: an int as IN parameter
        // (holding the qc_id of a QcSet) and as an
        // IN OUT parameter of the OracleTypes.CURSOR data type.
        // Use the Oracle CURSOR when the return type or input
        // parameter of a PL/SQL function or Procedure is the
        // Oracle REF CURSOR type. When using an Oracle JDBC driver,
        // the REF CURSOR type requires that you use the
        // OracleTypes.CURSOR as a register out parameter.
        // To get the data from the resulting cursor,
        // you must cast it to an OracleResultSet type.
        // The OracleResultSet type is similar to a
        // Java.sql.ResultSet.
        cstmt.registerOutParameter(2, OracleTypes.CURSOR);
        cstmt.execute();
} // End try
catch (SQLException e) {
    //  e.printStackTrace();throw e;
} // End catch
try {
        // Cast the OracleTypes.CURSOR to an OracleResultSet.

        // This statement casts the Oracle OracleTypes.CURSOR
        // type to an OracleResultSet type. This class also
        // includes a next() method. Like a Java ResultSet,
        // you empty the cursor using the next() method.
        rset =
            (OracleResultSet)cstmt.getObject(2);
        // Instantiate the obsList ArrayList
        obsList = new ArrayList();
        while (rset.next()) {
            ObsHelper oneObs = populateQcObsData(rset);
            // Insert oneObs object into the obsList ArrayList
            obsList.add(oneObs);
        }  // End while
        // Reduce obsList to the actual size
        obsList.trimToSize();
        // Return an ArrayList of ObsHelper
        // objects to the caller
        return obsList;
} // End try
catch (java.lang.NullPointerException e) {
    throw new java.lang.NullPointerException (e.getMessage());
} // End catch
catch (SQLException e) {

        // In Oracle 8.1.6, when you used the getObject() method of a
        // CallableStatement object to populate the
        // rset OracleResultSet, when this statement is executed,
```

```
        // you may get a SQLException if your PL/SQL code did not
        // open the cursor. The INVALID CURSOR SQLException is
        // thrown. You must catch this error and set the
        // OracleResultSet rset to null if you want to exit
        // the program gracefully.
        rset = null;
     // e.printStackTrace();
        throw new ObsException("No QcObs for this QcSet id: "
              +qcid );
  } // End catch
  // Clean up
  finally {
          if ( cstmt  != null ) cstmt.close();
          if ( rset  != null ) rset.close();
  } // End finally()
} // End getQcObsInfo(int qcid)

// This method populates the result set data
// to an ObsHelper object.
public ObsHelper populateQcObsData (ResultSet rset)
      throws SQLException {
  try {
      // Declare an ObsHelper object
      // using the default constructor.
      ObsHelper oneObs = new ObsHelper();
      // Set the member variables of the ObsHelper object.
      // Note that you could also use the parameterized
      // contructor1 defined in the ObsHelper class.
      oneObs.obs_id   = new BigDecimal(rset.getInt(1));
      oneObs.when_t   = rset.getString(2);
      oneObs.at_time  = rset.getString(3);
      rset.getInt(4);
      if  (rset.wasNull())
         oneObs.station_id = null;
      else
         oneObs.station_id = new BigDecimal(rset.getInt(4));
      rset.getInt(5);
      if  (rset.wasNull())
          oneObs.produced_id = null;
      else
          oneObs.produced_id = new BigDecimal(rset.getInt(5));
      rset.getInt(6);
      if  (rset.wasNull())
          oneObs.latitude = null;
      else
          oneObs.latitude = new BigDecimal(rset.getInt(6));
      rset.getInt(7);
      if  (rset.wasNull())
```

```
                oneObs.longitude = null;
        else
                oneObs.longitude = new BigDecimal(rset.getInt(7));
        rset.getInt(8);
        if  (rset.wasNull())
                oneObs.wdspd = null;
        else
                oneObs.wdspd = new BigDecimal(rset.getInt(8));
        rset.getInt(9);
        if  (rset.wasNull())
                oneObs.adj_wdspd = null;
        else
                oneObs.adj_wdspd = new BigDecimal(rset.getInt(9));
        rset.getInt(10);
        if  (rset.wasNull())
                oneObs.wddir = null;
        else
                oneObs.wddir = new BigDecimal(rset.getInt(10));
        rset.getInt(11);
        if  (rset.wasNull())
                oneObs.pressure = null;
        else
                oneObs.pressure = new BigDecimal(rset.getInt(11));
        return oneObs;
 } // End try
 catch (SQLException e) {
     throw e;
 }   // End catch
 catch (java.lang.NullPointerException e) {
     throw e;
 } // End catch
} // End populateQcObsData()


// This method is called by all methods that need
// to connect to the database using the internal JDBC driver
// Note that the code to obtain a Connection object
// could be placed in the ejbCreate() method.
public static Connection connectDb()
     throws SQLException, RemoteException {
   // Note that this method is only accessible
   // to the Bean class methods and NOT to clients
   // Create a java.sql.Connection variable
   Connection conn = null;
       DriverManager.registerDriver
         (new oracle.jdbc.driver.OracleDriver());
     // Instantiate using the Oracle8i internal JDBC driver
     conn =
       DriverManager.getConnection("jdbc:default:connection:");
```

```
         // Return a java.sql.Connection object
         return conn;
} // End connectDb()

public void ejbCreate()
    throws RemoteException, CreateException {
} // End ejbCreate()
public void ejbActivate()throws RemoteException {
} // End ejbActivate()
public void ejbPassivate() throws RemoteException {
} // End ejbPassivate()
public void ejbRemove() throws RemoteException {
} // End ejbRemove ()
public void setSessionContext(SessionContext ctxArg)
    throws RemoteException {
  ctx = ctxArg;
} // End setSessionContext()
} // End QcObsImpl class
```

The `QcSetBean` Session Bean

The `QcSetBean` Bean inserts data into the `QC_EVENT_LIST` table, retrieves data from the table, and invokes the `QcObsBean` methods to insert data into the `PASSED_OBSERVATION_LIST` table and retrieve data from that table. See Figure 5-3 for a high-level view of interactions between the `QcClient` application and the `ObservationBean`, `QcSetBean`, and `QcObsBean` session Beans.

The components of the `QcSetBean` Bean are as follows:

- The `ObsHelper` class

- The `QcObsHelper` class

- The `ObsException` class

- The `QcSetRemote` **interface**

- The `QcSetHome` **interface**

- The `QcSetImp` class

- The `QcSet.ejb` deployment descriptor

Creating the `QcSetRemote Interface`

The `QcSetRemote` **interface** advertises the methods that manipulate the `QC_EVENT_LIST` table. Note that the `insertQcObs ()` and `getQcObsInfo()` methods of this interface indirectly manipulate the `PASSED_OBSERVATION_LIST` table. Their invocation triggers the invocation of the `insertQcObs ()` and getQcObsInfo() methods of the QcObsBean Bean. The QcSetImp class provides the method bodies for the insertQcObs () and getQcObsInfo()methods listed in the QcSetRemote **interface**.

Here is the definition of the QcSetRemote **interface**:

```java
// Program Name: QcSetRemote.java
// Title:        Your Product Name
// Version:
// Copyright:    Copyright (c) 2000
// Author:       Your Name
// Company:      Your Company
// Description:
//
package obsserver;

// import helper classes
import helpers.QcSetHelper;
import helpers.QcObsHelper;
import helpers.ObsHelper;
import helpers.ObsException;

import java.util.ArrayList;
import java.rmi.*;
import javax.ejb.*;

import java.sql.SQLException;

public interface QcSetRemote extends EJBObject {

  // Insert a QcSetHelper object in an Oracle8i
  // database and its associated quality controlled observations
  public QcSetHelper insertQcSet(QcSetHelper qc,ArrayList qcObs)
        throws SQLException, RemoteException;

  // Get all QcSet information and return
  // the info in an ArrayList object of QcSetHelper objects
  // This method uses dynamic SQL to return
  // all data from the QC_EVENT_LIST table
  public ArrayList getAllQcInfo()
        throws SQLException, ObsException, RemoteException;

  // Get QcSet information and return
  // a QcSetHelper object based on qc id.
  public QcSetHelper getQcSetInfo(int qcid)
        throws SQLException, ObsException, RemoteException;

  // Insert new row of data into the PASSED_OBSERVATION_LIST table
```

```
// This method invokes the insertQcObs() of the QcObsBean Bean
public void insertQcObs (BigDecimal qc_id, ArrayList qcObs)
   throws SQLException, RemoteException;

// Get observation information and return
// an array of QcObsHelper objects based on qc id.
public ArrayList getQcObsInfo(int qcid)
   throws SQLException, ObsException, RemoteException;
}
```

Creating the `QcSetHome` Interface

Here is the definition of the `QcSetHome` **interface**:

```
// Program Name: QcSetHome.java
// Title:        Your Product Name
// Version:
// Copyright:    Copyright (c) 2000
// Author:       Your Name
// Company:      Your Company
// Description:
//
package obsserver;
import java.rmi.*;
import javax.ejb.*;

public interface QcSetHome extends EJBHome {
   // Create an instance of the QcSetRemote interface
   public QcSetRemote create()
        throws CreateException, RemoteException;
}
```

Creating the `QcSetImp` Class

The `QcSetImp` class is a typical example of a server-side client object illustrating how an EJB Bean starts up a new Oracle database session while executing in an existing session:

```
/* Program Name:  QcSetImp.java
** Version:
** Author:       Your Name
** Description:  An EJB Bean class that allows
**               client to insert a QcSetHelper
**               object, an ArrayList of QcSetHelper objects,
**               and retrieve an ArrayList of QcObsHelper objects.
**               The QcSetImp class manipulates data in the
**               Qc_event_list table and uses the QcObsBean Bean
**               to manipulate data in the Passed_Observation_List
```

```
**                 table.
*/
package obsserver;

// import helper classes
import helpers.QcSetHelper;
import helpers.ObsHelper;
import helpers.QcObsHelper;

// import the qcobserver objects.
// This statement and the one that follows it import
// the QcObsRemote and QcObsHome interfaces of the
// QcObsBean session Bean. The QcSetImp class is
// an EJB Bean client of the QcObsBean Bean. Note
// that standalone Java clients and EJB Beans must
// import the home and remote interfaces of any
// published object that they want to use
import qcobsserver.QcObsRemote;
import qcobsserver.QcObsHome;

import javax.ejb.SessionContext;
import javax.jts.UserTransaction;
import javax.naming.Context;
import javax.naming.InitialContext;
import javax.naming.NamingException;

import java.rmi.RemoteException;
import javax.ejb.*;

// import application-specific exception
import java.sql.SQLException;

import java.sql.*;
import oracle.sql.*;

// Import Oracle jdbc driver
import oracle.jdbc.driver.*;
// Import supporting Java classes
import java.math.BigDecimal;
import java.math.*;
import java.util.ArrayList;
import java.util.Hashtable;

public class QcSetImp implements SessionBean {

    // Create a variable of type SessionContext
    SessionContext ctx;
    // Create a global variable of type QcObsRemote
```

```java
// This statement creates the qcObsObj global
// variable of QcObsRemote type. The qcObsObj will
// hold a reference to the QcObsRemote interface.
// (See Note 1.)
 QcObsRemote qcObsObj = null;


// This method, non-callable by clients,
// connects to the database
// And calls the overloaded getNewQcSetId(conn)
// to get a new qc_id.
public QcSetHelper getNewQcSetId()
    throws SQLException, RemoteException {
        Connection conn = null;
        try {
                // Use the internal JDBC driver
                // to connect to the database
                conn = connectDb();
                QcSetHelper qc = getNewQcSetId(conn);
                return qc;
        } // End try
        catch(SQLException e) {
                throw e;
        }   // End catch()
} // End getNewQcSetId()

// This method is NOT callable by clients
// Therefore, it is not listed in the
// QcSetRemote interface
public QcSetHelper getNewQcSetId(Connection conn)
     throws SQLException, RemoteException {
   // Create a CallableStatement object
   CallableStatement cstmt  = null;

   // Call the getNewQcId() from the PL/SQL QcActions package
   // to get a new qc_id
   try {
       // Prepare a String for the call
       String sqlId =
         "{? = call QCACTIONS.GETNEWQCID}";
       // Prepare the call using the default JDBC connection
       cstmt = conn.prepareCall(sqlId);
       // Declare that the ? is a return value of type Integer
       cstmt.registerOutParameter (1, Types.INTEGER);
       // Get the new qcid by executing the query
       cstmt.execute ();
       BigDecimal anQcId = new BigDecimal(cstmt.getInt (1));
       // Return an QcSetHelper object using the new id
       return new QcSetHelper(anQcId);
```

```
    }  // End try
    catch (SQLException e) {
        throw e;
    }  // End catch
    // Clean up
    finally {
            if  ( cstmt  != null ) cstmt.close();
    } // End finally()
  } // End getNewQcSetId(conn)

  // CONTAINER-INITIATED TRANSACTION
  // This method gets a new qc_id and adds a new
  // QUALITY_CONTROL_EVENT in the QC_EVENT_LIST TABLE. Clients
  // invoke this method.
  public QcSetHelper insertQcSet( QcSetHelper inQc )
       throws SQLException, RemoteException {
   QcSetHelper qc = inQc;
   Connection conn = null;
   try {
        // Use the internal JDBC driver
        // to connect to the database
        conn = connectDb();
        // Get a new qc_id from the database
        QcSetHelper anQcid = getNewQcSetId(conn);
        // Update the input qc_id
        qc.qc_id = anQcid.qc_id;
        // Insert a new OCEANIC_OBSERVATION_TYPE
        anQcid = insertQcSet(qc,conn);

        // Return a QcSetHelper object
        // This statement returns the newly generated qc_id ID
        // to the caller.
        return new QcSetHelper(anQcid.qc_id);
    }  // End try
    catch (SQLException e) {
        throw e;
    }  // End catch
    catch (java.lang.NullPointerException e) {
       throw e;
    } // End catch
  } // End insertQcSet(qc)

public QcSetHelper insertQcSet(QcSetHelper qc, Connection conn)
       throws SQLException, RemoteException {
   // Create a CallableStatement object
   CallableStatement cstmt  = null;
   try {
        // Prepare the String to call the PL/SQL
```

```
        // QCACTIONS.INSERTQCSET() procedure.
        String sql =
           "{call QCACTIONS.INSERTQCSET(?,?,?,?,?)}";
        cstmt = conn.prepareCall(sql);
        cstmt.setInt(1, qc.qc_id.intValue());
        cstmt.setString(2, qc.when_t);
        cstmt.setString(3, qc.at_time);
        cstmt.setInt(4, qc.event_id.intValue());
        cstmt.setInt(5, qc.whom_id.intValue());
        cstmt.execute();
        // Return a QcSetHelper object
        return new QcSetHelper(qc.qc_id);
    }   // End try
    catch (SQLException e) {
        throw e;
    }   // End catch
    // Clean up
    finally {
            if ( cstmt != null ) cstmt.close();
    } // End finally()
} // End insertQcSet(qc,conn)

// This method uses dynamic SQL to return
// all data from the QC_EVENT_LIST table
public ArrayList getAllQcInfo()
    throws SQLException, ObsException, RemoteException {
    Connection conn = null;
    // Need a Java Vector to store the table rows since you
    // do not know how many rows are being retrieved.
    ArrayList qcList = null;
    // Declare a Java ResulSet object
    ResultSet rset = null;
    // Declare a PreparedStatement variable
    PreparedStatement pstmt = null;
    // Prepare the SQL SELECT statement
    String sql =
      "SELECT Q.qc_id, TO_CHAR(Q.when_t,'DD-MM-YYYY'),"
      + "Q.at_time, Q.event_id, Q.for_event.name, Q.whom_id, "
      + "Q.by_whom.lastname " + "FROM QC_EVENT_LIST Q";
    try {
        // Use the internal JDBC driver to connect to the database
        conn = connectDb();
        // Prepare the statement
        pstmt = conn.prepareStatement(sql);
        // Execute the query and store
        // the result in a Java ResultSet
        rset = pstmt.executeQuery();
        // Instantiate the qcList ArrayList
```

```
        qcList = new ArrayList();
        while (rset.next()) {
           // Declare a QcSetHelper object
           QcSetHelper oneQc = populateQcSetData(rset);
           // Insert oneObs object into the Java qcList
           // ArrayList
           qcList.add(oneQc);
        }  // End while
        // Check ArrayList size
        if  (qcList.size() == 0)
            throw new ObsException("No QcSet Data");
        // Trim the size of the qcList
        qcList.trimToSize();
        // Return the ArrayList object to the caller
        return qcList;
     } // End try
     catch (SQLException e) {
         throw e;
     }  // End catch
     catch (java.lang.Exception e) {
        throw e;
     }  // End catch
     // Clean up
     finally {
            if  ( rset  != null ) rset.close();
            if  ( pstmt != null ) pstmt.close();
     } // End finally()
}  // End getAllQcInfo

// Get observation info for a specific qc_id
public QcSetHelper getQcSetInfo(int qcid)
     throws SQLException, RemoteException {
  Connection conn = null;
  int qc_id = qcid;
  // Declare a Java ResultSet object
  ResultSet rset = null;
  // Declare a PreparedStatement variable
  PreparedStatement pstmt = null;
  // Prepare the SQL SELECT statement
  String sql =
    "SELECT Q.qc_id, TO_CHAR(Q.when_t,'DD-MM-YYYY'),"
    + "Q.at_time, Q.event_id, Q.for_event.name, Q.whom_id, "
    + "Q.by_whom.lastname " + "FROM QC_EVENT_LIST Q "
    + "WHERE Q.qc_id = ?";
  try {
       conn = connectDb();
       pstmt = conn.prepareStatement(sql);
       pstmt.setInt(1, qc_id);
```

```java
            rset = pstmt.executeQuery();
            QcSetHelper oneQc = null;
            while (rset.next()) {
                oneQc = populateQcSetData(rset);
            }  // End while
            return oneQc;
    }    // End try
    catch (SQLException e) {
       throw e;
    }  // End catch
    // Clean up
    finally {
            if  ( rset  != null ) rset.close();
            if  ( pstmt != null ) pstmt.close();
    }  // End finally()
}  // End getQcSetInfo()

// This method populates the result set data
// to a QcSetHelper object.
public QcSetHelper populateQcSetData (ResultSet rset)
     throws SQLException {
   try {
        // Declare a QcSetHelper object
        // using the default constructor.
        QcSetHelper oneQc = new QcSetHelper();
        // Set the member variables of the QcSetHelper object.
        // Note that you could also use the parameterized
        // contructor1 defined in the QcSetHelper class.
        oneQc.qc_id   = new BigDecimal(rset.getInt(1));
        oneQc.when_t  = rset.getString(2);
        oneQc.at_time = rset.getString(3);
        rset.getInt(4);
        if  (rset.wasNull())
            oneQc.event_id = null;
        else
            oneQc.event_id = new BigDecimal(rset.getInt(4));
        oneQc.evt_name  = rset.getString(5);
        rset.getInt(6);
        if  (rset.wasNull())
            oneQc.whom_id = null;
        else
            oneQc.whom_id = new BigDecimal(rset.getInt(6));
        oneQc.sc_name  = rset.getString(7);
        return oneQc;
   } // End try
   catch (SQLException e) {
      throw e;
   }  // End catch
```

```
 catch (java.lang.NullPointerException e) {
    throw e;
 } // End catch
} // End populateQcSetData()

// Insert new row of data into the PASSED_OBSERVATION_LIST table
public void insertQcObs (BigDecimal qc_id, ArrayList qcObs)
     throws SQLException, RemoteException {
  try {
       int arraySize = qcObs.size();
       // Create a new ArrayList object using qcObs.size().
       ArrayList arrayOfQcObsHelpers =
                     new ArrayList(arraySize);
       int loopVar = 0;
       while ( loopVar < arraySize ) {
         BigDecimal anObsid = (BigDecimal)qcObs.get(loopVar);
         // Create QcObsHelper objects using the qc_id and anObsid
         QcObsHelper aQcObsHelper =
               new QcObsHelper(qc_id,anObsid);
         // Put the QcObsHelper object into the ArrayList object
         arrayOfQcObsHelpers.add(aQcObsHelper);
         loopVar++;
       } // End while
       // Call insertQcObs (ArrayList qcObs) (See Note 2.)
       // This statement uses a reference to the QcObsRemote
       // interface to invoke the insertQcObs() method of the
       // QcObsImp class. This is a typical example of an
       // existing EJB Bean (server-side client object)
       // invoking another Bean and of implicit server-side
       // demarcated transactions.
       // In the QcObs.ejb deployment descriptor, you
       // use the TX_REQUIRED_NEW attribute value for
       // the QcObsBean Bean. Consequently, the QcObsBean Bean
       // will be invoked in a new transaction.

       qcObsObj.insertQcObs(qcObs);

  } // End try
  catch (SQLException e) {
     throw e;
  }  // End catch
  catch (java.lang.NullPointerException e) {
     throw e;
  } // End catch
} // End insertQcObs(BigDecimal qc_id, ArrayList qcObs)

// Get observation information and return an ArrayList of
// ObsHelper objects based on qc id.
```

```
  // This statement defines the getQcObsInfo() method of
  // the QcSetBean Bean. When called, this method will invoke the
  // getQcObsInfo() method of the QcObsBean session Bean.
public ArrayList getQcObsInfo(int qcid)
     throws SQLException, RemoteException {
  ArrayList obsList = null;
  try {
      // Call getQcObsInfo().
      // This statement invokes the getQcObsInfo() method
      // of the QcObsBean session Bean and returns an
      // ArrayList object of ObsHelper objects to the
      // QcSetBean Bean.
      obsList = qcObsObj.getQcObsInfo(qcid);

      // Return an ArrayList object
      return obsList;
  } // End try
  catch (java.lang.NullPointerException e) {
    throw e;
  } // End catch
  catch (SQLException e) {
    //  e.printStackTrace();
      throw e;
  } // End catch
} // End getQcObsInfo(int qcid)

  // This method is called by all methods that need
  // to connect to the database using the internal JDBC driver
public static Connection connectDb()
     throws SQLException, RemoteException {
  // Note that this method is only accessible
  // to the Bean class methods and NOT to clients
  // Create a java.sql.Connection variable
  Connection conn = null;
    DriverManager.registerDriver
        (new oracle.jdbc.driver.OracleDriver());
    // Instantiate using the Oracle8i internal JDBC driver
    conn =
       DriverManager.getConnection("jdbc:default:connection:");
    // Return a java.sql.Connection object
    return conn;
} // End connectDb()

 // (See Note 3.)
 public void ejbCreate()
    throws RemoteException, CreateException {
   try {
       // Create InitialContext  (See Note 4.)
```

```
        Hashtable env = new Hashtable();
        env.put (Context.URL_PKG_PREFIXES, "oracle.aurora.jndi");
        Context ic = new InitialContext(env);
        // Create the QcObsImp Bean (See Note 5.)
        String objectName = new String("/test/QcObsBean");

        // Start a new database session while
        // locating a reference to the QcObsBean home interface.
        // (See Note 6.)
        QcObsHome anQcObsHome =
            (QcObsHome)ic.lookup("sess_iiop://thisServer"
                    +objectName);

        // For better performance, use the same
        // database session instead. To do so, use the following:
        // QcObsHome anQcObsHome =
        // (QcObsHome)ic.lookup("sess_iiop://thisServer/:thisSession"
        //   +objectName);
        // (See Note 7.)
        qcObsObj = anQcObsHome.create();
    }   // End try
    catch (NamingException e) {
        // e.printStackTrace();
    } // End catch
} // End ejbCreate()
 public void ejbActivate()throws RemoteException {
 } // End ejbActivate()
 public void ejbPassivate() throws RemoteException {
 } // End ejbPassivate()
 public void ejbRemove() throws RemoteException {
 } // End ejbRemove ()
 // (See Note 8.)
 public void setSessionContext(SessionContext ctx)
     throws RemoteException {
   this.ctx = ctx;
 } // End setSessionContext()
}
```

Notes on the `QcSetImp` class:

I. The `qcObsObj` global variable will hold a reference to the `QcObsBean`
    Bean. A reference to the `QcObsBean` Bean is obtained when a client
    invokes the `create()` method of the `QcSetBean`. Recall that when a
    client invokes the `create()` method of a EJB home **interface**, the EJB
    container invokes the associated `ejbCreate()` method defined in the
    corresponding Bean class. In this example, when the QcClient application
    creates an instance of the `QcSetBean` Bean, the `QcSetImp` class
    automatically and transparently creates an instance of the `QcObsBean` Bean.

2. This statement uses a reference to the QcObsRemote **interface** to invoke the insertQcObs() method of the QcObsImp class. Recall that the QcSetBean Bean obtained a QcObsBean instance when the QcClient object invoked the create() method of the QcSetHome **interface**. This is a typical example of an existing EJB Bean (server-side client object) invoking another Bean and of implicit server-side demarcated transactions. In this example, the EJB container will create a new transaction context object. The QcObsBean Bean enters a transaction because the caller, the QcSetBean Bean, has a transaction in effect via the TX_SUPPORTS transaction attribute. Note that the transaction context opened in QcSetBean Bean is not propagated to QcObsBean. In the QcObs.ejb deployment descriptor, you are using the TX_REQUIRED_NEW attribute value for the QcObsBean Bean. The QcObsBean Bean will be invoked in a new transaction. While executing, the transaction that had started from the QcClient application and propagated to the QcSetBean will be suspended, and will resume after the execution of the insertQcObs() method of the QcObsImp class.

3. This statement defines the ejbCreate() method of the QcSetBean Bean. For STATELESS or STATEFUL Beans, the EJB container calls the following methods when a client program invokes the create() method of the EJB home **interface**:

- The newInstance() method allocates space and brings the Bean to existence.

- The setSessionContext() gives a session context. The SessionContext object that is passed points to a dynamic object that the EJB container updates each time a Bean's methods are invoked. The EJB container retains the SessionContext object for the entire life of the existing session Bean.

- The ejbCreate() method, like a Java constructor, creates an EJB instance and initializes an instance's internal state variables. As with the Java constructor, you can code the ejbCreate() method to initialize variables, connect to a database, or instantiate other Beans.

4. In this **try** block, the QcSetBean Bean will create a QcObsBean instance. Like Java standalone client programs, the QcSetBean Bean will use the JNDI lookup() method to obtain a reference to the desired published object—in this case, the QcObsBean Bean. The very first step is to set up the environment. Note that you only set the URL_PKG_PREFIXES variable. This is the only environment variable that you have to set because

the other had been previously set up for you by the very first client (that is, the `QcClient`) that had invoked the `create()` method of the `QcSetHome` **interface**. For more information regarding JNDI server-side object environment variable setup, see the "Server Object Starting a New Session" section of this chapter. After you set up the environment variables, you then create a JNDI `Context` object using the environment variables. The `QcSetBean` Bean will start up a new database session using a concatenation of the `sess_iiop://thisServer` URL and the `/test/QcObsBean` published object name; its transaction service will create a new transaction context, and the `QcObsBean` methods will be invoked using that transaction context. The execution of the `QcObsBean` methods will suspend any transaction initiated by the `QcClient` object and will resume after the `QcObsBean` methods complete. Note that here, for better performance, you could avoid creating a new database session and instead use the `sess_iiop://thisServer/:thisSession` as a URL. For more information regarding this notation, see the "Server Object Accessing the Same Session" section of this chapter.

5. This statement creates a Java `String` containing the `/test/QcObsBean` published object name.

6. This statement uses the `sess_iiop://thisServer` notation as a URL concatenated with the `/test/QcObsBean` name to obtain a reference to a Bean home **interface**. Recall that this URL creates a new database session. There now exist two database sessions: the first session was established by the `QcClient` application when it invoked the `QcSetBean`, and the second database session started when the EJB container executed the `ejbCreate()` method of the `QcSetImp` class.

7. This statement uses the `qcObsObj` global variable to store an instance of the `QcObsRemote` **interface**. Via the `qcObsObj` object, an instance of the `QcObsBean` session Bean is made visible at the class level—that is, an instance of the `QcObsBean` Bean is made available globally to all the methods of the `QcSetBean` Bean.

8. This statement defines the `setSessionContext()` method. Use this method to get the `SessionContext` object from the EJB container and save it in an instance variable.

The `QcSet.ejb` Deployment Descriptor File

The `QcSet.ejb` file contains instructions to deploy the `QcObsBean` and the `QcObs.ejb` file contains information to deploy the `QcSetObsBean` session Beans. Here is the definition of the `QcSet.ejb` file:

```
// File Name:   QcSet.ejb (See Note 1.)
// QcSet EJB deployment descriptor.
SessionBean obsserver.QcSetImp {
  BeanHomeName = "test/QcSetObsBean";
  HomeInterfaceClassName = obsserver.QcSetHome;
  RemoteInterfaceClassName = obsserver.QcSetRemote;
  AllowedIdentities = {PUBLIC};
  SessionTimeout = 0;
  StateManagementType = STATEFUL_SESSION;
  RunAsMode = CLIENT_IDENTITY;
  TransactionAttribute = TX_SUPPORTS; // (See Note 2.)
 } // End obsserver.QcSetImp
```

The `QcObs.ejb` Deployment Descriptor File

Here is the definition of the `QcObs.ejb` file:

```
// File Name:   QcObs.ejb (See Note 3.)
 // QcObs EJB deployment descriptor.
 SessionBean qcobsserver.QcObsImp {
   BeanHomeName = "test/QcObsBean";
   HomeInterfaceClassName = qcobsserver.QcObsHome;
   RemoteInterfaceClassName = qcobsserver.QcObsRemote;
   AllowedIdentities = {PUBLIC};
   SessionTimeout = 0;
   StateManagementType = STATEFUL_SESSION;
   RunAsMode = CLIENT_IDENTITY;
   TransactionAttribute = TX_REQUIRED_NEW; //(See Note 4.)
 }
```

Notes on the `QcSet.ejb` and the `QcObs.ejb` files:

1. The `obsserver.QcSetImp SessionBean` class defines the `QcSet.ejb` descriptor file for the `QcSetObsBean` session Bean.

2. This statement declares the transaction policy of the entire `QcSetBean` Bean. Recall that the `TX_SUPPORT` transaction attribute can be invoked in a client-supplied transaction context. Moreover, if the client does not supply a transaction context, it invokes the Bean method with no transaction context.

3. The `qcobsserver.QcObsImp SessionBean` class defines the `QcObs.ejb` descriptor file for the `QcObsBean` session Bean.

4. This statement declares the transaction policy of the entire `QcObsBean` Bean. `TX_REQUIRES_NEW` EJB Beans must always be invoked in a new transaction context whether or not the client supplies a transaction context. The EJB container creates a new one anyway, suspending the client transaction context until the Bean's transaction has been completed.

CAUTION
*The order in which you deploy the `QcSetObsBean` and `QcObsBean` session Beans is very important. You must deploy the `QcSetObsBean` enterprise Bean before you deploy the `QcObsBean` Bean. If you reverse the order, at invocation time the `QcSetObsBean` Bean will not be able to locate the `QcObsBean`'s home **interface**.*

The `QcClient` Transactional Application

The `QcClient` class is a standalone Java transactional client application that does the following:

- Initializes a client transaction service. It does so by invoking the `initialize()` method of `AuroraTransactionService` class.

- Demarcates and starts a new transaction (called `TX1`). This is done by invoking the JTS `begin()` method. In Figure 5-4, for illustration purposes, this transaction is named `TX1`.

- Gets an instance of the `ObservationBean` and `QcSetObsBean` session Beans.

- Uses the `TX1` transaction context (created in step 2) to invoke successively the `ObservationBean`'s `getAllObs()` method and the `QcSetObsBean`'s `insertQcSet()` method. Note that at the invocation of the `getAllObes()` method, the `TX1` transaction context is propagated to the `ObservationBean` Bean. When `QcClient` invokes the `insertQcSet()` method, `TX1` is also propagated to the `QcSAetObsBean` Bean.

- Terminates the `TX1` transaction initiated in step 2. This is done by invoking the JTS `commit()` method.

- Demarcates and starts a new transaction (called `TX2`). This is done by invoking the JTS `begin()` method again.

- Uses the `TX2` transaction context (created in step 3) to invoke the `QcSetObsBean`'s `insertQcObs()` method, which in turn invokes the `QcObsBean`'s `insertQcObs()` method. When the `QcSetObsBean` session Bean invokes the `QcObsBean`'s `insert QcObs()` method, the EJB container starts a new transaction (named `TX3`).

Figure 5-4 shows the various transaction scopes under which the Beans are invoked.

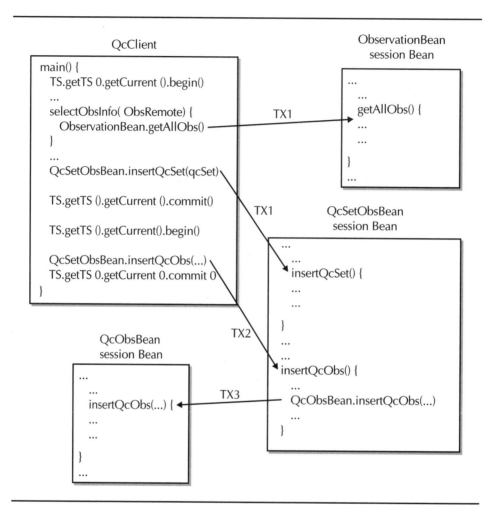

FIGURE 5-4. *Transaction scopes*

Notes on Figure 5-4:

1. In the local `selectObsInfo()` method, an instance of the `ObservationBean` Bean (denoted by `ObservationBean`) is used to invoke its `getAllObs()` method.

2. An instance of the `QcSetObsBean` Bean (denoted by `QcSetObsBean`) is used to invoke its `insertQcSet()` and `insertQcObs()` methods whereas and instance of the `QcObsBean` (denoted by `QcObsBean`) is used to call its `insertQcObs()` method.

The `QcClient` program is a typical client-side application with explicit transaction demarcation coded programmatically. In client-side demarcated applications, a transactional client explicitly encloses one or more Bean invocations or one or more method invocations on a specific Bean with demarcation methods such as `begin()` and `commit()` (or `rollback()`) that begin and end transactions. The beginning and ending *demarcators* are method calls on the client-side transaction service. When the client opens a transaction context, the transaction context is passed from the client object to the server object or from one server object to another. The transaction context carries the state of the transaction. After a client-side service is initialized, the transaction service implicitly creates a transaction context, and assigns a transaction ID number to the context. The client transaction service then propagates the transaction context to each participant—that is, to each EJB object that the client calls. On the client side, the transaction context is intercepted and then submitted on any method call to a server object. On the server side, the transaction context is extracted and made available to the server object. In the `QcClient` application, you use the `initialize()` method of the `AuroraTransactionService` class to initialize the transaction service. Once the transaction service is initialized, it implicitly creates a transaction context. The transaction is then demarcated with the execution of the appropriate `begin()` method, which starts a global transaction and associates the transaction with the calling thread. Note that the transaction-to-thread association is managed transparently. Once the transaction context is opened, the `QcClient` transaction service propagates it to the `ObservationBean` and the `QcSetBean` Beans, respectively.

Here is the definition of the `QcClient` class:

```
/* Program Name:  QcClient.java
** Version:
** Author:        Your Name
** Description:   A Java client application that allows
**                a user to get a list of atmospheric
**                observations, quality control them,
**                and simultaneously insert a new row
**                in the QC_EVENT_LIST table and insert a
**                new row in the PASSED_OBSERVATION_LIST.
**                After insertions are done, the client
**                calls the necessary methods to display
**                info from the PASSED_OBSERVATION_LIST table.
**
*/
// import helper classes
import helpers.QcSetHelper;
import helpers.ObsHelper;
import helpers.QcObsHelper;
```

```
// import the obsserver objects
import obsserver.ObsRemote;
import obsserver.ObsHome;
import obsserver.QcSetRemote;
import obsserver.QcSetHome;
import helpers.ObsException;

import oracle.aurora.jndi.sess_iiop.ServiceCtx;
// (See Note 1.)
import oracle.aurora.jts.client.AuroraTransactionService;
import oracle.aurora.jts.util.TS;

import javax.naming.Context;

import javax.naming.InitialContext;

// Import supporting Java classes
import java.math.BigDecimal;
import java.math.*;
import java.util.ArrayList;
import java.util.Hashtable;

public class QcClient {

  public static void main (String[] args) throws Exception {
    if (args.length != 5) {
        System.out.println ("usage: QcClient serviceURL "
        +" objectName user password");
        System.exit (1);
    }

    String serviceURL = args [0];
    String obsName = args [1]; // (See Note 2.)
    String qcSetName = args [2];
    String user = args [3];
    String password = args [4];

    Hashtable env = new Hashtable ();
    env.put (Context.URL_PKG_PREFIXES, "oracle.aurora.jndi");
    env.put (Context.SECURITY_PRINCIPAL, user);
    env.put (Context.SECURITY_CREDENTIALS, password);
    env.put (Context.SECURITY_AUTHENTICATION,
                         ServiceCtx.NON_SSL_LOGIN);
    // get a handle to the InitialContext
    Context ic = new InitialContext (env);

    // get handle to the TX-Factory (See Note 3.)
    AuroraTransactionService.initialize (ic, serviceURL);
```

```
ObsHome observationHome = null;
ObsRemote observationRemote = null;
QcSetHome qualityControlHome = null;
QcSetRemote qualityControlRemote = null;
try {
    // Demarcate the TX (named TX1 in Figure 5-4).(See Note 4.)
    TS.getTS ().getCurrent ().begin ();

    // Use the home interface to
    // locate the ObservationBean object
    // (See Note 5.)
    observationHome =
        (ObsHome)ic.lookup (serviceURL + obsName);

    // Create an ObservationBean instance
    observationRemote = observationHome.create();
    // Get observation info (See Note 6.)
    TX1 is propagated to the ObservationBean.
    ArrayList qcObsIds = selectObsInfo (observationRemote);

    // Use the home interface to
    // locate the QcObsBean object
    qualityControlHome =
        (QcSetHome)ic.lookup (serviceURL + qcSetName);

    // Create a QcSetObsBean instance (See Note 7.)
    qualityControlRemote = qualityControlHome.create();

    // Set variables to create a QcSetHelper object
    BigDecimal qc_id = null;
    String when_t = "04-AUG-2000";
    String at_time = "085500";
    BigDecimal event_id = new BigDecimal(1);
    BigDecimal whom_id = new BigDecimal(1);

    // Use the parameterized constructor
    // of the QcSetHelper class to create a QcSetHelper object
    QcSetHelper qcSet =
        new QcSetHelper(qc_id,when_t,at_time,event_id,whom_id);

    // Invoke the insertQcSet() method of
    // the QcSetBean session Bean (See Note 8.)
    TX1 is propagated to the QeSetObs Bean.
    QcSetHelper returnQcSetId =
        qualityControlRemote.insertQcSet(qcSet);

    //  (See Note 9.)
    // commit the changes made during the TX1 transaction
    TS.getTS ().getCurrent ().commit (true);
```

```
              // Start a new transaction named TX2
              // attached to the QcSet that you created
              // in the previous transaction. (See Note 10.)
              TS.getTS ().getCurrent ().begin ();

              TX2 is propagated to the QcSetObsBean by the invocation
              of its insertQcObs () method
              // Insert a new row into the PASSED_OBSERVATION_LIST table
              qualityControlRemote.insertQcObs(returnQcSetId.qc_id,
                                               qcObsIds);

              // Get all quality controlled observations
              // for a specific QcSet id. (See Note 11.)
              printQcObservations(returnQcSetId,qualityControlRemote);

              // Commit the changes

              // parameter of value true. (See Note 12.)
              TS.getTS ().getCurrent ().commit (true);

      } // End try ObsException
      catch (ObsException ex ) {
           System.err.println(ex.getMessage());
      } // End of catch
      catch ( Exception ex ) {
          System.out.println("Cannot locate" +" or create object");
          System.err.println("error : " + ex);
          System.exit(1);
      }  // End of catch
    } // end main

    // (See Note 13.)
    public static ArrayList selectObsInfo (ObsRemote observationRemote)
          throws Exception {
       try {
            // Get an ArrayList of observations  (See Note 14.)
            ArrayList arrayOfObs = observationRemote.getAllObs();

            // Select only two observations (See Note 15.)
            ArrayList returnArrayOfObs = new ArrayList(2);

            // Create the obs1 variable of type ObsHelper
            ObsHelper obs1 = null;

            int arraySize = arrayOfObs.size();

            // Retrieve an obs_id ID from the ArrayList
            obs1 = (ObsHelper)arrayOfObs.get(arraySize - 1);
```

```java
        // Get the last observation from the ArrayList object
        returnArrayOfObs.add(obs1.obs_id);

        // Get the first observation from the ArrayList object
        obs1 = (ObsHelper)arrayOfObs.get(arraySize - arraySize);
        returnArrayOfObs.add(obs1.obs_id);

        return returnArrayOfObs;

    } // End try
    catch (SQLException e) {
        System.err.println("selectObsInfo : " + e.getMessage());
        e.printStackTrace ();
        System.exit(1);
    } // End catch
} // End of selectObsInfo() method

// (See Note 16.)
public static void printQcObservations(QcSetHelper qcSet,
    QcSetRemote qualityControlRemote ) throws Exception {
    try {
        // Get all info for a specific qc_id
        int qc_id = qcSet.qc_id.intValue();
        // (See Note 17.)
        QcSetHelper returnQcSet =
          qualityControlRemote.getQcSetInfo(qcSet.qc_id);

        // Get all quality controlled observations
        // for the above qc_id. (See Note 18.)
        ArrayList returnQcObs =
            qualityControlRemote.getQcObsInfo(qc_id);

        // Print QcSet info
        System.out.println ("QcSet info:  ");
        System.out.println ("QcSet id:   " +returnQcSet.qc_id);
        System.out.println ("Date:    " +returnQcSet.when_t);
        System.out.println ("at_time:  " +returnQcSet.at_time);
        System.out.println ("Storm id:   " +returnQcSet.event_id );
        System.out.println ("Scientist id:   "
                    +returnQcSet.whom_id);
        System.out.println ("Storm Name:   " +returnQcSet.evt_name);
        System.out.println ("Scientist Name:   "
                    +returnQcSet.sc_name);
        System.out.println ("********************");
        System.out.println ("Quality Controlled Observations"
            +" for QcSet id: " +returnQcSet.qc_id);
        System.out.println (" ");
```

```
            int loopVar = 0;
            int arraySize = returnQcObs.size();
            while ( loopVar < arraySize ) {
                // Retrieve an ObsHelper object from
                // the ArrayList returnQcObs (See Note 19.)
                ObsHelper obs = (ObsHelper)returnQcObs.get(loopVar);
                System.out.println("id: " +obs.obs_id);
                System.out.println("when_t: " +obs.when_t);
                System.out.println("at_time: " +obs.at_time);
                System.out.println("station_id: " +obs.station_id);
                System.out.println("produced_id: " +obs.produced_id);
                System.out.println("latitude: " +obs.latitude);
                System.out.println("longitude: " +obs.longitude);
                System.out.println("wdspd: " +obs.wdspd);
                System.out.println("adj_wdspd: " +obs.adj_wdspd);
                System.out.println("wddir: " +obs.wddir);
                System.out.println("pressure: " +obs.pressure);

                loopVar++;
            } // End while
        } // End try
    }  // End of printQcObservations() method
}  // End QcClient class
```

Notes on the `QcClient` application:

1. This statement and the one that follows it import the appropriate classes from the `oracle.aurora.jts.client.*` and `oracle.aurora.jts.util.*` packages, respectively. If you want to use transaction demarcation in your standalone Java clients, you must import the `AuroraTransactionService` and the `TS` classes in your program. This is only valid for the Oracle8*i* database versions 8.1.5 and 8.1.6. With the new release of the Oracle database version 8.1.7, you will need to import the Java Transaction API (JTA) (`javax.transaction.*`) in your program.

2. This statement and the one that follows it retrieve the published object names of the session Beans that the client wants to use—that is, the `/test/ObservationBean` and the `/test/QcSetBean`, respectively.

3. Here, the `QcClient` program initializes the client-side transaction service. Clients that want to explicitly demarcate a transaction must initialize the transaction service prior to starting the transaction. If the transaction service is not initialized, the call to the `begin()` method will fail and the `NotTransactionService` exception will be thrown. At transaction initialization time, the transaction service creates implicitly a transaction context object and automatically assigns it a transaction ID number. This transaction context will be propagated to any other Beans participating

within the transaction (that is, to each EJB object that the `QcClient` will call). In this scenario, the `QcClient`'s transaction service will propagate the transaction context to the `ObservationBean` and the `QcSetBean` session Beans, respectively.

4. This statement explicitly demarcates the transaction with the call of the `begin()` method from the `oracle.aurora.jts.util.TS` class. Once you initialize the transaction service, you can invoke the `getCurrent()` static method on it to obtain the current transaction context. When you get the transaction context, you can invoke, begin, suspend, resume, commit, or rollback the current transaction on the current transaction context. During the execution of this method, the transaction service starts a global transaction and is managed transparently by the EJB container. Note that the transaction starts before retrieving the Beans. By beginning the transaction before retrieving the Beans, the Beans are automatically enlisted in the transaction. Both the `ObservationBean` and `QcSetBean` enterprise Beans are part of the same transaction from the time that they are created, through invocation of their methods, to the time that a `commit()` or a `rollback()` method gets executed. The idea here is to encapsulate the application in a transaction to ensure that all data updated is committed or all is rolled back.

5. This statement uses the JNDI `lookup()` method to obtain a reference to the `ObsHome` home **interface**. The statement that follows it gets an instance of the `ObservationBean` Bean.

6. This statement calls the `selectObsInfo()` method (a local method of the `QcClient` application). The `selectObsInfo()` method uses the `observationRemote` object as its input parameter and returns an `ArrayList` object to the `QcClient` consisting of a set of `ObsHelper` objects where each represents a row of atmospheric observations stored in the `OCEANIC_OBSERVATION_LIST` table. Note that the `selectObsInfo()` method will throw `ObsException` if there are no observations and no further processing will take place.

7. This statement creates an instance of the `QcSetBean` Bean. When the `QcClient` application invokes the `create()` method of the `QcSetBean` home **interface**, the EJB container invokes the associated `ejbCreate()` method of the `QcSetImp` class. The `ejbCreate()` method of the `QcSetImp` class then creates an instance of the `QcObsBean`. So, when the EJB container invokes the `ejbCreate()` method of the `QcSetImp` class, instances of `QcSetBean` and `QcObsBean` Beans are created.

8. This statement invokes the `insertQcSet()` method of the `QcSetBean`. The current transaction context previously created is propagated to the `QcSetBean` Bean.

9. The `commit()` demarcator method commits the changes to the database and ends the transaction. Note that the `commit()` method ends the transaction and takes an input parameter value of `true` if you want to commit the changes to the database. With a `false` parameter value, the transaction will terminate with no updates to the database.

10. This statement starts a new transaction. This example illustrates how you can start several transactions within the same program. The `QcClient`'s transaction service creates a new transaction context, which is propagated to the `QcSetBean`. The statement that follows it invokes the `insertQcObs()` method of the `QcSetBean`, which in turn invokes the `insertQcObs()` method of the `QcObsBean`. Recall that `QcObsBean` is a `TX_REQUIRED_NEW` session Bean. Consequently, the EJB container will always start a new transaction whenever a client uses the `QcObsBean` Bean.

11. This statement retrieves a set of atmospheric observations and displays them.

12. This statement ends the last transaction started in Note 10.

13. This statement defines the `selectObsInfo()` method. This method invokes the `getAllOBS()` method of the `ObservationBean` session Bean.

14. This statement invokes the `getAllOBS()` method of the `ObservationBean` session Bean. If the `getAllOBS()` method returns no data, the `ObsException` exception will be thrown and no other processing will take place.

15. This statement creates an `ArrayList` object to hold the quality controlled observations. The remaining statements select the observation IDs and store them in the `ArrayList` object.

16. This statement defines the `printQcObservations()` method that invokes the `getQcSetInfo()` and `getQcObsInfo()` methods of the `QcSetBean` and `QcObsBean` session Beans, respectively.

17. This statement invokes the `getQcSetInfo()` method of the `QcSetBean` Bean that returns data from the `QC_EVENT_LIST` table based on a specific `qc_id`.

18. This statement invokes the `getQcObsInfo()` method of the `QcSetBean` session Bean. Note that the `getQcObsInfo()` method, in turn, invokes the `getQcObs()` method of the `QcObsBean` Bean. The `getQcObs()` method returns an `ArrayList` object of `ObsHelper` objects where each `ObsHelper` object represents data from the `OCEANIC_OBSERVATION_LIST` table.

19. This statement casts each object from the `ArrayList` object into an `ObsHelper` object.

Conclusion

This chapter ends Part II of the book. Here, you learned how you to use the Java Transaction Service API to build reliable transactional applications. You developed the QcObsBean and QcSetObsBean session Beans. The former manipulates the PASSED_OBSERVATION_LIST table and the latter the QC_EVENT_LIST table. More importantly, you built the QcClient Java standalone transactional client application that uses three session Beans that reside in the Oracle8*i* database and the QcSetObsBean session Bean, an EJB Bean client that uses another Bean (the QcObsBean).

In Part III, you will learn how to build CORBA components that execute in the Oracle8*i* database.

PART
III

Building CORBA Components

CHAPTER

6

Introduction to CORBA

n this part of the book, you will learn how to use CORBA in the Oracle8*i* environment. In the current chapter, you will master the basics of CORBA. In particular you will consider

- CORBA overview

- IDL

- Deploying and using CORBA server objects

- CORBA callback mechanism

- CORBA tie mechanism

- Activating ORBs and server objects

- Coding CORBA interface specifications in Java

- Summary of some important tools

In Chapter 7, you will learn how Oracle8*i* enhances the standard CORBA model with the concept of database sessions, in which CORBA objects are activated.

In Chapter 8, you will learn the different ways of incorporating CORBA objects in transactions that guarantee the preservation of database consistency.

Finally, in Chapter 9, you will exercise your ability to implement components using CORBA server objects by constructing a number of CORBA components for the Purchase Order database.

CORBA Overview

CORBA (Common Object Request Broker Architecture) is a standard, published by the Object Management Group (OMG), for a distributed and heterogeneous network of objects. The network is distributed because the objects can exist on different computers. The network is heterogeneous because these computers can be running different operating systems and the objects can be implemented in different programming languages.

The interfaces for the objects are specified in a programming language–neutral specification language called Interface Definition Language (IDL), which is part of the CORBA standard.

A *CORBA client* refers to any software unit that makes use of the CORBA objects that are provided on the network (that is, units that make use of the CORBA *server objects*).

The CORBA Object Request Broker (ORB) is a software unit that mediates and directs requests from CORBA clients to CORBA server objects. The ORB makes the nitty-gritty details of such request handling transparent to the client. For example, method invocations on remote server objects in the network appear as local method invocations. The ORB is the fundamental part of a CORBA implementation. The ORB handles all communication between a client and a server object. Oracle8i provides an ORB within the JServer that is based on code from Inprise's VisiBroker for Java. There is an ORB that executes on the client side and an ORB that executes on the server side. Oracle8i makes ORB startup and interactions largely transparent to the implementation of both the client and server code.

The ORB implements a set of fully specified *services* that make it convenient to simply operate in the CORBA environment. For example, there are *naming services* that allow clients to simply reference server objects, *transaction services* that allow client code and server objects to be partitioned into atomic units called *transactions*, and *event services* that allow event data to be made available without requiring the originator of the event data to know the receivers of the data. Oracle8i CORBA clients use the Java Naming and Directory Interface (JNDI) as an interface in the lookup of server objects via a CORBA CosNaming service. In addition, Oracle8i provides a JNDI Service Provider Interface (SPI) to the CosNaming service. The Oracle8i transaction service APIs for CORBA are the Java Transaction Service (JTS) API and the Java Transaction API (JTA) that essentially replaces JTS in Oracle version 8.1.7. The use of JNDI is illustrated in this chapter, and is discussed in more detail in Chapter 7. JTS and JTA are discussed in Chapter 8.

Also, CORBA specifies the Internet Inter-ORB Protocol (IIOP) network protocol for transmission of ORB requests over a TCP/IP network. The use of IIOP is discussed in the next chapter.

IDL

In this section you will encounter the following:

- The IDL compiler
- IDL constructs

The IDL Compiler

One of the main advantages of CORBA is its language independence. CORBA objects written in one programming language can invoke methods in an object written in another programming language. This language independence is achieved through the use of the language-neutral Interface Definition Language (IDL). In IDL, you do not implement your object methods—you only specify them. More precisely, for each server object, you code an *IDL interface* that lists the constants, types, exceptions, attributes, and methods associated with the object. IDL was designed to be consistent with C++. You then compile the IDL file that specifies the interface, and afterward implement the interface in a specific programming languages such as Java. The IDL compiler you will use with Oracle8*i* is `idl2java`, which translates IDL interfaces into Java interfaces. After compiling your IDL interface into Java, you implement your Java interface to obtain the implementation of your server object. The following simple example illustrates this compilation and implementation procedure. The basic IDL compilation unit is the *module*, which consists of a logically related collection of interface (and other) definitions. The following module consists of a single interface containing a single method that takes no arguments and returns a string:

```
/* File Name: cool.idl
**
** Purpose:  Implementation will have cool() return the
**           string "Java is cool."
**
*/
module cool { interface Cool { wstring isCool(); }; };
```

wstring, a wide string, is an IDL type that corresponds to a Java **String**.

When you compile `cool.idl` using `idl2java`, you will get eight Java source files that are placed in a subdirectory named `cool` in the same directory as `cool.idl`. Thus, these Java source files then constitute a Java package named `cool`. The eight `.java` files are as follows:

- `Cool.java`
- `CoolHolder.java`
- `CoolHelper.java`
- `_st_Cool.java`
- `_CoolImplBase.java`
- `CoolOperations.java`
- `_tie_Cool.java`
- `_example_Cool.java`

`Cool.java` is the interface file:

```
package cool;
public interface Cool
  extends org.omg.CORBA.Object {
    public java.lang.String isCool(); }
```

Note that all CORBA basic interface classes are derived from `org.omg.CORBA.Object`.

A holder class and helper class are generated for each interface class in the module, and a holder class is used as a "wrapper class" when an interface method has parameters of modes *out* or *inout*.

A helper class is used to read and write the object to a stream.

The *stub file* `_st_Cool.java` defines a *stub class* that is installed on the client and acts as the interface between the client and the remote object.

The skeleton file `_CoolImplBase.java` defines a *skeleton class.* A skeleton class is a server-side class that communicates with the client-side stub class. The stub and skeleton classes hide remote invocation details from the developer, making the developer's job easier.

`_example_cool.java` provides you with an example of how you should implement the `Cool` interface. Of course, it leaves out the body of the `isCool()` method. You can rename the file (say, to `CoolImpl.java`), and add the code that implements the `isCool()` method. The `_example_Cool.java` file that is generated for you by the `idl2java` compiler, and the `CoolImpl.java` file that you might code, are as follows:

```
/* File Name: _example_Cool.java */

package cool;
public class _example_Cool extends _CoolImplBase {
  public _example_Cool( java.lang.String name ) { super( name ); }
  public _example_Cool() { super(); }
  public java.lang.String isCool() {}
}
```

```
/* Program Name: CoolImpl.java
**
** Purpose:  Implements server object.
**
*/
```

```
/* The implementor decided to store the implementation class in
   a package called coolServer.
*/
package coolServer;
import cool.*;
public class CoolEmpl extends _CoolImplBase {
  public String isCool() { return "Java is cool."; }
}
```

Note that the implementation class must extend the skeleton class.

The `CoolOperations` and `_tie_Cool` classes are used by the server for tie implementations of server objects. See the section "CORBA Tie Mechanism" of this chapter for a discussion of tie mechanisms.

The preceding Java classes must then be compiled by `javac` (or `sqlj`), the appropriate class files must be loaded into the JServer, and the server object must be published so that it can be accessed by clients. These steps are discussed in a subsequent section of this chapter titled "Deploying and Using CORBA Server Objects."

In the next section, you will learn about IDL by considering how IDL constructs are translated into Java.

IDL Constructs

In this section you will consider the following:

- IDL types

- IDL interfaces

- Generated holder and helper classes

- IDL exceptions

- Inheritance

- IDL modules

IDL Types

In this section you will consider the following:

- IDL basic types

- IDL *structs*

- IDL *enums*

- IDL *unions*

- IDL *sequences, arrays,* and *typedefs*

Basic Types   Table 6-1, taken from the *Oracle8i Enterprise JavaBeans and CORBA Developer's Guide Release 8.1.5* [52, pp. 3-11 – 3-12, Table 3.1], summarizes the correspondence between IDL and Java basic types, and indicates which CORBA exceptions can be raised on conversion between these types.

struct   There are three kinds of constructed types in IDL: *struct, enum,* and *union.* You will consider *structs* in this section and *enum* and *union* in the next two sections.

An IDL *struct* is analogous to a C++ `struct`, which contains only data members (that is, it does not contain any method members) and in which all the members are public. IDL *structs* are translated into Java classes that provide fields for the *struct* members and two constructors. Consider the following IDL module

CORBA IDL Data Type	Java Data Type	Exception
boolean	boolean	
char	char	CORBA:: DATA_CONVERSION
wchar	char	
octet	byte	
string	java.lang.String	CORBA::MARSHAL CORBA:: DATA_CONVERSION
wstring	java.lang.String	CORBA::MARSHAL
short	short	
unsigned short	short	
long	int	
unsigned long	long	
long long	long	
unsigned long long	long	
float	float	
double	double	

TABLE 6-1.   *IDL to Java Data Type Mappings*

that contains an IDL *struct*, which holds a *long* department number and a *long* project number:

```
module account {
    struct AccountInfo { long departmentno; long projectno; };
};
```

idl2java will translate the preceding module into the following Java source file:

```
package account;
final public class AccountInfo {
    public int departmentno;
    public int projectno;
    public AccountInfo() {}
    public AccountInfo ( int departmentno, int projectno ) {
        this.departmentno = departmentno;
        this.projectno = projectno;
    }
}
```

The first constructor allows the client to create a new uninitialized AccountInfo instance, and the second constructor allows the client to create and initialize a new AccountInfo instance.

enum   *enums*, the IDL enumerated types, are user-defined types in which the user specifies a set of identifiers that constitute the values of the type. For example, the following module contains a type declaration for an enumerated type employee:

```
module hit {
    enum employee { watchman, janitor, manager, ceo };
};
```

Such an *enum* type is translated into a Java **final** class with the same name as the *enum*, which defines a pair of static fields for each *enum* member. One of these fields is of type **final** int and is used as an index type when, for example, the *enum* type is used as an array index type. The other field is of the type of the generated Java class, and is used for parameter passing. There is also a **public** method value() that returns the int that corresponds to the current *enum* value, and a constructor that sets the int that corresponds to the current *enum* value. In addition, there is a **public static** method from_int(), which translates an int value into the corresponding generated class instance. For example, the preceding IDL *enum* type `employee` is translated into the following Java class `employee`:

```
final public class Employee {
   final public static int _watchman = 0;
   final public static int _janitor = 1;
   final public static int _manager = 2;
   final public static int _ceo = 3;
   final public static Employee watchman = new Employee( _watchman );
   final public static Employee janitor = new Employee( _janitor );
   final public static Employee manager = new Employee( _manager );
   final public static Employee ceo = new Employee( _ceo );
   private int_value;
   private Employee( int value ) { _value = value; }
   public int value(){
         return_value;}
   public static Employee from_int( int $value ) {
     switch( $value ) {
       case _watchman: return watchman;
       case _janitor: return janitor;
       case _manager: return manager;
       case _ceo: return ceo;
       default: throw new org.omg.CORBA.BAD_PARAM ( "enum out of range:
               + (4 - 1) + "]: " + $value );
     }
   }
}
```

union   *union*, the IDL discriminated union type, allows you to bundle several types into one type, where the discriminator for a particular union instance reference indicates which type is being used in the reference. For example, the following *union* bundles the *float* and *long* types together, with the `long` discriminator indicating whether a *float* or *long* is being used:

```
union FloatorInt switch( long ) {
   case 0: float floatval;
   case 1: long intval;
};
```

The discriminator can be either an *integer* type, *char* type, *boolean* type, or an *enum* type.

The IDL *union* is translated into a **final** Java class, with the same name as the IDL *union*, that provides a null constructor, an accessor method for the discriminator, an accessor method for each case that returns the value of the *union* object interpreted as being of the type for that case, and two modifier methods for each case that sets the value of the *union* object to a value of the type for that case. For example, the preceding *union* type is translated into the following Java class:

```java
final public class FloatorInt {

    // The current value of union object.
    private java.lang.Object _object;

    // The current discriminator value.
    private long _disc;

    // null constructor.
    public FloatorInt() {}

    // Discriminator accessor method.
    public long discriminator() { return _disc; }

    // Accessor method for float value.
    public float floatval() {
      if ( _disc != 0 ) {
        throw new org.omg.CORBA.BAD_OPERATION( "floatval" );
      }
      return( ( ( java.lang.Float ) _object).floatValue() );
    }

    // Accessor method for int value.
    public int intval() {
      if ( _disc != 1 ) {
        throw new org.omg.CORBA.BAD_OPERATION( "intval" );
      }
      return( ( ( java.lang.Int ) _object ).intValue() );
    }

    // Modifier method for int value.
    public void intvalue( int value ) {
      _disc = 1;
      _object = new java.lang.Integer( value );
    }

    /* Modifier method for int value in which discriminator
       value to be set is explicitly passed.
    */
    public void intval( int disc, int value ) {
      _disc = disc;
      _object = new java.lang.Integer( value );
    }

    //Modifier method for float value,
```

```
  public void floatval ( float value ){
    _disc = 0;
    _object = new java.lang.Float ( value ));

  /* Modifier method for float value in which discriminator
     value to be set is explicitly passed.
  */
  public void floatval( int disc, float value ) {
    _disc = disc;
    _object = new java.lang.Float( value );
  }
}
```

sequences, arrays, and typedefs   IDL supports two types of ordered collections: *sequences* and *arrays*. An IDL *sequence* is a one-dimensional array whose dimension does not have to be specified in the IDL definit-ion. An IDL *array* is a multidimensional array whose dimensions are specified in the IDL definition. In both cases, IDL *typedefs* are used to name the particular *sequence* and *array* types being defined. These *typedef* names provide aliases for the types that appear in them, just like in C. The following IDL module contains a *sequence* and an *array* type:

```
/* File Name: accounts.idl */

module accounts {
  struct AccountInfo { long departmentno; long projectno; }
  typedef sequence <AccountInfo> accountinfos;
  const long bound = 100;
  typedef AccountInfo AccountInfos2[bound];
  struct MyandYourAccounts {
    accountinfos myaccounts; accountinfos2 youraccounts;
  }
}
```

   idl2java will generate the following Java source file for the MyandYourAccounts *struct*:

```
package accounts;
final public class MyandYourAccounts {
  public AccountInfo[] myaccounts;
  public AccountInfo[] youraccounts;
  public MyandYourAccounts() {}
  public MyandYourAccounts (
    AccountInfo[] myaccounts, AccountInfo[] youraccounts ) {
    this.myaccounts = myaccounts;
    this.youraccounts = youraccounts;
  }
}
```

Note that the only reason for using the *typedef* in the IDL file is to provide the type alias it defines for referencing elsewhere in that IDL file. No Java class is generated for the *typedef*. Also note that the array-bound information is missing from the generated Java code.

IDL Interfaces

idl2java translates an IDL *interface* into a **public** Java **interface** that has the same name as the IDL **interface**. Such a Java **interface** is implemented on the client side by the generated stub class, and on the server side by the generated skeleton class together with the programmer-written server object class, which extends the skeleton class. If the IDL **interface** is named interfacename, the generated Java interface is also named interfacename, the generated stub class is named _st_interfacename, the generated skeleton class is named _interface-nameImplBase, and it is traditional for the programmer to name the server object class interfacenameImpl.

An IDL interface can contain type declarations, constant declarations, exception declarations, attribute declarations, and method declarations. *enum, union,* and *struct* declarations and *typedefs* are examples of type declarations. A constant that is defined within an interface is translated into a **final public static** field, with the same name as the constant, in the corresponding Java interface. The type of that field is the Java type that corresponds to the IDL type of the constant. For example,

```
interface hit { const long c = 10; };
```

gets translated into

```
public interface hit extends org.omg.CORBA.Object {
     final public static int c = 10;
}
```

An *exception* that is defined within an IDL interface is translated into a **final public** Java class definition that extends org.omg.UserException, as will be described in the subsequent section titled "Exception Declarations." This Java class definition is contained in the generated Java **interface** for the IDL **interface**.

Attributes are the instance data fields of an IDL **interface** (note that Java interfaces can only have **final** data fields). An *attribute* declaration consists of the keyword *readonly* (optional), followed by the keyword *attribute*, followed by an IDL type, followed by the *attribute* name:

```
[ readonly ] attribute type attributename;
```

An IDL *attribute* is translated into an accessor method (to get the *attribute* value) and a modifier method (to set the *attribute* value) in the corresponding generated

Java **interface** (if the *attribute* is declared *readonly*, only an accessor method is generated). For example, the IDL *interface* containing *attributes* in the following `account module` gets translated into the indicated Java **interface**:

```
module account {
   interface AccountInfo { long departmentno; long projectno; }
};
```

```
public interface AccountInfo extends org.omg.CORBA.Object {
   public void departmentno( int departmentno );
   public int departmentno();
   public void projectno( int projectno );
   public int projectno();
}
```

The preceding Java methods that have a **void** return type are the modifier methods, and the methods with **int** return type are the accessor methods. Note that the developer-written server object class that "implements" `AccountInfo` by extending the skeleton class generated for `AccountInfo` may or may not contain data fields for `departmentno` and `projectno`. It is the accessor method and modifier method that are considered to implement the *attribute*. It is the developer's choice as to whether Java data fields are to be used to aid that implementation.

IDL methods are called *operations* (although we use the more familiar term "methods" when referring to such operations). The syntax for an IDL method declaration is as follows:

```
return_type method_name ( list_of_parameters )
```

A `list_of_parameters` is either empty, or contains one `parameter_declaration`, or contains several `parameter_declarations` separated by commas ("**,**"). A `parameter_declaration` has the syntax:

```
[ mode ] type parameter_name
```

The possible modes are *in, out,* or *inout.* If the mode of the method parameter is *in,* the value of the actual parameter is passed in to the method parameter, but cannot be changed by the method. If the mode of the method parameter is *inout,* the value of the actual parameter is passed in to the method parameter, and the final value of the method parameter is passed back out to the actual parameter. If the mode of the parameter is *out,* the value of the actual parameter is not passed in to the method parameter, but the final value of the method parameter is passed back out to the actual parameter.

Since Java supports only call by value (that is, the *in* mode), `idl2java` generates a wrapper class called a holder class for each user-defined type such as *structs* and *interfaces*. These holder classes are then used for *inout* and *out* parameter types. Holder classes are also available for the IDL predefined types, such as *long*. For example, the following IDL interface method declaration is translated into the indicated Java method declaration:

```
interface account {
   void getAccountInfo(
     in long accountno, out long departmentno, out long projectno );
};
```

```
public interface account extends org.omg.CORBA.Object {
   public void getAccountInfo(
      int accountno,
      org.omg.CORBA.IntHolder departmentno,
      org.omg.CORBA.IntHolder projectno );
}
```

You will learn more about holder classes in the next section.

Holder Classes
Java holder classes for the basic IDL types can be found in the package `org.omg.CORBA`. For example, the following is the holder class for `int`:

```
final public class IntHolder {
   public int value;
   public Intholder () {}
   public Intholder( int initial ) { value = initial; }
}
```

Similar holder classes are generated for IDL user-defined types. Since any IDL **interface** method that has an *inout* or *out* parameter will have its Java **interface** method contain the appropriate holder class parameter, the Java code for the server object class for the interface will set the value of the parameter by setting the value field of the holder class parameter.

Note that holder classes are automatically generated for IDL **interfaces**, *structs*, *unions*, *enums*, and *exceptions*.

Exception Declarations
Exceptions are constructs that correspond to error conditions. IDL supports standard exceptions, called system exceptions, as well as user-defined exceptions.

System exceptions are translated into Java exceptions that are defined in the package `org.omg.CORBA`. An IDL user-defined exception is translated into a generated exception class (that is, a class that extends the class `org.omg.CORBA.UserException`). An IDL user-defined exception is defined with an *exception* declaration. An *exception* declaration has the same syntax as a *struct* declaration, except it starts with the keyword *exception* instead of the keyword *struct*. The exception attributes hold error messages and other values that are associated with the error. For example, the following IDL *exception* declaration is translated into the indicated Java class:

```
exception MyError { wstring mess; };
```

```
final public class MyError extends org.omg.CORBA.UserException {
  public java.lang.String mess;
  public MyError() {}
  public MyError( java.lang.String mess) { this.mess = mess; }
}
```

Note that `CORBA.UserException` is a subclass of `java.lang.Exception`, so that it behaves like a bona fide Java exception class.

IDL methods can be declared as capable of raising a particular exception via the *raises* clause:

```
void myfunc() raises( MyError );
```

Such a method declaration will get translated into a Java method declaration with a **throws** clause:

```
public void myfunc() throws MyError;
```

Inheritance
Although IDL allows multiple inheritance for interfaces, for simplicity only single inheritance will be considered in this section. For information on multiple inheritance, see *Java Programming with CORBA* [62].

Suppose that you have the following inheritance structure:

```
interface B:A { ... }
```

(where `B:A` designates that interface `B` is derived from interface `A`). Thus, interface `B` inherits all the constructs declared in interface `A`. The corresponding generated Java interfaces are also related by the subclass relation:

```
public interface B extends A { ... }
```

Modules

As you have seen, an IDL *module* is the compilation unit for IDL. The syntax of a module declaration is as follows:

```
module module_name {
   type declarations;
   constant declarations;
   exception declarations;
   interface declarations;
   module declarations;
};
```

The *type* declarations, *exception* declarations, and *constant* declarations in modules have the same syntax as when those declarations appear in interfaces. However, it should be mentioned that constant declarations are translated into Java somewhat differently. Constants within interfaces are translated into **final public static** fields within the corresponding Java interfaces. However, a constant directly contained within a module is translated into a Java **public interface** that contains a **final public static** field called value, which holds the value of the constant. For example,

```
const long MyConstant = 10;
```

is translated into:

```
public interface MyConstant {
   final public static int value = 10;
}
```

Deploying and Using CORBA Server Objects

In this section, you will use an account example to learn how to

- Code an IDL *module*

- Use the idl2java to appropriately generate Java source files from an IDL *module*

- Implement CORBA server objects in Java

- Compile the Java files and load the generated Java classes into the JServer

- Publish a name for each CORBA server object

■ Code and compile the Java client that invokes CORBA server object methods

■ Run the client

Code the IDL Module

The purpose of this application is to obtain the department number and project number for an indicated account number from the ACCOUNT_LIST table. You start by coding the following IDL module:

```
/* File Name: account.idl */

module account {
  struct AccountInfo { long departmentno; long projectno; };
  exception NoAccountError { wstring mess; };
  interface Account {
    AccountInfo getAccountInfo( in long accountno )
      raises( NoAccountError );
  };
};
```

getAccount is a method that will return an AccountInfo *struct* that contains the departmentno value and projectno for the ACCOUNT_LIST record that has the indicated accountno value. If no such ACCOUNT_LIST record exists, the NoAccountError exception will be raised.

Use idl2java to Generate Java Source Files from the IDL File

To compile account.idl into Java you merely enter the following:

```
idl2java _no_tie account.idl
```

The _no_tie option indicates that the tie mechanism will not be used, so that fewer Java source files will be generated. You will learn about the tie mechanism in a subsequent section of this chapter. idl2java will generate 12 Java source files for the module, all contained in the account directory:

■ A Java interface, helper, holder, stub, and skeleton file for the Account **interface**

■ A Java source file containing a class definition, as well as Java helper and holder files, for the AccountInfo *struct* and for the NoAccountError *exception*

■ The _example_Account file that contains an incomplete example of a Java implementation of the Account server object

Code the Java Implementation of the Server Object

Here you will find a SQLJ implementation of the server object. In a subsequent section of this chapter, you will be presented with a JDBC version of this code:

```
/* Program Name:  AccountImpl.sqlj
**
** Purpose:  Get account information for the given account number.
**
*/
package accountServer;
import account.*;
import java.sql.*;
public class AccountImpl extends _AccountImplBase {
  public AccountInfo getAccountInfo( int accountno )
    throws NoAccountError {
    try {

      // You must initialize variables to be selected into.
      int departmentno = 0;
      int projectno = 0;

      #sql {
        SELECT departmentno, projectno
          INTO :departmentno, :projectno
            FROM ACCOUNT_LIST
              WHERE accountno = :accountno
      };
      return new AccountInfo( departmentno, projectno );
    }
    catch( SQLException e ) {
      throw new NoAccountError( e.getMessage() );
    }
  }
}
```

Compile Java Files and Load Generated Class Files into the JServer

You first compile the Java source files:

```
javac account/Account.java\
  account/AccountHolder.java\
  account/AccountHelper.java
javac account/AccountInfo.java\
  account/AccountInfoHolder.java\
```

```
    account/AccountInfoHelper.java
javac account/NoAccountError.java\
    account/NoAccountErrorHolder.java\
    account/NoAccountErrorHelper.java
javac account/_EmployeeImplBase.java\
  account/_st_Account.java
sqlj -J-classpath\
  .:$(ORACLE_HOME)/lib/aurora_client.jar:\
  $(ORACLE_HOME)/jdbc/lib/classes111.zip:\
  $(ORACLE_HOME)/sqlj/lib/translator.zip$(ORACLE_HOME)/lib/vbjorb.jar:\
  $(ORACLE_HOME)/lib/vbjapp.jar$(JDK_HOME)/lib/classes.zip -ser2class\
  accountServer/AccountImpl.sqlj
```

Note that the `sqlj` command generates two additional class files, `AccountImpl_SJProfile0` and `AccountImpl_SJProfilekeys`, which must also be loaded into the server. You can then build a Java archive (`.jar`) file that contains all the classes that you wish to load into the server. This is preferable to loading each class, one at a time.

```
jar -cf0 accountjar.jar\
    account/Account*.class\
    account/NoAccountError*.class\
    account/_AccountImplBase.class\
    _st_Account.class\
    accountServer/AccountImpl*.class
```

Note that the wildcard (*****) is used assuming no other files in the directory have clashing names. Finally, you load all the classes in the `.jar` file into the JServer:

```
loadjava -oracleresolver -resolve -user scott/tiger accountjar.jar
```

The syntax of the `loadjava` command is given in the subsequent section of this chapter titled "Summary of Some Important Tools."

Publish the CORBA Server Object Name

The final step in preparing the server object is to publish a name for the object that a client program can look up. You accomplish this with the `publish` command:

```
publish -republish -user scott -password tiger -schema scott -service\
    sess_iiop://localhost:2481:ORCL\
    /test/Account AccountImpl account.AccountHelper
```

The options and arguments indicate the following:

- `-republish`: Overwrite a published object if it has the same name.
- `-user scott`: scott is the username of the schema doing the publishing.

- ■ -password tiger: tiger is the password for scott.

- ■ -schema scott: The name of the schema doing the publishing.

- ■ -service sess_iiop://localhost:2481:ORCL: This option specifies the URL that identifies the database whose session namespace is to be opened. The hostname (here, localhost) identifies the computer that hosts the database (localhost returns the hostname of the current computer), 2481 is the listener port for iiop, and ORCL is the SID of the database.

- ■ /test/Account: The name of the published object. The /test directory in the namespace is the place where most objects are published. The published name of the server object does not have to be the same as the interface name.

- ■ AccountImpl: This is the name of the Java class that implements the server object.

- ■ AccountHelper: This is the name of the helper class for Account.

The syntax of the publish command is given in the subsequent section of this chapter titled "Summary of Some Important Tools."

Code and Compile the Java Client

In order to access a server object by its published name, the client code must do the following:

- ■ Instantiate and populate a JNDI InitialContext object with the required connect properties.

- ■ Invoke the lookup() method on the InitialContext object, passing in a URL parameter that specifies the IIOP service name and the name of the server object to be found. The lookup() method then returns an object reference to the desired server object.

- ■ Invoke the desired server object method on the object reference.

The following client program AccountUser.java accomplishes these steps in order to invoke the getAccount() method on an object reference to the Account server object:

```
/* Program Name: AccountUser.java
**
** Purpose:  Use the Account server object to get account
```

```
**              information for the account 1056.
**
*/
import account.*;
import accountServer.*;

// Import JNDI property constants.
import oracle.aurora.jndi.sess_iiop.ServiceCtx;

/* Import the JNDI Context Interface.
   (See Note 1.)
*/
import javax.naming.Context;

/* Import the InitialContext class that implements the
   Context Interface.
   (See Note 2.)
*/
import javax.naming.InitialContext;

/* Import the hash table class to hold the initial context
   properties environment.
*/
import java.util.Hashtable;

public class AccountUser {

  // main throws instead of catching exceptions.
  public static void main( String[] args ) throws Exception {

    /* Instantiate and populate InitialContext object.
       (See Note 3).
    */
    Hashtable env = new Hashtable();
    env.put( Context.URL_PKG_PREFIXES, "oracle.aurora.jndi" );
    env.put( Context.SECURITY_PRINCIPAL, "scott" );
    env.put( Context.SECURITY_CREDENTIALS, "tiger" );
    env.put( Context.SECURITY_AUTHENTICATION,
      ServiceCtx.NON_SSL_LOGIN );
    Context ic = new InitialContext( env );

    // Lookup object name, obtaining object reference.
    Account account = ( Account )
      ic.lookup( "sess_iiop://localhost:2481:ORCL/test/Account" );

    // Invoke getAccountInfo() method.
    AccountInfo ai = account.getAccountInfo( 1056 );

    // Print account information.
```

```
System.out.println( "Department number = " + ai.departmentno +
                    " Project number = " + ai.projectno );
    }
}
```

Notes for `AccountUser.java`:

1. All Oracle8*i* EJB and CORBA clients that use JNDI methods to look up server objects must import the JNDI `Context` interface. This interface forms the basis for the JNDI operations you use to manage services and sessions in the Oracle8*i* ORB.

2. All naming operations are relative to a context. The initial context provides the starting point for the resolution of names.

3. You first create a new `Hashtable` in which to store environment properties. Specifically, `URL_PKG_PREFIXES` holds the name of the environment property for specifying the list of package prefixes to use when loading in URL Context features. In the current implementation, this property must be set to "`oracle.aurora.jndi.`" The other properties are for authentication:

   ■ `SECURITY_PRINCIPAL` holds the database username.

   ■ `SECURITY_CREDENTIAL` holds the database password.

   ■ `SECURITY_AUTHENTICATION` holds the type of authentication to use. There are three possible authentication values to use that are defined in the `ServiceContext` class: `NON_SSL_LOGIN`, `SSL_CREDENTIAL`, and `SSL_LOGIN`. The Secure Socket Layer (SSL) connection can, in general, provide two separate things: a secure channel (encrypted communication), which is always done, and authentication (verification of the client identity), which requires an SSL certificate for the client. If the client does not have a certificate, it cannot authenticate, but it can still use a secure connection. The `SSL_LOGIN` mode relies on the secure channel, but uses the login protocol (regular user's password) for authentication. However, the `SSL_CREDENTIAL` mode requires an SSL client certificate for authentication. The `NON_SSL_LOGIN` mode authenticates using the usual login protocol over TCP/IP, instead of using a Secure Socket Layer connection.

   Having coded the Java client, you can now compile it with `javac`:

```
javac AccountUser.java
```

Running the Client

You will use the `java` command on the client to run the client class `AccountUser`. In order to do this, you must set the `classpath` for the `java` command to include `classes.zip` (the standard Java library archive), classes such as those in `vbjapp.jar` and `vbjorb.jar` that are used by the client ORB, and the Oracle8*i*-supplied `.jar` file `aurora_client.jar`. The following `java` command line will appropriately run the desired Java class:

```
% java -classpath\
   .:$(ORACLE_HOME)/lib/aurora_client.jar:\
   $(ORACLE_HOME)/jdbc/lib/classes111.zip:\
   $(ORACLE_HOME)/sqlj/lib/translator.zip:\
   $(ORACLE_HOME)/lib/vbjorb.jar:\
   $(ORACLE_HOME)/lib/vbjapp.jar:$(JDK_HOME)/lib/classes.zipAccountUser
```

Here, `JDK_HOME` is the installation location of the Java Development Kit (JDK), and `ORACLE_HOME` is the Oracle home directory.

Implementation of CORBA Server Object Using JDBC

In this section, an implementation of `AccountImpl` that uses JDBC is provided:

```
/* Program Name:  AccountImpl.java */

package accountServer;
import account.*;
import java.sql.*;
public class AccountImpl extends _AccountImplBase {
  public AccountInfo getAccountInfo( int accountno )
    throws NoAccountError {
    try {
      Connection conn =
        new oracle.jdbc.driver.OracleDriver().defaultConnection();
      PreparedStatement ps = conn.prepareStatement
        ( "SELECT departmentno, projectno
            FROM ACCOUNT_LIST WHERE accountno = ?" );
      try {
        ps.setInt( 1, accountno );
        ResultSet rset = ps.executeQuery();
        if ( !rset.next() )
          throw new NoAccountError( "No such account." );
        return new AccountInfo( rset.getInt(1),
          rset.getInt(2) );
      }
```

```
      finally { ps.close(); }
    }
    catch( SQLException e ) {
      throw new NoAccountError( e.getMessage() );
    }
  }
}
```

CORBA Callback Mechanism

The callback service allows a server object to invoke a method in a client-side object. For a callback to be possible, you need the following:

■ A client callback object that contains the method that will be invoked by the server object when it does a "callback."

■ A server object that contains a method with a parameter that is an object reference to the client callback object. Refer to this method as the server callback method, since it is this method that will accomplish the callback.

■ An implementation of the client callback object.

■ An implementation of the server object.

■ Client code that invokes the server callback method.

Of course, the invocation of the client method does not have to be direct—that is, the server callback method can call another method that calls another method, and so on, that actually calls a method in the client callback object. However, the server callback method is the method that the client code invokes in order to pass the client callback object reference.

You will be introduced to the CORBA callback mechanism by the simple example provided in the following IDL and Java code in which the server method returns the string "Java is cool." and the client callback method returns the string "You said it."

Client Callback Object

The following IDL file defines the client callback object:

```
/* File Name:  clientcallback.idl
**
** Purpose:  Define the client callback object.
**
*/
```

```
module clientcallback {
  interface ClientCallback { wstring saidit(); };
};
```

Server Object

The following IDL file defines the server object:

```
/* File Name:  server.idl */

#include <clientcallback.idl>
module server {
  interface Server {
    wstring isCool( in clientcallback::ClientCallback objectref );
  };
};
```

Note that the server object can reference the `ClientCallback` object because, in true C++ style, the server IDL file includes the `clientcallback` IDL file. Also, note that the `ClientCallback` object is referenced using the C++ scope resolution operator (`::`).

Implementation of the Client Callback Object

The following Java file implements the `ClientCallback` object:

```
/* Program Name:  ClientCallbackImpl.java
**
** Purpose:  Implement ClientCallback object.
**
*/
import clientcallback.*;
public class ClientCallbackImpl extends _ClientCallbackImplBase {
  public String saidit() { return "You said it."; }
}
```

Note that the client callback object does not have to be loaded into the JServer, since it is running in the client.

Implementation of the Server Object

The following Java file implements the server object:

```
/* Program Name: ServerImpl.java */

package callServer;
```

```
import server.*;
import clientcallback.*;
public class ServerImpl extends _ServerImplBase {
  public String isCool( ClientCallback clientcallback) {
    return "Java is cool ." + clientcallback.saidit();
  }
}
```

Note that the Java classes from both the `clientcallback` and `server` packages (that were generated by running `javac` on the appropriate Java files) are required.

Client Code that Invokes the Server Callback Method

The following Java file contains the client code that starts the ball rolling by invoking the `isCool()` method in the server object. The additional required code for the callback creates the client callback object and publishes it to the ORB in the client. This code references the basic object adapter (BOA). The purpose of the BOA is to generate and interpret object references, and to activate and deactivate object implementations. The BOA is the component of the ORB that guarantees that an invocation on an object reference always reaches the activated object that can respond to it.

```
/* Program Name:  Client.java
**
** Purpose:  Invoke server callback method.
**
*/
import server.*;
import clientcallback.*;
import oracle.aurora.jndi.sess_iiop.ServiceCtx;
import javax.naming.Context;
import javax.naming.InitialContext;
import java.util.Hashtable;

public class Client {
  public static void main( String[] args ) throws Exception {
    Hashtable env = new Hashtable();
    env.put( Context.URL_PKG_PREFIXES, "oracle.aurora.jndi");
    env.put( Context.SECURITY_PRINCIPAL, "scott" );
    env.put( Context.SECURITY_CREDENTIALS, "tiger" );
    env.put( Context.SECURITY_AUTHENTICATION,
      ServiceCtx.NON_SSL_LOGIN );
    Context ic = new InitialContext( env );
```

```
    /*  In order to get the ORB initialized correctly, you have to get
        the server object before preparing the client callback object.
    */
    Server server = ( Server ) ic.lookup
      ( "sess_iiop://localhost:2481:ORCL/test/Server" );

    /* Create the client object and publish it to the ORB in
       the client.
    */
    /* Invoke the init() method on ORB pseudo-object to obtain a
       reference to the existing client-side ORB.  A pseudo-object
       does not necessarily involve CORBA types.
    */
    org.omg.CORBA.ORB orb = org.omg.CORBA.ORB.init();

    // Use the ORB reference to initialize the client-side BOA.
    org.omg.CORBA.BOA boa = orb.BOA_init();

    // Instantiate a new client callback object.
    ClientCallbackImpl clientcallback = new ClientCallbackImpl();

    // Register the client callback object with the client-side BOA.
    boa.obj_is_ready( clientcallback );

    // Invoke the server callback method.
    System.out.println( server.isCool( clientcallback ) );
  }
}
```

When the program is run, the user will see the following output:

```
Java is cool. You said it.
```

CORBA Tie Mechanism

The CORBA tie mechanism provides you with an alternative means to implement a server object, other than extending the generated skeleton class. When using the tie mechanism, you implement the Java **interface** *interfacenameOperations* that idl2java generated from the IDL **interface**, instead of directly extending the skeleton class. An advantage of using the tie mechanism is that you are free to have your server implementation class extend another class, since "implements" instead of "extends" is used. You cannot extend the usual server implementation class, because it already extends the skeleton class.

For example, consider the cool module from the section of this chapter titled "The IDL Compiler." If you were to implement the Cool object using the tie mechanism, you would have to recode your `CoolImpl.java` file. However, the rest of the IDL and Java files would remain exactly the same. Specifically, in the tie implementation of `CoolImpl`, you must implement the `oracle.aurora.AuroraServices.ActivateObject` interface, which contains one parameterless method, `_initializeAuroraObject()`. This method is usually implemented for tie classes by returning a new `_tie_objectname` instance, as indicated in the following example:

```
/* Program Name:  CoolImpl.java */

package coolServer;
import cool.*;
import oracle.aurora.AuroraServices.ActivatableObject;
public class CoolImpl implements CoolOperations, ActivatableObject {
  public String isCool() { return "Java is cool."; };
  public org.omg.CORBA.Object _initializeAuroraObject() {
    return new _tie_Cool( this );
  }
}
```

Of course, when you run `idl2java` on your server module, do not specify the `_no_tie` option.

Activating ORBs and Server Objects

In this section, you will consider the following:

- ORB activation
- Server object activation

ORB Activation

CORBA applications require that an ORB be active on both the client side and the server side. The following discusses ORB activation in Oracle8i.

The client-side ORB is activated when the client first invokes the `lookup()` method. If a reference to the client-side ORB is required, as it was in the previous callback example, the `init()` method on the ORB pseudo-object will return such a reference. Note that not all operations can be done on the reference returned by `ORB.init()`. This is particularly significant in the case of applets due to security considerations.

The server-side ORB is activated when the session is created, by the presentation that handles IIOP requests.

Server Object Activation

A server object is automatically activated when a client performs a `lookup` for it.

The JServer ORB automatically registers persistent objects with the BOA. However, *transient objects* (that is, objects that only last with the process that created them) that are generated by other objects must be registered with the BOA by invoking the `obj_is_ready()` method of the BOA object. Recall that this method was invoked by the client code in the callback example to register the "transient" client `Callback` object. The following example illustrates the creation of transient objects in which a server object method creates another server object method on the fly. The example consists of the following:

- An IDL module that defines two server objects, an object named `CoolMaker` that will create an instance of an object named `Cool`

- Implementations of these server objects

- Client code that invokes a method within the `CoolMaker` object (which will in turn, create a new `Cool` instance)

IDL Module

First, the IDL module is presented:

```
/* File Name:  maker.idl */

module maker {
    interface Cool { wstring isCool(); };
    interface CoolMaker { Cool make( in wstring mess ); };
};
```

The `make()` method will create a new `Cool` instance, initialized with the indicated message. Then the client can invoke the `isCool()` method within that instance to return the stored message.

Implementation of Server Objects

Next, the Java implementation of the server objects is presented:

```
/* Program Name:  CoolImpl.java
**
** Purpose:  Implement Cool object.
**
*/
package makerServer;
import maker.*;
```

```
public class CoolImpl extends _CoolImplBase {
  String mess;

  // Constructor to initiate object with message.
  public CoolImpl( String mess ) { this.mess = mess; }
  public String isCool() { return mess; }
}


/* Program Name:  CoolMakerImpl.java
**
** Purpose:  Implement CoolMaker object.
**
*/
package makerServer;
import maker.*;
import oracle.aurora.AuroraServices.ActivatableObject;
public class CoolMakerImpl extends _CoolMakerImplBase
  implements ActivatableObject {
  public Cool make( String mess ) {

    // Create transient Cool object.
    CoolImpl cool = new CoolImpl( mess );

    /* Register that object with the server-side BOA using
       the connect() method which is the portable version
       of obj_is_ready().
    */
    _orb().connect( cool );
    return cool;
  }
  public org.omg.CORBA.Object _initializeAuroraObject() {
    return this;
  }
}
```

Client Code
Finally, the client code is presented:

```
/* Program Name: CoolClient.java */

import maker.*;
import makerServer.*;
import oracle.aurora.jndi.sess_iiop.ServiceCtx;
import javax.naming.Context;
import javax.naming.InitialContext;
import java.util.Hashtable;
```

```
public class CoolClient {
  public static void main( String[] args ) throws Exception {
    Hashtable env = new Hashtable();
    env.put( Context.URL_PKG_PREFIXES, "oracle.aurora.jndi" );
    env.put( Context.SECURITY_PRINCIPAL, "scott" );
    env.put( Context.SECURITY_CREDENTIALS, "tiger" );
    env.put( Context.SECURITY_AUTHENTICATION,
      ServiceCtx.NON_SSL_LOGIN );
    Context ic = new InitialContext( env );

    // Set CoolMaker object.
    CoolMaker maker = ( CoolMaker )
      ic.lookup( "sess_iiop://localhost:2481:ORCL/test/CoolMaker" );

    /* Invoke make method to create cool objects that are initialized
       with appropriate messages.
    */
    Cool cool = maker.make( "Java is cool." );
    Cool cools = maker.make( "SQL is cool too." );

    // Invoke isCool() method in Cool instances to get messages.
    System.out.println( cool.isCool() );
    System.out.println( cools.isCool() );
  }
}
```

Coding CORBA Interface Specifications in Java

The Inprise Caffeine tools, `java2iiop` and `java2idl`, are available in the Oracle8*i* Java development environment. `java2iiop` will directly generate CORBA-compatible Java stubs and skeletons from interface specifications coded in Java. `java2idl` will generate IDL specifications from interface specifications coded in Java. See Chapter 6 of the *Oracle8i Enterprise JavaBeans and CORBA Developer's Guide* [52] for more information on these tools.

Summary of Some Important Tools

In this section you will consider the following tools that are executable from the system prompt:

■ `loadjava`

■ `dropjava`

- publish

- remove

loadjava

The loadjava utility is used to convert .class files into database library units, called *Java class schema objects*, that are stored in the server; to convert .ser files into similar units, called resource schema objects, that are also stored in the server; and to convert source files into library units, called source schema objects, that are stored in the server. A distinct schema object is created for each .class file, each .ser file, and each .java source file.

On the loadjava command line, you can specify each .class or .ser file separately, or you can first combine them into a .jar (Java archive) file and then just specify that .jar file on the loadjava command line. The jar utility is used to combine separate files into a .jar file. You can combine class and resource files into a .jar file, or source and resource files into a jar file, but source and class files cannot be combined in the same .jar file. The syntax for the loadjava tool is in *Oracle8*i *SQLJ Programming* [37, p. 525]:

```
loadjava {-user | -u} <user>/<password>[@<database>] [options]
{<file>.java | <file>.class | <file>.jar | <file>.zip | <file>.sqlj |
<resourcefile>} ...
```

The available options listed here are from *Oracle8*i *SQLJ Programming* [37, pp.526-527]:

Option	Description
\<filenames\>	You can specify any number and combination of .java, .class, .sqlj, .jar, .zip, and resource filenames in any order.
-andresolve	Directs loadjava to compile sources if they have been loaded and to resolve external references in each class as it is loaded. -andresolve and -resolve are mutually exclusive.
-debug	Directs the Java compiler to generate debugging information.
-definer	By default, class schema objects run with the privileges of their invoker. This option confers definer privileges on classes instead.
-grant \<grants\>	Grants the EXECUTE privilege on loaded classes to the listed users and roles. Any number and combination of user and role names can be specified, separated by commas but not spaces (-grant Bob,Betty not -grant Bob, Betty).

Option	Description
`-oci8`	Uses the OCI JDBC driver; `-oci8` and `-thin` are mutually exclusive; if neither is specified, `-oci8` is used by default.
`-oracle` `resolver`	Uses a resolver that requires all referred to classes to be found.
`-resolve`	Compiles (if necessary) and resolves external references in classes after all classes on the command line have been loaded. `-andresolve` and `-resolve` are mutually exclusive.
`-resolver` `<resolver>`	Uses a resolver that requires all referred to classes to be found.
`-schema`	Designates the schema where schema objects are created. If not specified, the logon schema is used. To create a schema object in a schema that is not your own, you must have the CREATE PROCEDURE or CREATE ANY PROCEDURE privilege.
`-synonym`	Creates a PUBLIC synonym for loaded classes making them accessible outside the schema into which they are loaded. You must have the CREATE PUBLIC SYNONYM privilege.
`-thin`	Uses the thin JDBC driver. `-oci8` and `-thin` are mutually exclusive; if neither is specified, `-oci8` is used by default.
`-user, -u`	Specifies a user, password, and database connect string. The argument has the form `<username>/<password>[@<database>]`.
`-verbose`	Directs `loadjava` to emit detailed status messages while running.

dropjava

The `dropjava` utility is used to remove Java schema objects from the server. The `dropjava` command is the inverse of the `loadjava` command as appears in *Oracle8*i *SQLJ Programming* [37, p. 527]:

```
dropjava {-u | -user} <user>/<password>[@<database>] [options]
{<file>.java | <file>.class | <file>.sqlj | <file>.jar | <file>.zip |
<resourcefile>} ...
```

The available options listed here are described in *Oracle8*i *SQLJ Programming* [37, p. 528]:

Option	Description
-user	Specifies a user, password, and optional database connect string.
<filenames>	You can specify any number and combination of .java, .class, .sqlj, .jar, .zip, and resource filenames in any order. .jar and .zip files must be uncompressed.
-oci8	Uses the OCI JDBC driver. -oci8 and -thin are mutually exclusive; if neither is specified, -oci8 is used by default.
-schema	Designates the schema from which schema objects are dropped. If not specified, the logon schema is used. To drop a schema object from a schema that is not your own, you need the DROP ANY PROCEDURE system privilege.
-thin	Uses the thin JDBC driver. The -oci8 and -thin options are mutually exclusive; if neither is specified, -oci8 is used by default.
-verbose	Directs dropjava to emit detailed status messages while running.

publish

Each database instance running the JServer software has a session namespace, which the Oracle8*i* ORB uses to activate CORBA server objects. A *session namespace* is a hierarchical collection of objects known as PublishedObjects and PublishingContexts.

PublishedObjects are the bottom level of the hierarchy, and PublishingContexts are upper-level nodes analogous to UNIX system files and directories. Each PublishedObject corresponds to a class schema object that represents a CORBA object implementation. To activate a CORBA server object, a client references the name of the corresponding published object.

Creating a PublishedObject is known as *publishing*, and can be accomplished with the publish utility (which is described in this section), or the interactive session shell (which is described in Appendix F). CORBA published objects are created with these utilities after the corresponding object implementations have been loaded into the server with the loadjava utility.

A `PublishedObject` has the following attributes as listed in the *Oracle8i Enterprise JavaBeans and CORBA Developer's Guide Release 8.1.5* [52, p. 6-18]:

- **Schema object name**   The name of the Java class schema object associated with the `PublishedObject`.

- **Schema**   The name of the schema containing the corresponding class schema object.

- **Helper schema object name**   The name of the helper class the Oracle8i ORB uses to automatically narrow a reference to an instance of the CORBA object.

`PublishedObjects` and `PublishingContexts` have owners and privileges. An owner can be a username or a role name. Only the owner of a `PublishedObject` or `PublishingContext` can change the ownership of privileges of that `PublishedObject` or `PublishingContext`. Table 6-2 is taken from the *Oracle8i Enterprise JavaBeans and CORBA Developer's Guide Release 8.1.5* [52, p. 6-18, Table 6-4] describes session namespace rights.

Oracle8*i* creates a session namespace automatically when the Oracle8i ORB is configured. The `PublishingContexts` contained in Table 6-3 from the *Oracle8*i *Enterprise JavaBeans and CORBA Developer's Guide Release 8.1.5* [52, p. 6-18, Table 6-5] are present in all session namespaces.

Since, by default, only `/test` is writable by `PUBLIC`, you will usually create `PublishingContexts` and `PublishedObjects` under `/test`. The `publish` utility creates or replaces (*republishes*) a `PublishedObject` in a `PublishingContext`. It is not necessary to republish when you update a Java class schema object. You only have to republish when you change the attributes of

Right	Meaning for PublishingContext	Meaning for PublishedObject
read	List contents and attributes (type, rights, and creation time).	List object attributes (type, schema object, schema, helper rights, and creation time).
write	Create a `PublishedObject` or `PublishingContext` in the `PublishingContext`.	Republish object.
execute	Use contents to resolve a name.	Activate associated class.

TABLE 6-2.   *PublishingContext and PublishingObject Rights*

Name	Owner	Read	Write	Execute
/	SYS	PUBLIC	SYS	PUBLIC
/bin	SYS	PUBLIC	SYS	PUBLIC
/etc	SYS	PUBLIC	SYS	PUBLIC
/test	SYS	PUBLIC	PUBLIC	PUBLIC

TABLE 6-3. *Initial Publishing Contexts and Rights*

a published object. The syntax of the publish command is as follows in the *Oracle8*i *Enterprise JavaBeans and CORBA Developer's Guide Release 8.1.5* [52, p. 6-19]:

```
publish <name> <class> [<helper>] -user <username> -password <password>
-service <serviceURL> [options]
    [-describe]
    [{-g | -grant} {<user> | <role>}[,{<user> | <role>}]...]
    [{-h | -help}]
    [-iiop]
    [-role <role>]
    [-republish]
    [-schema <schema>]
    [-ssl]
    [-version]
```

The publish command-line arguments are summarized in Table 6-4 (from the *Oracle8*i *Enterprise JavaBeans and CORBA Developer's Guide Release 8.1.5* [52, pp. 6-19 – 6-21, Table 6-6]):

remove

The remove utility removes a PublishedObject or PublishingContext from a session namespace. Note that it does not remove the corresponding Java object from the server; the dropjava utility accomplishes that. The syntax of the remove command is as appears in the *Oracle8*i *Enterprise JavaBeans and CORBA Developer's Guide Release 8.1.5* [52, p. 6-21]:

```
remove <name> -user <username> -password <password>
-service <serviceURL> [options]
    [{-d | -describe}]
    [{-h | -help}]
    [iiop]
    [{-r | -recurse}]
    [-role role]
    [-ssl]
    [-version]
```

Option	Description
<name>	Name of the `PublishedObject` being created or republished; `PublishingContexts` are created if necessary.
<class>	Name of the class schema object that corresponds to <name>.
<helper>	Name of the Java class schema object that implements the `narrow()` method for <class>.
-user	Specifies identity with which to log into the database instance named in `-service`.
-password	Specifies authenticating password for the username specified with `-user`.
-service	URL identifying database whose session namespace is to be "opened" by `sess_sh`. The `serviceURL` has the form: `sess_iiop://<host>:<lport>:<sid>.` <host> is the computer that hosts the target database; <lport> is the listener port that has been configured to listen for session IIOP; <sid> is the database instance identifier. Example: `sess_iiop://localhost:2481:ORCL` which matches the default installation on the invoker's machine.
-describe	Summarizes the tool's operation, and then exits.
-grant	After creating or republishing the `PublishedObject`, grants `read` and `execute` rights to the sequence of <user> and <role> names. When republishing, replace the existing users/roles that have read/execute rights with the <user> and <role> names. To selectively change the rights of a `PublishedObject`, use the `sess_sh`'s `chmod` command. Note that to activate a CORBA object or EJB, a user must have the `execute` right for both the `PublishedObject` and the corresponding class schema object.
-help	Summarizes the tool's syntax, and then exits.
-iiop	Connects to the target database with IIOP instead of the default session IIOP. Use this option when publishing to a database server that has been configured without session IIOP.
-role	Role to assume for the `publish`; no default.

TABLE 6-4.   *Publish Tool Argument Summary*

Option	Description
-republish	Directs `publish` to replace an existing `PublishedObject`; without this option, the `publish` tool rejects an attempt to publish an existing name. If the `PublishedObject` does not exist, `publish` creates it. Republishing deletes non-owner rights; use the `-grant` option to add `read`/`execute` rights when republishing.
-schema	The schema containing the Java `<class>` schema object. If you do not specify, the `publish` tool uses the invoker's schema.
-ssl	Connects to the database with SSL server authentication. You must have configured the database for SSL to use this option, and you must specify an SSL listener port in `-service`.
-version	Shows the tool's version, and then exits.

TABLE 6-4. *Publish Tool Argument Summary* (continued)

Table 6-5 (from the *Oracle8i Enterprise JavaBeans and CORBA Developer's Guide Release 8.1.5* [52, pp. 6-21 – 6-22, Table 6-7]) summarizes the `remove` arguments:

An example of a `remove` invocation is shown here:

```
remove /test/Account -user scott -password tiger\
   -service sess_iiop://localhost:2481:ORCL
```

This command will remove the `PublishedObject` named `/test/Account` from the session namespace.

Conclusion

In this chapter you were provided with the information you need to deploy and use simple CORBA server objects. You saw that the main advantages of using CORBA server objects include heterogeneity—for example, server objects, which are specified in the programming language neutral IDL, can be implemented in different programming languages—and location transparency; that is, the client does not have to be aware of the location of the server object it uses.

Option	Description
`<name>`	Name of `PublishingContext` or `PublishedObject` to be removed.
`-user`	Specifies identity with which to log into the instance named in `-service`.
`-password`	Specifies authenticating password for the `<username>` you specified with `-user`.
`-service`	URL identifying database whose session namespace is to be "opened" by `sess_sh`. The `serviceURL` has the form:

`sess_iiop://<host>:<lport>:<sid>`.

`<host>` is the computer that hosts the target database; `<lport>` is the listener port that has been configured to listen for session IIOP; `<sid>` is the database instance identifier. Example:

`sess_iiop://localhost:2481:ORCL`

which matches the default installation on the invoker's machine. |
`-describe`	Summarizes the tool's operation, and then exits.
`-help`	Summarizes the tool's syntax, and then exits.
`-iiop`	Connects to the target database with IIOP instead of the default session IIOP. Use this option when removing from a database server that has been configured without session IIOP.
`-recurse`	Recursively removes `<name>` and all subordinate `PublishingContexts`; required to remove a `PublishingContext`.
`-role`	Role to assume for the `remove`; no default.
`-ssl`	Connects to the database with SSL server authentication. You must have configured the database for SSL to use this option.
`-version`	Shows the tool's version, and then exits.

TABLE 6-5. *remove* Argument Summary

Specific CORBA coding techniques you considered include the CORBA callback mechanism, which allows a server object to invoke a method in the client, the CORBA tie mechanism, which provides you with an alternative means to implement a server object (other than extending the generated skeleton class), and the technique of activating transient objects by first registering them with the BOA.

In the subsequent chapter, you will learn a lot more about creating and managing sessions that involve CORBA objects.

CHAPTER
7

CORBA Sessions

lthough standard CORBA does not support the session concept, the session concept is fundamental to the Oracle8*i* database and the JServer ORB. Every Oracle8*i* CORBA server object executes in a particular session. Frequently, all server objects are activated in a single session. If this is the case, the standard IIOP service is sufficient for session management. However, if the server objects are to be activated in a variety of sessions, the session IIOP service is required. In this chapter you will learn about those topics that are related to sessions. In particular, you will consider:

- Connection services: TTC and IIOP

- Review of JNDI

- Oracle8*i* CORBA sessions

- Session management

- Authentication

- Non-JNDI clients

Connection Services: TTC and IIOP

In Oracle, a *presentation* refers to a service protocol that accepts incoming network requests and activates routines in the database kernel layer or in the Java VM to handle the requests. A *service* implements a service protocol. There are three services supported by the Oracle8*i* JServer: the two-task common (TTC) layer, inherited from Oracle version 8.0.5; the CORBA session Internet Inter-ORB Protocol (session IIOP) service; and the standard IIOP service. In Oracle version 8.1.7, there is a fourth presentation, HTTP, used for servlets. Also, Oracle8*i* allows users to define their own presentations.

The TTC service handles incoming Net8 requests for database SQL services from Oracle tools, such as SQL*PLUS, and customer-written applications implemented using such tools as Oracle Forms, PRO*C, and SQLJ. The IIOP services handle TCP/IP requests that are routed to the service entry point by the listener and the dispatcher. These IIOP services start, control, and terminate Oracle8*i* database sessions that access CORBA objects in the same way that the TTC service starts, controls, and terminates upon receiving requests from a tool such as SQL*PLUS. Tools such as `publish`, `deployejb`, and the `session shell` access CORBA objects, and thus connect to the database using an IIOP port. In addition, EJB and CORBA clients, as well as distributed objects that access other distributed objects, use an IIOP port when sending requests to Oracle. However, tools such as `loadjava` and `dropjava`, that do not access distributed objects, connect using a

TTC port. Note that `1521` is the default port number for TTC and `2481` is the default port number for IIOP.

The standard and session IIOP services differ in only one major respect: the standard IIOP service only allows a client to access server objects that run in a single session, whereas the session IIOP service permits a client to access server objects in multiple sessions. The session IIOP supports connection to multiple sessions by embedding a session identifier in object references, permitting different object references to be associated with different sessions simultaneously.

Review of JNDI

In this section, you will review the use of the Java Naming and Directory Interface (JNDI) to look up and activate published objects in the session namespace. JNDI is supplied by Sun Microsystems. If you are using JNDI in your client code or server object implementation code, you must include the following import statements in each such source file:

```
// the JNDI Context interface.
import javax.naming.Context;

/* Import the InitialContext class that implements the
   Context interface.
*/
import javax.naming.InitialContext;

//JNDI property constants.
import oracle.aurora.jndi.sess_iiop.ServiceCtx;

// Hash table for the initial context environment.
import java.util.Hashtable;
```

In this section, you will consider the following:

- The JNDI `Context` **interface**
- The JNDI `InitialContext` class

The JNDI Context Interface

All Oracle8*i* EJB and CORBA clients that use JNDI methods to look up and activate server objects must import the `javax.naming.Context` **interface**. This interface forms the basis for the JNDI operations that are used to manage services and sessions in the Oracle8*i* ORB.

Before you can use JNDI to connect your client program to an Oracle8*i* server, you must set up an environment for the JNDI context. The environment properties are typically stored in a hash table, although a properties list can also be used for this purpose. A hash table is created in your Java program by executing this statement:

```
Hashtable environment = new Hashtable();
```

Please see Note 3 following the program code in the section of Chapter 6 entitled "Code and Compile the Java Client" for a discussion of the environment properties and how to set them.

The Context **interface** contains several methods that are implemented in the ServiceCtx, SessionCtx, and InitialContext classes. These classes are discussed in the next session.

The JNDI InitialContext Class

InitialContext is a class in the javax.naming package that implements the Context **interface**. An InitialContext object is created for an environment, and the lookup() method that can return an object reference for a published object can be invoked on an InitialContext object. For example, the following code fragment is from the program AccountUser.java in Chapter 6:

```
Hashtable env = new Hashtable();
env.put(Context.URL_PKG_PREFIXES, "oracle.aurora.jndi");
env.put(Context.SECURITY_PRINCIPAL, "scott");
env.put(Context.SECURITY_CREDENTIALS, "tiger");
env.put(Context.SECURITY_AUTHENTICATION, ServiceCtx.NON_SSL_LOGIN);
Context ic = new InitialContext(env);
Account account = (Account) ic.lookup(
  "sess_iiop://localhost:2481:ORCL/test/Account" );
```

Also, lookup() can be invoked on an InitialContext object to return a new service context object.

```
ServiceCtx service = (ServiceCtx)ic.lookup(
  "sess_iiop://localhost:2481:ORCL" );
```

In this case, there is no object named in the URL (such a URL is called a serviceURL), and the object returned by lookup() is cast to ServiceCtx. The preceding code would start the session IIOP service. The service context object represents the service name of the service that was started by the lookup() invocation. The ServiceCtx class extends the Context class. Similarly, the SessionCtx class extends the Context class, and a SessionCtx object represents a session.

Oracle8*i* CORBA Sessions

A *session* is a specific connection of a client to a service. For example, when a tool such as SQL*PLUS makes a connection through Net8 to a listener TTC port, Oracle8*i* establishes a new database session to handle the connection and provide SQL support. In the same way, when an incoming request from a CORBA client program is generated—say, by the execution of the context `lookup()` method, which establishes a new connection—a new session might be established by Oracle8*i* to handle the request. Whenever `InitialContext.lookup()` activates a server object, the activation will occur either within a new or an existing session. Since server objects are thusly activated within sessions, the ORB and the database need a way of distinguishing objects within the same server process based on the sessions in which they are activated.

In the standard IIOP, a connection is identified by its host and port number, which are also encoded into object references. However, with the session IIOP, a client can connect to multiple sessions within a service. Thus, the session IIOP service needs a way to distinguish among sessions as well as services. The session IIOP *component tag*, `SessionIIOP`, provides such a way. `SessionIIOP` contains information that uniquely identifies the session in which the object was activated. This information is used by the client ORB runtime to send requests to the right objects in the right session. Note, however, that the only difference between the session and the standard IIOP is the inclusion of session ID information.

When client code makes an IIOP connection to the database, the server code must decide if a new session should be started to handle the connection, or if the connection should be handled in an existing session. If the client is making a new request for a connection via the `lookup()` method, and no session is active for that connection, a new session is automatically started.

The session IIOP is not needed to route a connection request to an existing session; the standard IIOP is sufficient for that purpose. The session IIOP is required only if the same client is to have access to server objects residing in multiple sessions (for example, when a middle-tier server connects to Oracle8*i* on behalf of multiple clients).

Next, you will consider the following:

- Database listeners and dispatchers

- URL syntax for services and sessions

- URL components and classes

- The service context class

- The session context class

- Sample application

Database Listeners and Dispatchers

Upon receiving a client request for an IIOP connection, the listener assigns an IIOP dispatcher to the client request, and sends an IIOP reply to ask the client to reconnect to the dispatcher.

When a shared server services a new IIOP connection, it first creates a new database session for the connection, and then activates the ORB in the session. In that session, the ORB handles the reading of incoming IIOP messages, authenticating the client, finding and activating the corresponding server-side objects, and sending appropriate IIOP messages to the client.

Further, IIOP messages from the same client are sent directly to the existing session, and are handled similarly by the ORB.

When a listener is configured to accept both Net8 and IIOP connections, there is no distinguishing between session IIOP and standard IIOP. They are both handled by the listener on the same port. However, a separate port is required for Secure Socket Layer (SSL) connections. Some information on SSL connections is provided in the section of Chapter 6 titled "Code and Compile the Java Client."

URL Syntax for Services and Sessions

Oracle8*i* provides universal resource locator (URL) syntax that lets the user employ JNDI requests to start up services and sessions, and to access server objects that are published in the database instance. You have already seen URLs passed as arguments to the `InitialContext` class `lookup()` method. A `serviceURL` is used to start a service such as `sess_iiop`. Such a URL consists of the following:

- The service name followed by a colon and two slashes: `sess_iiop://`.

- The system name (hostname). You can use either the explicit hostname, or `localhost` (that evaluates to the local hostname), or the numeric form of the IP address for the host.

- The listener port number for IIOP services (the default is `2481`).

- The SID (such as ORCL).

Colons are used to separate the hostname, port, and SID. For example,

```
sess_iiop://localhost:2481:ORCL
```

is the `serviceURL`. A URL to activate a server object has the form of a `serviceURL` with the addition of a server object name:

```
sess_iiop://localhost:2481:ORCL/test/Account
```

URL Components and Classes

As you saw in the preceding section, when you make a connection to Oracle and look up a published object using JNDI, you use a URL that specifies the service (service name, host, port, and SID), in addition to the name of the published object to look up and activate. The session name can also be placed in such a URL:

```
sess_iiop://localhost:2481:ORCL/:default/test/Account
```

Here, `sess_iiop://localhost:2481:ORCL` specifies the service name, `:default` specifies the default session (if a session has already been established), and `/test/Account` gives the full path in the namespace of the server object to be looked up. In the client, the first session established is considered the default session and is automatically named `:default`. Any server object that is subsequently activated from the client by an `InitialContext.lookup()` invocation is automatically activated in the default session, unless a different session name is explicitly specified in the URL passed to the `lookup()` method. Note that if no session name is specified on a URL that contains a server object name, the server object is still activated in the default session. Thus, it is not necessary to explicitly specify `:default` in the URL.

Each of these URL components represents a Java class—for example, the service name is represented by a `ServiceCtx` object, and the session by a `SessionCtx` object.

You will next consider the following:

- The service context class

- The session context class

The Service Context Class

The `ServiceCtx` class extends the JNDI Context class. The `ServiceCtx` class defines several **final public static** variables (that is, constants), as you have already seen. Table 7-1 taken from *Oracle8i Enterprise JavaBeans and CORBA Developer's Guide, Release 8.1.5* [pp. 4-14 - 4-15, Table 4-1] summarizes these.

The following **public** methods in `ServiceCtx` are available for use from CORBA and EJB applications.

- `public Context createSubcontext( String name )`

This method creates a new named session. The name parameter provides the name of the session, and the context object returned represents that session. This method, in combination with the `SessionCtx.activate()` method to be discussed in the next section, is used to activate a server object in a new session, instead of in the default session.

String Name	Value
DEFAULT_SESSION	`":default"`
NON_SSL_CREDENTIAL	`"Credential"`
NON_SSL_LOGIN	`"Login"`
SSL_CREDENTIAL	`"SecureCredential"`
SSL_LOGIN	`"SecureLogin"`
SSL_30	`"30"`
SSL_20	`"20"`
SSL_30_WITH_20_HELLO	`"30_WITH_20_HELLO"`
THIS_SERVER	`":thisServer"`
THIS_SESSION	`":thisSession"`

Integer Name	Integer Constructor
SESS_IIOP	`new Integer(2)`
IIOP	`new Integer(1)`

TABLE 7-1. *ServiceCtx Public Variables*

- ```
  public static org.omg.CORBA.ORB init(
      String username,
      String password,
      String role,
      boolean ssl,
      java.util.Properties props )
  ```

This method returns a reference to the ORB created when you did a lookup. Set the `ssl` parameter to `true` for SSL authentication. This method is used by non-JNDI clients. See the subsequent section titled "Non-JNDI Clients."

- ```
  public synchronized SessionCtx login()
  ```

This method authenticates the caller using the properties in the initial context environment, and then activates a new session and returns the session context object.

- ```
  public Object lookup( String name )
  ```

This method looks up a server object in the database instance associated with the service context, and returns an activated instance of the object. Thus, a
  ```

lookup() invocation on an InitialContext object with a serviceURL can activate the service and return a ServiceCtx object, and a subsequent lookup() invocation on that ServiceCtx object can activate the indicated server object (instead of doing both these steps with one lookup() invocation).

- ■ public Object _lookup(String name)

This method is identical to the lookup() method, except that the server object is not activated.

The Session Context Class

The SessionCtx class extends the JNDI Context class. SessionCtx objects represents sessions and contain methods that allow you to perform session operations such as authenticating the client or activating objects.

- ■ public synchronized boolean login()

This method authenticates the client using the initial context environment properties that were passed to InitialContext constructor: username, password, and role.

- ■ public synchronized boolean login(
  String username, String password, String role)

This method authenticates the client using the username, password, and role passed as parameters (the role is optional and is often passed as null), and is typically used to authenticate a client for a session that was explicitly started, using Context.createSubcontext().

- ■ .public Object activate(String name)

This method looks up and activates a server object having the indicated name, and is commonly used to activate a server object in a session that was explicitly started using Context.createSubcontext().

Sample Application

In this section, you will see a sample application in which a lookup is done with a serviceURL, a session is explicitly created with the SessionCtx.createSubcontext() method, the client is authenticated with SessionCtx.login() method, and a server object is explicitly activated with the SessionCtx.activate() method. The particular server object used will be Account from Chapter 6. For completeness, we include the IDL file for that server object:

```
/* File Name: account.idl */
```

```
module account {
  struct AccountInfo { long departmentno; long projectno; };
  exception NoAccountError { wstring mess; };
  interface Account {
    AccountInfo getAccountInfo( in long accountno )
      raises( NoAccountError );
  };
};
```

AccountImpl.sqlj must be coded so that Account objects can be explicitly activated. In order for this to be the case, AccountImpl has to implement the oracle.aurora.AuroraServices.ActivatableObject interface and the _intializeAuroraObject() method of that interface must be implemented. See the section "Server Object Activation" in Chapter 6 for a discussion of this.

```
/* Program Name:  AccountImpl.sqlj
**
** Purpose:  Get account information for the given account number.
**
*/
package accountServer;
import account.*;
import java.sql.*;
import oracle.aurora.AuroraServices.ActivatableObject;
public class AccountImpl extends _AccountImplBase
  implements ActivatableObject {
  public AccountInfo getAccountInfo( int accountno )
    throws NoAccountError {
    try {

      // You must initialize variables to be selected into.
      int departmentno = 0;
      int projectno = 0;

      #sql {
        SELECT departmentno, projectno
          INTO :departmentno, :projectno
            FROM ACCOUNT_LIST
              WHERE accountno = :accountno
      };
      return new AccountInfo( departmentno, projectno );
    }
    catch( SQLException e ) {
      throw new NoAccountError( e.getMessage() );
    }
  }
```

```
  // Implement ActivatableObject._intializeAuroraObject().
  public org.omg.CORBA.Object _initializeAuroraObject() {return this;}
}


/* Program Name: ExplicitAccountUser.java
**
** Purpose:  Use the Account server object to get account
**           information for the account 1056, illustrating
**           explicit creation, activation, and authentication
**           steps.
**
*/
import account.*;
import accountServer.*;

// Import ServiceCtx class and SessionCtx class.
import oracle.aurora.jndi.sess_iiop.ServiceCtx;
import oracle.aurora.jndi.sess_iiop.SessionCtx;

// Import the JNDI Context Interface.
import javax.naming.Context;

/* Import the InitialContext class that implements the
   Context interface.
*/
import javax.naming.InitialContext;

/* Import the hash table class to hold the initial context
   properties environment.
*/
import java.util.Hashtable;

public class ExplicitAccountUser {

  // main throws instead of catching exceptions.
  public static void main( String[] args ) throws Exception {

    /* Prepare simplified initial context.  Since session is
       explicitly started, authentication must be explicitly done.
    */
    Hashtable env = new Hashtable();
    env.put( Context.URL_PKG_PREFIXES, "oracle.aurora.jndi" );
    Context ic = new InitialContext( env );

    /* Get SessionCtx object that represents database instance,
       using serviceURL.
    */
    ServiceCtx service = ( ServiceCtx )
```

```
      ic.lookup( "sess_iiop://localhost:2481:ORCL" );

   // Create a session named :mysession in the instance.
   SessionCtx session = ( SessionCtx )
     service.createSubcontext( ":mysession" );

   // Authenticate.
   session.login( "scott", "tiger", null );

   // Activate the Account object.
   Account account = ( Account )
     session.activate( "/test/Account" );

   // Invoke getAccountInfo() method.
   AccountInfo ai = account.getAccountInfo( 1056 );

   // Print account information.
   System.out.println( "Department number = " + ai.departmentno +
                       " Project number = " + ai.projectno );
 }
}
```

Session Management

In this section, you will learn about the explicit control of sessions. In particular, you will learn about

- Session start up from a server object

- Starting a named session from a client

- A two-session sample program

- A sample program with URLs that contain session names

- Controlling session duration and ending a session

Session Start-up from a Server Object

When a server object activates another server object using the same URL a client would use, the new server object is activated in a separate session from the session in which the server object that did the lookup is running:

```
Hashtable env = new Hashtable();
env.put( Context.URL_PKG_PREFIXES, "oracle.aurora.jndi" );
env.put( Context.SECURITY_PRINCIPAL, "scott" );
```

```
env.put( Context.SECURITY_CREDENTIALS, "tiger" );
env.put( Context.SECURITY_AUTHENTICATION, ServiceCtx.NON_SSL_LOGIN );
Context ic = new InitialContext( env );
Account = ( Account ) ic.lookup(
    "sess_iiop://localhost:2481:ORCL/test/Account );
```

However, if you want the new server object to run in the same session as the invoking server object, you should use the `thisServer/:thisSession` notation in place of `hostname:port:SID` in the URL. Thus, you would recode the preceding `lookup()` invocation as follows:

```
Hashtable env = new Hashtable();
env.put( Context.URL_PKG_PREFIXES, "oracle.aurora.jndi" );
Context ic = new InitialContext( env );
Account myObj = ( Account ) ic.lookup(
    "sess_iiop://thisServer/:thisSession/test/Account );
```

Note that there is no need to supply login authentication, as the client (a server object in this case) is already authenticated. Remember that clients, not objects, are authenticated to a session. Whenever a separate session is to be started, which does not happen in this case, either login or SSL credential authentication must be performed.

Starting a Named Session from a Client

If you specify a server object name, but you don't specify an explicit name for your session, in the URL that you pass to an `InitialContext.lookup()` invocation (or you specify the default session), the server object is activated in the `:default` session. If you subsequently activate additional server objects in the client, they will run in that same default session. If, however, you want a server object to be activated in a separate session, you do this as follows:

1. Create a new service context by doing a `lookup()` invocation with a serviceURL:

   ```
   ServiceCtx service = ( Servicectx ) ic.lookup(
       "sess_iiop://localhost:2481:ORCL" );
   ```

2. Create a new session context by invoking the `createSubcontext()` method on the service context:

   ```
   SessionCtx newsess = ( SessionCtx )
       service.createSubcontext ( ":mysession" );
   ```

3. Authenticate the client by invoking the `login()` method on the new session:

   ```
   newsess.login( "scott", "tiger", "null" );
   ```

In the next section, you will see a fully coded example that explicitly starts two sessions.

A Two-Session Sample Program

In this example, a client explicitly starts two different sessions, and explicitly activates a server object in each session. The example is very similar to the previous sample application, except that two sessions instead of one session are started. Again, you will use the `Account` object from Chapter 6. For completeness, the IDL file is repeated here.

```
/* File Name: account.idl */

module account {
  struct AccountInfo { long departmentno; long projectno; };
  exception NoAccountError { wstring mess; };
  interface Account {
    AccountInfo getAccountInfo( in long accountno )
      raises( NoAccountError );
  };
};


/* Program Name:  AccountImpl.sqlj
**
** Purpose:  Get account information for the given account number.
**
*/
package accountServer;
import account.*;
import java.sql.*;
import oracle.aurora.AuroraServices.ActivatableObject;
public class AccountImpl extends _AccountImplBase
  implements ActivatableObject {
  public AccountInfo getAccountInfo( int accountno )
    throws NoAccountError {
    try {

      // You must initialize variables to be selected into.
      int departmentno = 0;
      int projectno = 0;

      #sql {
        SELECT departmentno, projectno
          INTO :departmentno, :projectno
            FROM ACCOUNT_LIST
              WHERE accountno = :accountno
```

```
      };
      return new AccountInfo( departmentno, projectno );
    }
    catch( SQLException e ) {
      throw new NoAccountError( e.getMessage() );
    }
  }

  // Implement ActivatableObject._initializeAuroraObject().
  public org.omg.CORBA.Object _initializeAuroraObject() {return this;}
}

/* Program Name: AccountUser2.java
**
** Purpose:  Use the Account server object to get account
**           information for accounts 1056 and 2001.
**
*/
import account.*;
import accountServer.*;

// Import ServiceCtx class and SessionCtx class.
import oracle.aurora.jndi.sess_iiop.ServiceCtx;
import oracle.aurora.jndi.sess_iiop.SessionCtx;

// Import the JNDI Context Interface.
import javax.naming.Context;

/* Import the InitialContext class that implements the
   Context Interface.
*/
import javax.naming.InitialContext;

/* Import the hash table class to hold the initial context
   properties environment.
*/
import java.util.Hashtable;

public class AccountUser2 {

  // main throws instead of catching exceptions.
  public static void main( String[] args ) throws Exception {
    Hashtable env = new Hashtable();

    /* Prepare simplified initial context.  Since session is
       explicitly started, authentication must be explicitly done.
    */
    env.put( Context.URL_PKG_PREFIXES, "oracle.aurora.jndi" );
```

```
Context ic = new InitialContext( env );

// Get SessionCtx object that represents database instance.
ServiceCtx service = ( ServiceCtx )
  ic.lookup( "sess_iiop://localhost:2481:ORCL" );

// Create a session in the instance named :mysession1.
SessionCtx session1 =
  ( SessionCtx ) service.createSubcontext( ":mysession1" );

// Authenticate.
session1.login( "scott", "tiger", null );

// Create another session in the instance named :mysession2.
SessionCtx session2 =
  ( SessionCtx ) service.createSubcontext( ":mysession2" );

// Authenticate.
session2.login( "scott", "tiger", null );

// Activate an Account object in :mysession1.
Account account1 =
  ( Account ) session1.activate( "/test/Account" );

// Activate an Account object in :mysession2.
Account account2 =
  ( Account ) session2.activate( "/test/Account" );

// Invoke getAccountInfo() method on account1 and account2.
AccountInfo ai1 = account1.getAccountInfo( 1056 );
AccountInfo ai2 = account2.getAccountInfo( 2001 );

// Print account information.
System.out.println( "For account 1056: " +
                    "Department number = " + ai1.departmentno +
                    " Project number = " + ai1.projectno );
System.out.println( "For account 2001: " +
                    "Department number = " + ai2.departmentno +
                    " Project number = " + ai2.projectno ); }
}
```

Sample Program with URLs That Contain Session Names

This example is similar to the previous one, except that the
`InitialContext.lookup()` method, instead of the `SessionCtx activate()`
method, is used to activate the server objects. For completeness, the IDL file is again
repeated:

```
/* File Name: account.idl */

module account {
  struct AccountInfo { long departmentno; long projectno; };
  exception NoAccountError { wstring mess; };
  interface Account {
    AccountInfo getAccountInfo( in long accountno )
      raises( NoAccountError );
  };
}
```

```
/* Program Name:  AccountImpl.sqlj
**
** Purpose:  Get account information for the given account number.
**
*/
package accountServer;
import account.*;
import java.sql.*;

/* Note that AccountUser3 does not require the ActivatableObject class
   since it activates server object within the lookup() invocations.
*/
import oracle.aurora.AuroraServices.ActivatableObject;

public class AccountImpl extends _AccountImplBase
  implements ActivatableObject {
  public AccountInfo getAccountInfo( int accountno )
    throws NoAccountError {
    try {

      // You must initialize variables to be selected into.
      int departmentno = 0;
      int projectno = 0;

      #sql {
        SELECT departmentno, projectno
          INTO :departmentno, :projectno
            FROM ACCOUNT_LIST
              WHERE accountno = :accountno
      };
      return new AccountInfo( departmentno, projectno );
    }
    catch( SQLException e ) {
      throw new NoAccountError( e.getMessage() );
    }
  }

  // Implement ActivatableObject._initializeAuroraObject().
```

```
   /* Note that AccountUser3 does not require this method, since
      it activates server object with lookup() invocation.
   */
   public org.omg.CORBA.Object _initializeAuroraObject() {return this;}
}


/* Program Name: AccountUser3.java
**
** Purpose:  Use the Account server object to get account
**           information for accounts 1056 and 2001.
*/
import account.*;
import accountServer.*;

// Import ServiceCtx class and SessionCtx class.
import oracle.aurora.jndi.sess_iiop.ServiceCtx;
import oracle.aurora.jndi.sess_iiop.SessionCtx;

// Import the JNDI Context Interface.
import javax.naming.Context;

/* Import the InitialContext class that implements the
   Context Interface.
*/
import javax.naming.InitialContext;

/* Import the hash table class to hold the initial context
   properties environment.
*/
import java.util.Hashtable;

public class AccountUser3 {

  // main throws instead of catching exceptions.
  public static void main( String[] args ) throws Exception {

    /* Prepare simplified initial context.  Since session is
       explicitly started, authentication must be explicitly done.
    */

    Hashtable env = new Hashtable();
    env.put( Context.URL_PKG_PREFIXES, "oracle.aurora.jndi" );
    Context ic = new InitialContext( env );

    // Get SessionCtx object that represents database instance.
    ServiceCtx service = ( ServiceCtx )
      ic.lookup( "sess_iiop://localhost:2481:ORCL" );
```

```
// Create a session in the instance named :mysession1.
SessionCtx session1 =
    ( SessionCtx ) service.createSubcontext( ":mysession1" );

// Authenticate.
session1.login( "scott", "tiger", null );

// Create another session in the instance named :mysession2.
SessionCtx session2 =
    ( SessionCtx ) service.createSubcontext( ":mysession2" );

// Authenticate.
session2.login( "scott", "tiger", null );

/* Activate the objects by using the fully specified URL
   that contains the session name.
*/
/* Note that the initial context need not contain
   authentication information, since the client has
   already been authenticated in the sessions.
*/
Account account1 = ( Account ) ic.lookup(
    "sess_iiop://localhost:2481:ORCL/:mysession1/test/Account" );
Account account2 = ( Account ) ic.lookup(
    "sess_iiop://localhost:2481:ORCL/:mysession2/test/Account" );

// Invoke getAccountInfo() method on account1 and account2.
AccountInfo ai1 = account1.getAccountInfo( 1056 );
AccountInfo ai2 = account2.getAccountInfo( 2001 );

// Print account information.
System.out.println( "For account 1056: " +
                    "Department number = " + ai1.departmentno +
                    " Project number = " + ai1.projectno );
System.out.println( "For account 2001: " +
                    "Department number = " + ai2.departmentno +
                    " Project number = " + ai2.projectno );
  }
}
```

Controlling Session Duration and Ending a Session

A session normally ends when the last client connection terminates. However, the `oracle.aurora.net.Presentation.sessionTimeout()` method provides the server object with a way of controlling the session duration. This method takes as its parameter the session timeout value in seconds. The session timeout clock starts ticking when the last client requests complete. Thus, if the timeout parameter is 30, the session will be terminated whenever 30 seconds has elapsed since the last client request:

```
oracle.aurora.net.Presentation.sessionTimeout(30);
```

Note that when you use the `sessionTimeout()` method, you must add

```
$(ORACLE_HOME)/lib/aurora.zip to your classpath.
```

The `exitSession()` method in `oracle.aurora.vm.OracleRuntime` will terminate a database session, much as `System.exit()` will terminate a program:

```
oracle.aurora.vm.OracleRuntime.exitSession(1);
```

The **int** parameter for this method is an exit value, similar to the value supplied for `System.exit()`.

Authentication

Since the Oracle server is a secure server, a client cannot access data stored in the database without first being authenticated by the Oracle server. Because Oracle8*i* CORBA server objects and Enterprise JavaBeans execute within the Oracle server, the following conditions must be satisfied in order for a client to be able to activate a server object and invoke methods on it:

- The client must be able to authenticate itself to the server by passing a username and password.

- The client must have access rights to any object that it activates.

- In some cases, the client must have `execute` privileges on the method itself. For example, in EJB, access rights can be established on a method-to-method basis.

In this section you will consider the following:

- Client authentication techniques
- Access rights to database objects

Client Authentication Techniques

There are three ways that a client can authenticate itself to the server:

- By using the Oracle8*i* login protocol over a standard (not Secure Socket Layer) TCP/IP connection

- By using the login protocol over a Secure Socket Layer connection

- By using credential-based authentication over a Secure Socket Layer connection

The authentication technique that the client uses is determined by the value set in the `javax.naming.Context.SECURITY_AUTHENTICATION` attribute when the JNDI initial context is established. There are the following three possible values:

- `ServiceCtx.NON_SSL_LOGIN` establishes the use of the Oracle8*i* login protocol over a standard TCP/IP connection.

- `ServiceCtx.SSL_LOGIN` establishes the use of the login protocol over a Secure Socket Layer connection

- `ServiceCtx.SSL_CREDENTIAL` establishes the use of the credential protocol over a Secure Socket Layer connection

If no value is specified for the `javax.naming.Context.SECURITY_AUTHENTICATION` attribute, the client will have to activate the login protocol directly.

You will next take a closer look at

- The login protocol

- The credential protocol

The Login Protocol

You can use the login protocol either with or without Secure Socket Layer (SSL) encryption. If your application requires an SSL connection for data security, specify the `SSL_LOGIN` value for the `SECONDARY_AUTHENTICATION` attribute. Otherwise, specify the `NON_SSL_LOGIN` value for that attribute. In the latter case, the login handshaking is secured by encryption, but the remainder of the client/server interaction may be less secure.

When you specify a value for each of the four JNDI Context variables (`URL_PKG_PREFIXES`, `SECURITY_PRINCIPAL`, `SECURITY_CREDENTIALS`,

SECURITY_AUHENTICATION), the first invocation of the `Context.lookup()` method performs the login automatically.

Note that the login protocol requires two components: a client component and a server component. `Login`, the client component, implements the client side of the login handshaking protocol, and acts as a proxy object for calling the server login object. The `Login` object resides in the `oracle.aurora.client` package.

The login server object is called `LoginServer` and resides in the `oracle.aurora.AuroraServices` package. The following version of `AccountUser` shows how to explicitly authenticate a client using these login objects, instead of invoking the `Sessionctx.login()` method that automatically invokes the login objects:

```java
/* Program Name: AccountUser4.java
**
** Purpose:  Use the Account server object to get account
**           information for the account 1056.
**
*/
import account.*;
import accountServer.*;
import oracle.aurora.jndi.sess_iiop.ServiceCtx;
import oracle.aurora.jndi.sess_iiop.SessionCtx;
import oracle.aurora.AuroraServices.LoginServer;
import oracle.aurora.client.Login;
import javax.naming.Context;
import javax.naming.InitialContext;
import java.util.Hashtable;
public class AccountUser4 {

  // main throws instead of catching exceptions.
  public static void main( String[] args ) throws Exception {

    // Prepare simplified initial context.
    Hashtable env = new Hashtable();
    env.put( Context.URL_PKG_PREFIXES, "oracle.aurora.jndi" );
    Context ic = new InitialContext( env );

    // Get SessionCtx object that represents database instance.
    ServiceCtx service = ( ServiceCtx )
      ic.lookup( "sess_iiop://localhost:2481:ORCL" );

    // Create a session in the instance named :mysession.
    SessionCtx session =
      ( SessionCtx ) service.createSubcontext( ":mysession" );

    // Activate the LoginServer object at the standard name etc/login.
    LoginServer login_server =
      ( LoginServer ) session.activate( "etc/login" );
```

```
/* Create the login client and authenticate with the login
   protocol.
*/
Login login = new Login( login_server );
login.authenticate( "scott", "tiger", null );

// Activate the Account object.
Account account = ( Account ) session.activate( "/test/Account" );

// Invoke getAccountInfo() method.
AccountInfo ai = account.getAccountInfo( 1056 );

// Print account information.
System.out.println( "Department number = " + ai.departmentno +
                    " Project number = " + ai.projectno );
  }
}
```

The Credential Protocol

Using the `ServiceCtx.SSL_CREDENTIAL` authentication type means that the username, password, and role are passed to the server on the first method invocation through an SSL connection. Since the SSL connection causes the password to be encrypted by the transfer protocol, there is no need for the handshaking that the login protocol uses, so the credential protocol is slightly more efficient for SSL connections.

Access Rights to Database Objects

Only users that have been granted `EXECUTE` rights to the Java class of an object stored in the database can activate the object and invoke methods on it.

You can use the `-grant` argument to the `loadjava` command in order to control `EXECUTE` rights on the Java classes being loaded.

Also, you can use the SQL `GRANT` command to grant `EXECUTE` permission on a Java class that has already been loaded into the database:

```
GRANT EXECUTE on "Account" to George
```

Published objects can be accessed by all users unless permissions are explicitly controlled. There are two ways to thusly control permissions:

- Use the `-grant` option on the `publish` tool. See Chapter 6 for a description of the `publish` tool.

- Use the `chmod` and `chown` commands within the session shell. See Appendix F for a description of the session shell.

Note that published objects have permissions that can differ from the underlying classes. A user must have EXECUTE permission on the published object as well as on the underlying classes in order to be able to activate the object.

Non-JNDI Clients

It is possible for clients to bypass JNDI completely and to connect to the Oracle server by directly using CosNaming methods. Note that in this scenario, the Login class must be used for authentication. The following example shows how to do this:

```
/* Program Name:  AccountUser5.java */

// Import CORBA Object and CosNaming classes.
import org.omg.CORBA.Object;
import org.omg.CosNaming.*;

import oracle.aurora.AuroraServices.*;
import oracle.aurora.client.Login;
import account.*;
import org.omg.CORBA.SystemException;
import accountServer.*;

public class AccountUser5 {
  public static void main( String[] args ) throws Exception {

    // Get the Name Service object reference.
    PublishingContext pc = null;
    pc = VisiAurora.getNameService( "localhost", 2481, "ORCL" );

    // Get the pre-published login object reference.
    PublishedObject lob = null;
    LoginServer serv = null;
    NameComponent[] name = new NameComponent[2];
    name[0] = new NameComponent( "etc", "" );
    name[1] = new NameComponent( "login", "" );

    // Lookup this object in the name service.
    Object l = pc.resolve( name );

    // Make sure it is a published object.
    lob = PublishedObjectHelper.narrow(l);

    // Create and activate this object.
    l = lob.activate_no_helper();
    serv = LoginServerHelper.narrow(l);
```

```
    // Create a client login proxy object and authenticate.
    Login login = new Login( serv );
    login.authenticate( "scott", "tiger", null );

    // Create and get Account object reference.
    PublishedObject accountObj = null;
    name[0] = new NameComponent( "test", "" );
    name[1] = new NameComponent( "Account", "" );

    // Lookup this object in Name Service.
    Object a = pc.resolve( name );

    // Make sure it is a published object.
    accountObj = PublishedObjectHelper.narrow(a);

    // Create and activate this object.
    a = accountObj.activate_no_helper();

    /* Use narrow() method of helper class to cast Object a into
       Account object account.  This invocation is done automatically
       for you when you use JNDI InitialContext.lookup() method to get
       Account reference.
    */
    Account account = null;
    account = AccountHelper.narrow(a);

    // Invoke getAccountInfo() method.
    AccountInfo ai = account.getAccountInfo( 1056 );

    // Print account information.
    System.out.println( "Department number = " + ai.departmentno +
                        " Project number = " + ai.projectno );
  }
}
```

Conclusion

In this chapter you considered different scenarios for authenticating clients and activating server objects. In particular, you learned how to cause server objects to be executed in a variety of session configurations. You also learned how to bypass JNDI by directly locating objects using `CosNaming` methods, and how authentication must be done in this scenario using the `Login` class.

In the next chapter, you will learn about transaction management for CORBA applications, which guarantees that your CORBA applications leave your database in a consistent state. This transaction management will be very sensitive to the session configurations in which your server objects are running. In particular, when JTS is employed as the transaction API, all the server objects in a transaction must be running in the same session.

CHAPTER

8

CORBA Transaction Management

n this chapter, you will consider transaction management for CORBA applications. You have already learned about transaction management for EJB applications in Part II of this book. Transaction management for CORBA and EJB applications is fundamentally similar, but there are some differences. In particular, EJBs have *declarative transactional* capability in that the transactional properties of the application can be declared at Bean deployment time, eliminating the need for the developer to write any transaction code. However, the CORBA developer must code calls to a transaction service to enable transactional properties for the server objects. This is done using the transactional APIs provided. Such a transactional API is usually a mapping of a subset of the OMG Object Transaction Service (OTS) API. Two such mappings are supplied by the Oracle8*i* server: the Java Transaction Service (JTS), to be used with Oracle versions 8.1.5 and 8.1.6, and the Java Transaction API (JTA) that essentially replaces JTS in Oracle 8.1.7, and is specified by Sun Microsystems. In this chapter you will learn about JTS, and the differences between JTA and JTS.

A *transaction* is a unit of database work that is

- **Atomic**   All changes to the database made in a transaction are rolled back if any change fails.

- **Consistent**   A transaction preserves consistency—that is, it takes the database from one consistent state to another.

- **Isolated**   Concurrently executed transactions do not interfere with each other, in that intermediate steps in a transaction are not visible in another concurrently executing transaction.

- **Durable**   When a transaction is committed, its effects persist in the database.

These so-called ACID properties are implemented in a relational DBMS by a combination of crash recovery and concurrency control mechanisms. In this chapter, you will learn how to manage CORBA transactions in Oracle8*i*. Specifically, you will consider the following:

- The limitations of JTS

- Transaction demarcation and transaction context

- Transaction Service interfaces

- Java Transaction Service methods

- Using JTS methods in CORBA client code

- A client-side demarcation example

- Using JTS methods in CORBA server code

- A server-side demarcation example

- A CORBA server object component

- A client that accesses an EJB component with transaction demarcation through the `TransactionService` class

- A CORBA client that accesses an EJB component and CORBA server object component

- JTA

Limitations of JTS

The Oracle8*i* implementation of JTS suffers from several limitations because it is intended to support mostly client-side transaction demarcation. These limitations are as follows:

- **No transactions with multiple resources**   An Oracle8*i* JTS transaction cannot involve multiple databases, multiple sessions, or multiple servers. However, an Oracle8*i* JTS transaction can involve multiple CORBA server objects and multiple EJBs, as long as they are running in the same session and on the same server.

   The scope of a transaction is defined by a *transaction context*. A transaction can involve many objects, and the transaction context for the transaction is shared by those objects. However, transaction contexts are never propagated outside a server. If a server object calls out to an object in another server, the transaction context is not carried along.

   It should be pointed out that the Java Transaction API (JTA), to be discussed subsequently, does support transactions involving multiple databases and multiple servers.

- **No nested transactions**   If you attempt to begin a new transaction before committing or rolling back the current transaction, the `SubtransactionsUnavailable` exception is thrown.

- **No timeouts**   JTS methods that support timeouts, such as `set_timeout()`, behave as "no ops"—that is, you can invoke them from your code, and no exception is thrown, but they have no effect. However, timeouts do work in JTA.

- **No interoperability**   The transaction services do not interoperate with other OTS implementations.

Transaction Demarcation and Transaction Context

A transaction has the property that it is *demarcated*—that is, it has a definite beginning and a definite end. A JTS transaction is initiated by a call to the `TS.begin()` method and terminated with a call to the `TS.commit()` method or the `TS.rollback()` method. These methods are discussed in a subsequent section of this chapter titled "Java Transaction Service Methods."

Note that every SQL `INSERT`, `DELETE`, and `UPDATE` statement in a server object must be executed within an active transaction. These transactions must be committed or rolled back with the JTS `commit()` and `rollback()` methods. They cannot be committed and rolled back with the SQL `COMMIT` and `ROLLBACK` statements, which do not apply to the "global" transaction consisting of CORBA and EJB server objects. However, an `INSERT`, `DELETE`, or `UPDATE` statement explicitly executed in the client is not part of the global transaction (it is executing in a separate session from the server objects), and hence must be committed and rolled back with the SQL `COMMIT` and `ROLLBACK` statements.

Transactions can be described as being client-side demarcated or server-side demarcated. In client-side demarcation, a transactional client explicitly executes demarcation methods that begin and end transactions. The begin and end demarcations are method calls on the client-side transaction service. See the section of this chapter titled "Using JTS Methods in CORBA Client Code," and the subsequent client-side demarcation example, for details. Remember that even if the global transaction—the statements to which the JTS methods apply—is client-side demarcated, it contains only the `INSERT`, `DELETE`, and `UPDATE` statements that appear in the server objects, and not such statements that appear directly by the client.

With server-side demarcation, the server object begins and ends a transaction. See the sections of this chapter titled "Using JTS Methods in CORBA Server Code" and "A Server-Side Demarcation Example," for details. Note that a transaction can span several objects, any one of which can end that transaction.

The *transaction context* is a pseudo-object that is passed to the server object from the client, or from one server object to another (when a server object is acting like a client by invoking a method in another server object). The transaction context records the state of the transaction.

After a client-side transaction service is initialized, and a begin transaction method is invoked, the transaction service implicitly creates a transaction context and assigns a transaction ID number to the context. The client transaction service then propagates the transaction context to each object that the client invokes.

The transaction contexts are propagated transparently from the transaction initiator to the server object. On the client side, an interceptor is engaged to submit the transaction context on any method call to a server object. A server-side interceptor extracts the transaction context information and makes it available to the server object.

Note that if your client invokes several CORBA and EJB server objects, and a transaction begins in one of those server objects, there is no propagation of the transaction context to the other server objects. Therefore, a transaction that begins in one server object that is invoked by a client does not contain the updates executed in other server objects that are invoked by that client.

Transaction Service Interfaces

There are two classes that an application developer can use to interface with JTS:

- `TransactionService`.

- `UserTransaction`, implemented by `oracle.aurora.jts.client.AuroraTransactionService`. The `UserTransaction` class is used with EJBs, and so was discussed in Chapter 4 of this book.

You use the `TransactionService` class to initialize a transaction on the client. To do this, you must import several classes in your Java client source code:

```
import oracle.aurora.jts.client.AuroraTransactionService;
import javax.jts.*;
import oracle.aurora.jts.util.*;
```

These classes are included in the library file `aurora_client.jar`, which must be in the `classpath` when compiling and executing all source files that use the JTS.

The one method in `AuroraTransactionService` that you can call is

```
public synchronized static void initialize(
    Context initialContext, String serviceName )
```

The purpose of this method is to initialize the transaction context on a client. The `initialContext` parameter is a context object returned by a JNDI `Context` constructor. The `serviceName` parameter is a complete service name, such as

```
sess_iiop://localhost:2481:ORCL
```

For example, the following code fragment includes the invocation of the `initialize()` method:

```
Hashtable env = new Hashtable();
env.put( Context.URL_PKG_PREFIXES, "oracle.aurora.jndi" );
env.put( Context.SECURITY_PRINCIPAL, "scott" );
env.put( Context.SECURITY_CREDENTIALS, "tiger" );
```

```
env.put( Context.SECURITY_AUTHENTICATION, ServiceCtx.NON_SSL_LOGIN );
Context initialContext = new InitialContext( env );
AuroraTransactionService.initialize(
  initialContext, "sess_iiop://localhost:2481:ORCL" );
```

Java Transaction Service Methods

The jts package contains methods that a client or server object can use to begin transactions, commit transactions, roll back transactions, and perform utility functions such as setting the transaction timeout. These JTS methods can be used in CORBA clients, EJB clients, and CORBA server objects. EJB developers who need transaction control with Beans should use the UserTransaction **interface** in a Bean-managed state. See Chapter 4 for details.

In order to use the JTS methods, you must include the following **import** statements in your source code:

```
import oracle.aurora.jts.util.TS;
import javax.jts.util*;
import org.omg.CosTransactions.*;
```

The oracle.aurora.jts.util package is included in the library file aurora_client.jar, which must be in the classpath for all Java sources that use the jts package.

The transaction service is provided by the following **static** methods in the TS class.

public static synchronized TransactionService getTS( )

The getTS() method returns a transaction service object. The getCurrent() method is then invoked on that transaction service object to return a Current pseudo-object, which is the transaction context. It is that Current pseudo-object on which you invoke methods such as commit() and rollback() to accomplish the actual transaction processing.

The following code fragment illustrates the beginning of a new transaction on a client, starting with obtaining the JNDI initial context:

```
import oracle.aurora.jndi.sess_iiop.ServiceCtx;
import oracle.aurora.jts.client.AuroraTransactionService;
import javax.naming.Context;
import javax.naming.InitialContext;
import java.util.Hashtable;
...
Context ic = new InitialContext( env );
```

```
...
AuroraTransactionService.initialize(
  ic, "sess_iiop://localhost:2481:ORCL" );
...
Account account = ( Account )ic.lookup(
  "sess_iiop://localhost:2481:ORCL/test/Account" );
oracle.aurora.jts.util.TS.getTS().getCurrent().begin();
```

If no transaction service is available, `getTS()` throws a `NoTransactionService` exception.

The following methods can be invoked on the `Current` class.

public void begin()

This method begins a new transaction. `begin()` can throw the following exceptions:

- `NoTransactionService` is thrown if you have not initialized a transaction context.

- `SubtransactionsUnavailable` is thrown if you call `begin()` before the current transaction has been committed or rolled back.

public Control suspend()

This method suspends the current transaction in the session, enabling a new transaction to be initiated. `suspend()` returns a `Control` pseudo-object on which you will invoke any subsequent `resume()` calls. The following illustrates a `suspend()` invocation:

```
org.omg.CosTransactions.Control control =
    oracle.aurora.jts.util.TS.getTS().getCurrent().suspend();
```

`suspend()` can throw the following exceptions:

- `NoTransactionService` is thrown if you have not initialized a transaction context.

- `TransactionDoesNotExist` is thrown if you do not have an active transaction context. This can occur if a `suspend()` call follows a previous `suspend()` call, with no intervening `resume()` call.

public void resume(Control control)

This method resumes a suspended transaction. `resume()` is invoked after a suspend, in order to resume the specified transaction context. The `control` parameter must be the transaction `Control` object that was returned by the previous matching `suspend()` invocation in the same session. The following code fragment illustrates the invocation of the `resume()` method:

```
org.omg.CosTransactions.Control control =
  oracle.aurora.jts.util.TS.getTS().getCurrent().suspend();
...
oracle.aurora.jts.util.TS.getTS().getCurrent().resume( control );
```

`resume()` can throw the `InvalidControl` exception if the `control` parameter is `null` or not valid.

public void commit(boolean report_heuristics)

This method commits the current transaction. You must set the `report_heuristics` parameter to `false`. You would set the `report_heuristics` parameter to `true` if you wanted extra information on two-phase commits. However, since the JServer does not currently support the two-phase commit protocol for distributed objects, you must currently set the `report_heuristics` to `false`. This parameter is included for compatibility with future releases of the JServer.

`commit()` can throw the following exceptions:

- `HeuristicMixed` is thrown if `report_heuristics` was set to `true`, a two-phase commit is in progress, a heuristic decision has been made, and some relevant updates in the transaction have been committed, while some others have been rolled back.

- `HeuristicHazard` is thrown if `report_heuristics` was set to `true`, a two-phase commit is in progress, and some relevant updates have been rolled back.

- `NoTransaction` is thrown if there is no active transaction.

public void rollback()

This method rolls back the effects of the current transaction. Because invoking `rollback()`, just like invoking `commit()`, will end the current transaction, invoking any JTS method except `begin()` after a `rollback()`, will throw a `NoTransaction` exception.

`rollback()` will throw the `NoTransaction` exception if you are not in a transaction context.

public void rollback_only()

This method modifies the transaction associated with the current thread so that the only possible outcome is to roll back the transaction. `rollback_only()` will throw the `NoTransaction` exception if you are not in a transaction context.

public void set_timeout(int seconds)

This method is currently not supported, and has no effect if invoked. The default timeout value is 60 seconds in all cases.

public Status get_status()

This method is invoked to discover the status of the current transaction. Some of the possible return values are as follows:

- `javax.transaction.Status.StatusActive`
- `javax.transaction.Status.StatusMarkedRollback`
- `javax.transaction.Status.StatusNoTransaction`

The complete set of status `int` values is defined in `javax.transaction.Status`.

public String get_transaction_name()

This method returns the name of the current transaction. If `get_transaction_name()` is invoked when no transaction is active, or outside of a transaction context, a null string is returned.

Using JTS Methods in CORBA Client Code

You should employ the following steps to use JTS methods in your CORBA client code:

1. Import the following packages:

   ```
   oracle.aurora.jts.client.AuroraTransactionService
   oracle.aurora.jts.util.TS
   org.omg.CosTransactions
   ```

2. Invoke the `AuroraTransactionService.initialize()` method, passing it the `serviceURL` and JNDI initial context parameters.

3. Begin a transaction by invoking:

   ```
   oracle.aurora.jts.util.TS.getTS().getCurrent().begin()
   ```

4. End the transaction by invoking `TS.getTS().getCurrent().commit( false )` or `TS.getTS().getCurrent().rollback()`.

The following code fragment illustrates these steps:

```
import oracle.aurora.jndi.sess_iiop.ServiceCtx;
import oracle.aurora.jts.client.AuroraTransactionService;
import oracle.aurora.jts.util.TS;
import org.omg.CosTransactions.*;
...
// Initialize a transaction context.
AuroraTransactionService.initialize( ic,
  "sess_iiop://localhost:2481:ORCL" );

// Begin a transaction.
TS.getTS().getCurrent().begin();
...
// Commit the transaction.
TS.getTS().getCurrent().commit( false );
```

A complete client-side demarcation example is contained in the subsequent section.

A Client-Side Demarcation Example

In this example, a `deleteAccount()` method is added to the `Account` object from Chapter 6. This method deletes an account row from the `ACCOUNT_LIST` table, given the account number of that row. The `deleteAccount()` method is implemented in SQLJ. A CORBA client is then coded that invokes the `deleteAccount()` method within a transaction context.

The first step is to code the IDL file:

```
/* File Name: account.idl */

module account {
  struct AccountInfo { long departmentno; long projectno; };

  exception NoAccountError { wstring mess; };
  exception DeleteAccountError { wstring mess; };

  interface Account {
    AccountInfo getAccountInfo( in long accountno )
      raises( NoAccountError );
    void deleteAccount( in long accountno )
      raises( NoAccountError, DeleteAccountError );
  };
};
```

The next step is to implement the `Account` object in SQLJ. An implementation in JDBC is provided on the CD for this book, and on the Web sites referenced in the introduction to this book.

```
/* Program Name:  AccountImpl.sqlj
**
** Purpose:  Implement Account object.  Two methods are provided:
**           one to return account information and one to delete
**           an ACCOUNT_LIST row.
**
*/

package accountServer;

import account.*;
import java.sql.*;

public class AccountImpl extends _AccountImplBase {
  public AccountInfo getAccountInfo( int accountno )
    throws NoAccountError {
    try {

      // You must initialize variables to be selected into.
      int departmentno = 0;
      int projectno = 0;

      #sql {
        SELECT departmentno, projectno
          INTO :departmentno, :projectno
            FROM ACCOUNT_LIST
              WHERE accountno = :accountno
      };
      return new AccountInfo( departmentno, projectno );
    }

    catch( SQLException e ) {
      throw new NoAccountError( e.getMessage() );
    }
  }

  // Delete desired account.
  public void deleteAccount( int accountno )
    throws NoAccountError, DeleteAccountError {
    try {
      int acctno = 0;
      #sql {
```

```
                    SELECT accountno
                      INTO :acctno
                        FROM ACCOUNT_LIST
                          WHERE accountno = :accountno
                  };
                }

                // SELECT INTO failed (probably) due to nonexistent row.
                catch( SQLException e ) {
                  throw new NoAccountError( e.getMessage() );
                }

                try {
                  #sql {
                    DELETE FROM ACCOUNT_LIST
                      WHERE accountno = :accountno
                  };
                }

                // Delete failed.
                catch( SQLException e ) {
                  throw new DeleteAccountError( e.getMessage() );
                }
              }
            }
```

Finally, the client program is coded:

```
/* Program Name: AccountUser6.java
**
** Purpose:  Use the Account server object to delete
**           account 1056 from the ACCOUNT_LIST table.
**
*/
import account.*;
import accountServer.*;

// Import JNDI property constants.
import oracle.aurora.jndi.sess_iiop.ServiceCtx;

// Import the JNDI Context Interface.
import javax.naming.Context;

/* Import the InitialContext class that implements the
   Context Interface.
```

```
*/
import javax.naming.InitialContext;

/* Import the hash table class to hold the initial context
   properties environment.
*/
import java.util.Hashtable;

// Import classes for transaction processing.
import oracle.aurora.jts.util.*;
import org.omg.CosTransactions.*;
import oracle.aurora.jts.client.AuroraTransactionService;

public class AccountUser6 {

  // main throws instead of catching exceptions.
  public static void main( String[] args ) throws Exception {

    // Instantiate and populate InitialContext object.
    Hashtable env = new Hashtable();
    env.put( Context.URL_PKG_PREFIXES, "oracle.aurora.jndi" );
    env.put( Context.SECURITY_PRINCIPAL, "scott" );
    env.put( Context.SECURITY_CREDENTIALS, "tiger" );
    env.put( Context.SECURITY_AUTHENTICATION,
      ServiceCtx.NON_SSL_LOGIN );
    Context ic = new InitialContext( env );

    // Initialize Aurora transaction service.
    AuroraTransactionService.initialize(
      ic, "sess_iiop://localhost:2481:ORCL" );

    // Lookup object name, obtaining object reference.
    Account account = ( Account )
      ic.lookup( "sess_iiop://localhost:2481:ORCL/test/Account" );

    // Begin transaction.
    TS.getTS().getCurrent().begin();

    // Delete 1056 account.
    account.deleteAccount( 1056 );

    // Commit transaction.
    TS.getTS().getCurrent().commit( false );
  }
}
```

Using JTS Methods in CORBA Server Code

The following steps indicate how to use JTS methods in your CORBA server code:

1. Import `oracle.aurora.jts.TS` and `org.omg.CosTransactions.*`.

2. You need not initialize the aurora transaction service by invoking `AuroraTransactionService.initialize()` in the server, since the server does this for you.

3. Begin a transaction by invoking `TS.getTS().getCurrent().begin()`. You can do this in a separate method, or in the method that executes the first SQL DML command using SQLJ or JDBC. A transaction spans methods, as its scope is within the session where it began.

4. End the transaction by invoking `TS.getTS().getCurrent().commit( false )` or `TS.getTS.getCurrent().rollback()`.

A complete server-side demarcation example is contained in the subsequent section.

A Server-Side Demarcation Example

In this example, all the transaction processing methods are invoked in the implementation of the server object. The IDL from the previous example is modified so as to provide an exception that will pass messages back to the client that were reported to the server object because of transaction method failures.

```
/* File Name: account.idl */

module account {

  struct AccountInfo { long departmentno; long projectno; };

  exception NoAccountError { wstring mess; };
  exception DeleteAccountError { wstring mess; };
  exception TransactionError { wstring mess; };

  interface Account {
    AccountInfo getAccountInfo( in long accountno )
      raises( NoAccountError );
    void deleteAccount( in long accountno )
      raises( NoAccountError, DeleteAccountError, TransactionError );
  };
};
```

The server object is then implemented so as to accomplish transaction processing. The following implementation is coded in SQLJ. An implementation in JDBC is provided on the CD for this book, and on the Web sites referenced in the introduction to this book.

```
/* Program Name:  AccountImpl.sqlj
**
** Purpose:  Implement Account object.  Two methods are provided:
**           one to return account information and one to delete
**           an ACCOUNT_LIST row.  The delete method invokes
**           transaction processing methods.
**
*/

package accountServer;

import account.*;
import java.sql.*;

// Import classes for transaction processing.
import oracle.aurora.jts.util.*;
import org.omg.CosTransactions.*;
import oracle.aurora.jts.client.AuroraTransactionService;

public class AccountImpl extends _AccountImplBase {
  public AccountInfo getAccountInfo( int accountno )
    throws NoAccountError {
    try {

      // You must initialize variables to be selected into.
      int departmentno = 0;
      int projectno = 0;

      #sql {
        SELECT departmentno, projectno
          INTO :departmentno, :projectno
            FROM ACCOUNT_LIST
              WHERE accountno = :accountno
      };

      return new AccountInfo( departmentno, projectno );
    }

    catch( SQLException e ) {
      throw new NoAccountError( e.getMessage() );
    }
  }
```

```java
// Delete desired account.
public void deleteAccount( int accountno )
  throws NoAccountError, DeleteAccountError, TransactionError {

  // Begin transaction.
  try {
    TS.getTS().getCurrent().begin();
  }

  // Begin failed.
  catch( Exception e ) {
    throw new TransactionError( "Begin failed: " + e );
  }

  try {
    int acctno = 0;
    #sql {
      SELECT accountno
        INTO :acctno
          FROM ACCOUNT_LIST
            WHERE accountno = :accountno
    };
  }

  // SELECT INTO failed (probably) due to nonexistent row.
  catch( SQLException e ) {
    throw new NoAccountError( e.getMessage() );
  }

  try {
    #sql {
      DELETE FROM ACCOUNT_LIST
        WHERE accountno = :accountno
    };
  }

  // Delete failed.
  catch( SQLException e ) {
    throw new DeleteAccountError( e.getMessage() );
  }

  // Commit transaction.
  try {
    TS.getTS().getCurrent().commit( false );
  }

  // Commit failed.
  catch( Exception e ) {
```

```
            throw new TransactionError( "Commit failed: " + e );
        }
    }
}
```

The client code is now relieved of invoking transaction processing methods:

```
/* Program Name: AccountUser7.java
**
** Purpose:  Use the Account server object to delete
**           account 1056 from the ACCOUNT_LIST table.
**
*/
import account.*;
import accountServer.*;

// Import JNDI property constants.
import oracle.aurora.jndi.sess_iiop.ServiceCtx;

// Import the JNDI Context Interface.
import javax.naming.Context;

/* Import the InitialContext class that implements the
   Context Interface.
*/
import javax.naming.InitialContext;

/* Import the hash table class to hold the initial context
   properties environment.
*/
import java.util.Hashtable;

public class AccountUser7 {

    // main throws instead of catching exceptions.
    public static void main( String[] args ) throws Exception {

        // Instantiate and populate InitialContext object.
        Hashtable env = new Hashtable();
        env.put( Context.URL_PKG_PREFIXES, "oracle.aurora.jndi" );
        env.put( Context.SECURITY_PRINCIPAL, "scott" );
        env.put( Context.SECURITY_CREDENTIALS, "tiger" );
        env.put( Context.SECURITY_AUTHENTICATION,
          ServiceCtx.NON_SSL_LOGIN );
        Context ic = new InitialContext( env );

        // Lookup object name, obtaining object reference.
```

```
    Account account = ( Account )
      ic.lookup( "sess_iiop://localhost:2481:ORCL/test/Account" );

    // Delete 1056 account.
    account.deleteAccount( 1056 );
  }
}
```

A CORBA Server Object Component

In this section you will create a CORBA server object component to manipulate the ACCOUNT_LIST table. This server object extends and refines the server object defined in the preceding section. As was the case in the previous section, all transaction processing is accomplished in the server object.

What is a component? As you have seen in previous chapters of this book, a *component* is a unit of composition with contractually specified interfaces and explicit context dependencies. A component can be deployed independently or can be subject to composition by third parties (see *Oracle8i SQLJ Programming* [37, p. 308]). What this means is that a component is a unit of software which is sufficiently well-specified and self-contained that it can be easily deployed by itself, as well as being easily integrated with other software units. A CORBA component may be implemented as a single CORBA server object, or a logically related collection of server objects.

In this section, a component to manipulate the ACCOUNT_LIST table will be implemented as a single server object called AccountList. This server object will provide methods for retrieving a row from the ACCOUNT_LIST table, inserting a row into the ACCOUNT_LIST table, deleting a row from the ACCOUNT_LIST table, beginning a transaction, committing a transaction, and rolling back a transaction (see Figure 8-1). Also, a sample CORBA client that uses the component will be presented.

You will encounter in this section:

- An accountlist.idl file for the AccountList server object
- An implementation of the AccountList server object
- A CORBA client that uses the AccountList server object

```
┌─────────────────────────────────────────────────────────┐
│                                                         │
│   AccountList Interface                                 │
│   ───────────────────────────────────────────────      │
│   Operations:                                           │
│                                                         │
│   getAccount( in int accountno )                        │
│     raises( NoAccountError ) :AccountInfo               │
│                                                         │
│   deleteAccount( in int accountno )                     │
│     raises( NoAccountError ) :                          │
│                                                         │
│   insertAccount( in int accountno, in int departmentno, │
│     in int projectno ) raises( DuplicateAccountError ) :│
│                                                         │
│   beginTrans() raises( TransactionError ) :             │
│                                                         │
│   commitTrans() raises( TransactionError ) :            │
│                                                         │
│   rollbackTrans() raises( TransactionError ) :          │
│                                                         │
└─────────────────────────────────────────────────────────┘
```

FIGURE 8-1. *AccountList Interface*

accountlist.idl

The following is the IDL file for the AccountList server object:

```
/* File Name: accountlist.idl */

module accountlist {

  struct AccountInfo { long departmentno; long projectno; };

  exception NoAccountError { wstring mess; };
  exception TransactionError { wstring mess; };
  exception DuplicateAccountError { wstring mess; };
  exception DeleteAccountError { wstring mess; };
```

```
interface AccountList {
  AccountInfo getAccountInfo( in long accountno )
    raises( NoAccountError );
  void deleteAccount( in long accountno )
    raises( NoAccountError, DeleteAccountError );
  void insertAccount(
    in long accountno, in long departmentno, in long projectno )
      raises( DuplicateAccountError );
  void beginTrans() raises( TransactionError );
  void commitTrans() raises( TransactionError );
  void rollbackTrans() raises( TransactionError );
};
};
```

AccountListImpl.sqlj

The following is the implementation class for the `AccountList` server object coded in SQLJ. An implementation in JDBC is provided on the CD with this book and on the Web sites referenced in the introduction to this book.

```
/* Program Name:  AccountListImpl.sqlj
**
** Purpose:  Implement an AccountList object for manipulating
**           the ACCOUNT_LIST table.
**
*/

package accountlistServer;

import accountlist.*;
import java.sql.*;

import oracle.aurora.jts.util.*;
import org.omg.CosTransactions.*;

public class AccountListImpl extends _AccountListImplBase {

  // Retrieve desired account.
  public AccountInfo getAccountInfo( int accountno )
    throws NoAccountError {
    try {

      // You must initialize variables to be selected into.
      int departmentno = 0;
      int projectno = 0;

      #sql {
        SELECT departmentno, projectno
          INTO :departmentno, :projectno
```

```
            FROM ACCOUNT_LIST
                WHERE accountno = :accountno
        };
        return new AccountInfo( departmentno, projectno );
    }

    // Retrieval failed (probably) due to nonexistent row.
    catch( SQLException e ) {
      throw new NoAccountError( e.getMessage() );
    }
}

// Delete desired account.
public void deleteAccount( int accountno )
throws NoAccountError, DeleteAccountError {
    try {
        int acctno = 0;
        #sql {
          SELECT accountno
            INTO :acctno
              FROM ACCOUNT_LIST
                WHERE accountno = :accountno
        };
    }

    // SELECT INTO failed (probably) due to nonexistent row.
    catch( SQLException e ) {
      throw new NoAccountError( e.getMessage() );
    }

    try {
      #sql {
        DELETE FROM ACCOUNT_LIST
          WHERE accountno = :accountno
      };
    }

    // Delete failed.
    catch( SQLException e ) {
      throw new DeleteAccountError( e.getMessage() );
    }
}

// Insert new account.
public void insertAccount(
  int accountno, int departmentno, int projectno )
    throws DuplicateAccountError {
    try {
      #sql {
```

```
          INSERT INTO ACCOUNT_LIST
            VALUES(:accountno, :departmentno, :projectno )
       };
     }

     /* Insert failed (probably) due to account number
        already being in table.
     */
     catch( SQLException e ) {
       throw new DuplicateAccountError( e.getMessage() );
     }
   }

   // Begin transaction.
   public void beginTrans() throws TransactionError {
     try {
       TS.getTS().getCurrent().begin();
     }
     // Begin failed.
     catch( Exception e ) {
       throw new TransactionError( e.getMessage() );
     }
   }

   // Commit transaction.
   public void commitTrans() throws TransactionError {
     try {
       TS.getTS().getCurrent().commit( false );
     }
     // Commit failed.
     catch( Exception e ) {
       throw new TransactionError( e.getMessage() );
     }
   }

   // Rollback transaction.
   public void rollbackTrans() throws TransactionError {
     try {
       TS.getTS().getCurrent().rollback();
     }
     // Rollback failed.
     catch( Exception e ) {
       throw new TransactionError( e.getMessage() );
     }
   }
}
```

CORBA Client for AccountList Component

The following is a CORBA client for the `AccountList` server object.

```
/* Program Name: AccountListUser.java
**
** Purpose:  Use the AccountList component to get account
**           information for the account 1056, delete
**           account 1056, and insert an account 2056.
**
*/
import accountlist.*;
import accountlistServer.*;

// Import JNDI property constants.
import oracle.aurora.jndi.sess_iiop.ServiceCtx;

// Import the JNDI Context Interface.
import javax.naming.Context;

/* Import the InitialContext class that implements the
   Context Interface.
*/
import javax.naming.InitialContext;

/* Import the hash table class to hold the initial context
   properties environment.
*/
import java.util.Hashtable;

public class AccountListUser {

  // main throws instead of catching exceptions.
  public static void main( String[] args )
    throws Exception {

    // Instantiate and populate InitialContext object.
    Hashtable env = new Hashtable();
    env.put( Context.URL_PKG_PREFIXES, "oracle.aurora.jndi" );
    env.put( Context.SECURITY_PRINCIPAL, "scott" );
    env.put( Context.SECURITY_CREDENTIALS, "tiger" );
    env.put( Context.SECURITY_AUTHENTICATION,
      ServiceCtx.NON_SSL_LOGIN );
    Context ic = new InitialContext( env );

    // Lookup object name, obtaining object reference.
```

```
AccountList account = ( AccountList )
  ic.lookup( "sess_iiop://localhost:2481:ORCL/test/AccountList" );


// Invoke getAccountInfo() method to get info for account 1056.
AccountInfo ai = account.getAccountInfo( 1056 );

// Print account information.
System.out.println( "Department number = " + ai.departmentno +
                    " Project number = " + ai.projectno );

// Begin transaction.
account.beginTrans();

// Delete 1056 account.
account.deleteAccount( 1056 );

// Insert 2056 account.
account.insertAccount( 2056, 200, 200 );

// Commit transaction consisting of delete and insert.
account.commitTrans();
  }
}
```

An Example Involving the Suspension and Resumption of a Transaction

This example illustrates the suspension of the current transaction, the initiation and committing of a new transaction, and the resumption and committing of the original transaction. The example consists of a client program that uses the AccountList component that was implemented in the preceding section to insert some ACCOUNT_LIST rows. Then the client uses that component to insert another ACCOUNT_LIST row in a second transaction, and finally the client uses that component to insert an ACCOUNT_LIST row in the original transaction.

The client program cannot use the beginTrans() and the commitTrans() methods from the AccountList server object because the JTS suspend() and resume() methods do not work with server-side demarcation.

```
/* Program Name: AccountListUser2.java
**
** Purpose:  Use the AccountList server object to insert
**           rows into the ACCOUNT_LIST table within
**           a transaction, suspend that transaction,
**           begin a second transaction, insert an
```

```
**          ACCOUNT_LIST row in that second
**          transaction, resume the first transaction,
**          and insert a row into the ACCOUNT_LIST table
**          within the first transaction.
**
*/
import accountlist.*;
import accountlistServer.*;

// Import classes for transaction processing.
import oracle.aurora.jts.util.*;
import org.omg.CosTransactions.*;
import oracle.aurora.jts.client.AuroraTransactionService;

// Import JNDI property constants.
import oracle.aurora.jndi.sess_iiop.ServiceCtx;

// Import the JNDI Context Interface.
import javax.naming.Context;

/* Import the InitialContext class that implements the
   Context Interface.
*/
import javax.naming.InitialContext;

/* Import the hash table class to hold the initial context
   properties environment.
*/
import java.util.Hashtable;

public class AccountListUser2 {

  // main throws instead of catching exceptions.
  public static void main( String[] args )
    throws Exception {

    // Instantiate and populate InitialContext object.
    Hashtable env = new Hashtable();
    env.put( Context.URL_PKG_PREFIXES, "oracle.aurora.jndi" );
    env.put( Context.SECURITY_PRINCIPAL, "scott" );
    env.put( Context.SECURITY_CREDENTIALS, "tiger" );
    env.put( Context.SECURITY_AUTHENTICATION,
      ServiceCtx.NON_SSL_LOGIN );
    Context ic = new InitialContext( env );

    // Initialize Aurora transaction service.
    AuroraTransactionService.initialize(
      ic, "sess_iiop://localhost:2481:ORCL" );
```

```
         // Lookup object name, obtaining object reference.
         AccountList account = ( AccountList )
           ic.lookup( "sess_iiop://localhost:2481:ORCL/test/AccountList" );

         // Begin ACCOUNT_LIST transaction.
         TS.getTS().getCurrent().begin();

         //Insert three ACCOUNT_LIST records.
         account.insertAccount( 3056, 200, 200 );
         account.insertAccount( 4056, 200, 200 );
         account.insertAccount( 5056, 200, 200 );

         // Suspend first transaction.
         Control c = TS.getTS().getCurrent().suspend();

         // Begin second transaction.
         TS.getTS().getCurrent().begin();

         // Insert ACCOUNT_LIST row.
         account.insertAccount( 7056, 200, 200 );

         // Commit second transaction.
         TS.getTS().getCurrent().commit( false );

         // Resume suspended ACCOUNT_LIST transaction.
         TS.getTS().getCurrent().resume(c);

         // Insert ACCOUNT_LIST row.
         account.insertAccount( 6056, 200, 200 );

         // Commit first ACCOUNT_LIST transaction.
         TS.getTS().getCurrent().commit( false );
      }
   }
```

A Client that Accesses an EJB Component

In this section you will encounter a client program that uses the EJB
ObservationBean component from Chapter 4 to insert a row into the
OCEANIC_OBSERVATION_LIST table. This client program will accomplish all the
transaction processing for the insert, using the CORBA TransactionService
instead of the EJB UserTransaction.

```
/* Program Name: ObsRemoteUser.java
**
** Purpose:  Use the ObsRemote interface to insert an
```

```
**              OCEANIC_OBSERVATION_LIST row.
**
*/
import java.sql.*;
import oracle.aurora.jts.util.*;
import org.omg.CosTransactions.*;
import oracle.aurora.jts.client.AuroraTransactionService;

// Import helper classes.
import helpers.ObsHelper;

import obsserver.ObsRemote;
import obsserver.ObsHome;

// Import JNDI property constants.
import oracle.aurora.jndi.sess_iiop.ServiceCtx;

// Import the JNDI Context Interface.
import javax.naming.Context;

/* Import the InitialContext class that implements the
   Context Interface.
*/
import javax.naming.InitialContext;

/* Import the hash table class to hold the initial context
   properties environment.
*/
import java.util.Hashtable;

public class ObsRemoteUser {

  // main throws instead of catching exceptions.
  public static void main( String[] args ) throws Exception {

    // Instantiate and populate InitialContext object.
    Hashtable env = new Hashtable();
    env.put( Context.URL_PKG_PREFIXES, "oracle.aurora.jndi" );
    env.put( Context.SECURITY_PRINCIPAL, "scott" );
    env.put( Context.SECURITY_CREDENTIALS, "tiger" );
    env.put( Context.SECURITY_AUTHENTICATION,
      ServiceCtx.NON_SSL_LOGIN );
    Context ic = new InitialContext( env );

    // Initialize Aurora transaction service.
    AuroraTransactionService.initialize(
      ic, "sess_iiop://localhost:2481:ORCL" );

    ObsHome myObsHome = null;
```

```
        ObsRemote myObservationBean = null;

        // Use the home interface to locate the EJB object.
        myObsHome = ( ObsHome )
          ic.lookup(
            "sess_iiop://localhost:2481:ORCL/test/ObservationBean" );

        // Create a Bean instance.
        myObservationBean = myObsHome.create();

        /* Invoke the Bean class method to retrieve the
           OCEANIC_OBSRVATION_LIST row for specified obs_id = 2.
           Pressure will be 0, instead of null.
        */
        ObsHelper obs = myObservationBean.getObsInfo(2);

        // Change date.
        obs.when_t="07-JUN-2000";

        // Begin transaction.
        TS.getTS().getCurrent().begin();

        /* Invoke insertObj() method to get a new obs_id and insert a
           new row with that obs_id into the OCEANIC_OBSERVATION_LIST
           table that is otherwise the same as the row for obs_id = 2,
           except for a different date and a pressure of zero.
        */
        ObsHelper oh = myObservationBean.insertObs( obs );

        // Commit transaction.
        TS.getTS().getCurrent().commit( false );
    }
}
```

A CORBA Client that Accesses an EJB Component and CORBA Server Object Component

In this section you encounter a CORBA client program that uses an EJB
`ObservationBean` component, as in the previous example, as well as uses the
`AccountList` CORBA component (see Figure 8-2). All transaction processing will
be done in the client, instead of being done through the `AccountList` transaction
methods, because invocation of the EJB from the client would not work if JTS
server-side transaction demarcation was accomplished in the invoked CORBA

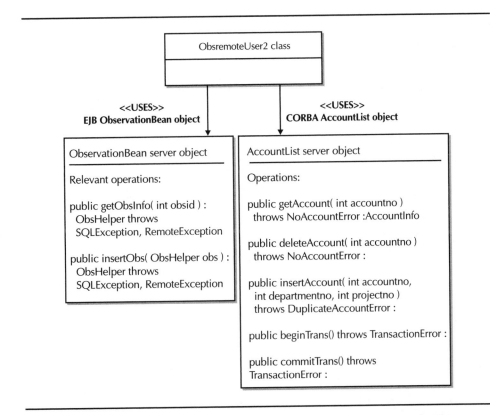

FIGURE 8-2. *ObsRemoteUser2 client uses EJB and CORBA server objects*

server object. It would not work because the transaction context will not be propagated from the server object to the EJB.

```
/* Program Name: ObsRemoteUser2.java
**
** Purpose:  Use the ObsRemote Interface to insert an
**           OCEANIC_OBSERVATION_LIST row, and use the
**           AccountList server object to insert an
**           ACCOUNT_LIST row.
**
*/
import accountlist.*;
import accountlistServer.*;

import java.sql.*;
```

```java
import oracle.aurora.jts.util.*;
import org.omg.CosTransactions.*;
import oracle.aurora.jts.client.AuroraTransactionService;

// Import helper classes.
import helpers.ObsHelper;

import obsserver.ObsRemote;
import obsserver.ObsHome;

// Import JNDI property constants.
import oracle.aurora.jndi.sess_iiop.ServiceCtx;

// Import the JNDI Context Interface.
import javax.naming.Context;

/* Import the InitialContext class that implements the
   Context Interface.
*/
import javax.naming.InitialContext;

/* Import the hash table class to hold the initial context
   properties environment.
*/
import java.util.Hashtable;

public class ObsRemoteUser2 {

  // main throws instead of catching exceptions.
  public static void main( String[] args ) throws Exception {

    // Instantiate and populate InitialContext object.
    Hashtable env = new Hashtable();
    env.put( Context.URL_PKG_PREFIXES, "oracle.aurora.jndi" );
    env.put( Context.SECURITY_PRINCIPAL, "scott" );
    env.put( Context.SECURITY_CREDENTIALS, "tiger" );
    env.put( Context.SECURITY_AUTHENTICATION,
      ServiceCtx.NON_SSL_LOGIN );
    Context ic = new InitialContext( env );

    // Initialize Aurora transaction service.
    AuroraTransactionService.initialize(
      ic, "sess_iiop://localhost:2481:ORCL" );

    // Lookup AccountList object name, obtaining object reference.
    AccountList account = ( AccountList )
      ic.lookup( "sess_iiop://localhost:2481:ORCL/test/AccountList" );
    ObsHome myObsHome = null;
    ObsRemote myObservationBean = null;
```

```
// Use the home interface to locate the EJB object.
myObsHome = ( ObsHome )
  ic.lookup(
    "sess_iiop://localhost:2481:ORCL/test/ObservationBean" );

// Create a Bean instance.
myObservationBean = myObsHome.create();

/* Invoke the Bean class method to retrieve the
   OCEANIC_OBSERVATION_LIST row for specified obs_id = 2.
   Pressure will be 0, instead of null.
*/
ObsHelper obs = myObservationBean.getObsInfo(2);

// Change date.
obs.when_t="07-JUN-2000";

// Begin transaction.
TS.getTS().getCurrent().begin();

/* Invoke insertObj() method to get a new obs_id and insert a
   new row with that obs_id into the OCEANIC_OBSERVATION_LIST
   table that is otherwise the same as the row for obs_id = 2,
   except for a different date and a pressure of zero.
*/
ObsHelper oh = myObservationBean.insertObs( obs );

// Insert 7056 account.
account.insertAccount( 7056, 200, 200 );

// Commit transaction.
TS.getTS().getCurrent().commit( false );
  }
}
```

JTA

In Oracle version 8.1.7, JTA replaces JTS as the primary transaction API. You encountered some advantages of JTA over JTS in the section of this chapter titled "Limitations of JTS." In this section, you will learn how to implement client-side and server-side transaction demarcation using JTA. In particular, you will encounter the following:

■ The structure of a client with JTA client-side demarcation

■ A JTA client-side demarcation example

■ The structure of a server object implementation with JTA server-side demarcation

The Structure of a Client with JTA Client-Side Demarcation

When using the JTA transaction API for CORBA applications, as well as for EJB applications, you employ the `UserTransaction` class. Before the client can be started, you must first bind the `UserTransaction` object in the namespace. You can bind the `UserTransaction` object in the namespace through the `bindut` command of the `sess_sh` tool. For example, if you want to bind a `UserTransaction` object to the name "`/test/hit`" in the namespace located on the host data-i.com, you would execute the following:

```
sess_sh -service jdbc:oracle:thin:@data-i.com:2481:ORCL
-user SCOTT -password TIGER & bindut /test/hit -url

jdbc:oracle:thin@data-i.com:2481:ORCL
```

The client has the following structure with respect to JTA transaction processing:

1. Specify the location of the namespace where the transaction object is bound. This is inserted into the hash table that will be used to initialize the `InitialContext` object:

   ```
   Hashtable env = new Hashtable();
   env.put( jdbc_accessURLContextFactory.CONNECTION_URL_PROP,
     "jdbc:oracle:thin:data-i.com:2481:ORCL" );
   ...
   Context ic = new InitialContext( env );
   ```

2. Register the JDBC `OracleDriver`:

   ```
   DriverManager.registerDriver( new
   oracle.jdbc.driver.OracleDriver() );
   ```

3. Retrieve the `UserTransaction` object from the JNDI namespace:

   ```
   UserTransaction ut = ( UserTransaction )
     ic.lookup( "jdbc_access:/test/hit" );
   ```

4. Begin the transaction:

   ```
   ut.begin()
   ```

5. Retrieve server objects and execute their methods. This is done the same way as with JTS.

6. Commit the transaction:

   ```
   ut.commit();
   ```

A JTA Client-Side Demarcation Example

You will learn differences between JTA client-side transaction demarcation and the corresponding JTS client-side transaction demarcation by considering the following modification of the JTS client given in this chapter in the section titled "A Client-Side Demarcation Example."

```
/* Program Name: AccountUserJTA.java
**
** Purpose:  Use the Account server object to delete
**           account 1056 from the ACCOUNT_LIST table.
**
*/
import account.*;
import accountServer.*;

import java.sql.DriverManager;
import javax.transaction.UserTransaction;
import javax.naming.NamingException;
import oracle.aurora.jndi.jdbc_access.jdbc_accessURLContextFactory;
import oracle.aurora.jndi.sess_iiop.ServiceCtx;

// Import JNDI property constants.
import oracle.aurora.jndi.sess_iiop.ServiceCtx;

// Import the JNDI Context Interface.
import javax.naming.Context;

/* Import the InitialContext class that implements the
   Context Interface.
*/
import javax.naming.InitialContext;

/* Import the hash table class to hold the initial context
   properties environment.
*/
import java.util.Hashtable;

public class AccountUserJTA {

  // main throws instead of catching exceptions.
  public static void main( String[] args ) throws Exception {

    // Instantiate and populate InitialContext object.
    Hashtable env = new Hashtable();
    env.put( Context.URL_PKG_PREFIXES, "oracle.aurora.jndi" );
    env.put( Context.SECURITY_PRINCIPAL, "scott" );
```

```
env.put( Context.SECURITY_CREDENTIALS, "tiger" );
env.put( Context.SECURITY_AUTHENTICATION,
  ServiceCtx.NON_SSL_LOGIN );
env.put( jdbc_accessURLContextFactory.CONNECTION_URL_PROP,
  "jdbc:oracle:thin:@data-i.com:2481:ORCL" );
Context ic = new InitialContext( env );

// Register a JDBC OracleDriver.
DriverManager.registerDriver(
  new oracle.jdbc.driver.OracleDriver() );

// Retrieve the UserTransaction object from JNDI namespace.
UserTransaction ut = ( UserTransaction )
  ic.lookup ( "jdbc_access:/test/hit" );

// Lookup server object name, obtaining object reference.
Account account = ( Account )
  ic.lookup( "sess_iiop://localhost:2481:ORCL/test/Account" );

// Begin transaction.
ut.begin();

// Delete 1056 account.
account.deleteAccount( 1056 );

// Commit transaction.
ut.commit( false );
  }
}
```

The Structure of a Server Object Implementation with JTA Server-Side Demarcation

The structure of a server object implementation with server-side JTA demarcation is identical to the structure of the preceding program, except that if the `UserTransaction` object is bound locally, only the JNDI name of the `UserTransaction` object needs to be supplied, and the initial context can be created without any set environment because the environment values are already known:

```
InitialContext ic = new InitialContext();
UserTransaction ut = ( UserTransaction ) ic.lookup( "/test/hit" );
```

In the preceding sections on JTA, you have encountered JTA transaction processing for a local database. You are encouraged to consult the *CORBA*

Developer's Guide, version 8.1.7 [32] for information on JTA transaction processing involving multiple remote databases.

Conclusion

In this chapter, you learned about the transaction management of components through CORBA. In particular, you were first presented with the limitations of the JTS API (some of which are removed in JTA that will be available in Oracle version 8.1.7), and were then presented with examples illustrating client-side and server-side transaction demarcation in JTS. Finally, you learned about JTA that will essentially replace JTS in Oracle version 8.1.7, especially for server-side demarcation applications.

In the next chapter, you will gain further insight into CORBA components by implementing a suite of CORBA components for the Purchase Order Schema.

CHAPTER

9

Purchase Order
Components

n this chapter, you will increase your skills at designing and implementing CORBA components by developing a suite of components for processing most of the tables in the Purchase Order Schema that was presented in Chapter 1. There will be one component for each table dealt with. If a table contains a foreign key, one of its component methods will return the full information for the designated table row, including the information contained in the row referenced by the foreign key value in that table row. In addition, the component for the `PURCHASE_LIST` table will contain a method that will return the full information for the purchase order, including the set of line item records for that purchase order. The latter is based on the one-to-many inverse of the foreign key relationship between line items and purchases.

For each component, you will consider the user requirements for the component and high-level view that specifies the design of the component, as well as considering the implementation and a sample client for the component. Note that all transaction demarcation will be accomplished in the client programs, due to the deficiencies of server-side demarcation (see the sections of Chapter 8 titled "Transaction Demarcation and Transaction Context" and "An Example Involving the Suspension and Resumption of a Transaction").

A component will be provided for each table in the purchase order schema, except for the `CREDITCARD_LIST`, `CHECKACCOUNT_LIST`, and `ACCOUNT_LIST` tables (a component for the `ACCOUNT_LIST` table was presented in the section of Chapter 8 titled "A CORBA Server Object Component"). Components for these latter tables can be produced in a manner similar to the production of components for the other tables, and is left as an exercise for the reader.

Therefore, in this chapter, you will consider the production of the following:

- A `DepartmentList` CORBA component
- An `EmployeeList` CORBA component
- A `VendorList` CORBA component
- A `ProjectList` CORBA component
- `PurchaseList` and `LineItemList` CORBA components

A `DepartmentList` CORBA Component

In this section, you will consider the production of a `DepartmentList` component as a CORBA server object. The production and use of such a component involves at least the following:

- Obtaining user requirements for the component

■   Developing a high-level view of the component that specifies the component

■   Implementing the high-level view

■   Developing clients that use the component

Even though a component is not bound to any one application, it does arise out of the needs of a community of users for a specific task to be performed (in this section, the task of processing the DEPARTMENT_LIST table). The user requirements express those needs for the task.

Because each component presented in this chapter will be implemented as a CORBA server object, the high-level view will specify the operations (methods) that the server object interface must provide, as well as specifying the relationship between the server object interface for the current component and the server object interfaces for the other components that the current component requires.

Next, the materialization of the server object is provided by the production of the IDL file for the server object and by the production of the server object implementation class. The IDL file specifies the server object as an interface that supports the methods given in the high level view (along with fully specifying the types that are required by the interface), and the server object implementation class implements those methods in Java.

Finally, the component can be used by a Java client.

This chapter provides the following:

■   The user requirements for DepartmentList

■   The high-level view of DepartmentList

■   The IDL file for DepartmentList

■   The server object implementation for DepartmentList

■   A client for DepartmentList

The User Requirements for DepartmentList

Assume that your users wish to be able to perform the following operations on the DEPARTMENT_LIST table:

■   Given a department number, get the non-primary key column values of the DEPARTMENT_LIST row that matches that department number.

■   Given a department number, delete the DEPARTMENT_LIST row that matches that department number.

■   Insert a row into the DEPARTMENT_LIST table that contains the specified column values.

The High-Level View of `DepartmentList`

Clearly, Figure 9-1 presents the high-level view of a component that satisfies the user requirements given in the preceding section. Note that exceptions corresponding to error conditions can be specified at this stage.

The IDL File for `DepartmentList`

The following IDL file expresses the specification of the `DepartmentList` component given in Figure 9-1:

```
/* File Name: departmentlist.idl */

module departmentlist {
  struct DepartmentInfo { wstring shortname; wstring longname; };

  exception NoDepartmentError { wstring mess; };
  exception DuplicateDepartmentError { wstring mess; };
  exception DeleteDepartmentError { wstring mess; };

  interface DepartmentList {
    DepartmentInfo getDepartmentInfo( in long departmentno )
      raises( NoDepartmentError );
    void deleteDepartment( in long departmentno )
      raises( NoDepartmentError, DeleteDepartmentError );
    void insertDepartment( in long departmentno,
      in wstring shortname, in wstring longname )
        raises( DuplicateDepartmentError );
  };
};
```

The Server Object Implementation for `DepartmentList`

The following SQLJ file contains the code for the `DepartmentListImpl` class that implements the operations specified in the IDL file from the preceding section.

```
┌─────────────────────────────────────────────────────────┐
│ DepartmentList Interface                                  │
├─────────────────────────────────────────────────────────┤
│ Operations:                                               │
│                                                           │
│  getDepartment( in long departmentno )                    │
│   raises( NoDepartmentError, DeleteDepartmentError )      │
│                                                           │
│  deleteDepartment( in long departmentno )                 │
│   raises( NoDepartmentError ) :                           │
│                                                           │
│  insertDepartment(                                        │
│    in long departmentno,                                  │
│     in wstring shortname,                                 │
│      in wstring longname )                                │
│        raises( DuplicateDepartmentError ) :               │
│                                                           │
└─────────────────────────────────────────────────────────┘
```

FIGURE 9-1. *High-level view of* `DepartmentList`

```
/* Program Name:  DepartmentListImpl.sqlj
**
** Purpose:  Implement a DepartmentList server object for
**           manipulating the DEPARTMENT_LIST table.
**
*/

package departmentlistServer;

import departmentlist.*;
import java.sql.*;

public class DepartmentListImpl extends _DepartmentListImplBase {

  // Retrieve desired department.
  public DepartmentInfo getDepartmentInfo( int departmentno )
    throws NoDepartmentError {
    try {
```

```
    // You must initialize variables to be selected into.
    String shortname = null;
    String longname = null;

    #sql {
      SELECT shortname, longname
        INTO :shortname, :longname
          FROM DEPARTMENT_LIST
            WHERE departmentno = :departmentno
    };
    return new DepartmentInfo( shortname, longname );
  }

  // Retrieval failed (probably) due to nonexistent row.
  catch( SQLException e ) {
    throw new NoDepartmentError( e.getMessage() );
  }
}

// Delete desired department.
public void deleteDepartment( int departmentno )
  throws NoDepartmentError, DeleteDepartmentError {
  try {
    int deptno = 0;
    #sql {
      SELECT departmentno
        INTO :deptno
          FROM DEPARTMENT_LIST
            WHERE departmentno = :departmentno
    };
  }

  // SELECT INTO failed (probably) due to nonexistent row.
  catch( SQLException e ) {
    throw new NoDepartmentError( e.getMessage() );
  }

  try {
    #sql {
      DELETE FROM DEPARTMENT_LIST
        WHERE departmentno = :departmentno
    };
  }

  // Delete failed.
  catch( SQLException e ) {
    throw new DeleteDepartmentError( e.getMessage() );
  }
```

```
    }

    // Insert new department.
    public void insertDepartment(
      int departmentno, String shortname, String longname )
        throws DuplicateDepartmentError {
      try {
        #sql {
          INSERT INTO DEPARTMENT_LIST
            VALUES( :departmentno, :shortname, :longname )
        };
      }

      /* Insert failed (probably) due to department number
         already being in table.
      */
      catch( SQLException e ) {
        throw new DuplicateDepartmentError( e.getMessage() );
      }
    }
  }
}
```

A Client for `DepartmentList`

The following Java source file contains a Java class that uses the `DepartmentList`
component by invoking the `getDepartmentInfo()`, `deleteDepartment()`,
and `insertDepartment()` methods:

```
/* Program Name: DepartmentListUser.java
**
** Purpose:  Use the DepartmentList component to get department
**           information for the department 200, delete
**           department 200, and insert a department 2056.
**
*/

// Import component classes.
import departmentlist.*;
import departmentlistServer.*;

// Import classes for transaction processing.
import oracle.aurora.jts.util.*;
import org.omg.CosTransactions.*;
import oracle.aurora.jts.client.AuroraTransactionService;

// Import JNDI property constants.
import oracle.aurora.jndi.sess_iiop.ServiceCtx;
```

```java
// Import the JNDI Context Interface.
import javax.naming.Context;

/* Import the InitialContext class that implements the
   Context Interface.
*/
import javax.naming.InitialContext;

/* Import the hash table class to hold the initial context
   properties environment.
*/
import java.util.Hashtable;

public class DepartmentListUser {

  // main throws instead of catching exceptions.
  public static void main( String[] args )
    throws Exception {

    // Instantiate and populate InitialContext object.
    Hashtable env = new Hashtable();
    env.put( Context.URL_PKG_PREFIXES, "oracle.aurora.jndi" );
    env.put( Context.SECURITY_PRINCIPAL, "scott" );
    env.put( Context.SECURITY_CREDENTIALS, "tiger" );
    env.put( Context.SECURITY_AUTHENTICATION,
      ServiceCtx.NON_SSL_LOGIN );
    Context ic = new InitialContext( env );

    // Initialize Aurora transaction service.
    AuroraTransactionService.initialize(
      ic, "sess_iiop://localhost:2481:ORCL" );

    // Lookup object name, obtaining object reference.
    DepartmentList department = ( DepartmentList )
      ic.lookup(
        "sess_iiop://localhost:2481:ORCL/test/DepartmentList" );

    /* Invoke getDepartmentInfo() method to get info for
       department 200.
    */
    DepartmentInfo di = department.getDepartmentInfo( 200 );

    // Print department information.
    System.out.println( "Short Name = " + di.shortname +
                        " Long Name = " + di.longname );

    // Begin transaction.
    TS.getTS().getCurrent().begin();
```

```
    // Delete 200 department.
    department.deleteDepartment( 200 );

    // Insert 2056 department.
    department.insertDepartment( 2056, "M", "Morgue" );

    // Commit transaction consisting of delete and insert.
    TS.getTS()..getCurrent().commit( false );
  }
}
```

An `EmployeeList` CORBA Component

The `EmployeeList` component is somewhat more complicated than the `DepartmentList` component presented previously in this chapter in that the information for the department referenced by the employee record through the `departmentno` foreign key must also be retrieved. This operation is requested in the user requirements.

In this section, you will see, in particular, how this operation is specified and implemented by considering:

- The user requirements for `EmployeeList`

- The high-level view of `EmployeeList`

- The IDL file for `EmployeeList`

- The server object implementation for `EmployeeList`

- A client for `EmployeeList`

The User Requirements for `EmployeeList`

Your users want you to provide the following operations in your component:

- Given an employee number, return the other values in the row for that employee in the `EMPLOYEE_LIST` table.

- Given an employee number, return the full information for the employee, including the non-primary key column values in the matching `EMPLOYEE_LIST` row, and the non-primary key values in the `DEPARTMENT_LIST` row that is referenced by the `departmentno` field in that `EMPLOYEE_LIST` row.

- Given an employee number, delete the matching `EMPLOYEE_LIST` row.

- Insert an `EMPLOYEE_LIST` row containing the specified column values.

The High-Level View of `EmployeeList`

Figure 9-2 contains the high-level view that specifies an `EmployeeList` component that satisfies the given user requirements. At this stage, you have decided that the operation that returns the full employee information will do this by returning an object that contains a reference to the `DepartmentInfo` object that was defined for the `DepartmentList` component, and will invoke the `getDepartmentInfo()` method from `DepartmentList` to obtain that `DepartmentInfo` object.

EmployeeList Interface	FullEmployeeInfo	DepartmentList Interface
Operations:	<<USES>>	Operations:
	DepartmentInfo	
getFullEmployeeInfo(		
in long employeeno)	getFullEmployeeInfo	getDepartmentInfo(
raises(NoEmployeeError)	<<USES>>	in long departmentno)
:FullEmployeeInfo	getDepartmentInfo	raises(NoDepartmentError)
		:DepartmentInfo
getEmployeeInfo(		
in long employeeno)		
raises(NoEmployeeError)		
:EmployeeInfo		
deleteEmployee(		
in long employeeno)		deleteDepartment(
raises(NoEmployeeError) :		in long departmentno)
DeleteEmployeeError)		raises(NoDepartmentError,
		DeleteDepartmentError) :
insertEmployee(		
in long employeeno,		
in long departmentno,		insertDepartment(
in wstring type,		in long departmentno,
in wstring lastname,		in wstring shortname,
in wstring firstname,		in wstring longname)
in wstring phone)		raises(
raises(		DuplicateDepartmentError) :
DuplicateEmployeeError) :		

FIGURE 9-2. *High-level view of* `EmployeeList`

The IDL File for `EmployeeList`

The following IDL file expresses most of the specification of the `EmployeeList` component given in Figure 9-2 (the fact that `getFullEmployeeInfo()` invokes `getDepartmentInfo()` is not expressed in the IDL file).

Because the `getFullEmployeeInfo()` method of the `EmployeeList` component requires the `DepartmentInfo` struct of the `DepartmentList` component, the IDL file for the `EmployeeList` component must include the IDL file for the `DepartmentList` component.

```
/* File Name: employeelist.idl */

// Include IDL file for referenced object.
#include <departmentlist.idl>

module employeelist {

  struct EmployeeInfo {
    long departmentno; wstring type;
      wstring lastname; wstring firstname; wstring phone;
  };

  /* FullEmployeeInfo holds reference to DepartmentInfo
     object for employee plus EMPLOYEE_LIST information.
  */
  struct FullEmployeeInfo {
    departmentlist::DepartmentInfo dinfo;
      long departmentno;
        wstring type; wstring lastname;
          wstring firstname; wstring phone;
  };

  exception NoEmployeeError { wstring mess; };
  exception DuplicateEmployeeError { wstring mess; };
  exception DeleteEmployeeError { wstring mess; };

  interface EmployeeList {
    EmployeeInfo getEmployeeInfo( in long employeeno )
      raises( NoEmployeeError );
    FullEmployeeInfo getFullEmployeeInfo( in long employeeno )
      raises( NoEmployeeError );
    void deleteEmployee( in long employeeno )
      raises( NoEmployeeError, DeleteEmployeeError );
    void insertEmployee(
      in long employeeno, in long departmentno, in wstring type,
        in wstring lastname, in wstring firstname, in wstring phone )
          raises( DuplicateEmployeeError );
  };
};
```

The Server Object Implementation for `EmployeeList`

The most complex method to implement in `EmployeeListImpl.sqlj` is the `getFullEmployeeInfo()` method. This method accesses another server object—namely, the `DepartmentList` object—so as to invoke the `getDepartmentInfo()` method of that server object to obtain the department information for the employee's department. Note that the `serviceURL` specified in the lookup for `DEPARTMENT_LIST` specifies `thisServer`, causing the `DepartmentList` server object to run in the same session as the `EmployeeList` server object. See the section of Chapter 7 titled "Session Startup from a Server Object" for more on this. This example would not work if `thisServer` was not specified, since a JTS transaction cannot span sessions.

```
/* Program Name:  EmployeeListImpl.sqlj
**
**
** Purpose:  Implement an EmployeeList server object for
**           manipulating the EMPLOYEE_LIST table.
**
*/

package employeelistServer;

import java.sql.*;
import employeelist.*;

// Import classes for DepartmentList component.
import departmentlist.*;
import departmentlistServer.*;

// Import JNDI property constants.
import oracle.aurora.jndi.sess_iiop.ServiceCtx;

// Import the JNDI Context Interface.
import javax.naming.Context;

/* Import the InitialContext class that implements the
   Context Interface.
*/
import javax.naming.InitialContext;

/* Import the hash table class to hold the initial context
   properties environment.
*/
```

```java
import java.util.Hashtable;

public class EmployeeListImpl extends _EmployeeListImplBase {

  // Retrieve desired employee information.
  public EmployeeInfo getEmployeeInfo( int employeeno )
    throws NoEmployeeError {
    try {

      // You must initialize variables to be selected into.
      int departmentno = 0;
      String type = null;
      String lastname = null;
      String firstname = null;
      String phone = null;

      #sql {
        SELECT departmentno, type, lastname, firstname, phone
          INTO :departmentno, :type, :lastname, :firstname, :phone
            FROM EMPLOYEE_LIST
              WHERE employeeno = :employeeno
      };
      return new EmployeeInfo(
        departmentno, type, lastname, firstname, phone );
    }

    // Retrieval failed (probably) due to nonexistent row.
    catch( SQLException e ) {
      throw new NoEmployeeError( e.getMessage() );
    }
  }

  /* Retrieve desired full employee information, including
     department information for the employee.
  */
  public FullEmployeeInfo getFullEmployeeInfo( int employeeno )
    throws NoEmployeeError {
    try {

      // Get employee info.
      EmployeeInfo ei = getEmployeeInfo( employeeno );

      // Get department info for employee.

      // Instantiate and populate InitialContext object.
      Hashtable env = new Hashtable();
      env.put( Context.URL_PKG_PREFIXES, "oracle.aurora.jndi" );
      Context ic = new InitialContext( env );
```

```
      /* Lookup DepartmentList object name, obtaining object
         reference.
      */
      DepartmentList department = ( DepartmentList )
        ic.lookup( "sess_iiop://thisServer/test/DepartmentList" );

      // Invoke getDepartment() method to get info for department.
      DepartmentInfo di =
        department.getDepartmentInfo( ei.departmentno );

      /* Return FullEmployeeInfo object that includes reference to
         DepartmentInfo object for the employee's department.
      */
      return(
        new FullEmployeeInfo(
          di, ei.departmentno, ei.type,
            ei.lastname, ei.firstname, ei.phone ) );
    }

    // Catch any exceptions raised.
    catch( Exception e ) {
      throw new NoEmployeeError( e.getMessage() );
    }
  }

  // Delete desired employee.
  public void deleteEmployee( int employeeno )
    throws NoEmployeeError, DeleteEmployeeError {
    try {
      int empno = 0;
      #sql {
        SELECT employeeno
          INTO :empno
            FROM EMPLOYEE_LIST
              WHERE employeeno = :employeeno
      };
    }

    // SELECT INTO failed (probably) due to nonexistent row.
    catch( SQLException e ) {
      throw new NoEmployeeError( e.getMessage() );
    }
    try {
      #sql {
        DELETE FROM EMPLOYEE_LIST
          WHERE employeeno = :employeeno
      };
    }
```

```
    // Delete failed.
    catch( SQLException e ) {
      throw new DeleteEmployeeError( e.getMessage() );
     }
  }

  // Insert new employee.
  public void insertEmployee(
    int employeeno, int departmentno, String type,
      String lastname, String firstname, String phone )
        throws DuplicateEmployeeError {
    try {
      #sql {
        INSERT INTO EMPLOYEE_LIST
          VALUES( :employeeno, :departmentno, :type,
            :lastname, :firstname, :phone )
      };
    }

    /* Insert failed (probably) due to employee number
      already being in table.
    */
    catch( SQLException e ) {
      throw new DuplicateEmployeeError( e.getMessage() );
    }
  }
}
```

A Client for `EmployeeList`

The following CORBA client program accesses the `EmployeeList` server object,
invokes the `getFullEmployee()` method to obtain employee information for a
specific employee (including the information concerning the employee's department),
deletes that same employee from the `EMPLOYEE_LIST` table, and inserts a new
employee into the `EMPLOYEE_LIST` table:

```
/* Program Name: EmployeeListUser.java
**
** Purpose:  Use the EmployeeList component to get full
**           employee information for the employee 104,
**           delete employee 104, and insert an employee 2056.
**
*/

// Import component classes.
import employeelist.*;
import employeelistServer.*;
```

```
// Import classes for transaction processing.
import oracle.aurora.jts.util.*;
import org.omg.CosTransactions.*;
import oracle.aurora.jts.client.AuroraTransactionService;

// Import JNDI property constants.
import oracle.aurora.jndi.sess_iiop.ServiceCtx;

// Import the JNDI Context Interface.
import javax.naming.Context;

/* Import the InitialContext class that implements the
   Context Interface.
*/
import javax.naming.InitialContext;

/* Import the hash table class to hold the initial context
   properties environment.
*/
import java.util.Hashtable;

public class EmployeeListUser {

  // main throws instead of catching exceptions.
  public static void main( String[] args )
    throws Exception {

    // Instantiate and populate InitialContext object.
    Hashtable env = new Hashtable();
    env.put( Context.URL_PKG_PREFIXES, "oracle.aurora.jndi" );
    env.put( Context.SECURITY_PRINCIPAL, "scott" );
    env.put( Context.SECURITY_CREDENTIALS, "tiger" );
    env.put( Context.SECURITY_AUTHENTICATION,
      ServiceCtx.NON_SSL_LOGIN );
    Context ic = new InitialContext( env );

    // Initialize Aurora transaction service.
    AuroraTransactionService.initialize(
      ic, "sess_iiop://localhost:2481:ORCL" );

    // Lookup object name, obtaining object reference.
    EmployeeList employee = ( EmployeeList )
      ic.lookup(
        "sess_iiop://localhost:2481:ORCL/test/EmployeeList" );

    /* Invoke getFullEmployeeInfo() method to get info for
```

```
        employee 104.
    */
    FullEmployeeInfo fi = employee.getFullEmployeeInfo( 104 );

    // Print employee information.
    System.out.println( "Type = " + fi.type +
                        " Last name = " + fi.lastname +
                        " First name = " + fi.firstname +
                        " Phone = " + fi.phone );

    // Print department info for employee.
    System.out.println( "Department number = " + fi.departmentno +
                        " Short name = " + fi.dinfo.shortname +
                        " Long name = " + fi.dinfo.longname );

    // Begin transaction.
    TS.getTS().getCurrent().begin();

    // Delete 104 employee.
    employee.deleteEmployee( 104 );

    // Insert 2056 employee.
    employee.insertEmployee( 2056, 200, "Surgeon",
      "Smith", "Garrett", "999-9999" );

    // Commit transaction consisting of delete and insert.
    TS.getTS().getCurrent().commit( false );
  }
}
```

A `VendorList` **CORBA Component**

Because the VENDOR_LIST table does not contain any foreign keys, the
VendorList component is simple, and similar to the DepartmentList
component. In this section you will see:

- The user requirements for VendorList

- The high-level view of VendorList

- The IDL file for VendorList

- The server object implementation for VendorList

- A client for VendorList

The User Requirements for `VendorList`

The user requirements for `VendorList` are similar to the user requirements for `DepartmentList`. The user wants the following operations to be provided:

- Given a vendor number, get the non-primary key column values of the `VENDOR_LIST` row that matches that vendor number.

- Given a vendor number, delete the `VENDOR_LIST` row that matches that vendor number.

- Insert a row into the `VENDOR_LIST` table that contains the specified column values.

The High-Level View of `VendorList`

From the previous user requirements, Figure 9-3 is easily seen to provide a reasonable high-level view for `VendorList`.

The IDL File for `VendorList`

The following IDL file expresses the high-level view of the `VendorList` component given in the previous section.

VendorList Interface
Operations:

  getVendorInfo(in long vendorno)
   raises(NoVendorError) :VendorInfo

  deleteVendor(in long vendorno)
   raises(NoVendorError, DeleteVendorError) :

  insertVendor(
   in long vendorno, in wstring name,
    in wstring address, in wstring city,
     in wstring state, in wstring vzip,
      in wstring country)
       raises(DuplicateVendorError) :

FIGURE 9-3. *High-level view of* `VendorList`

```
/* File Name: vendorlist.idl */

module vendorlist {

  struct VendorInfo {
    wstring name; wstring address; wstring city;
      wstring state; wstring vzip; wstring country;
  };

  exception NoVendorError { wstring mess; };
  exception DuplicateVendorError { wstring mess; };
  exception DeleteVendorError { wstring mess; };

  interface VendorList {
    VendorInfo getVendorInfo( in long vendorno )
      raises( NoVendorError );
    void deleteVendor( in long vendorno )
      raises( NoVendorError, DeleteVendorError );
    void insertVendor(
      in long vendorno, in wstring name, in wstring address,
        in wstring city, in wstring state, in wstring vzip,
          in wstring country )
            raises( DuplicateVendorError );
  };
};
```

The Server Object Implementation
of VendorList

The following SQLJ file contains the VendorListImpl class that implements the server object:

```
/* Program Name:  VendorListImpl.sqlj
**
** Purpose:  Implement a VendorList object for
**           manipulating the VENDOR_LIST table.
**
*/

package vendorlistServer;

import vendorlist.*;
import java.sql.*;

public class VendorListImpl extends _VendorListImplBase {
```

```
// Retrieve desired vendor.
public VendorInfo getVendorInfo( int vendorno )
  throws NoVendorError {
  try {

    // You must initialize variables to be selected into.
    String name = null;
    String address = null;
    String city = null;
    String state = null;
    String vzip = null;
    String country = null;

    #sql {
      SELECT name, address, city, state, vzip, country
        INTO :name, :address, :city, :state, :vzip, :country
          FROM VENDOR_LIST
            WHERE vendorno = :vendorno
    };
    return new VendorInfo(
      name, address, city, state, vzip, country );
  }

  // Retrieval failed (probably) due to nonexistent row.
  catch( SQLException e ) {
    throw new NoVendorError( e.getMessage() );
  }
}

// Delete desired vendor.
public void deleteVendor( int vendorno )
  throws NoVendorError, DeleteVendorError {
  try {
    int vendno = 0;
    #sql {
      SELECT vendorno
        INTO :vendno
          FROM VENDOR_LIST
            WHERE vendorno = :vendorno
    };
  }

  // SELECT INTO failed (probably) due to nonexistent row.
  catch( SQLException e ) {
    throw new NoVendorError( e.getMessage() );
  }
  try {
    #sql {
```

```
      DELETE FROM VENDOR_LIST
        WHERE vendorno = :vendorno
    };
  }

  // Delete failed.
  catch( SQLException e ) {
    throw new DeleteVendorError( e.getMessage() );
  }
}

// Insert new vendor.
public void insertVendor(
  int vendorno, String name, String address, String city,
    String state, String vzip, String country )
      throws DuplicateVendorError {
  try {
    #sql {
      INSERT INTO VENDOR_LIST
        VALUES( :vendorno, :name, :address,
            :city, :state, :vzip, :country  )
    };
  }

  /* Insert failed (probably) due to vendor number
     already being in table.
  */
  catch( SQLException e ) {
    throw new DuplicateVendorError( e.getMessage() );
  }
}
}
```

A Client for `VendorList`

The following Java program uses the `VendorList` component:

```
/* Program Name: VendorListUser.java
**
** Purpose:  Use the VendorList component to get vendor
**           information for the vendor 401 and insert
**           a vendor 2056.
**
*/

// Import component classes.
import vendorlist.*;
```

```
import vendorlistServer.*;

// Import classes for transaction processing.
import oracle.aurora.jts.util.*;
import org.omg.CosTransactions.*;
import oracle.aurora.jts.client.AuroraTransactionService;

// Import JNDI property constants.
import oracle.aurora.jndi.sess_iiop.ServiceCtx;

// Import the JNDI Context Interface.
import javax.naming.Context;

/* Import the InitialContext class that implements the
   Context Interface.
*/
import javax.naming.InitialContext;

/* Import the hash table class to hold the initial context
   properties environment.
*/
import java.util.Hashtable;

public class VendorListUser {

  // main throws instead of catching exceptions.
  public static void main( String[] args )
    throws Exception {

    // Instantiate and populate InitialContext object.
    Hashtable env = new Hashtable();
    env.put( Context.URL_PKG_PREFIXES, "oracle.aurora.jndi" );
    env.put( Context.SECURITY_PRINCIPAL, "scott" );
    env.put( Context.SECURITY_CREDENTIALS, "tiger" );
    env.put( Context.SECURITY_AUTHENTICATION,
      ServiceCtx.NON_SSL_LOGIN );
    Context ic = new InitialContext( env );

    // Initialize Aurora transaction service.
    AuroraTransactionService.initialize(
      ic, "sess_iiop://localhost:2481:ORCL" );

    // Lookup object name, obtaining object reference.
    VendorList vendor = ( VendorList )
      ic.lookup( "sess_iiop://localhost:2481:ORCL/test/VendorList" );

    // Invoke getVendorInfo() method to get info for vendor 401.
    VendorInfo vi = vendor.getVendorInfo( 401 );
```

```
    // Print vendor information.
    System.out.println( "Name = " + vi.name +
                        " Address = " + vi.address +
                        " City = " + vi.city +
                        " State = " + vi.state +
                        " Zip = " + vi.vzip +
                        " Country = " + vi.country );

    // Begin transaction.
    TS.getTS().getCurrent().begin();

    // Insert 2056 vendor.
    vendor.insertVendor( 2056, "Shell Shop",
                         "105 S. Ocean Drive",
                         "Miami Beach", "Florida",
                         "77777", "USA" );

    // Commit transaction.
    TS.getTS().getCurrent().commit( false );
  }
}
```

A `ProjectList` **CORBA Component**

This component is similar to the `DepartmentList` and `VendorList` components. Both `VendorList` and `ProjectList` will be used by the components developed in the last section of this chapter.

In this section you will consider

- The user requirements for `ProjectList`

- The high-level view of `ProjectList`

- The IDL file for `ProjectList`

- The server object implementation for `ProjectList`

- A client for `ProjectList`

The User Requirements for `ProjectList`

Again, we assume that the user requirements for `ProjectList` are similar to those for `DepartmentList`. The users desire the following operations:

- Given a project number, get the non-primary key column values of the `PROJECT_LIST` row that matches that project number.

■ Given a project number, delete the PROJECT_LIST row that matches that project number.

■ Insert a row into the PROJECT_LIST table that contains the specified column values.

The High-Level View of `ProjectList`

The high-level view given in Figure 9-4 specifies a `ProjectList` component that satisfies the user requirements given in the preceding section.

The IDL File for `ProjectList`

The following IDL file expresses the `ProjectList` specification that is pictorially represented in Figure 9-4:

```
/* File Name: projectlist.idl */

module projectlist {

  struct ProjectInfo {
    wstring projectname; wstring startdate; long amtoffunds;
  };

  exception NoProjectError { wstring mess; };
  exception DuplicateProjectError { wstring mess; };
  exception DeleteProjectError { wstring mess; };

  interface ProjectList {
    ProjectInfo getProjectInfo( in long projectno )
      raises( NoProjectError );
    void deleteProject( in long projectno )
      raises( NoProjectError, DeleteProjectError );
    void insertProject(
      in long projectno, in wstring projectname,
        in wstring startdate, in long amtoffunds )
          raises( DuplicateProjectError );
  };
};
```

The Server Object Implementation for `ProjectList`

The methods specified in `ProjectList.idl` are implemented in `ProjectListImpl.sqlj`.

```
ProjectList Interface
Operations:

  getProjectInfo( in long projectno )
   raises( NoProjectError ) :ProjectInfo

  deleteProject( in long projectno )
   raises( NoProjectError DeleteProjectError ) :

  insertProject(
    in long projectno, in wstring projectname,
     in wstring startdate, in long amtoffunds )
       raises( DuplicateProjectError ) :
```

FIGURE 9-4. *High-level view of* `ProjectList`

```
/* Program Name:  ProjectListImpl.sqlj
**
** Purpose:  Implement a ProjectList object for
**           manipulating the PROJECT_LIST table.
**
*/

package projectlistServer;

import projectlist.*;
import java.sql.*;

public class ProjectListImpl extends _ProjectListImplBase {

  // Retrieve desired project.
  public ProjectInfo getProjectInfo( int projectno )
    throws NoProjectError {
    try {

      // You must initialize variables to be selected into.
      String projectname = null;
      String startdate = null;
      int amtoffunds = 0;

      #sql {
        SELECT projectname, start_date, amt_of_funds
          INTO :projectname, :startdate, :amtoffunds
            FROM PROJECT_LIST
```

```
              WHERE projectno = :projectno
    };
    return new ProjectInfo( projectname, startdate, amtoffunds );
  }

  // Retrieval failed (probably) due to nonexistent row.
  catch( SQLException e ) {
    throw new NoProjectError( e.getMessage() );
  }
}

// Delete desired project.
public void deleteProject( int projectno )
  throws NoProjectError, DeleteProjectError {
  try {
    int projno = 0;
    #sql {
      SELECT projectno
        INTO :projno
          FROM PROJECT_LIST
            WHERE  projectno = :projectno
    };
  }

  // SELECT INTO failed (probably) due to nonexistent row.
  catch( SQLException e ) {
    throw new NoProjectError( e.getMessage() );
  }
  try {
    #sql {
      DELETE FROM PROJECT_LIST
        WHERE projectno = :projectno
    };
  }

  // Delete failed.
  catch( SQLException e ) {
    throw new DeleteProjectError( e.getMessage() );
  }
}

// Insert new project.
public void insertProject(
  int projectno, String projectname,
    String startdate, int amtoffunds )
      throws DuplicateProjectError {
  try {
    #sql {
      INSERT INTO PROJECT_LIST
```

```
        VALUES(
            :projectno, :projectname, :startdate, :amtoffunds )
        };
    }

    /* Insert failed (probably) due to project number already
       being in table.
    */
    catch( SQLException e ) {
      throw new DuplicateProjectError( e.getMessage() );
    }
  }
}
```

A `ProjectList` Client

The following Java program uses the `ProjectList` component:

```
/* Program Name: ProjectListUser.java
**
** Purpose:   Use the ProjectList component to get project
**            information for the project 300, delete
**            project 300, and insert a project 2056.
**
*/

// Import component classes.
import projectlist.*;
import projectlistServer.*;

// Import classes for transaction processing.
import oracle.aurora.jts.util.*;
import org.omg.CosTransactions.*;
import oracle.aurora.jts.client.AuroraTransactionService;

// Import JNDI property constants.
import oracle.aurora.jndi.sess_iiop.ServiceCtx;

// Import the JNDI Context Interface.
import javax.naming.Context;

/* Import the InitialContext class that implements the
   Context Interface.
*/
import javax.naming.InitialContext;

/* Import the hash table class to hold the initial context
   properties environment.
```

```
*/
import java.util.Hashtable;

public class ProjectListUser {

  // main throws instead of catching exceptions.
  public static void main( String[] args )
    throws Exception {

    // Instantiate and populate InitialContext object.
    Hashtable env = new Hashtable();
    env.put( Context.URL_PKG_PREFIXES, "oracle.aurora.jndi" );
    env.put( Context.SECURITY_PRINCIPAL, "scott" );
    env.put( Context.SECURITY_CREDENTIALS, "tiger" );
    env.put( Context.SECURITY_AUTHENTICATION,
      ServiceCtx.NON_SSL_LOGIN );
    Context ic = new InitialContext( env );

    // Initialize Aurora transaction service.
    AuroraTransactionService.initialize(
      ic, "sess_iiop://localhost:2481:ORCL" );

    // Lookup object name, obtaining object reference.
    ProjectList project = ( ProjectList )
      ic.lookup( "sess_iiop://localhost:2481:ORCL/test/ProjectList" );

    // Invoke getProjectInfo() method to get info for project 300.
    ProjectInfo pi = project.getProjectInfo( 300 );

    // Print project information.
    System.out.println( "Project name = " + pi.projectname +
                        " Start date = " + pi.startdate +
                        " Amount of funds = " + pi.amtoffunds );

    // Begin transaction.
    TS.getTS().getCurrent().begin();

    // Delete 300 project.
    project.deleteProject( 300 );

    // Insert 2056 project.
    project.insertProject(
      2056, "Neonatal Expansion", "07-Jun-2000", 0 );

    // Commit transaction consisting of delete and insert.
    TS.getTS().getCurrent().commit( false );
  }
}
```

`PurchaseList` and `LineItemList` **CORBA Components**

Because these components are so interrelated, they are presented together. In particular, since they both reference each other, if they were specified in separate IDL files, both these IDL files would have to be generated before either of their implementation files could be compiled. Therefore, both components are specified in the same IDL file.

You will now consider how these components reference each other. Each purchase order has a set of line items associated with it. The `LINEITEM_LIST` record contains a `requestno` column that is a foreign key, which refers to the `PURCHASE_LIST` record for the line item. The user requirements for `LineItemList` specify that the component provides an operation that returns, among other things, the `PURCHASE_LIST` information for the referenced `PURCHASE_LIST` record (a similar operation was done in the `EmployeeList` component). On the other hand, the user requirements for `PurchaseList` specify that a `PurchaseList` operation returns, among other things, the `LINEITEM_LIST` information for all the line items pertaining to the indicated purchase order. The high-level view specifies that these two user requirements are implemented in such a way as to make the components mutually referential. Note that the second operation is based on the one-to-many inverse of the foreign key relationship between line items and purchases.

In this section you will consider the following:

- The user requirements for `PurchaseList` and `LineItemList`

- The high-level view of `PurchaseList` and `LineItemList`

- The IDL file for `PurchaseList` and `LineItemList`

- The server object implementation for `PurchaseList`

- The server object implementation for `LineItemList`

- A client for `PurchaseList`

The User Requirements for `PurchaseList` and `LineItemList`

First consider the operations that the users require for `PurchaseList`:

- Given a request number, return the values of the other columns in the `PURCHASE_LIST` row that match the request number.

■ Given a request number, return the full information for the purchase order, including the non-primary key information in the matching employee row, the non-primary key information in the matching vendor row, as well as the information in the line item rows for the purchase order.

■ Given a request number, delete the matching PURCHASE_LIST row.

■ Insert a new PURCHASE_LIST row with the designated column values.

Next, consider the required operations for the LineItemList component:

■ Given a request number, line number, and project number, return the non-primary key column values for the line item.

■ Given a request number, line number, and project number, return the full information for the line item, including the non-primary key column values for the matching PURCHASE_LIST row and the non-primary key column values for the matching PROJECT_LIST row.

■ Given a request number, line number, and project number, delete the matching LINEITEM_LIST row.

■ Insert a new LINEITEM_LIST row containing the designated column values.

■ Given a request number, return the non-requestno column values in the matching LINEITEM_LIST rows.

The High-Level View of `PurchaseList` and `LineItemList`

These components are more complicated than the other ones you have seen in this chapter. Therefore, several figures are used to represent the common high-level view of these components. Figure 9-5 specifies the relationship between PurchaseList and LineItemList.

Figure 9-6 specifies the relationships among PurchaseList, EmployeeList, and VendorList.

Finally, Figure 9-7 specifies the relationship between LineItemList and ProjectList.

The IDL File for `PurchaseList` and `LineItemList`

The IDL file contains two sections—one for the PurchaseList types and one for the LineItemList types. However, the typedef, the PurchaseInfo definition, and the POLineItemInfo definition are of relevance to both components.

PurchaseList Interface		LineItemList Interface
Operations:	FullPurchaseInfo <<USES>> LineItemInfo	Operations:
getFullPurchaseInfo(in long requestno) raises(NoPurchaseError) :FullPurchaseInfo	getFullPurchaseInfo <<USES>> getLineItems	getLineItems(in long requestno) raises(LineItemError) :LineItemInfos
		getLineItemInfo(in long requestno, in long lineno, in long projectno) raises(NoLineItemError) :LineItemInfo
deletePurchase(in long requestno) raises(NoPurchaseError, DeletePurchaseError) :		deleteLineItem(in long requestno, in long lineno, in long projectno) raises(NoLineItemError DeleteLineItemError)
insertPurchase(in long requestno, in long employeeno, in long vendorno, in wstring purchasetype, in long checkno, in wstring whenpurchased) raises(DuplicatePurchaseError) :		insertLineItem(in long requestno, in long lineno, in long projectno, in long quantity, in wstring unit, in float estimatedcost, in float actualcost, in wstring description) raises(DuplicateLineItemError) :
	FullLineItemInfo <<USES>> PurchaseInfo	getFullLineItemInfo(in long requestno, in long lineno, in long projectno) raises(NoLineItemError) :FullLineItemInfo
getPurchaseInfo(in long requestno) raises(NoPurchaseError) :PurchaseInfo	getFullLineItemInfo <<USES>> getPurchaseInfo	

FIGURE 9-5. *High-level view of relationship between* PurchaseList *and* LineItemList

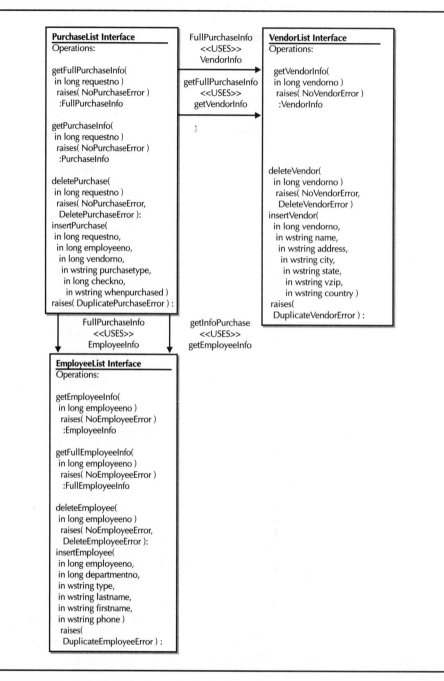

FIGURE 9-6. *High-level view of relationships between* `PurchaseList` *and* `VendorList` *and* `PurchaseList` *and* `EmployeeList`

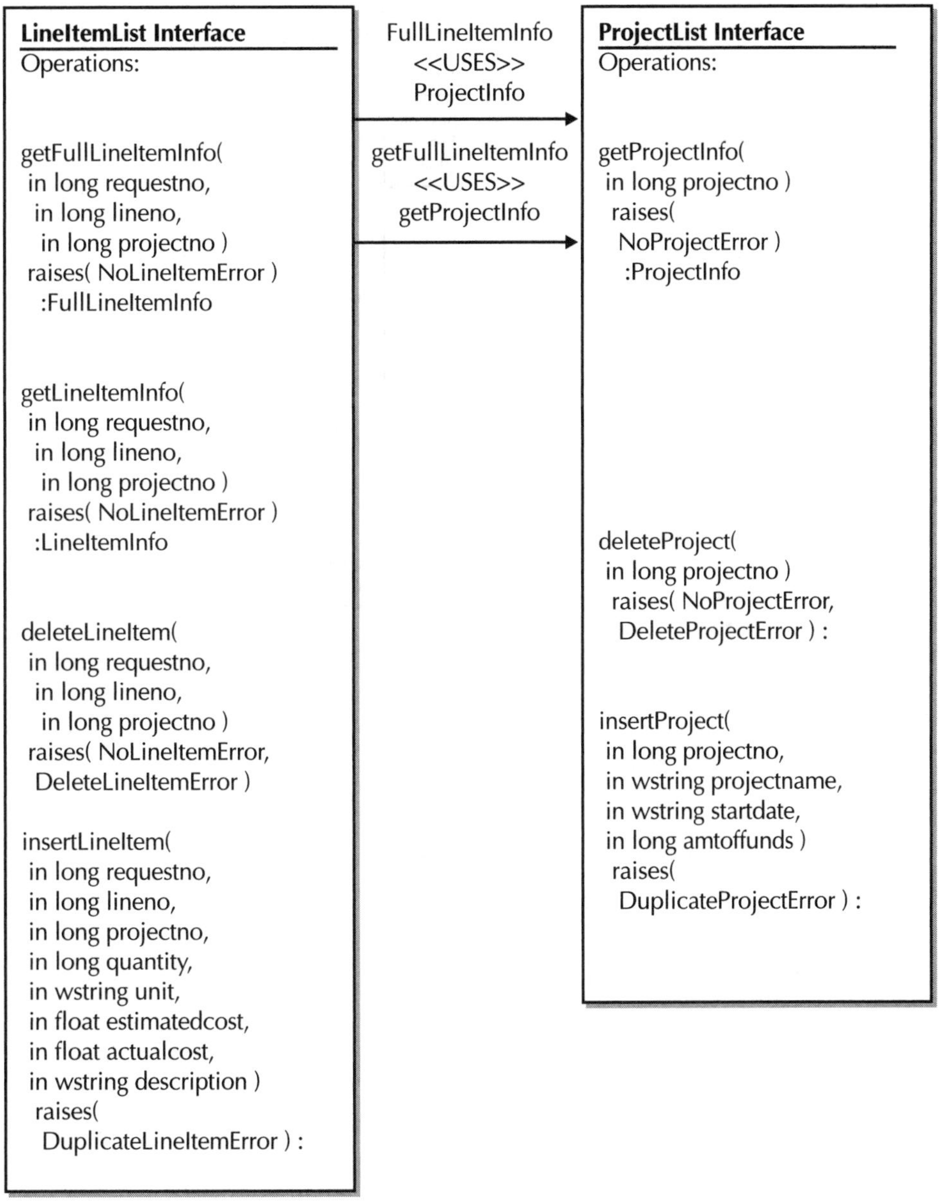

LineItemList Interface

Operations:

getFullLineItemInfo(
 in long requestno,
 in long lineno,
  in long projectno)
 raises(NoLineItemError)
 :FullLineItemInfo

getLineItemInfo(
 in long requestno,
 in long lineno,
  in long projectno)
 raises(NoLineItemError)
 :LineItemInfo

deleteLineItem(
 in long requestno,
 in long lineno,
  in long projectno)
 raises(NoLineItemError,
 DeleteLineItemError)

insertLineItem(
 in long requestno,
 in long lineno,
 in long projectno,
 in long quantity,
 in wstring unit,
 in float estimatedcost,
 in float actualcost,
 in wstring description)
 raises(
  DuplicateLineItemError) :

FullLineItemInfo
<<USES>>
ProjectInfo

getFullLineItemInfo
<<USES>>
getProjectInfo

ProjectList Interface

Operations:

getProjectInfo(
 in long projectno)
 raises(
  NoProjectError)
  :ProjectInfo

deleteProject(
 in long projectno)
  raises(NoProjectError,
  DeleteProjectError) :

insertProject(
 in long projectno,
 in wstring projectname,
 in wstring startdate,
 in long amtoffunds)
  raises(
  DuplicateProjectError) :

FIGURE 9-7. *High-level view of relationship between* LineItemList
and ProjectList

The set of line item information contained in the `FullPurchaseInfo` type, and returned by the `getLineItems()` method, is specified as being an array of `POLineItemInfo` objects. A `POLineItemInfo` object contains all the information in a `LINEITEM_LIST` row:

```
/* File Name: purchaseorder.idl */

// Include IDL files for referenced types.
#include <employeelist.idl>
#include <vendorlist.idl>
#include <projectlist.idl>

module purchaseorder {

  // PurchaseList section.
  struct PurchaseInfo {
    long employeeno; long vendorno;
      wstring purchasetype; long checkno;
        wstring whenpurchased;
  };

  /* POLineItemInfo holds info in LineItemInfo plus the three
     primary key field values from LINEITEM_LIST table.
  */
  struct POLineItemInfo {
    long requestno; long lineno; long projectno;
      long quantity; wstring unit; float estimatedcost;
        float actualcost; wstring description;
  };

  /* typedef for array of line item information objects for
     purchase order.
  */
  typedef sequence <POLineItemInfo> LineItemInfos;

  /* FullPurchaseInfo holds references to EmployeeInfo and
     VendorInfo objects for purchase order, as well as holding
     a reference to array of line item information for purchase
     order objects and holding PURCHASE_LIST information.
  */
  struct FullPurchaseInfo {
    employeelist::EmployeeInfo einfo;
      vendorlist::VendorInfo vinfo;
        LineItemInfos linfo; long employeeno; long vendorno;
          wstring purchasetype; long checkno; wstring whenpurchased;
  };
```

```
exception NoPurchaseError { wstring mess; };
exception DuplicatePurchaseError { wstring mess; };
exception DeletePurchaseError { wstring mess; };

interface PurchaseList {
  PurchaseInfo getPurchaseInfo( in long requestno )
    raises( NoPurchaseError );
  FullPurchaseInfo getFullPurchaseInfo( in long requestno )
    raises( NoPurchaseError );
  void deletePurchase( in long requestno )
    raises( NoPurchaseError, DeletePurchaseError );
  void insertPurchase(
    in long requestno, in long employeeno, in long vendorno,
      in wstring purchasetype, in long checkno,
        in wstring whenpurchased )
          raises( DuplicatePurchaseError );
};

// LineItemList section.
struct LineItemInfo {
  long quantity; wstring unit; float estimatedcost;
    float actualcost; wstring description;
};

/* FullLineItemInfo holds references to PurchaseInfo
   and ProjectInfo objects for the line item, as well
   as holding LINEITEM_LIST information.
*/
struct FullLineItemInfo {
  PurchaseInfo pinfo;
    projectlist::ProjectInfo prinfo;
      long quantity; wstring unit; float estimatedcost;
        float actualcost; wstring description;
};

exception NoLineItemError { wstring mess; };
exception DeleteLineItemError { wstring mess; };
exception DuplicateLineItemError { wstring mess; };
exception LineItemError { wstring mess; };

interface LineItemList {
  LineItemInfo getLineItemInfo(
    in long requestno, in long lineno, in long projectno )
      raises( NoLineItemError );
  FullLineItemInfo getFullLineItemInfo(
    in long requestno, in long lineno, in long projectno )
      raises( NoLineItemError );
```

```
      void deleteLineItem(
        in long requestno, in long lineno, in long projectno )
          raises( NoLineItemError, DeleteLineItemError );
      void insertLineItem(
        in long requestno, in long lineno, in long projectno,
          in long quantity, in wstring unit, in float estimatedcost,
            in float actualcost, in wstring description )
              raises( DuplicateLineItemError );

      /* getLineItems returns array of line items information
         for purchase order.
      */
      LineItemInfos getLineItems( in long requestno )
        raises( LineItemError );
    };
};
```

The Server Object Implementation for PurchaseList

The getFullPurchaseInfo() method is the most complex method to implement for the component. In this method, the EMPLOYEE_LIST information is obtained by accessing the EmployeeList component. The VENDOR_LIST information is obtained by accessing the VendorList component. The LINEITEM_LIST information is obtained by accessing the LineItemList component. The EMPLOYEE_LIST and VENDOR_LIST information are stored in objects of types EmployeeInfo and VendorInfo, respectively. The LINEITEM_LIST information is stored in an array (of POLineItemInfo objects). References to all three of these are returned by getFullPurchaseInfo() in a FullPurchaseInfo object:

```
/* Program Name:  PurchaseListImpl.sqlj
**
** Purpose:  Implement a PurchaseList object for
**           manipulating the PURCHASE_LIST table.
**
*/

package purchaseorderServer;

import java.sql.*;
import purchaseorder.*;

/* Import classes for EmployeeList, VendorList,
   and LineIntemList components.
*/
import employeelist.*;
```

```java
import employeelistServer.*;
import vendorlist.*;
import vendorlistServer.*;
import lineitemlist.*;

// Import JNDI property constants.
import oracle.aurora.jndi.sess_iiop.ServiceCtx;

// Import the JNDI Context Interface.
import javax.naming.Context;

/* Import the InitialContext class that implements the
   Context Interface.
*/
import javax.naming.InitialContext;

/* Import the hash table class to hold the initial context
   properties environment.
*/
import java.util.Hashtable;

public class PurchaseListImpl extends _PurchaseListImplBase {

  // Retrieve desired purchase order information.
  public PurchaseInfo getPurchaseInfo( int requestno )
    throws NoPurchaseError {
    try {

      // You must initialize variables to be selected into.
      int employeeno = 0;
      int vendorno = 0;
      String purchasetype = null;
      int checkno = 0;
      String whenpurchased = null;

      #sql {
        SELECT employeeno, vendorno, purchasetype,
               checkno, whenpurchased
          INTO :employeeno, :vendorno, :purchasetype,
               :checkno, :whenpurchased
            FROM PURCHASE_LIST
              WHERE requestno = :requestno
      };
      return new PurchaseInfo(
        employeeno, vendorno, purchasetype,
          checkno, whenpurchased );
    }
```

```
      // Retrieval failed (probably) due to nonexistent row.
      catch( SQLException e ) {
        throw new NoPurchaseError( e.getMessage() );
      }
    }

    /* Retrieve desired full purchase order information,
       including employee, vendor, and line items information
       for the purchase order.
    */
    public FullPurchaseInfo getFullPurchaseInfo( int requestno )
      throws NoPurchaseError {
      try {

        // Get purchase info.
        pi = getPurchaseInfo( requestno );

        // Instantiate and populate InitialContext object.
        Hashtable env = new Hashtable();
        env.put( Context.URL_PKG_PREFIXES, "oracle.aurora.jndi" );
        Context ic = new InitialContext( env );

        // Get employee info for purchase order.

        // Lookup EmployeeList object name, obtaining object reference.
        EmployeeList employee = ( EmployeeList )
          ic.lookup( "sess_iiop://thisServer/test/EmployeeList" );

        // Invoke getEmployeeInfo() method to get info for employee.
        EmployeeInfo ei = employee.getEmployeeInfo( pi.employeeno );

        // Get vendor info for purchase order.

        // Lookup vendorlist object name, obtaining object reference.
        VendorList vendor = ( VendorList )
          ic.lookup( "sess_iiop://thisServer/test/VendorList" );

        // Invoke getVendorInfo() method to get info for vendor.
        VendorInfo vi = vendor.getVendorInfo( pi.vendorno );

        // Get line items info for purchase order.

        // Lookup lineitemlist object name, obtaining object reference.
        LineItemList lineitem = ( LineItemList )
          ic.lookup( "sess_iiop://thisServer/test/LineItemList" );

        // Invoke getLineItems() method to get info for line items.
        POLineItemInfo[] lis = lineitem.getLineItems( requestno );
```

```
      return new FullPurchaseInfo(
        ei, vi, lis, pi.employeeno, pi.vendorno,
          pi.purchasetype, pi.checkno, pi.whenpurchased );
    }

    // Get failed.
    catch( Exception e ) {
      throw new NoPurchaseError( e.getMessage() );
    }
  }

// Delete desired purchase record.
public void deletePurchase( int requestno )
  throws NoPurchaseError, DeletePurchaseError {
  try {
    int reqno = 0;
    #sql {
      SELECT requestno
        INTO :reqno
          FROM PURCHASE_LIST
            WHERE requestno = :requestno
    };
  }

  // SELECT INTO failed (probably) due to nonexistent row.
  catch( SQLException e ) {
    throw new NoPurchaseError( e.getMessage() );
  }
  try {
    #sql {
      DELETE FROM PURCHASE_LIST
        WHERE requestno = :requestno
    };
  }

  // Delete failed.
  catch( SQLException e ) {
    throw new DeletePurchaseError( e.getMessage() );
  }
}

// Insert new purchase record.
public void insertPurchase(
  int requestno, int employeeno, int vendorno,
    String purchasetype, int checkno, String whenpurchased )
      throws DuplicatePurchaseError {
  try {
```

```
      #sql {
        INSERT INTO PURCHASE_LIST
          VALUES( :requestno, :employeeno, :vendorno,
            :purchasetype, :checkno, :whenpurchased )
      };
    }

    /* Insert failed (probably) due to request number already
       being in table.
    */
    catch( SQLException e ) {
      throw new DuplicatePurchaseError( e.getMessage() );
    }
  }
}
```

The Server Object Implementation for `LineItemList`

The two most complex methods to implement in this class are `getFullLineInfo()` and `getLineItems()`. However, `getFullLineInfo()` has an identical structure to the `getFullEmployeeInfo()` method given in a previous section of this chapter titled "The Server Object Implementation for `EmployeeList`." We therefore concentrate on `getLineItems()`.

First, the line item information for the desired purchase order is moved into an iterator. Then, row by row, that information is moved into a `Vector`. A `Vector` is a dynamic array. We use a `Vector` instead of a "fixed bound" array because it is too costly to compute up front, with a `SELECT INTO` statement, how many rows were loaded into the iterator. The `Vector` increases in size as elements are inserted into it.

After all the rows from the iterator have been loaded into the `Vector`, an array of the appropriate size is created, and the `Vector` information is copied into the array. A reference to that array is what is returned by the method:

```
/* Program Name:  LineItemListImpl.sqlj
**
** Purpose:  Implement a LineItemList object for
**           manipulating the LINEITEM_LIST table.
**
*/

package purchaseorderServer;

import lineitemlist.*;

/* Import classes for EmployeeList, PurchaseList,
```

```
      and ProjectList components.
*/
import employeelist.*;
import purchaseorder.*;
import projectlist.*;
import projectlistServer.*;

import java.sql.*;
import java.util.Vector;

// Import JNDI property constants.
import oracle.aurora.jndi.sess_iiop.ServiceCtx;

// Import the JNDI Context Interface.
import javax.naming.Context;

/* Import the InitialContext class that implements the
   Context Interface.
*/
import javax.naming.InitialContext;

/* Import the hash table class to hold the initial context
   properties environment.
*/
import java.util.Hashtable;

// LIter will hold line item records for purchase order.
#sql iterator LIter (
   int lineno, int projectno, int quantity, String unit,
     float estimatedcost, float actualcost, String description );

public class LineItemListImpl extends _LineItemListImplBase {

   // Retrieve desired line item information.
   public LineItemInfo getLineItemInfo(
     int requestno, int lineno, int projectno )
       throws NoLineItemError {
     try {

        // You must initialize variables to be selected into.
        int quantity = 0;
        String unit = null;
        float estimatedcost = (float)0.0;
        float actualcost = (float)0.0;
        String description = null;

        #sql {
          SELECT quantity, unit, estimatedcost,
```

```
                  actualcost, description
           INTO :quantity, :unit, :estimatedcost,
                :actualcost, :description
             FROM LINEITEM_LIST
               WHERE requestno = :requestno
                 AND lineno = :lineno
                   AND projectno = :projectno
      };
      return new LineItemInfo(
        quantity, unit, estimatedcost, actualcost, description );
    }

    // Retrieval failed (probably) due to nonexistent row.
    catch( SQLException e ) {
      throw new NoLineItemError( e.getMessage() );
    }
  }

  /* Retrieve desired full line item information, including
     purchase and project information for the line item.
  */
  public FullLineItemInfo getFullLineItemInfo(
    int requestno, int lineno, int projectno )
      throws NoLineItemError {
    try {

      // Get line item info.
      LineItemInfo li = getLineItemInfo(
        requestno, lineno,  projectno );

      // Get purchase info for line item.

      // Instantiate and populate InitialContext object.
      Hashtable env = new Hashtable();
      env.put( Context.URL_PKG_PREFIXES, "oracle.aurora.jndi" );
      Context ic = new InitialContext( env );

      // Lookup purchase object name, obtaining object reference.
      PurchaseList purchase = ( PurchaseList )
        ic.lookup( "sess_iiop://thisServer/test/PurchaseList" );

      // Invoke getPurchaseInfo() method to get info for purchase.
      PurchaseInfo pi = purchase.getPurchaseInfo( requestno );

      // Get project info for line item.

      // Lookup project object name, obtaining object reference.
      ProjectList project = ( ProjectList )
        ic.lookup( "sess_iiop://thisServer/test/ProjectList" );
```

```
      // Invoke getProjectInfo() method to get info for project.
      ProjectInfo pri = project.getProjectInfo( projectno );

      return(
        new FullLineItemInfo(
          pi, pri, li.quantity, li.unit, li.estimatedcost,
            li.actualcost, li.description )
      );
    }

  // Get failed.
  catch( Exception e ) {
    throw new NoLineItemError( e.getMessage() );
  }
}

// Delete desired line item.
public void deleteLineItem(
  int requestno, int lineno, int projectno )
    throws NoLineItemError, DeleteLineItemError {
  try {

    // You must initialize variables to be selected into.
    int quantity = 0;
    String unit = null;
    float estimatedcost = (float)0.0;
    float actualcost = (float)0.0;
    String description = null;

    #sql {
      SELECT quantity, unit, estimatedcost,
             actualcost, description
        INTO :quantity, :unit, :estimatedcost,
             :actualcost,:description
          FROM LINEITEM_LIST
            WHERE requestno = :requestno
              AND lineno = :lineno
                AND projectno = :projectno
    };
  }

  // SELECT INTO failed (probably) due to nonexistent row.
  catch( SQLException e ) {
    throw new NoLineItemError( e.getMessage() );
  }
  try {
    #sql {
```

```
        DELETE FROM LINEITEM_LIST
          WHERE requestno = :requestno
            AND lineno = :lineno
              AND projectno = :projectno
      };
    }

    // Delete failed.
    catch( SQLException e ) {
      throw new DeleteLineItemError( e.getMessage() );
    }
  }

  // Insert new line item.
  public void insertLineItem(
    int requestno, int lineno, int projectno,
      int quantity, String unit, float estimatedcost,
        float actualcost, String description )
          throws DuplicateLineItemError {
    try {
      #sql {
        INSERT INTO LINEITEM_LIST
          VALUES( :requestno, :lineno, :projectno,
            :quantity, :unit, :estimatedcost,
              :actualcost, :description )
      };
    }

    /* Insert failed (probably) due to line item already
       being in table.
    */
    catch( SQLException e ) {
      throw new DuplicateLineItemError( e.getMessage() );
    }
  }

  // Get line items information for desired purchase order.
  public POLineItemInfo[] getLineItems( int requestno )
    throws LineItemError {
    try {

      /* Place retrieved line item information in Vector,
         since it is too time consuming to compute the number
         of line items for a purchase order.
      */
      Vector polineitemVector = new Vector();
      LIter anLIter = null;
      #sql anLIter =
```

```
          { SELECT lineno, projectno, quantity, unit,
             estimatedcost, actualcost, description
               FROM LINEITEM_LIST
                 WHERE requestno = :requestno
          };

      // Add retrieved record to Vector.
      while( anLIter.next() ) {
        polineitemVector.addElement(
          new POLineItemInfo(
            requestno,
            anLIter.lineno(),
            anLIter.projectno(),
            anLIter.quantity(),
            anLIter.unit(),
            anLIter.estimatedcost(),
            anLIter.actualcost(),
            anLIter.description() ) );
      }
      anLIter.close();

      // Move records from Vector to array.
      POLineItemInfo[] returnarray =
        new POLineItemInfo[ polineitemVector.size() ];
      polineitemVector.copyInto( returnarray );

      // Return array reference.
      return returnarray;
    }

    // Get failed.
    catch( SQLException e ) {
      throw new LineItemError( e.getMessage() );
    }
  }
}
```

A Client for `PurchaseList`

For illustrative purposes, it suffices to provide a client that uses only the
`PurchaseList` component, since `PurchaseList` itself uses the
`LineItemList` component.

The client accesses the `PurchaseList` component, and invokes
the `getFullPurchaseInfo()` method on it. This method returns a
`FullPurchaseInfo` object that contains the non-primary key column values
of the desired PURCHASE_LIST row, as well as references to the matching

EMPLOYEE_LIST row information, VENDOR_LIST row information, and an array of POLineItemInfo references that contains the appropriate line item information for the purchase order. The client then prints this information. A for loop is used to print the information in the array.

Finally, the client uses the PurchaseList component to delete a row from, and insert a row into, the PURCHASE_LIST table:

```
/* Program Name: PurchaseListUser.java
**
** Purpose:   Use the PurchaseList component to get purchase
**            order information for the purchase record 500,
**            delete purchase record 500, and insert a purchase
**            record 2056.
**
*/

import java.util.Vector;

// Import component classes.
import purchaseorder.*;
import purchaseorderServer.*;

// Import classes for transaction processing.
import oracle.aurora.jts.util.*;
import org.omg.CosTransactions.*;
import oracle.aurora.jts.client.AuroraTransactionService;

// Import JNDI property constants.
import oracle.aurora.jndi.sess_iiop.ServiceCtx;

// Import the JNDI Context Interface.
import javax.naming.Context;

/* Import the InitialContext class that implements the
   Context Interface.
*/
import javax.naming.InitialContext;

/* Import the hash table class to hold the initial context
   properties environment.
*/
import java.util.Hashtable;

public class PurchaseListUser {

  // main throws instead of catching exceptions.
  public static void main( String[] args )
    throws Exception {
```

```
// Instantiate and populate InitialContext object.
Hashtable env = new Hashtable();
env.put( Context.URL_PKG_PREFIXES, "oracle.aurora.jndi" );
env.put( Context.SECURITY_PRINCIPAL, "scott" );
env.put( Context.SECURITY_CREDENTIALS, "tiger" );
env.put( Context.SECURITY_AUTHENTICATION,
  ServiceCtx.NON_SSL_LOGIN );
Context ic = new InitialContext( env );

// Initialize Aurora transaction service.
AuroraTransactionService.initialize(
  ic, "sess_iiop://localhost:2481:ORCL" );
  Vector polineitemVector = new Vector();

// Lookup object name, obtaining object reference.
PurchaseList purchase = ( PurchaseList )
  ic.lookup(
    "sess_iiop://localhost:2481:ORCL/test/PurchaseList" );

/* Invoke getFullPurchaseInfo() method to get info for
   purchase record 500, including employee, vendor, and
   line item information.
*/
FullPurchaseInfo fi = purchase.getFullPurchaseInfo( 500 );

// Print purchase order information.
System.out.println(
  "Employee number = " + fi.employeeno +
  " Vendor number = " + fi.vendorno +
  " Purchase type = " + fi.purchasetype +
  " Check number = " + fi.checkno +
  " Purchase date = " + fi.whenpurchased );

// Print employee info for purchase order.
System.out.println(
  "Last name = " + fi.einfo.lastname +
  " First name = " + fi.einfo.firstname +
  " Type = " + fi.einfo.type +
  " Department number = " + fi.einfo.departmentno +
  " Phone = " + fi.einfo.phone );

// Print vendor info for purchase order.
System.out.println(
  "Name = " + fi.vinfo.name +
  " Address = " + fi.vinfo.address +
  " City = " + fi.vinfo.city +
  " Zip = " + fi.vinfo.vzip +
  " Country = "+ fi.vinfo.country );
```

```
    // Print line item info for purchase order.
    for( int i = 0; i < fi.linfo.length; i++ ) {
      System.out.println(
        "Line number = " + fi.linfo[i].lineno +
        " Project number = " + fi.linfo[i].projectno +
        " Quantity = " + fi.linfo[i].quantity );

      System.out.println(
        "Unit = " + fi.linfo[i].unit +
        " Estimated cost = " + fi.linfo[i].estimatedcost +
        " Actual cost = " + fi.linfo[i].actualcost +
        " Description = " + fi.linfo[i].description );
    }

    // Begin transaction.
    TS.getTS().getCurrent().begin();

    // Delete 500 purchase record.
    purchase.deletePurchase( 500 );

    // Insert 2056 purchase record.
    purchase.insertPurchase(
      2056, 102, 402, null, 0, "07-JUN-2000" );

    // Commit transaction consisting of delete and insert.
    TS.getTS().getCurrent().commit( false );
  }
}
```

Conclusion

This ends Part III of this book, the part dealing with CORBA.

In Chapter 6, you learned the basics of implementing and using CORBA server objects in Java. In Chapter 7, you considered the various ways in which CORBA server objects could be invoked in database sessions. In Chapter 8, you mastered the intricacies of invoking CORBA server objects in global transactions. In Chapter 9, you exercised your ability to design and implement CORBA components that are related to each other in a quite natural way—namely, through foreign key and one-to-many relationships.

In Part IV, you will learn how to implement JavaServer Pages (JSP) that access EJB and CORBA components.

PART
IV

Building Web Applications with JavaServer Pages

CHAPTER
10

Introduction to Programming with JavaServer Pages

n Chapter 2, you were introduced to Web programming with servlets and JSPs. You learned about the difference between the two models and the general architecture of Web applications. Recall that a JSP supports Java-based scripting in an HTML page, so that you can easily build Web pages with dynamic content. For example, using a JSP, you can query a database and output the results as an HTML table. JSPs are based on servlets, which are pure Java programs that can be executed in a Web server to create dynamic pages. The primary goal of the JSP specification is to provide a higher level of abstraction over servlets, and a more convenient programming model. By design, JSPs are intended for component-based programming through scripting tags and JavaBeans. They support clean separation of the static content of a Web page from the program logic that generates dynamic content. JSPs are translated to Java programs and use the same execution framework as servlets, with productivity extensions such as automatic retranslation of JSP files that aid in the rapid development of your Web application.

In this part of the book, which consists of Chapters 10–12, you will delve more deeply into JSP programming. Chapter 10 gives you the necessary background on basic program development with JSPs. In Chapter 11, you will learn about component-based programming with JavaBeans and JSPs. The emphasis is on database applications using JavaBean components written in SQLJ and JDBC. Chapter 12 focuses on other types of components, such as Enterprise JavaBeans (EJBs) and Java CORBA objects deployed in Oracle 8*i*, and JSP tag libraries. You will explore different ways in which these components can be combined in JSPs and understand how to effectively utilize the capabilities of Oracle8*i* and Java to build modular and powerful Web-based database applications.

The purpose of this chapter is to introduce some key concepts in JSP programming and provide a broad overview of JSP programming techniques. You will learn about basic JSP syntax and the application development process through several sample programs. You will also understand how to use JSPs with other JSPs and servlets. In particular, you will learn how to do the following:

- Write a `Hello` JSP using scripting elements, implicit objects, and an HTML form

- Learn more about the JSP translation and execution mechanism

- Use directives to import Java packages and include other pages at JSP translation time

- Use the `<jsp:include>` and `<jsp:forward>` standard action tags to call other pages from a JSP at runtime

■ Learn how to invoke a servlet from a JSP and vice versa, so that you can mix and match the two types of code in your Web application

■ Use error pages to handle runtime errors in a JSP

■ Use SQLJ code in your JSP to execute a static SQL query on the Oracle database

■ Use the command-line translator in Oracle's JSP implementation

Most of the examples illustrate standard features in the JSP 1.0 and 1.1 specifications, except for the command-line JSP translator and use of SQLJ in JSP files. These features are useful extensions provided in Oracle's JSP implementation.

In addition to the tags mentioned previously, there are several other standard tags available in a JSP. Tags for component-based programming with JavaBeans, such as `<jsp:useBean>` and `<jsp:setProperty>`, are discussed in the next chapter. The complete set of JSP tags appears in Appendix D. Besides the set of standard tags, JSP 1.1 defines a tag extension framework for *custom* tags. This feature is the main difference between the JSP 1.0 and JSP 1.1 specifications. It provides a powerful mechanism for JSP extensibility through third-party *tag libraries*. You will learn about the JSP 1.1 tag extension scheme in the section in Chapter 12 titled "Using JSP Tag Libraries."

The JSP specification in theory allows scripting languages other than Java; however, Java is the basis for understanding JSP and servlet programming. In this book, you will use either Java or SQLJ (which is an extension of Java for embedding SQL statements) as the scripting language. The JSP and servlet specifications also allow communication protocols other than HTTP. HTTP is assumed in this book, as most servlet and JSP implementations are based on HTTP.

Basic JSP Programming

There are two categories of programming elements available to build a JSP application:

■ JSP *scripting elements* that are used to embed Java code in your JSP file

■ JSP *implicit objects* that are automatically available within a JSP for accessing the underlying Java objects, such as the HTTP request and HTTP response

You will now learn about these two features in a JSP and use them to write a simple JSP program that prints out a "Hello" greeting along with the current date and time. This example shows how quick and easy it is to develop a basic JSP application using the built-in facilities.

JSP Scripting Elements

There are three types of scripting elements available in a JSP:

- Declarations
- Scriptlets
- Expressions

The JSP specification provides two forms of syntactic notation for each type of scripting element. One notation uses delimiters such as `<%` and `%>` to start and terminate a scripting element, while the other uses XML-compatible syntax for the same purpose. The reason for providing equivalent XML notation is to allow JSPs to be written using XML document authoring tools. Here, you will learn about both types of syntax.

Following is a brief description of each type of JSP scripting element.

Declarations

These are declarations of Java variables and methods that you will use in the Java code of your JSP file. They appear within `<%!` and `%>` tags and can be used in the entire page. For example, the following block declares two string-valued Java variables, `firstName` and `lastName`:

```
<%! String firstName;
    String lastName;
%>
```

Using the alternate XML-compatible notation, the preceding declarations can be written as follows:

```
<jsp:declaration>
    String firstName;
    String lastName;
</jsp:declaration>
```

Variables declared as above are initialized when the JSP page is loaded and initialized (refer to Chapter 2 for a description of JSP execution steps). These variable and method declarations do not directly produce any output in the page, but they are used by other elements in the JSP, such as expressions and scriptlets to create dynamic content.

Expressions

These are Java expressions that are dynamically evaluated at runtime and printed as strings in the output page. They appear embedded within `<%=` and `%>` tags that are interleaved with the static content. For example, the following statement embeds the Java expression `firstName` within some HTML code to print a greeting:

```
Hello  <%= firstName %> !  Have a nice day!
```

In the alternate XML notation, the preceding code is written as follows:

```
Hello  <jsp:expression> firstName </jsp:expression> ! Have a nice day!
```

When this code fragment is executed, the value of the `firstName` variable is evaluated and the string value is inserted at the proper position in the generated output. Note that an embedded expression does *not* end with a semicolon; this is because the generated code uses it as an argument in a `print(…)` method call.

Scriptlets

JSP scriptlets are fragments of Java code that are executed when the JSP is invoked. They appear within `<%` and `%>` tags interleaved with the static content. For example, the following code checks if the value of the variable `itemCount` is greater than 0, and prints out a message on the screen accordingly:

```
<%  if (itemCount > 0) { %>
      <B> You selected <%= itemCount %> items. </B>
<%  }  else  { %>
      <B> You have not selected any items. </B>
<%     } %>
```

Three different Java scriptlets are used in the preceding example: the **if** statement, the **else** statement, and the terminating curly brace for the **if** statement. An embedded JSP expression is also used to print out the value of `itemCount`. The scriptlets and the expression appear interleaved with HTML code in the order in which they are to be executed. Notice that the scriptlets are not necessarily complete blocks of Java code—the first scriptlet starts the **if** statement and ends with an opening curly brace. This scriptlet is followed by some static HTML code with a JSP expression embedded in it, which in turn is followed by an **else** statement that continues the **if** statement of the previous scriptlet. When the JSP page is translated, these separate code fragments are combined together to yield a block of Java code. This block of code must be syntactically valid in order to compile successfully. Therefore, you must end a scriptlet with a semicolon or omit the semicolon depending on Java syntax rules.

Using alternate XML notation, the previous scriptlet can be written as follows:

```
<jsp:scriptlet>  if (itemCount > 0) { </jsp:scriptlet>
 <B>You selected <jsp:expression>itemCount</jsp:expression> items.</B>
<jsp:scriptlet>  } else { </jsp:scriptlet>
     <B>You have not selected any items.</B>
<jsp:scriptlet>     } </jsp:scriptlet>
```

Note that all JSP tags are case sensitive. The complete set of JSP scripting elements is given in Appendix D. You will write a simple JSP program, `Hello.jsp`, that uses all three types of scripting elements you learned earlier. But before you do that, you need to know about objects that are implicitly available in a JSP.

JSP Implicit Objects

For programming convenience, there are several Java objects that are automatically defined for use within JSP scriptlets and expressions without requiring explicit declarations of program variables. Included among these objects are the following:

- `request` This object represents the HTTP request for the client call. It is an instance of the type `javax.servlet.http.HttpServletRequest`. It provides methods such as `getParameter()`, `getParameterNames()`, and `getParameterValues()` to retrieve invocation parameters from the HTTP request.

- `response` This object represents the HTTP response from the server. It is an instance of the `javax.servlet.http.HttpServletResponse` type. It provides methods such as `setContentType()` to set the character encoding of the output.

- `session` This object represents the HTTP session (if any) associated with the client request. It is available if the JSP is part of an HTTP session (an optional property of the Web page). This object is an instance of the `javax.servlet.http.HttpSession` type and provides methods such as `setMaxInactiveInterval()` to set the session timeout.

- `application` This object represents the Web application (servlet context) within which the JSP is running. It is an instance of the `javax.servlet.ServletContext` type and provides methods such as `log()` to write errors and other messages to the log file.

- `out` This object represents the output stream for the JSP. It is used to write out the static and dynamic data. It is an instance of the `javax.servlet.jsp.JspWriter` type and provides methods such as `print()`, `println()`, `clear()`, `flush()`, and `close()` for writing data.

The JSP specification defines other implicit objects such as `exception`, `pageContext`, `config`, and `page`. You will learn how to use the `exception` object in the "Handling JSP Errors" section later in this chapter. The complete set of JSP implicit objects is listed in Appendix D. Definitions for the corresponding types in the Servlet 2.2 API appear in Appendix A.

The following is an example of a JSP scriptlet that uses the implicit `request` object:

```
<% String user = request.getParameter("username"); %>
```

This scriptlet calls the `getParameter()` method of the `request` object to populate the string-valued Java variable `user`. The argument to the `getParameter()` method is the string representing the parameter, which is `username` here. This method call returns a string value if the parameter is present in the list of JSP request parameters, and `null` otherwise. Note that this parameter name-value lookup operation is case sensitive.

Writing `Hello.jsp`

You can now put together what you have learned so far in this chapter into a complete JSP. The purpose of this program is to print out a greeting to the client, along with the current date and time. The code for this JSP (using non-XML `<% … %>` notation) is shown next. The code is annotated with comments that refer to explanatory notes following the program. Notice the convention for comments—they can be written using HTML syntax, Java convention, or JSP tags. Comments using HTML and XML syntax appear within `<!--` and `--` > tags, and they can have embedded JSP expressions in them. These comments are part of the generated output page. Within Java code, a comment can follow the Java convention of `/* … */` or `//` as appropriate; such comments do not appear in the generated page. You can also use the JSP comment tags `<% -- … -- %>`. These comments are not interpreted by the JSP translator.

```
<%-- Program name: Hello.jsp
  -- Purpose:       Print a greeting and the current time
  --%>
<HTML>                                    <%-- (See Note 1.) --%>
  <HEAD> <TITLE> The Hello JSP </TITLE>
  </HEAD>
  <!-- This JSP body prints a hello message to the user
    -- with the current time --!>
  <BODY  BGCOLOR="white">                 <%-- (See Note 2.) --%>
    <%! String defaultName = "there";  /* (See Note 3.) */ %>
    <%  String name = request.getParameter("username");
                                    /* (See Note 4.) */ %>
    <H3> Hello  <%=  (name == null)? defaultName : name %> ! </H3>
                                    <%-- (See Note 5.) --%>
```

```
<P><B> The current time is <%= new java.util.Date() %>.
                           <%-- (See Note 6.) --%>
</B></P>
<B>May I have your name?</B>
<FORM METHOD=GET>                <%-- (See Note 7.) --%>
  <INPUT TYPE="text"
         NAME="username"
         SIZE=15>                <%-- (See Note 8.) --%>
  <INPUT TYPE="submit"
         VALUE="Submit name">   <%-- (See Note 9.) --%>
</FORM>
<P><B> Have a good day! :-) </B></P>
</BODY>
</HTML>
```

Notes on the `Hello.jsp` program:

1. The `<HTML>` tag defines the start of the HTML code. The next three statements are regular HTML constructs that define the start of the page and its title through the `<HEAD>` and `<TITLE>` tags.

2. The `<BODY>` tag defines the start of the HTML body segment. Here, it uses the `BGCOLOR` attribute to specify the background color as white.

3. This statement is a JSP declaration of a string variable called `defaultName` that is initialized to the constant value `"there"`. In this example, `defaultName` could also have been declared within a scriptlet since it is only being used in the main body of the page (there are no other Java methods explicitly declared).

4. This statement sets the value of the `name` variable to the value of the request parameter `username` by calling the method `getParameter()` on the implicit `request` object.

5. This statement uses an embedded Java expression to print out a "Hello" message with the user name if it is not `null`, or "Hello there" if the user name is not provided (the method call `request.getParameter("username")` returns `null` in this case).

6. This statement obtains the current time through another embedded Java expression: `new java.util.Date()`. The result returned by this constructor is automatically converted to a Java string value representing the date and time, and placed in the output page.

7. This statement indicates the start of an HTML form segment. Forms are frequently used in HTML programming to get data from the client browser,

as you learned in Chapter 2. Briefly, here is how an HTML form works (for further details you can refer to any standard book on HTML). A form segment is defined within the <FORM> and </FORM> start and end tags. The form can define one or more input fields and one or more buttons. Each input field has a name associated with it, and may optionally have TYPE and SIZE fields denoting the data type and the size of the input box. Clicking on an action button sends a new HTTP request to the server. Where and how the new request is sent is determined by the following:

■ The ACTION attribute of the <FORM> tag, which is specified as a URL for the program that is to be invoked at the server. If omitted, as in the Hello.jsp program, the default is to send the request to the same page—that is, to Hello.jsp.

■ The METHOD field, which is an optional attribute of the <FORM> tag to specify the HTTP method for transmitting data to the Web server. Its value can be either POST or GET. If the attribute is omitted, the default value is GET. The GET method appends the form data entered (also known as the *query string*) to the action URL as *key=value* pairs. Multiple form fields (if present) are separated by the '&' character, each space is converted to the '+' character, and any special character is represented by its hexadecimal equivalent. In contrast, the POST method sends the form data as part of the HTTP request body, which is not directly visible in the request URL.

In the Hello.jsp example, the GET method is used in the <FORM> tag to illustrate how the form data entered on the screen is sent as part of the request URL. This URL can be bookmarked and directly invoked. However, the GET method is not suitable for sending large amounts of data or confidential information such as the social security number; the POST method is more appropriate in these cases. For both GET and POST methods, the form data can be retrieved from the HTTP request object through the getParameter() method. Accordingly, in the Hello.jsp program, the method call request.getParameter("username") is used to retrieve the user name entered through the screen (see Note 4).

8. This <INPUT> tag defines a text input field called username that is 15 characters wide.

9. This <INPUT> tag defines an action button called "Submit name". When you type a name (say, Pam) in the text box and click the button on the screen, a new request is sent to the Web server along with the entered data. Since the form method is GET (see Note 7), the new URL has the query string username=Pam appended to the original URL.

Running `Hello.jsp`

First, install the `Hello.jsp` program on your Web server. These installation steps vary depending on which Web server you are using. Appendix E gives the setup steps required for some popular Web servers. Assume that the JSP file is installed as `examples/jsp/chapter10/Hello.jsp` with respect to the default application root of your Web server. Then, you can run this JSP by just pointing your browser to the appropriate URL, such as the following:

```
http://localhost:8080/examples/jsp/chapter10/Hello.jsp
```

This request causes the JSP engine to automatically run the JSP translator, if it is the first time that this page is being invoked. The generated code is compiled by a Java compiler, and the resulting Java bytecode is executed by the Web server. Unless the `Hello.jsp` file is modified, subsequent requests to the same page do not retranslate the JSP, but directly execute the previously compiled Java bytecode. Figure 10-1 shows a typical browser output for this page.

For the case shown in Figure 10-1, the request URL does not have a `username` parameter. Therefore, the `Hello.jsp` program just prints a "Hello there" message with the current time, and displays the text field and submit button for the data entry form. If the page is invoked with the same URL again, the output page will show a different timestamp.

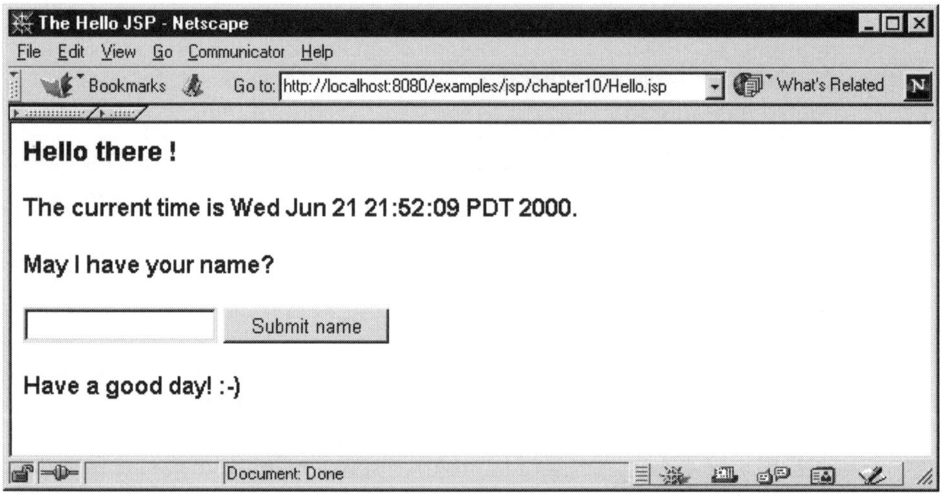

FIGURE 10-1. *Output of `Hello.jsp`*

Now, if you enter the name **Pam** in the text box of the form and click the "Submit name" button, the following new request is sent to the Web server as a result of executing the HTML form action:

```
http://localhost:8080/examples/jsp/chapter10/Hello.jsp?username=Pam
```

Notice how the original URL for invoking `Hello.jsp` is augmented with a '?' and the query string `username=Pam`, in accordance with the rules of the `GET` method of the form. The '?' character acts as the separator between the URL for the page and the HTTP request parameters. Figure 10-2 shows the output in the browser generated by this request. You can see that the JSP successfully retrieved the parameter `username` from the request URL, and printed "Hello Pam" instead of the "Hello there" greeting of Figure 10-1.

Peeking Behind the Scenes

Now that you have seen how easy it is to write and run the `Hello.jsp` program, it is worth looking briefly at what goes on behind the scenes. As described in Chapter 2, the JSP engine (also known as the JSP container) is the entity in charge of managing and executing JSP programs. It usually operates as an extension-mapped servlet, which means that it is invoked by the underlying Web server and servlet engine if the request URL ends in a `.jsp` extension. The JSP engine performs several steps automatically for you, hiding many details and speeding up the development of your application. Upon first invocation of the page, the JSP program

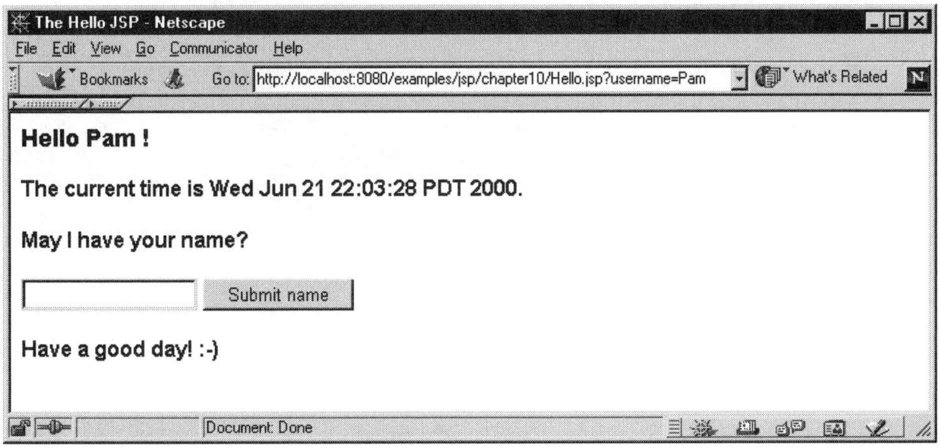

FIGURE 10-2. *Output of `Hello.jsp` after entering Pam in the text box*

is translated into Java servlet code, which is then compiled with a Java compiler to generate bytecode of the servlet class. Next, the generated servlet class is loaded, initialized, and run, producing the output page that is sent back to the HTTP client. The servlet class may be reloaded or unloaded at a later point by the JSP engine.

Note that it is also possible to pretranslate the JSP file before it is first invoked. This prevents any delays in response due to translation overhead when a JSP is first invoked. The Oracle JSP implementation provides a command-line tool called `ojspc` for this purpose. Usage of this tool is described in the "Oracle's JSP Implementation" section of this chapter.

It is instructive to look at the Java code `Hello.java` generated for the `Hello.jsp` program. Parts of the generated code are implementation dependent, but the essential contracts defined in the JSP specification must be satisfied by all compliant JSP engines. Listing 10-1 shows the code generated by the Oracle JSP 1.0 translator. The code has been annotated with references to detailed explanatory notes that follow the listing. Note that the generated code uses Oracle JSP libraries to handle implementation-specific tasks. The code is also different in Oracle JSP 1.1, although the conceptual structure remains the same. The significant points in Listing 10-1 are as follows:

- **A Java class is generated for the JSP** The generated class name is implementation specific—assume for explanatory purposes that it is named `Hello`. This class may be placed in a package whose name is also implementation dependent—the JSP specification does not mandate a specific algorithm for it. Generally, the package name is used only by the JSP engine and is not directly relevant for the JSP programmer.

- **The generated class defines a method `_jspService()`** This method is the main entry point for JSP invocation and contains code to write both the static and the dynamic content in the JSP page to the output stream. In particular, all JSP scriptlets and expressions are part of this method body. The method name and signature follow the standard contract defined by the JSP specification. It takes two arguments, which are the HTTP `request` and `response` objects, and can throw exceptions when executed.

Listing 10-1: Code generated from `Hello.jsp`

```
package examples.jsp.chapter10;  // (See Note 1.)

import oracle.jsp.runtime.*; // (See Note 2.)
import javax.servlet.*;
import javax.servlet.http.*;
import javax.servlet.jsp.*;
import java.io.*;
import java.util.*;
import java.lang.reflect.*;
```

```java
import java.beans.*;

public class Hello extends oracle.jsp.runtime.HttpJsp {
                                    // (See Note 3.)
    public final String _globalsClassName = null;
    // ** Begin Declarations
    String defaultName = "there";  // (See Note 4.)
    // ** End Declarations
    public void _jspService(HttpServletRequest request,
                            HttpServletResponse response)
                    throws IOException, ServletException {
                                    // (See Note 5.)
      /* set up the intrinsic variables using the pageContext :
      ** session = HttpSession
      ** application = ServletContext
      ** out = JspWriter
      ** page = this
      ** config = ServletConfig
      ** all session/app beans declared in globals.jsa
      */
       JspFactory factory = JspFactory.getDefaultFactory();  // (See Note 6.)
       PageContext pageContext = factory.getPageContext(this, request,
                    response, null, true, JspWriter.DEFAULT_BUFFER, true);
       // Note: this is not emitted if the session directive == false
       HttpSession session = pageContext.getSession();
       ServletContext application = pageContext.getServletContext();
       JspWriter out = pageContext.getOut();
       Hello page = this;
       ServletConfig config = pageContext.getServletConfig();
       try {
         out.println( "<HTML>");  // (See Note 7.)
       out.println( "  <HEAD> ");
         out.println( "     <TITLE> The Hello JSP </TITLE> ");
         out.println( "  </HEAD> ");
         out.println( "  <BODY  BGCOLOR=\"white\">");
         out.print( "      ");
         out.println( "");
         out.print( "      ");
         String name = request.getParameter("username"); // (See Note 8.)
         out.println( "");
         out.print( "    <H3> Hello  ");
         out.print(   (name == null)? defaultName : name );
                                                // (See Note 9.)
         out.println( " ! </H3>");
         out.print( "    <P><B> The current time is ");
         out.print(  new java.util.Date() );  // (See Note 10.)
         out.println( ".  ");
         out.println( "    </B></P>");
         out.println( "    <B>May I have your name?</B>");
         out.println( "    <FORM METHOD=GET> ");
         out.println( "       <INPUT TYPE=\"text\"");
         out.println( "             NAME=\"username\"");
         out.println( "             SIZE=15>");
         out.println( "       <INPUT TYPE=\"submit\"");
```

```
        out.println( "                    VALUE=\"Submit name\">");
        out.println( "       </FORM>");
        out.println( "     <P><B> Have a good day! :-) </B></P>");
        out.println( "  </BODY>");
        out.println( "</HTML>");
        out.flush();  // (See Note 11.)
    }
  catch( Exception e) {  // (See Note 12.)
    try { if (out != null) out.clear();}
    catch( Exception clearException) {
    }
    pageContext.handlePageException( e);
  }
  finally {  // (See Note 13.)
    if (out != null) out.close();
    factory.releasePageContext(pageContext);
  }
 }
}
```

Notes on the `Hello.java` code generated from `Hello.jsp`:

1. This statement is the package declaration for the `Hello.jsp` program. In the case of Oracle JSP 1.0, it is derived from the path name where JSP is installed on the Web server.

2. These `import` statements are generated automatically by the JSP translator to import the necessary JSP and servlet libraries, and other utility packages.

3. This statement declares a public Java class named `Hello`, which in the case of the Oracle JSP 1.0 implementation is the base name of the JSP file `Hello.jsp`. The `Hello` class extends the `oracle.jsp.runtime.HttpJsp` class, which is an abstract class defined in the JSP runtime library provided by Oracle. It provides default (empty) implementations of methods such as `jspInit()` and `jspDestroy()` that are called by the JSP engine to initialize and dispose of the JSP page instance as necessary. These methods may in fact be overridden by the programmer through explicit Java method declarations in the JSP page, although this is seldom done. The exact definition of the `HttpJsp` abstract class is implementation specific, but it must implement the standard interface `javax.servlet.jsp.HttpJspPage` as defined in the Servlet 2.2 API specification (refer to Appendix A for details of the Servlet 2.2 API).

4. This statement corresponds to declaration of the Java variable `defaultName` that appears within the `<%! … %>` tags in the `Hello.jsp` program. Notice that this declaration is a class-level declaration—that is, the variable name is accessible to all methods of the `Hello` class.

5. This statement defines a public method called `_jspService()` that is called to process the HTTP request from a client. The body of this method is automatically generated by the JSP translator based on the contents of the JSP page. Typically, the method body has three parts:

- **Setup code**, where the necessary HTTP and JSP runtime objects are initialized.

- **User code**, which is based on the JSP page. In Listing 10-1, this code appears in a series of `out.print()` and `out.println()` statements. Note that other code generation schemes are possible; in fact, Oracle JSP 1.1 optimizes the code by using character arrays instead of strings for the constant HTML code. Despite differences in the exact form of the generated code, the essential characteristic is the same across different JSP implementations: The static content and the dynamic scriptlets and expressions are placed in the same order as they appear in the original JSP page. Exceptions (such as `javax.servlet.ServletException` and `java.io.IOException`) may be thrown if runtime errors are encountered.

- **Exception handling and finalization code**, where the output stream is cleared or flushed before exit, and internal resources are cleaned up.

6. This statement is part of the setup code. It gets the default factory from the `javax.servlet.jsp.JspFactory` class (for details of the JSP API, refer to Appendix D). This factory is then used to create the `pageContext` object associated with the JSP page. The `pageContext` object encapsulates various implementation-dependent features of the JSP engine, and manages the scope namespaces (`request`, `page`, `session`, and `application`). The next five statements are also part of the JSP setup phase, where runtime objects such as the HTTP session and the output stream writer are initialized from the page context data by calling appropriate methods.

7. This statement is the start of the HTML code in the JSP. It is written to the output stream.

8. This statement is generated from the JSP scriptlet that reads the value of the `username` parameter from the `request` object.

9. This statement is generated from the JSP expression that is embedded in the hello message.

10. This statement is generated from the JSP expression that prints the current time.

11. This statement indicates the end of user code and flushes the output buffer.

12. This statement is part of the third and final section of the `_jspService()` method. It is automatically generated to catch any exceptions that may arise during JSP execution. In case an error occurs, the output buffer is cleared and the exception is passed to the `pageContext` object for processing and error reporting.

13. This is finalization code that runs before the JSP exits. The output buffer is closed and the `pageContext` object is released.

While writing JSP applications, most of the time you will not need to know details of the generated code as explained here. Oracle JDeveloper supports source-level debugging of JSP code—you can set breakpoints in the JSP page source and run it on a local servlet engine. This functionality is available in JDeveloper 3.1 and higher versions.

JSP Directives

In the previous section you have seen how to use JSP declarations, scriptlets, and expressions to embed Java code. Now you will learn about JSP directives. These directives are used to pass information required for JSP translation, such as the following:

- Java `import` statements
- Files to be included statically during JSP translation
- Content type (MIME type and character set) of the JSP and the output page

You will learn about each of these uses in this section. Other uses of JSP directives will be demonstrated in subsequent sections of this chapter.

A JSP directive is written within `<%@ ... %>` tags using the following general syntax:

```
<%@ directive attribute1="value1"  attribute2="value2" … … %>
```

The purpose of a JSP directive is to provide some information to the JSP translator. It affects the code generated for the JSP, but does not directly produce any content in the output page. The value of an attribute cannot use runtime parameters from the HTTP request.

There are three types of JSP directives: the `page` directive, the `include` directive, and the `taglib` directive. The set of allowed attributes depends on the type of directive you are using. In the following two sections, you will see how to use the `page` and `include` directives and their attributes. The `taglib` directive is discussed in the "Using JSP Tag Libraries" section in Chapter 12. A description of all the JSP directives and their attributes appears in Appendix D.

The `page` Directive

The `page` directive is used to specify information to the JSP translator that applies throughout the page. It has several attributes—you will learn about the important ones in this section, such as `import` and `contentType`. The complete set of attributes for the `page` directive is listed in Appendix D .

One or more page directives may appear in a JSP page and other pages that are included statically within it. However, each attribute, except for the `import` attribute, may occur only once. Here is a description of the attributes that are most frequently used:

- `import`   This attribute specifies one or more Java classes that are to be imported in the translated code. For example, the `page` directive listed here imports the `java.sql.*` libraries:

  ```
  <%@ page import="java.sql.*" %>
  ```

  This directive can also be written using alternate XML-based notation, as follows:

  ```
  <jsp:directive.page import="java.sql.*"  />
  ```

  Following the Java convention, `page` directives to import packages are generally placed in the top section of the JSP. Multiple packages may be imported in the same `page` directive by using a comma-separated list of Java classes and packages, as follows:

  ```
  <%@ page import="java.sql.*,sqlj.runtime.ref.DefaultContext" %>
  ```

  The same effect can also be achieved through multiple `page` directives appearing on different lines with separate `import` attributes, for example:

  ```
  <%@ page import="java.sql.*" %>
  <%@ page import="sqlj.runtime.ref.DefaultContext" %>
  ```

- `language`   This attribute defines the scripting language used in the JSP. The standard default value for this attribute is `java`. Oracle's JSP implementation also allows the value `sqlj`:

  ```
  <%@ page language="sqlj" %>
  ```

The effect of this directive is to allow `#sql` statements in the JSP for writing embedded SQL statements. In this case, the JSP translator calls the SQLJ translator during page translation. The use of SQLJ statements within a JSP is demonstrated in the "Using SQLJ in a JSP" section later in this chapter.

■ `buffer` This attribute defines whether the output stream used to write the final page contents is buffered. The default behavior is to buffer the output stream, which is generally desirable. The value `none` is used to specify no buffering. The `page` directive below specifies a buffer size of 20 kilobytes:

```
<%@ page buffer="20kb" %>
```

The default buffer size depends on the implementation, but must be 8 kilobytes or larger.

■ `autoFlush` This `boolean` attribute is related to the `buffer` attribute described earlier, and defines the behavior of a buffered output stream. It specifies whether the buffer is automatically flushed when full, or whether an exception is raised to indicate overflow. The default value for this attribute is `true`.

■ `isErrorPage` This `boolean` attribute indicates whether this JSP page can access the exception that occurred in another page, and this page is invoked as a result of that exception. The default value is `false`, in which case the implicit `exception` object cannot be used in the JSP (it will cause a translation error). If the value of this attribute is set to `true`, information about an exception is available to the scriptlets and expressions in that JSP through the implicitly defined `exception` object. This attribute is related to the `errorPage` attribute described next.

■ `errorPage` This attribute defines the URL of another JSP for error handling. If an error is encountered in the JSP page where this directive appears, processing is forwarded to the specified URL along with the details of the exception raised. The JSP to which the error is forwarded is usually defined as an error page—that is, it has a `page` directive with the `isErrorPage` attribute (described earlier) set to `true`. The default URL for error handling depends on the JSP implementation. The Oracle JSP implementation defines its own error page to process uncaught exceptions. You will see an example of using the `errorPage` and `isErrorPage` attributes in the "Handling JSP Errors" section of this chapter.

■ `contentType` This attribute defines the MIME type and character set of the JSP page. It applies to the page text during translation as well as for output during runtime. The default value for the MIME type is `text/html,` and the default character set encoding is ISO-8859-1 (also known as Latin-1). The value of the character set is in terms of the IANA name (IANA stands for Internet Assigned Numbers Authority, and IANA names for various character sets are available through the Web page `http://www.iana.org/numbers.htm`). For example, the following statement sets the character encoding to Japanese 'Shift_JIS':

```
<%@ page contentType="text/html;charset=Shift_JIS" %>
```

For correct translation, a `page` directive with a `contentType` setting must appear near the top of the JSP, before any non-Latin-1 characters are used or the output buffer is flushed (when the output stream is initialized with character set information).

The `include` Directive

The `include` directive is used to physically insert the contents of another file during JSP translation. Be careful not to confuse this directive with the `<jsp:include>` action tag, which is used to include files at JSP runtime. You will learn about the `include` tag in the "Calling Other Pages from a JSP" section of this chapter. The `include` directive is sometime referred to as the *static* include, while the `include` action tag is referred to as the *dynamic* include.

Syntax for the `include` directive is shown here:

```
<%@ include  file="fileURL" %>
```

In XML-complaint JSP notation, the `include` directive is written as follows:

```
<jsp:directive.include file="fileURL" />
```

This directive has a single mandatory attribute—the file to be included. The file is specified in terms of a *relative* URL, which can be in one of the following two forms:

- **Page-relative**, where it does not start with a '/' character. In this case, the file path is relative to the location of the current JSP.

- **Application-relative or context-relative**, where it starts with a '/' character. This URL syntax implies that the file path is relative to the root of the JSP application. As discussed in the section titled "The Servlet Context" in Chapter 2, the Servlet 2.2 specification defines the notion of a Web application root, which is associated with the servlet context for that application. For file-system–based servlet environments (such as the Apache Web server with the Tomcat servlet engine), the application root corresponds to a directory on the file system. All files belonging to the Web application are placed under that directory.

The `include` directive causes the JSP translator to insert the contents of the specified file in the position where this directive appears. In other words, this directive is substituted with the file contents during JSP translation. This directive is generally used for common "header" text or code, such as copyright notices and banner information. The included file can also be conveniently used to hold `page` directives that are common to a set of JSP pages, such as imported Java classes and packages.

The example here shows a simple JSP program, `StaticInclude.jsp`, that uses the `include` directive to insert two files, `Imports.jsp` and `Banner.htm`, in the main JSP code:

```
<%-- Program name: StaticInclude.jsp
  -- Purpose:      Include other pages at translation time
  --%>
<HTML>
  <HEAD> <TITLE> The StaticInclude JSP </TITLE> </HEAD>
  <BODY>
     <%@ include file="Imports.jsp"%>
<H3> Hello! The current time is: <%= new Date() %> </H3> <BR><HR>
     <%@ include file="common/Banner.htm" %>
  </BODY>
</HTML>
```

Notice that the `Imports.jsp` file is assumed to be in the same directory as the main JSP, while the `Banner.htm` file is in the subdirectory `common` with respect to the location of the `StaticInclude.jsp` file. To run this example, a simple file, `Banner.htm`, is defined below:

```
<!-- Banner.htm -->
<H2><I> … Here goes the banner information …  </I></H2>
```

The `Imports.jsp` file is intended to hold common imports, for example:

```
<!-- Imports.jsp  -->
<%@ page import="java.sql.*, java.util.Date" %>
<%@ page import="sqlj.runtime.ref.DefaultContext" %>
```

Figure 10-3 shows the browser output upon executing `StaticInclude.jsp`. Note how the banner information has been inserted at the bottom of the page.

Calling Other Pages from a JSP

In this section, you will learn how a JSP program can call other pages. There are two JSP action tags available for this purpose:

- The `<jsp:include>` tag, which calls another page and then returns control to the caller JSP.

- The `<jsp:forward>` tag, which transfers execution control to the forwarded page and terminates the caller JSP.

These tags are generally used to switch to different pages based on dynamic conditions. In the following examples, you will learn how to use these tags in your JSP application.

The `<jsp:include>` Tag

The `<jsp:include>` tag is used to send the HTTP request to another page from the main JSP. The included page may be a static text or HTML file, or a dynamic program such as another JSP or a servlet. The included page processes the request and presumably generates some data, which is inserted in the output stream as part of the final page. The caller JSP resumes its execution after the `include` action is complete. The basic syntax of the `include` tag is as follows:

```
<jsp:include  page ="includeURL" flush="true" />
```

Notice that the `include` tag syntax is XML compatible. This tag has two attributes: `page` and `flush`. The `page` attribute specifies the relative URL of the page to be invoked. This URL could be either a constant string or computed at runtime through an embedded JSP expression. The `boolean`-valued `flush` attribute must always be set to `true`, indicating that the output stream buffer of the main JSP is to be flushed before control is transferred to the included page. Flushing

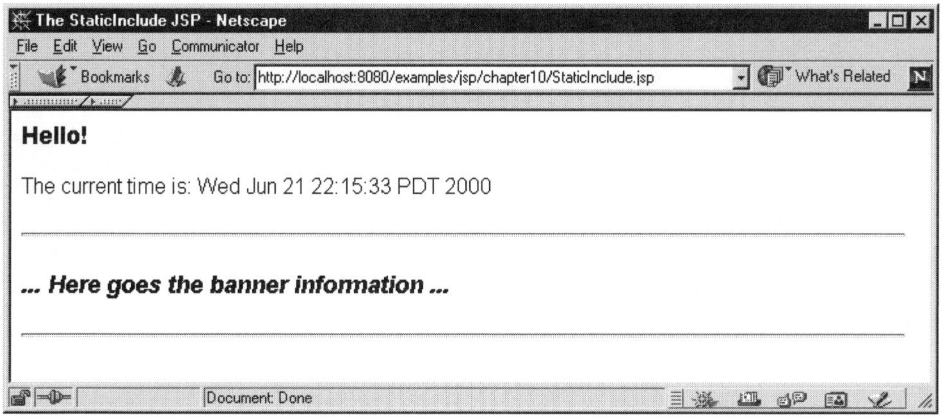

FIGURE 10-3. *Output of executing `StaticInclude.jsp`*

the buffer is necessary so that the included page can insert its own output in the proper position in the HTTP response.

You will now see an example program, `DynamicInclude.jsp`, that includes the output of an HTML page, `Included.htm`, and of a JSP program, `Included.jsp`, by calling them through the include tag. The code for this program is shown here:

```
<%-- Program name: DynamicInclude.jsp
  -- Purpose:      Call other pages at runtime
  --%>
<HTML>
  <HEAD> <TITLE> The Dynamic Include JSP </TITLE> </HEAD>
  <BODY BGCOLOR="white">
    <% String includedHtml = "include/IncludedHello.htm"; %>
    <P> <jsp:include page="<%= includedHtml %>" flush="true"/>
    <B> <jsp:include page="Time.jsp" flush="true"/>  </B>
  </BODY>
</HTML>
```

Notice that the URL for the included HTML page is set dynamically through a JSP expression, based on the value assigned to the `includedHtml` variable in the JSP scriptlet. The assigned value is the constant string "`include/IncludedHello.htm`" in this example, but can in general be computed from some dynamic condition. This capability to dynamically determine the URL of the included page is a basic distinction between the `<jsp:include>` tag and the translation-time `include` directive discussed in the preceding section.

The `IncludedHello.htm` file must be available in the `include` subdirectory with respect to the location of the `DynamicInclude.jsp`. A simple `IncludedHello.htm` file is given here:

```
<!-- Program name: IncludedHello.htm
  -- Purpose:      Print some static text
  --!>
<H2> Hello! How are you? </H2>
<P><B> I am the IncludedHello HTML page.
<P>The current time is: </B>
```

Based on the page URL used in the `include` tag, the `Time.jsp` file must be installed in the same directory as the main JSP file. The `Time.jsp` page contains the following code:

```
<%-- Program name: Time.jsp   --%>
<%= new java.util.Date() %>
```

If you now point your browser to the URL for `DynamicInclude.jsp`, the output page will include the contents of the `IncludedHello.htm` file, followed by the current time as computed by the `Time.jsp` program. Note that the included JSP will be automatically translated before invocation, in case it has not been translated before. A typical browser output of calling the `DynamicInclude.jsp` is shown in Figure 10-4.

Although not shown in this example, multiple levels of `include` action are allowed in a JSP application. This is left as a programming exercise for you.

In some applications, the HTTP request needs to be augmented with additional information before it is sent to the included page for processing. The JSP 1.1 specification provides a special `<jsp:param>` tag for this purpose (note that this tag is not available in JSP 1.0). It can be used to specify additional request parameters as *name=value* pairs that are appended to the original HTTP `request` object from the caller JSP. The syntax for the `<jsp:param>` tag is as follows:

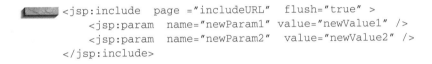

```
<jsp:param   name="paramName"   value="paramValue" />
```

The syntax of the `include` tag when using additional request parameters is as follows:

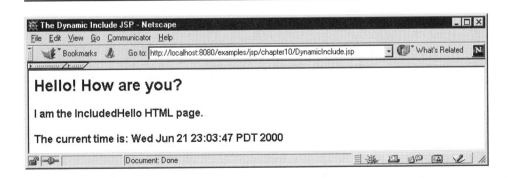

```
<jsp:include  page ="includeURL"  flush="true" >
     <jsp:param  name="newParam1" value="newValue1" />
     <jsp:param  name="newParam2"  value="newValue2" />
</jsp:include>
```

The Dynamic Include JSP - Netscape

File Edit View Go Communicator Help

Bookmarks   Go to: `http://localhost:8080/examples/jsp/chapter10/DynamicInclude.jsp`   What's Related

Hello! How are you?

I am the IncludedHello HTML page.

The current time is: Wed Jun 21 23:03:47 PDT 2000

Document: Done

FIGURE 10-4. *Output of running* `DynamicInclude.jsp`

Writing a JSP that uses additional request parameters to invoke an included page is left as an exercise for you.

The `<jsp:forward>` Tag

The syntax of the action tag for request forwarding is as follows:

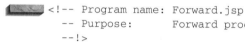

```
<jsp:forward   page="forwardedURL"  />
```

The effect of this action is to dispatch the HTTP request to the specified page URL and to terminate execution of the current page. The page forwarded to could be a static HTML or text file, or a JSP or servlet program. If the caller JSP has already written some data into the output buffer, the buffer is cleared before forwarding the request. If you need to add additional parameters to the HTTP request before forwarding it, you can use nested `<jsp:param>` tags using similar syntax as shown earlier for the `<jsp:include>` tag.

The following is a `Forward.jsp` page that illustrates the concept of forwarding a request:

```
<!-- Program name: Forward.jsp
  -- Purpose:        Forward processing conditionally to other pages
  --!>
<HTML>
  <HEAD><TITLE> The Forward JSP </TITLE></HEAD>
  <BODY>
     <%  if (request.getParameter("username") == null) { %>
          <jsp:forward page="forward/ForwardedHello.htm" />
     <% } else { %>
          <jsp:forward page="forward/WelcomeUser.jsp" />
     <% } %>
  </BODY>
</HTML>
```

The `Forward.jsp` application checks if the HTTP request has a parameter called `username`. If this parameter is not present or has a `null` value, the request is forwarded to the static HTML file `ForwardedHello.htm` in the subdirectory `forward` with respect to the current page. If the `username` parameter has a non-`null` value, the request is forwarded to the `WelcomeUser.jsp` program in the `forward` subdirectory. The `ForwardedHello.htm` file is shown here:

```
<!-- Program name:  ForwardedHello.htm
  -- Purpose:        Print some static text
  --!>
<HTML>
  <HEAD><TITLE> The ForwardedHello Page </TITLE></HEAD>
```

```
<BODY BGCOLOR="white">
  <H2> Hello, There!  </H2>
  <P> I am the ForwardedHello HTML Page.
</BODY>
</HTML>
```

The purpose of the `WelcomeUser.jsp` page is to print out the name of the user in a greeting message. The code for this JSP is shown here:

```
<%-- Program name: WelcomeUser.jsp
  -- Purpose:      Print a welcome message for the username parameter
  --%>
<HTML>
  <HEAD><TITLE>The WelcomeUser JSP </TITLE></HEAD>
  <BODY>
    <H2> Welcome <%= request.getParameter("username") %> ! </H2>
  </BODY>
</HTML>
```

To run this JSP, you should install the `Forward.jsp` file in the `examples/jsp/chapter10` directory on your Web server and the `ForwardedHello.htm` and `WelcomeUser.jsp` files in the subdirectory `forward` with respect to `Forward.jsp` (refer to Appendix E for installation steps). If you then point your browser to the URL for `Forward.jsp`, the output page shown in Figure 10-5 is displayed by the browser.

There are two significant points to observe in the output generated by `Forward.jsp`:

■ Because the invocation URL has no request parameters, execution control is transferred to the `ForwardedHello.htm` page, whose contents are displayed by the browser.

■ The title of the output page appears as "The ForwardedHello Page". Notice the caller JSP (that is, `Forward.jsp`) has the title line as "The Forward JSP", which appears positionally before the `forward` action. However, in accordance with the semantics of `forward`, the output buffer is cleared before forwarding. Thus, the title of the final page is determined by the page forwarded to, which in this case is the title specified in `ForwardedHello.htm`. If you examine the source of the generated page, you will see that it consists only of the contents of this page.

To try the other case of forwarding to `WelcomeUser.jsp`, you invoke `Forward.jsp` with a request parameter called `username` that has a non-`null` value. This can be tested by pointing your browser to the appropriate URL, for example:

```
http://localhost:8080/examples/jsp/chapter10/Forward.jsp?username=Tara
```

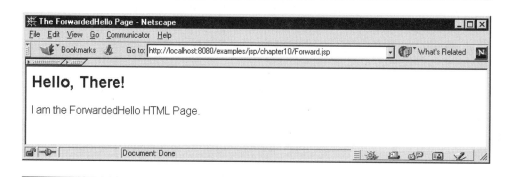

FIGURE 10-5. *Output of executing* `Forward.jsp` *without request parameters*

Notice that the request parameter and its value is appended to the base URL as a *name=value* pair after the '?' separator character, in accordance with the convention of the HTTP GET method. The browser output in this case is shown in Figure 10-6. Notice again that the title displayed in the header of the browser window is the title of the forwarded page and not that of the caller JSP.

Using JSPs with Servlets

It is important to understand how JSPs and servlets can work together. In some cases, writing a servlet is preferable to a JSP (see the "JSP vs. Servlet" section in Chapter 2). For example, if you want to return some binary data, a JSP is not a suitable mechanism. This is because JSP uses a `javax.servlet.jsp.JspWriter` object to write out data, and its methods only apply well for plain text (which is what JSPs are primarily designed to handle). Therefore, you will generally have to use a servlet if you are returning binary data. In this case, the `getOutputStream()`

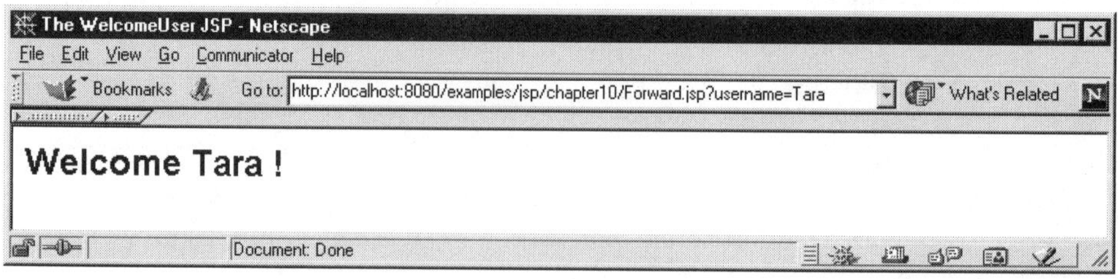

FIGURE 10-6. *Output of executing* `Forward.jsp` *with a username parameter*

method of the HTTP `response` object can be used to obtain an output stream, which you can use to write out binary data. Thus, there are cases where you will need to use both servlets and JSPs in your Web application.

In this section, you will learn how to call a JSP from a servlet and vice versa. The examples in this section assume that you are using a servlet engine that supports the Servlet 2.1 API or higher versions, such as JSWDK or Tomcat. This assumption is necessary because certain features are missing in the Servlet 2.0 specification (which is the version implemented by the JServ servlet runner for Apache). Specifically, the `javax.servlet.RequestDispatcher` **interface** is not available in the Servlet 2.0 API specification; it was added only in Servlet 2.1 API.

Calling a Servlet from a JSP

You can use the `<jsp:include>` and `<jsp:forward>` standard tags to invoke a servlet from a JSP for servlet implementations that conform to Servlet 2.1 and higher versions. The following is the code for a JSP program, `CallServlet.jsp`, that includes output generated by a servlet class named `CalledServlet`. By now, the general structure of the JSP code should look very familiar to you. Note that output from the servlet is included in between output from the JSP through the `<jsp:include>` tag, which functions like a method call:

```
<%-- Program name: CallServlet.jsp
  -- Purpose:       Call a servlet from the JSP
  --%>
<HTML>
  <HEAD> <TITLE> The CallServlet JSP </TITLE> </HEAD>
  <BODY BGCOLOR="white">

<H3> Hello, I am the CallServlet JSP. </H3>
<p> <b>Below I will include output generated by a servlet.</b><br>
<br><hr><i>
<jsp:include page="/servlet/chapter10.CalledServlet" flush="true" />
</i><br><hr>

<p> <b>You are now back to the CallServlet JSP.</b>
  </BODY>
</HTML>
```

The code for the `CalledServlet.java` program is shown here. This servlet gets the `PrintWriter` object from the `response` argument and prints out a message:

```
/** Program name: CalledServlet.java
 ** Purpose:       Print out a greeting message
 **/
```

```
package chapter 10;

import javax.servlet.*;
import javax.servlet.http.*;
import java.io.PrintWriter;
import java.io.IOException;

public class CalledServlet extends HttpServlet {
    public void doGet (HttpServletRequest request,
                       HttpServletResponse response)
                throws IOException {
        PrintWriter out= response.getWriter();
        out.println("Hello, I am CalledServlet.");
        out.println("<BR>The current time is:"+ new java.util.Date()
              +"<BR>");
        out.println("Now returning to calling page..");
    }
}
```

Install these JSP and servlet programs on your Web server (see Appendix E for Web server setup). Figure 10-7 shows the output generated when you invoke `CallServlet.jsp`.

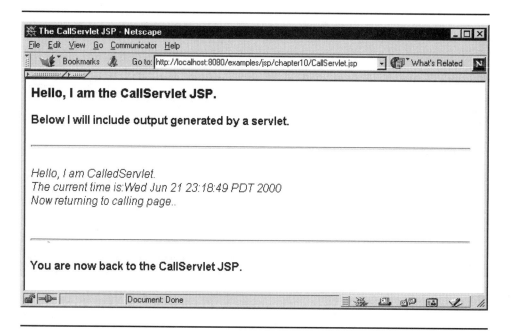

FIGURE 10-7. *Output of CallServlet.jsp*

Likewise, you can use the `<jsp:forward>` tag to forward execution control from a JSP to a servlet. Recall the difference between `include` and `forward`: for a `forward`, the output contains data from the forwarded page only and no data from the originating page. In contrast, output from a `<jsp:include>` statement is physically placed in the position where the statement appears in your JSP, and is only a part of the final response sent to the browser. The calling program continues its execution after control returns from the included program, just like a method call.

You may be wondering at this point how you can pass information to the included or forwarded page from the caller page. One way is to use the `<jsp:param>` tag discussed in the preceding section. This tag is available in JSP 1.1 implementations. There are several other ways to do this, for example, using the HTTP `session` or `request` objects, or through a JavaBean. Using the attributes of the `request` object to pass data is discussed in the next section, and you can use this technique when a JSP calls a servlet or another JSP page. Data sharing between pages through an appropriately scoped JavaBean is illustrated in the next chapter.

Calling a JSP from a Servlet

You can also include or forward the HTTP request to a JSP from a servlet. This requires using the `javax.servlet.RequestDispatcher` **interface** introduced in the Servlet 2.1 API specification. In the next section you will learn about this **interface** and how to use its methods. The `<jsp:include>` and `<jsp:forward>` tags discussed in the preceding section are implemented using this **interface**. Therefore, much of the discussion in this section also applies to the `include` and `forward` action tags. Although most of the steps are done by the JSP runtime and generally not written directly by the JSP programmer, knowing about the `RequestDispatcher()` **interface** will help you to better understand the operation of the `<jsp:include>` and `<jsp:forward>` tags.

The `RequestDispatcher` Interface

The `RequestDispatcher` **interface** provides a mechanism to invoke other Web application resources from a servlet or a JSP. Methods in this **interface** can be called to pass the current HTTP request to another program, typically a servlet or JSP, for further processing. The methods of `RequestDispatcher` and other Servlet 2.2 interfaces are listed in Appendix A. Dispatching to another program through this **interface** typically consists of the following four steps:

1. First, get a `ServletContext` object. This can be obtained from the HTTP servlet instance through its `getServletContext()` method, as follows:

```
javax.servlet.ServletContext sc = getServletContext();
```

2. Next, obtain a `RequestDispatcher` object from the `ServletContext` object by calling its `getRequestDispatcher()` method with the application-relative URL of the called program as the argument:

```
javax.servlet.RequestDispatcher rd =
            sc.getRequestDispatcher("/jsp/chapter10/CalledJSP.jsp")
```

3. You will often want to share data between the included or forwarded page and the calling page. There are several ways to do this:

   ■ You can append a query string to the page URL in the `getRequestDispatcher()` method call using the '?' convention and name-value pairs, for example,

   ```
   javax.servlet.RequestDispatcher rd =
     sc.getRequestDispatcher(
             "/jsp/chapter10/CalledJSP.jsp?username=jspuser");
   ```

   In this case, the parameter `username` and its value become part of the HTTP request and can be retrieved using the `request.get-Parameter()` method call. You can use the same technique in the `<jsp:include>` and `<jsp:forward>` tags. Note, however, that the extra information passed is restricted to be a string in this method as it is part of the URL.

   ■ You can use the method call `request.setAttribute()` to attach any Java object to the HTTP `request` object before you call the other page. For example,

   ```
   Order o = new Order();
   request.setAttribute("cart", o);
   ```

   This attribute is then available in an included or forwarded page via the `request.getAttribute()` method call. For example,

   ```
   Order o = (Order) request.getAttribute("cart");
   ```

   ■ You could also share the data through the HTTP session object by calling the `session.setAttribute()` and `session.getAttribute()` methods. These methods are analogous to the corresponding methods in the `request` object, with the important difference that they are accessible to any page invoked within the same HTTP session and not just for the same HTTP request.

   ■ You could alternatively use a session-scoped JavaBean that is shared by all pages in the HTTP session. This approach is illustrated in the next chapter.

Which of these approaches you should use depends on the requirements and structure of your Web application. If the information is to be shared only for the duration of the HTTP request, you should use the `request` object to hold the data. If the information is relevant for all pages in the application, use the session object or a session-scoped JavaBean.

4. Finally, after the shared data and the request dispatcher are set up, you invoke the `include()` or `forward()` method on the `RequestDispatcher` object with the HTTP `request` and `response` objects as parameters:

```
rd.include(request, response); // including a page
rd.forward(request, response); // forwarding to a page
```

In contrast to the `include()` method, execution control is transferred to the called program and the calling program is terminated for the `forward()` method.

You can now put these steps together to write a complete servlet that invokes a JSP and passes it some information. The following is the code for the `CallJSP` servlet, which sets the `username` attribute in the `request` object and then calls the `CalledJSP` program, including its output in the generated page:

```
/** Program name: CallJSP Servlet
 ** Purpose:      Call a JSP from a servlet
 **/
import javax.servlet.*;
import javax.servlet.http.*;
import java.io.PrintWriter;
import java.io.IOException;
public class CallJSP extends HttpServlet {
    public void doGet (HttpServletRequest request,
                  HttpServletResponse response)
      throws IOException, ServletException {
        response.setContentType("text/html");
        PrintWriter out = response.getWriter();
        out.println("<html><body bgcolor=\"white\">");
        out.println("<head><title>The CallJSP Servlet</title>");
        out.println("</head><body>");

        out.println("<H3>I am the CallJSP Servlet.</H3>");
        out.println("<B>I will now include the CalledJSP page..</B>");
        out.println("<BR><BR><HR><i>");

        request.setAttribute("username", "jspuser");
        getServletContext().
          getRequestDispatcher("/jsp/chapter10/CalledJSP.jsp").
          include(request, response);
```

```
        out.println("</I><HR><BR>");
        out.println("<P><B>Now you are back to CallJSP servlet.</B>");
        out.println("</body>");
        out.println("</html>");
    }
}
```

The code for the `CalledJSP` program is shown here. This page simply prints out a greeting message and the current time. It uses the `getAttribute()` method in the HTTP `request` object to retrieve the value of `username` that was set by the `CallJSP` servlet.

```
/** Program name: CalledJSP.jsp
 ** Purpose:      Retrieve the username attribute from the request and
 **               print a greeting and the current time
 **/
<P>Hello <%= request.getAttribute("username") %>, I am CalledJSP.
<P>Hello, I am CalledJSP.
<BR>The current time is: <%= new java.util.Date() %>
<BR>Now returning to calling page..<P>
```

Output of invoking the `CallJSP` servlet is shown in Figure 10-8. Notice that control is returned back to this servlet after execution of the `CalledJSP` program is complete. Writing a servlet program that forwards to (instead of including) a JSP is left as an exercise for you.

Considerations for Servlet 2.0 Environments

Some popular servlet runners, such as JServ, implement only the Servlet 2.0 API. In these environments, such as in the Oracle Internet Application Server version 1.0 based on the Apache Web server and JServ, the `RequestDispatcher` **interface** is not available. Oracle's JSP implementation still supports the `<jsp:include>` and `<jsp:forward>` tags by emulating some functionality of the `RequestDispatcher` **interface** in the Servlet 2.0 environment. However, a restriction is that only JSP pages can be invoked through these tags (Oracle JSP 1.1 will also support calling HTML pages through action tags in Servlet 2.0 environments–this functionality was being added at the time of writing). The HTML pages could be renamed or copied to have `.jsp` extensions relatively easily. The workaround for servlets is to "wrap" your servlet in a JSP so that you can conveniently invoke them from JSPs through the `include` and `forward` action tags. The following code fragment shows such a JSP page, `ServletWrapper.jsp`, that calls an underlying servlet program, `CalledServlet` (which you wrote earlier in this section), when the JSP page is invoked. It initializes and destroys the wrapped servlet in the `jspInit()` and `jspDestroy()` methods, respectively, and calls the

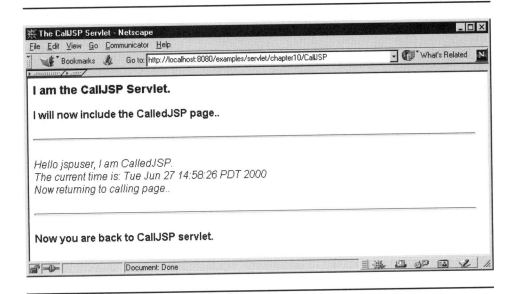

FIGURE 10-8.   *Output of* `CallJSP` *servlet*

`doGet()` method of `CalledServlet` through a JSP scriptlet as part of the JSP service request.

```
<%-- Program name: ServletWrapper.jsp
  -- Purpose:        Invoke a servlet program without JSP tags or
  --                 the RequestDispatcher interface.  Useful in
  --                 Servlet 2.0 environments.
  --%>
<%@ page isThreadSafe="true" import="CalledServlet" %>
<%! CalledServlet calledServlet = null;
    public void jspInit() {
      calledServlet = new CalledServlet();
      try {
       calledServlet.init(this.getServletConfig());
      } catch (ServletException se) {
         calledServlet = null;
      }
    }
    public void jspDestroy() {
        if (calledServlet != null)
          calledServlet.destroy();
    }
%>
```

```
<% if (calledServlet != null) {
    calledServlet.doGet(request, response);
}
else {
    throw new JspException("Error initializing servlet!!");
}
%>
```

Note the use of the `isThreadSafe` attribute in the `page` directive in `ServletWrapper.jsp`. This attribute is `true` by default, but it should be set to `false` if the underlying servlet is not thread safe. You can now call the `ServletWrapper.jsp` page through the `<jsp:include>` tag as follows:

```
<jsp:include page="ServletWrapper.jsp">
```

This `include` statement will work in all JSP and servlet environments, including Apache/JServ with a Servlet 2.0 implementation.

Handling JSP Errors

In this section, you will learn how to use JSP error pages to handle exceptions that occur during JSP execution. Because JSPs can have Java code in scriptlets, you could write a **try...catch** block to catch exceptions and print appropriate error messages. JSP also provides a clean way to create modular error pages that are specifically meant for formatting and reporting exceptions. This facility uses the `errorPage` and `isErrorPage` attributes of the `page` directive. You learned about the syntax of these attributes in the "JSP Directives" section earlier in this chapter. Now, you will see them in action.

The following code is a JSP page, `ErrorGenerator.jsp`, that generates an error message if the HTTP `request` object has no parameter called `username`. Such a scenario could arise, for example, in a login page that has a form for entering the user's name and password. A friendly error message is needed in case this information is not supplied.

Parts of the code in `Errorgenerator.jsp` that are related to error handling are shown in bold. The essential JSP feature being illustrated here is the use of the `page` directive to specify an `ErrorHandler.jsp` page. The HTTP request will be forwarded to this error page whenever an error is encountered in the main JSP page. The same error-handler page can be used for multiple JSPs, although only one is shown here.

```
<%-- Program name: ErrorGenerator.jsp
  -- Purpose:      Generate an error to illustrate use of error page
  --%>
```

```
<%@ page errorPage="ErrorHandler.jsp" %>
<HTML>
  <HEAD> <TITLE> The ErrorGenerator JSP  </TITLE>
  </HEAD>
  <BODY  BGCOLOR="white">
     <%  // check if username provided, else throw an exception
         String user = request.getParameter("username");
         if (user == null) {
           throw new Exception("You gave no user name!!"); }
         else %>
     Hello <%= user %>!
  </BODY>
</HTML>
```

The code for the `ErrorHandler.jsp` page that actually formats and reports the error message is shown here:

```
<%-- Program name: ErrorHandler.jsp
  -- Purpose:       To report errors with user-friendly output
  --%>
<%@ page isErrorPage="true" %>
<HTML>
 <HEAD> <TITLE>The ErrorHandler JSP </TITLE></HEAD>
 <BODY BGCOLOR="white">
  <P><B> Hello! I am the ErrorHandler JSP.
  <P>    Sorry, there was a problem:
                <%= exception.getLocalizedMessage() %> </B>
 </BODY>
</HTML>
```

The main point to note in the `ErrorHandler.jsp` program is that it is declared to be an error-handling page by setting the `isErrorPage` attribute to `true` in the `page` directive. Recall from the earlier section titled "JSP Directives" in this chapter that the effect of this setting is to make the `exception` object implicitly available in the page. The `ErrorHandler.jsp` program accesses this object to extract and print out the error message that was generated by the main JSP page. It does so by calling the `getLocalizedMessage()` method on the `exception` object. It could also call the `getMessage()` method if locale is not important for error reporting. Figure 10-9 shows the output of invoking the `ErrorGenerator.jsp` page without a `username` parameter, thus raising an exception that is reported by the `ErrorHandler.jsp` page.

A final point about error pages: Are the generated exceptions also available to servlets that are part of the same Web application? The answer is yes. Besides using the implicit `exception` variable in the error page, the same `exception` object

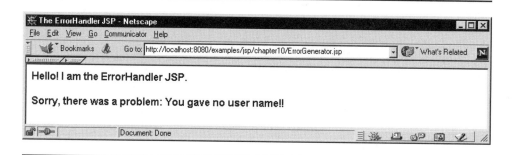

FIGURE 10-9. *Output of invoking* `ErrorGenerator.jsp` *with no parameter*

can be accessed via an attribute named `javax.servlet.jsp.jspException` in the HTTP `request` object, as shown in the following code fragment:

```
<% Exception e = (Exception)
            request.getAttribute("javax.servlet.jsp.jspException");  %>
<P> Sorry, there was a problem: <%= e.getLocalizedMessage() %>
```

In order to invoke a JSP error page, a servlet needs to call the `request.setAttribute()` method with the generated exception, and then forward request processing to the JSP error page by using the `forward()` method in the `RequestDispatcher` **interface** (as described in the previous section). Writing a servlet that forwards errors to a JSP error-handler page using this technique is left as a programming exercise for you.

Oracle's JSP Implementation

Oracle has its own implementation of the JSP 1.0 and 1.1 specifications. The implementation is freely downloadable from Oracle Technology Network (`http://technet.oracle.com/tech/java/servlets`). A distinguishing feature of the Oracle JSP engine is that it works with different versions of the Servlet API (2.0, 2.1, and 2.2). Therefore, the same Oracle JSP libraries will work with JServ as the servlet runner (Servlet 2.0 API) on the Apache Web server, and will also work with Tomcat (Servlet 2.2). This independence from the Servlet API version makes Oracle JSP a portable JSP engine across many different servlet runners. Refer to Appendix E for the steps to install Oracle JSP in the popular Web server environments.

In the Oracle 8.1.7 release, servlets and JSPs can be executed within the embedded Java Virtual machine in the database (JServer). This functionality also uses Oracle's JSP engine, which runs optimized JSP code in the database. This product is under development at the time of writing, and is expected to be available by early fall of 2000.

In addition to being fully compliant with the JSP specifications, the Oracle JSP implementation also has several extensions for programming convenience. Of these extensions, two major ones are as follows:

- Support for using SQLJ code in a JSP scriptlet

- A translator tool `ojspc` to pretranslate JSP files from the command line

You will now learn about these two extensions through examples.

Using SQLJ in a JSP

SQLJ is an ANSI/ISO standard for embedding static SQL statements in a Java program through special `#sql` notation. The `#sql` statements are converted to Java code by the SQLJ translator. The compiled program can be run against a database with the help of a JDBC driver. The advantage of using SQLJ is that the shorthand notation makes programming more convenient and less error prone. SQLJ code is generally much shorter than a JDBC program, and takes less time to write and maintain. SQLJ also has the capability of checking your static SQL statements against the database, catching SQL syntax errors and type mismatches at compile time instead of at runtime (refer to the book *Oracle 8i SQLJ Programming*, OMH, November 1999 for details). However, direct JDBC calls still need to be used if your SQL command is dynamic—that is, it is not known statically before runtime.

You can indicate that your JSP uses SQLJ code in one of the following two ways:

- Use the `.sqljsp` extension for your source file instead of the `.jsp` extension.

- Specify `language="sqlj"` in a `page` directive in your JSP. Refer to the "The `page` Directive" section earlier in this chapter for syntax details.

Although the Oracle JSP implementation supports SQLJ code in the JSP scriptlets for convenience, you should understand that a much better programming practice is to use JavaBean components to access the database. You can write SQLJ code in a JavaBean, making the code more modular and reusable. This also eliminates cumbersome program logic in the JSP that is interwoven with the static text. Using JavaBeans with JSP is explored in depth in the next chapter.

The following code is for a page, `SQLJQuery.jsp`, that uses SQLJ to access the database and display the results of a static SQL query. Given an employee number as the query parameter, the purpose of this program is to retrieve the full name, job description, and department name of the employee from the purchase order database. The schema for this database is defined in the "Introduction" chapter at the beginning of this book. The relevant tables EMPLOYEE_LIST and DEPARTMENT_LIST are reproduced below for convenience:

```
CREATE TABLE EMPLOYEE_LIST(
      employeeno     NUMBER(7),
      departmentno NUMBER(5),
      type     VARCHAR2(30),
      lastname VARCHAR2(30),
      firstname VARCHAR2(30),
      phone VARCHAR2(10));
CREATE TABLE DEPARTMENT_LIST(
      departmentno NUMBER(5),
      shortname VARCHAR2(6),
      longname VARCHAR2(20));
```

Assume that these tables are installed in the jspuser account with password jsp. Then, you can write the following program to retrieve the desired information using SQLJ:

```
<%-- Program name:  SQLJQuery.jsp
     -- Purpose:        Query information from the purchase order database
     --                 using SQLJ in JSP
     --%>
<%@ page language="sqlj" %>   <!-- (See Note 1.) -->
<%@ page import="sqlj.runtime.ref.DefaultContext" %>
<%@ page import="oracle.sqlj.runtime.Oracle" %>
<HTML> <HEAD> <TITLE> The SQLJQuery JSP  </TITLE> </HEAD>
<BODY BGCOLOR="white">
  <H3> Hello, I can do a SQLJ query to get employee data...</H3>
  <%   String empno = request.getParameter("empno"); // (See Note 2.)
       if (empno != null) { %>
  <H2> Employee # <%=empno %> Details: </H2>
  <%   DefaultContext dctx = null;            <!-- (See Note 3.) -->
       try { // set up database connection
         dctx = Oracle.getConnection("jdbc:oracle:oci8:@",
                                     "jspuser", "jsp"); // (See Note 4.)
         String job = null;
         String deptName = null;
         String empName = null;
         #sql [dctx] {  /* (See Note 5.) */
                    SELECT type, department_list.longname,
                           lastname||','||firstname
                    INTO  :job, :deptName, :empName
                    FROM EMPLOYEE_LIST, DEPARTMENT_LIST
                    WHERE employeeno= :empno
                    AND  DEPARTMENT_LIST.deptno =
```

```
                    EMPLOYEE_LIST.deptno}; %>
  <H3><BLOCKQUOTE><PRE>
    Name        : <%= empName %>   <!-- (See Note 6.) -->
    Job         : <%= job %>
    Department : <%= deptName %>
  </PRE></BLOCKQUOTE></H3>
<%
} catch (java.sql.SQLException e) {  %>  <!-- (See Note 7.) -->
   <P> SQL error: <PRE> <%= e %> </PRE> </P>
<%   } finally { if (dctx != null) dctx.close(); } }  %>
<HR><BR>
<B>Enter an Employee Number:</B>
<FORM METHOD=GET>     <!-- (See Note 8.) -->
   <INPUT TYPE="text" NAME="empno" SIZE=15 VALUE="111">
   <INPUT TYPE="submit" VALUE="Ask Oracle">
</FORM>
</BODY>
</HTML>
```

Notes on the `SQLJQuery.jsp` program:

1. This `page` directive declares that SQLJ code is being used in the JSP. The next two lines also use the `page` directive to import the necessary SQLJ classes.

2. This scriptlet gets the value of the parameter named `empno` from the `request` object. If the value of this parameter is not `null`, the JSP will execute the SQL query.

3. This statement is part of the main JSP scriptlet, and declares an explicit `DefaultContext` object to represent a SQLJ connection to the database. Although SQLJ supports the notion of a default connection for executing SQL, it should not be used for JSP or servlet programming. The reason is that the default connection is represented as a static variable in the SQLJ runtime, and concurrently executing servlets and JSPs running in the same Java Virtual Machine would overwrite this single static variable. The solution to this problem is to use an explicit `DefaultContext` object for executing SQL statements, as shown in this program.

4. This Java statement initializes the SQLJ `DefaultContext` with a database connection. Note that the JDBC-OCI driver is being used to connect to the `jspuser/jsp` account.

5. This statement is the static SQL query written in SQLJ. It uses `dctx` as the connection context to execute the query. The query uses the request parameter `empno` in the `WHERE` clause to retrieve data for the matching

employee from the EMPLOYEE_LIST and DEPARTMENT_LIST tables. The fetched data is placed in three Java variables, namely, job, deptName, and empName that have been declared earlier in this scriptlet.

6. This HTML statement displays the value of the empName variable as assigned by the preceding SQL query. The next two lines of HTML code display the job and department name, respectively.

7. This Java statement is used to catch any SQL exceptions that may be thrown by the SQLJ code. The action of the **catch** block is to print out this exception. It is followed by a **finally** block that closes the connection context previously opened.

8. This statement indicates the start of an HTML form segment. It is used to get the employee number from the user as data entered through the screen. This parameter is subsequently used in the SQL query. Note that the form specifies 111 as the default employee number.

Figure 10-10 shows the browser output from the SQLJQuery.jsp if it is invoked with no parameters.

If you enter an employee number in the text box and click the Ask Oracle button on the screen, the SQLJQuery.jsp program will be invoked with the request parameter empno set to 111. This causes the SQL query to be submitted to the database, and the output page shown in Figure 10-11 is displayed by the browser.

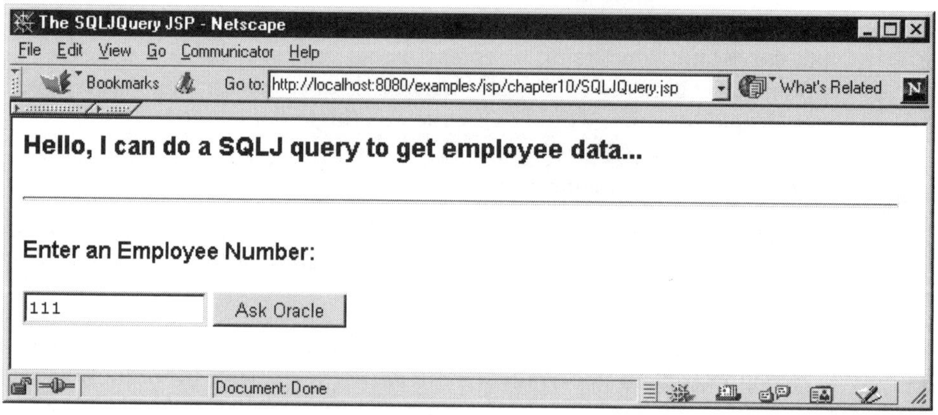

FIGURE 10-10. *Output of executing* SQLJQuery.sqljsp *with no parameters*

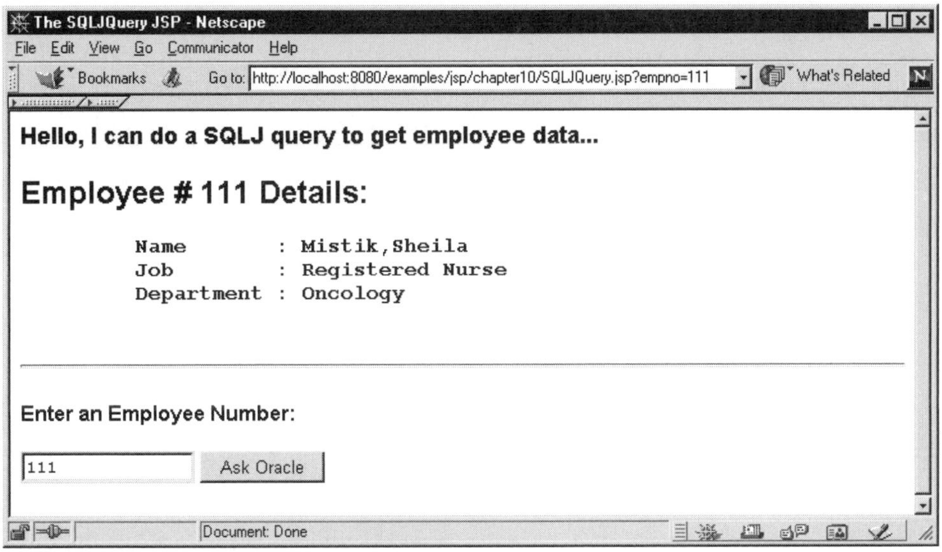

FIGURE 10-11. *Result of querying for employee 111 through* `SQLJQuery.jsp`

Using the `ojspc` Command-Line Translator

JSP engines support automatic translation of installed JSPs as they are invoked. This facility is very useful while developing JSP applications. However, for JSP application deployment, it is often undesirable for a JSP to be translated when it is first invoked by the end user. There is a time overhead associated with JSP translation, and it may slow down the response of the application compared to pages that are already compiled. Therefore, after the application has been developed, it would be useful if you could pretranslate the JSPs to avoid translation at runtime. Oracle's JSP implementation provides a command-line translator tool, `ojspc`, exactly for this purpose. In this section, you will learn about the syntax and options of this tool.

The `ojspc` command is simply a shell script on UNIX (and a bat file on Windows) that invokes the Java class `oracle.jsp.tools.Jspc`. This class is part of the Oracle JSP libraries. You need to have these libraries as well as the servlet libraries in the CLASSPATH environment variable in order to use this tool. Additionally, if you translate `.sqljsp` files using `ojspc`, make sure that the JDBC classes (`classes111.zip` or `classes12.zip`, depending on whether you are using JDK 1.1 or JDK 1.2), and the SQLJ libraries (`translator.zip`) are available in your CLASSPATH. The syntax to call `ojspc` is as follows:

```
ojspc [options] file_list
```

Wildcards are acceptable in the source file list for UNIX shell environments. Allowed extensions for source files are `.jsp`, `.sqljsp`, `.sqlj`, and `.java`. The `.sqljsp` files may contain static SQL statements in `#sql` notation. The JSP translator automatically invokes the SQLJ translator for these files. Any SQLJ and Java files given on the command line are used to resolve type references during JSP and SQLJ translation. The `ojspc` tool also calls the Java compiler (`javac` by default) to directly produce bytecode; there is a `-noCompile` option to turn off this automatic Java compilation of the generated code.

To see the list of options available for `ojspc`, you can type the following:

```
ojspc -help
```

The main options are as follows:

- `-addclasspath` This option specifies additional CLASSPATH entries for Java compilation of generated code. If not specified, it uses the system CLASSPATH setting.

- `-appRoot` This option specifies an application root directory for files that are included statically via application-relative URLs in the JSP `include` directive. This option was named `-includePath` in Oracle JSP version 1.0, and has been renamed to `-appRoot` in version 1.1 and higher. The default value for this option is the current directory.

- `-d`, `-dir` This option specifies an output directory for the generated bytecode. By default, the bytecode is placed in the current directory.

- `-extres` This flag specifies that an external resource file should be generated for the static text in the JSP source. This flag is useful for working around the 64K length limitation on the body of Java methods (recall that the static text is placed in the `_jspService()` method in the generated code). It also speeds up the Java compilation since the constant strings are placed in the external resource file.

- `-noCompile` This flag indicates that Java compilation of the generated code is not required. You can subsequently compile the generated files yourself in an additional step, perhaps using a Java compiler other than the default `javac`.

- `-packageName` This option specifies a package name for the generated class. The package name generally corresponds to the page path where the JSP is installed on the Web server. Therefore, for a JSP page installed under `examples/jsp/chapter10` under the doc root of your Web server, you would specify the package name `examples.jsp.chapter10` during pretranslation through `ojspc`. This is how the Oracle JSP engine maps page paths in the request URL to Java package names. The exact scheme for this mapping is not defined by the JSP specification, and is implementation dependent.

■ `-S-sqljoption` This option only applies for JSPs that have SQLJ code in them, and is used to specify options for the SQLJ translator. The `-S` prefix must be followed by a valid SQLJ option name, a space character, and then the option value (if any).

■ `-srcdir` This option specifies the directory where generated source files are to be placed. Do not confuse this option with the `-d` option discussed above, which controls the location of the generated bytecode.

■ `-verbose` This flag is used to get detailed information on the translation steps.

■ `-version` This flag displays the version number of the Oracle JSP library.

Following are some examples that illustrate the use of the `ojspc` tool. Note that spaces are used to delimit an option from its value (if any). String values for options such as package names and directory paths should be enclosed in double quotes and are case sensitive. However, option names are not case sensitive.

To get information on the translation steps while compiling the JSP file `Foo.jsp`, you can type the following:

```
ojspc -verbose Foo.jsp
```

To compile the files `Bar.jsp` and `Query.sqljsp`, you can type the following:

```
ojspc Bar.jsp Query.sqljsp
```

The source file paths may be specified either relative to the current directory in which `ojspc` is invoked or as an absolute path on the file system. The default output directory for the generated classes is the current directory where `ojspc` is called. The location of the generated source and compiled bytecode may be changed through the `-d` and `-srcdir` options as follows:

```
ojspc -d _pages -srcdir /home/mywebpages *.jsp
```

You can specify options to the SQLJ translator by prefixing the option with the `-S` flag. For example, to instruct the SQLJ translator to read the options from the file `sqlj.properties`, you can type the following:

```
ojspc -S-props sqlj.properties Query.sqljsp
```

For a complete list of options available for `ojspc`, refer to *Oracle JSP Developer Guide and Reference, Release 8.1.7.*

Conclusion

In this chapter, you have learned about JSP scripting elements and other essential JSP programming techniques. You saw how easy it is to write and run JSP programs. The JSP engine automatically translates, loads, and runs the JSP pages, providing a rapid development framework for your Web applications. JSP declarations, scriptlets, and expressions allow you to conveniently embed Java code in your JSPs and generate sections of the Web page dynamically. You can use the JSP `page` directive to pass page-related information such as the character encoding to the JSP translator. Special `errorPage` and `isErrorpage` attributes are provided in the `page` directive to handle runtime errors in your JSP. The JSP `include` directive is used to include the contents of other pages statically at compile time. You also learned how to use the standard JSP action tags `<jsp:include>` and `<jsp:forward>` to call other JSP and servlets programs from a JSP page. You understood how to use the `RequestDispatcher` **interface** to call JSPs and other Web resources from a servlet.

Finally, you learned about Oracle's JSP implementation and the extra features that it supports in addition to full compliance with the JSP specification. Java is the only scripting language in most JSP implementations. Oracle's JSP implementation also supports the use of SQLJ in JSP scriptlets so that database programming is made easier. A command-line translator tool, `ojspc`, is provided for pretranslating your JSP pages before deployment.

After reading this chapter, you should be able to write JSP pages that use JSP scripting elements, declarations, expressions, and implicit objects for computing the page contents dynamically based on request parameters entered through HTML forms. You should also understand the JSP translation and execution process that generates the output page. You learned how to write JSP pages that call other HTML pages, JSPs, or servlets, and servlets that call JSPs. You also wrote a JSP that performs a static SQL query on the Oracle database, and you learned how to invoke the `ojspc` command-line translator to pre-translate JSP program files.

Now that you have mastered the basics of JSP programming, you can write simple but useful Web pages. The next chapter shows you how to use JavaBean components in your JSP programs to cleanly separate static text from dynamic content. You will learn about bean-related tags such as `<jsp:useBean>` and `<jsp:setProperty>`, which are standard JSP tags for easy creation and manipulation of JavaBeans and their properties. You can combine the JSP programming techniques that you learned in this chapter with JavaBean components to create versatile Web applications that are compact and modular, and also easy to write and maintain.

CHAPTER
11

Using JSP with JavaBeans

n the previous chapter, you learned about the basic syntax and features of JSP. In this chapter, you will understand how to use JSPs for component-based programming with JavaBeans. First, you will learn about the basic concepts of JavaBeans. Then, you will understand how to effectively use the Oracle database in your JavaBean components. You will also learn how to generate XML using JSPs and JavaBeans. Specifically, you will learn how to

- Use a JavaBean component through convenient built-in JSP tags

- Develop a session-based JSP application that uses a "shopping cart" for order entry

- Execute database updates based on user data entered through HTML forms

- Execute a static SQL query using SQLJ to interact with the database

- Execute dynamic SQL queries using JDBC, and format the query result into an HTML table

- Generate XML from SQL query results

- Optimize the performance of database access by using application-level connection pooling

Developing JSP Applications with JavaBean Components

As you learned in Chapter 2, the JSP framework has been designed for use with modular and reusable software components such as JavaBeans. Using JavaBeans in a JSP allows clean separation of the Java code that generates dynamic content from the presentation logic in HTML. The Java code that computes the dynamic content can be conveniently placed in one or more JavaBeans, and these beans can be "plugged into" a JSP for easy manipulation. This separation allows the Java programmer to develop the computing logic in JavaBean components, and the Web designer to write the presentation format. Then, the components can be integrated cleanly in a JSP.

In this section, you will learn how to write simple JavaBeans and use them in your JSP programs through compact and powerful syntax.

Introducing JavaBeans

A JavaBean is a Java class that follows a certain design pattern. The pattern has a well-defined semantics in order to allow the structure of the JavaBean to be discovered through introspection of its compiled class using the Java *reflection* API. The essential requirements of a JavaBean are as follows:

■ It is a **public** Java class.

■ It has a **public** constructor with no arguments.

■ Typically, a JavaBean also has one or more *properties* (or attributes) that can be manipulated through public *accessor* methods.

The properties of a bean are generally implemented as **private** Java variables or fields, and the accessor methods are used to assign and retrieve their values. By default, the accessor methods are associated with their respective properties by a simple naming convention—the accessor methods for a property declared as int x are getX() and setX(int newX), respectively. Such implicit design rules support easy application development, as well as dynamic discovery and manipulation of the bean properties in external environments in which the bean is embedded, such as within a GUI development tool or as a component in a JSP.

Besides having properties, a JavaBean can also define methods like any other Java class. Keep in mind that a JavaBean is a regular Java class with some special characteristics.

Another common feature of a bean is that it may react to *events* in the embedding environment by implementing *event listener* interfaces. For example, a bean that performs a database query would need to close the underlying cursor when the HTTP session terminates. The bean can be notified of the session termination event by registering itself on a list of objects that are interested in this event. You will learn more about event listeners in the "Events and Event Listener Interfaces" section of this chapter.

In relatively rare cases, you may need to use non-default names for the accessor methods, or some other non-default design pattern for the bean. The JavaBeans framework is flexible enough so that you can write such a JavaBean, but you must then write an additional bean *descriptor* class to provide information on the structure of the bean. This descriptor class is named by appending the suffix BeanInfo to the bean class name, and it must implement the java.beans.BeanInfo **interface**. This interface provides methods to get the necessary information on the attributes, methods, and events for the JavaBean. For details, you can refer to any book on JavaBeans, such as *Developing JavaBeans* by Robert Englander, O'Reilly Press. The examples in this book follow the standard get and set naming pattern for the accessor methods of a JavaBean.

Writing a Simple JavaBean

As a first step, you will see a very simple JavaBean, UserNameBean, that consists of a single string-valued property userName to represent the user's name. The accessor methods for this property are defined using the default naming convention. The basic structure of this bean component is shown diagrammatically in Figure 11-1.

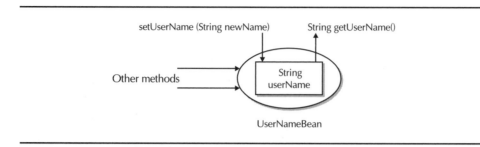

FIGURE 11-1. *Structure of the* `UserNameBean` *component*

The following code shows a such a bean—the `UserNameBean` class has a **private** field called `userName`, and provides methods `getUserName()` and `setUserName(String newName)` to retrieve and assign the value of this property. It defines an additional convenience method—`noUser()`—that returns `true` if the user name is `null` or is just the empty string.

```
package mybeans;

public class UserNameBean {
  private String userName = "";
  public String getUserName() {
     return userName;
  }
  public void synchronized setUserName(String newName) {
     userName = newName;
  }
  public boolean noUser() {
    return ((userName == null) || (userName.equals("")));
  }
}
```

In the preceding code, the `UserNameBean` class has been placed in the package `mybeans`. Providing a package name is optional for a JavaBean, just as for any other Java class. There is no explicit constructor, which means that the default class constructor is used. Remember that a JavaBean is a regular Java class with some additional structural rules, so you follow the usual Java syntax and semantic rules in writing the bean class. Note also that both `get` and `set` methods need not be provided for a property of a bean used in a JSP; depending on how the property is used, one or the other accessor method may be omitted. Typically, the `set` method is protected against multithreaded access by declaring it as a **synchronized** method.

The bean can be compiled like any other Java class. In order to use a bean in your JSP application, remember that the bean class must installed on your Web server (refer to Appendix E for setup steps).

Standard JSP Tags for JavaBeans

After you have written a JavaBean, you can easily plug it into a JSP through standard tags. Three built-in tags are defined by the JSP specification for easy manipulation of beans, namely:

- `<jsp:useBean>`
- `<jsp:setProperty>`
- `<jsp:getProperty>`

These tags are used to integrate the Java logic in beans with the static HTML code in your JSP. You will now learn about the syntax and semantics of these tags, and see how to use them effectively in your JSP applications.

The `<jsp:useBean>` Tag

This tag indicates that a certain bean is being used in the JSP. The general format of this tag is as follows:

```
<jsp:useBean id="variable" other_attributes />
```

where `other_attributes` includes `class` and `scope`, among others. Here, you will learn about the usage of the `id`, `scope`, and `class` attributes, which are the most frequently used.

The `class` attribute provides the fully qualified class name for the JavaBean—for example `mybeans.UserNameBean`.

The `id` attribute defines a Java identifier for the bean instance. You can refer to the bean instance using this identifier within the Java scope in which the `<jsp:useBean>` tag appears. For example, you can have the following statement in your JSP program to specify that it uses an instance of the bean class `mybeans.UserNameBean`:

```
<jsp:useBean  id= "userBean" class="mybeans.UserNameBean" />
```

In the preceding statement, the identifier `userBean` denotes the name of the bean instance. Subject to Java scoping rules for variables, you can write a JSP expression or scriptlet involving the given identifier—for example,

```
<%= userBean.getUserName() %>
```

The `scope` attribute is optional, but it is an important one. This attribute controls the *lifetime* of a bean component used in the JSP—that is, the duration of its existence as a program variable. It can have one of four values:

- page

- `request`
- `session`
- `application`

The default value for scope is `page`. The following is a description of what the four values mean:

- `page` scope   At the time the `<jsp:useBean>` statement is executed, the JSP container looks in the `page` object (discussed in the "JSP Implicit Objects" section in Chapter 10) for a bean instance with the same identifier. If such a bean is not found, a new bean instance is created and associated with the `page` object using the identifier specified in the `id` attribute. This lookup rule implies that you cannot access a `page`-scoped bean in other pages called from this JSP—for example, in the pages invoked through the `<jsp:include>` and `<jsp:forward>` tags (described in Chapter 10). If you reinvoke the same JSP, the same identifier will refer to an entirely new and different instance of the bean.

- `request` scope   This scope behaves in a manner similar to the `page` scope, with the important difference that the bean instance gets associated with the HTTP `request` object. Therefore, you can access a `request`-scoped bean in a different page that is called (included or forwarded to) by the current JSP. The identifier for a bean with `request` scope should be unique among all pages that handle the same HTTP request.

- `session` scope   In this case, the bean instance is associated with the `session` object and exists during the HTTP session in which this JSP is invoked. When the `<jsp:useBean>` tag is executed, an instance of the bean is created if it is not already present in the `session` object. The identifier for a bean with `session` scope should be unique among all pages invoked within the same HTTP session. Beans with `session` scope are very commonly used for session-tracking applications, such as those implementing "shopping cart" functionality. You will see an example of such a bean later in this chapter.

- `application` scope   This scope operates in a manner similar to the other scopes, but associates the bean instance with the `application` object (discussed in Chapter 10). Using this scope makes the bean instance accessible to all pages that execute in the same Java Virtual Machine and are part of the same Web application as the current JSP.

Besides having attributes, a `<jsp:useBean>` tag may also have a body. The body can contain other JSP tags and scriptlets to manipulate the bean instance. For example

```
<jsp:useBean id="userBean" class="mybeans.UserNameBean" >
    Initial value of user name is: <%= userBean.getUserName() %>
</jsp:useBean>
```

The `<jsp:setProperty>` Tag

The `<jsp:setProperty>` standard tag is used to set the properties of a JavaBean component used in a JSP. The general format of this tag is as follows:

```
<jsp:setProperty name="beanName" property_expression />
```

where *beanName* is the identifier of a JavaBean instance, which is generally defined in a `<jsp:useBean>` tag earlier in the JSP. The *property_expression* clause can have one of the following four formats:

- `property="propertyName"` This format specifies the name of a single property of the JavaBean, and its value is set from the matching parameter in the HTTP `request` object. That is, the `set` method of this property will be called with the matching request parameter value as the argument. For example, to set the `userName` property of the previously defined `UserNameBean` from the corresponding HTTP request parameter, you can write the following:

  ```
  <jsp:setProperty  name="userBean" property="userName" />
  ```

- `property="*"`   This expression provides a shorthand to denote that the properties of the JavaBean will be set from the values of the corresponding request parameters by matching their names. That is, each parameter in the HTTP `request` object is examined, and if there is a matching bean property, its `set` method is called with the request parameter value as the argument.

- `property="propertyName"` `param="parameterName"` This format is used to specify a property and request a parameter pair. The bean property is assigned from the specified request parameter by calling the appropriate `set` method with the parameter value as the argument. For example, if the HTTP `request` object uses a different identifier—say, newName—to represent the user's name, then to assign the bean property userName from this parameter you can write the following:

  ```
  <jsp:setProperty name="userBean"  property="userName"
                                parameter="newName" />
  ```

- `property="propertyName"` `value="newValue"`   This format is used to assign the specified value to the given property of the bean. The *newValue* may be a constant string, or a JSP expression that is computed at request time.

The `<jsp:getProperty>` Tag

This statement displays the value of a named JavaBean property. The effect is to call the `get` method for the property, convert the returned value to a string, and then write it to the `out` object (which represents the response stream). The general format of this tag is as follows:

```
<jsp:getProperty name="beanName" property="propertyName" />
```

Here, the `name` attribute refers to the identifier of a bean that previously appeared in a `<jsp:useBean>` tag within the JSP, and the `property` attribute specifies a property of this bean. For example, to display the `userName` property of the `UserNameBean`, you can write the following:

```
<jsp:getProperty name="userBean" property="userName" />
```

At this point, you may be wondering about the necessity of having the `<jsp:getProperty>` tag. After all, it seems that an equivalent JSP expression would have the same effect. For example, you could rewrite the preceding statement as follows to generate the same output:

```
<%= userBean.getUserName() %>
```

So, what is the difference between the two statements? In some cases, the `<jsp:getProperty>` tag provides a more flexible way to get the property value. For example, the bean may use non-default names for the accessor methods (as specified in the `BeanInfo` descriptor class), and the accessor method names may not be known to the JSP programmer. The actual name of the accessor method corresponding to the specified property would be discovered during JSP translation by introspecting the bean class and the corresponding bean descriptor class. In this case, using the `<jsp:getProperty>` tag is convenient. The names of the accessor methods could also be changed without requiring modifications to the JSP code.

Indexed Properties

Indexed properties associate multiple values with a single property name. An indexed property is declared as an array—for example,

```
private String[] phones;
```

The JavaBean specification defines a standard design pattern for the accessor methods of indexed properties. The accessor methods may take an extra attribute—namely, the integer index in the array—to access individual values in the array. Other forms of the accessor methods may `set` and `get` the entire array. For example, the following method signatures are the default accessor pattern for the `phones` property declared earlier:

```
public String[] getPhones();
public void setPhones(String[] newPhones);
public String getPhones(int index);
public void setPhones(int index, String newPhone);
```

The JSP 1.1 specification supports indexed properties in the `<jsp:setProperty>` standard tag. For example, assume that the indexed property `phones` is declared as part of a bean instance named `addrBean`. Then, the following statements can be used in a JSP to `set` and `get` the values of this indexed property:

```
<% String[] thePhones = new String[]{"123-4567", "456-7890"}; %>
<jsp:setProperty name="addrBean" property="phones"
                 value="<%= thePhones %>" />
<%=addrBean.getPhones(0)%>,<%+addrBean.getPhones(1)%>
```

Writing `HelloBean.jsp` Using `UserNameBean`

You are now ready to write a JSP that uses the `UserNameBean` component defined earlier. This JSP, called `HelloBean.jsp`, essentially performs the same function as the `Hello.jsp` program you wrote in Chapter 10, with the difference that `HelloBean.jsp` uses a JavaBean and standard JSP bean tags instead of Java code in JSP scriptlets. The code for this JSP is shown here:

```
<!-- Program name: HelloBean.jsp
  -- Purpose:        To store and retrieve the user's name through
  --                 the UserNameBean component, and print a greeting
-->
<!-- (See Note 1.) -->
<jsp:useBean id="nameBean" class="mybeans.UserNameBean" />
<!-- (See Note 2.) -->
<jsp:setProperty name="nameBean" property="*" />

<HTML>
  <HEAD>
    <TITLE> The HelloBean JSP  </TITLE>
  </HEAD>
  <BODY  BGCOLOR="white">
                  <!- (See Note 3.) ->
    <H3> Hello  <%= nameBean.getUserName() %> ! </H3>
    <P><B> The current time is <%= new java.util.Date() %>.
          Have a nice day! </B></P>
    <B>Please type in your user name:</B>
      <!- (See Note 4.) ->
      <FORM METHOD=GET>
        <INPUT TYPE="text" NAME="username" SIZE=15>
```

```
            <INPUT TYPE="submit" VALUE="Enter name">;
        </FORM>
    </BODY>
</HTML>
```

Notes on HelloBean.jsp:

1. The `<jsp:useBean>` tag declares that the JSP is using an instance of the bean class `mybeans.UserNameBean`, and associates it with the identifier `nameBean`. Since no scope is specified, the default `page` scope is implied.

2. This statement sets the `userName` property of `nameBean` to the value of the corresponding request parameter. Notice that the shorthand "`*`" is used to denote the bean property that matches the HTTP request parameter.

3. In the "Hello" greeting, the value of the `userName` property is retrieved from the bean by calling the accessor `getUserName()`.

4. The last part of the JSP uses an HTML form to accept a name from the user, and then invokes the same JSP (the default action of the form). Notice that the name of the input text field in the form is `userName`. This name intentionally matches the bean property name, and provides the implicit "wiring" between the HTTP request parameters and the bean attributes. In other words, the value entered in this text field becomes part of the HTTP request, which is then used to set the matching bean property through the `<jsp:setProperty>` tag.

Running HelloBean.jsp

First, install `HelloBean.jsp` source file on your Web server, following the steps outlined in Appendix E. You must also compile the `UserNameBean` class and install it on your Web server. These steps are described in Appendix E for different Web servers. For example, for the Tomcat server running on a UNIX system, you can use the shell script shown in Listing 11-1 to compile the bean class, and to place it in the `webapps/examples/WEB-INF/classes` subdirectory under the root directory of the Tomcat installation.

Listing 11-1 Shell script `buildbeans.sh` for compiling `UserNameBean` class

```
#!/bin/sh
# buildbeans.sh
TOMCAT_HOME=/private/jakarta-tomcat
JDK_HOME=/usr/local/packages/jdk1.2.2
APP_HOME=${TOMCAT_HOME}/webapps/examples
exec ${JDK_HOME}/bin/javac -d ${APP_HOME}/WEB-INF/classes \
    ${APP_HOME}/jsp/chapter11/mybeans/*.java
```

After the bean has been compiled, you can run the JSP through your browser. Invoking the page with no parameters displays the hello message with no user name, the current time, and the form for entering the user name.

Now, suppose that you type in the name **Pam** in the text box on the screen and then click the "Enter name" button. This action sends the HTTP request over to the same JSP page (as the default action of the HTML form), and sets the value of the `userName` property of the `UserNameBean` instance associated with the JSP page (which is the default scope for the bean instance). The subsequent method called `nameBean.getUserName()` retrieves and displays this value. The output produced in the browser is shown in Figure 11-2.

Using JavaBeans in Different Scopes

You will now program a JSP application that uses JavaBean components in different scopes. The example shows not only the use of modular beans and their properties, but also the effect of lifetime scoping. The application consists of two JSP pages, `BeanScoping.jsp` and `BeanScopingIncluded.jsp`. The second JSP is called by the first JSP using a `<jsp:include>` tag (described in Chapter 10), so that they are both executed as part of a single HTTP request. The intent is to illustrate that the bean instances with `request` and `session` scopes can be accessed from an included (or forwarded) JSP page, whereas a `page`-scoped bean is local to a JSP page.

Figure 11-3 illustrates the structure of this application, showing the two JSP pages and the component beans that are used by them. The request and session beans are shared by the two pages (through the HTTP request and the HTTP session respectively), while the page bean instances are distinct to each JSP page.

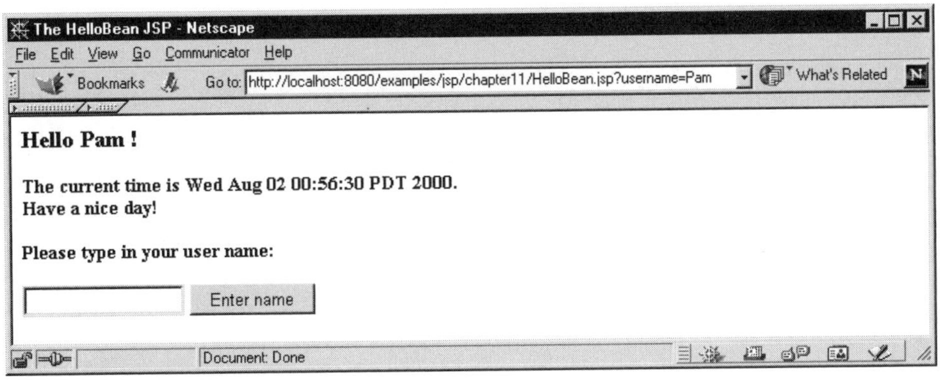

FIGURE 11-2. *Output of* `HelloBean.jsp` *after entering* `Pam` *as input*

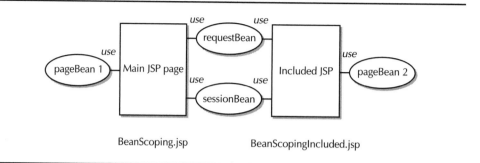

BeanScoping.jsp   BeanScopingIncluded.jsp

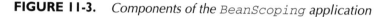

FIGURE 11-3. *Components of the* `BeanScoping` *application*

The following is the code for `BeanScoping.jsp` program, which uses three instances of the same `UserNameBean` class (defined earlier in this section) in the `page`, `request`, and `session` scopes. The JSP can be divided into four parts:

- The first part creates and sets the properties of the three bean instances.

- The second part reads and prints the property values of the bean instances.

- The third part includes another JSP as part of the same HTTP request.

- The fourth and final part has data entry forms for specifying the value of the `userName` property in the beans.

```
<!-- Program name: BeanScoping.jsp
  -- Purpose:      Use JavaBean components in page, request
  --               and session scopes.
  --!>
<!-- (See Note 1.) -->
<!-- Use the bean instance in the current page -->
<jsp:useBean id="pageBean"
            class="mybeans.UserNameBean"
            scope="page" />
<jsp:setProperty name="pageBean"
                 property="*" />

<!-- Use the bean instance in the current request  -->
<jsp:useBean id="requestBean"
            class="mybeans.UserNameBean"
            scope="request" />
<jsp:setProperty name="requestBean"
                 property="*" />
```

```
<!-- Use the bean instance in the current HTTP session -->
<jsp:useBean id="sessionBean"
             class="mybeans.UserNameBean"
             scope="session" />
<jsp:setProperty name="sessionBean"
                 property="*" />


<HTML>
<HEAD> <TITLE> The BeanScoping JSP </TITLE> </HEAD>
<BODY BGCOLOR="white">
<H2> Welcome to the BeanScoping JSP! </H2>
<B> Printing bean properties…
<!-- (See Note 2.) -->
<% if (pageBean.noUser())
    {  /* user name not set in page-scoped bean */ %>
        <BR> No user name in page-scoped bean!
<% } else {
      /* get the user name property from pageBean */  %>
        <BR>  User name in pageBean: <%= pageBean.getUserName() %>
<%  } %>


<% if (requestBean.noUser())
     {  /* user name not set in request-scoped bean */ %>
        <BR> No user name in request-scoped bean!
<% } else {
        /* get the user name property from requestBean */ %>
        <BR> User name in requestBean: <%= requestBean.getUserName() %>
<% } %>


<% if (sessionBean.noUser())
     {  /* user name not set in session-scoped bean */ %>
        <BR> No user name in session-scoped bean!
<% } else {
        /* get the user name property from sessionBean */ %>
        <BR> User name in sessionBean: <%= sessionBean.getUserName() %>
<% } %>


<P>Now printing output from an included page..
<BR><HR>
<!--  (See Note 3.) -->
   <jsp:include page="BeanScopingIncluded.jsp" flush="true" />
<BR><BR><HR><BR>
<!--  (See Note 4.) -->
<P><H3>Please enter your user name:</H3>
  <FORM METHOD="GET">
    <INPUT TYPE=TEXT name="userName" size = 20>
    <INPUT TYPE=SUBMIT VALUE="Submit new user name">
```

```
  </FORM>
  <FORM METHOD="GET" >
    <INPUT TYPE=SUBMIT VALUE="Use previous name"> <BR><BR>
  </FORM>
  </BODY>
</HTML>
```

Notes on `BeanScoping.jsp`:

1. The first part of the JSP has three `<jsp:useBean>` tags that use different instances of the same bean class in different scopes, namely `page`, `request`, and `session`. Following each of the three `<jsp:useBean>` statements are `<jsp:setProperty>` tags that set the properties of these bean instances from the corresponding request parameter (`userName`) in the HTTP request.

2. This part of the JSP retrieves and displays the property value from each bean. If the value is `null` or the empty string, as determined by calling the `noUser()` method on the beans, then a message is printed saying so. Otherwise, the property value obtained by calling the `getUserName()` accessor method is displayed.

3. This statement includes another JSP page, `BeanScopingIncluded.jsp`. You will write this page next.

4. The last part of the JSP has two HTML forms:

   - The first form segment lets you enter the user name, which becomes a parameter in the HTTP `GET` request when the "Submit new user name" button is clicked. It is no coincidence that the name of the text input field in this form matches the `userName` attribute of the `UserNameBean` class—name matching is the mechanism by which the request parameter and the bean properties are "wired" together in this JSP.

   - The second HTML form's submit action invokes the same JSP, but with no `userName` parameter. The intent of this action is to retrieve and reuse the value of `userName` saved in the `session`-scoped bean from the previous invocation of the JSP.

The following is the code for the `BeanScopingIncluded.jsp` program, which is called `BeanScoping.jsp` by the main JSP page. The `BeanScopingIncluded.jsp` page is in fact very similar to `BeanScoping.jsp`; the main differences are that the included JSP page does not set any bean properties through `<jsp:setProperty>` tags, and does not have any HTML forms for data entry. It simply uses three appropriately-named bean instances in the `page`, request, and `session` scopes, so that the `request`- and `session`-scoped beans are shared with the main page `BeanScoping.jsp`. As shown in Figure 11-3, the `page`-scoped bean instance is its own local component, not shared with the other page.

```jsp
<!-- Program name: BeanScopingIncluded.jsp
  -- Purpose:       Use beans created in the main page BeanScoping.jsp
  -->

<!-- Use the bean instance in the current page -->
<jsp:useBean id="pageBean"
class="mybeans.UserNameBean"
scope="page" />

<!-- Use the bean instance in the current request -->
<jsp:useBean id="requestBean"
class="mybeans.UserNameBean"
scope="request" />

<!-- Use the bean instance in the current HTTP session -->
<jsp:useBean id="sessionBean"
class="mybeans.UserNameBean"
scope="session" />

<% if (pageBean.noUser())
    {  /* user name is not set in page-scoped bean */ %>
      <BR> BeanScopingIncluded.jsp: No user name in page-scoped bean!
<% } else {
     /* get the user name property from pageBean */  %>
      <BR> BeanScopingIncluded.jsp: User name in pageBean:
                        <%= pageBean.getUserName() %>
<% } %>

<% if (requestBean.noUser())
     {  /* user name is not set in request-scoped bean */ %>
      <BR> BeanScopingIncluded.jsp: No user name in
                                  request-scoped bean!
<% } else {
     /* get the user name property from requestBean */ %>
      <BR> BeanScopingIncluded.jsp: User name in requestBean:
                        <%= requestBean.getUserName() %>
<% } %>

<% if (sessionBean.noUser())
     {  /* user name is not set in session-scoped bean */ %>
      <BR> BeanScopingIncluded.jsp: No user name in
                                  session-scoped bean!
```

```
<% } else {
      /* get the user name property from sessionBean */ %>
      <BR> BeanScopingIncluded.jsp: User name in sessionBean:
                          <%= sessionBean.getUserName() %>
<% } %>
```

Running the `BeanScoping` JSP

You can best understand the operation of the `BeanScoping` JSP by seeing it in action. Figure 11-4 shows the browser output produced when you invoke this JSP for the first time and without any request parameters. In this case, the `<jsp:useBean>` tags cause new instances of the three beans to be created in the appropriate scopes. However, there is no matching HTTP parameter for their `userName` property, and hence calls to the `noUser()` method return `true` initially. Thus, "no user name" messages are printed by the JSP, as shown in Figure 11-4.

Next, suppose that you enter the name **Rita** through the HTML form and click the "Submit new user name" button. This constitutes a new HTTP request, and

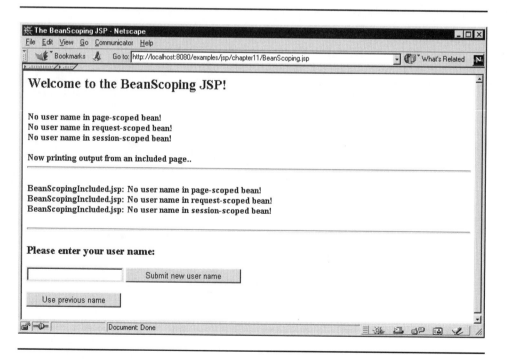

FIGURE 11-4. *Initial output of BeanScoping.jsp*

causes new instances of the page bean and the request bean to be created in the main `BeanScoping.jsp` page. Assuming the HTTP session has not expired, the same instance of the session bean is used. The `userName` property of these new instances of the page and request beans, and of the same session bean, are all set to the input value Rita. Then, all the beans in the main page print this user name, as shown in the first part of Figure 11-5. The next part in this figure shows the output generated by the included page, `BeanScopingIncluded.jsp`. This page does not set any bean properties, and therefore no user name is found in its page bean. On the other hand, the request and session beans have their property set by the main page, and the value of the user name is correctly read and printed by the included page from these shared bean instances.

To see how the session bean retains its property settings across invocations, you can reinvoke the same JSP with no request parameters by clicking the "Use previous name" button before the HTTP session times out. As shown in Figure 11-6, the `session`-scoped bean retains the setting of its `userName` property from the previous call, while the new page bean and request bean instances do not have the user name set.

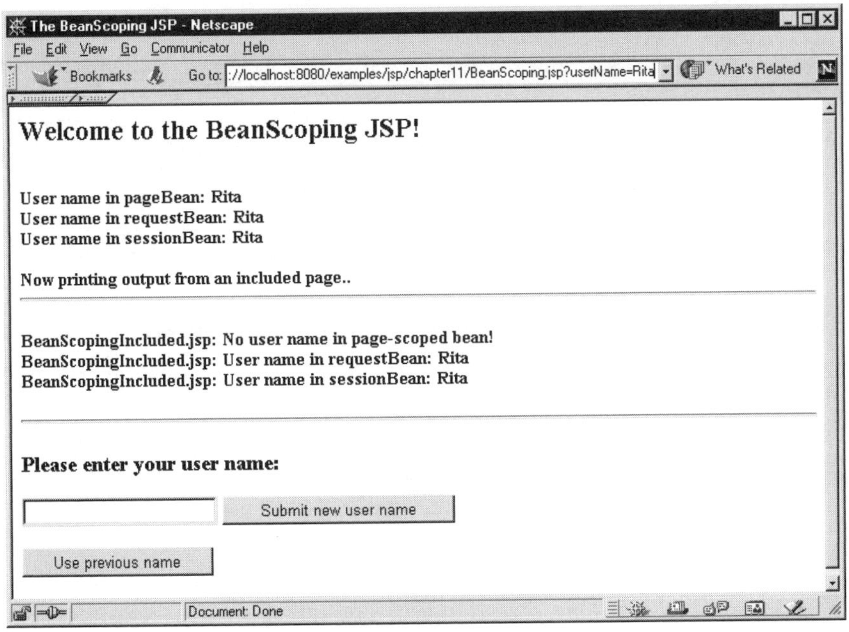

FIGURE 11-5. *Output of* `BeanScoping.jsp` *after entering user name "Rita"*

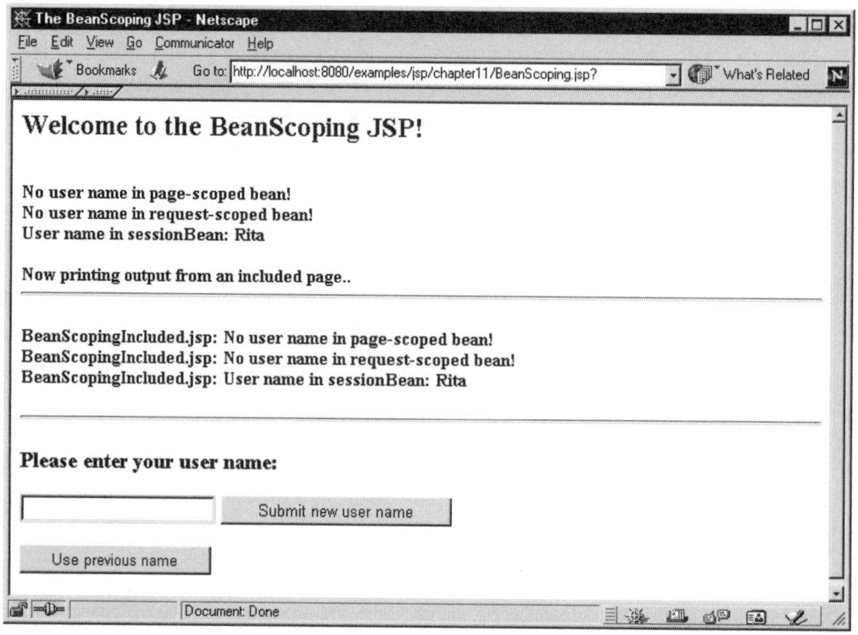

FIGURE 11-6. *Output of reinvoking* `BeanScoping.jsp` *with no parameters*

Using JavaBeans in the `application` scope is very similar to the example shown earlier. You will see how to use a bean in the `application` scope for database connection caching in the "Connection Pooling" section later in this chapter.

Developing a Session-Tracking JSP Application

You are now ready to try a more complex example of using JavaBeans in a JSP that tracks user actions in a given HTTP session. This example is modeled after a very common Web application—an online order entry system. Suppose that your application program, called Order Online, needs to provide the following functionality:

■ You can select one or more items from a set of items.

■ The selected items are placed in a "shopping cart."

■ You may add or remove any item from the cart, or clear the cart as you make your selections.

■ At the end of the item selection process, you can submit your order to the system. This will insert the order information into the database tables.

■ Finally, you can query the details of an order from the database.

You will now understand the steps in developing such an application using JSPs and JavaBeans.

Order Online Application Architecture

The first step is to design the components of the JSP application. Figure 11-7 illustrates a modular architecture for the Order Online JSP application. There are three JSP pages: `EnterOrder.jsp`, `InsertOrder.jsp`, and `QueryOrder.jsp`. These JSPs will serve as the user **interface** for the interactive processes of item selection, order submission, and order inquiry, respectively. The shopping cart is represented by the `cartBean` component. It will contain the current list of selected items, and will be shared by the `EnterOrder.jsp` and `InsertOrder.jsp` pages. The `InsertOrder.jsp` page has an additional component, `DBInsertBean`, which will execute the SQL INSERT operations for storing the submitted order in the purchase order database. The `QueryOrder.jsp` page will have its own JavaBean component, `DBQueryBean`. This JavaBean will query the purchase order database to retrieve order information.

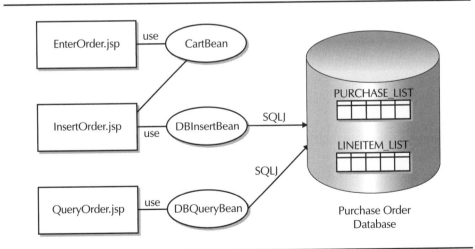

FIGURE 11-7. *Architecture of the Order Online application*

Writing the `CartBean` Class

As the first step of this programming task, you will define the JavaBean `CartBean` to model the shopping cart. It will manage the list of items selected by the user and will support add, remove, and clear operations on this list. That is, the current contents of the cart will be modified based on the parameters of the HTTP requests submitted by the user within the same HTTP session.

The code for the `CartBean` class is shown as follows. It uses an instance of the `java.util.ArrayList` class, which is a new utility class defined in JDK 1.2, to represent the shopping cart. If you are using a JDK 1.1 environment, you will need to modify the code to use another data type such as `java.util.Vector`.

```
/** Program name: CartBean.java
 ** Purpose:       Implement a shopping cart component to which items
 **                may be added and removed, or the cart may be cleared.
 **/
package mybeans;

import java.util.ArrayList; // requires JDK 1.2

public class CartBean {
    // (See Note 1.)
    private String[] itemsSelected = null; // items selected
    private String   action = null;        // action selected
    // (See Note 2.)
private ArrayList itemsList = new ArrayList();  // cart contents

    /* method to set the action: add, remove, or clear */
    public synchronized void setAction (String newAction) {
        // (See Note 3.)
        action = newAction;
        if (action.startsWith("Clear")) {  // empty the cart
            itemsList.clear();
        }
    }
    /* method to process a new list of selected items */
    public synchronized void setItemsSelected (String[] newItems) {
        // (See Note 4.)
        if (newItems != null) {  // some items selected
            for (int i = 0; i < newItems.length; i++) {
                if (action.startsWith("Add")) {  // add to cart
                    itemsList.add(newItems[i]);
                } else if (action.startsWith("Remove")) {  // remove
                    // find the last occurrence of this item in cart
                    int index = itemsList.lastIndexOf(newItems[i]);
                    if (index != -1) {
                        itemsList.remove(index); // delete from list
```

```
                    }
                }
            }
        }
    }
    // (See Note 5.)
    /* method to return the current number of ordered items */
    public int countItems () {
        return itemsList.size();
    }

    /* method to return a particular item */
    public Object getItem(int index) {
        return  itemsList.get(index);
    }

    /* method to return the entire list of items ordered */
    public ArrayList getOrder() {
        return  itemsList;
    }
} // end CartBean
```

Notes on `CartBean.java`:

1. The bean has two properties, namely, `itemsSelected` and `action`. The `itemsSelected` property denotes the list of items selected by the user on the screen, while the `action` property denotes the nature of the operation: add items, remove items, or clear the cart. The bean provides `set` methods for both of its properties. The values of these properties are only written and not read externally, so the `get` methods are omitted.

2. The variable `itemsList` denotes the current contents of the cart.

3. The `setAction()` method sets the value of the `action` attribute. Also, if the action is "Clear the cart," then the `itemsList.clear()` method is called to empty the cart contents.

4. The `setItemsSelected()` method executes logic to set the cart contents depending on the action chosen:

   ■ If some items have been selected and the action is "Add to cart," `itemsList` is augmented with the selected items by calling the method `itemsList.add()`.

   ■ If some items have been selected and the action is "Remove from cart," the last occurrence of each selected item is deleted from the `itemsList` array.

5. The bean provides three other **public** methods, namely, countItems(), getItem(), and getOrder(). These methods are used, respectively, to return the total number of items currently in the cart, to return an item at a specific position in the list of items in the cart, and to return the list of items accumulated in the cart. You will use these methods in the EnterOrder.jsp program that you will write next.

Writing the EnterOrder.jsp program

Now you will write the EnterOrder.jsp page that uses the CartBean class defined earlier. This JSP will integrate the HTML presentation code and the computing logic in the bean to handle the order placement process. The actual entry of the order into the purchase order database is handled by another JSP named InsertOrder.jsp, which you will define in the next section.

The code for the EnterOrder.jsp program is shown here:

```
<!-- Program name: EnterOrder.jsp
  -- Purpose:       Page for selecting items for an order
  -->
<HTML>
 <HEAD> <TITLE> The EnterOrder JSP </TITLE> </HEAD>
 <BODY BGCOLOR="white">
  <H2> Welcome to Order Online! </H2>
  <!-- Use a cart bean in session scope -->  <!-- (See Note 1.) -->
  <jsp:useBean id="cart" class="mybeans.CartBean" scope="session" />
  <jsp:setProperty name="cart" property="action" />
  <jsp:setProperty name="cart" property="itemsSelected"
                               parameter="item"/>

  <HR><BR>
  <BLOCKQUOTE>   <!--  (See Note 2.) -->
   <H3>Please choose from the following items:</H3>
   <FORM METHOD="GET">
     <INPUT TYPE="Checkbox" NAME="item" VALUE="Book Shelf">
       Book Shelf <BR>
     <INPUT TYPE="Checkbox" NAME="item" VALUE="File Cabinet">
       Filing Cabinet <BR>
     <INPUT TYPE="Checkbox" NAME="item" VALUE="Office Desk">
       Office Desk <BR>
     <INPUT TYPE="Checkbox" NAME="item" VALUE="PC">
       Personal Computer <BR>
     <INPUT TYPE="Checkbox" NAME="item" VALUE="Wastebasket">
       Wastebasket <BR> <BR>
    <P> <INPUT TYPE=SUBMIT NAME="action" VALUE="Add to cart">
        <INPUT TYPE=SUBMIT NAME="action" VALUE="Remove from cart ">
        <INPUT TYPE=SUBMIT NAME="action" VALUE="Clear cart">
   </FORM>
```

```
</BLOCKQUOTE>
<CENTER>
 <!-- (See Note 3.) -->
 <FORM ACTION="InsertOrder.jsp" METHOD="GET">
   <INPUT TYPE="SUBMIT" NAME="insert" VALUE="Submit my order">
 </FORM>
</CENTER>
 <!-- (See Note 4.) -->
<HR><BR>
<% int numItems = cart.countItems(); %>
<H3>Your cart now contains
     <%= numItems %> item<%= (numItems > 1) ? "s" : "" %>.
</H3>
<UL>
 <% for (int i = 0; i < numItems; i ++ ) { %>
     <LI>  <%=  cart.getItem(i) %>
 <% }  %>
</UL>
</BODY>
</HTML>
```

Notes on `EnterOrder.jsp`:

1. The JSP uses the previously defined bean class `CartBean` in `session` scope. The two properties of this bean, namely `action` and `itemsSelected`, are set from the HTTP request parameters named `action` and `item`, respectively.

2. The page consists of two HTML form segments. The first form provides a list of items with checkboxes beside them for selection. There are three action buttons named "Add to cart," "Remove from cart," and "Clear cart." When clicked, these action buttons set the value of the request parameter named `action` to the appropriate value, and invoke the same JSP program (that is, `EnterOrder.jsp`) through the HTTP GET method.

3. The second HTML form consists of a single submit button named "Submit my order." When this button is clicked, the action of the form is to send an HTTP request to the `InsertOrder.jsp` page. This request is intended to be part of the same HTTP session as `EnterOrder.jsp`, so that the same instance of `CartBean` can be accessed from the `session` scope by the other JSP. The significance of this point will be evident when you write the `InsertOrder.jsp` program in the next section.

4. The last part of the `EnterOrder.jsp` page displays the list of items currently in the cart by calling the appropriate methods on the `CartBean` instance.

Running the Order Online JSP Application

After you have installed the `EnterOrder.jsp` file and the compiled class for `CartBean.java` on your Web server (see the `buildbeans.sh` script in the previous section, and the installation steps in Appendix E), you can invoke the `EnterOrder.jsp` program through the appropriate URL. Figure 11-8 shows the initial browser output of the first invocation of this page.

Now, suppose that you choose the items "Book Shelf" and "Office Desk" through the checkboxes on the screen, and then click the "Add to cart" button. Figure 11-9 shows the browser output after these steps.

Similarly, you can remove items from the cart by choosing the appropriate checkboxes and then clicking the "Remove from cart" button. Clicking the "Clear cart" button removes all items from the cart. You can alternate between the "Add to cart," "Remove from cart," and "Clear cart" actions as often as you like, provided that the HTTP session does not expire in between these operations.

At the end of the selection phase, you are ready to place the order! You can now click the "Submit my order" button, which will invoke the action of the second HTML form, and take you to the `InsertOrder.jsp` page. This is the page that you will write next.

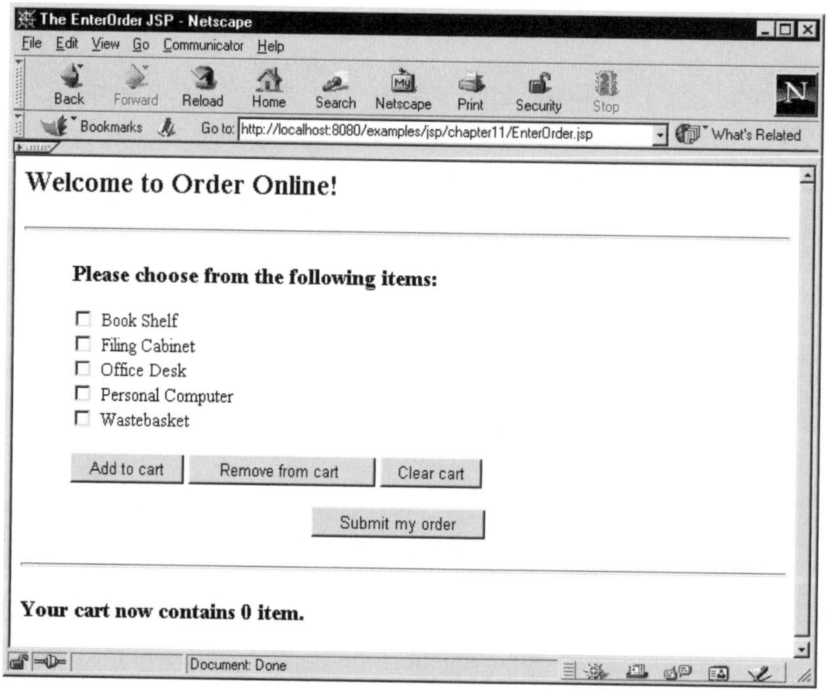

FIGURE 11-8. *Initial output of* `EnterOrder.jsp`

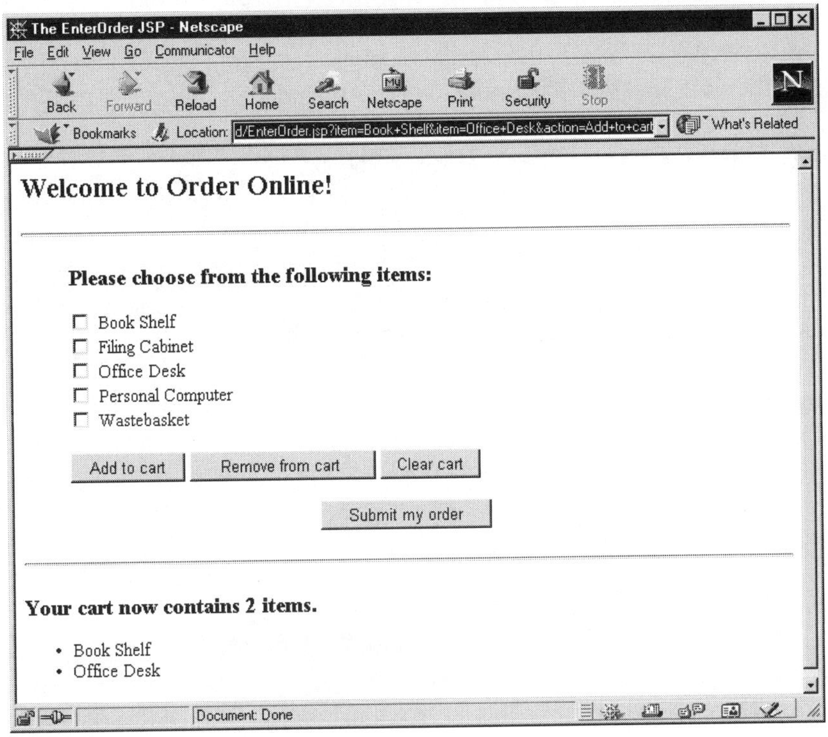

FIGURE 11-9. *Output of* `EnterOrder.jsp` *after selecting some items*

Executing Database Operations Using JavaBeans

In the previous section, you learned how to program the order entry process using a JSP and a shopping cart JavaBean. In this section, you will learn how to execute database operations in your JSP application. Specifically, you will complete the final step of the order entry process by inserting the appropriate data in the Purchase Order database.

As you learned in Chapter 10, it is possible to write JDBC or SQLJ code directly in your JSP to access the database. However, having a lot of Java logic in your JSP is not a good programming practice for any sizable JSP application. As discussed in Chapter 2, modularity is the basic design premise of component-based programming. From that viewpoint, it is a much better programming style to place your Java code in a separate JavaBean component, and then invoke it from your JSP. This effectively separates the Java logic for dynamic processing from the static HTML code. You will now learn how to access the Oracle database through a JavaBean, and how to integrate the bean into your JSP application.

Executing Database Inserts

In the Order Online JSP application, the request for order submission is sent via the "Submit my order" action of the HTML form to the `InsertOrder.jsp` page, which inserts the details of the order in the Purchase Order database. You will now write this JSP, and then develop the JavaBean `DBInsertBean` that actually executes the SQL `INSERT` operations for the data gathered by your `EnterOrder.jsp` program.

Writing `InsertOrder.jsp`

The code for the `InsertOrder.jsp` program is shown next. Explanatory notes appear after the code. A major point to note is that the JSP uses two JavaBeans to process the order information:

- The `session`-scoped `cartBean` instance created earlier by the `EnterOrder` JSP. This bean contains the list of items selected by the user of the Order Online application.

- A `page`-scoped instance of the bean `DBInsertBean` that is a local component for this JSP. This bean will connect to the Oracle database to execute the necessary SQL operations.

```
<%-- Program name: InsertOrder.jsp
  -- Purpose:      Page for inserting the order created through the
  --               EnterOrder JSP into the Purchase Order database
  --%>
<HTML>
<!-- Use the cart bean existing in the session scope -->
 <jsp:useBean id="cart" class="mybeans.CartBean"
                    scope="session" />   <!-- (See Note 1.) -->
 <HEAD> <TITLE> The InsertOrder JSP </TITLE> </HEAD>
 <BODY BGCOLOR="white">
  <H2> Ready to Order! </H2>     <!-- (See Note 2.) -->
  <B> You have selected: </B>    <%= cart.getOrder() %>
<%   if ((request.getParameter("DBInsert")) != null) {
%>
   <!-- (See Note 3.) -->
   <jsp:useBean id="dbInsert" class="mybeans.DBInsertBean"
              scope="page" />
   <jsp:setProperty name="dbInsert" property="*" />
<H3> Result of processing order: </H3>
```

```
<PRE>   <!--  (See Note 4.) -->
<%= dbInsert.processOrder(cart.getOrder()) %>
</PRE>
<!-- Clear the previous contents of the cart -->
<!--  (See Note 5.) -->
<% cart.setAction("Clear"); }
   else {
 %>
 <HR><BR>
 <BLOCKQUOTE>  <!--  (See Note 6.) -->
 <P><H3>Please fill in the following information:</H3>
 <FORM METHOD="POST" >
  <P> <b>Employee Number:</b> <INPUT TYPE="TEXT" NAME="empNum" SIZE=20>
      <b>Project Number:</b> <INPUT TYPE="TEXT" NAME="projNum" SIZE=20>
  <P>    <INPUT TYPE="SUBMIT" NAME="DBInsert" VALUE="Submit Order">
 </FORM>
<% } %>
<BR><BR>
<FORM METHOD="GET" ACTION="EnterOrder.jsp">
  <P>    <INPUT TYPE="SUBMIT" VALUE="Back to Order Entry">
 </FORM>
 </BLOCKQUOTE>
 </BODY>
</HTML>
```

Notes on `InsertOrder.jsp`:

1. The `InsertOrder` JSP assumes that it was invoked from the `EnterOrder` JSP after the item selection process was complete. This implies that an instance of `CartBean` was already created by the `EnterOrder` JSP and placed in `session` scope. Therefore, the first `<jsp:useBean>` tag in the `InsertOrder` JSP retrieves this instance of `CartBean` from the `session` scope, and makes it available to the rest of the code.

2. This statement prints the list of items that are currently in the cart. It is done by calling the method `getOrder()` on the `CartBean` instance.

3. The second `<jsp:useBean>` tag is executed conditionally only when the HTTP request has a parameter named `DBInsert`. This tag creates an instance of the bean class `mybeans.DBInsertBean` (which is to be defined shortly) with the identifier `dbInsert`. This bean is created in the `page` scope, since the database operation is not pertinent outside the scope of this JSP. The properties of the `dbInsert` bean instance are set from the HTTP request parameters.

4. The following JSP expression calls the `processOrder()` method on the `dbInsert` bean with the order retrieved from the `CartBean` instance as argument. The result of this method call is displayed on the screen.

5. This statement clears the contents of the cart in order to reset the purchase list.

6. The latter part of the `InsertOrder` JSP uses two HTML form segments:

   ■ The first form segment has two text input fields that accept an employee number (`empNum`) and a project number (`projNum`) for the order. Once you provide the appropriate data in these fields, you can click the "Submit my order" button to reinvoke the same JSP but with the `DBInsert` parameter set in the HTTP request. As explained in the previous notes, the presence of this parameter causes the order to be sent to the `dbInsert` bean for processing.

   ■ The second form segment has no input fields but just has a "Back to Order Entry" button that returns the user to the initial order entry screen by calling `EnterOrder.jsp` as the form action.

Writing `DBInsertBean.sqlj`

The purpose of the `DBInsertBean` class is to insert the list of items selected into the Purchase Order database. Hence, it must perform the necessary SQL operations on the tables. The schema for these tables was defined in the Introduction of this book. There are two relevant tables, `PURCHASE_LIST` and `LINEITEM_LIST`, which are reproduced here for convenience:

```
CREATE TABLE PURCHASE_LIST (
     requestno       NUMBER(10),
     employeeno      NUMBER(7),
     vendorno        NUMBER(6),
     purchasetype    VARCHAR2(20),
     checkno         NUMBER(11),
     whenpurchased DATE);

CREATE TABLE LINEITEM_LIST (
     requestno       NUMBER(10),
     lineno          NUMBER(5),
     projectno       NUMBER(5),
     quantity        NUMBER(5),
     unit            VARCHAR2(2),
     estimatedcost NUMBER(8,2),
     actualcost      NUMBER(8,2),
     description     VARCHAR2(30));
```

The JavaBean must provide two properties named `empNum` and `projNum` to accept the data entered through the form in the `InsertOrder` JSP. The code for this JavaBean is shown as follows. It is written using SQLJ code to execute the database operations conveniently.

```
/** Program name: DBInsertBean.sqlj
 ** Purpose:      Insert order into tables of purchase order database
 **/

package mybeans;

import java.util.ArrayList;
import java.sql.*;
import oracle.sqlj.runtime.Oracle;
import sqlj.runtime.ref.DefaultContext;

public class DBInsertBean {
  // (See Note 1.)
  private String empNum = null;   // employee number
  private String projNum= null;   // project number

  // Method to set the empNum property
  public synchronized void setEmpNum(String empNum) {
    this.empNum = empNum;
  }

  // Method to set the projNum property
  public synchronized void setProjNum(String projNum) {
    this.projNum = projNum;
  }

  private DefaultContext dctx = null;  // database connection context
  private int requestno;               // request number for the order

  // Method to process the submitted order
  // (See Note 2.)
  public synchronized String processOrder (ArrayList order) {
    if ((order == null) || (order.size() == 0)) {
      return ("No order items to insert!");
    }
    try {
      // Connect to the database
      // (See Note 3.)
      dctx = Oracle.getConnection("jdbc:oracle:oci8:@",
                                  "jspuser", "jsp");
      // Insert the order into database
      DBInsert(order);
```

```
            // No errors occurred!
            return ("Purchase order processed successfully! <BR> " +
                    "Your request number is: " + requestno);
        } catch (SQLException e) {
            return ("SQL Error:" + e.getMessage());
        } finally {
            // Disconnect from the database
            try {
              dctx.close();    // (See Note 4.)
            } catch (Exception e) {}
        }
    }

    private void DBInsert(ArrayList order) throws SQLException {
        // (See Note 5.)
        // First, get the next sequence number for the request
        #sql [dctx] { SELECT requestno_seq.NEXTVAL
                        INTO :requestno
                        FROM DUAL      };

        // Next, insert the request into the PURCHASE_LIST table
        #sql [dctx] { INSERT INTO
                        PURCHASE_LIST( requestno,
                                        employeeno,
                                        whenpurchased)
                        VALUES( :requestno,
                                :empNum,
                                SYSDATE
                               )
        };

        // Now, insert each line items from the submitted order
        for (int i = 0; i < order.size(); i++) {
            #sql [dctx] {  INSERT INTO
                        LINEITEM_LIST ( requestno,
                                        lineno,
                                        projectno,
                                    quantity,
                                    description
                                )
                    VALUES (:requestno,

                            lineno_seq.NEXTVAL,
                            :projNum,
                            1,
                        :(order.get(i))
                        )
            };
```

```
        #sql [dctx] { COMMIT }; // commit the row insertion
    }
  }
}
```

Notes on `DBInsertBean.sqlj`:

1. The `DBInsertBean` has two properties: `empNum` and `projNum`. It provides methods to set the values of these two properties. The values of these properties are only written and not read, so the `get` methods are omitted.

2. The central method of the bean is `processOrder()`, which accepts an order of type `java.util.ArrayList` as an argument. The order is processed as follows:

   ■ If there are no items in the order, the method returns immediately with an appropriate message.

   ■ Otherwise, it connects to the database, using the method `Oracle.getConnection()`. Then, it calls the method `DBInsert()` to actually insert the order in the database, and returns the number for the order just entered. Finally, it disconnects from the database.

3. There is an important point to note about setting up the database connection. The method `getConnection()` on the class `oracle.sqlj.runtime.DefaultContext` is called to get back a SQLJ connection context `dctx`. This connection context is used explicitly in each subsequent SQL statement through **`#sql`** `[dctx]` syntax. The reason for using an explicit connection context in each SQL operation is a bit subtle. Remember that there could be multiple concurrent users of your JSP application running on the same Java Virtual Machine of your Web server, and they could be connecting to the database simultaneously for order insertion. Setting and using the SQLJ default connection context (which is implemented through a static variable in the SQLJ runtime) is clearly not correct in this scenario—it would cause different users to step over each other's connection. *Therefore, you must always use an explicit connection context in the SQLJ statements to avoid concurrency problems.*

4. A final word of caution about database connections: In this bean, a database connection is opened and closed for each order that is submitted. In practice, opening and closing of connections are fairly expensive operations and should be minimized. Furthermore, connecting for each HTTP session can easily lead to too many database connections being open, especially if the number of concurrent users of the Order Online application is large. To avoid these problems, you can use *connection*

pooling to share physical connections to the database. You will learn more about connection management in the "Performance Tuning SQL Operations" section later in this chapter.

5. The DBInsert() method uses SQLJ to perform the following database operations:

■ Inserts one record into the table PURCHASE_LIST for the purchase request. The request number is obtained from the request sequence by using a SQLJ SELECT-INTO statement to fetch the next sequence number requestno_seq.NEXTVAL.

■ Inserts records into the table LINEITEM_LIST for each item in the list of items ordered, using the request number selected previously from the request sequence. The line numbers are generated from the line number sequence lineno_seq.

Running InsertOrder.jsp

First, you must install the InsertOrder.jsp program on your Web server, following the steps outlined in Appendix E. Remember to compile the code for DBInsertBean.sqlj, and to make the compiled class accessible to your Web server. After these steps are complete, you can invoke the InsertOrder JSP through the "Submit my order" button in the EnterOrder.jsp page of the Order Online application. Figure 11-10 shows the initial screen of the InsertOrder.jsp page that is displayed after you select the items "Book Shelf" and "Office Desk" through the EnterOrder.jsp.

If you now enter an employee number and a project number in the form displayed by the InsertOrder JSP, and then click "Submit Order," an instance of the DBInsertBean class is created and initialized with these two request parameters. The processOrder() method call causes the bean to execute the necessary INSERT operations on the database, and for a successful order entry the output shown in Figure 11-11 is generated. At this point, you may choose to return to the EnterOrder JSP by clicking the "Back to Order Entry" button.

Executing Static SQL Queries

Now that you have successfully entered data in the purchase order database, you will learn how to execute a static SQL query and display the results from a JSP. In particular, you will use a SQLJ iterator to fetch the details of a purchase order in the database. But before you write this program, you first need to learn the basic concepts about events and event listener interfaces. These interfaces can be implemented by JavaBeans to effectively manage shared resources such as database connections.

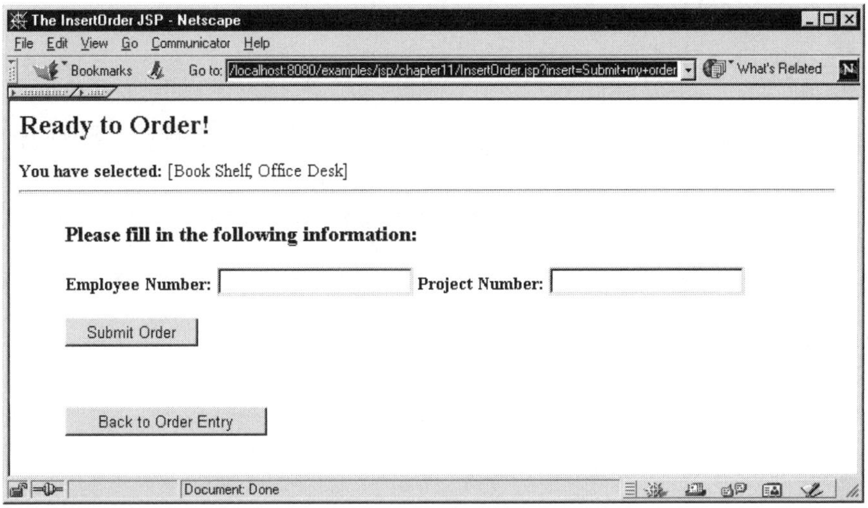

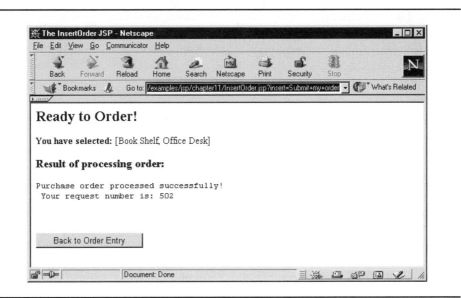

FIGURE 11-10. *Initial screen of the* `InsertOrder` *JSP*

FIGURE 11-11. *Final screen of* `InsertOrder` *JSP after successful order submission*

Events and Event Listener Interfaces

An *event* is a general Java term for a notification mechanism involving various components in a Java application. For example, a mouse click constitutes an event. Using the event notification mechanism, any Java object may register its interest in one or more events generated by other objects. It is then said to be *listening* for the events. The objects generating events are called *event sources*, and the objects being notified of the events are called *event listeners*.

The event notification mechanism is based on implementing methods in *event listener interfaces*. Each event corresponds to a specific method in an event listener interface. Any Java class can implement such an interface. An event listener object registers itself with the event source to enable event notification. When the event takes places, then the event source object invokes the associated method on all objects that have registered themselves as listeners for that event. The event itself is represented by an event object, which contains a reference to the event source, and is passed as a parameter to the method being invoked. Figure 11-12 shows a diagram of the event notification model.

Note that the event model is not specific to JavaBeans, but is a general feature of the Java programming language. The Java package `java.util` defines several classes and interfaces to support the event model.

As a concrete example, consider a `session`-scoped JavaBean class. This bean may be interested in being notified when it is being stored in (bound) and removed (unbound) from the HTTP `session` object, so that it can manage its resources such as database cursors and connections. The servlet API defines an event listener interface for this purpose. It is of the type `javax.servlet.http.HttpSessionBindingListener`, and has two methods, `valueBound()` and `valueUnbound()`, with the following signatures:

```
public interface HttpSessionBindingListener
                extends java.util.EventListener {
  public void valueBound(HttpSessionBindingEvent event);
  public void valueUnbound(HttpSessionBindingEvent event);
}
```

A `session`-scoped JavaBean can implement this event listener interface. The `valueBound()` method is invoked when the bean is stored in the HTTP `session` object, as part of the actions taken by the `<jsp:useBean>` tag with `session` scope. The `valueUnbound()` method is called when the bean is removed from the `session` object.

Figure 11-13 illustrates the method calls involved in the lifetime of the JavaBean `DBQueryBean` that you will write next. This bean implements the `HttpSessionBindingListener` **interface** in order to be notified of session-related events. Suppose that the bean is instantiated through the

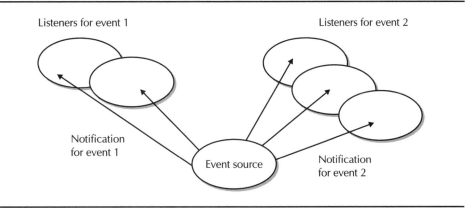

FIGURE 11-13. *The event model with event sources and listeners*

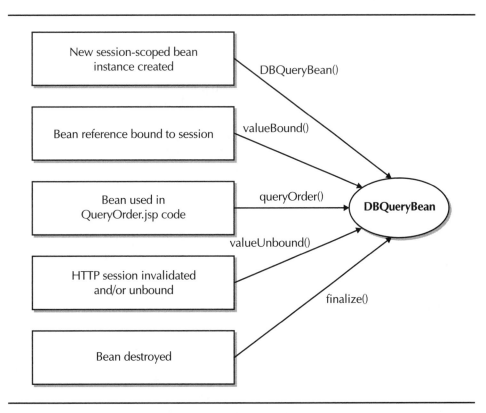

FIGURE 11-12. *A session-scoped JavaBean listening for session events*

`<jsp:useBean>` tag with `session` scope. Then, it is automatically bound to the HTTP `session` object after instantiation (using the `session.setAttribute()` method call). This bind step causes the `valueBound()` method to be invoked on the bean through the event listener **interface**. After that, the JSP page has access to the bean instance, and can call methods such as `queryOrder()` on it. When the HTTP session is terminated (for example, through a `session.invalidate()` method call) or the bean reference is explicitly removed from the session (by calling the `session.remove()` method), then the `valueUnbound()` method is invoked on the bean. The bean may also provide a `finalize()` method that is called when the bean instance is destroyed.

Why does the bean need to implement the special session listener methods? Could you not close the database connection in the `finalize()` method for the bean that would be called when it is garbage collected? It certainly seems simpler to program. But the answer is no—the effect of the `finalize()` method is not quite the same as that of the session listener methods. Specifically, the session listener **interface** has a much more well-defined behavior compared to the `finalize()` method. It is true that when the HTTP session terminates, the reference to a `session`-scoped bean is no longer available. Presumably, the bean would then be garbage collected, thereby invoking its `finalize()` method. However, the frequency of garbage collection depends on the memory consumption pattern in the entire Java Virtual Machine where one or more applications are executing. It is therefore uncertain when the bean would actually be garbage collected, and the database connection would be held open until it is. For performance reasons, holding on to a connection for such an unpredictable time interval is simply not a good idea. The HTTP session listener interfaces provide well-defined callbacks for event notification precisely for this purpose.

Writing `DBQueryBean.sqlj`

You will now write the JavaBean, `DBQueryBean`, that executes a static SQL query to fetch the details of a particular order in the purchase order database. This bean will implement the HTTP session-related event listener **interface** to release the database connection upon session termination or timeout. The `DBQueryBean` will perform a SQLJ query based on the value of its `requestNum` property, and format the query result for displaying in the browser. There are two important points to note about the logic in this bean:

■ It implements the `javax.servlet.http.HttpSessionBinding Listener` **interface**, and is intended for use in `session` scope.

■ It uses the instance variable `dctx` to remember the SQLJ connection context for the duration of the HTTP session. The database connection represented by `dctx` is closed when the `valueUnbound()` event listener method is called.

The code for `DBQueryBean.sqlj` program is shown as follows:

```
/** Program name: DBQueryBean.sqlj
 ** Purpose:       Retrieve information for an order from
 **                the Purchase Order database using SQLJ
 **/

package mybeans;

import java.sql.*;
import javax.servlet.http.*;
import oracle.sqlj.runtime.Oracle;
import sqlj.runtime.ref.DefaultContext;

public class DBQueryBean
            implements HttpSessionBindingListener { // (See Note 1.)

  String requestNum = null; // (See Note 2.)
  // Method to set the requestNum property
  public synchronized void setRequestNum(String requestNum) {
    this.requestNum = requestNum;
    result = null;
  }

private StringBuffer result = null;  // the query result
  private DefaultContext dctx = null;  // database connection context

  // Method to fetch the order details
  public synchronized String queryOrder () {  // (See Note 3.)

   if (result != null)  // same query done earlier, so reuse the result!
      return result.toString();

   try {
    // Connect to the database if necessary
    if (dctx == null)
      dctx = Oracle.getConnection("jdbc:oracle:oci8:@",
                                  "jspuser", "jsp");  // (See Note 4.)
    // Query the order from database tables
    DBQuery();

    return result.toString();
    // But do not close the database connection!

} catch (SQLException e) {
        return("Error in querying: " + e.getMessage());
    }
```

```java
}

// SQLJ iterator declaration for line items
// (See Note 5.)
#sql iterator LineItems (int lineno, int projectno,
                         int quantity, String description);
private LineItems  li = null;

// Method to select purchase order and line items data for a new order
private String DBQuery() {
  int empNum;
  String empName;

  try {      // (See Note 6.)
    #sql [dctx] { SELECT PURCHASE_LIST.employeeno,
                         firstname || ' ' || lastName
                  INTO :empNum,
                       :empName
                  FROM PURCHASE_LIST, EMPLOYEE_LIST
                   WHERE requestno = :requestNum
                         AND EMPLOYEE_LIST.employeeno =
                             PURCHASE_LIST.employeeno
    };

    result = new StringBuffer();
    result.append("Employee: " + empName +
                  " , number: " + empNum + "<BR><BR>");

    // Now, query the line items for the order
    // (See Note 7.)
    #sql [dctx] li = {
                       SELECT  lineno,
                               projectno,
                               quantity,
                               description
                        FROM  LINEITEM_LIST
                        WHERE requestno =  :requestNum
           };
  formatHTML();
  li.close();  // close the iterator
    return result.toString();
  } catch (SQLException e) {
      return("Error on DB Query: " + e.getMessage()) ;
  }
}

private void formatHTML () throws SQLException {  // (See Note 8.)
  if (li == null || !li.next()) {
    result.append("<P> No matching rows.<P>\n");
```

```
      return;
    }

    // Print the header for the table with order details
    result.append("<TABLE BORDER>\n");
    result.append("<TH><I> Line # </I></TH>");
    result.append("<TH><I> Project # </I></TH>");
    result.append("<TH><I> Quantity </I></TH>");
    result.append("<TH><I> Description </I></TH>");

      do {  // Print the data for each item ordered
      result.append("<TR>\n");
        result.append("<TD>" + li.lineno() + " </TD>");
        result.append("<TD>" + li.projectno() + " </TD>");
        result.append("<TD>" + li.quantity() + " </TD>");
        result.append("<TD>" + li.description() + " </TD>");
        result.append("</TR>");
      } while (li.next());
      result.append("</TABLE>");
    }
  // (See Note 9.)
  // Method executed when HTTP session starts
  public void valueBound(HttpSessionBindingEvent event) {
    // Do nothing here!
    // Database connection will be opened only if a query is submitted.
  }

  // Method executed when HTTP session exits
  public synchronized void valueUnbound(HttpSessionBindingEvent event) {
    if (dctx != null) {
        try { dctx.close();
      } catch (SQLException e) {}
    }
  }
}
```

Notes on `DBQueryBean.sqlj`:

1. `DBQueryBean` implements the `HttpSessionBindingListener`
interface, and is intended to be invoked through a `<jsp:useBean>`
tag with `session` scope. The `QueryOrder` JSP (which you will write next)
will use a `session`-scoped instance of this bean.

2. The `DBQueryBean` has a single property named `requestNum` that
represents the order number of the order that you wish to query. It provides
a method `setRequestNum()` to set the value of this property. This
method also resets the result of any query that was previously executed.

3. The `QueryOrder` JSP page will call the `queryOrder()` method of the bean only when the user provides a search parameter (that is, an order number) in the HTML form. So, in order to minimize the connection duration, the bean does not connect to the database in its `valueBound()` method, which is called when the bean is created and bound to the HTTP `session` object. Rather, the database connection is opened in the `queryOrder()` method when it is invoked for the first time with a request number. This connection is held open for the remaining lifetime of the bean, which is the duration of the HTTP session. A valid alternate approach is to place the `<jsp:useBean>` tag under conditional logic that executes only when a request number is first entered, and open the database connection when the bean is instantiated.

4. This statement sets up a SQLJ connection context using the JDBC-OCI driver.

5. This statement declares a SQLJ named iterator `LineItems` for fetching line item information.

6. A SQLJ `SELECT-INTO` statement is used to fetch the employee number and name corresponding to the order.

7. An instance of the `LineItems` iterator is populated with the appropriate SQL query using the value of the request number property.

8. The `formatHTML()` method takes the result of the query and formats it into an HTML table with the appropriate column headers.

9. Note that the bean implements the two methods, `valueBound()` and `valueUnbound()`, of the `HttpSessionBindingListener` **interface**. The `valueBound()` method is invoked when the bean is created and associated with the HTTP session. However, this method is not required to do anything because the database connection is opened only when a query is submitted. The `valueUnbound()` method simply closes the database connection if it is not `null`.

Writing `QueryOrder.jsp`

Now you can write the `QueryOrder.jsp` program that uses the `DBQueryBean` class defined earlier. This bean is used in `session` scope, because it implements the `HttpSessionBindingListener` **interface**. The code for this JSP is shown next with the significant parts in bold font. The general pattern of the JSP logic should seem quite familiar to you by now. An HTML form is used to accept a request number from the user. If this request number is not `null`, the `queryOrder()` method is invoked on the `DBQueryBean` instance to display the details of the particular order.

```
<%-- Program name: QueryOrder.jsp
  -- Purpose:       Accept an order number and query details for it
  --                from the purchase order database
  --%>
<jsp:useBean id="queryBean" class="mybeans.DBQueryBean" scope="session" />
<jsp:setProperty name="queryBean" property="requestNum" />
<HTML>
<HEAD> <TITLE> The Query Order JSP  </TITLE> </HEAD>
<BODY BGCOLOR="white">
<%  String requestNum = request.getParameter("requestNum");
if (requestNum != null) { %>
      <H3>Details of order number: <%= requestNum %> </H3>
      <CENTER><B>
<%=  queryBean.queryOrder() %>
      </CENTER><B><BR>
      <HR>
<%  }  %>

<P><B>Enter an order number:</B></P>
<FORM METHOD=get>
<INPUT TYPE="text" NAME="requestNum" SIZE=10>
<INPUT TYPE="submit" VALUE="Submit Query");
</FORM>
</BODY>
</HTML>
```

Running `QueryOrder.jsp`

You will need to install the `QueryOrder` JSP program and the compiled `DBQueryBean` class on your Web server (see Appendix E for setup steps). After that, you can invoke the JSP through the appropriate URL. Figure 11-14 shows the output of inquiring for order #502 through the `QueryOrder` JSP.

Executing Dynamic SQL Queries

In the `QueryOrder.jsp` example, the SQL query is static. That is, you know at program development time which columns you wish to fetch from which tables, and the search condition to use for the SQL SELECT statement. For some applications, not all of this information is available until runtime. In these cases, you must use the JDBC API since SQLJ can only execute static SQL queries and updates. Keep in mind that SQLJ and JDBC are interoperable, so you can mix and match SQLJ and JDBC as necessary in your application.

In this section, you will write a JavaBean that uses JDBC to perform a dynamic SQL query. This JavaBean, written as the `DynamicQueryBean` class, will be used as a component in the `AnyQuery.jsp` program, to dynamically execute any SQL query text that is posted through an HTML form. First you will develop the JavaBean, and then write the `AnyQuery.jsp` page that calls this bean.

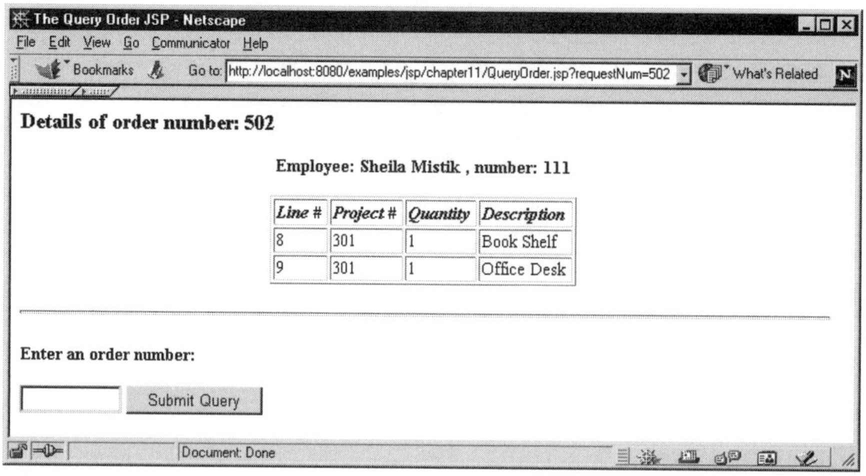

FIGURE 11-14. *Output of retrieving an order through* `QueryOrder.jsp`

Writing `DynamicQueryBean.java`

The function of this query bean is to execute any query on the Purchase Order database. The code for this program is shown as follows, with the significant parts in bold font. Notice that this bean also implements the `HttpSessionBindingListener` **interface**, like the `DBQueryBean.sqlj` program you wrote in the previous section. Thus, this bean will be used in the `session` scope in your JSP, and will close its database connection when the HTTP session terminates.

A major point to note in the `DynamicQuerybean` program is how to format the result of a general SQL query into an HTML table. This function is performed by the `formatResult()` method that takes a JDBC result set and generates an HTML table with the appropriate headers and rows. The logic of this method is further explained here.

```
/** Program name: DynamicQueryBean.java
 ** Purpose:      Execute a dynamic JDBC query on the
 **               Purchase Order database
 **/

package mybeans;

import java.sql.*;
import javax.servlet.http.HttpSessionBindingListener;
import javax.servlet.http.HttpSessionBindingEvent;

public class DynamicQueryBean implements HttpSessionBindingListener  {
```

```java
public void DynamicQueryBean() {
}
private String query = "";      // (See Note 1.)
private String result = null;   // (See Note 2.)
public synchronized void setQuery(String newQuery) {
    result = null;
    query = newQuery;
}

// Main method to return the query result
public String getResult() throws SQLException { // (See Note 3.)
  if (result != null) return result;
  else return (runQuery());
}

private Connection conn = null;
private synchronized String runQuery() {  // (See Note 4.)
  try {
    if (conn == null) {
      DriverManager.registerDriver(
                  new oracle.jdbc.driver.OracleDriver());
      conn = DriverManager.getConnection("jdbc:oracle:oci8:@",
                                         "jspuser", "jsp");
    }
    Statement stmt = conn.createStatement();
    ResultSet rset = stmt.executeQuery (query);
    result = formatResult(rset));
    if (rset!= null) rset.close();
    if (stmt!= null) stmt.close();
    return result;
  } catch (SQLException e) {
    return ("<P> SQL error for query: <PRE> " +
            query + "<BR>" + e + " </PRE> </P>\n");
  }
}

private String formatResult(ResultSet rs) // (See Note 5.)
              throws SQLException {
  StringBuffer sb = new StringBuffer();
  if (rs == null || !rs.next()) {
    sb.append("<P> No matching rows found.<P>\n");
    return sb.toString();
  }
  sb.append("<TABLE BORDER>\n");
  ResultSetMetaData md = rs.getMetaData();
  int numCols = md.getColumnCount();
  for (int i=1; i<= numCols; i++) {
    sb.append("<TH><I>" + md.getColumnLabel(i) + "</I></TH>");
  }
```

```
do {
     sb.append("<TR>\n");
     for (int i = 1; i <= numCols; i++) {
      sb.append("<TD>");
      Object obj = rs.getObject(i);
      if (obj != null)  sb.append(obj.toString());
            sb.append("</TD>");
     }
     sb.append("</TR>");
   } while (rs.next());
   sb.append("</TABLE>");
   return sb.toString();
 }

 // Method executed when session starts
 public void valueBound(HttpSessionBindingEvent event) {
   // nothing to be done here. Bean will create connection only when
   // a query is submitted.
 }

 // Method executed when session exits
 public synchronized void valueUnbound(HttpSessionBindingEvent event)
 {
   try {
      if (conn != null) conn.close();  // (See Note 6.)
    }  catch (SQLException e)  {  }
 }
}
```

Notes on `DynamicQueryBean.java`:

1. The `DynamicQueryBean` has a single property named `query`. This property represents the text of the SQL query to be executed, and is set by the user through an HTML form.

2. The local variable `result` denotes the result returned by the previous query execution, if any. This value is cached by the bean, so that it can be reused in case the same query is reexecuted. Accordingly, the `setQuery()` action also invalidates this cached copy of the result by setting it to `null`.

3. The method `getResult()` is the **public** method that is called to execute the query and return the formatted result as an HTML table. This method returns the cached query result if it is available (from a previous execution with the same request parameter), or else calls the `runQuery()` method of the bean.

4. The runQuery() method is a **private** method that contains the code for the actual execution of the query. It first opens a database connection using JDBC, if one is not already open. Then, a statement handle is obtained on the connection and the query is executed to create a result set. This result set is formatted by calling the formatResult() method.

5. The formatResult() method is quite interesting to program. The method takes a JDBC result set as its argument, and formats the rows into an HTML table. First, it checks if the result set is empty. If so, it simply returns a message that no rows were found; otherwise, it uses the getColumnLabel() method call in the ResultSetMetadata object of the JDBC ResultSet argument to determine the names of the columns returned by the query. Using these column names, it constructs the header of the HTML table. Next, it traverses each row in the result set, and formats it into an HTML table using appropriate HTML tags and the toString() method call on each fetched object.

6. Finally, the valueUnbound() method of the HttpSessionBinding Listener **interface** closes the JDBC connection handle upon termination of the HTTP session.

Writing AnyQuery.jsp

The code for this JSP is shown as follows. Notice that the code uses the DynamicQueryBean class in session scope, and setting its query property from the SQL query text entered in a text area of the HTML form. The JSP checks if the HTTP request has a parameter named query, and if so, it calls the getResult() method of DynamicQueryBean to execute the query and output the formatted result. The text area contains a default query to start with. If a new query is entered by the user, the default query is replaced with the current user query.

```
<%-- Program name: AnyQuery.jsp
  -- Purpose:      Accept and execute any user query on the purchase order
  --               database, displaying the results as an HTML table.
  --%>

<jsp:useBean id="queryBean" class="mybeans.DynamicQueryBean"
scope="session" />
<jsp:setProperty name="queryBean" property="*" />

<HTML>
<HEAD> <TITLE> The AnyQuery JSP  </TITLE> </HEAD>
<BODY BGCOLOR="white">

<%  String query = request.getParameter("query");
    if (query != null) { %>
```

```
        <H3>Result of your query:  </H3>
        <CENTER><B>
        <%=  queryBean.getResult() %>
        </CENTER><B><BR>
        <HR>
<%  }  %>


<H4> Hello! Here you can execute any query on the
           Order database. </H4>
<H4>Please enter your query below:</H4>

<FORM METHOD=post>
<TEXTAREA NAME="query" rows="8" cols="50">
<% if (query != null ) { %>
<%= query %>
<% } else { %>
  SELECT firstname || ' ' || lastname AS "Name",
         employeeno AS "Employee #",
         deptno AS "Depart #"
    FROM EMPLOYEE_LIST
     WHERE lastname LIKE 'A%'
       ORDER BY lastname
  <% } %>
</TEXTAREA>
<INPUT TYPE="submit" VALUE="Submit Query">
</FORM>
</BODY>
</HTML>
```

Running `AnyQuery.jsp`

Figure 11-15 shows the initial output of invoking the `AnyQuery.jsp` page. The
screen has a text box for entering a query, and it also contains a default query on
the `EMPLOYEE_LIST` table of the purchase order database.

Suppose that you now modify the default query by changing the search condition
in the `WHERE` clause of the `SELECT` statement to `lastname LIKE M%` and then click
the "Submit Query" button. As a result of this action, the `getResult()` method
on the `DynamicQueryBean` JavaBean is invoked. This method takes the query text
entered through the input box and executes it via JDBC. The result is formatted into an
HTML table and sent back to the browser. Figure 11-16 shows the result of executing
this query. Notice that the default query in the text box has been replaced with the
modified query that was submitted.

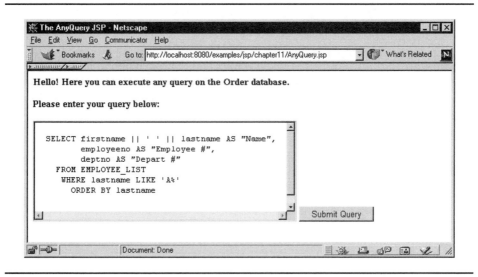

FIGURE 11-15. *Initial output of* `AnyQuery.jsp`

Database Access Beans in Oracle JSP 1.1

Oracle JSP 1.1 provides a set of database access beans as convenient prebuilt components to execute SQL operations in your Web application. In this section, you will learn about these beans, and write a JSP page that uses such a bean to execute a SQL query and generate results in XML.

Oracle JSP Bean Library

There are four different JavaBeans provided in the Oracle JSP bean library. These beans can be created and used in different scopes in your JSP page through the `<jsp:useBean>` tag. They use JDBC to connect to the database and execute SQL operations. However, many details of SQL execution are hidden by the beans, which provide a simpler interface than JDBC for database interaction. For example, a bean for connection management can automatically close the database connection when it goes out of scope (`page`, `request`, `session`, or `application`). Thus, the connection is always closed properly, and programmer errors are avoided. The same connection bean can be used in different scopes, because the bean class implements the `oracle.jsp.event.JspScopeListener` **interface**, which is a general event listener mechanism supported in Oracle JSP for different JSP scopes.

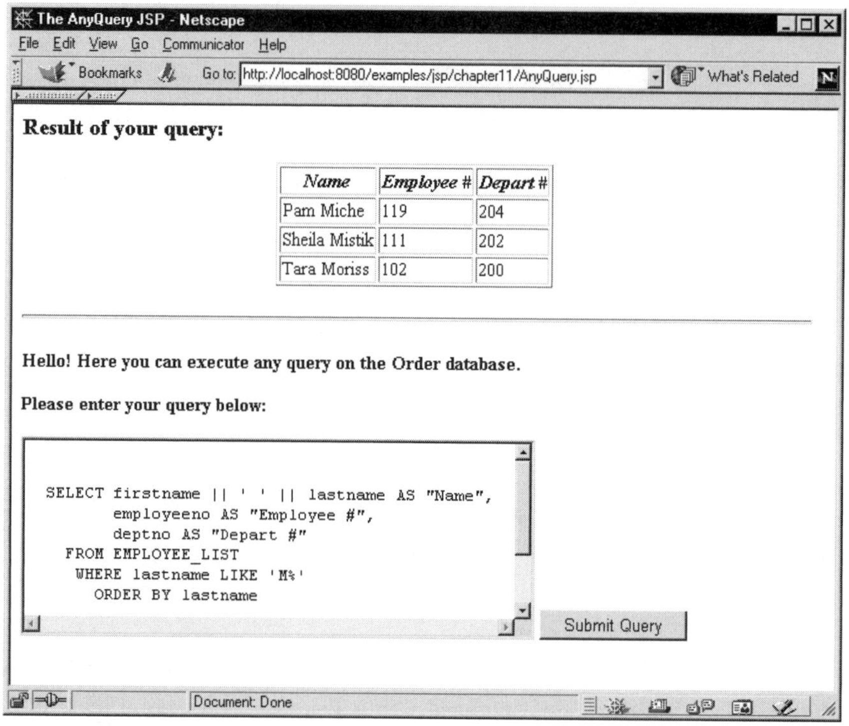

FIGURE 11-16. *Output of* `AnyQuery.jsp` *after executing a query*

The following beans are available in the `oracle.jsp.dbutil` package that is part of the Oracle JSP 1.1 libraries (`ojsputil.jar`):

- `ConnBean` This bean is used to get a simple database connection without connection pooling.

- `ConnCacheBean` This bean uses Oracle's connection caching facilities for efficiently sharing database connections among multiple users.

- `DBBean` This bean is used to execute a database query, and to print the results either as an HTML table or as XML.

- `CursorBean` This bean can call stored procedures, and execute general SQL DML statements (`UPDATE`, `INSERT`, and `DELETE`) as well as SQL queries.

In the next section, you will learn how to use the DBBean. This bean can connect to a database and execute a SQL operation. The bean manages the connection efficiently, closing it automatically when going out of scope. Another useful capability of the DBBean is to return the result of a SQL query in XML format. In the next section, you will get an overview of XML, and then write a JSP that uses the DBBean to generate XML.

Later in this chapter, you will also see an example of another predefined bean, the ConnCacheBean, which is used to manage a shared pool of connections. This example appears in the "Performance Tuning SQL Operations" section in this chapter.

Generating XML Pages with JSP and JavaBeans

The JSP specification supports the creation of XML pages with JSPs. As you learned in Chapter 10, there is XML-compatible notation for each of the JSP tags, so that JSP pages can be conveniently written using XML authoring tools. The output generated by a JSP page can also be XML. Before you learn about the details of XML generation with a JSP, you first need to know what XML is and why it is useful.

What Is XML?

XML stands for *Extensible Markup Language*. It is based on Standard Generalized Markup Language (SGML), which has been used for a number of years for general documents. XML is a simpler version of SGML, having eliminated several of its complexities. However, XML retains much of the power of SGML by being extensible (unlike HTML, which has a predefined set of tags). What this implies is that you can define your own tags (also known as *elements*) and their syntax rules for your XML document through a *document type definition* (DTD). This DTD can be used to check the XML document for "well formedness" and validity by the XML *parser*, which is a program that reads in an XML document and applies the syntax rules for element construction.

Tags in XML are used to define the hierarchical structure of a document, and can be nested to arbitrary depths. For example, a purchase order can be represented in XML by the following nested structure:

```
<order>
  <employeeInfo>
    <employeeName> name </employeeName>
    <employeeNumber> 1234 </employeeNumber>
  </employeeInfo>
  <itemList>
    <item>
      <itemNumber> 1 </itemNumber>
      <itemName> XXX </itemName>
      <quantity> 123 </quantity>
```

```
        <description> This item is for XXX purpose. </description>
      </item>
      <item>
        <itemNumber> 2 </itemNumber>
        <itemName> YYY </itemName>
        <quantity> 345 </quantity>
        <description> This item is for YYY purpose. </description>
      </item>
    </itemList>
  </order>
```

As shown in this example, the structure of an XML document is hierarchical or tree-based. The "top-level" `<order>` tag represents the purchase order element. Its termination is denoted by the matching end tag `</order>`. The order element has two nested elements, `employeeInfo` and `itemList`, which themselves contain other subelements. Notice that an `item` element is repeated within the `itemList` tag for each of the items in the purchase order. An element such as `quantity` is just a simple integer number, with no further subelements. These types of elements are the "leaf" elements that hold the actual data in the XML document. The non-leaf elements define the nesting structure, and may contain other leaf and non-leaf elements within them.

Unlike HTML, an XML document does not necessarily provide any formatting information. That is, in XML there is no specification of fonts or colors in which an element should be displayed. This omission is quite intentional, and separates content from presentation. You must be wondering at this point how an XML document is displayed by the browser. It can be done through the application of XSL *style sheets*. XSL stands for *Extensible Stylesheet Language*. It is a companion specification to the XML standard. XSL is a powerful tree-transformation and formatting tool with template-matching rules for processing XML elements, and for defining their visual presentation format for browser display.

Because of its flexibility and extensibility, XML has rapidly grown in popularity. It is now a W3C standard (W3C stands for the World Wide Web Consortium; their home site is http://www.w3.org). XML technology is being adopted by a growing number of companies for widely different purposes, from structured data representation to message communication protocols. Its use is certain to be even more widespread in future.

Writing `XMLQuery.jsp`

An interesting aspect of database applications is how to generate structured XML representation of SQL query results. Oracle provides several utilities for such XML generation and manipulation. Oracle's XML utilities are packaged as the Oracle XML Developer's Kit (XDK), which is downloadable from the Web site for Oracle Technology Network (http://technet.oracle.com/tech/xml). The XDK includes an

XML parser, XSL processor, and the Oracle XML-SQL utility to generate XML data from JDBC result sets. The Oracle XML-SQL utility is in fact used by the database access beans (such as DBBean) to convert SQL results to XML in a transparent manner, hiding much of the details of XML generation. You will now see an example of a JSP page that generates XML results for a SQL query through the DBBean.

The following is a JSP program—XMLQuery.jsp—that uses a page-scoped instance of the DBBean class (described earlier) to execute a query entered through the text input box in the HTML form. The significant parts of the code are shown in bold font.

```jsp
<%-- Program name: XMLQuery.jsp
  -- Purpose:       Generate XML results for a SQL query
  --%>
<%@ page import="java.sql.*" %>
<jsp:useBean id="dbbean" class="oracle.jsp.dbutil.DBBean"
scope="page">
<jsp:setProperty name="dbbean" property="user" value="jspuser"/>
<jsp:setProperty name="dbbean" property="password" value="jsp"/>
<jsp:setProperty name="dbbean" property="URL"
value="jdbc:oracle:oci8:@"/>
</jsp:useBean>

<HTML>
  <HEAD> <TITLE> XMLQuery JSP </TITLE> </HEAD>
 <BODY BGCOLOR="white">
<%  String query = request.getParameter("query");
    if (query != null) { %>
      <H3>Result of your query in XML:  </H3>
 <P>
<%    dbbean.connect(); /* connect to the database */ %>
<PRE> <%= dbbean.getResultAsXMLString(query) %> </PRE>
<%    dbbean.close();  /* close the database connection */
     } %>
<H4>Please enter your query below:</H4>
 <FORM METHOD=post>
  <TEXTAREA NAME="query" rows="8" cols="50">
  <% if (query != null ) { %>
  <%= query %>
  <% } else { %>
    SELECT firstname || ' ' || lastname AS "Name",
           employeeno AS "Employee #",
           deptno AS "Depart #"
      FROM EMPLOYEE_LIST
     WHERE lastname LIKE 'A%'
     ORDER BY lastname
    <% } %>
```

```
</TEXTAREA>
<INPUT TYPE="submit" VALUE="Submit Query">
</FORM>
</BODY>
</HTML>
```

The DBBean has three properties that are usually required to set up a database connection, namely, user, password, and URL. These properties are typically set through <jsp:setProperty> calls, or less commonly, by calling their set methods directly. If there is a query in the request parameters, then the database connection is established using the dbbean.connect() call. There are two methods available in this bean to execute a SQL query. They have the following signatures:

```
String getResultAsHTMLTable (String queryText);
String getResultAsXMLString(String queryText);
```

The first method executes the given query, and formats the rows into an HTML table (using an algorithm similar to the DynamicQueryBean you wrote earlier in this chapter). The SQL column names or aliases are used as column headers for the HTML table. The second method also executes the query, but formats the rows into XML. The SQL column names or aliases are used as XML tags.

In the XMLQuery.jsp program, the second method, getResultAsXMLString(), is called to execute the user's query on the purchase order database, and generate XML output. Finally, the database connection is closed by calling the dbbean.close() method. The DBBean instance also closes the connection automatically, if it is not closed already, when the JSP page execution completes and it goes out of scope.

Running XMLQuery.jsp

Install this JSP page on your Web server, and remember to add the ojsputil.jar library from Oracle JSP 1.1, as well as xsu12.jar (for JDK 1.2) or xsu111.jar (for JDK 1.1) to the CLASSPATH. The latter libraries are part of the Oracle XDK download (from the Oracle Technology Network site http://technet.oracle.com), and are also available in your Oracle 8.1.7 or Oracle Internet Application Server installation.

When you invoke XMLQuery.jsp, an HTML page with an embedded XML block in it is produced. The source for the page generated by executing XMLQuery.jsp appears in Listing 11-2, with the XML parts marked in boldface.

Listing 11-2 HTML/XML page generated by XMLQuery.jsp

```
<HTML>
  <HEAD> <TITLE> XMLQuery JSP </TITLE> </HEAD>
  <BODY BGCOLOR="white">
```

```
      <H3>Result of your query in XML:   </H3>
 <P>
<?xml version="1.0"?>
<ROWSET>
<ROW num="1">
 <Name>Pam Miche</Name>
 <Employee #>119</Employee #>
 <Depart #>204</Depart #>
</ROW>
<ROW num="2">
 <Name>Sheila Mistik</Name>
 <Employee #>111</Employee #>
 <Depart #>202</Depart #>
</ROW>
<ROW num="3">
   <Name>Tara Moriss</Name>
   <Employee #>102</Employee #>
   <Depart #>200</Depart #>
</ROW>
</ROWSET>
<H4>Please enter your query below:</H4>
<FORM METHOD=post>
   <TEXTAREA NAME="query" rows="8" cols="50">

    SELECT firstname || ' ' || lastname AS "Name",
          employeeno AS "Employee #",
          deptno AS "Depart #"
      FROM EMPLOYEE_LIST
       WHERE lastname LIKE 'M%'
         ORDER BY lastname
   </TEXTAREA>
   <INPUT TYPE="submit" VALUE="Submit Query">
   </FORM>
 </BODY>
</HTML>
```

In this page generated by XMLQuery.jsp, the statement <?xml version="1.0"?> denotes the start of the XML data. The "top-level" element generated for the result is named ROWSET by default, and each nested row is named ROW. The rows are also numbered sequentially through the num attribute of the ROW element. This is the default behavior of the Oracle XML-SQL routines.

Your browser (such as Netscape 4.6) might not display any of the XML tags in the generated page, because it does not directly understand the XML notation. You can apply an XSL style sheet to format the XML result into an HTML table for displaying in the browser. There are several ways in which a style sheet could be applied. One convenient way is to use the <jml:transform> custom tag provided in Oracle JSP 1.1. Use of this tag is illustrated in the next chapter.

Performance Tuning SQL Operations

In the earlier sections of this chapter you have learned how to effectively use JavaBeans to program database operations in your Web application. In this section you will consider the performance issues associated with SQL execution in the Web environment.

Web applications are unique in that they are often expected to serve thousands of concurrent requests in real time. The response time of a Web application is very critical, since it is almost always interacting with a human being waiting impatiently for a response at the other end. This unique requirement implies that special design techniques should be considered in building your Web application. Now, you will learn about some of the important performance issues and design techniques for executing SQL operations in the Web environment.

Using JDBC Prepared Statements

If your Web application executes the same SQL operation with different parameters in each invocation, reparsing and reoptimizing the SQL statement every time is very inefficient. The execution plan of a SQL statement generally does not depend on the bind parameters, which are just arguments to the SQL operation. It is possible to save time by parsing the SQL statement only once, and then simply reexecuting it over and over again with different bind parameters. The JDBC `PreparedStatement` type provides exactly such a mechanism. The `java.sql.PreparedStatement` type is a subtype of `java.sql.Statement`, and provides parameter binding methods for repeated execution.

The SQLJ runtime also makes use of JDBC prepared statements—in Oracle 8.1.6 and later versions, they are cached and reused for execution in a loop. So remember that *you automatically get the benefit of JDBC prepared statements whenever you use SQLJ.*

As an example, consider a SQL statement that inserts 100 line items in the `LINEITEM_LIST` table of the purchase order database. The same `INSERT` statement is to be executed 100 times in a loop with different data for each row. The code fragment in Listing 11-3 shows how to use JDBC prepared statements for this case.

Listing 11-3 Using JDBC prepared statements

```
public void insertLineItems(java.sql.Connection conn)
    throws java.sql.SQLException   {
  java.sql.PreparedStatement pstmt =
      conn.prepareStatement( // prepare the insert statement once
      "INSERT INTO LINEITEM_LIST (requestno, lineno, projectno, " +
                          " quantity, description) VALUES( " +
                          " ?, ?, ?, ?, ?)" );
    for (int i=1; i<100; i++) { // insert 100 rows
```

```
    // Bind the parameter values
    pstmt.setInt(1,requestno);
    pstmt.setInt(2, i);
    pstmt.setInt(3, projectno);
    pstmt.setInt(4, quantity[i]);
    pstmt.setString(5, description[i]);
    pstmt.executeUpdate();         // insert the row
  }
  pstmt.close();
}
```

Notice that the prepared statement object is created only once by calling the method `prepareStatement()` on the JDBC connection with the SQL command as the argument. The '"?" character in the text of the SQL statement represents each bind parameter positionally. The SQL `INSERT` operation is performed in a loop to enter 100 rows into the `LINEITEM_LIST` table. Each insert uses different data values for the `lineno`, `quantity`, and `description` columns. The appropriate data values are bound to the "?" placeholders in the prepared statement through the `setInt()` and `setString()` calls. The `PreparedStatement` type provides such `set` calls for all data types supported by JDBC. After binding the parameters, the prepared statement is executed. No reparsing of the SQL command will occur on successive iterations of the loop.

Batching of Updates

In Oracle 8.1.6 and later versions, SQL `INSERT`, `DELETE`, and `UPDATE` operations may be *batched* in JDBC 2.0 and SQLJ. Batching is a performance optimization that works as follows: if you are inserting or updating data through the same DML statement in a loop, then the parameter bindings can be collected locally on the client side until they are explicitly sent to the server via the `executeBatch()` method call. At this time, the DML statement is executed once with an array bind of the collected parameter values. Thus, batching saves round trips to the database. The JDBC 2.0 API provides explicit methods on the `java.sql.Statement` object to add rows to a batch and execute it.

SQLJ also supports batching of updates through *execution contexts*. A `#sql` statement may specify a certain execution context. This execution context defines the "environment," such as batching and other execution parameters of the SQL operation. Methods can be called on an execution context instance to set up these execution parameters, and in particular to turn on batching and to set a batch size limit. A pending batch may be sent to the database explicitly by calling the `executeBatch()` method of the execution context, or it will be implicitly sent by the SQLJ runtime when the specified batch size is reached or when a different SQLJ statement is executed in your program. Thus, you can take full advantage of the JDBC 2.0 batching facilities in SQLJ code.

Caching Statement Handles

Oracle SQLJ provides automatic caching of JDBC-prepared statement handles in Oracle 8.1.6 and later versions. That is, the prepared statement objects for SQL statements appearing in the SQLJ program are stored and reused as long as the database connection is open.

Oracle 8.1.7 JDBC drivers also provide transparent statement caching based on a "least recently used" scheme. When statement caching is enabled in JDBC, a close on the `Statement` object doesn't necessarily close the underlying database cursor. Instead, it is cached and can be reused later if the same SQL is reexecuted. An alternative to this scheme is to use a `session`-scoped SQL bean that explicitly reuses a prepared statement handle without closing it for the duration of the HTTP session.

Connection Pooling

Connection pooling is an important framework for optimizing database access from multiple sessions of a Web application. The idea is to share physical connections from a common connection cache in order to minimize the cost of creating and closing database connections, which are generally quite expensive operations. Closing a "logical" database connection actually returns the physical connection to the shared connection pool instead of terminating it. Connection pooling is a common feature of application servers running in the middle tier to optimize database access.

The JDBC 2.0 API introduces the concept of JNDI-based *data sources* for connecting to databases (as an alternative to the JDBC `DriverManager` scheme in JDBC 1.0). JDBC 2.0 also defines a standard connection pooling framework through the `javax.sql.ConnectionPoolDataSource` and related interfaces. These interfaces are implemented by different JDBC drivers to provide efficient connection pooling. Oracle's JDBC 2.0 drivers also support the connection pooling interfaces. Refer to the *Oracle8i JDBC Developer's Guide and Reference, Release 8.1.6*, Oracle Corporation, for details on data sources and connection pooling.

Using Connection Pooling in a JSP

You can use the connection pooling facilities provided by JDBC 2.0 in your JSP application. The shared pool of database connections (connection cache) can be attached to the `application` object so that it can be shared by all HTTP sessions running on the same Java Virtual Machine. This approach is particularly beneficial if different HTTP sessions use the same database schema, as in the Order Online application you wrote earlier in this chapter. The connection cache can also handle connections to different schemas. In this case, it returns the connection object with the correct schema based on the user's name, password, and database URL information.

The bean library in Oracle JSP 1.1 provides a prebuilt JavaBean component called `ConnCacheBean` for convenient use of the connection caching facility in a JSP. This JavaBean can be used in the `application` scope of your Web application to efficiently manage a shared pool of physical connections to the database. This bean has the following properties:

- `user` Schema name in the database.

- `password` Password for the schema.

- `URL` Database URL for making a JDBC connection.

- `maxLimit` Maximum number of open database connections in this cache.

- `minLimit` Minimum number of open database connections in this cache.

- `stmtCacheSize` Size of the Oracle JDBC statement cache (default is no statement caching).

- `cacheScheme` Policy for cache management. This property can have one of the following three values: DYNAMIC_SCHEME, FIXED_WAIT_SCHEME, or FIXED_RETURN_NULL_SCHEME.

These cache schemes implement different policies when the maximum limit on open connections is exceeded for the cache. In the DYNAMIC_SCHEME, the number of pooled connections is allowed to be more than the maximum limit, but each extra physical connection is closed as soon as the logical connection is freed. When the maximum number of open connections is reached in the FIXED_WAIT_ SCHEME, then a request for a new connection waits for some connection to be freed up instead of creating a new one. In contrast, the FIXED_RETURN_NULL_SCHEME returns a `null` connection when the maximum limit is reached, until some connections are released.

The `oracle.jsp.dbutil.ConnCacheBean` class extends the Oracle JDBC class `oracle.jdbc.pool.OracleConnectionCacheImpl`, which in turn extends the Oracle JDBC class `oracle.jdbc.pool.OracleDataSource`. The `ConnCacheBean` class inherits the following properties and their accessor methods from the `oracle.jdbc.pool.OracleDataSource` class: `databaseName`, `dataSourceName`, `description`, `networkProtocol`, `portNumber`, `serverName`, and `driverType`. For more information about these properties and their usage semantics, refer to the *Oracle8i JDBC Developer's Guide and Reference, Release 8.1.6*, Oracle Corporation.

Using the `ConnCacheBean` is illustrated in the `ConnectionCaching.jsp` program in Listing 11-4. The JSP first sets the `MaxLimit`, `CacheScheme`, `user`, `password`, and `URL` properties of the bean to appropriate values. These are constant strings in this program, but can also be set from HTTP request parameters. The `connCacheBean.getConnection()` method call is used to get a logical connection from the cache. Next, a statement is created and the query is executed. After the query results are printed, the result set and statement objects are closed. The connection is closed by calling the `connCacheBean.close()` method, but in effect this method only returns the connection handle to the cache.

Listing 11-4 Using the `ConnCacheBean` in a JSP

```
<!-- Program name: ConnectionCaching.jsp
  -- Purpose:       Uses ConnCacheBean from the bean library
  --                in OracleJSP to connect to the database
  --                and execute a SQL query.
  -->
<%@ page import="java.sql.*" %>
<%@ page import="javax.sql.*" %>
<%@ page import="oracle.jsp.dbutil.ConnCacheBean" %>

<jsp:useBean id="connCacheBean" class="oracle.jsp.dbutil.ConnCacheBean"
                               scope="application">
  <jsp:setProperty name="connCacheBean" property="MaxLimit"
                                         value="50"  />
  <jsp:setProperty name="connCacheBean" property="CacheScheme"
        value="<%= ConnCacheBean.FIXED_RETURN_NULL_SCHEME %>"  />
  <jsp:setProperty name="connCacheBean" property="user"
        value="jspuser"/>
  <jsp:setProperty name="connCacheBean" property="password"
        value="jsp"/>
  <jsp:setProperty name="connCacheBean" property="URL"
                   value="jdbc:oracle:oci8:@"  />
</jsp:useBean>
<HTML>
 <HEAD> <TITLE> The Connection Caching JSP </TITLE> </HEAD>
 <BODY BGCOLOR="white">
<%
      // get a connection from the cache
      Connection conn = connCacheBean.getConnection();
      // create a statement
      Statement stmt = conn.createStatement ();
      // execute the query
      ResultSet rset = stmt.executeQuery (
                        "SELECT * FROM EMPLOYEE_LIST" );
      if (rset.next()) {
%>
        <!- print the query results ->
        Result of your query:
      ... ...
<%      } else {  %>
        <P> No rows found that match your query. </P>
```

```
<%      }
        rset.close();   // close the result set
        stmt.close();   // close the statement
        conn.close();   // return the connection to the pool
  %>
 </BODY>
</HTML>
```

Caching Query Results

It is sometimes possible to efficiently reuse SQL query results within or across different HTTP sessions. For example, consider a Web site that is promoting some merchandise for a certain week. The query to determine which items are on sale can be shared across different users and sessions. Analogous to the connection pooling mechanism, such caching can be achieved by using SQL query beans in appropriate scopes (session or application) through the <jsp:useBean> tag. The bean would cache the query result once it is computed. Clients of the bean instance would be able to share this result without reexecuting the query.

Caching of query results also involves the question of invalidating and maintaining them. That is, if the underlying data changes or the acceptable time lag for a result expires, the query must be re-executed to refresh the results. Automatic invalidation or refreshing of cached query results upon data update is a complex problem and requires the use of database triggers. Implementing such functionality "under the covers" without any explicit programming may not be efficient. However, providing an API that the programmer can call to specify his or her caching requirements easily is certainly feasible. At press time, Oracle was considering such "programmable" Web caching functionality for its servlet and JSP environments. The feature may be available in a future release of Oracle JSP.

Conclusion

This chapter shows you how to use JavaBean components in your JSP programs. A JavaBean is a general-purpose Java class following a special design pattern that allows easy manipulation of its properties and clean integration with a JSP. As such, it can be used as a modular Java component to execute dynamic logic. The JSP specification has special built-in tags for easy use of JavaBeans, not only separating HTML and Java code cleanly, but also providing the means to integrate them easily. Thus, Web designers can focus on writing user-friendly JSP pages using HTML or XML, while Java programmers develop the JavaBeans. Finally, the dynamic logic can be easily "plugged into" the JSP using the simple but powerful bean tags.

In this chapter, you developed several different programs using JSPs and JavaBeans. You studied various issues in writing JavaBean components, with particular emphasis on database applications. Specifically, you learned how to write

JavaBean classes, set and get their properties, and associate them with different JSP scopes. You developed a session-tracking JSP application for an order entry system with a shopping cart, which enters the submitted order into the purchase order database using SQLJ in a JavaBean component. You also wrote a JavaBean that performs a static query using SQLJ and displays the query results as an HTML table. For dynamic SQL queries that are not known until runtime, you wrote a JavaBean using JDBC, and formatted the results into an HTML table using the JDBC ResultSetMetaData object. You also learned how to generate XML from SQL tables in the database using JavaBean components from the Oracle JSP bean library. Finally, you understood how to optimize the performance of database access from your Web application.

In Chapter 12, you will learn how to work with EJB and CORBA components for modular development of your JSP applications. You will see that JavaBeans can be used to conveniently access the EJB and CORBA objects, keeping the Java code in your JSP to a minimum. Chapter 12 will also cover the use of tag libraries that provide custom tags for JSP extensibility. You can use these different technologies in conjunction with each other to write powerful and versatile Web applications.

CHAPTER
12

Using JSP with EJB, CORBA, and Tag Libraries

Web application is generally composed of a variety of resources. They may be static resources such as HTML pages and GIF images, and dynamic modules such as JSPs and servlets, JavaBeans, Enterprise JavaBeans, and CORBA objects. The dynamic components can be used in combination with one another to build up powerful enterprise-level applications.

In the previous two chapters, you learned how to use a JSP with other JSPs and servlets, and how to use JavaBean components in your JSP. In Part II of this book, you learned about EJBs—how to deploy them in Oracle 8*i* and invoke them from your client code. Part III of this book showed you how to define and deploy CORBA components in Oracle8*i*. In this chapter, you will learn how to use these component programming techniques in JSP-based Web applications.

The JSP 1.1 specification also introduces the concept of extending the set of JSP tags through *tag libraries*. The tag extension scheme is a modular and portable framework to define and use custom tags that are conveniently packaged in a tag library. Using this framework, you can define your own custom tag to encapsulate some action in a component. You can also use tag libraries provided by different vendors. Tag libraries can be used in JSPs along with other Java components such as JavaBeans and EJBs to build sophisticated and modular Web applications.

Using detailed examples, this chapter will show you how to do the following:

■ Invoke an EJB from a JSP application

■ Call a CORBA component from a JSP

■ Use Oracle's JSP tag library to execute SQL queries

■ Use Oracle's JSP tag library to generate XML results for a SQL query, and transform them using XSL stylesheets

■ Write your own JSP custom tag to print the current date and time

■ Write your own JSP custom tag to execute a SQL query and create an HTML menu of items

By the end of this chapter, you will understand how to exploit the full power and capability of Java component programming model from JSP applicaitons.

Developing Web Applications with EJB Components

Enterprise JavaBean is an important part of the component model in the Java programming framework. In Part II of this book, you learned how to write and deploy EJBs in the Oracle8*i* database. Now you will see how you can invoke such

EJB components from JSPs and servlets. The EJB effectively encapsulates business logic, while the JSP and servlet provide the "front-end" logic for interactive data entry, EJB invocation, and result presentation logic. First, you will implement an EJB component, and then write JSPs and JavaBeans that use this component.

A Session EJB for Orders

In this section, you will develop a simple session EJB to handle order inquiries on the Purchase Order database (described in the "Introduction" of this book). Recall that in Chapter 11 you wrote a JavaBean—DBQueryBean.sqlj—to query order information from the database. You will now code similar functionality using an EJB instead of a JavaBean. You have learned about EJB session beans in Part II of this book. In comparison to a JavaBean, an EJB provides much greater power and flexibility in terms of transaction and security specifications of business logic, although it can be more complex to code and deploy. Using a JavaBean that executes SQL queries will be adequate in cases of simple data manipulation; more advanced business logic and usage scenarios will require that you use an EJB.

The following steps are required to develop the OrderEJB session bean and deploy it in Oracle8*i*. If you are not already familiar with the EJB model, refer to Part II of this book to learn about the structure of an EJB and how to program it.

1. Define the home interface OrderHome for the OrderEJB.

2. Define the remote interface Order for the OrderEJB.

3. Write the Java class OrderHeader to return top-level header information for an order.

4. Write the Java class LineItem to return information for an item in the order.

5. Write the implementation class for OrderEJB.

6. Define the EJB deployment descriptor.

7. Deploy the EJB in Oracle8*i*.

You will carry out these steps in the following sections. After you have written and deployed the EJB, you will learn how to call it from your Web application.

Writing the Home Interface

First, you will define the home **interface** OrderHome for the OrderEJB session bean. This code is shown here. It extends the standard **interface** EJBHome, and has a method—create()—that would be called to create an instance of the EJB.

```
/** Program name: OrderHome.java
 * Purpose:      Home interface for the OrderEJB
 **/
```

```
package order;

import javax.ejb.*;
import java.rmi.RemoteException;

public interface OrderHome extends EJBHome {
  public Order create()
        throws CreateException, RemoteException;
}
```

Writing the Remote Interface

Now you will define the remote **interface** Order for the OrderEJB. It consists of two methods: getOrder() and getItems(). The purpose of the getOrder() method is to return header information such as the name and number of the employee who placed the order, and the total number of items. This information is encapsulated in a Java class named OrderHeader. You will write this class in the next step. The getItems() method returns details of the items ordered; the return value is an array of LineItem objects. You will write the LineItem class shortly.

The getOrder() method is intended to be invoked first, causing the order number to be stored in the (stateful) EJB, and the getItems() method is intended to be called subsequently to get the line item details. The code for the Order **interface** appears here:

```
/** Program name: Order.java
 * Purpose:       Remote interface for the OrderEJB
 **/

package order;

import javax.ejb.EJBObject;
import java.rmi.RemoteException;

public interface Order extends EJBObject  {

  public OrderHeader getOrder (int orderNumber)
        throws java.sql.SQLException, RemoteException;

  public LineItem [] getItems ()
        throws java.sql.SQLException, RemoteException;
}
```

Writing the Java Class for Order Header Information

Next, you will define the Java class OrderHeader. This class is intended to hold the top-level information associated with an order. An instance of this class will be used by the OrderEJB session bean to return to the client the results of querying an order. The fields `empName` and `empNum` denote the name and number of the employee placing the order, and `itemCount` is the total number of items ordered. The code for `OrderHeader.java` is shown here:

```
/** Program name: OrderHeader.java
 * Purpose:      Hold the top-level information for a purchase order
 **/

package order;

public class OrderHeader implements java.io.Serializable {
  public String empName;   // employee name
  public int empNum;       // employee number
  public int itemCount;    // total number of items
  // constructor


public OrderHeader (String empName,
                    int empNum,
                    int itemCount) {
    this.empName = empName;
    this.empNum = empNum;
    this.itemCount = itemCount;
  }
}
```

Writing the Java Class for Line Item Information
You will now define the Java class `LineItem`. This class is intended to hold line information for an order—specifically the line number, project number, quantity, and description of a line item in the purchase order. The code for `LineItem.java` is shown here:

```
/** Program name: LineItem.java
 * Purpose:       Hold line item information for the order
 **/
package order;

public class LineItem implements java.io.Serializable {
  public int lineno;
  public int projectno;
  public int quantity;
  public String description;
  // constructor
  public LineItem(int lineno, int projectno, int quantity,
                  String description){
    this.lineno = lineno;
```

```
      this.projectno = projectno;
      this.quantity = quantity;
      this.description = description;
   }
}
```

Writing the EJB Implementation Class

You will finally define an implementation class OrderEJBImpl.sqlj that
executes SQLJ queries to return order header and items information. Notice
that this class implements two methods—getOrder() and getItems()—as
defined earlier in the Order **interface**. These methods fetch the header and
line information for an order through SQL queries on the PURCHASE_LIST,
EMPLOYEE_LIST, and LINEITEM_LIST tables in the Purchase Order database.
Refer to the "Introduction" of this book for the definition of the tables in the
purchase order schema. Explanatory notes on the OrderEJBImpl.java class
are provided after the code listing.

```
/** Program name: OrderEJBImpl.sqlj
 * Purpose:       Implementation class for the OrderEJB
 *                Queries the database for order and lines information
 **/

package order;

import order.OrderHeader;
import order.LineItem;
import java.sql.*;
import java.rmi.RemoteException;
import javax.ejb.*;

public class OrderEJBImpl implements SessionBean {
  SessionContext ctx;
  public void ejbCreate() throws CreateException, RemoteException {
  }

  public void ejbActivate() {  }
  public void ejbPassivate() {  }
  public void ejbRemove() {  }

  public void setSessionContext(SessionContext ctx) {
    this.ctx = ctx;
  }
  private int orderNumber = 0; // store the order number
  private int itemCount = 0;   // and the item count for getOrder()
                               // They may be used later by getItems()
```

```
  // method to get header info for an order
public OrderHeader getOrder (int orderNumber)
  throws SQLException, RemoteException  // (See Note 1.)
{
  String empName;
  int empNum;
  this.orderNumber = orderNumber;        // (See Note 2.)
  // fetch the name and number of the employee who placed the order
  #sql { SELECT PURCHASE_LIST.employeeno,
               firstname || ' ' || lastName
          INTO :empNum,
               :empName
          FROM PURCHASE_LIST, EMPLOYEE_LIST
         WHERE requestno = :orderNumber
               AND EMPLOYEE_LIST.employeeno =
                   PURCHASE_LIST.employeeno
    }; // (See Note 3.)
  return new OrderHeader (empName, empNum, getItemCount());
}
// Count the number of items ordered
private int getItemCount () throws SQLException { // (See Note 4.)
    #sql { SELECT COUNT(*)
            INTO :itemCount
            FROM LINEITEM_LIST
           WHERE requestno =  :orderNumber };
    return itemCount;
}
// SQLJ iterator for fetching line item details
#sql iterator LineItemsIter (int lineno,
                             int projectno,
                             int quantity,
                             String description); // (See Note 5.)

// method to fetch line item details
public LineItem [] getItems() throws SQLException {
                                            // (See Note 6.)
  // SQLJ iterator declaration for line items
  LineItemsIter  li = null;
  // fetch the line info through a SQL query
    #sql li = {   SELECT  lineno,
                          projectno,
                          quantity,
                          description
                    FROM  LINEITEM_LIST
                   WHERE  requestno =  :orderNumber
                ORDER BY lineno
```

```
      };  // (See Note 7.)
   LineItem[] items = new LineItem [itemCount];  // (See Note 8.)
   for (int i = 0; i < itemCount; i++) {
     li.next();
     items[i] = new LineItem(li.lineno(),
                             li.projectno(),
                             li.quantity(),
                             li.description());  // (See Note 9.)
   }
   li.close();  // close the iterator           // (See Note 10.)
   return items;
 }
}
```

Notes on `OrderEJBImpl.sqlj`:

1. This method implements the `getOrder()` method for the remote **interface** `Order`.

2. This statement stores the `orderNumber` argument to the `getOrder()` method in an instance variable of the EJB class. This EJB will be used as a stateful session bean, and the stored order number and item count will be reused subsequently when the `getItems()` method is called.

3. This SQL statement joins the `PURCHASE_LIST` and `EMPLOYEE_LIST` tables to fetch the full name and number of the employee who placed the order. The `orderNumber` argument is used in the `WHERE` clause of the `SELECT` statement.

4. This method computes the total number of items in the order by doing a SQL query on the `LINEITEM_LIST` table. The `WHERE` clause of the SQL `SELECT` statement uses `orderNumber` to select the correct set of rows.

5. This statement declares a SQLJ named iterator class `LineItemsIter` for fetching line item details.

6. This method implements the `getItems()` method declared in step 2 for the remote **interface** `Order`.

7. This SQLJ statement initializes the SQLJ iterator instance `li` with the result of a SQL query. This query fetches details of the items in the particular order from the `LINEITEM_LIST` table.

8. This statement creates an array of `LineItem` objects that will be populated from the SQLJ iterator and returned as the result of the `getItems()` method call.

9. This statement constructs a new instance of the `LineItem` class from the data in a row in the `li` iterator instance.

10. This statement closes the `li` iterator instance, releasing the cursor for the SQL query.

Writing the EJB Deployment Descriptor

In order to deploy the EJB, you must write a deployment descriptor. The deployment descriptor `order.ejb` for the `OrderEJB` component is shown in Listing 12-1. The `OrderEJBImpl` bean is declared as a session bean with the home name `/test/OrderEJB`, and the appropriate home and remote interfaces.

Listing 12-1   The `OrderEJB` deployment descriptor

```
SessionBean order.OrderEJBImpl {
    BeanHomeName = "/test/OrderEJB";
    RemoteInterfaceClassName = order.Order;
    HomeInterfaceClassName = order.OrderHome;
    AllowedIdentities = {PUBLIC};
    StateManagementType = STATEFUL_SESSION;
    RunAsMode = CLIENT_IDENTITY;
    TransactionAttribute = TX_REQUIRED;
}
```

Deploying the EJB

You have now completed writing the code for `OrderEJB`. Next, you must compile the source files (a Makefile is provided with the code), and create a `.jar` file `OrderEJB.jar`. Then, load and deploy the `OrderEJB` in Oracle8*i*. The following command is an example of this step:

```
deployejb -republish -temp temp \
    -u jspuser -p jsp -s sess_iiop://data-i:2481:ORCL \
    -descriptor order.ejb orderEJB.jar
```

Invoking the `OrderEJB` from Your Web Application

You learned about the various architectural choices for writing Web applications in the "Web Application Architecture" section in Chapter 2. Indeed, there are several different ways that you can invoke the `OrderEJB` from your JSP or servlet code. Among the various possibilities are the following:

1. Call the EJB directly from your JSP. This requires having the Java code for EJB lookup, initialization, and method calls in the JSP itself. This approach is not generally recommended, because JSPs are intended primarily for presentation and not for computing logic. A lot of Java code in a JSP makes maintenance difficult.

2. Write a JavaBean wrapper for your EJB, and invoke its methods from a JSP. This approach cleanly hides the details of EJB manipulation from the JSP author, and allows convenient use of the JavaBean through the `<jsp:useBean>` standard tag. In this section, you will use this approach to call `OrderEJB`. This approach can be extended to writing JSP custom tags for the EJB component.

3. Call the EJB from a servlet. You can directly call the EJB from the servlet code, or define a JavaBean wrapper for the EJB as in option 2, and call the bean from the servlet. In fact, there is no restriction that JavaBeans can be invoked only by JSPs—you can easily reuse the JavaBean code from a servlet. JSP supports some convenient shortcuts for setting the properties and scope of a JavaBean, which you will need to code explicitly in your servlet. The benefit of using a servlet is that it can contain more complex Java code (if needed by your Web application), and be written and maintained by a Java programmer.

4. Use a servlet to look up and initialize the EJB, and use a JSP for the data presentation logic. This approach is known as the *model-view-controller* or MVC design pattern (discussed in Chapter 2). The EJB or JavaBean represents the component model, and the servlet is the controller that accepts the HTTP request, validates request parameters, initializes the EJB, and, finally, forwards to the JSP, which provides the user view of the computed data. The servlet code is written by a Java developer and not by an HTML author, and therefore it can contain the details of EJB manipulation and exception handling. Developing such a servlet-EJB-JSP Web application to call the `ObservationBean` EJB that you wrote in Chapter 3 is left as an exercise for you.

Invoking `OrderEJB` Through a JavaBean Wrapper

You will now develop a JSP-based application that uses `OrderEJB` to fetch order information. The various components of this Web application are shown in Figure 12-1. The application uses a JavaBean class `OrderEJBWrapper` as the "wrapper" program through which `OrderEJB` is accessed. The use of a JavaBean for this purpose greatly reduces the amount of Java code that must be written in the JSP itself. There are two JSP pages—`CallOrderEJB.jsp` and `CallOrder EJBForLines.jsp`—that will serve as the entry points to this application. These two JSP pages will share the same instance of the JavaBean through the HTTP `session` object.

Writing the `OrderEJBWrapper` JavaBean   In this section, you will write the `OrderEJBWrapper` JavaBean to call the `OrderEJB` component. The JavaBean is to be used in `session` scope. The function of the `OrderEJBWrapper` JavaBean is as follows:

- Look up `OrderEJB` in the Oracle8*i* JNDI namespace and create an instance for it. The instance of the EJB should be destroyed when the JavaBean goes out of `session` scope.

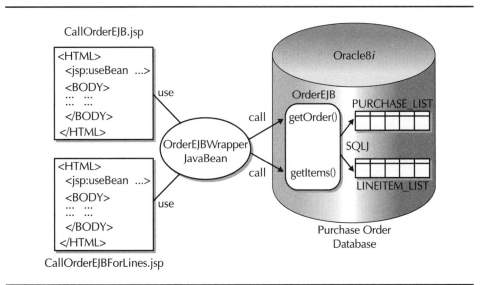

FIGURE 12-1.   *Architecture of the Web application using the OrderEJB component*

■ To provide wrapper methods for the `getOrder()` and `getItems()` methods supported by `OrderEJB`.

■ To allow the `getOrder()` and `getItems()` methods to be called in any sequence. Notice that the `OrderEJB` requires `getOrder()` to be called before `getItems()`, so that an order number is available for fetching the line items. The JavaBean wrapper can work around this requirement by calling `getOrder()` first if `getItems()` is directly invoked.

■ To provide some performance benefit by "caching" data fetched for an order. For example, if an order being queried about is the same as the previous request in the HTTP session, then the cached result is returned instead of reinvoking the `getOrder()` or `getItems()` method of the `OrderEJB`. Of course, this caching type of will be useful only if the order information in underlying SQL tables is not being updated concurrently.

The code for this JavaBean is shown below. Significant parts of the code are shown in bold font. It has a single property named `orderNumber`, and methods to `set` and `get` this attribute. An instance of the `OrderEJB` instance is stored locally after creation in the `getOrder()` method, and is reused for the lifetime the `OrderEJBWrapper` JavaBean. The JavaBean implements the `HttpSessionBindingListener` **interface** (refer to the "Events and Event Listener Interfaces" section in Chapter 11), because it is intended to be used by the JSP in `session` scope. It discards the EJB instance when the HTTP `session` scope expires.

Notice that setting the order number to a different value from the previous one causes the cached order information to be discarded. If the order number is the same as before, the cached value will be returned. In case the cached value is not desired, you can invoke the same JSP in a different HTTP session, when a different instance of the JavaBean (and consequently of `OrderEJB`) will be created and the latest order information can be retrieved. Another alternative is to provide a different order number to discard the cached value.

```
/** Program name: OrderEJBWrapper.java
  * Purpose:       JavaBean to access OrderEJB
  **/

package mybeans;

import order.Order;
import order.OrderHome;
import order.OrderHeader;
import order.LineItem;
import oracle.aurora.jndi.sess_iiop.ServiceCtx;
```

```java
import javax.naming.Context;
import javax.naming.InitialContext;
import javax.servlet.http.HttpSessionBindingListener;
import javax.servlet.http.HttpSessionBindingEvent;
import java.util.Hashtable;

public class OrderEJBWrapper
            implements HttpSessionBindingListener
{
  public OrderEJBWrapper() {}            // the bean constructor
  private int orderNumber = 0;           // the bean property

  // Cache the instance of OrderEJB and fetched order and line details
  private Order orderEJB = null;
  private OrderHeader orderHeader = null;
  private LineItem[] itemsArray = null;

    // method to set the orderNumber property
    public synchronized void setOrderNumber (int orderNum) {
  if (this.orderNumber != orderNum) {
     orderHeader = null;  // discard cached value
     itemsArray = null;    // discard cached value
     this.orderNumber = orderNum;
   }
  }

  public int getOrderNumber () {
    return orderNumber;
  }

  public synchronized OrderHeader getOrder () throws Exception {
    if (orderHeader != null)
    return orderHeader;  // Reuse cached value if available
      if (orderEJB == null) { // create the EJB instance
      String serviceURL = "sess_iiop://data-i:2481:ORCL";
      String objectName = "/test/OrderEJB";
      String user = "jspuser";
      String password = "jsp";

      // Client code to lookup the EJB and create an instance
      Hashtable env = new Hashtable();
      env.put(Context.URL_PKG_PREFIXES, "oracle.aurora.jndi");
      env.put(Context.SECURITY_PRINCIPAL, user);
      env.put(Context.SECURITY_CREDENTIALS, password);
      env.put(Context.SECURITY_AUTHENTICATION,
        ServiceCtx.NON_SSL_LOGIN);
      Context ic = new InitialContext(env);
```

```
        OrderHome home = (OrderHome)ic.lookup (serviceURL + objectName);
        orderEJB = home.create ();  // create an instance of the EJB
      }
     orderHeader = orderEJB.getOrder (orderNumber);  // get order info
     return orderHeader;
   }

  public synchronized LineItem[] getItems() throws Exception {
      if (itemsArray != null)
        return itemsArray;  // Reuse cached value
      if (orderEJB == null)
        orderHeader = getOrder(); // lookup+create the EJB instance
      itemsArray = orderEJB.getItems(); // then fetch item details
      return (itemsArray);
   }
   // Method executed when bean is placed in HTTP session
   public void valueBound(HttpSessionBindingEvent event) {
      // Do nothing here!
      // EJB will be created only if a query is submitted.
   }
   // Method executed when bean is removed from session
   public synchronized void valueUnbound(
                        HttpSessionBindingEvent event) {
      if (orderEJB != null) {
        try {
           orderEJB.remove ();  // destroy the bean instance
        } catch (Exception ignore) {}
      }
   }
}
```

After you write the JavaBean class `OrderEJBWrapper`, you must compile it, and install the compiled class on your Web server (refer to Appendix E for the setup steps). Then, you can invoke its methods from one or more JSPs. Following, you will write the `CallOrderEJB.jsp` and `CallOrderEJBForLines.jsp` pages, which will share the same instance of this JavaBean through the same HTTP `session` object.

Writing `CallOrderEJB.jsp`   The following code is for `CallOrderEJB.jsp`, which is used as the initial screen of the application. Significant parts of the code are shown in bold font. This code uses an instance of the `OrderEJBWrapper` bean in HTTP `session` scope. The JSP page has an HTML form to input the order number that is to be looked up in the database. When you enter an order number in the text box and click the Submit Query button, a new HTTP request is generated to the same

JSP with the input order number. This order number is used to set the corresponding property of the OrderEJBWrapper JavaBean, and then its getOrder() method is invoked. The JSP uses another HTML form to display a Show Items button for fetching line items. When this button is clicked, the CallOrderEJBForLines.jsp program is invoked as the action of the form. You will write this JSP in the next section.

```
<!-- Program name: CallOrderEJB.jsp
  -- Purpose:     To accept an order number from the user and
  --              query the order information.
  -->
<%@ page import="order.*" %>
<jsp:useBean id="orderBean" class="mybeans.OrderEJBWrapper"
             scope="session" />

<HTML>
<HEAD> <TITLE> The CallOrderEJB JSP  </TITLE> </HEAD>
<BODY BGCOLOR="white">
<%  String orderNumber = request.getParameter("orderNumber");
    if (orderNumber != null) { %>
        <jsp:setProperty name="orderBean" property="orderNumber" />
        <H3>Details of order number: <%= orderNumber %> </H3>
        <CENTER><B>
        <% OrderHeader oh = orderBean.getOrder(); %>
        <P>Employee: <%= oh.empName %>, Emp #: <%= oh.empNum %>
        </B><BR><BR>
        <FORM METHOD=get ACTION="CallOrderEJBForLines.jsp">
          <INPUT TYPE="submit" VALUE="Show Items">
        </FORM>
        </CENTER><BR>
        <HR>
<%  }  %>

<P><B>Please enter an order number:</B></P>
  <FORM METHOD=get ACTION="CallOrderEJB.jsp">
    <INPUT TYPE="text" NAME="orderNumber" SIZE=10>
    <INPUT TYPE="submit" VALUE="Submit Query">
  </FORM>
 </BODY>
</HTML>
```

Seeing the Web application in action is the best way to understand its operation. Output of running CallOrderEJB.jsp is shown in Figure 12-2. This page displays the information about which employee placed the order and the employee number. It also provides a Show Items button that can invoke CallOrderEJBForLines.jsp (which you will write next) to retrieve the details of line items. The intention is that line items for an order are not automatically displayed, but are displayed only when the Show Items button is clicked by the user.

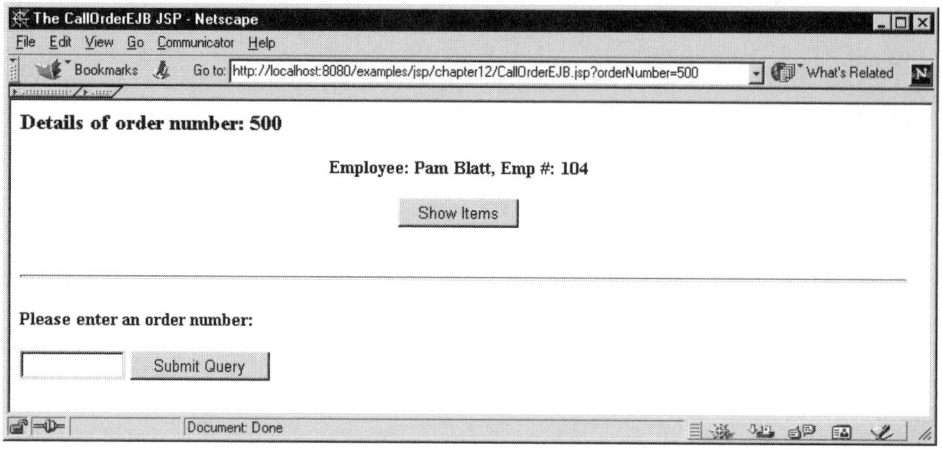

FIGURE 12-2. *Output of CallOrderEJB.jsp*

Writing `CallOrderEJBForLines.jsp`   The `CallOrderEJB.jsp` page
works in conjunction with `CallOrderEJBForLines.jsp`, which is shown below.
This JSP can be invoked either directly or by clicking the Show Items button in
`CallOrderEJB.jsp`, and shows all the line items for a particular purchase order.

Notice that the `<jsp:useBean>` tag of this JSP uses the same name `orderBean`
in `session` scope for the `OrderEJBWrapper` bean. Recall from Chapter 11 that
a `session`-scoped JavaBean is placed in the HTTP `session` object, and can be
looked up by any program participating in the same HTTP session. Therefore, the
`<jsp:useBean>` tag in the `CallOrderEJBForLines.jsp` code looks up the
object (if any) by name `orderBean` that was previously created by the `CallOrder`
`EJB.jsp` program. In other words, these two JSPs can share the order information
fetched during the same HTTP session through the same instance of the `OrderEJB`
`Wrapper` JavaBean.

```
<!-- Program Name: CallOrderEJBForLines.jsp
   -- Purpose:      Use the orderBean JavaBean, and display
   --               line information for the order
   -->
<%@ page import="order.*" %>
<jsp:useBean id="orderBean" class="mybeans.OrderEJBWrapper"
            scope="session" />

<HTML>
  <HEAD> <TITLE> The CallOrderEJBForLines JSP  </TITLE> </HEAD>
<BODY BGCOLOR="white">
    <CENTER><B>
```

```
    <% OrderHeader oh = orderBean.getOrder(); %>
    <P>Employee: <%= oh.empName %>,
       Emp #: <%= oh.empNum %>,
       Order #: <%= orderBean.getOrderNumber() %>
    </B><BR><BR>
  <%
     LineItem[] li  = orderBean.getItems();
     if (oh.itemCount > 0) { %>
        <TABLE BORDER>
        <TH><I> Line # </I></TH>
        <TH><I> Project # </I></TH>
        <TH><I> Quantity </I></TH>
        <TH><I> Description </I></TH>
<%      for (int i=0; i < oh.itemCount; i++) {   %>
         <TR>
           <TD> <%= li[i].lineno %> </TD>
           <TD> <%= li[i].projectno %> </TD>
           <TD> <%= li[i].quantity %> </TD>
           <TD> <%= li[i].description %> </TD>
         </TR>
     <% } %>
        </TABLE>
   <% }
        </CENTER><B><BR>
        <HR>

<P><B>Please enter an order number:</B></P>
  <FORM METHOD=get ACTION="CallOrderEJB.jsp">
    <INPUT TYPE="text" NAME="orderNumber" SIZE=10>
    <INPUT TYPE="submit" VALUE="Submit Query">
  </FORM>
 </BODY>
</HTML>
```

Output of submitting the Show Items request is shown in Figure 12-3. This page has a Submit Query button that, when clicked, will take you back to the CallOrderEJB.jsp page.

Invoking the `OrderEJBWrapper` Bean from a Servlet

It is also possible to use a servlet to call the JavaBean wrapper for `OrderEJB`, and display the data using a JSP. This approach follows the model-view-controller paradigm, which is a good architecture for complex Web applications (as discussed in the "Web Application Architecture" section in Chapter 2). The tasks of the "controller" servlet would be as follows:

■ Initializing an instance for the `OrderEJBWrapper` JavaBean, or the `OrderEJB` component directly.

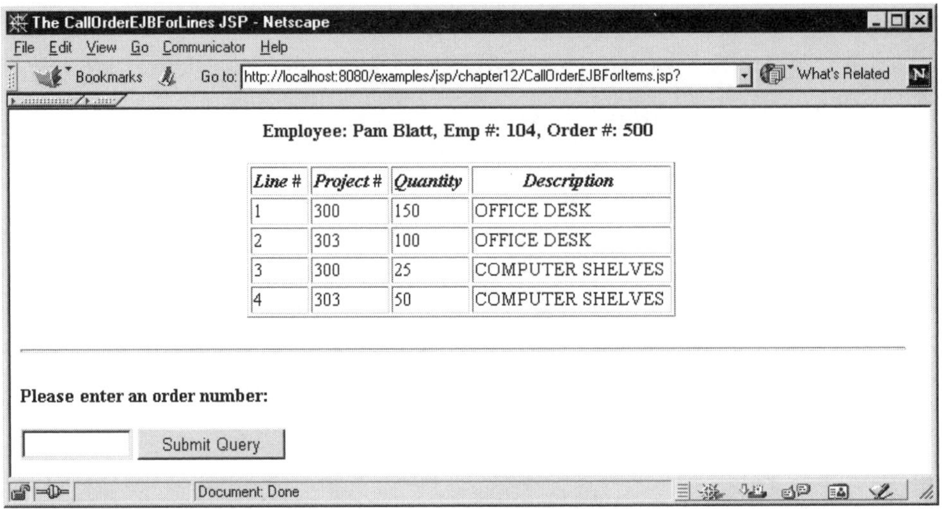

FIGURE 12-3. *Output of* `CallOrderEJBForLines.jsp`

- Calling the `getOrder()` method to fetch information for a particular order

- Associating the retrieved `OrderHeader` object or the bean with the HTTP session, by using a `session.setAttribute()` method call

- Forwarding execution control to a JSP for presentation

The JSP can retrieve the `OrderHeader` object from the (shared) HTTP session and display its data appropriately, and likewise for the `getItems()` call for showing the items in the order. Writing an application using this type of component architecture is left as an exercise for you.

Developing Web Applications with CORBA Components

In Part III of this book you learned how to develop and deploy CORBA components in the Oracle8*i* database. In this section, you will use that knowledge to write a CORBA component that fetches order data stored in the Purchase Order database, and you will invoke an instance of this CORBA object from your Web application.

The functionality of this component will be similar to the `OrderEJB` JSP that you defined in the preceding section, but will be coded and deployed using CORBA techniques. First, you will write the CORBA component for getting order information from the database, and then develop the Web application around this component.

A CORBA Object for Orders

There are three steps to defining and deploying a CORBA object:

1. Write and compile the IDL file for the CORBA module.

2. Define the server implementation class.

3. Deploy the CORBA object in Oracle8*i*.

You will now see how to do these steps for the CORBA module for orders.

Writing the CORBA IDL File

First, you must define the `orderCorba.idl` file. It consists of the module `orderCorba` that defines the structures of order header information and the line items. You can define two structs: `LineItem` and `OrderInfo`, where `OrderInfo` contains a sequence of `LineItem` objects. The `Order` **interface** defines a single method `getOrder()` to fetch the entire information associated with an order. This scheme is intentionally different from the `OrderEJB` implementation you saw earlier in this chapter, where there are two methods `getOrder()` and `getItems()`; the purpose is to illustrate a different way to fetch order information.

```
// Program name: orderCorba.idl
// Purpose:      Define the structure of the CORBA object using IDL
//
module orderCorba {
   struct LineItem {
     long lineno;
     long projectno;
     long quantity;
     wstring description;
   };

   struct OrderInfo {
     wstring empName;
     long empNum;
     long itemCount;
     sequence <LineItem> items;
   };
```

```
exception SQLError {
  wstring message;
};

interface Order {
  OrderInfo getOrder (in long orderNumber) raises (SQLError);
};
};
```

This IDL file can be compiled with the `idl2java` utility to generate the necessary Java classes. The generated files will include Java class definitions for `orderCorba.OrderInfo` and `orderCorba.LineItem` for the `OrderInfo` and `LineItem` structs, respectively, and other helper and holder classes required for communication between the client and the server. The generated `orderCorba.OrderInfo` class will have a Java array `LineItem[]` to represent the sequence of line items.

Writing the Server Implementation Class

Next, you will define the server implementation class `OrderCorbaImpl`. This class must implement the public `getOrder()` method following the signature that you defined in the `orderCorba` IDL file. You can conveniently use SQLJ to do your static SQL queries to fetch order information. The file `OrderCorbaImpl.sqlj` is shown here, with explanatory notes following the code listing. The SQLJ iterator declaration and queries must seem very familiar to you by now. The schema for the Purchase Order database is given in the "Introduction" of this book.

```
/** Program name: OrderCorbaImpl.sqlj
 * Purpose:      Server implementation class for orderCorba module
 **/
package orderCorbaServer;

import orderCorba.*;
import oracle.aurora.AuroraServices.ActivatableObject;
import java.sql.*;

public class OrderCorbaImpl
       extends _OrderImplBase
       implements ActivatableObject  {

  public OrderInfo getOrder (int orderNumber)
                   throws SQLError {  // (See Note 1.)
    try {
```

```
    String empName = null;
    int empNum = 0;

    // Select employee information for the order
    #sql { SELECT PURCHASE_LIST.employeeno,
                      firstname || ' ' || lastName
                INTO :empNum,
                     :empName
              FROM PURCHASE_LIST, EMPLOYEE_LIST
              WHERE requestno = :orderNumber
                AND EMPLOYEE_LIST.employeeno =
                        PURCHASE_LIST.employeeno
    };

  return new OrderInfo (empName, empNum, getItemCount(orderNumber),
                        getItems(orderNumber));  // (See Note 2.)

  } catch (SQLException e) {
    throw new SQLError (e.getMessage ());
  }
}

private int itemCount = 0;
// method to select the total item count for an order
private int getItemCount (int orderNumber) throws SQLException {
    #sql { SELECT COUNT(*)
             INTO :itemCount
             FROM  LINEITEM_LIST
            WHERE requestno =  :orderNumber
    };
     return itemCount;
}

 // SQLJ iterator declaration for line items
 #sql iterator LineItemsIter (int lineno, int projectno,
                              int quantity, String description);

// method to select the items corresponding to a certain order
private LineItem[] getItems(int orderNumber) throws SQLException {
  LineItemsIter  li = null;
  // (See Note 3.)
  #sql li = {
                     SELECT  lineno,
                             projectno,
                             quantity,
                             description
```

```
                      FROM  LINEITEM_LIST
                     WHERE  requestno =  :orderNumber
                  ORDER BY  lineno
        };

  LineItem[] items = new LineItem [itemCount];
  for (int i = 0; i < itemCount; i++) {
    li.next();
    items[i] = new LineItem(li.lineno(),
                            li.projectno(),
                            li.quantity(),
                            li.description());
  }
  li.close();
  return items;
}

public org.omg.CORBA.Object _initializeAuroraObject () {
  return this;
}
}
```

Notes on `OrderCorbaImpl.sqlj`:

1. This is the implementation of the `getOrder()` method defined in the `orderCorba` module. It selects the header information for the order from the `PURCHASE_LIST` and `EMPLOYEE_LIST` tables, and then calls the `getItems()` method to retrieve line information.

2. This statement constructs a new `OrderInfo` object for the given order, and returns it.

3. This method uses a SQLJ named iterator to retrieve the items for the given order from the `LINEITEM_LIST` table.

Compiling and Deploying the CORBA Component

You can compile and load the classes into Oracle8*i* using the `loadjava` utility (a Makefile is provided with the code). Then, you must publish the CORBA object in the JNDI namespace through the Oracle8*i* session shell tool. Following is an example of this step:

```
publish -republish -u jspuser -p jsp -schema JSPUSER \
    -s sess_iiop://data-i:2481:ORCL \
      /test/OrderCorba orderCorbaServer.OrderCorbaImpl \
      orderCorba.OrderHelper
```

Calling the CORBA Object from a Web Application

As in the case of EJBs, there are several architectural choices for a Web application that uses a CORBA component. The most direct, but not necessarily the best, approach is to call it from your JSP. This involves writing a significant amount of Java code in your JSP, which makes code maintenance difficult. A much better approach is to invoke the CORBA object through a JavaBean or a servlet, and to use a JSP only for data entry and display of output data to the user. This is the approach you will take here. You will define a JavaBean wrapper `OrderCorbaWrapper` for the `OrderCorba` object, and use the bean in your JSP.

Invoking the `OrderCorba` Object Through a JavaBean Wrapper

You will now write a JSP-based application that uses `OrderCorba` to fetch order information. The components of this Web application are shown in Figure 12-4. The application uses a JavaBean class `OrderCorbaWrapper` to access the `OrderCorba` component. The use of a JavaBean component reduces the amount of Java code that must be written in the JSP itself. The JSP page `CallOrderCorba.jsp` is the entry point to this application.

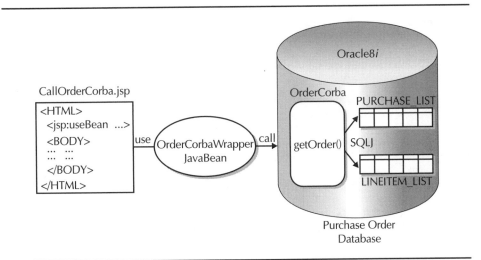

FIGURE 12-4.   *Architecture of the Web application using the `OrderCorba` component*

Writing the OrderCorbaWrapper JavaBean   The following code is for the
OrderCorbaWrapper JavaBean that looks up and activates the CORBA object,
and provides a wrapper method for its getOrder() method. An added function of
the getOrder() method is to try to reuse the cached order information if the order
number has not changed since the last invocation of this method. The logic of this
JavaBean is quite similar to the OrderEJBWrapper that you wrote in the previous
section. The significant parts of the code are shown in bold.

```java
/** Program name: OrderCorbaWrapper.java
 * Purpose:       To access the OrderCorba object and
 *                fetch order information
 */
package mybeans;

import orderCorba.*;
import oracle.aurora.jndi.sess_iiop.ServiceCtx;
import javax.naming.Context;
import javax.naming.InitialContext;
import java.util.Hashtable;
import javax.servlet.http.*;

public class OrderCorbaWrapper
           implements HttpSessionBindingListener
{

  public OrderCorbaWrapper() {}

  private Order order = null;         // the CORBA object
  private OrderInfo orderInfo = null; // fetched order info

  private int orderNumber;
  public void setOrderNumber (int orderNum) {
    if (this.orderNumber != orderNum) {
      orderInfo = null;  // discard previously cached value
      this.orderNumber = orderNum;
    }
      }

  public OrderInfo getOrder () throws Exception {
    if (orderInfo != null)
      return orderInfo;  // reuse previously cached value

    if (order == null) {  // lookup the object
      String serviceURL = "sess_iiop://data-i:2481:ORCL";
      String objectName = "/test/OrderCorba";
      String user = "jspuser";
      String password = "jsp";
```

```
        Hashtable env = new Hashtable();
        env.put(Context.URL_PKG_PREFIXES, "oracle.aurora.jndi");
        env.put(Context.SECURITY_PRINCIPAL, user);
        env.put(Context.SECURITY_CREDENTIALS, password);
        env.put(Context.SECURITY_AUTHENTICATION,
          ServiceCtx.NON_SSL_LOGIN);

        Context ic = new InitialContext(env);

        order = (Order)ic.lookup (serviceURL + objectName);
      }
      OrderInfo orderInfo = order.getOrder(orderNumber);
      return orderInfo;
  }
  // Method executed when bean is placed in HTTP session
  public void valueBound(HttpSessionBindingEvent event) {
      // Do nothing here!
      // CORBA object will be created only if a query is submitted
  }
  // Method executed when bean is removed from session
  public synchronized void valueUnbound(
                      HttpSessionBindingEvent event) {
      if (order != null) {
        try {
          order.deactivate();
        } catch (Exception e) {}
      }
    }
}
```

Writing `CallOrderCorba.jsp`   In the final step, you will write the `CallOrderCorba.jsp` program. This JSP will use the `OrderCorbaWrapper` JavaBean defined above to invoke the `OrderCorba` object. The code for this program is shown here. Significant parts of the code are in boldface. The JSP has an HTML form for entering the order number, and a Submit Query button for fetching order details that trigger a call to the `OrderCorba` component through the JavaBean. The data is formatted and displayed in an HTML table to the user.

```
<!-- Program name: CallOrderCorba.jsp
    -- Purpose:        Fetch order information using the
    --                 OrderCorbaWrapper JavaBean to access the
    --                 OrderCorba object
    -->
<%@ page import="orderCorba.*" %>

<jsp:useBean id="orderWrapper"
```

```
                class="mybeans.OrderCorbaWrapper"
                scope="session" />
<jsp:setProperty name="orderWrapper"
                property="orderNumber" />

<HTML>
<HEAD> <TITLE> The CallOrderCorba JSP  </TITLE> </HEAD>
<BODY BGCOLOR="white">
<%  String orderNumber = request.getParameter("orderNumber");
    if (orderNumber != null) { %>
      <H3>Details of order number: <%= orderNumber %> </H3>
      <CENTER><B>
    <%  OrderInfo oi = orderWrapper.getOrder(); %>
      Employee: <%= oi.empName %>,  Emp #:  <%= oi.empNum %>
      <BR><BR>
    <% LineItem[] li  = oi.items;
      if (oi.itemCount > 0) { %>
        <TABLE BORDER>
        <TH><I> Line # </I></TH>
        <TH><I> Project # </I></TH>
        <TH><I> Quantity </I></TH>
        <TH><I> Description </I></TH>
    <%    for (int i=0; i < oi.itemCount; i++) {  %>
         <TR>
          <TD> <%= li[i].lineno %> </TD>
          <TD> <%= li[i].projectno %> </TD>
          <TD> <%= li[i].quantity %> </TD>
          <TD> <%= li[i].description %> </TD>
         </TR>
      <% } %>
        </TABLE>
      <% } %>
        </CENTER><B><BR> <HR>
<%  }   %>

<P><B>Please enter an order number:</B></P>
  <FORM METHOD=get>
  <INPUT TYPE="text" NAME="orderNumber" SIZE=10>
  <INPUT TYPE="submit" VALUE="Submit Query">
  </FORM>
 </BODY>
</HTML>
```

Figure 12-5 shows the result of invoking this JSP. Although it is not directly visible in the output, entering the same order number as the previous one in the form will reuse the value locally cached in the `session`-scoped JavaBean, instead of reinvoking the `getOrder()` method of the remote CORBA object.

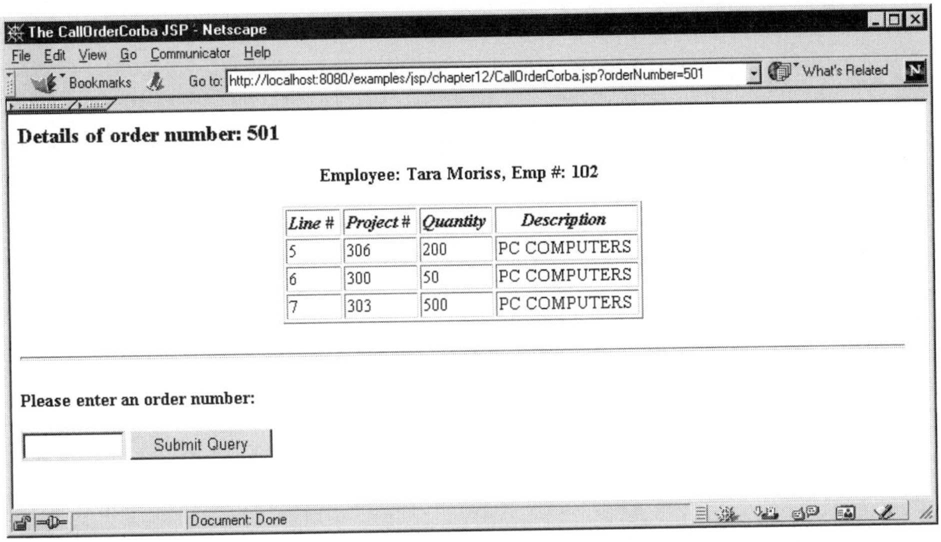

FIGURE 12-5. *Output of* `CallOrderCorba.jsp`

Invoking the `OrderCorbaWrapper` Bean from a Servlet

Note that it is also possible to use a servlet to call the JavaBean wrapper, and display the data using a JSP. This approach follows the model-view-controller paradigm, which is a good architecture for complex Web applications. The task of the "controller" servlet would be as follows:

■ Initialize an instance of the `OrderCorbaWrapper` JavaBean or the `OrderCorba` object directly

■ Call the `getorder()` method on it to fetch information for a particular order

■ Associate the retrieved `OrderInfo` object with the HTTP session, by using a `session.setAttribute()` method call.

■ Forwarding execution control to a JSP for presentation.

The JSP can retrieve the `OrderInfo` object from the (shared) HTTP session object, and display its data. Writing a program using this model is left as an exercise for you.

Using JSP Tag Libraries

In this section, you will learn about using tag libraries in your JSP programs. The JSP 1.1 specification introduces a standard and portable tag extension scheme for defining and using *tag libraries*. A tag library consists of a collection of custom tags, where each tag provides some specific functionality. For example, you can write a Java component and expose its functionality through convenient JSP tag syntax. This keeps your JSP from being cluttered with Java code and can hide a lot of complexity as part of the tag action. The name of the tag, its attributes, and the body are part of the definition of the custom tag. The set of custom tags that are available in a tag library is described in a *tag library descriptor* file (TLD file in short) using XML notation. You can import a tag library through the `taglib` directive in your JSP, and then use the tags that are defined in the library.

Tag libraries are typically implemented by JSP vendors, but you can also define your own custom tags and package them as one or more tag libraries. The tag extension framework extends the set of standard of standard action tags like `<jsp:useBean>` in a modular way that is portable between different JSP implementations.

Oracle's JSP 1.1 implementation provides two tag libraries:

- The SQL tag library, which can be used to execute SQL queries and format results.

- The JML tag library (JML stands for *JSP Markup Language*), which provides general tags for convenient scripting, including application of XSL stylesheets to XML documents.

Using these tags, you can, for example, execute and format SQL queries conveniently through compact syntax, and apply a stylesheet to convert dynamically generated XML into an HTML table. In the next section, you will learn about some useful tags from these two libraries (full details for all of these tags can be found in *Oracle JSP Developer's Guide and Reference, Release 8.1.7,* Oracle Corporation). First, you will learn how to import tag libraries through the `taglib` directive. Next, you will write JSP pages that use tag libraries provided with the Oracle JSP 1.1 implementation. Finally, you will learn how to write a simple custom tag of your own.

The `taglib` Directive

The `taglib` directive is used to specify that a custom tag library will be used in a JSP page. The purpose of this directive is twofold: to specify a location for the TLD (tag library descriptor) file, and to define a local prefix for these tags. The syntax of this directive is as follows:

```
<%@ taglib uri="tldURI" prefix="prefix" %>
```

The `taglib` directive has two attributes: `uri` and `prefix`. The prefix specified in the directive is used to distinguish tags in this library from other tags. The `uri` attribute defines the name and location of the TLD file (URI stands for *Universal Resource Indicator*, and is a more generic term than URL). There are different ways to specify the TLD, depending on how you have deployed the tag library and your Web application. For example, you can fully specify the path to the TLD file, as follows:

```
<%@ taglib uri="/WEB-INF/tlds/sqltaglib.tld" prefix="ora" %>
```

Here, the location is an application-relative path (starting with the "/" character), and the TLD file must be available in that location. Alternatively, you can specify a `.jar` file instead of a `.tld` file, where the `.jar` file must contain the TLD file as `META-INF/taglib.tld`. In this case, the `taglib` directive might appear as follows:

```
<%@ taglib uri="/WEB-INF/tlds/sqltags.jar" prefix="ora" %>
```

It is also possible to use a "shortcut" URI in the `taglib` directive, where the shortcut is defined in the `web.xml` deployment descriptor (refer to the Servlet 2.2 and JSP 1.1 specifications from Sun Microsystems for details on the `web.xml` deployment descriptor and its use for TLD files). JSP pages can use this file to specify locations and short names for TLD files, and these shortcuts can then be used in the `taglib` directive.

The `taglib` directive must appear before any of the custom tags in the imported tag library are used.

The SQL Tags

Oracle JSP 1.1 includes a tag library that provides custom tags for executing SQL operations conveniently. Underlying the tags are JDBC routines that execute the SQL operations. The following tags are available in this library:

- `dbOpen`
- `dbClose`
- `dbQuery`
- `dbCloseQuery`
- `dbNextRow`
- `dbExecute`

The following is a description of the tags, followed by examples of their use.

The dbOpen Tag

This tag is used to open a database connection. The general syntax of this tag is as follows:

```
<ora:dbOpen [ connId="connection-id" ]
             user="username"
             password="password"
             URL="databaseURL" >
        … optional nested body that uses this connection …
</ora:dbOpen>
```

The prefix ora corresponds to the prefix specified in the taglib directive for the JSP. The attribute connId is optional, and denotes a connection identifier. If the connection identifier is omitted, then the database connection is automatically closed when the end tag </ora:dbOpen> is encountered. The connection handle is implicitly available for tags such as dbQuery (described later) that appear nested within the body. If the connection identifier is specified, then the connection handle can be referenced through that name elsewhere in the JSP page, such as in the dbQuery tag. SQL operations using that connection identifier do not need to be nested between the dbOpen start and end tags. In this case, the connection must be closed explicitly with a dbClose tag after the SQL operations are over.

The user, password, and URL for the database are mandatory attributes. They can be set to constant strings in the JSP, or, more commonly, to request-time expressions that typically involve the HTTP request or session objects. The example here shows the use of computed expressions for the user and password attributes:

```
<ora:dbOpen connId="conn"
             user="<%=request.getParameter(\"username\") %>"
             password="<%=request.getParameter(\"mypassword\") %>"
             URL="jdbc:oracle:oci8:@" />
```

In this example, the dbOpen tag does not have a body, and therefore the end tag is />. The tag opens a database connection with the given username, password, and URL parameters, and assigns the name conn to this connection handle. Subsequently, other statements in the JSP page can refer to the connection conn, till the end of the JSP page.

At this point, you are very likely wondering about the conn object. What is its type? Recall the database access beans that you learned about in Chapter 11. These are prebuilt components in Oracle's JSP bean utility library to help execute SQL operations in your JSP. Underlying the SQL tags are these beans. For example, the dbOpen tag uses a ConnBean object to represent the connection. If necessary, in your JSP you can set additional ConnBean properties such as stmtCacheSize, preFetch, and batchSize to use these Oracle JDBC features. Refer to the "The Oracle JSP Bean Library" section in Chapter 11 for usage details of this bean.

The `dbClose` Tag

The `dbClose` tag has a single mandatory attribute—`connId`—which corresponds to the connection identifier previously specified in a `dbOpen` tag (described earlier). The effect of the `dbClose` tag is to close the database connection represented by the given connection identifier. If the `dbOpen` tag did not specify a connection identifier, then the database connection is closed automatically when the end tag for `dbOpen` is found. In that case, the `dbClose` tag is not required. The example below closes a connection represented by the identifier `conn`:

```
<ora:dbClose connId="conn" />
```

The `dbQuery` Tag

The `dbQuery` tag is used to execute a SQL query. The result can be obtained as a JDBC result set, as an HTML table, or as an XML string. The `SELECT` statement is placed in the body of this tag, between the start and end tags for `dbQuery`. The syntax is as follows:

```
<ora:dbQuery
        [ connId="connection name" ]
        [ output="HTML"|"XML"|"JDBC" ]
        [ queryId="query identifier" ] >
     … a SELECT statement …
     </ora:dbQuery>
```

This tag has three optional attributes: `connId`, `queryId`, and `output`. The tag can be nested within the `dbOpen` tag, and in that case, the `connId` attribute is omitted, and the connection established by the enclosing `dbOpen` tag is implicitly used to execute the query.

The `output` attribute is used to specify in what form you want to obtain the query result. The following three different forms are available for the query result:

- **HTML table** In the simplest case, you may just want to print the results as an HTML table, with the SQL column names or aliases as the headers for the table. This is the default behavior.

- **XML string** You can also obtain the result as an XML string that is generated by calling the Oracle XML-SQL utility (introduced in Chapter 11).

- **JDBC result set** Lastly, you can obtain a JDBC result set and process its rows using the `dbNextRow` tag (described later). In this case, you must use the `queryId` attribute to specify an identifier for the generated result set.

If the `queryId` attribute is used, you must explicitly close the underlying cursor with a `dbCloseQuery` tag (described next) after you have processed the rows. When the `queryId` attribute is absent, the cursor is automatically closed when the `</ora:dbQuery>` end tag is seen.

The object represented by the identifier in `queryId` is actually a `CursorBean` object. This object is a prebuilt bean component in Oracle's bean library (refer to the "Oracle JSP Bean Library" section in Chapter 11 for a discussion of the database access beans).

The `dbCloseQuery` Tag

The `dbCloseQuery` tag closes a cursor that corresponds to the `queryId` attribute specified in a `dbQuery` tag (described earlier). The `dbCloseQuery` tag is not required if the `queryId` attribute is not used in the `dbQuery` tag; in that case, the cursor is closed automatically when the end tag for `dbQuery` is reached. The syntax of the `dbCloseQuery` tag is as follows:

```
<ora:dbCloseQuery queryId="query identifier" />
```

The `dbNextRow` Tag

The `dbNextRow` tag is used in conjunction with the `dbQuery` tag (described earlier) to process each row of a result set. The result set is referenced by the `queryId` specified in `dbQuery` tag, which must also have `output="JDBC"` in its attributes. The code to process the rows in the result set is nested between the `dbNextRow` start and end tags, and this code is executed for each row in the result set. The general syntax of the tag is as follows:

```
<ora:dbNextRow queryId="query identifier" >
… Code to process each row in the query result set …
</ora:dbNextRow >
```

For example, the following code fragment prints the second and fourth columns of the JDBC result set named `query1` (specified in a `dbQuery` tag earlier) in each line:

```
… …
<br>
<jml:dbNextRow queryId="query1">
    <%= query1.getString(2) %>
    <%= query1.getString(4) %> <br>
</jml:dbNextRow>
```

The `dbExecute` Tag

You can use the `dbExecute` tag to execute any SQL DDL or DML statement, including stored programs. The SQL statement appears nested within the tag body, between the `dbExecute` start and end tags. The general format of this tag is as follows:

```
<ora:dbExecute
      [connId="connection identifier"]
      [output="yes"|"no"] >
  ... a nested SQL DDL or DML statement ...
</ora:dbExecute >
```

This tag has two optional attributes, namely `connId` and `output`. If the tag is nested within the `dbOpen` tag (described earlier), the database connection opened by that tag is implicitly used; otherwise, a connection identifier must be specified, and it should reference a connection opened by a previous `dbOpen` tag. The `output` attribute is used to denote whether the result of the operation should be sent to the browser as part of the generated Web page. By default, no output is generated by this tag.

Writing `DBQuery.jsp`

Now, you will write a JSP page `DBQuery.jsp` that uses the `dbOpen` and `dbQuery` SQL tags described earlier to execute a SQL query and display the result automatically as an HTML table. The architecture of this application is illustrated in Figure 12-6. The tag handler classes effectively act as modular components that encapsulate some specific functionality, such as database access.

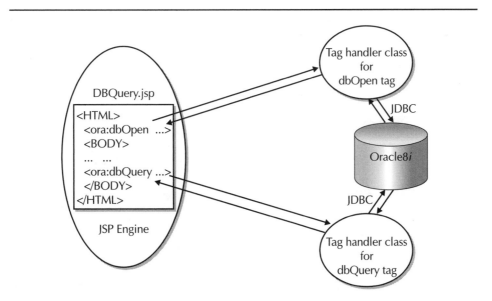

FIGURE 12-6.   *Architecture of a JSP with SQL tags*

The code for `DBQuery.jsp` is shown here, with the significant parts in bold font:

```
<!-- Program name: DBQuery.jsp
  -- Purpose:       Use dbOpen and dbQuery tags to query a table
  -->
<%@ taglib uri="/WEB-INF/sqltaglib.tld" prefix="ora" %>
<HTML>
<HEAD> <TITLE> The DBQuery JSP  </TITLE> </HEAD>
<BODY BGCOLOR="white">
<H3>You can query any table using this page.</H3>
<%
   String tableName = request.getParameter("tableName");
   String condition = request.getParameter("searchCond");
   if ((condition != null) && (condition.length() != 0))
       condition = "WHERE " + condition; else condition"";
   if (tableName != null) { %>
     <ora:dbOpen URL="jdbc:oracle:oci8:@"
                 user="<%= request.getParameter(\"userName\") %>"
                 password="<%= request.getParameter(\"password\") %>" >
        <H3> Search results for table: <%= tableName %>,
                        condition: <%= condition %>
        <ora:dbQuery>
          SELECT * FROM <%= tableName %>
                   <%= condition %>
        </ora:dbQuery>
        </ora:dbOpen>
<% } %>
<BR><HR>
   <B>Enter the following information:</B>
   <FORM METHOD="POST">
    <TABLE>
     <TR> <TD> User Name </TD>
          <TD> <INPUT TYPE="text" NAME="userName" SIZE=30> </TD>
     </TR>
     <TR> <TD> Password </TD>
          <TD> <INPUT TYPE="password" NAME="password" SIZE=30> </TD>
     </TR>
     <TR> <TD> Table Name </TD>
          <TD> <INPUT TYPE="text" NAME="tableName" SIZE=30> </TD>
     </TR>
     <TR> <TD> Search Condition </TD>
          <TD> <INPUT TYPE="text" NAME="searchCond" SIZE=30> </TD>
     </TR>
    </TABLE>
     <INPUT TYPE="submit" VALUE="Lookup rows">
   </FORM>
 </BODY>
</HTML>
```

In the DBQuery.jsp program, an HTML form is used to accept the user's name and password for logging in to the database, as well as a table name and search condition for doing the query. The database connection is opened with the dbOpen tag. The query is executed by the dbQuery tag, which is nested within the dbOpen tag, so that the connection opened by the dbOpen tag can be implicitly used to execute the SQL query. As you can see from this example, using the SQL tags greatly simplifies your database access code.

Running DBQuery.jsp   Before you can run the DBQuery.jsp program, you must first ensure that the required libraries are set up as follows:

- ojsputil.jar   This library comes with the Oracle JSP distribution, and contains the bean and tag libraries. This library must be accessible to your Web server and the servlet engine—by including it in your CLASSPATH environment variable, for example.

- sqltaglib.tld   This TLD file is part of the Oracle JSP distribution, and contains the description of the SQL and other tags. Place this file in the location specified by the taglib directive of your JSP page, which is /WEB-INF/sqltaglib.tld in the DBQuery.jsp page.

- oraclexmlsql.jar   This jar is required if you are using XML output in the dbQuery tag. This library is part of the Oracle XDK distribution (downloadable from the Oracle Technology Network Web site http://technet.oracle.com), and contains the XML SQL utility classes to format the rows of a JDBC result set using XML notation. Make this library accessible via the CLASSPATH of your Web server.

You must also install and configure Oracle JSP for your Web server, following the steps outlined in Appendix E. Figure 12-7 shows the output of running DBQuery.jsp after the setup steps have been properly completed.

The JML Tags

In addition to the SQL tags, Oracle JSP also provides other utility tags for convenient scripting and iteration. These tags are called *JML tags*, where JML stands for *JSP Markup Language*. Here, you will learn about one of these tags: the transform tag.

The transform Tag

This tag is used to conveniently transform an XML document using an XSL stylesheet (refer to any good book on XML, such as *Professional XML* by Mark Birbeck et al, Wrox Press Inc., to learn more about XML and XSL stylesheets). Briefly, XSL stands for *Extensible Stylesheet Language*, and it is a companion specification to the XML

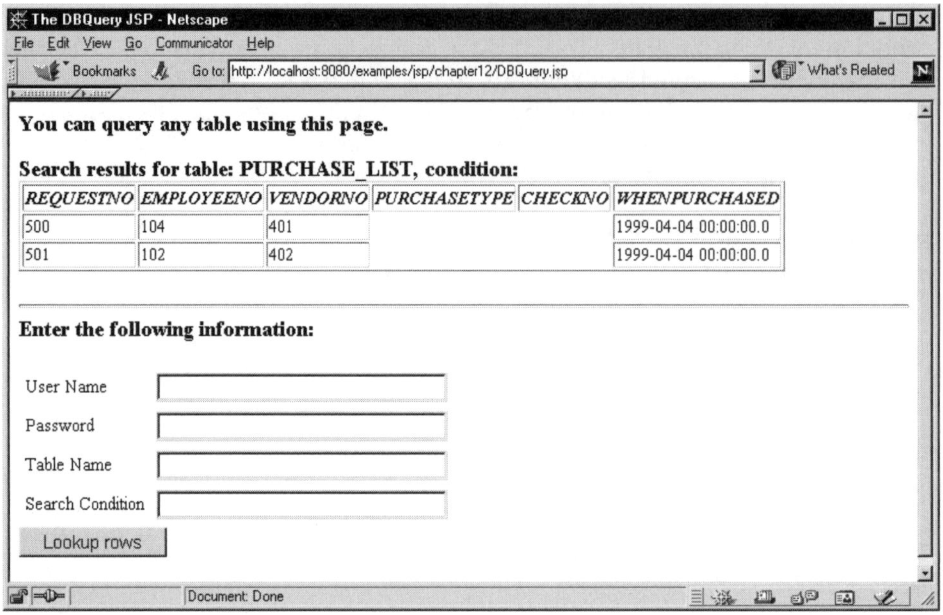

FIGURE 12-7. *Output of running* `DBQuery.jsp`

standard. An XSL stylesheet is itself an XML document that is used to format or restructure another XML document, typically for visual presentation in the browser. It uses tree-based template matching rules to manipulate the structure of the XML document. For example, XML output generated as the result of executing a SQL query through the `dbQuery` tag described earlier can be formatted with an XSL stylesheet into an HTML table with rows and columns for browser display.

The `transform` tag is used to apply an XSL stylesheet to the part of a JSP page that it encloses between the start and end tags. The syntax of this tag is as follows:

```
<jml:transform href="reference to an XSL stylesheet" >
… Nested body that contains or generates XML …
</jml:transform >
```

The tag has one mandatory attribute, `href`. This attribute refers to an XSL stylesheet, which can be either a static file or a dynamically generated one (for example, through another JSP or servlet). The stylesheet can be specified using an application-relative or page-relative path, or as a fully qualified URL. The name of the stylesheet can also be a request-time expression that is computed dynamically using JSP expression syntax. The `jml` prefix is used here, assuming this was the prefix specified in the `taglib` directive of your JSP page.

A JSP page can have multiple XML blocks within a page, and you can use the `transform` tag to apply stylesheets to one or more such blocks. The XML string can be a constant. More typically, it is dynamically generated, such as by doing a SQL query through the `dbQuery` tag with `output="XML"`. An example of using the `transform` tag in this manner is shown in Listing 12-2.

Listing 12-2   Applying an XSL stylesheet with the transform tag

```
<!-- The ApplyXSL JSP
  -- Applies stylesheets to XML blocks in the JSP page
  -- using the transform tag from Oracle's JSP tag library
  -->

<?xml version="1.0"?>
<%@ taglib uri="/WEB-INF/jml.tld" prefix="jml" %>
<%@ taglib uri="/WEB-INF/sqltaglib.tld" prefix="ora" %>
  <ora:dbOpen URL="jdbc:oracle:oci8:@"
              user="jspuser"
              password="jsp" >
    <jml:transform href="mystyle1.xsl" >
      <ora:dbQuery output="XML">
          SELECT * FROM PURCHASE_LIST
      </ora:dbQuery>
    </jml:transform>
    ... ...
    <jml:transform href="/styles/mystyle2.xsl" >
       <!-- another static or dynamic XML block -->
       ... ...
    </jml:transform>
  </ora:dbOpen>
```

In this code, tags from both the SQL tag library and JML tag library are being used, as declared by the `taglib` directives in the page. There are two XML blocks in the JSP. The first one is generated through the `dbQuery` tag, and is processed with the stylesheet `mystyle1.xsl` from the same directory as the JSP. The second XML block is processed with the file `mystyle2.xsl` that is located in the directory `styles` with respect to the Web application root.

How Is a Custom Tag Implemented?

As you have seen in the previous examples, using a custom tag is a good way to write modular applications. You can define a Java component that performs a certain function, and allow it to be invoked through a JSP custom tag. The custom tags are typically packaged as a tag library that is portable across different JSP implementations. In this section, you will learn how custom tags work, and write your own simple custom tags.

The Tag Library Framework

The tag extension framework defined by the JSP 1.1 specification works as follows. Each custom tag corresponds to a *tag handler* Java class, which executes the appropriate action for the custom tag. The code for the tag handler class varies depending on whether the tag has a body. An example of a tag with just attributes and no body is the dbClose tag described earlier. The dbQuery tag does have a body, which is the SQL query; the action of the tag is to execute this query. Depending on the need to process a body, a tag handler class implements one of the following two standard interfaces:

- javax.servlet.jsp.tagext.Tag **interface**, if the tag does not need to process a body.

- javax.servlet.jsp.tagext.BodyTag **interface**, if the tag needs to process a body between its start and end tags. This class extends the Tag **interface**.

The Tag **interface** has methods such as doStartTag() and doEndTag() that are called by the JSP engine when the start and end tags are encountered. The BodyTag **interface** has additional methods, such as doInitBody() and doAfterBody(), that are invoked at appropriate points during body processing. There are also methods such as setPageContext() and setParent() that are called by the JSP to set the corresponding properties of the tag handler instance to the current PageContext object for the JSP, and the parent tag handler instance (for the enclosing tag, if any).

After the tag handler class has been written, it must be deployed through *a tag library descriptor* (TLD) file, which is specified in your JSP through the taglib directive. This file is written in XML and has a .tld extension by convention. It contains information about the tag library being deployed, and about each tag in the library. This information is used by the JSP translator in order to determine what action to take when it finds a tag from the library in the JSP page. Each tag has an entry in the TLD file that specifies usage information for the tag, such as the following:

- Name of the tag

- The corresponding tag handler class name

- Names of the attributes and their characteristics (such as optional or mandatory)

- Information on how the tag body (if any) should be processed

- A TagExtraInfo (TEI) class for any variables set by the tag

You will see an example of a TLD file in the next section.

At request time, a tag handler instance is created when the custom tag is found. The properties of this instance are set by the JSP engine, including the `PageContext` object for the JSP page in which the custom tag appears, and a parent tag handler object if this custom tag is nested within an outer custom tag.

You will now learn how to implement and deploy two simple tags—one that has no body and one that does.

Implementing a Tag Without a Body   For a tag with no body, the tag handler class implements the `Tag` **interface**. This interface has two methods— `doStartTag()` and `doEndTag()`—that are called by the JSP when the start and end tags are encountered. The signatures of these methods are as follows:

```
public int doStartTag()
     throws javax.servlet.jsp.tagext.JspTagException;
public int doEndTag()
     throws javax.servlet.jsp.tagext.JspTagException;
```

In addition to these methods, the `Tag` **interface** has other methods for interaction of the tag handler class with the JSP. These methods are `setPageContext()`, `setParent()`, `getParent()`, and `release()`. The `setPageContext()` method sets the current `PageContext` object in the tag handler and is called by the JSP before the `doStartTag()` method. The `setParent()` and `getParent()` methods are used to `set` and `get` the parent tag instance (that is, the enclosing tag, if any) of the tag handler. The `release()` method is called after the `doEndTag()` method to clean up any state in the tag handler class. The signatures of these methods appear in Appendix D.

The tag handler class, which is written by the tag developer, must implement these methods appropriately. The action of the tag is implemented in the `doStartTag()` method, and any postprocessing or cleanup code appears in the `doEndTag()` method. The `doStartTag()` method returns an integer value, which can be of the following three constants:

- `SKIP_BODY`, if the tag has no body or if processing of the body should be skipped. This is the value returned by the default implementation of the `doStartTag()` method in the `TagSupport` class.

- `EVAL_BODY_INCLUDE`, if the tag has a body but it does not need to be processed by the tag handler. This return value indicates that the body text should be included in the output stream of the JSP.

- `EVAL_BODY_TAG`, if the tag body needs to be processed by the tag handler itself. This constant is actually defined in the `BodyTag` **interface** (described later), and returning this value from the `doStartTag()` method is illegal for a tag that has no body.

The `doEndTag()` method can return one of the following two integer constants:

- `SKIP_PAGE`, if the rest of the page should be skipped.

- `EVAL_PAGE`, if evaluation of the page should continue after the tag. This is the value returned by the default implementation of the `doEndTag()` method of the `TagSupport` class.

The tag handler class typically extends a standard utility class—`javax.servlet.jsp.tagext.TagSupport`—that is defined in the JSP specification. Use of this class is illustrated in the next section where you will write your own custom tag.

Writing the `dateTime` Custom Tag   You will now design, implement, deploy, and run a custom tag that displays the date or the time when invoked. The general syntax of this tag can be written as follows:

```
<mytag:dateTime [ output="DATE"|"TIME"|"DATETIME" ]
                [ format="SHORT"|"MEDIUM"|"FULL"|"LONG" ] />
```

This tag is named `dateTime`, and has two attributes, `output` and `format`. The `output` attribute indicates whether the date, or the time, or both are to be printed. The default is to print the date only. The `format` attribute denotes the style in which the date and the time are to be reported. The possible values for `format` are SHORT, MEDIUM, FULL, and LONG, which correspond to the constants defined in the `java.text.DateFormat` class. SHORT will format the output into a numeric value, such as 09.15.00 for the date. MEDIUM uses a longer style, such as Aug 15, 2000. The LONG format is longer than MEDIUM, such as August 15, 2000, and FULL is a complete specification of the date or time, including the time zone. The default formatting style is MEDIUM.

The code for the tag handler class `DateTimeTag.java` is shown here:

```
/* Program name: DateTimeTag.java
 * Purpose:      Print the date and/or time in given format
 */
package chapter12;

import javax.servlet.jsp.*;          // standard jsp library
import javax.servlet.jsp.tagext.*;   // standard jsp tag extension lib
import java.util.Date;
import java.text.DateFormat;

public class DateTimeTag
   extends TagSupport
```

```
{
  private String output = "DATE";           // DATE is default
  private int format = DateFormat.MEDIUM; // MEDIUM style is default

  public void setOutput(String output)
  { // set the output - whether TIME or DATE or DATETIME
    this.output = output;
  }

  public void setFormat(String format)
  { // set the format - whether SHORT, MEDIUM, FULL or LONG
    if (format.equalsIgnoreCase("MEDIUM"))
      this.format = DateFormat.MEDIUM;
    else if (format.equalsIgnoreCase("SHORT"))
      this.format = DateFormat.SHORT;
    else if (format.equalsIgnoreCase("LONG"))
      this.format = DateFormat.LONG;
    else if (format.equalsIgnoreCase("FULL"))
      this.format = DateFormat.FULL;
  }

  public int doStartTag() throws JspTagException
  { // this tag has no body
  return SKIP_BODY;
  }

  public int doEndTag() throws JspTagException
  {
    try {
      // first set the format
      DateFormat df = null;
      if (output.equalsIgnoreCase("DATE"))
          df = DateFormat.getDateInstance(format);
      else if (output.equalsIgnoreCase("TIME"))
        df = DateFormat.getTimeInstance(format);
      else if (output.equalsIgnoreCase("DATETIME"))
        df = DateFormat.getDateTimeInstance(format, format);

      // print the date or time to output stream
      pageContext.getOut().write(df.format(new Date()));
    }
    catch (java.io.IOException e) {
      throw new JspTagException ("Error in datetime tag:" +
                      e.getMessage());
    }
    return EVAL_PAGE; // continue evaluation of the page
  }
}
```

The `DateTimeTag` class extends the `TagSupport` utility class, and implements the methods `setOutput()` and `setFormat()` for setting its two attributes, and the methods `doStartTag()` and `doEndTag()` for executing the tag action. The method `doStartTag()` simply returns the constant `SKIP_BODY`, as this tag has no body. The method `doEndTag()` creates a `DateFormat` object accordingly to the specified style, and prints the current date or time to the output stream of the `PageContext` object.

Compiling, Deploying, and Testing the `dateTime` Tag   To run the `DateTime` tag, you need to compile it, placing the generated class in an appropriate location of your Web server. You must then write the tag library descriptor (TLD) file for the tag. Finally, you can write a JSP to invoke your tag. These steps are illustrated below for the TOMCAT server:

1. Compile the `DateTimeTag.java`.

   The following shell script can be used to compile the `DateTimeTag.java` file. The script assumes that the Tomcat server is being used, and places the generated class file in the directory `$TOMCAT_HOME/webapps/examples/WEB_INF/classes` (refer to Appendix E to learn how to set up the Tomcat server).

   ```
   #!/bin/sh
   TOMCAT_HOME=/private/jakarta-tomcat
   JDK_HOME=/usr/local/packages/jdk1.2.2
   APP_HOME=${TOMCAT_HOME}/webapps/examples
   CLASSPATH=${TOMCAT_HOME}/lib/servlet.jar:${CLASSPATH}
   exec ${JDK_HOME}/bin/javac -d ${APP_HOME}/WEB-INF/classes \
           -classpath ${CLASSPATH} \
           ${APP_HOME}/jsp/chapter12/DateTimeTag.java
   ```

2. Describe the `dateTime` tag in a tag library descriptor file.

   The following is an XML file—`mytaglib.tld`—that describes the `dateTime` tag and its attributes. The relevant parts of the TLD file are shown in bold. The first part of the TLD file follows the standard format defined by the JSP specification. The latter part of the file provides information on the tag, such as the name of the tag, the names of its attributes, and whether the attributes are mandatory or optional. You must place this file in an appropriate location on your Web server, as specified in the `taglib` directive of your JSP page that calls this tag. You will shortly write such a JSP page as the final step of testing the `dateTime` tag.

   ```
   <?xml version="1.0" encoding="ISO-8859-1" ?>
   <!DOCTYPE taglib
       PUBLIC "-//Sun Microsystems, Inc.//DTD JSP Tag Library 1.1//EN"
   ```

```
        "web-jsptaglib_1_1.dtd">
<!-- tab library descriptor for the dateTime tag -->
<taglib>
  <tlibversion>1.0</tlibversion>
  <jspversion>1.1</jspversion>
  <shortname>mytags</shortname>
  <info>
    My simple tab library
  </info>
  <!-- Entry for the dateTime tag -->
  <tag>
    <name>dateTime</name>
    <tagclass>chapter12.DateTimeTag</tagclass>
    <bodycontent>empty</bodycontent>
    <info>
       Prints the current date and/or the time in different formats.
    </info>
    <attribute>
      <name>output</name>
      <required>false</required>
    </attribute>
    <attribute>
      <name>format</name>
      <required>false</required>
    </attribute>
  </tag>
</taglib>
```

3. Test the dateTime tag.

The following simple JSP—TestDateTime.jsp—first imports the mytaglib.tld file for the dateTime tag through the taglib directive, and then invokes the tag in three separate places with different parameters:

```
<!-- Program name: TestDateTime.jsp
  -- Purpose:       Test the dateTime custom tag
  -->

<%@ taglib uri="/WEB-INF/mytaglib.tld" prefix="mytag" %>
<HTML>
  <HEAD><TITLE> The TestDateTime JSP </TITLE></HEAD>
  <BODY>
   <H3>
    Today's date is: <mytag:datetime /> <BR>
    The time is:   <mytag:datetime output="TIME" format="SHORT" /> <BR>
    The full date and time is:
```

```
              <mytag:datetime output="DATETIME" format="FULL" />
    </H3>
    </BODY>
</HTML>
```

Install the JSP on your Web server following the steps outlined in Appendix E. Output of running `TestDateTime.jsp` is shown in Figure 12-8. As you can see from this example, custom tags can successfully hide much computing logic from the JSP, using the tag handler class as a component.

Writing a Tag with a Body   Now that you have written a tag without a body, consider a custom tag whose body must be processed by the tag handler. Such a tag handler class must implement the `javax.servlet.jsp.tagext.BodyTag` standard **interface**, which extends the `javax.servlet.jsp.tagext.Tag` **interface**. The `BodyTag` **interface** specifies a `doInitBody()` method and a `doAfterBody()` method in addition to the methods in the `Tag` **interface**. The `doInitBody()` method is called by the JSP before the tag body is evaluated, and the `doAfterBody()` method is called each time the tag body is evaluated (the body could, in fact, be evaluated multiple times, such as for an iterative tag). The signatures of these methods are as follows:

```
public void doInitBody()
            throws javax.servlet.jsp.tagext.JspTagException;
public int doAfterBody()
            throws javax.servlet.jsp.tagext.JspTagException;
```

Custom tags that must process the body typically extend the standard support class `javax.servlet.jsp.tagext.BodyTagSupport`. As for tags without bodies, the `doStartTag()` method is generally defined in the tag handler class to execute the appropriate starting action for the tag, and the `doEndTag()` method is

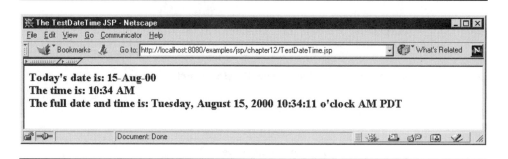

FIGURE 12-8.   *Output of* `TestDateTime.jsp`

also overridden to provide postprocessing logic for tag. The return value EVAL_BODY_ INCLUDE is illegal from the doStartTag() method for a tag handler class that processes a body (that is, implements the BodyTag **interface**). The methods doInitBody() and doAfterBody() are also implemented by the tag handler class, and are used to process the body. The sequence of method calls is as follows:

- The doStartTag() method is executed. It may return one of the values SKIP_BODY or EVAL_BODY_TAG.

- If doStartTag() returns EVAL_BODY_TAG, then the doInitBody() and doAfterBody() methods are called. Otherwise, SKIP_BODY is returned, and these methods are not called (for example, for a custom tag that includes the body conditionally, and the condition is determined to be false in the doStartTag() method call). Instead, the doEndTag() method is called.

- If the doAfterBody() method returns the value EVAL_BODY_TAG, then it is reinvoked for another iteration over the body. Thus, the doAfterBody() method is called multiple times for iterative tags, until it returns SKIP_BODY.

- The doEndTag() method is executed after body processing is over, when the end tag is reached. This method can return either SKIP_PAGE or EVAL_PAGE, depending on whether page processing should end or continue.

- The release() method is always invoked to clean up the state of the tag handler instance, irrespective of whether the doEndTag() method call returns the value SKIP_PAGE or EVAL_PAGE.

The BodyTag **interface** has an additional method—setBodyContent()— that takes as argument a BodyContent object that can be used in processing the tag body (the BodyTag **interface** and the BodyContent class are listed in Appendix D). This method can be used by the JSP engine to pass a BodyContent handle to a tag handler instance. The corresponding get method is getBodyContent(), which returns a BodyContent object. You will use this object to process the body in the makeMenu custom tag that you will write next.

Writing the makeMenu Custom Tag   You will now design and implement a custom tag—makeMenu—that creates an HTML selection menu from a column of a SQL query appearing in its body. This menu can be used within an HTML form to select a certain value, such as an order number from the PURCHASE_LIST table in the Purchase Order schema. The steps to be performed by the makeMenu tag are as follows:

- Read the SQL query text that is nested between its start and end tags.

■ Get a database connection and execute the SQL query.

■ Construct a list of option values for the HTML menu from the first column of the query.

■ Print this list in the output stream.

The code for the `MenuTag.java` program is shown here. A key point to note is that this class extends the `BodyTagSupport` class described earlier, and inherits the default implementations of most of the methods from it, except for the method `doAfterBody()`. This method is used to process the body text to perform the tag-specific steps just outlined.

```
/* Program name: MenuTag.java
 * Purpose:      Create a HTML selection menu from a database query
 */

package chapter12;

import javax.servlet.jsp.*;          // standard jsp library
import javax.servlet.jsp.tagext.*;   // standard jsp tag extension lib
import java.sql.*;

public class MenuTag
  extends BodyTagSupport
{
  int maxRows = 100;                 // (See Note 1.)
  public void setMaxRows(int maxRows) {
    this.maxRows = maxRows;
  }

  /** Extract the String from the nested body, get a connection,
   * do a query, and print the HTML menu.
   */
  public int doAfterBody() throws JspTagException
  { // get the tag body as a string
    BodyContent body = getBodyContent();      // (See Note 2.)
    String query = body.getString().trim();
    try {
      DriverManager.registerDriver(
          new oracle.jdbc.driver.OracleDriver());
      Connection conn = DriverManager.getConnection( // (See Note 3.)
                          "jdbc:oracle:oci8:@", // URL
                          "jspuser", "jsp");  // User/password
      Statement stmt = conn.createStatement();
      ResultSet rset = stmt.executeQuery(query);
      if (rset.next()) {  // the result set is not empty
        body.getEnclosingWriter().println(makeMenu(rset));
                                // (See Note 4.)
```

```
    }
  } catch (Exception e) {
    throw new JspTagException("Error in Menu tag: " +
                             e.getMessage());
  }
  finally {try {conn.close();} catch (Exception e) {}}
  return EVAL_PAGE; // continue with page processing
}

/* Create the list of items in the menu */
private String makeMenu(ResultSet rset) throws Exception {
  int num = 0;
  StringBuffer sb = new StringBuffer();
  do {  // (See Note 5.)
    sb.append("<OPTION> " + rset.getString(1) + " </OPTION>\n");
    num++;
  } while (rset.next() && (num <= maxRows)); rset.close();
  return sb.toString();
  }
}
```

Notes on `MenuTag.java`:

1. The `makeMenu` tag has one optional attribute—`maxRows`—which denotes the number of rows to be fetched from the result set for the query. The `setMaxRows()` method is used to set the value of this property from the JSP.

2. This statement gets the `BodyContent` object for the tag, as set previously by the JSP runtime. This object is used to get the text for the body through the `getString()` method call. The body text is trimmed of trailing spaces to get the SQL query text.

3. This statement creates a connection to the database. In practice, it is much more likely that a connection will be obtained through a connection bean in the HTTP `session` object, or through a connection manager bean at the `application` scope, instead of being opened directly in the `MenuTag` class. It is coded like this in the previous example in order to keep the logic simple.

4. This statement gets a `Writer` object from the `BodyContent` object using the method call `getEnclosingWriter()`. This `Writer` object is used to output the result of processing the tag body.

5. This statement is the loop that processes each row in the result set, and puts the value of the first column between the `<OPTION>` and `</OPTION>` HTML tags for printing the menu in a HTML `SELECT` statement. You will shortly see this statement in action when you write the `OrderMenu.jsp` program.

Compiling, Deploying, and Testing the `makeMenu` **Custom Tag**   As with the
`dateTime` tag you wrote in the previous section, you must compile and deploy the
`makeMenu` tag before you can call it from your JSP. You must place the compiled class
in the appropriate location of your Web server, and write the tag library descriptor
(TLD) entry for the tag. These steps are given below for the Tomcat server:

I. Compile `MenuTag.java`.

    The following shell script can be used to compile the `MenuTag.java` file in
    the Tomcat environment (refer to Appendix E to set up the Tomcat server):

    ```
    #!/bin/sh
    TOMCAT_HOME=/private/jakarta-tomcat
    JDK_HOME=/usr/local/packages/jdk1.2.2
    APP_HOME=${TOMCAT_HOME}/webapps/examples
    CLASSPATH=${ORACLE_HOME}/jdbc/lib/classes12.zip
    CLASSPATH=${TOMCAT_HOME}/lib/servlet.jar:${CLASSPATH}
    exec ${JDK_HOME}/bin/javac -d ${APP_HOME}/WEB-INF/classes \
        -classpath ${CLASSPATH} \
        ${APP_HOME}/jsp/chapter12/DateTimeTag.java
    ```

2. Describe the `makeMenu` tag in the `mytaglib.tld` file.

    You can add the following tag entry to the `mytaglib.tld` file that you
    created for the `dateTime` tag written earlier. The entry appears between
    the enclosing `<taglib>` and `</taglib>` elements in the file. The main
    difference between this tag entry and the one for the `dateTime` tag is the
    value for the `<bodycontent>` element. It is set to the value `JSP` here
    instead of `empty` in the `dateTime` tag. The value `JSP` indicates that the
    body will contain JSP code, possibly including scriptlets and expressions
    that should be evaluated. Therefore, the SQL query in the body of
    `makeMenu` tag can be constructed at request time.

    ```
    <taglib>
    ...

    <!-- makeMenu tag -->
      <tag>
        <name>makeMenu</name>
        <tagclass>chapter12.MenuTag</tagclass>
        <bodycontent>JSP</bodycontent>
        <info>
           Makes an HTML menu out of the first column of a
           SQL query in the tag body
        </info>
        <attribute>
    ```

```
      <name>maxRows</name>
      <required>false</required>
    </attribute>
   </tag>
  </taglib>
```

3. Write a JSP to call the makeMenu tag.

The third and final step is to write a JSP that will call the new makeMenu custom tag. The following is a JSP page—OrderMenu.jsp—that uses this tag to create a menu of the requestno column values in the PURCHASE_LIST table. This menu is placed between the <SELECT> and </SELECT> HTML tags within an HTML form, and used to pick a value from the displayed list. The selected value is given the name orderNumber, and is passed through the HTML form action to the CallOrderEJB.jsp page (that you wrote at the beginning of this chapter) to query the details for the selected order number. You could execute any other action here; the CallOrderEJB.jsp page is used just as an illustration. Note that the SQL query is being formulated at request time, which makes the tag really flexible.

```
<!-- Program name: OrderMenu.jsp
  -- Purpose:       Use the Menu custom tag to select an order
  -->
<%@ taglib uri="/WEB-INF/mytaglib.tld" prefix="mytag" %>
<HTML>
  <HEAD><TITLE> The OrderMenu JSP </TITLE></HEAD>
  <BODY>
   <% String columnName = "requestno"; %>
   <H3> Pick an order number: </H3>
   <FORM ACTION="CallOrderEJB.jsp">
    <SELECT Name="orderNumber" >
       <mytag:makeMenu>
         SELECT <%= columnName %> FROM PURCHASE_LIST
       </mytag:makeMenu>
    </SELECT>
    <INPUT TYPE="submit" Name="Query order" >
   </FORM>
  </BODY>
</HTML>
```

The output of executing OrderMenu.jsp is shown in Figure 12-9.

Creating Scripting Variables in Custom Tags   It is possible for custom tag handlers to create *scripting variables* that can be used by this or other tags, and by other JSP scripting elements in the page. For example, the dbOpen tag described earlier introduces a scripting variable through its connId attribute. This variable can be subsequently used in the dbQuery tag to obtain a connection handle.

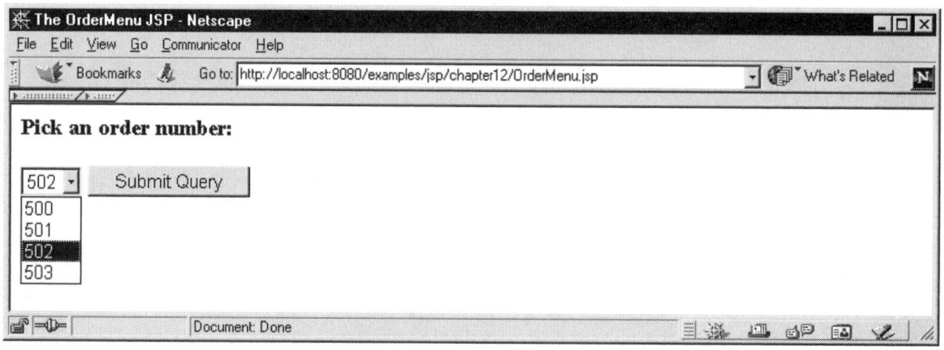

FIGURE 12-9. *Output of* `OrderMenu.jsp`

Any scripting variables that a custom tag defines have to be specified in a *tag extra information* (or TEI) class, which is a subclass of the standard `javax.servlet.jsp.tagext.TagExtraInfo` abstract class. The TEI class used by a custom tag is given in the TLD file for the tag, as specified in the `taglib` directive in the JSP page. The JSP engine uses the TEI instances during translation. A TEI class has a `getVariableInfo()` method to retrieve the names and types of the scripting variables that will be defined at request time. While compiling the JSP, this method is called by the JSP translator to obtain the name, the Java type, and the scope of the scripting variable, and whether it is newly declared. For more information on scripting variables and their use in custom tags, refer to the "JavaServer Pages 1.1 Specification" from Sun Microsystems.

As a simple example, consider an enhanced `dateTime` tag that stores the computed date and time in a scripting variable, so that other tags can use the value subsequently:

```
<mytag:dateTime theTime="var_name"
                [ output="DATE"|"TIME"|"DATETIME" ]
                [ format="SHORT"|"MEDIUM"|"FULL"|"LONG" ] />
```

Writing such a custom tag and its TEI class is left as a programming exercise for you. You could also write JSP custom tags for easy use of EJB and CORBA components. Other advanced examples of custom tags include nested tags and cooperating tags. For further information and examples, refer to the Tag Library tutorial from Sun Microsystems: http://java.sun.com/products/jsp/tutorial/TagLibrariesTOC.html.

Conclusion

In this chapter, you learned how to build JSP-based Web applications that use different software components such as Enterprise JavaBeans and CORBA objects deployed in Oracle8*i*. You developed JSP pages that accept input parameters through the browser screen, invoke the EJB and CORBA objects to execute business logic with these parameters, and present the results to the user. The business components effectively encapsulate the processing logic, such as executing database operations, while the JSP page handles the presentation and use of these objects.

You also learned how to use JSP tag libraries. The tag library framework allows you to extend the set of JSP tags with your own custom tags, or to plug in third-party custom tag libraries in a standard way. Using this framework, you can use write modular Java components and then expose their functionality through convenient tag syntax. Oracle's JSP implementation provides a set of utility tags to open database connections, execute SQL queries, format generated XML results using XSL stylesheets, and so on. You learned how to import and use these tags in your JSP. Finally, you came to understand how the tag extension scheme works, and wrote your own custom tags to display the time in a specified format and make an HTML menu from a SQL query column.

As you have seen in the last three chapters, you can build up smart Web applications using "pluggable" software components effectively in your JSPs and servlets. You can easily combine the different component programming technologies in your Web application, and thus exploit the full power and versatility of the Java platform.

PART V

Appendices

APPENDIX A

Servlet Quick Reference and API Summary

his appendix discusses the Servlet Quick Reference Guide and gives a summary of the Servlet 2.2 API.

Servlet Quick Reference Guide

To implement and run a Java servlet, you need to perform the following steps:

- Write the servlet code
- Compile the servlet code into Java bytecode
- Deploy the compiled servlet class on your Web server
- Invoke the deployed servlet through your browser

In this section, you will write two servlets, `HelloServlet` and `JDBCQueryServlet`, and go through the above tasks step by step for these two programs, running them in the final step. Recall that you developed the `HelloServlet` program in the "Writing a Simple Servlet" section of Chapter 2. The `JDBCQueryServlet` will do a SQL query on the Oracle database using JDBC.

Since the steps to install a servlet are different for different Web environments (see Appendix E), the Tomcat server is used here to illustrate the deployment steps. Appendix E describes installation and configuration steps for Tomcat and other Web servers.

Writing the Servlets

A servlet that handles HTTP requests generally extends the `javax.servlet.http.HttpServlet` abstract class, which in turn extends the abstract class `javax.servlet.GenericServlet` (refer to the latter part of this appendix for definitions of these and other types in the Servlet API). A servlet class typically defines the following methods:

- `init()` method to initialize the servlet instance. If omitted, a default (trivial) implementation of this method is inherited from the ancestor class `javax.servlet.GenericServlet`.

- `destroy()` method to destroy the servlet instance. If omitted, a default (trivial) implementation of this method is inherited from the ancestor class `javax.servlet.GenericServlet`.

- doGet() and/or doPost() methods to process HTTP GET and PUT requests. Less common methods are doPut() and doHead() for the HTTP PUT and HEAD requests respectively. Depending on the HTTP request, the appropriate do...() method is dispatched by the service() method in the parent class javax.servlet.http.HttpServlet. All of these methods take the HTTP request and response objects as arguments.

Writing the `HelloServlet`

HelloServlet is a very simple servlet that prints a greeting to the user, along with the time. The HTTP GET method is used by default. The user's name is provided as a request parameter in the URL, and can therefore be retrieved through the request.getParameter() method call. This method takes the parameter name as argument and returns its value. Because it is so simple, the HelloServlet does not need any special actions to be executed during initialization or shutdown. Therefore, the init() and destroy() methods are not required; you will only write the doGet() method. Here is the code for HelloServlet:

```java
/** Program name: HelloServlet.java
 ** Purpose:      Say hello to the user and print the current time
 **/
package appendixA;

import javax.servlet.*;
import javax.servlet.http.*;
import java.io.PrintWriter;
import java.io.IOException;

public class HelloServlet extends HttpServlet {
    public void doGet (HttpServletRequest request,
                       HttpServletResponse response)
               throws ServletException, IOException {
    // Get the output writer from the response
    PrintWriter out= response.getWriter();
    // Set the content type of the response to HTML text
    response.setContentType("text/html");
    // Generate the contents of the response
    out.println("<HTML>");
    out.println("<BODY>");
    out.println("<B><P>Hello " + request.getParameter("user") +
                ", how are you? ");
    out.println("<P>The current time is " + new java.util.Date());
    out.println("<P>Have a nice day!</B>");
    out.println("</BODY>");
    out.println("</HTML>");
    out.close();
    }
}
```

Writing the JDBCQueryServlet

Now you will write the `JDBCQueryServlet` servlet. This servlet illustrates two points:

- How to use HTML forms to enter request parameters
- How to use the HTTP request parameters to do a JDBC query on the Oracle database

Specifically, the function of this servlet will be to accept a search condition from the user, and look up the name and phone number from the `EMPLOYEE_LIST` table in the Purchase Order schema. This schema is defined in the "Introduction" chapter at the beginning of this book, and is reproduced here for convenience:

```
CREATE TABLE EMPLOYEE_LIST(
    employeeno      NUMBER(7),
    deptno          NUMBER(5),
    type            VARCHAR2(30),
    lastname        VARCHAR2(30),
    firstname       VARCHAR2(30),
    phone           VARCHAR2(10));
```

The servlet code will be divided into several methods:

- `init()`   This method sets up the database connection.
- `destroy()`   This method disconnects from the database.
- `doPost()`   This method handles the HTTP `POST` request.
- `doQuery()`   This **private** method executes the SQL query with the given condition.
- `printResults()`   This **private** method prints the query result as an HTML table.
- `printForm()`   This **private** method prints the HTML form for entering the search condition.

The `JDBCQueryServlet` will also define a `doGet()` method, so that it can be invoked through HTTP `GET` requests. This type of request is generated when you type in the URL for the servlet in the browser. The `doGet()` method will simply call the `doPost()` method with the `request` and `response` objects as parameters. The code for `JDBCQueryServlet` that does phone lookup is given here:

```
/** Program name: JDBCQueryServlet.java
 ** Purpose:      Do a JDBC query with request parameters
 **               entered through an HTML form
```

```
**/

package appendixA;

import javax.servlet.*;
import javax.servlet.http.*;
import java.io.PrintWriter;
import java.io.IOException;
import java.sql.*;

public class JDBCQueryServlet extends HttpServlet {
  // instance variable for the database connection
  Connection conn = null;

  // method to initialize the servlet - set up database connection
  public void init()
    throws ServletException {
      try { // connect using the JDBC-OCI driver
            // to the schema jspuser/jsp
            DriverManager.registerDriver(new
                oracle.jdbc.driver.OracleDriver());
            conn = DriverManager.getConnection("jdbc:oracle:oci8:@",
                                                "jspuser", "jsp");
        } catch (SQLException e) {
            conn = null;
            throw new ServletException(e.getMessage());
        }
    }

  // method to destroy the servlet - disconnect from database
  public void destroy() {
    try {
          if (conn!= null) conn.close();
        } catch (SQLException ignore) {}
    }

  // method to process HTTP POST requests
  public void doPost (HttpServletRequest request,
                      HttpServletResponse response)
        throws ServletException, IOException {

        // get the output writer from the response
        PrintWriter out= response.getWriter();

        // set the content type of the response to HTML text
        response.setContentType("text/html");

        // Now print the HTML content
```

```
        out.println("<HTML>");
        out.println("<HEAD> <TITLE> The JDBCQueryServlet" +
                    "  </TITLE> </HEAD>");
        out.println("<BODY>");
        String condition = request.getParameter("cond");
        if (condition != null) {
          out.println("<H3> Search results for  <I>" +
                      condition + " </I> </H3><B>");

          // Do the query and print search results
          doQuery(condition, out);

          out.println(" </B> <HR><BR>");
        }

        // Print the HTML form for entering search condition
        printForm(out);

        // Lastly, close the output writer
        out.close();
    }

  // method to process HTTP GET requests
  public void doGet (HttpServletRequest request,
                     HttpServletResponse response)
      throws ServletException, IOException
  { // simply call the POST method
    doPost(request, response);
  }

// Method to execute the SQL query
// It is synchronized to control access to database connection -
// only one thread may use it at a time.
private synchronized void doQuery(String condition,
                                  PrintWriter out) {
   if (conn == null) {
     out.println("No database connection!");
     return;
   }
   Statement stmt = null;
   ResultSet rs = null;
   try {
     stmt = conn.createStatement();
     rs = stmt.executeQuery ("SELECT firstname, lastname, phone" +
                             " FROM employee_list " +
                             (condition.length() == 0?
                             "" : ("WHERE " + condition)) +
                             " ORDER BY firstname" );
```

```
        // format the result rows into an HTML table
        printResult(rs, out);
    } catch (SQLException e) {
        out.println ("<P> SQL error: <PRE> " + e + " </PRE> </P>\n");
    } finally {  // clean up
        try {
            if (rs!= null) rs.close();        // close the result set
            if (stmt!= null) stmt.close();    // close the statement
        } catch (SQLException ignore) { }
    }
}

// Method to print the query results as an HTML table
private void printResult (ResultSet rs, PrintWriter out)
        throws SQLException {
  if (!rs.next()) { // no rows found
      out.println("<P> No such employee!<P>\n");
      return;
  }

  // Format the rows into an HTML table
  out.println("<TABLE BORDER>");
  // First, print the headers
  out.println("<TH>First Name</TH>");
  out.println("<TH>Last Name</TH>");
  out.println("<TH>Phone</TH>");

  // Then print the table rows, looping through the result set
  do {  out.println("<TR>" + "<TD>" + rs.getString(1) + "</TD>"
                         + "<TD>" + rs.getString(2) + "</TD>"
                         + "<TD>" + rs.getString(3) + "</TD>"
                  + "</TR>");
  } while (rs.next());
  out.println("</TABLE>");
}

// method to print the HTML form for entering the search condition
private void printForm(PrintWriter out) {
      out.println("<B>Search condition:</B>");
      out.println("<FORM METHOD=POST> ");
      out.println("<INPUT TYPE=\"text\" NAME=\"cond\" SIZE=30" +
                      " VALUE=\"firstname like 'A%'\">");
      out.println("<INPUT TYPE=\"submit\" VALUE=\"Lookup Phone\">");
      out.println(" </FORM>");
      out.println(" </BODY>");
      out.println("</HTML>");
  }
}
```

The `doPost()` method checks to see if there is a parameter `cond` present in the HTTP `request` object. If so, it calls the `doQuery()` method to execute the phone lookup query with this search condition. The `doQuery()` method appends the given condition to the SQL `SELECT` statement, and generates a result set for the query. If the query executes successfully, it calls the `printResult()` method to format the rows in the result set into an HTML table. The `printResult()` method iterates through all the rows, printing out the data. Finally, the `printForm()` method is called by `doPost()` to provide a text input box through which the user can enter a search condition for phone lookup. This text input box has a default condition of `firstname like 'A%'` printed in it.

Note that the method `doQuery()` is *synchronized*. This is done so that only one invoker of the servlet has access to the shared database connection at a time (recall from Chapter 2 that concurrent HTTP requests for a servlet are typically handled by spawning multiple threads). The `conn` variable representing the shared database connection is initialized in the `init()` method of the servlet, and it is closed in the `destroy()` method. Access to the database is effectively serialized during request processing. In practice, better performance may be obtained by using a shared pool of database connections.

The search condition for the SQL query is entered by the user through an HTML form. The form is printed by the `printForm()` method in the servlet. This form defines a single input text box named `cond` for typing in the condition and an action button for submitting the query. The default action is to invoke the same program, here `JDBCQueryServlet`. When the button is clicked by the user, the value entered in the `cond` field is included in a new HTTP request to invoke the `JDBCQueryServlet` program through the HTTP `POST` method. Refer to any standard book on HTML and HTTP to learn further details about how HTML forms work.

Compiling the Servlets

In the UNIX environment, use the following steps to compile the servlet code. The steps on a Windows NT system are analogous. The Tomcat server is used to illustrate the steps.

Compiling `HelloServlet.java`

You must first install JDK and the Tomcat server (refer to Appendix E for the installation and configuration steps for Tomcat). Set the environment variable `JDK_HOME` to point to the root of the JDK installation, and the environment variable `TOMCAT_HOME` to point to the root of the Tomcat installation. Then, you can use the commands shown in Listing A-1 to compile `HelloServlet.java` on a UNIX system.

Listing A-1 UNIX commands to compile `HelloServlet`

```
# At the Unix prompt:
${JDK_HOME}/bin/javac -g \
```

```
-d ${TOMCAT_HOME}/webapps/examples/WEB-INF/classes \
-classpath ${TOMCAT_HOME}/lib/servlet.jar \
HelloServlet.java
```

Compiling `JDBCQueryServlet.java`

This servlet connect to the database using JDBC, and hence requires the JDBC libraries. These libraries are available in your Oracle installation. Use the commands shown in Listing A-2 to compile `JDBCQueryServlet.java` on a UNIX system that is using JDK 1.2.

Listing A-2   UNIX commands to compile `JDBCQueryServlet` using JDK 1.2

```
# At the UNIX prompt:
${JDK_HOME}/bin/javac -g \
    -d ${TOMCAT_HOME}/webapps/examples/WEB-INF/classes \
    -classpath ${ORACLE_HOME}/jdbc/lib/classes12.zip:\
${TOMCAT_HOME}/lib/servlet.jar \
  JDBCQueryServlet.java
```

If your system uses JDK 1.1, you must use the JDBC libraries ${ORACLE_HOME}/jdbc/lib/classes111.zip instead of classes12.zip.

Deploying the Servlets on Tomcat

To deploy the servlets you must place the compiled classes in the appropriate directory on your Web server. This directory depends on the root of your Web application. For example, for Tomcat, the `${TOMCAT_HOME}/webapps/examples` directory is preconfigured as the root directory of the `examples` application. So, in Tomcat you can place the compiled class files `HelloServlet.class` and `JDBCQueryServlet.class` under the directory `$TOMCAT_HOME/webapps/examples/WEB-INF/classes`. This can be conveniently done in the compilation step through the `-d` option in the `javac` compiler (see Listings A-1 and A-2).

Invoking the Servlets

After the deploying the servlets, you can invoke them through your browser. Assuming that your Tomcat server is running on port 8080 on the local machine, you can invoke the servlets through the following URLs: http://localhost:8080/examples/servlet/appendixA.HelloServlet?user=Pat or http://localhost:8080/examples/servlet/appendixA.JDBCQueryServlet

Notice that the URLs use the fully qualified class name for the servlets, such as `appendixA.HelloServlet`. The browser output of executing `HelloServlet` is shown in Figure A-1.

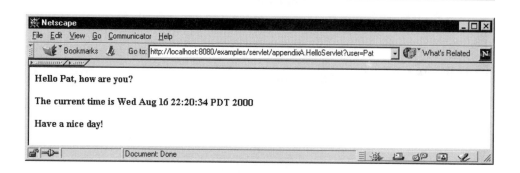

FIGURE A-1. *Output of executing* `HelloServlet`

You can see the actual HTML code for the generated page through the page source viewing facility in your browser. For example, for the Netscape browser you can choose the View button from the top menu followed by Page Source to see the generated HTML. This code is shown in Listing A-3.

Listing A-3 HTML page generated by `HelloServlet`

```
<HTML>
<BODY>
<B><P>Hello Pat, how are you?
<P>The current time is Wed Aug 16 22:20:34 PDT 2000
<P>Have a nice day! </B>
</BODY>
</HTML>
```

The browser output of executing `JDBCQueryServlet` is shown in Figure A-2. You can change the search condition through the HTML form, and execute another query. The page source for the output HTML page is shown in Listing A-4.

Listing A-4   HTML page generated by `JDBCQueryServlet`

```
<HTML>
<HEAD> <TITLE> The JDBCQueryServlet  </TITLE> </HEAD>
<BODY>
<H3> Search results for  <I>firstname like 'A%' </I> </H3><B>
<TABLE BORDER>
<TH>First Name</TH>
<TH>Last Name</TH>
<TH>Phone</TH>
<TR><TD>Alice</TD><TD>Sunset</TD><TD>1004</TD></TR>
</TABLE>
  </B> <HR><BR>
<B>Search condition:</B>
<FORM METHOD=POST>
<INPUT TYPE="text" NAME="cond" SIZE=30 VALUE="firstname like 'A%'">
<INPUT TYPE="submit" VALUE="Lookup Phone">
  </FORM>
  </BODY>
</HTML>
```

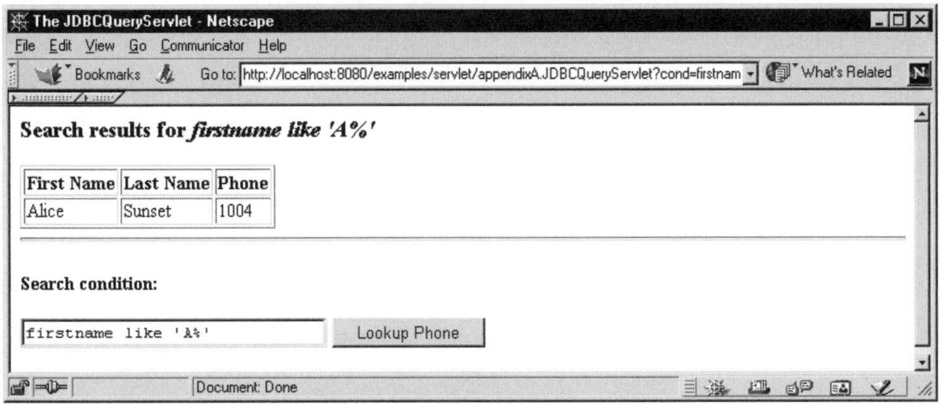

FIGURE A-2.   *Output of executing the default query in* `JDBCQueryServlet`

Servlet API 2.2

The following sections briefly list the classes and interfaces in the Servlet 2.2 API. The servlet API consists of two packages: `javax.servlet` and `javax.servlet.http`. The `javax.servlet` package deals with the generic protocol-independent API for servlets, and the `javax.servlet.http` package deals with the API for HTTP-based servlets. First, the class and **interface** hierarchy of the types in both of these packages are shown. Then, the individual classes and interfaces in each of the packages are listed.

Class Hierarchy

The hierarchy of classes in the `javax.servlet` and `javax.servlet.http` packages is shown here:

```
class java.lang.Object
  class javax.servlet.http.Cookie (implements java.lang.Cloneable)
  class java.util.EventObject (implements java.io.Serializable)
    class javax.servlet.http.HttpSessionBindingEvent
  class javax.servlet.GenericServlet (implements java.io.Serializable,
            javax.servlet.Servlet, javax.servlet.ServletConfig)
    class javax.servlet.http.HttpServlet (implements
                                java.io.Serializable)
  class javax.servlet.http.HttpUtils
  class java.io.InputStream
    class javax.servlet.ServletInputStream
  class javax.servlet.jsp.JspEngineInfo
  class javax.servlet.jsp.JspFactory
  class java.io.OutputStream
    class javax.servlet.ServletOutputStream
  class javax.servlet.jsp.PageContext
  class javax.servlet.jsp.tagext.TagAttributeInfo
  class javax.servlet.jsp.tagext.TagData (implements
                                java.lang.Cloneable)
  class javax.servlet.jsp.tagext.TagExtraInfo
  class javax.servlet.jsp.tagext.TagInfo
  class javax.servlet.jsp.tagext.TagLibraryInfo
  class javax.servlet.jsp.tagext.TagSupport (implements
            java.io.Serializable, javax.servlet.jsp.tagext.Tag)
    class javax.servlet.jsp.tagext.BodyTagSupport (implements
                            javax.servlet.jsp.tagext.BodyTag)
```

```
class java.lang.Throwable (implements java.io.Serializable)
  class java.lang.Exception
    class javax.servlet.jsp.JspException
      class javax.servlet.jsp.JspTagException
    class javax.servlet.ServletException
      class javax.servlet.UnavailableException
class javax.servlet.jsp.tagext.VariableInfo
class java.io.Writer
  class javax.servlet.jsp.JspWriter
    class javax.servlet.jsp.tagext.BodyContent
```

Interface Hierarchy

The hierarchy of interfaces in the `javax.servlet` and `javax.servlet.http` packages is shown here:

```
interface java.util.EventListener
  interface javax.servlet.http.HttpSessionBindingListener
interface javax.servlet.http.HttpSession
interface javax.servlet.http.HttpSessionContext
interface javax.servlet.RequestDispatcher
interface javax.servlet.Servlet
  interface javax.servlet.jsp.JspPage
    interface javax.servlet.jsp.HttpJspPage
interface javax.servlet.ServletConfig
interface javax.servlet.ServletContext
interface javax.servlet.ServletRequest
  interface javax.servlet.http.HttpServletRequest
interface javax.servlet.ServletResponse
  interface javax.servlet.http.HttpServletResponse
interface javax.servlet.SingleThreadModel
interface javax.servlet.jsp.tagext.Tag
  interface javax.servlet.jsp.tagext.BodyTag
```

Classes and Interfaces

This section provides a listing of the interfaces, classes, and exceptions that compose the Servlet API. Signatures of the methods in these classes and interfaces are briefly listed in Table A-1. For detailed descriptions of these types and their methods, please see the Java Servlet Specification, v2.2, from Sun Microsystems.

Package `javax.servlet`	**Package `javax.servlet.http`**
RequestDispatcher	HttpServletRequest
Servlet	HttpServletResponse
ServletConfig	HttpSession
ServletContext	HttpSessionBindingListener
ServletRequest	HttpSessionContext
ServletResponse	Cookie
SingleThreadModel	HttpServlet
GenericServlet	HttpSessionBindingEvent
ServletInputStream	HttpUtils
ServletOutputStream	
ServletException	
UnavailableException	

TABLE A-1. *Servlet API Package Summary*

Package `javax.servlet`

The `javax.servlet` package deals with protocol-independent servlet programming. It consists of the following interfaces and classes:

```
interface RequestDispatcher
interface Servlet
interface ServletConfig
interface ServletContext
interface ServletRequest
interface ServletResponse
interface SingleThreadModel

class GenericServlet
class ServletInputStream
class ServletOutputStream
class ServletException
class UnavailableException
```

Each of these interfaces and classes are briefly described here.

RequestDispatcher   The RequestDispatcher **interface** is used to include and forward requests to other resources, such as other servlets and JSPs, HTML pages, and so on. The RequestDispatcher **interface** is shown here:

```
public interface RequestDispatcher

public void forward(ServletRequest req, ServletResponse res);
public void include(ServletRequest req, ServletResponse res);
```

Servlet   The Servlet **interface** is the basic **interface** implemented by all servlets and JSP programs. There are methods to initialize and destroy a servlet instance and to service requests. The Servlet **interface** is shown here:

```
public interface Servlet

public void init(ServletConfig config) throws ServletException;
public ServletConfig getServletConfig();
public void service(ServletRequest req, ServletResponse res)
    throws IOException, ServletException;
public String getServletInfo();
public void destroy();
```

ServletConfig   Initialization parameters can be passed to a servlet using a ServletConfig object. The ServletConfig **interface** is shown here:

```
public interface ServletConfig

public ServletContext getServletContext();
public String getInitParameter(String name);
public Enumeration get InitParameterNames();
public String getServletName();
```

ServletContext   The ServletContext **interface** can be used to obtain information about the Web server environment in which a servlet or JSP is executing. The ServletContext **interface** is shown here:

```
public interface ServletContext

public String getMimeType(String filename);
public URL getResource(String path) throws MalformedURLException;
```

```
public InputStream getResourceAsStream(String path);
public RequestDispatcher getRequestDispatcher(String path);
public RequestDispatcher getNamedDispatcher(String name);
public String getRealPath(String path);
public ServletContext getcontext(String uripath);
public String getServerInfo();
public String getInitParameter(String name);
public Enumeration getInitParameterNames;
public Object getAttribute(String name);
public Enumeration getAttributeNames();
public void setAttribute (String name, Object attribute);
public void removeAttribute(String name);
public int getMajorVersion();
public int getMinorVersion();
public void log(String message);
public void log(String message, Throwable cause);

//deprecated methods
public Servlet getServlet(String Name) throws ServletException;
public Enumeration getServlets();
public Enumeration getServletNames();
public void log(Exception exception, String messages);
```

ServletRequest   A ServletRequest object contains client request information such as parameter names and values. The ServletRequest **interface** is shown here:

```
public interface ServletRequest

public Object getAttribute(String name);
public Object setAttribute(String name,Object attribute);
public Enumeration getAttributeNames();
public void removeAttribute(String name);
public Locale getLocale();
public Enumeration getLocales();
public String getCharacterEncoding();
public int getContentLength();
public String getContentType();
public ServletInputStream getInputStream() throws IOException;
public String getParameter(String name);
public String getParameterNames();
public String getParameterValues();
public String getProtocol();
public String getScheme();
public String getServerName(0;
public int getServerport();
public BufferedReader getReader() throws IOException;
public String getRemoteAddr();
```

```
public String getRemoteHost();
public boolean isSecure();
public RequestDispatcher getRequestDispatcher(String path);

//depreciated methods
public String getRealPath();
```

ServletResponse   A `ServletResponse` object represents the response to a client request. The `ServletResponse` **interface** is shown here:

```
public interface ServletResponse

public String getCharacterEncoding();
public ServletOutputStream getServletOutputStream()
        throws IOException;
public PrintWriter getWriter throws IOException;
public void setContentLength (int length);
public void setContentType(String type);
public void setBufferSize(int size);
public int getBuffersize();
public void reset();
public boolean isCommitted();
public void flushBuffer() throws IOException;
public void setLocale(Locale  locale);
public Locale getLocale();
```

SingleThreadModel   A servlet can implement the `SingleThreadModel` **interface** to indicate that only one thread at a time may execute its `service()` method (see discussion on this topic in Chapter 2). This **interface** has no methods; it only serves as an indicator of the single-thread execution scheme. The `SingleThreadModel` **interface** is shown here:

```
public interface SingleThreadModel

//no methods
```

GenericServlet   The `GenericServlet` abstract class represents a protocol-independent servlet. It implements the `Servlet` **interface**. The `GenericServlet` class is shown here:

```
public abstract class GenericServlet implements Servlet

public GenericServlet();
public String getInitParameter();
public Enumeration getInitParameterNames();
```

```
public ServletConfig getServletConfig();
public ServletContext getServletContext();
public String getServletInfo();
public void init();
public void init(ServletConfig config) throws ServletException;
public void log(String message);
public void log(String message, Throwable cause);
public abstract void service (ServletRequest req,
                                   ServletResponse res)
       throws ServletException, IOException;
public void destroy();
```

ServletInputStream   A `ServletInputStream` object can be used to read binary data from a client request. The `ServletInputStream` abstract class is shown here:

```
public abstract class ServletInputStream extends InputStream

public ServletInputStream();
public int readLine(byte[] buffer, int offset, int length)
    throws IOException;
```

ServletOutputStream   A `ServletOutputStream` object can be used to send binary data to a client. The `ServletOutputStream` class extends the `java.io.OutputStream` class, and defines overloaded methods to print scalar and `String` data types. The `ServletOutputStream` abstract class is shown here:

```
public abstract class ServletOutputStream extends OutputStream

public ServletOutputStream();
public void print(String s) throws IOException;
public void print(boolean b) throws IOException;
public void print(char c) throws IOException;
public void print(int i ) throws IOException;
public void print(long l) throws IOException;
public void print(float f) throws IOException;
public void print(double d) throws IOException;
public void println() throws IOException;
public void println(String s) throws IOException;
public void println(boolean b) throws IOException;
public void println(char c) throws IOException;
public void println(int i) throws IOException;
public void println(long l) throws IOException;
public void println(float f) throws IOException;
public void println(double d) throws IOException;
```

ServletException   A `ServletException` object represents a general exception thrown by a servlet or a JSP. The `ServletException` class is shown here:

```
public class ServletException extends Exception;

public ServletException();
public ServletException(String message);
public ServletException(String message, Throwable cause);
public ServletException(Throwable cause);
public Throwable getRootCause();
```

UnavailableException   The `UnavailableException` class extends the `ServletException` class. It is used to indicate that a servlet is temporarily or permanently unavailable. The `UnavailableException` class is shown here:

```
public class UnavailableException extends ServletException

public UnavailableException(String message);
public UnavailableException(String message, int sec);
public int getUnavailableException();
public boolean isPermanent();

//newly deprecated methods
public UnavailableException(Servlet servlet, String message);
public UnavailableException(int sec, Servlet servlet, String msg);
public Servlet getServlet();
```

Package javax.servlet.http

The `javax.servlet` package deals with servlet programming using the HTTP protocol. It consists of the following interfaces and classes:

```
interface HttpServletRequest
interface HttpServletResponse
interface HttpSession
interface HttpSessionBindingListener
interface HttpSessionContext

class Cookie
class HttpServlet
class HttpSessionBindingEvent
class HttpUtils
```

Each of these interfaces and classes are briefly described here.

HttpServletRequest An `HttpServletRequest` object represents a servlet request sent through HTTP. The `HttpServletRequest` **interface** is shown here:

```
public interface HttpServletRequest extends ServletRequest;

public String getAuthType();
public Cookie[] getCookies();
public long getDateHeader(String name);
public String getHeader(String name);
public Enumeration getHeaders(String name);
public Enumeration getHeaderNames();
public int getIntHeader(String name);
public String getMethod();
public String getContextPath();
public String getPathInfo();
public String getPathTranslated();
public String getQueryString();
public String getRemoteUser();
public boolean isUserInRole(String role);
public java.security.Principal getUserPrincipal();
public String getRequestedSessionId();
public boolean isRequestedSessionIdValid();
public boolean isRequestedSessionIdFromCookie();
public boolean isRequestedSessionIdFromURL();
public String getRequestURI();
public String getServletPath();
public HttpSession getSession();
public HttpSession getSession(boolean create);

// deprecated methods
public boolean isRequestSessionIdFromUrl();
```

HttpServletResponse The `HttpServletResponse` **interface** provides methods for HTTP-specific features such as headers and cookies. This **interface** is shown here:

```
public interface HttpServletResponse extends ServletResponse
<<< STATUS CODES 416 AND 417 REPORTED MISSING>>>

public static final int SC_CONTINUE;
public static final int SC_SWITCHING_PROTOCOLS;
public static final int SC_OK;
public static final int SC_CREATED;
public static final int SC_ACCEPTED;
public static final int SC_NON_AUTHORITATIVE_INFORMATION;
```

```
public static final int SC_NO_CONTENT;
public static final int SC_RESET_CONTENT;
public static final int SC_PARTIAL_CONTENT;
public static final int SC_MULTIPLE_CHOICES;
public static final int SC_MOVED_PERMANENTLY;
public static final int SC_MOVED_TEMPORARILY;
public static final int SC_SEE_OTHER;
public static final int SC_NOT_MODIFIED;
public static final int SC_USE_PROXY;
public static final int SC_BAD_REQUEST;
public static final int SC_UNAUTHORIZED;
public static final int SC_PAYMENT_REQUIRED;
public static final int SC_FORBIDDEN;
public static final int SC_NOT_FOUND;
public static final int SC_METHOD_NOT_ALLOWED;
public static final int SC_NOT_ACCEPTABLE;
public static final int SC_PROXY_AUTHENTICATION_REQUIRED;
public static final int SC_REQUEST_TIMEOUT;
public static final int SC_CONFLICT;
public static final int SC_GONE;
public static final int SC_LENGTH_REQUIRED;
public static final int SC_PRECONDITION_FAILED;
public static final int SC_REQUEST_ENTITY_TOO_LARGE;
public static final int SC_REQUEST_URI_TOO_LONG;
public static final int SC_UNSUPPORTED_MEDIA_TYPE;
public static final int SC_REQUESTED_RANGE_NOT_SATISFIABLE;
public static final int SC_EXPECTATION_FAILED;
public static final int SC_INTERNAL_SERVER_ERROR;
public static final int SC_NOT_IMPLEMENTED;
public static final int SC_BAD_GATEWAY;
public static final int SC_SERVICE_UNAVAILABLE;
public static final int SC_GATEWAY_TIMEOUT;
public static final int SC_VERSION_NOT_SUPPORTED;
public void addCookie(Cookie cookie);
public boolean containsHeader(String name);
public String encodeURL(String url);
public String encodeRedirectURL(String url);
public void sendError(int status) throws IOException;
public void sendError(int status, String message)
    throws IOException;
public void sendRedirect(String location) throws IOException;
public void setDateHeader(String headername, long date);
public void setHeader(String headername, String value);
public void addHeader(String headername, String value);
public void addDateHeader(String headername, long date);
public void addIntHeader(String headername, int value);
public void setIntHeader(String headername, int value);
public void setStatus(int statuscode);
```

```
//deprecated methods
public void setStatus(int statuscode, String message);
public String encodeUrl(String url);
public String encodeRedirectUrl(String url);
```

HttpSession   The HttpSession **interface** defines methods for session-based interaction between a client and the server, such as for an online order entry application. The HttpSession **interface** is shown here:

```
public interface HttpSession

public long getCreationTime();
public String getId();
public long getLastAccessedTime();
public boolean isNew();
public int getMaxInactiveInterval();
public void setMaxInactiveInterval(int interval);
public Object getAttribute(String name);
public Enumeration getAttributeNames();
public void setAttribute(String name, Object attribute);
public void removeAttribute(String name);
public void invalidate();

// deprecated methods
public Object getValue(String name);
public String[] getValueNames();
public void putValue(String name, Object value);
public void removeValue(String name);
public HttpSessionContext getSessionContext();
```

HttpSessionBindingListener   The HttpSessionBindingListener **interface** is an event listener **interface** (refer to the "Events and Event Listener Interfaces" section in Chapter 2). The methods in this **interface** are called when an object is bound to and unbound from an HTTP session. The HttpSessionBindingListener **interface** is shown here:

```
public interface HttpSessionBindingListener extends EventListener

public void valueBound(HttpSessionBindingEvent event);
public void valueUnbound(HttpSessionBindingEvent event);
```

HttpSessionContext   The HttpSessionContext **interface** has been deprecated because of security reasons. The definition of this **interface** is shown here:

```
// deprecated
public abstract interface HttpSessionContext
```

```
// deprecated methods
public void Enumeration getIds();
public HttpSession getSession(String id);
```

Cookie   A `Cookie` object represents state information for a client. It can be sent by a servlet to the browser and can be used to track HTTP sessions. The `Cookie` class is shown here:

```
public class Cookie implements Cloneable

public Cookie(String name, String value);
public void setComment(String comment);
public String getComment();
public void setDomain(String domain);
public String getDomain();
public void setMaxAge(int expiry);
public int getMaxAge();
public void setPath(String uriPath);
public String getPath();
public void setSecure();
public boolean getSecure();
public String getName();
public void setValue(String value);
public String getValue();
public int getVersion();
public void setVersion(int version);
public Object clone();
```

HttpServlet   The `HttpServlet` abstract class provides HTTP-specific functionality for servlets. For example, it defines `doGet()` and `doPost()` methods for servicing HTTP `GET` and `POST` requests. The `HttpServlet` abstract class is shown here:

```
public abstract class HttpServlet extends GenericServlet
        implements Serializable

public HttpServlet();
protected void doGet(HttpServletRequest req,
                     HttpServletResponse res)
    throws ServletException, IOException;
protected void doPost(HttpServletRequest req,
                      HttpServletResponse res)
    throws ServletException, IOException;
protected void doPut(HttpServletRequest req,
                     HttpServletResponse res)
```

```
    throws ServletException, IOException;
protected void doDelete(HttpServletRequest req,
                        HttpServletResponse res)
    throws ServletException, IOException;
protected void doOptions(HttpServletRequest req,
                         HttpServletResponse res)
    throws ServletException, IOException;
protected void doTrace(HttpServletRequest req,
                       HttpServletResponse res)
    throws ServletException, IOException;
protected void service(HttpServletRequest req,
                       HttpServletResponse res)
    throws ServletException, IOException;
public void service(ServletRequest req, ServletResponse res)
    throws ServletException, IOException;
protected long getLastModifed(HttpServletRequest req);
```

HttpSessionBindingEvent   An HttpSessionBindingEvent object represents the events of binding and unbinding of an object to an HTTP session. It is passed as an argument in the methods of the HttpSessionBindingListener **interface**. The HttpSessionBindingEvent class is shown here:

```
public class HttpSessionBindingEvent extends EventObject

public HttpSessionBindingEvent(HttpSession session, String name);
public String getName();
public HttpSession getSession();
```

HttpUtils   The HttpUtils class defines static utility methods for servlet programming. The HttpUtils class is shown here:

```
public class HttpUtils

public HttpUtils();
public static Hashtable parseQueryString(String queryString);
public static Hashtable parsePostData(int length,
                                      ServletInputStream in);
public static StringBuffer getRequestURL(HttpServletRequest req);
```

APPENDIX B

Enterprise JavaBeans
Quick Reference
and API

n this appendix, you will find a step-by-step walkthrough that demonstrates how to create, compile, and deploy Enterprise JavaBeans. This walkthrough is presented in the "Enterprise JavaBeans Quick Reference Guide" section of this appendix. This appendix also summarizes the Enterprise JavaBeans API (versions 1.0 and 1.1).

Enterprise JavaBeans Quick Reference Guide

To implement a client/server application that uses an enterprise Bean, you need to perform the following tasks:

- Write the enterprise Bean.
- Compile the components of the enterprise Bean.
- Package the enterprise Bean.
- Write the deployment descriptor file.
- Deploy the enterprise Bean.
- Write the client application.
- Compile the client application.
- Run the client application.

In this section, you will use the `My8iEJB` session Bean as an example to perform all the above tasks. Recall that you developed the `My8iEJB` Bean in the "Writing Your First Enterprise JavaBean" section of Chapter 3.

Writing the Enterprise Bean (Session Bean)

Every enterprise Bean requires the following components:

- Remote `interface`
- Home `interface`
- Enterprise Bean class

Writing the Remote Interface

An EJB remote **interface** defines the business methods callable by a client. In this **interface**, an EJB developer provides a list of method signatures whose implementations reside in an enterprise Bean class. All EJB remote interfaces must extend the `javax.ejb.EJBObject` **interface**, and the method signatures must include the `java.rmi.RemoteException` exception in their **throws** clause. Additionally, method definitions may include any application-specific exceptions. Here is the definition of the `My8iEJB` remote **interface**:

```
// Program Name: My8iEJB.java

package server;

// Mandatory Java and ejb packages
// for EJB remote interfaces
import java.rmi.*;
import javax.ejb.*;

// Define a public interface that extends the
// javax.ejb.EJBObject interface
public interface My8iEJB extends EJBObject {

  // Define the public method that matches
  // exactly the method defines in the Bean class
  // Business method signature
  public String getFirst8iEJB() throws RemoteException;
}
```

Writing the Home Interface

All EJB home **interfaces** must extend the `javax.ejb.EJBHome` **interface**. A home **interface** defines the methods that allow a client to create, find, or remove an enterprise Bean. Note that a home **interface** for a session Bean can only define one `create()` method, whereas a home **interface** for an entity Bean may define one or more `create()` methods and one `find()` method. The `create()` method of the home **interface** returns an object of the remote **interface** type and must include in its **throws** clause `java.rmi.Remote-Exception` and `javax.ejb.CreateException`. Here is the definition of the `My8iEJBHome` home **interface**:

```
// Program Name:   My8iEJBHome.java

package server;
```

```
import java.rmi.*;
import javax.ejb.*;

// This interface must be public and
// must extend the java.ejb.EJBHome interface
public interface My8iEJBHome extends EJBHome {

// The definition of the developer's home interface
// must include one or more create() methods.
// Each create() method listed here must have a
// matching ejbCreate() method listed in the Bean class.

  My8iEJB create() throws CreateException, RemoteException;
}
```

Writing the Enterprise Bean Class

All session Bean classes must implement the `javax.ejb.SessionBean`
interface. All entity Bean classes must implement the `javax.ejb-`
`.EntityBean` **interface**. Here, you will use the `My8iEJBClass` class that
you wrote in Chapter 3, and you will deploy it as a `STATELESS` session Bean.
This Bean implements one business method, the `getFirst8iEJB()` method that
the `My8iEJB` remote **interface** defines. Remember that business methods
implemented in the Bean class must match exactly the method signatures advertised
in the remote **interface**. When a client invokes the `getFirst8iEJB()` method,
it returns a Java `String` to the caller. In addition to the business methods, all
enterprise Bean classes must include the following methods: the `ejbCreate()`,
`ejbActivate()`, `ejbPassivate()`, `ejbRemove()`, and `setSession-`
`Context(SessionContext ctx)` methods. Here is the definition of the
`My8iEJBClass` Bean class:

```
// Program Name:  My8iEJBClass.java

package server;

import java.rmi.RemoteException;
import javax.ejb.*;

public class My8iEJBClass implements SessionBean {
  public String getFirst8iEJB() throws RemoteException {
    String aString =
            "First EJB application stored in the "
            + " Oracle8i database on data-i.com server "
            + " from the Oracle8i Java Component Programming "
            + " with EJB, CORBA, and JSP book.";
    return aString;
```

```
// Note the ejbCreate() method that
// corresponds to the create() method in the
// definition of the home interface.
public void ejbCreate()
    throws RemoteException, CreateException {
} // End of ejbActivate()

public void ejbActivate()
    throws RemoteException {
} // End of ejbActivate()

public void ejbPassivate()
    throws RemoteException {
} // End of ejbPassivate()

public void ejbRemove()
    throws RemoteException {
} // End of ejbRemove()

public void setSessionContext(SessionContext ctx)
    throws RemoteException {
} // End of setSessionContext()

} // End of My8iEJBClass
```

Compiling the Bean's Source Code

In the UNIX environment use the MAKEFILE, and in Windows use the
SetupJDK1EnvMy8iBean.bat or SetupJDK2EnvMy8iBean.bat to set your
CLASSPATH and compile the source code. Listing B-1 illustrates how to set the
environment to compile the Java source code:

Listing B-1:   Compiling the Bean's source code in DOS

```
// At the Dos prompt:
set ORACLE_HOME=G:\Oracle\Ora81
set ORACLE_SERVICE=sess_iiop://data-i.com:2481:ORCL
REM Using JDK1.1.x
set JDK_CLASSPATH=J:\JDeveloper30\java\lib\classes.zip
REM Using JDK1.2.x: set JDK_CLASSPATH=C:\jdk1.2.1\lib\dt.jar
set CLASSPATH=.;I:\donnai;%ORACLE_HOME%\lib\aurora_client.jar;
%ORACLE_HOME%\jdbc\lib\classes12.zip;
%ORACLE_HOME%\sqlj\lib\translator.zip;
%ORACLE_HOME%\lib\vbjorb.jar;
%ORACLE_HOME%\lib\vbjapp.jar;%JDK_CLASSPATH%
```

Compile the Source Code   Use the following code fragment to compile the Bean's source code:

```
javac -g My8iEJB.java
javac -g My8iEJBHome.java
javac  -g My8iEJBClass.java
```

Packaging the Enterprise Bean
Use the `jar` command to package your enterprise Bean:

```
jar cvf0 server/My8iEJB.jar server/*.class
```

Writing the Deployment Descriptor File
Use a text editor to write the deployment descriptor file for EJB 1.0-compliant Beans and XML for EJB 1.1-compliant Beans. However, the upcoming release of the Oracle8*i* version 8.1.7 will support a text and XML format for the deployment descriptor file. Here, we present the text format as an example:

```
// File Name:    My8iEJB.ejb
SessionBean server.My8iEJBClass {
    BeanHomeName = "test/My8iEJB";
    HomeInterfaceClassName = server.My8iEJBHome;
    RemoteInterfaceClassName = server.My8iEJB;
    AllowedIdentities = {PUBLIC};
    SessionTimeout = 0;
    StateManagementType = STATELESS_SESSION;
    RunAsMode = CLIENT_IDENTITY;
}
```

Deploying the Enterprise Bean
Use the Oracle `deployejb` tool to deploy the `My8iEJB` session Bean. When you use the `deployejb` tool, it generates the stub classes that allow the client to communicate with the enterprise Bean instance that is running in the EJB container. In this example, the Oracle tool generates the stub classes and stores them in the `My8iEJBClient.jar` file:

```
deployejb -republish -keep -temp temp -u scott -p tiger
-s %ORACLE_SERVICE% -verbose -descriptor My8iEJB.ejb
-generated My8iEJBClient.jar My8iEJB.jar
```

Writing the Client Application
The `MyFirstEJBClient` program is a standalone Java application. The `MyFirstEJBClient` illustrates the basic tasks performed by a client of an enterprise Bean:

- Locate the home **interface**.

- Create an enterprise Bean instance.

- Invoke a business method.

Locate the Home Interface   Use the following steps to locate a Bean's home **interface**:

1. Set up environment variables and create a JNDI naming context:

```
// Create a Hashtable object to store the
   // environment variables
   Hashtable env = new Hashtable();

   // Required Setup of JNDI security environment properties
   // to be passed to a Context object.
   env.put(Context.URL_PKG_PREFIXES, "oracle.aurora.jndi");
   env.put(Context.SECURITY_PRINCIPAL, 'SCOTT');
   env.put(Context.SECURITY_CREDENTIALS, 'tiger');
   env.put(Context.SECURITY_AUTHENTICATION,
       ServiceCtx.NON_SSL_LOGIN);

   // Create an instance of the Context class
   Context ic = new InitialContext (env);
```

2. Use the `lookup()` method of the Context **interface** to obtain a reference to the Bean's home **interface**. The `lookup()` method takes one input parameter, which is the concatenation of a URL address and the name of the published object:

```
My8iEJBHome my8iEJBHome =
   (My8iEJBHome)ic.lookup ("sess_sh://data-i.com:2481:orcl"
                           +"/test/My8iEJB");
```

Create an Enterprise Bean Instance   Use the `create()` method of the home **interface** to create an instance of the `My8iEJB` Bean. The `create()` method returns an object whose type is `My8iEJB`. The remote `My8iEJB` **interface** defines the method in the `My8iEJBClass` class that the client may call. When the client invokes the `create()` method, the EJB container instantiates `My8iEJBClass`, and then invokes the `My8iEJBClass.ejbCreate()` method:

```
my8iEJBBean = my8iEJBHome.create();
```

Invoke a Business Method   Invoke the method on the `My8iEJB` object. When the client invokes a Bean method, the EJB container invokes the corresponding method on the `My8iEJBClass` instance that is running in the server. The following code fragment illustrates how a client invokes the `getFirst8iEJB()` method:

```
String outputFromBean = my8iEJBBean.getFirst8iEJB();
```

Here is the full source code for the `MyFirstEJBClient` program:

```
/*      Program Name: MyFirstEJBClient.java
*/

package client;

// Import the Bean's remote interface
import server.My8iEJB;

// Import the Bean's home interface
import server.My8iEJBHome;

// import the ServiceCtx class from the Oracle package
import oracle.aurora.jndi.sess_iiop.ServiceCtx;

// import the Java mandatory classes to use JNDI
import javax.naming.Context;
import javax.naming.InitialContext;

// import application-specific Java classes
import java.util.Hashtable;
import java.sql.*;

public class MyFirstEJBClient {
  public static void main(String[] args)
      throws Exception  {
  // Check input parameter
  if (args.length != 4) {
      System.out.println("usage: Client "
            +"serviceURL objectName user password");
      System.exit(1);
  }  // End if

  // Create String objects to store input parameters
  // which contains:
  // args [0] = sess_sh://data-i.com:2481:orcl;
  // args [1] = /test/My8iEJB;
  // args [2] = scott;
  // args [3] = tiger;
  String serviceURL = args [0];
  String objectName = args [1];
```

```java
String user = args [2];
String password = args [3];

// Create a Hashtable table to store the
// environment variables
Hashtable env = new Hashtable();

// Required Setup of JNDI security environment properties
// to be passed to a Context object.
env.put(Context.URL_PKG_PREFIXES, "oracle.aurora.jndi");
env.put(Context.SECURITY_PRINCIPAL, user);
env.put(Context.SECURITY_CREDENTIALS, password);
env.put(Context.SECURITY_AUTHENTICATION,
     ServiceCtx.NON_SSL_LOGIN);

 // Create an instance of the Context class
 Context ic = new InitialContext (env);

// Create an instance of the EJB object home interface
My8iEJBHome my8iEJBHome = null;

// Create a remote object.
My8iEJB my8iEJBBean = null;

System.out.println("Variable Created Properly");
System.out.println("serviceURL : " + serviceURL);
System.out.println("objectName : " + objectName);

try {
    // Use the home interface to
    // locate the EJB object
    my8iEJBHome =
        (My8iEJBHome)ic.lookup (serviceURL + objectName);
    System.out.println("Home Lookup Properly");

    // Create a Bean instance
    my8iEJBBean = my8iEJBHome.create();

    System.out.println("Bean Created Properly");

} // End of try
catch ( Exception ex ) {
    System.out.println("Cannot locate"
        +" or create My8iEJB object");
    System.err.println("error : " + ex);
    System.exit(1);
} // End of catch
```

```
// Create a Java String to store the result from
// invoking the Bean's method
String outputFromBean = null;

// Invoke the EJB Remote Method: getFirst8iEJB().
// Use the my8iEJBBean remote instance to
// invoke the Bean's method and store the result
// in the outputFromBean Java variable.
try {
    outputFromBean = my8iEJBBean.getFirst8iEJB();
    System.out.println("Method Invocation went well: "
            + outputFromBean);
}  // End of try
 catch (Exception ex) {
 System.err.println(" Unable to invoke "
 + " the getFirst8iEJB() method : " + ex);
        System.exit(1);
}  // End of catch
}
} // End of MyFirstEJBClient class
```

Compiling the Client Application   To compile your client, use Listing B-1 and
add the My8iEJB.jar and My8iEJBClient.jar files to the CLASSPATH
variable. Recall that you generated the My8iEJB.jar and My8iEJBClient.jar
files in the "Packaging the Enterprise Bean" and "Deploying the Enterprise Bean"
sections of this appendix. For example,

```
...
...
set CLASSPATH=.;I:\donnai;%ORACLE_HOME%\lib\aurora_client.jar;
%ORACLE_HOME%\jdbc\lib\classes12.zip;
%ORACLE_HOME%\sqlj\lib\translator.zip;
%ORACLE_HOME%\lib\vbjorb.jar;
%ORACLE_HOME%\lib\vbjapp.jar;%JDK_CLASSPATH%;
My8iEJB.jar;My8iEJBClient.jar
// Compile the client
javac -g MyFirtsEJBClient.java
```

Running the Client Application   To run the client, use the setup described in
the "Compiling the Client Application" section of this appendix:

```
java MyFirtsEJBClient %ORACLE_SERVICE% /test/My8iEJB scott tiger
```

Enterprise JavaBeans API

In this section, we present a summary of the EJB API (1.0 and 1.1). To learn more about the Enterprise JavaBeans API, see http://www.java.sun.com/products/ejb/javadoc-1.1/.

Hierarchy for Package javax.ejb

The Enterprise JavaBeans API consists of several interfaces and classes. In the first two sections of this appendix, we present the class and **interface** hierarchies. The remainder of the appendix presents the definition of the Java classes and interfaces comprising the EJB API.

Class Hierarchy

The class hierarchy is as follows:

```
class java.lang.Object
    class java.lang.Throwable (implements java.io.Serializable)
      class java.lang.Exception
        class javax.ejb.CreateException
          class javax.ejb.DuplicateKeyException
        class javax.ejb.FinderException
          class javax.ejb.ObjectNotFoundException
        class javax.ejb.RemoveException
        class java.lang.RuntimeException
          class javax.ejb.EJBException
            class javax.ejb.NoSuchEntityException
```

Interface Hierarchy

Here is the **interface** hierarchy:

```
interface javax.ejb.EJBContext
    interface javax.ejb.EntityContext
    interface javax.ejb.SessionContext
interface javax.ejb.EJBMetaData
interface java.rmi.Remote
    interface javax.ejb.EJBHome
    interface javax.ejb.EJBObject
interface java.io.Serializable
    interface javax.ejb.EnterpriseBean
      interface javax.ejb.EntityBean
```

```
    interface javax.ejb.SessionBean
  interface javax.ejb.Handle
  interface javax.ejb.HomeHandle
interface javax.ejb.SessionSynchronization
```

Package: javax.ejb

This package consists mostly of interfaces, many of which are implemented by your EJB vendor, and a number of exceptions that are thrown by the enterprise Beans.

CreateException

All create() methods defined in the home **interface** must include the CreateException in their **throws** clause:

```
public class javax.ejb.CreateException
     extends java.lang.Exception{
  public CreateException();
  public CreateException(String message);
}
```

DuplicateKeyException

All create() methods of the home **interface** of entity Beans must include the DuplicateKeyException in their **throws** clause:

```
public class javax.ejb.DuplicateKey
     extends javax.ejb.CreateException{
  public DuplicateKeyException();
  public DublicateKeyException(String message);
}
```

EJBContext

This is the parent **interface** of both EntityContext and SessionContext. EJBContext provides information about the security identity, transaction status, and access to environmental variables and the Bean's EJB home:

```
public interface javax.ejb.EJBContext {
    // The getCallerPrincipal() is new in EJB 1.1
    public abstract Principal getCallerPrincipal();
    public abstract EJBHome getEJBHome();
    public abstract boolean getRollbackOnly();
    public abstract UserTransaction getUserTransaction();
    // The getEnvironment() is deprecated in 1.1
    public abstract Properties getEnvironment();
```

```
    // The getCallerIdentity() is deprecated in 1.1
    public abstract Identity getCallerIdentity();
    // The isCallerInRole is deprecated in 1.1
    public abstract boolean isCallerInRole(Identity role);
    // new in 1.1
    public abstract boolean isCallerInRole(String roleNames);
    public abstract void setRollbackOnly();
}
```

EJBException (version 1.1)
Here is the `EJBException` class as defined by the EJB Specification version 1.1:

```
public class javax.ejb.EJBException
    extends java.lang.RuntimeException{
    public EJBException();
    public EJBException(String message);
    public EJBException(Exception exception);
    public Exception getCausedException();
}
```

EJBHome
All Bean's home **interfaces** must extend this **interface**:

```
public interface javax.ejb.EJBHome
    extends java.rmi.Remote{
    // The getHomeHandle() method is new in 1.1
    public abstract HomeHandle getHomeHandle();
    public abstract EJBMetaData getEJBMetaData();
    public abstract void remove(Handle handle);
    public abstract void remove(Object primaryKey);
}
```

EJBMetaData
The container vendor implements this **interface**. The EJB container provides a `Serializable` class that contains information about the enterprise Beans:

```
public interface javax.ejb.EJBHome{
    public abstract EJBHome();
    public abstract Class getHomeInterfaceClass();
    public abstract Class getPrimaryKeyclass();
    public abstract Class getRemoteInterfaceClass();
    public abstract boolean isSession();
    // The isStatelessSession() method is new in 1.1
    public abstract boolean isStatelessSession();
}
```

EJBObject
All remote **interfaces** must extend the EJBObject **interface**:

```
public interface javax.ejb.EJBObject
        extends java.rmi.Remote {
  public abstract EJBHome getEJBHome();
  public abstract Handle getHandle();
  public abstract Object getPrimaryKey();
  public abstract boolean isIdentical(EJBObject obj);
  public abstract void remove();
}
```

EnterpriseBean
All EntityBean and SessionBean **interfaces** extend this **interface**:

```
public interface javax.ejb.EnterpriseBean
  extends java.io.Serializable{
}
```

EntityBean
All entity Bean classes must implement this **interface**:

```
public interface javax.ejb.Entitybean
        extends javax.ejb.EnterpriseBean{
  public abstract void ejbActivate();
  public abstract void ejbLoad();
  public abstract void ejbPassivate();
  public abstract void ejbRemove();
  public abstract void ejbStore();
  public abstract void setEntityContext(EntityContext ctx);
  public abstract void unsetEntityContext();
}
```

EntityContext
The Entitycontext provides the Bean instance with an **interface** to the container:

```
public interface javax.ejb.EntityContext
        extends javax.ejb.EJBcontext{
  public abstract EJBObject getEJBObject();
  public abstract Object getPrimaryKey();
}
```

FinderException

This standard application exception is thrown by find methods defined in the home **interface** of an entity Bean:

```
public class javax.ejb.FinderException
       extends java.lang.Exception{
    public FinderException();
    public FinderException(String message);
}
```

Handle

This **interface** provides the client with a serializable object that can be used to store a Bean's remote reference and reobtain the reference when necessary:

```
public interface javax.ejb.Handle
       extends java.io.Serializable{
    public abstract EJBHome getEJBHome();
}
```

HomeHandle (version 1.1)

Here is the HomeHandle class as defined by the EJB Specification (version 1.1):

```
public class javax.ejb.NoSuchEntityException
       extends javax.ejb.EJBException{
    public NoSuchEntityException();
    public NoSuchEntityException(String message);
    public NoSuchEntityException(Exception exception);
}
```

ObjectNotFoundException

Here is the definition of the ObjectNotFoundException class:

```
public class javax.ejb.ObjectNotFoundException
       extends javax.ejb.FinderException{
    public ObjectNotFoundException();
    public ObjectNotFoundException(String message);
}
```

RemoveException

Here is the RemoveException class:

```
public class javax.ejb.RemoveException
       extends java.lang.Exception{
```

```
        public RemoveException();
        public RemoveException(String message);
}
```

SessionBean
All session Bean classes must implement this **interface**:

```
public interface javax.ejb.SessionBean
        extends javax.ejb.EnterpriseBean{
    public abstract void ejbActivate();
    public abstract void ejbPassivate();
    public abstract void ejbRemove();
    public abstract void setSessionContext(SessionContext ctx);
}
```

SessionContext
This **interface** provides methods for obtaining the SessionBean's EJB object reference. SessionContext provides the Bean instance with an **interface** to the container:

```
public interface javax. ejb.SessionContext
        extends javax.ejb.EJBContext{
    public abstract EJBObject getEJBObject();
}
```

SessionSynchronization
Here is the SessionSynchronization **interface**:

```
public interface javax.ejb.SessionSynchronization{
    public abstract void afterBegin();
    public abstract void afterCompletion(boolean commited);
    public abstract void beforeCompletion();
}
```

Package: javax.ejb.deployment (EJB 1.0 Only)
The javax.ebj.deployment package contains a number of classes used to deploy enterprise Beans in a container. This package and all of its classes no longer exist in EJB 1.1.

AccessControlEntry
Here is the AccessControlEntry class:

```
public class javax.ejb.deployment.AccessControlEntry
      extends java.lang.Object
      implements java.io.Serializable{
   public AccessControlEntry();
   public AccessControlEntry(Method method);
   public AccessControlEntry(Method method,
                    Identity identities);
   public Identity[] getAllowedIdentities();
   public Identity getAllowedIdentities(int index);
   public Method getMethod();
   public void setAllowedIdentities(Identity values[]);
   public void setAllowedIdentities (int index, Identity values);
   public void setMethod(Method value);
}
```

ControlDescriptor

An object of this class is used to specify transactional and runAs attributes associated with the Bean's methods:

```
public class javax.ejb.deployment.ControlDescriptor
        extends java.lang.Object implements java.io.Serializable{
   public final static int CLIENT_IDENTITY;
   public final static int SPECIFIED_IDENTITY;
   public final static int SYSTEM_IDENTITY;
   public final static int TRANSACTION_READ_COMMITTED;
   public final static int TRANSACTION_READ_UNCOMMITTED;
   public final static int TRANSACTION_REPEATABLE_READ;
   public final static int TRANSACTION_SERIALIZABLE;
   public final static int TX_BEAN_MANAGED;
   public final static int TX_MANDATORY;
   public final static int TX_NOT_SUPPORTED;
   public final static int TX_REQUIRED;
   public final static int TX_REQUIRES_NEW;
   public final static int TX_SUPPORTS;
   public ControlDescriptor();
   public ControlDescriptor(method method);
   public int getIsolationLevel();
   public Method getMethod();
   public Identity getRunAsIdentity();
   public int get RunAsMode();
   public int get TransactionAttribute();
   public void setIsolationLevel();
   public void setMethod(Method method);
   public void setRunAsIdentity(Identity value);
   public void setRunAsMode(int value);
   public void setTransactionAttribute(int value);
}
```

DeploymentDescriptor

At deployment time, an object of this class is used to describe the Bean to the container. The `DeploymentDescriptor` class is a base class for the `EntityDescriptor` and the `SessionDescriptor` classes, which are used by `EntityBean` and `SessionBean` types, respectively. An object of the `DeploymentDescriptor` class contains all the `AccessControlEntry` and `ControlDescriptor` objects for the Bean, descriptions of the remote **interface**, the home **interface**, the Bean class names, and the name binding (published object name) of the Bean:

```
public class javax.ejb.deployment.DeploymentDescriptor
        extends java.lang.Object implements java.io.Serializable {
    protected int versionNumber;
    public DeploymentDescriptor();
    public AccessControlEntry[] getAccessControlEntries();
    public AccessControlEntry getAccessControlEntries(int index);
    publicName getBeanHomeName();
    public ControlDescriptor[] getControlDescriptors();
    public ControlDescriptor getControlDescriptors(int index);
    public String getEnterpriseBeanClassName();
    public Properties getEnvironmentProperites();
    public String getHomeInterfaceClassName();
    public boolean getReentrant();
    public String getRemoteInterfaceClassName();
    public boolean isReentrant();
    public void setAccessControlEntries(AccessControlEntry value[]);
    public void setAccessControlEntries(int i, AccessControlEntry v);
    public void setBeanHomeName(Name value);
    public void setControlDescriptors(ControlDescriptor values[]);
    public void setControlDescriptors(int index,
                                ControlDescriptor value);
    public void setEnterpriseBeanClassName(String value);
    public void setEnvironmentProperties(Properties value);
    public void setHomeInterfaceClassName(String value);
    public void setReentrant(boolean value);
    public void setRemoteInterfaceClassName(String value);
}
```

EntityDescriptor

This class extends the `DeploymentDescriptor` class and provides methods specific to entity Beans:

```
public class javax.ejb.deployment.EntityDescriptor
        extends javax.ejb.deployment.DeploymentDescriptor {
    public EntityDescriptor();
```

```
    public Field[] getContainerManagedFields(int index);
    public Field getContainerManagedFields(int, index);
    public String getPrimaryKeyClassName();
    public void setContainerManagedFields(Fields values[]);
    public void setContainerManagedFields(int index, Field value);
    public void setPrimaryKeyClassName(String value);
}
```

SessionDescriptor

This class extends the `DeploymentDescriptor` class and provides methods specific to session Beans:

```
public class javax.ejb.deployment.SessionDescriptor
        extends javax.ejb.deployment.DeploymentDescriptor {
    public final static int STATEFUL_SESSION;
    public final static int STATELESS_SESSION;
    public SessionDescriptor();
    public int getSessionTimeout();
    public int getStateManagementType();
    public void setSessionTimeout(int value);
    public void setStateManagementType(int value);
}
```

APPENDIX

C

Oracle8*i* CORBA
Quick Reference
Guide for Java

n this appendix you will revisit the `Account` server object from the section of Chapter 6 titled "Deploying and Using CORBA Server Objects," so as to, indeed, obtain an illustrated and concise summary of the necessary steps in deploying and using a server object.

These steps are as follows:

- Code an IDL module

- Use the `idl2java` to appropriately generate Java source files from an IDL module

- Implement CORBA server objects in Java

- Compile the Java files and load the generated Java classes into the JServer

- Publish a name for each CORBA server object

- Code and compile the Java client that invokes CORBA server object methods

- Run the client

Code the IDL Module

The purpose of this server object is to obtain the department number and project number for an indicated account number from the `ACCOUNT_LIST` table. You start by coding the following IDL module:

```
/* File Name: account.idl */

module account {
  struct AccountInfo { long departmentno; long projectno; };
  exception NoAccountError { wstring mess; };
  interface Account {
    AccountInfo getAccountInfo( in long accountno )
      raises( NoAccountError );
  };
};
```

`getAccount` is a method that will return an `AccountInfo` *struct* that contains the `departmentno` value and `projectno` for the `ACCOUNT_LIST` record that has the indicated `accountno` value. If no such `ACCOUNT_LIST` record exists, the `NoAccountError` exception will be raised.

Use idl2java to Generate Java Source Files from the IDL File

To compile `account.idl` into Java you merely enter the following:

```
idl2java _no_tie account.idl
```

The `_no_tie` option indicates that the tie mechanism will not be used, so that fewer Java source files will be generated. You can learn about the tie mechanism by reading the section titled "CORBA Tie Mechanism" in Chapter 6. With the `_no_tie` option, `idl2java` will generate 12 Java source files for the module, all contained in the `account` directory:

■ A Java interface, helper, holder, stub, and skeleton file for the `Account` interface

■ A Java source file containing a class definition, as well as Java helper and holder files, for the `AccountInfo` *struct* and for the `NoAccountError` *exception*

■ The `_example_Account` file that contains an incomplete example of a Java implementation of the `Account` server object

Code the Java Implementation of the Server Object

Here, you will find a SQLJ implementation of the server object. In the section of Chapter 6 titled "Implementation of CORBA Server Object Using JDBC," you were presented with a JDBC version of this code:

```
/* Program Name:  AccountImpl.sqlj
**
** Purpose:  Get account information for the given account number.
**
*/
package accountServer;
import account.*;
import java.sql.*;
public class AccountImpl extends _AccountImplBase {
  public AccountInfo getAccountInfo( int accountno )
    throws NoAccountError {
    try {
```

```
      // You must initialize variables to be selected into.
      int departmentno = 0;
      int projectno = 0;

      #sql {
        SELECT departmentno, projectno
          INTO :departmentno, :projectno
            FROM ACCOUNT_LIST
              WHERE accountno = :accountno
      };
      return new AccountInfo( departmentno, projectno );
    }
    catch( SQLException e ) {
      throw new NoAccountError( e.getMessage() );
    }
  }
}
```

Compile Java Files and Load Generated Class Files into the JServer

First, you compile the Java source files:

```
javac account/Account.java\
  account/AccountHolder.java\
  account/AccountHelper.java
javac account/AccountInfo.java\
  account/AccountInfoHolder.java\
  account/AccountInfoHelper.java
javac account/NoAccountError.java\
  account/NoAccountErrorHolder.java\
  account/NoAccountErrorHelper.java
javac account/_EmployeeImplBase.java\
 account/_st_Account.java
sqlj -J-classpath\
 .:$(ORACLE_HOME)/lib/aurora_client.jar:\
 $(ORACLE_HOME)/jdbc/lib/classes111.zip:\
 $(ORACLE_HOME)/sqlj/lib/translator.zip$(ORACLE_HOME)/lib/vbjorb.jar:\
 $(ORACLE_HOME)/lib/vbjapp.jar$(JDK_HOME)/lib/classes.zip -ser2class\
 accountServer/AccountImpl.sqlj
```

Note that the `sqlj` command generates two additional class files, `AccountImpl_SJProfile0` and `AccountImpl_SJProfilekeys`, which must also be loaded into the server. You can then build a Java archive (`.jar`) file that contains all the classes that you want to load into the server. This is preferable to loading each class, one at a time.

```
jar -cf0 accountjar.jar\
    account/Account*.class\
    account/NoAccountError*.class\
    account/_AccountImplBase.class\
    _st_Account.class\
    accountServer/AccountImpl*.class
```

Note that the wildcard (*) is used, assuming no other files in the directory have clashing names. Finally, you load all the classes in the .jar file into the JServer:

```
loadjava -oracleresolver -resolve -user scott/tiger accountjar.jar
```

Publish the CORBA Server Object Name

The final step in preparing the server object is to publish a name for the object that a client program can look up. You accomplish this with the publish command:

```
publish -republish -user scott -password tiger -schema scott -service\
    sess_iiop://localhost:2481:ORCL\
    /test/Account AccountImpl account.AccountHelper
```

The options and arguments indicate the following:

- -republish: Overwrite a published object if it has the same name.

- -user scott: scott is the username of the schema doing the publishing.

- -password tiger: tiger is the password for scott.

- -schema scott: The name of the schema doing the publishing.

- -service sess_iiop://localhost:2481:ORCL: This option specifies the URL that identifies the database whose session namespace is to be opened. The hostname (here, localhost) identifies the computer that hosts the database (localhost returns the hostname of the current computer), 2481 is the listener port for iiop, and ORCL is the SID of the database.

- /test/Account: The name of the published object. The published name of the server object does not have to be the same as the interface name. The

/test publishing context in the namespace is an initially existing publishing context that is open to the public for publishing.

■ AccountImpl: This is the name of the Java class that implements the server object.

■ AccountHelper: This is the name of the helper class for Account.

Code and Compile the Java Client

In order to access a server object by its published name, the client code must do the following:

■ Instantiate and populate a JNDI InitialContext object with the required connect properties.

■ Invoke the lookup() method on the InitialContext object, passing in a URL parameter that specifies the IIOP service name and the name of the server object to be found. The lookup() method then returns an object reference to the desired server object.

■ Invoke the desired server object method on the object reference.

The following client program, AccountUser.java, accomplishes these steps in order to invoke the getAccount() method on an object reference to the Account server object:

```
/* Program Name: AccountUser.java
**
** Purpose:  Use the Account server object to get account
**           information for the account 1056.
**
*/
import account.*;
import accountServer.*;

// Import JNDI property constants.
import oracle.aurora.jndi.sess_iiop.ServiceCtx;

// Import the JNDI Context Interface.
import javax.naming.Context;

/* Import the InitialContext class that implements the
```

```
      Context Interface.
   */
   import javax.naming.InitialContext;

   /* Import the hash table class to hold the initial context
      properties environment.
   */
   import java.util.Hashtable;

   public class AccountUser {

     // main throws instead of catching exceptions.
     public static void main( String[] args ) throws Exception {

       // Instantiate and populate InitialContext object.
       Hashtable env = new Hashtable();
       env.put( Context.URL_PKG_PREFIXES, "oracle.aurora.jndi" );
       env.put( Context.SECURITY_PRINCIPAL, "scott" );
       env.put( Context.SECURITY_CREDENTIALS, "tiger" );
       env.put( Context.SECURITY_AUTHENTICATION,
                ServiceCtx.NON_SSL_LOGIN );
       Context ic = new InitialContext( env );

       // Lookup object name, obtaining object reference.
       Account account = ( Account )
       ic.lookup( "sess_iiop://localhost:2481:ORCL/test/Account" );

       // Invoke getAccountInfo() method.
       AccountInfo ai = account.getAccountInfo( 1056 );

       // Print account information.
       System.out.println( "Department number = " + ai.departmentno +
                           " Project number = " + ai.projectno );
     }
   }
```

Having coded the Java client, you can now compile it with `javac`:

```
javac AccountUser.java
```

Running the Client

You will use the `java` command on the client to run the client class
`AccountUser`. In order to do this, you must set the `classpath` for the `java`

command to include `classes.zip` (the standard Java library archive), classes such as those in `vbjapp.jar` and `vbjorb.jar` that are used by the client ORB, and the Oracle8*i*-supplied `.jar` file `aurora_client.jar`. The following `java` command line will appropriately run the desired Java class:

```
% java -classpath\
    .:$(ORACLE_HOME)/lib/aurora_client.jar:\
   $(ORACLE_HOME)/jdbc/lib/classes111.zip:\
   $(ORACLE_HOME)/sqlj/lib/translator.zip:\
   $(ORACLE_HOME)/lib/vbjorb.jar:\
   $(ORACLE_HOME)/lib/vbjapp.jar:$(JDK_HOME)/lib/classes.zipAccountUser
```

Here, `JDK_HOME` is the installation location of the Java Development Kit (JDK), and `ORACLE_HOME` is the Oracle home directory.

APPENDIX

D

JavaServer Pages Quick Reference Guide

his appendix presents a summary of the syntax for JavaServer Pages (JSP) Specification 1.1 and JSP API. For more information, see the JSP Specifications 1.0 and 1.1 and the PDF syntax cards at http://java.sun.com/products/jsp.

- JavaServer Pages (JSP) syntax reference
- JSP API includes the `javax.servlet.jsp` and `javax.servlet.jsp.tagext` packages

JSP Syntax Reference

This section provides a quick reference on JSP syntax.

The `page` Directive

The page directive defines the attributes of a page. All the attributes are optional:

```
<%@ page page_directive_attr_list %>
page_directive_attr_list ::= { language=" scriptingLanguage"}
{ extends=" className"}
{ import=" importList"}
{ session="true|false" }
{ buffer="none| sizekb" }
{ autoFlush="true| false" }
{ isThreadSafe="true|false" }
{ info=" info_text" }
{ errorPage=" error_url" }
{ content_type="text/html;charset=IANA-Charset-name" }
{ isErrorPage="true|false" }
```

`taglib` Directive

This directive defines a tag library namespace for the page:

```
<%@ taglib uri=" tagLibraryURI" prefix=" tagPrefix" %>
...
<tagPrefix:tagName attributeName="attributeValue" >
  JSP content
</tagPrefix:tagName>
<tagPrefix:tagName attributeName="attributeValue" >
```

The Tag Library Descriptor

The tag library descriptor (TLD) is an XML document that describes a tag library. It includes documentation on the library as a whole and on its individual tags, version information on the JSP container and on the tag library, and information on each of the actions defined in the tag library. The DTD for LTD is defined in http://java.sun.com/j2ee/dtds/web-jsptaglibrary_1_.dtd.

The include Tags

Two include tags exist: the include directive and the jsp:include. The include directive includes a static file specified by a URL. Here is the syntax:

```
<%@ include file=" relativeURLspec" %>
```

The jsp:include tag includes a static or dynamically-referenced file. Here is the syntax:

```
<jsp:include page="relativeURL"flush="true"/>
```

JavaBean Tags

There are three tags to handle JavaBeans from a page:

- jsp:useBean

- jsp:setProperty

- jsp:getProperty

The jsp:useBean Tag

This tag checks for an instance of a bean of the given class and scope. Here is the syntax:

```
<jsp:useBean id="nameOfBean"
    class=" package.className"
    scope="page|request|session|application"
/>
```

Other less commonly-used attributes include type="typeName" and beanName="someBean".

The jsp:setProperty Tag

This tag sets the property of the bean referenced by name:

```
<jsp:setProperty name="anotherBeanName"
    property="*|propertyName"
    value="newValue"
/>
```

The jsp:getProperty Tag

This tag gets the named property and outputs its value. This value gets included in the page as a String:

```
<jsp:getProperty name="anotherBeanName"
    property="propertyName"
/>
```

Comments

JSP allows you to include comments in your source code in addition to comments in Java code. There are two types of comments—JSP and HTML comments—as shown here:

```
<%-- JSP comments --%>
<!-- HTML comments -->
```

Variable and Function Declarations

JSP allows you to declare variables and functions for the page:

```
<%!
  int k = 0;
  int calculateSum (int a, int b) {
     // Perform the calculation
  }
%>
```

Scriptlets

Use scriptlets to embed Java code in JSP programs. For example,

```
<%
    // include here Java code
%>
```

Expressions

JSP allows you to use expressions in JSP programs. Expressions return a value from Java code as a `String` to the page:

```
<br> Hello, <%=username %> <br>
```

The `jsp:plugin` Tag

This tag enables JSP programs to include beans or applets in the client page:

```
<jsp:plugin type="bean|applet"
code=" objectCode"
codebase=" objectCodebase"
{ align=" alignment" }
{ archive=" archiveList" }
{ height=" height" }
```

```
{ hspace=" hspace" }
{ jreversion=" jreversion" }
{ name=" componentName" }
{ vspace=" vspace" }
```

The `jsp:forward` Tag

This tag allows you to forward a client request to another URL. This URL can be an HTML, `.jsp`, or servlet file:

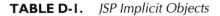

```
<jsp:forward page="relativeURL" />

<jsp:forward page="relativeURL" >
  <jsp:param name="parameterName" value="parameterValue" />
</jsp:forward>
```

Implicit Objects

An implicit object is a server-side object that is defined by the JSP container. The implicit objects are shown in Table D-1.

Implicit Objects	Type	Scope
request	javax.servlet.ServletRequest	Request
response	javax.servlet.ServletResponse	Page
pageContext	javax.servlet.jsp.PageContext	Page
session	javax.servlet.HttpSession	Session
application	javax.servlet.ServletContext	Application
out	javax.servlet.jsp.JspWriter	Page
config	javax.servlet.ServletConfig	Page
exception	java.lang.Throwable	Page
page	java.lang.Object	Page

TABLE D-I.   *JSP Implicit Objects*

JSP API Reference

This section presents a summary of the JSP API. For detail explanations on the various packages, interfaces, and classes, see http://java.sun.com/j2ee/j2sdkee/techdocs/api/javax/servlet/jsp/package-summary.html and http://java.sun.com/j2ee/j2sdkee/techdocs/api/javax/servlet/jsp/tagext/package-summary.html, respectively.

The JSP API consists of two packages:

■ The `javax.servlet.jsp`

■ The `javax.servlet.jsp.tagext`

The `javax.servlet.jsp` Package

The `javax.servlet.jsp` package consists of several interfaces and classes. Listing D-1 presents the JSP interfaces and their methods.

Listing D-1: JSP Interfaces

```
// HttpJspPage interface
public interface HttpJspPage extends JspPage {
    public void _jspService (HttpServletRequest request,
                             HttpServletResponse response)
        throws ServletException, IOException;
} // End of HttpJspPage interface

// JspPage interface
public interface JspPage extends Servlet {
    public void jspDestroy();
    public void jspInit();
} // End JspPage interface
```

Listing D-2 presents the JSP classes and their methods.

Listing D-2: JSP Classes

```
// JspEngineInfo class
public abstract class JspEngineInfo extends Object {
    // Constructor
    public JspEngineInfo();
    // Method
    public abstract String getSpecificationVersion();
} // End JspEngineInfo class
```

```
// JspFactory class
public abstract class JspFactory extends Object {
    // Contructor
    public JspFactory();

    // Methods
    public static getDefaultFactory();
    public static void setDefaultFactory (JspFactory aJspFactory);
    public abstract JspEngineInfo getEngineInfo();

    // PageContext methods
    public abstract PageContext getPageContext
            (Servlet requestServlet,
             ServletRequest request,
             ServletResponse response,
             String errorPageUrl,
             boolean needsSession, int buffer,
             boolean autoFlush);
    public abstract void releasePageContext (PageContext pc);
} // End JspFactory

// JspWriter class
public abstract class JspWriter extends Writer {
    // Constructor
    protected JspWriter (int bufferSize, boolean autoFlush);

    // Methods
    public abstract void clear() throws IOException;
    public abstract void clearBuffer() throws IOException;
    public abstract void close() throws IOException;
    public abstract void flush() throws IOException;
    public int getBufferSize();
    public abstract int getRemaining();
    public boolean isAutoFlush();
    public abstract void newLine()throws IOException;

    // Print methods
    public abstract void print (boolean b) throws IOException;
    public abstract void print (char c) throws IOException;
    public abstract void print (char[] charArray) throws IOException;
    public abstract void print (double d) throws IOException;
    public abstract void print (float f) throws IOException;
    public abstract void print (int i) throws IOException;
    public abstract void print (long l) throws IOException;
    public abstract void print (Object obj) throws IOException;
    public abstract void print (String str) throws IOException;
```

```
   // println methods
   public abstract void println () throws IOException;
   public abstract void println (boolean b) throws IOException;
   public abstract void println (char c) throws IOException;
   public abstract void println (char[] charArray) throws IOException;
   public abstract void println (double d) throws IOException;
   public abstract void println (float f) throws IOException;
   public abstract void println (int i) throws IOException;
   public abstract void println (long l) throws IOException;
   public abstract void println (Object obj) throws IOException;
   public abstract void println (String str) throws IOException;
} // End JspWriter

// PageContext class
public abstract class PageContext extends Object {
   // constructor
   public PageContext();

   // Scope constants
   public static final int APPLICATION_SCOPE;
   public static final int PAGE_SCOPE;
   public static final int REQUEST_SCOPE;
   public static final int SESSION_SCOPE;

   // Attribute methods
   public abstract Object findAttribute(String name);
   public abstract Object getAttribute(String name);
   public abstract Object getAttribute(String name, int scope);
   public abstract Enumeration
       getAttributeNamesInScope(int scope);
   public abstract int getAttributeScope(String name);
   public abstract void removeAttribute(String name);
   public abstract void removeAttribute (String name, int scope);
   public abstract void setAttribute (String name, Object obj);
   public abstract void setAttribute (String name,
                                      Object obj,
                                      int scope);
   // Exception methods
   public abstract Exception getException();
   public abstract void handlePageException(Exception e )
        throws ServletException, IOException;

   // Forward methods
   public abstract void forward(String relativePath)
        throws ServletException, IOException;

   // getOut method
  public abstract  JspWriter getOut( );
```

```
// include method
public abstract void include(String relativePath)
   throws ServletException, IOException;

// Initialize method
public abstract void include
        (Servlet requestServlet,
         ServletRequest request,
         ServletResponse response,
         String errorPageUrl,
         boolean needsSession, int buffer,
         boolean autoFlush)
      throws IOException, IllegalStateException,
             IllegalArgumentException;

// popBody method
public JspWriter popBody();

// pushBody method
public BodyContent pushBody();

// release method
public abstract void release();

// Methods to return Servlet components
public abstract Object getPage();
public abstract ServletRequest getRequest();
public abstract ServletResponse getResponse();
public abstract ServletConfig getServletConfig();
public abstract ServletContext getServletContext(;
public abstract HttpSession getSession();
} // End PageContext
```

The `javax.servlet.jsp.tagext` Package

This package consists of several interfaces and classes. Listing D-3 presents the interfaces and their methods, whereas Listing D-4 presents the classes and their methods.

Listing D-3: Tag Interfaces

```
// BodyTag interface
public interface BodyTag extends Tag {
   // constant
   public static final int EVAL_BODY_TAG;
```

```
    // Methods
    public int doAfterBody() throws JspTagException;
    public int doInitBody() throws JspTagException;
    public void setBodyContent(BodyContent bc);
} // End BodyTag

// Tag interface
public interface Tag {
    // constants
    public static final int SKIP_BODY;
    public static final int EVAL_BODY_INCLUDE;
    public static final int SKIP_PAGE;
    public static final int EVAL_PAGE;

    // Methods
    public int doEndTag() throws JspTagException;
    public int doStartTag() throws JspTagException;
    public Tag getParent();
    public void release();
    public void setPageContext(PageContext pc);
    public void setParent(Tag tag);
} // End Tag interface
```

Listing D-4   Tag Classes

```
// BodyContent class
public abstract class BodyContent extends JspWriter {
    // constructor
    protected BodyContent();

    // Methods
    public void clearBody();
    public void flush() throws IOException;
    public JspWriter getEnclosingWriter();
    public abstract Reader getReader();
    public abstract String getString();
    public abstract void writeOut(Writer out)
        throws IOException;

} // End BodyContent class

// BodyTagSupport class
public class BodyTagSupport extends TagSupport
        implements BodyTag {
    // Constructor
    public BodyTagSupport();
```

```
    // Methods
    public int doAfterBody() throws JspTagException;
    public int doEndTag() throws JspTagException;
    public int doInitBody();
    public BodyContent getBodyContent();
    public JspWriter getPreviousOut();
    public void release();
    public void setBodyContent(BodyContent bc);

} // End BodyTagSupport class

// TagAttributeInfo class
public class TagAttributeInfo extends Object {
    // Constructor
    public TagAttributeInfo(String name,
                            boolean required,
                            boolean rtexprvalue,
                            String type,
                            boolean reqTime);

    // Methods
    public boolean canBeRequestTime();
    public static TagAttributeInfo
    getIdAttribute(TagAttributeInfo[] lists);
    public String getName();
    public String getTypeName();
    public boolean isRequired();
    public String toString();

} // End TagAttributeInfo class

// TagData class
public class TagData extends Object
    implements Cloneable {
    // Constructor
    public TagData(Object[][] attrs);
    public TagData(Hashtable attrs);

    // Methods
    public Object getAttribute(String name);
    public String getAttributeString(String name);
    public String getId();
    public void setAttribute(String name, Object value);

} // End TagData class
```

```java
// TagExtraInfo class
public abstract class TagExtraInfo extends Object {
  // Constructor
  public TagExtraInfo();

  // Methods
  public TagInfo getTagInfo();
  public VariableInfo[] getVariableInfo(TagData td);
  public boolean isValid(TagData td);
  public void setTagInfo(TagInfo ti);

} // End TagExtraInfo class

// TagInfo class
public class TagInfo extends Object

  public static final int BODY_CONTENT_JSP;
  public static final int BODY_CONTENT_TAG_DEPENDENT;
  public static final int BODY_CONTENT_EMPTY;
  // Contructor
  public TagInfo(String name, String class,
                 String content, String infoString,
                 TagLibraryInfo lib, TagExtraInfo tsi,
                 TagAttributeInfo[] attr);

  // Methods
  public TagAttributeInfo[] getAttributes();
  public String getBodyContent();
  public String getInfoString();
  public String getTagClassName();
  public TagExtraInfo getTagExtraInfo();
  public TagLibraryInfo getTagLibraryInfo();
  public String getTagName();
  public VariableInfo[] getVariableInfo(TagData td);
  public boolean isValid(TagData td);
  public String toString();

} // End TagInfo class

// TagLibraryInfo class
public class TagInfo extends Object {
  //constructor
  public TagLibraryInfo(String LibraryPrefix,
                        String libraryURI);
```

```
  // Methods
  public String getInfoString();
  public String getPrefixString();
  public String getReliableURN();
  public String getRequiredVersion();
  public String getShortName();
  public TagInfo getTag(String tagName);
  public TagInfo[] getTags();
  public String getURI();

} // End TagLibraryInfo class

// TagSupport class
public class TagSupport extends Object
  implements Tag, Serializable {
  // Constructor
  public TagSupport();

  // Methods
  public int doEndTag() throws JspTagException;
  public int doStartTag() throws JspTagException;
  public String getTagId();
  public void setTagId(String id);
  public Tag getParent();
  public void setParent(Tag t);
  public void release();
  public void setPageContext(PageContext pc);
  public Object getValue(String name);
  public Enumeration getValue();
  public void removeValue(String name);
  public void setValue(String name, Object value);

} // End TagSupport class

// VariableInfo class
public class VariableInfo extends Object {
  // Constructor
  public VariableInfo(String varName, String className
                      boolean declare, int scope);

  // Methods and Constants
  public static final int NESTED;
  public static final int AT_BEGIN;
  public static final int AT_END;
  public String getVarName();
```

```
public String getClassName();
public boolean getDeclare();
public int getScope();

} // End TagSupport class
```

To learn more about JSP, see Chapters 2, 10–12, http://java.sun.com/products/jsp, and the Bibliography at the end of this book.

APPENDIX
E

Web Server Installation and Configuration for Oracle JSP

his appendix describes how to install and configure the following Web servers and servlet engines to run Oracle JSP:

- Tomcat (Servlet 2.2 API)

- Java Web Server (Servlet 2.1 API)

- Apache and JServ (Servlet 2.0 API)

Oracle Internet Application Server (iAS) release 1.0 uses the Apache/JServ environment. The Oracle JSP engine is set up as part of the iAS installation. Oracle release 8.1.7 also has the capability to run servlets and JSPs within the database. The Oracle JSP engine is installed as part of the database install, in this case. Oracle 8.1.7 additionally includes the Oracle HTTP Server, which runs outside the database and is powered by Apache/JServ and the Oracle JSP engine. You can also edit and debug JSP programs on Oracle JDeveloper (see Appendix F).

Installing Oracle JSP on Tomcat

Tomcat is the open source Servlet 2.2 API and JSP 1.1 reference implementation that has been developed cooperatively by Apache Software Foundation, Sun Microsystems, and other industry partners. Tomcat can be easily configured to run Oracle JSP. This section outlines the steps to install and configure Tomcat and Oracle JSP.

Installation Steps

It is possible to run Tomcat with the Apache Web server, or just standalone as a lightweight Web server. Here, you will learn the steps to install and run Tomcat standalone. Refer to the Tomcat documentation to learn how to set up Tomcat with Apache in the alternative configuration.

The following steps are involved in running JSP programs using Oracle JSP and Tomcat:

- Install the JDK

- Install Tomcat

- Install Oracle JSP

- Install Oracle database with JDBC and SQLJ

- Install Oracle XML utilities (optional)

These steps are further described here.

Installing the JDK

Download and install JDK 1.1 or higher from http://java.sun.com. JDK 1.2 (Java 2 is recommended, as it includes JDBC 2.0 connection pooling and other new useful libraries). Assume that it is installed in the ${JDK_HOME} directory on your system. Then, augment the CLASSPATH environment variable to include the `javac` compiler—it will be required for compilation of Java source code generated for JSP files. This step depends on the version of JDK you installed:

- For JDK 1.2, include ${JDK_HOME}/lib/tools.jar in the CLASSPATH.

- For JDK 1.1.*, include ${JDK_HOME}/lib/classes.zip in the CLASSPATH.

For NT, use the appropriate file separator character (\\) and path separator (;) in the directory paths.

Installing Tomcat

Download and install the latest release of Tomcat for your platform from the Web site http://jakarta.apache.org. Set the ${TOMCAT_HOME} environment variable to point to the root directory of the install. This variable is used by the startup and shutdown scripts in Tomcat (its default value is the current or parent directory relative to where the scripts are invoked).

If you wish to use Tomcat with Apache and not as a standalone Web server, refer to the instructions in the file "Tomcat+Apache-HOWTO" in the directory ${TOMCAT_HOME}/docs.

Installing Oracle JSP

Download the latest release (1.1 or higher) of Oracle JSP from Oracle Technology Network (http://technet.oracle.com/tech/servlets). Set the environment variable ${OJSP_HOME} appropriately. Oracle JSP 1.1 libraries are also available as part of the Oracle 8.1.7 installation.

Installing Oracle with JDBC and SQLJ

If your servlets and JSPs communicate with the database, you will also need access to a database instance. Evaluation copies of Oracle 8*i* for NT and Linux are downloadable from the Oracle Technology Network site (http://technet.oracle.com/). Follow the steps outlined there to set up the database. Set the environment variable ${ORACLE_HOME} to point to the root of this installation. The JDBC and SQLJ libraries are available as part of the Oracle installation. You can also download them separately from the Oracle Technology Network site (http://technet.oracle.com/tech/java/sqlj_jdbc).

Installing Oracle XML Utilities

If you are using XML in your JSPs, you must download and install the Oracle XML libraries. These libraries include the Oracle XML parser (version 2) and the Oracle XML-SQL utility (XSU). They are included in the Oracle 8.1.7 installation, and can also be downloaded separately from the Oracle Technology Network site (http://technet.oracle.com/tech/xml) as part of the Oracle XML Developer's Kit (XDK). Set the environment variable ${XML_HOME} appropriately.

Configuration Steps

Tomcat has its own JSP engine, but you can easily configure Tomcat to run Oracle JSP. You can set the Oracle JSP parameters according to the needs of your environment. You might also want to modify the default Tomcat configuration (such as change the default listener port from 8080 to some other port). There are two types of files on Tomcat that you can use to configure it: `server.xml` and `web.xml`.

This section covers these configuration steps. The following steps are involved:

- Configuring the Tomcat Server using `server.xml`
- Configuring Tomcat with Oracle JSP using `web.xml`

Configuring Tomcat Server

The behavior of the Tomcat engine can be customized through an XML file: `${TOMCAT_HOME}/conf/server.xml`. For example, to change the default port number from 8080 to 8085, you need to modify this file as follows (the line is shown in bold font):

```
<Connector className="org.apache.tomcat.service.SimpleTcpConnector">
  <Parameter name="handler"
    value="org.apache.tomcat.service.http.HttpConnectionHandler"/>
    <Parameter name="port" value="8085" />
</Connector>
```

Using Oracle JSP With Tomcat

Tomcat comes with its own JSP engine (called Jasper). However, the Tomcat server can be reconfigured to use Oracle JSP, which comes with value-added database access beans and tag libraries, and other enhancements. Instructing Tomcat to use the Oracle JSP engine consists of three steps:

- Adding the `oracle.jsp.JspServlet` to the set of servlets. This servlet is the entry point for the Oracle JSP engine.

- Mapping the JSP extensions in a URL to this servlet. This is referred to as *extension mapping.*

- Adding the required libraries to the CLASSPATH.

For Tomcat, the first two steps are done through the `web.xml` file. It contains the names of the servlets and their URL mappings, along with session configuration information such as the timeout, tag library mappings, and so on. There is a global `web.xml` file in the `${TOMCAT_HOME}/conf` directory. To use different settings for a Web application that you install, update the `web.xml` file in the `WEB-INF` directory under the particular application root. For example, you can modify the file `${TOMCAT_HOME}/webapps/examples/WEB-INF/web.xml` to run Oracle JSP on Tomcat.

Adding oracle.jsp.JspServlet   Add the following entries for the Oracle JSP servlet under the `<web-app>` section in the `web.xml` file:

```
<servlet>
  <servlet-name>
    ojsp
  </servlet-name>
  <servlet-class>
    oracle.jsp.JspServlet
  </servlet-class>
        <init-param>
            <param-name>
                external_resource
            </param-name>
            <param-value>
                true
            </param-value>
            <param-name>
                unsafe_reload
            </param-name>
            <param-value>
                true
            </param-value>
        </init-param>
</servlet>
```

This declaration adds the servlet named `oracle.jsp.JspServlet` to the set of servlets in this application. It is given the short name `ojsp`, which can be used as an alias (see the next step). Here, two initialization parameters—

external_resource and unsafe_reload—are defined for the Oracle JSP
servlet through the <init-param> element. The parameter name and value are
specified through the <param-name> and <param-value> elements that are
enclosed in the <init-param> block. For a description of the Oracle JSP
configuration parameters and their values, refer to the "Oracle JSP
configuration Parameters" section later in this appendix.

Mapping the JSP Extensions   You must map the JSP servlet to URLs that
reference JSP files. To do this, map the oracle.jsp.JspServlet to the four
different URL patterns, namely *.jsp, *.JSP, *.sqljsp, and *.SQLJSP,
indicating that this servlet is to be invoked by the Web server for all request URLs
that end with a .jsp, .JSP, .sqljsp, or .SQLJSP extension. This can be done by
adding the following lines to the servlet mapping section in the web.xml file:

```
<servlet-mapping>
    <servlet-name>
        ojsp
</servlet-name>
    <url-pattern>
        *.jsp
    </url-pattern>
</servlet-mapping>
 <servlet-mapping>
    <servlet-name>
        ojsp
    </servlet-name>
    <url-pattern>
        *.JSP
    </url-pattern>
    </servlet-mapping>
    <servlet-mapping>
    <servlet-name>
        ojsp
    </servlet-name>
    <url-pattern>
        *.sqljsp
    </url-pattern>
    </servlet-mapping>
 <servlet-mapping>
    <servlet-name>
        ojsp
    </servlet-name>
    <url-pattern>
        *.SQLJSP
    </url-pattern>
 </servlet-mapping>
```

This mapping uses the short name `ojsp` for the `oracle.jsp.JspServlet` class (you set up this alias in Step 2a) and specifies that it is to be invoked for the four file suffixes.

Adding the Libraries   There are three different types of libraries to be considered:

- Oracle JSP

- JDBC and SQLJ

- XML

The steps for adding these libraries to the Tomcat environment are outlined here.

- **Add Oracle JSP libraries**   For UNIX-based systems, copy (or symbolically link) the Oracle JSP libraries `${OJSP_HOME}/lib/ojsp.jar` and `${OJSP_HOME}/lib/ojsputil.jar` to the `${TOMCAT_HOME}/lib` directory. The jar files in this directory are automatically included in the CLASSPATH of the Tomcat server. For Windows-based systems, edit the `tomcat.bat` file in the `${TOMCAT_HOME}\bin` directory to include these two jar files in the CLASSPATH environment variable.

Alternatively, you could add these libraries in the CLASSPATH before you start up the Tomcat server.

- **Add Oracle JDBC and SQLJ libraries**   If you are doing database operations in your servlets and JSPs, you will also need to add the JDBC and SQLJ libraries to the CLASSPATH. Typically, they are placed in the `${TOMCAT_HOME}/lib` directory as in Step 3a. You can either copy these libraries directly or point to them through a symbolic link to the Oracle installation. The JDBC libraries are located at `${ORACLE_HOME}/lib/classes111.zip` (for JDK 1.1) and `${ORACLE_HOME}/lib/classes12.zip` (for JDK 1.2). The SQLJ translator libraries are located at `${ORACLE_HOME}/lib/translator.zip`. You will also need to add the appropriate SQLJ runtime classes in one of the following libraries:

  - `runtime12.zip` (for use with JDK 1.2 and Oracle JDBC 8.1.7)

  - `runtime12ee.zip` (for JDK 1.2.* Enterprise Edition with Oracle JDBC 8.1.7)

  - `runtime11.zip` (for JDK 1.1.* with Oracle JDBC 8.1.7)

  - `runtime.zip` (generic: for JDK 1.2 or 1.1 with any Oracle JDBC version)

The JDK 1.2 Enterprise Edition (ee) version of the SQLJ libraries supports JDBC 2.0 *datasources* in compliance with the SQLJ ISO specification.

- **Add Oracle XML libraries**   If you are using XML in your JSPs, add the ORACLE XML libraries `${XML_HOME}/lib/xmlparserv2.jar` and `${XML_HOME}/lib/oraclexmlsql.jar` to `${TOMCAT_HOME}/lib` following the same procedure as in Step 3a and Step 3b. Alternatively, you may add them to the CLASSPATH before you start up the Tomcat server.

Starting the Tomcat Server

Once the setup steps are complete, go to the `${TOMCAT_HOME}/bin` directory and start up the Tomcat server. On a UNIX system, you use the `startup.sh` script to start the server, and the `shutdown.sh` script to stop it. On Windows systems, you use the batch files `startup.bat` and `shutdown.bat` to start and stop the server. After the server starts up, you can get to the welcome page by typing in the appropriate URL in your browser, such as http://localhost:8085/.

Running JSPs on Tomcat

Tomcat comes with several JSP examples. These examples are linked off the Tomcat welcome page, and it is a good idea to run them before trying your own JSPs. Here, you will see how to run the `Hello.jsp` program from Chapter 10, and the Order Online application that you wrote in Chapter 11 on Tomcat.

Running `Hello.jsp`

Place the `Hello.jsp` file that you wrote in Chapter 10 in the following directory: `${TOMCAT_HOME}/webapps/examples/jsp/chapter10/Hello.jsp`. Then, you can run the JSP simply by pointing your browser to the URL http://localhost:8085/examples/jsp/chapter10/Hello.jsp.

You can also set up your own Web application on Tomcat, and install the `Hello.jsp` file there. Steps to do this are in the installation steps for the Order Online application (discussed next).

Running the Order Online Application

You developed the Order Online application in Chapter 11. This application consists of the following files:

- JSP pages `EnterOrder.jsp`, `InsertOrder.jsp`, `QueryOrder.jsp`
- Beans `CartBean.java`, `DBInsertBean.sqlj`, and `DBQueryBean.sqlj`, which are all in the Java package `mybeans`

There are two ways you can deploy this application on Tomcat:

- As part of the existing examples application
- As a new OrderOnline application

In the first case, you can simply place the three JSP files in the directory `${TOMCAT_HOME}/webapps/examples/jsp/chapter11/`, and compile the JavaBean classes and place them under `${TOMCAT_HOME}/webapps/examples/WEB-INF/classes`. To compile the beans, you can use the following commands on a UNIX system and JDK 1.2 environment:

```
${JDK_HOME}/bin/javac -g \
     -d ${TOMCAT_HOME}/webapps/examples/WEB-INF/classes \
     -classpath ${TOMCAT_HOME}/lib/servlet.jar \
     CartBean.java

${ORACLE_HOME}/bin/sqlj -g \
     -d ${TOMCAT_HOME}/webapps/examples/WEB-INF/classes \
     -classpath ${ORACLE_HOME}/jdbc/lib/classes12.zip:\
${ORACLE_HOME}/sqlj/lib/translator.zip:\
${ORACLE_HOME}/sqlj/lib/runtime.zip:${TOMCAT_HOME}/lib/servlet.jar \
     DBInsertBean.sqlj DBQueryBean.sqlj
```

Use corresponding commands on a Windows NT system. In these commands, the compiled bean classes are placed in the directory `${TOMCAT_HOME}/webapps/examples/WEB-INF/classes` through the `-d` option in `javac`. This directory is included in the CLASSPATH for the Tomcat Web server for the examples application.

Once you have completed this setup, you can invoke the first screen of the application by typing in the appropriate URL in your browser, such as the following: http://localhost:8085/examples/jsp/chapter11/EnterOrder.jsp.

In the second case, where you want to create a separate Web application named OrderOnline, you will need to insert a context entry in the `server.xml` file (discussed earlier in the Tomcat configuration steps). This entry appears here:

```
<Context path="/OrderOnline"
          docbase="webapps/OrderOnline"
          reloadable="true" >
</Context>
```

In this declaration, the URL path to the application is specified as `/OrderOnline`, and the application root as the directory `${TOMCAT_HOME}/webapps/OrderOnline`. You can place the three JSP files in the jsp subdirectory. The `reloadable` parameter specifies that the beans and other classes should be automatically reloaded (without restarting the Tomcat server) in order to speed up the development time. Compiled JavaBean classes would typically be placed in the directory `${TOMCAT_HOME}/webapps/OrderOnline/WEB-INF/classes`. The `WEB-INF` directory is not accessible through the browser URL, and this directory is included by default in the CLASSPATH of the Tomcat server. Other supporting classes (if any) should be placed under the directory `${TOMCAT_HOME}/webapps/OrderOnline/WEB-INF/lib` directory. Any jar and zip files in this directory are automatically added to the CLASSPATH of the server.

Once you have completed this setup, you can invoke the first screen of the Order Online application through the appropriate URL, such as,

`http://localhost:8085/OrderOnline/jsp/EnterOrder.jsp`

Installing and Configuring the Java Web Server

The Java Web Server (JWS) is part of the Java Server Web Development Kit (JSWDK), which serves as the reference implementation for the Servlet 2.1 API and the JSP 1.0 specification. This implementation has mostly been superseded by the Tomcat implementation. It is considered here for the sake of completeness, and because there are existing users on this environment.

Installation Steps

1. **Install JDK**   Refer to step 1 in the Tomcat installation steps given earlier. Remember to include the `javac` compiler libraries in your CLASSPATH, as noted there.

2. **Install JSWDK**   Download and install the JSWDK from the Web site http://java.sun.com/products/servlet/index.html. Suppose that it is installed under the `${JWS_HOME}` directory.

3. **Install Oracle JSP**   Refer to step 3 in the Tomcat installation steps given earlier.

4. **Install Oracle with JDBC and SQLJ**   Refer to step 4 in the Tomcat installation steps given earlier.

5. **Install Oracle XML**   Refer to step 5 in the Tomcat installation steps given earlier.

Configuration Steps

This section outlines the steps involved in running Oracle JSP on the Java Web Server (JWS).

Using Oracle JSP With JWS

Like Tomcat, JWS comes with its own JSP engine. However, it can be easily configured to run Oracle JSP instead. This procedure in similar to the one for Tomcat, and involves three steps:

- Adding the Oracle JSP servlet to JWS

- Mapping the JSP extensions

- Adding the required libraries to the JWS environment

These steps are further described here.

Add Oracle JSP Servlet   Modify the `servlets.properties` file in the `WEB-INF` directory of each servlet context to specify `oracle.jsp.JspServlet` as the servlet that handles JSP processing. Also, comment out the previously defined mapping for the JSP reference implementation. For example, you can modify the file `${JWS_HOME}/examples/WEB-INF/servlets.properties` as follows:

```
#remove: jsp.code=com.sun.jsp.runtime.JspServlet
#remove: jsp.initparams=keepgenerated=true
jsp.code=oracle.jsp.JspServlet
jsp.initparams=external_resource=true,unsafe_reload=true
```

You can control the behavior of the Oracle JSP engine through the `jsp.initparams` line. Here, two initialization parameters—`external_resource` and `unsafe_reload`—are specified. You can find a description of these and other configuration parameters for Oracle JSP at the end of this appendix.

Mapping the JSP Extension   Edit the `mappings.properties` file in the `WEB-INF` directory of each servlet context to map the JSP extensions as follows:

```
# Map the JSP extensions
.jsp=jsp
.JSP=jsp
.sqljsp=jsp
.SQLJSP=jsp
```

Adding the Libraries   You need to add Oracle JSP libraries, Oracle JDBC and SQLJ libraries, and optionally the Oracle XML libraries as follows:

- **Add Oracle JSP libraries**   Place the Oracle JSP libraries, `${OJSP_HOME}/lib/ojsp.jar` and `${OJSP_HOME}/lib/ojsputil.jar` in the `${JWS_HOME}/lib` directory. You must also modify the `startserver` script in the `${JWS_HOME}` root directory to add the libraries `ojsp.jar` and `ojsputil.jar` to the `jspJars` environment variable:

```
set jspJars=./lib/ojsp.jar:/lib/ojsputil.jar
```

■ **Add Oracle JDBC and SQLJ libraries**   Place the JDBC and SQLJ libraries (the set of required libraries is defined in the Tomcat configuration steps given earlier) in the `${JWS_HOME}/lib` directory. Additionally, you must modify the `startserver` script in the `${JWS_HOME}` root directory to add these libraries to the `miscJars` environment variable:

```
miscJars=./lib/translator.zip;./lib/runtime.zip:./lib/classes12.zip
```

■ **Add Oracle XML libraries**   Copy the Oracle XML libraries you downloaded (`${XML_HOME}/xmlparserv2.jar` and `${XML_HOME}/lib/oraclexmlsql.jar`) into the `${JWS_HOME}/lib` directory. You must also modify the `startserver` script in the `${JWS_HOME}` root directory to add these libraries to the `miscJars` environment variable, as in the previous step (for JDBC and SQLJ libraries).

Running JSPs on JWS

The JWS has several JSP examples that you can run through your browser. These examples are linked off the JWS welcome page, and it is a good idea to run them before you try your own JSPs. Once you have checked that the Java Web server is working properly, here is what you need to do to run `Hello.jsp` and the Order Online application that you wrote on JWS.

Running `Hello.jsp`

Place the `Hello.jsp` file that you wrote in Chapter 10 in the directory `${JWS_HOME}/examples/jsp/chapter10/Hello.jsp`. You can now run the JSP simply by pointing your browser to the appropriate URL, such as http://localhost:8080/examples/jsp/chapter10/Hello.jsp.

Running the Order Online Application

You can place three JSP files in the directory `${JWS_HOME}/webapps/examples/jsp/chapter11/`. Compiled JavaBean classes would typically be placed in the directory `${JWS_HOME}/examples/jsp/beans/classes`. This directory is included in the CLASSPATH for JWS. Now, you can invoke the first screen of this application through an appropriate URL, such as http://localhost:8080/examples/jsp/chapter11/EnterOrder.jsp.

Alternatively, you can set up the Order Online application as a separate Web application. Refer to JSWDK documentation on how to set up your own Web application.

Installing and Configuring Apache and JServ

Apache is a popular Web server that is open source and freely available. JServ is a servlet engine that implements the Servlet 2.0 API and works with the Apache Web server through the `mod_jserv` module. Apache and JServ are used in the Oracle Internet Application Server (iAS) release 1.0, which also includes the Oracle JSP engine for executing JavaServer Pages. In this section, you will learn how to set up Apache and JServ, assuming you are downloading the individual software modules yourself. If you instead use the Oracle Internet Application Server, installation and configuration of the Apache Web server, JServ servlet engine, and Oracle JSP are done as part of the iAS install. The latter approach is recommended.

Installation Steps

The steps to install Apache, JServ, and Oracle JSP individually are given here:

1. **Install JDK**   Refer to step 1 in the Tomcat installation steps given earlier.

2. **Install Apache**   Go to the Apache site (http://www.apache.org/dist) and download the latest release of the Apache Web server for your platform. Run the installation program. Assume that it is installed in the `${APACHE_HOME}` directory. Then, edit the configuration file `${APACHE_HOME}/conf/httpd.conf` and uncomment the line

   `#ServerName localhost`

   This modification will allow your server to be referenced through the URL http://localhost in your Web browser.

3. **Install JServ and mod_jserv**   Download and install the JServ servlet runner and the module `mod_jserv` from the Apache Web site http://java.apache.org/jserv/dist. Set the environment variable `${JSERV_HOME}` appropriately.

4. **Install Oracle JSP**   Refer to step 4 in the Tomcat installation steps given earlier.

5. **Install Oracle with JDBC and SQLJ**   Refer to step 5 in the Tomcat installation steps.

6. **Install Servlet 2.0 and 2.2 libraries**   The JServ servlet runner implements the Servlet 2.0 API, which is packaged as the `jsdk.jar` library that is downloadable as part of JSDK 2.0 (from http://www.javasoft.com/ products/servlet/index.html). Although JServ only uses Servlet 2.0, the

Oracle JSP 1.1 engine also needs the Servlet 2.2 libraries for its internal operation. Download the `servlet.jar` file from the Web site http://www.javasoft.com/servlet/index.html, and then follow the configuration steps here.

Configuration Steps

1. **Configure JServ with Apache**   Follow the instructions in the JServ documentation to have the JServ servlet engine work with the Apache Web server.

2. **Map JSP extensions to the Oracle JSP servlet**   Update either the file `${JSERV_HOME}/conf/jserv.conf` or the file `${JSERV_HOME}/conf/mod_jserv.conf` (depending on which one is included in the file `${APACHE_HOME}/conf/httpd.conf`) to add `ApJServAction` commands to perform the JSP extension mappings as follows:

```
# JSP extension mappings
ApJServAction .jsp /servlets/oracle.jsp.JspServlet
ApJServAction .JSP /servlets/oracle.jsp.JspServlet
ApJServAction .sqljsp /servlets/oracle.jsp.JspServlet
ApJServAction .SQLJSP /servlets/oracle.jsp.JspServlet
```

3. **Add the libraries**   You will need to add appropriate `wrapper.classpath` commands to the `${JSERV_HOME}/conf/jserv.properties` file. Files for your JDK environment should also already be in the CLASSPATH. The following example (which happens to use UNIX directory paths) includes files for Servlet 2.0 and 2.2, Oracle JSP, JDBC, SQLJ, and XML libraries:

```
# servlet 2.0 APIs (required by Apache/JServ, from Sun JSDK 2.0):
wrapper.classpath=${JSDK_HOME}/lib/jsdk.jar
# servlet 2.2 APIs (included as part of Oracle JSP download):
wrapper.classpath=${OJSP_HOME}/lib/servlet.jar
# OracleJSP packages:
wrapper.classpath=${OJSP_HOME}/lib/ojsp.jar
wrapper.classpath=${OJSP_HOME}/lib/ojsputil.jar
# JDBC 2.0 (JDK 1.2) libraries
wrapper.classpath=${ORACLE_HOME}/lib/classes12.zip
# SQLJ translator and runtime classes
wrapper.classpath=${ORACLE_HOME}/lib/translator.zip
wrapper.classpath=${ORACLE_HOME}/lib/runtime12.zip
# Oracle XML libraries (used for XML/XSL)
wrapper.classpath=${XML_HOME}/lib/xmlparserv2.jar
wrapper.classpath=${XML_HOME}lib/oraclexmlsql.jar
```

Running JSPs on Apache/JServ

Apache/JServ is a Servlet 2.0 environment, so it does not have a formal notion of Web applications (unlike Tomcat, which is a Servlet 2.2 implementation). However, JServ does have a concept of servlet *zones*. A servlet zone is conceptually similar to a servlet context. You can set up Oracle JSP pages to run in a separate zone. Refer to the JServ documentation for information on how to set up a servlet zone.

Running `Hello.jsp`

In order to run the Hello.jsp program, you can place the JSP file under the directory ${APACHE_HOME}/htdocs/examples/jsp/. After that, you can invoke the JSP by visiting the appropriate URL through your browser, such as http://localhost:8080/examples/jsp/Hello.jsp.

Running the Order Online Application

Place the three JSP files—`EnterOrder.jsp`, `InsertOrder,jsp`, and `QueryOrder.jsp`—under the directory `${APACHE_HOME}/htdocs/examples/jsp/OrderOnline`. In this application, you have the following `useBean` command in the `EnterOrder.jsp` file:

```
<jsp:useBean id="cartBean"
             class="mybeans.CartBean"
             scope="session" />
```

You can add the following `wrapper.classpath` entry to the `jserv.properties` file:

```
wrapper.classpath=${APACHE_HOME}/beans/
```

Then, compile and place the bean class in the directory `${APACHE_HOME}/beans/mybeans/`.

You can now invoke the first page `EnterOrder.jsp` of this application through the appropriate URL, such as http://localhost:8080/examples/jsp/OrderOnline/EnterOrder.jsp.

Oracle JSP Configuration Parameters

This section describes the configuration parameters for Oracle JSP release 1.1.0.0.0. The Oracle JSP engine is invoked as a servlet—`oracle.jsp.JspServlet`—which has several configuration parameters to control its behavior. These parameters are set as servlet initialization parameters for `oracle.jsp.JspServlet`, following the rules for your Web server and servlet engine (see the Web server configuration steps described earlier). The list of Oracle JSP parameters and a brief description appear below. Some of the parameters are relevant only in specific environments, such as on Apache/JServ. These parameters are noted as such.

alias_translation

This parameter is Apache/JServ-specific. It is a `boolean`-valued parameter that allows OracleJSP to work around limitations in the way Apache/JServ handles directory aliasing. For example, the following directory aliasing command may be specified in the file `${APACHE_HOME}/conf/httpd.conf`:

```
alias /images/ "/home/apache/images/"
```

For Oracle JSP to correctly handle references to such aliased paths, you must set the value of the `alias_translation` configuration parameter to `true`. The default value of this parameter is `false`.

bypass_source

This `boolean`-valued parameter controls whether Oracle JSP will check for a `.jsp` source file. This option is useful when the developer wants to deploy only the compiled JSP classes and not the JSP source. If you set this parameter to `true`, the Oracle JSP engine will load and execute the compiled JSP class even if the JSP source file is absent. If the source is available, its timestamp will still be checked for determining whether retranslation is necessary (assuming the parameter `developer_mode`, which is described below, is set to `true`). The default value of this parameter is `false`.

classpath

This parameter is used to add entries to the default CLASSPATH of Oracle JSP. The Oracle JSP engine loads classes from its own CLASSPATH (including entries from this CLASSPATH parameter), the system CLASSPATH, the Web server CLASSPATH, the page repository, and other predefined locations relative to JSP application root directories. Note that classes specified in this parameter are loaded by the JSP class loader, and not by the system (JDK) class loader. The implication of adding an entry is twofold:

- These classes (loaded by the JSP class loader) cannot refer to classes loaded by the system or other class loaders, and vice versa.

- Automatic class reloading is performed by Oracle JSP upon modification of a jar file in this CLASSPATH.

The default value for this parameter is `null`.

developer_mode

This `boolean`-valued parameter controls whether the timestamp of JSP source files should be compared against compiled JSP class files when a JSP page is invoked. If this flag is `false`, Oracle JSP will not do the timestamp checking, speeding up JSP request processing. Therefore, set this flag to `false` when your JSP pages are not changing—that is, in a deployment environment. In this case, Oracle JSP will only check timestamps for the first request for the page, and it will simply re-execute the compiled JSP class for subsequent invocations. The default value of this parameter is `true`.

emit_debuginfo

This `boolean`-valued parameter can be used to instruct the Oracle JSP translator to generate a line map to the JSP source file for debugging purposes. This parameter is enabled for source-level JSP debugging in JDeveloper. The default value of this parameter is `false`.

external_resource

This `boolean`-valued parameter controls the code generated by the Oracle JSP translator. If this flag is set to `true`, the static content in the JSP page (that is, the HTML or XML code) is placed in a Java resource file instead of in the `_jspService()` method of the generated JSP class. The name of this file is based on the name of the JSP file, but has the `.res` extension. The resource file is placed in the same directory as class files. Using such an external resource file can speed the translation and execution of the JSP, especially if there is a lot of static code. It may also help prevent the `_jspService()` method from exceeding the 64K size limit in Java. The default value of this parameter is `false`.

javaccmd

This parameter specifies a command for compiling the Java class generated for a JSP. It is useful if you want to use a compiler other than the standard `javac` in the JDK (which is the default compiler used by Oracle JSP), or to specify command-line options for `javac`, such as

javac -verbose -O

Using this parameter causes Oracle JSP to call the alternate compiler through a separate process, instead of invoking the default compiler within the same Java Virtual Machine where Oracle JSP is executing. You can give the fully qualified path or the unqualified path for the compiler executable; in the latter case, Oracle JSP looks for the executable through the system path. This parameter is not set by default.

page_repository_root

This parameter specifies the fully qualified root directory for JSP pages. The default root directory is the documentation root directory for the Apache Web server/JServ environment, and in Servlet 2.1 and 2.2 environments it is the servlet context root of the application that the JSP page belongs to. You can use this parameter to specify a different root directory. JSP pages must reside in this root directory or in some subdirectory. This parameter is not set by default.

session_sharing

This parameter is Apache/JServ-specific. This parameter comes into play when using the `globals.jsa` file as an application marker in Servlet 2.0 environments such as Apache/JServ (refer to the Oracle JSP documentation for details on the use of `globals.jsa`). If this parameter is set to `true`, which is the default, then for each JSP invocation the Oracle JSP engine creates a wrapper object over the servlet `session` object provided by the servlet engine. In this case, the JSP session data (such as a value attached to the JSP session through the `session.putValue()` call) will be propagated to the underlying servlet session. This allows session data to be shared between JSPs and servlets in the same application. On the other hand, if the `session_sharing` parameter is `false`, JSP session data is not propagated to the servlet session, and cannot be accessed by the servlets. This parameter has no effect if `globals.jsa` is not being used for the JSP application.

sqljcmd

This parameter specifies a command for invoking the SQLJ translator. It is useful if you want to use a different SQLJ translator than the default one, or if you want to specify SQLJ command-line options, such as for SQL semantics checking:

```
sqljcmd= sqlj -ser2class -user scott -password tiger
```

Using this parameter also provides better error reporting in some (JDK 1.1) environments. Oracle JSP invokes the SQLJ translator in a separate process (and thus, in a separate Java Virtual Machine), instead of calling it within the same Java Virtual Machine. You can give either the fully qualified path for the SQLJ executable, or let the executable be located through the system path. This parameter is not set by default.

translate_params

This `boolean`-valued parameter controls the encoding of multibyte (NLS) parameters in the HTTP `request` object. Most servlet engines do not consider NLS encodings of request parameters, so the JSP programmer must code the translation to the correct encoding. If you set this parameter to `true`, this task is automatically handled by the Oracle JSP engine. That is, it translates the HTTP request parameters and bean property settings according to the encoding of the HTTP `request` object.

The default value of this parameter is `false`, in which case Oracle JSP returns the HTTP request parameters just as they are obtained from the underlying servlet engine (without any additional NLS processing).

`unsafe_reload`

This parameter controls the behavior of the Oracle JSP engine when a JSP page is dynamically modified as the JSP application is running. In this case, the default behavior of the Oracle JSP engine is to restart the application and the servlet sessions, which invalidates existing sessions. This behavior may not always be desirable. If you set this parameter to `true`, Oracle JSP will not restart the application after dynamic retranslations of JSP pages. This prevents existing sessions from becoming invalid. Note, however, that this behavior is unsafe in that incompatible changes made to a JSP class may cause class cast exceptions and other execution errors. Therefore, this parameter is intended in development mode only, and *not* recommended for deployment environments. The default value of this parameter is `false`.

For more information on Oracle JSP configuration parameters, refer to the *OracleJSP Developer's Guide and Reference, Release 8.1.7*, Oracle Corporation.

APPENDIX
F

Oracle8*i* EJB and
CORBA Tools and JSP
Support in JDeveloper

his appendix consists of two parts: Oracle8*i* tools for EJB and CORBA and JSP support in JDeveloper. The tools for EJB and CORBA are placed in the same part because of the significant overlap between those two sets of tools.

Oracle8*i* Tools for EJB and CORBA

This part consists of three sections:

- Oracle8*i* tools used for EJB
- Oracle8*i* tools used for both EJB and CORBA
- Oracle8*i* tools used for CORBA

Oracle8*i* Tools Used for EJB

In this section, you will encounter descriptions of the following:

- `deployejb`
- `ejbdescriptor`

deployejb

The `deployejb` tool makes an EJB component ready for clients to use it. It uses the deployment descriptor for the Bean and the `.jar` file that contains the EJB interfaces, classes, and their dependent classes. The tool converts the deployment descriptor file that you create for your enterprise Beans to a Java serialized object, and generates and compiles classes that enable communication between clients and published objects. Remember that you must have specific Oracle system privileges to publish objects in the database. More than likely, the Oracle DBA will have set the privileges for you. For an excellent example of how to use the tool, see step 9 of the "Writing an Enterprise JavaBean Application" section of Chapter 3. In Oracle version 8.1.7, the `deployejb` tool accepts the XML deployment descriptor required by the new EJB 1.1 specification.

Here is the syntax for the `deployejb` tool:

```
deployejb -user <username> -password <password>
-service <serviceURL> -descriptor <file>
-temp <dir> <beanjar>
  [-addclasspath <dirlist>]
  [-describe]
  [-generated <clientjar>]
```

```
[-help]
[-iiop]
[-keep]
[-republish]
[-role <role>]
[-ssl]
[-useServiceName]
[-verbose]
[-version]
```

Here is an example of the `deployejb` tool:

```
deployejb -temp temp -u scott -p tiger
-s %ORACLE_SERVICE%
-descriptor My8iEJB.ejb -generated My8iEJBClient.jar My8iEJB.jar
```

Table F-1, taken from *Oracle8i Enterprise JavaBeans and CORBA Developer's Guide, Release 8.1.5* [52, pp. 6-37 - 6-38, Table 6-18], summarizes the `deployejb` arguments.

Argument	Description and Values
`-user`	Specifies the schema into which the EJB classes will be loaded.
`-password`	Specifies the password for `<username>`.

`-service`	URL identifying database in whose session namespace the EJB is to be published. The `serviceURL` has the form:
	`sess_iiop://<host>:<lport>:<sid>`
	`<host>` is the computer that hosts the target database; `<lport>` is the listener port configured to listen for session IIOP; `<sid>` is the database instance identifier. For example,
	`sess_iiop://localhost:2481:ORCL`
	matches the default installation on the invoker's machine.

TABLE F-1. *deployejb Argument Summary*

Argument	Description and Values
`-descriptor`	Specifies the text file containing the EJB deployment descriptor.
`-temp`	Specifies a temporary directory to hold intermediate files `deployejb` creates. Unless you specify `-keep`, `deployejb` removes the files and the directory when it completes.
`<beanjar>`	Specifies the name of the `.jar` file containing the bean interface and implementation files.
`-addclasspath`	Specifies directories containing interface and/or implementation dependency classes not contained in `<beanjar>`. Format of `<dirlist>` is the same as `javac`'s `classpath` argument. Required for `-beanonly`.
`-beanonly`	Skips generation of interface files. This is useful if you change only the bean implementation.
`-describe`	Summarizes the tool's operation, and then exits.
`-generated`	Specifies the name of the output (generated) `.jar` file, which contains communication files bean clients need. If you do not specify it, the output `.jar` file has the name of the input `.jar` file with `-generated` appended.
`-help`	Summarizes the tool's syntax, and then exits.
`-iiop`	Connects to the target database with IIOP instead of the default session IIOP. Use this option when deploying to a database server that has been configured without session IIOP.
`-keep`	Do not remove the temporary files generated by the tool. This option may be useful for debugging because it provides access to the source files `deployejb` generates.

TABLE F-1. *deployejb Argument Summary* (continued)

Argument	Description and Values
-republish	Replaces the published BeanHomeName attributes if the BeanHomeName has already been published; otherwise, it publishes it.
-role	Specifies role to assume when connecting to the database; no default.
-ssl	Connects to the database with SSL authentication and encryption.
-verbose	Emits detailed status information while running.
-version	Shows the tool's version, and then exits.

TABLE F-1.   *deployejb Argument Summary* (continued)

ejbdescriptor

The ejbdescriptor tool allows a developer to convert a deployment descriptor file from ASCII readable (.txt) format to non-readable (.ejb) format. The syntax is as follows:

```
ejbdescriptor {-parse | -dump} <infile> <outfile>
```

Use the -parse option to create a serialized deployment descriptor <outfile> from <infile>:

```
ejbdescriptor -parse My8iEJB.txt My8iEJB.ejb
```

Use the -dump option to create the text file <outfile> from the serialized deployment descriptor <infile>:

```
ejbdescriptor -dump My8iEJB.ejb My8iEJB.txt
```

In Oracle version 8.1.7, the ejbdescriptor tool translates between Oracle's proprietary textual descriptor, compatible with previous versions of Oracle8*i*, and the XML descriptor prescribed by the EJB 1.1 specification.

Oracle8*i* Tools Used for Both EJB and CORBA

In this section, you will encounter descriptions of the following:

- `sqlj`
- `dropjava`
- `remove`
- `sess_sh`

sqlj

The Oracle `sqlj` tool is used for translating SQLJ source code and invoking the Java compiler. The syntax used for executing the `sqlj` tool on the command line is as follows:

 `sqlj <option_list> file_list`

The `option_list` is a list of SQLJ option settings separated by spaces. The `file_list` is the list of files—`.sqlj`, `.java`, `.ser`, or `.jar`—separated by spaces. The * wildcard entry can be used in filenames. Table F-2, taken from *Oracle8i SQLJ Programming* [37, pp. 520-521], summarizes the SQLJ options.

Option	Description	Default
`-C<option>`	Pass `-<option>` to `javac` compiler	N/A
`-classpath` (`command line only`)	Option to specify `classpath` to Java VM and Java compiler (passed to `javac`)	None
`-compile=false`	Do not compile generated Java files	`true`
`-d=<directory>`	Set output directory for generated `.ser` and `.class` binary files	Empty
`-dir`	Option to set output directory for SQLJ-generated `.java` files	Empty

TABLE F-2.   *sqlj Option List*

Option	Description	Default
`-driver`	Option to specify JDBC driver to register	`oracle.jdbc.driver.OracleDriver`
`-P<option>`	Prefix that marks options to pass to SQLJ profile customizer	N/A
`password=<password>`	Option to set user password for database connection for online semantics checking	None
`-profile=false`	Do not customize generated `*.ser` profile files	`true`
`-props`	Option to specify properties file	None
`-ser2class`	Convert generated `*.ser` files to `*.class` files	`false`
`-status, -v`	Print status during translation	`false`
`-url=<url>`	Specify URL for online checking	`jdbc:oracle:oci8:@`
`-user, -u`	Enable online checking	None (no online semantics checking)
`-verbose (command line only)`	Passed to `javac`; enables status	N/A
`-warn`	Comma-separated list of flags to enable or disable various warnings - individual flags are `precision/noprecision`, `nulls/nonulls`, `portable/noportable`, `strict/nostrict`, and `verbose/noverbose`; global flag is `all/none`.	`precision nulls noportable strict noverbose`

TABLE F-2. *sqlj* Option List (continued)

The following example does not run the customize profile; it converts the `.ser` files to `.class` files and sets the output directory for the `.class` files to "dist":

```
sqlj -profile=false -ser2class -d=dist PIManager.sqlj
SqljInJavaApplet.java
```

dropjava

The `dropjava` utility is used to remove Java schema objects from the server. The `dropjava` command is the inverse of the `loadjava` command. Here is the syntax used to execute `dropjava` at the command line (as it appears in *Oracle8i SQLJ Programming* [37, p. 527]):

```
dropjava {-u | -user} <user>/<password>[@<database>] [options]
{<file>.java | <file>.class | <file>.sqlj | <file>.jar | <file>.zip |
<resourcefile>} ...
```

The available arguments are listed in Table F-3, which is taken from *Oracle8i SQLJ Programming* [37, p. 528].

Option	Description
-user	Specifies a user, password, and optional database connect string.
<filenames>	You can specify any number and combination of `.java`, `.class`, `.sqlj`, `.jar`, `.zip`, and resource filenames in any order. `.jar` and `.zip` files must be uncompressed.
-oci8	Use the OCI JDBC driver. -oci8 and -thin are mutually exclusive; if neither is specified, -oci8 is used by default.
-schema	Designates the schema from which schema objects are dropped. If not specified, the logon schema is used. To drop a schema object from a schema that is not your own, you need the DROP ANY PROCEDURE system privilege.
-thin	Use the thin JDBC driver. The -oci8 and -thin options are mutually exclusive; if neither is specified, -oci8 is used by default.
-verbose	Directs `dropjava` to emit detailed status messages while running.

TABLE F-3. *dropjava Argument Summary*

remove

The `remove` utility removes a `PublishedObject` or `PublishingContext` from a session namespace. Note that it does not remove the corresponding Java object from the server; the `dropjava` utility accomplishes that. The syntax of the `remove` command is given as it appears in the *Oracle8i Enterprise JavaBeans and CORBA Developer's Guide, Release 8.1.5* [52, p. 6-21]:

```
remove <name> -user <username> -password <password>
-service <serviceURL> [options]
   [{-d | -describe}]
   [{-h | -help}]
   [iiop]
   [{-r | -recurse}]
   [-role role]
   [-ssl]
   [-version]
```

Table F-4 (from the *Oracle8i Enterprise JavaBeans and CORBA Developer's Guide, Release 8.1.5* [52, pp. 6-21 – 6-22, Table 6-7]) summarizes the `remove` arguments.

Option	Description
`<name>`	Name of `PublishingContext` or `PublishedObject` to be removed.
`-user`	Specifies identity with which to log into the instance named in `-service`.
`-password`	Specifies authenticating password for the `<username>` you specified with `-user`.
`-service`	URL identifying database whose session namespace is to be "opened" by `sess_sh`. The `serviceURL` has the form: `sess_iiop://<host>:<lport>:<sid>`. `<host>` is the computer that hosts the target database; `<lport>` is the listener port that has been configured to listen for session IIOP; `<sid>` is the database instance identifier. For example, `sess_iiop://localhost:2481:ORCL` matches the default installation on the invoker's machine.

TABLE F-4.   *remove Argument Summary*

Option	Description
-describe	Summarizes the tool's operation, and then exits.
-help	Summarizes the tool's syntax, and then exits.
-iiop	Connects to the target database with IIOP instead of the default session IIOP. Use this option when removing from a database server that has been configured without session IIOP.
-recurse	Recursively removes <name> and all subordinate PublishingContexts; required to remove a PublishingContext.
-role	Role to assume for the remove; no default.
-ssl	Connects to the database with SSL server authentication. You must have configured the database for SSL to use this option.
-version	Shows the tool's version, and then exits.

TABLE F-4. *remove Argument Summary* (continued)

An example of a remove invocation is shown here:

```
remove /test/Account -user scott -password tiger\
    -service sess_iiop://localhost:2481:ORCL
```

This command will remove the PublishedObject named /test/Account from the session namespace.

sess_sh

The session shell (sess_sh) is an interactive interface tool that allows you to submit commands that are similar to UNIX shell commands, in order to process a database instance's session namespace—that is, process PublishedContexts and PublishedObjects. For example,

```
ls /test
```

will list all the PublishedObjects and PublishedContexts in the test PublishedContext.

You specify database connection arguments when you execute the sess_sh command. Here is the syntax for the sess_sh command:

```
sess_sh [options] -user <user>
-password <password> -service <serviceURL>
[-d | -describe]
[-h | -help]
[-iiop] [-role <rolename>]
[-ssl] [-useServiceName] [-version]
```

Here is an example of an execution of the sess_sh command:

```
sess_sh -user scott -password tiger
  -service sess_iiop://data-i.com:2481:ORCL
```

Table F-5 (from *CORBA Developer's Guide, Release 2 (8.1.7)* [32, p. 7-9, Table 7-5]) summarizes the arguments for the sess_sh command.

Table F-6 summarizes the commands that can be submitted to sess_sh, as is given in *CORBA Developer's Guide, Release 2 (8.1.7)* [32, pp. 7-10 – 7-18] .

Option	Description
-user	Specifies user's name for connecting to the database.
-password	Specifies user's password for connecting to the database.
-service	URL identifying database whose session namespace is to be "opened" by sess_sh. The serviceURL has the form: sess_iiop://<host>:<lport>:<sid> <host> is the computer that hosts the target database; <lport> is the listener port configured to listen for session IIOP; <sid> is the database instance identifier. For example, sess_iiop://localhost:2481:ORCL matches the default database installation on the invoker's machine.
-describe	Summarizes the tool's operation, and then exits.
-help	Summarizes the tool's syntax, and then exits.

TABLE F-5.   *sess_sh Argument Summary*

Option	Description
-iiop	Connects to the target database with plain IIOP instead of the default session IIOP. Use this option for a database server configured without session IIOP.
-role	Role to pass to database; there is no default.
-ssl	Connects to the database with SSL server authentication. You must have configured the database for SSL and specify an SSL port to use this option.
-useServiceName	If you are using a service name instead of an SID in the URL, you must specify this flag. Otherwise, the tool assumes the last string in the URL is the SID.
-version	Shows the command's version, and then exits.

TABLE F-5. *sess_sh Argument Summary* (continued)

Command	Purpose
cd	The cd command is analogous to a UNIX shell's cd command; it changes the working PublishingContext.
chmod	The chmod command is analogous to a UNIX shell's chmod command; it changes the users or roles that have rights for a PublishingContext or PublishedObject.
chown	The chown command is analogous to the UNIX chown command; it changes the ownership of a PublishingContext or PublishedObject. The owner of a newly created PublishingContext or PublishedObject is the user who publishes it.
exit	The exit command terminates sess_sh.

TABLE F-6. *Commands that Can Be Submitted to sess_sh*

Command	Purpose
help	The help command summarizes the syntax of the session shell commands.
java	The java command is analogous to the JDK java command; it invokes a class's **static** main() method. The class must have been loaded with loadjava.
lcd	The lcd (local cd) command changes the local working directory, just as executing cd outside of the session shell would.
lls	The lls (local ls) command lists the contents of the working directory, just as executing ls outside of the session shell would.
ln	The ln (link) command is analogous to the UNIX ln command. A link is a synonym for a PublishingContext or PublishedObject. A link can prevent a reference to a PublishingContext or PublishedObject from becoming invalid when you move a PublishingContext or PublishedObject (see mv command); creating a link with the old name makes the object accessible by both its old and new names.
lpwd	The lpwd (local print working directory) command displays the name of the working directory, just as executing pwd outside of the session shell would.
ls	The ls (list) command shows the contents of the PublishingContexts as the UNIX ls command shows the contents of directories.
mkdir	The mkdir command is analogous to the UNIX shell mkdir command; it creates a PublishingContext. You must have the write right for the target PublishingContext to use mkdir in it.
mv	The mv (move) command is analogous to the UNIX shell mv command.

TABLE F-6.   *Commands that Can Be Submitted to* sess_sh (continued)

Oracle8*i* Tools Used for CORBA

In this section, you will encounter descriptions of loadjava and publish.

loadjava

The loadjava utility is used to convert .class files into database library units (called *Java class schema objects*), that are stored in the server to convert .ser files into similar units; (called *resource schema objects*), that are also stored in the server; and to convert source files into library units (called *source schema objects*) that are stored in the server. A distinct schema object is created for each .class file, each .ser file, and each .java source file.

On the loadjava command line, you can specify each .class or .ser file separately, or you can first combine them into a .jar (Java archive) file and then just specify that .jar file on the loadjava command line. The jar utility is used to combine separate files into a .jar file. You can combine class and resource files into a .jar file, or source and resource files into a .jar file, but source and class files cannot be combined in the same .jar file. The syntax for executing the loadjava tool on the command line is given as in *Oracle8i SQLJ Programming* [37, p. 525]:

```
loadjava {-user | -u} <user>/<password>[@<database>] [options]
{<file>.java | <file>.class | <file>.jar | <file>.zip | <file>.sqlj |
<resourcefile>} ...
```

The available arguments listed in Table F-7 are taken from *Oracle8i SQLJ Programming* [37, pp. 526-527].

Option	Description
<filenames>	You can specify any number and combination of .java, .class, .sqlj, .jar, .zip, and resource filenames in any order.
-andresolve	Directs loadjava to compile sources if they have been loaded and to resolve external references in each class as it is loaded. -andresolve and -resolve are mutually exclusive.

TABLE F-7. *loadjava Argument Summary*

Option	Description
`-debug`	Directs the Java compiler to generate debugging information.
`-definer`	By default, class schema objects run with the privileges of their invoker. This option confers definer privileges on classes instead.
`-grant<grants>`	Grants the EXECUTE privilege on loaded classes to the listed users and roles. Any number and combination of user and role names can be specified, separated by commas but not spaces (`-grant Bob,Betty` not `-grant Bob, Betty`).
`-oci8`	Use the OCI JDBC driver; `-oci8` and `-thin` are mutually exclusive; if neither is specified, `-oci8` is used by default.
`-oracleresolver`	Use a resolver that requires all referred to classes to be found.
`-resolve`	Compiles (if necessary) and resolves external references in classes after all classes on the command line have been loaded. `-andresolve` and `-resolve` are mutually exclusive.
`-resolver<resolver>`	Use a resolver that requires all referred to classes to be found.
`-schema`	Designates the schema where schema objects are created. If not specified, the logon schema is used. To create a schema object in a schema that is not your own, you must have the CREATE PROCEDURE or CREATE ANY PROCEDURE privilege.
`-synonym`	Creates a PUBLIC synonym for loaded classes, making them accessible outside the schema into which they are loaded. You must have the CREATE PUBLIC SYNONYM privilege.

TABLE F-7.   *loadjava Argument Summary* (continued)

Option	Description
`-thin`	Use the thin JDBC driver. `-oci8` and `-thin` are mutually exclusive; if neither is specified, `-oci8` is used by default.
`-user, -u`	Specifies a user, password, and database connect string. The argument has the form `<username>/<password>` `[@<database>]`.
`-verbose`	Directs `loadjava` to emit detailed status messages while running.

TABLE F-7. *loadjava Argument Summary* (continued)

publish

Each database instance running the JServer software has a session namespace, which the Oracle8*i* ORB uses to activate CORBA server objects. A *session namespace* is a hierarchical collection of objects known as `PublishedObjects` and `PublishingContexts`.

`PublishedObjects` are the bottom level of the hierarchy, and `PublishingContexts` are upper-level nodes, analogous to UNIX system files and directories. Each `PublishedObject` corresponds to a class schema object that represents a CORBA or EJB implementation. To activate a CORBA server object, a client references the name of the corresponding published object.

Creating a `PublishedObject` is known as *publishing* and can be accomplished with the `publish` utility (which is described in this section) or the interactive session shell (which is described in the section of this appendix titled "sess_sh"). CORBA published objects are created with these utilities after the corresponding object implementations have been loaded into the server with the `loadjava` utility.

The syntax of the `publish` command is as follows (this is taken from *Oracle8i Enterprise JavaBeans and CORBA Developer's Guide, Release 8.1.5* [52, p. 6-19]):

```
publish <name> <class> [<helper>] -user <username> -password <password>
-service <serviceURL> [options]
   [-describe]
   [{-g | -grant} {<user> | <role>}[,{<user> | <role>}]...]
   [{-h | -help}]
   [-iiop]
   [-role <role>]
   [-republish]
   [-schema <schema>]
   [-ssl]
   [-version]
```

The `publish` command-line arguments are summarized in Table F-8 (this is taken from the *Oracle8i Enterprise JavaBeans and CORBA Developer's Guide, Release 8.1.5* [52, pp. 6-19 – 6-21, Table 6-6]).

Option	Description
`<name>`	Name of the `PublishedObject` being created or republished; `PublishingContexts` are created if necessary.
`<class>`	Name of the class schema object that corresponds to `<name>`.
`<helper>`	Name of the Java class schema object that implements the `narrow()` method for `<class>`.
`-user`	Specifies identity with which to log into the database instance named in `-service`.
`-password`	Specifies authenticating password for the username specified with `-user`.
`-service`	URL identifying database whose session namespace is to be "opened" by `sess_sh`. The `serviceURL` has the form: `sess_iiop://<host>:<lport>:<sid>`. `<host>` is the computer that hosts the target database; `<lport>` is the listener port that has been configured to listen for session IIOP; `<sid>` is the database instance identifier. For example, `sess_iiop://localhost:2481:ORCL` matches the default installation on the invoker's machine.
`-describe`	Summarizes the tool's operation, and then exits.
`-grant`	After creating or republishing the `PublishedObject`, grants `read` and `execute` rights to the sequence of `<user>` and `<role>` names. When republishing, replace the existing users/roles that have read/execute rights with the `<user>` and `<role>` names. To selectively change the rights of a `PublishedObject`, use the `sess_sh`'s `chmod` command. Note that to activate a CORBA object or EJB, a user must have the `execute` right for both the `PublishedObject` and the corresponding class schema object.

TABLE F-8. *publish Argument Summary*

Option	Description
-help	Summarizes the tool's syntax, and then exits.
-iiop	Connects to the target database with IIOP instead of the default session IIOP. Use this option when publishing to a database server that has been configured without session IIOP.
-role	Role to assume for the publish; no default.
-republish	Directs publish to replace an existing PublishedObject; without this option, the publish tool rejects an attempt to publish an existing name. If the PublishedObject does not exist, publish creates it. Republishing deletes nonowner rights; use the -grant option to add read/execute rights when republishing.
-schema	The schema containing the Java <class> schema object. If you do not specify it, the publish tool uses the invoker's schema.
-ssl	Connects to the database with SSL server authentication. You must have configured the database for SSL to use this option, and you must specify an SSL listener port in -service.
-version	Shows the tool's version, and then exits.

TABLE F-8. *publish Argument Summary* (continued)

JSP Support in JDeveloper

Oracle provides a complete family of application development and business intelligence tools for building Internet applications, called the *Oracle Internet Developer Suite*. This set of tools is based on Internet standards such as Java, XML, EJB, Servlet, JSP, and CORBA. The components of the Oracle Internet Developer Suite are as follows:

- **The Oracle Designer** provides a task-oriented environment to model and generate server DDL, client/server, and Web-based applications that exploit the power and portability of Java and HTML user interfaces.

- **The Oracle Forms Developer** provides an environment for building enterprise-class, database-centric Internet applications. Oracle Forms Developer is the foundation of Oracle Applications 11*i*.

- **The Oracle JDeveloper** is an application development tool that offers integrated support for building end-to-end e-business applications for the Internet. JDeveloper offers an integrated environment for developing, debugging, deploying, reusing, and customizing multitier, component-based Java, Servlet, JSP, and XML applications.

- **The Oracle Reports Developer** allows you to build and publish dynamically generated Web reports. Reports may be published throughout the enterprise via a standard Web browser in any chosen format, including HTML, HTMLCSS, PDF, delimited text, RTF, PostScript, PCL, and XML.

- **The Oracle Discoverer** is an ad hoc query, reporting, analysis, and Web publishing tool that enables business users at all levels of the organization to access information from relational data warehouses, data marts, or online transaction processing systems.

- **The Oracle Portal** is a Web-based application for building and deploying enterprise portals. It provides a manageable environment for delivering network-based software services and information resources.

For more information regarding Oracle development tools, see http://technet.oracle.com.

In this section, we provide a walkthrough that teaches you step by step how to create and run a JSP application using the Oracle JDeveloper tool. To learn more about developing JavaServer Pages (JSP) applications, see Chapter 2 and Part IV (Chapters 10–12).

In the "Writing Hello.jsp" section of Chapter 10, you developed your first JSP program. Here, you will use the Oracle JDeveloper tool, version 3.1 to create a simple JSP program called `Hello.jsp`. This program will print out a greeting to the client along with the current date and time.

Developing a new JSP application using JDeveloper is quite simple. The steps are as follows:

1. Create a project.

2. Add a JSP file to your project to create the source code file.

3. Run the program.

Creating a New JavaServer Pages Application

Launch JDeveloper (see Figure F-1). If you have previously used JDeveloper, when you launch the tool, it will automatically open the `Workspace` of the last application that you created. If you want to create a new project, you must create a new workspace. Therefore, if the tool had opened the workspace of another application, you must first close the workspace before proceeding. To close the workspace, click File, Close Workspace.

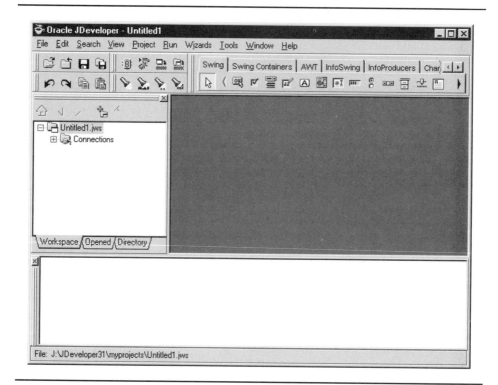

FIGURE F-1. *Oracle JDeveloper - Untitled*

1. Create a new project: click File and then New Project as shown here. When you create a new project, JDeveloper automatically creates a new `workspace` for the project.

```
File
  New...
  New Project...
  New Empty Project
  New Workspace
  Open...                 Ctrl+U
  Reopen                       ▶
  Close Workspace

  Save                    Ctrl+S
  Save As...
  Save Project
  Save Workspace
  Save All

  Remove File
  Rename...

  Printer Setup...
  Print...

  Exit
```

2. Use the Project Wizard to create a new application (see Figure F-2).

3. In the Project Wizard Welcome window, click the Next button (see Figure F-3). In this window, you can either accept the default of the tool or you can enter a path, a filename, or a combination of both. The default is "`J:\JDeveloper31\myprojects\MyProject1.jpr`".

4. Use the `Browse` button to select the path and type a name of your choice (see Figure F-4). To select a path, click Browse and select the path of your choice. Replace `MyProject1` with `MyFirstJspApp` and click Open.

5. When you click Open on the Select Project window, the tool takes you back to Project Wizard window. Click Empty Project and then Next (see Figure F-5).

6. At this time, you can click the Finish button and accept the remaining default offered by JDeveloper, or you can click the Next Button to continue your setting. Click the Next button. In step 2 of the Project Wizard window, the tool allows you to enter a new package name and select the directories under which you want to store your Java or JSP source code and `.class` files (see Figure F-6).

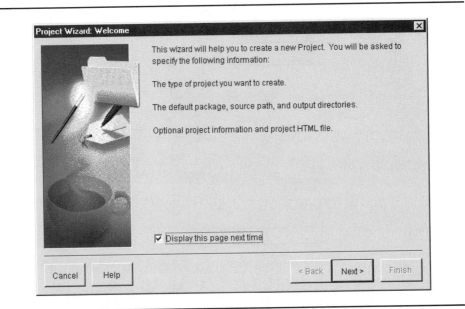

FIGURE F-2.   *Project Wizard Welcome screen*

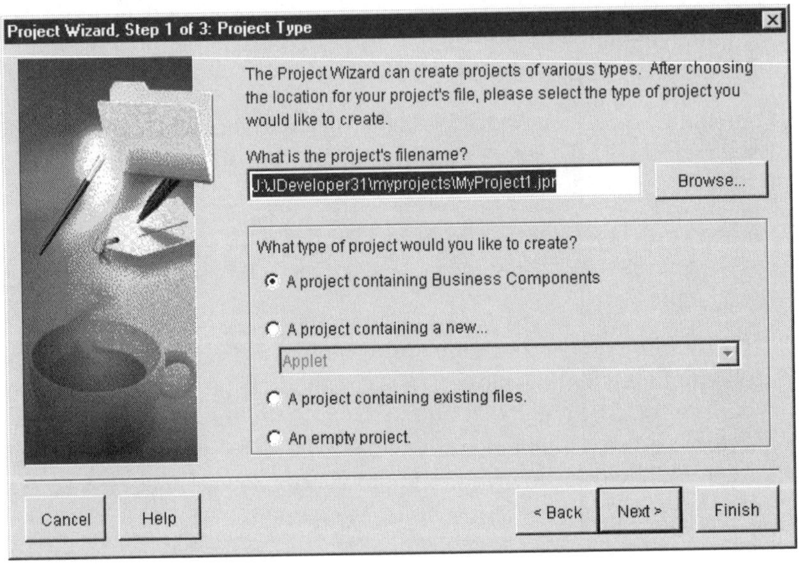

FIGURE F-3.   *Project Wizard, step 1 of 3*

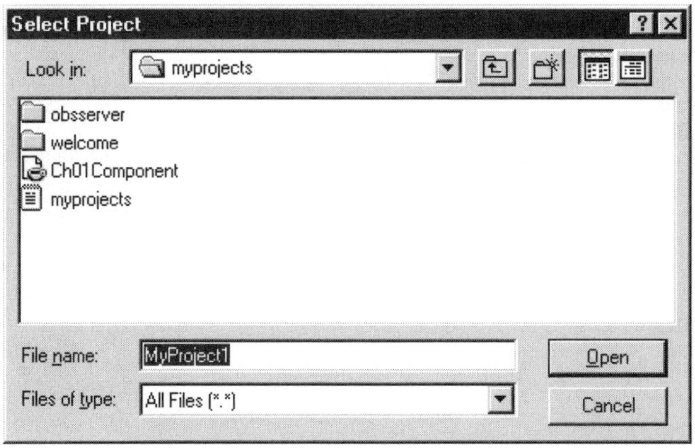

FIGURE F-4. *Select project using the Browse button to choose your file path*

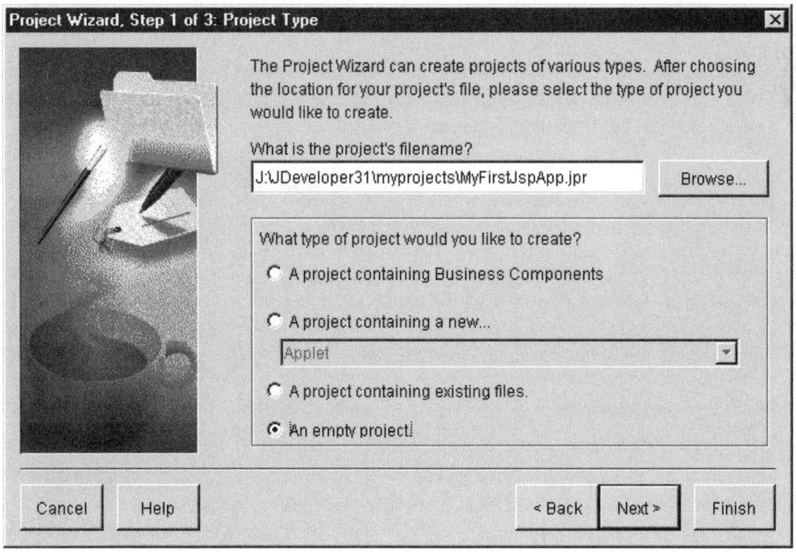

FIGURE F-5. *Selecting a project's file name*

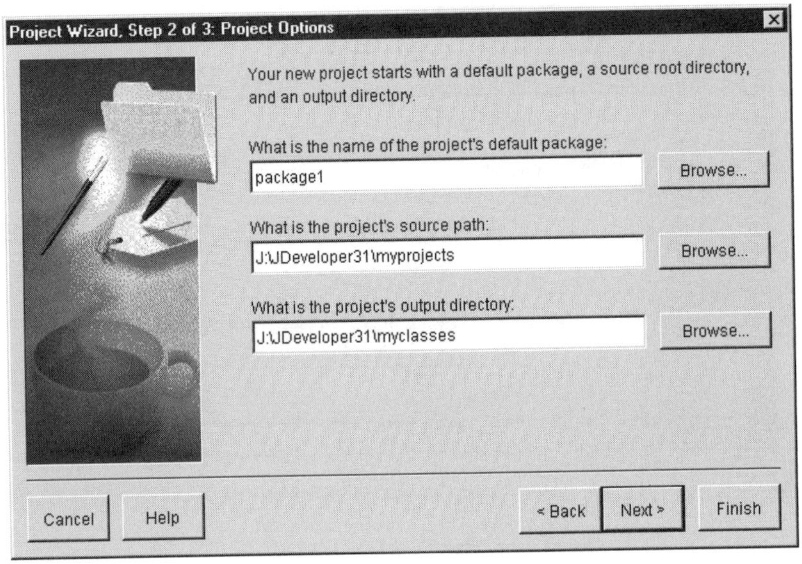

FIGURE F-6. *Selecting the package name and file path*

7. Accept the default shown in Figure F-6 and click the Next button. In step 3 of the Project Wizard window, you can enter your name, your company name, and other relevant information (see Figure F-7). Here, you can request that JDeveloper generate an HTML file for your project. To do so, click "Generate project HTML file" and then Next.

8. When you click the Next button, JDeveloper lists the options that you have selected for your project (see Figure F-8).

9. When you click the Finish button shown in Figure F-8, JDeveloper returns you to the Navigator panel. As you can see, the window shown in Figure F-9 is the same as Figure F-1 with the exception that it includes the information as recorded by the Project Wizard window.

10. Rename your project from Untitled1 to MyFirstJspApp. To do so, highlight the Untitled1.jws name, click File from the toolbar, and then rename it. Replace Untitled1 with MyFirstJspApp and then click

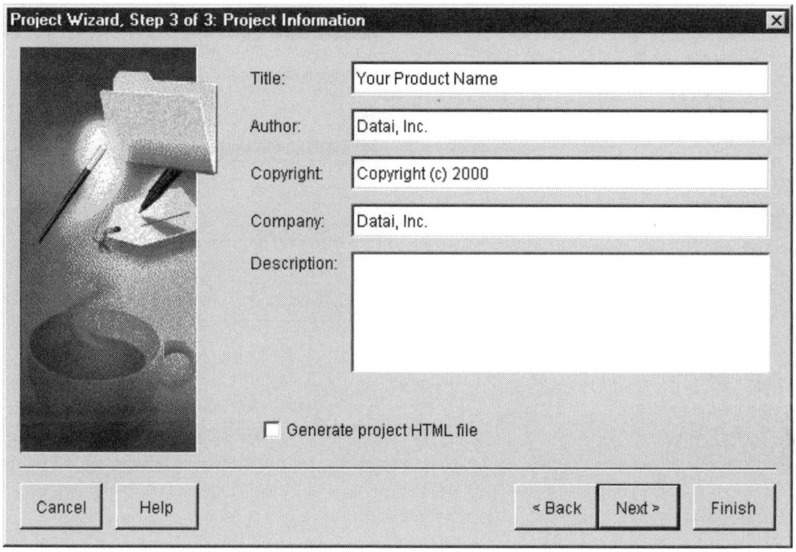

FIGURE F-7. *Project information*

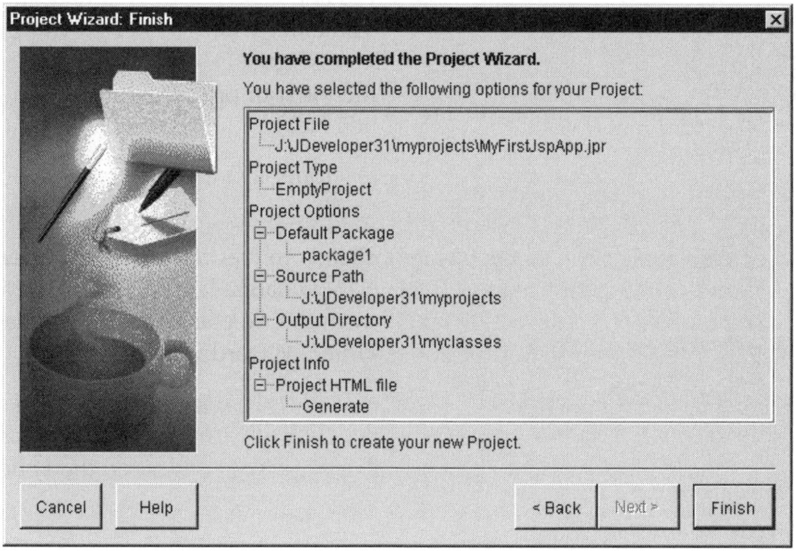

FIGURE F-8. *The Finish screen*

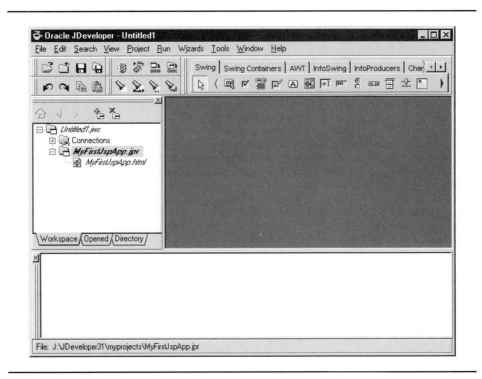

FIGURE F-9. *Oracle JDeveloper - Untitled1*

Save. JDeveloper automatically updates the Navigator panel for you (see Figure F-10).

11. You are now ready to create your first JSP application. To do so, click File, New. Click the Web Objects tab. This wizard allows you to select the type of Web application that you want to build. As you can see, JDeveloper allows you to create "pure" HTML, JSP, HTTP Servlet, DBServlet, Web Bean, and business component JSP applications. Here, you will build a simple JSP

```
Save Untitled1.jws As                                    ? X

Save in:    🗀 myprojects              ▼  🔁  🗀*  📰 📑

  🗀 obsserver
  🗀 welcome




File name:    MyFirstJspApp                          Save

Save as type:  JDeveloper Workspace (*.jws)    ▼      Cancel
```

FIGURE F-10.   *Save Untitled.jws As MyFirstJspApp*

application. So, highlight JSP and click OK. Here we show the updated
Navigator panel. Note that the tool has created the `untitled1.jsp` file
for you to double-click.

12. Now rename the `untitled1.jsp` file. To do so, highlight the
    `untitled1.jsp`, click File, and then rename it.

13. Replace the code generated by JDeveloper with the `Hello.jsp` program presented in the "`Writing Hello.jsp`" section of Chapter 10. Figure F-11 shows the updated JSP file.

14. Replace `untitled1.jsp` with `Hello.jsp` and click the Save button. Figure F-12 shows the changes as recorded by JDeveloper.

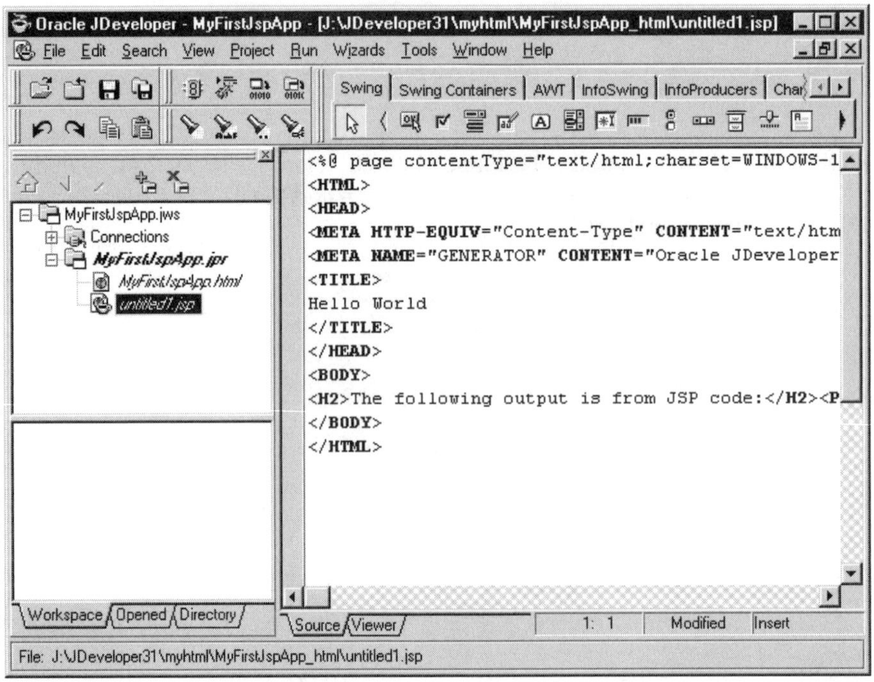

FIGURE F-11. *A new* `.jsp` *file created by JDeveloper*

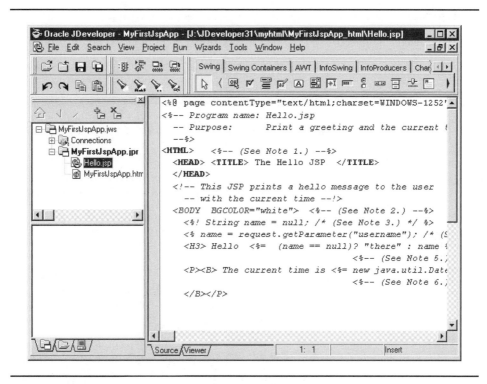

FIGURE F-12.   *Replacing JDeveloper's default JSP program*

15. Run the JSP `Hello` application. Right-click the `Hello.jsp` program and click Run, as shown here.

16. Figure F-13 shows the output after you have executed the
`Hello.jsp` program.

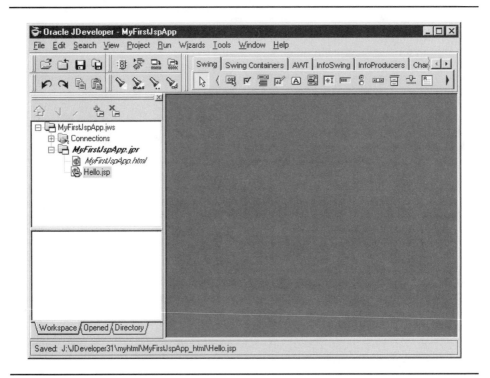

FIGURE F-13. *Navigator panel with the* `Hello.jsp` *file*

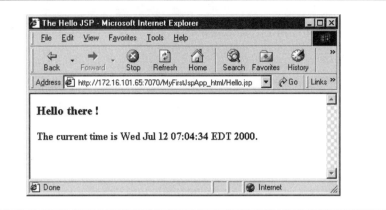

FIGURE F-14. *Output from the* `Hello.jsp` *program*

Bibliography

1. Ai-Ashmad, W. and Steegmans, E., *Inheritance in Object-Oriented Languages: Requirements and Supporting Mechanisms*, Journal of Object-Oriented Programming (JOOP), January 2000, pp. 15–24

2. Ambler, Scott, *Architectural Modeling*, Software Development Online, http://www.sdmagazine.com/uml/articles/s9910dc1.shtml, October 1999

3. Anderson, Richard, *Professional XML*, Wrox Press, January 2000

4. Avedal, Karl et al, *Professional JSP: Using JavaServer Pages, Servlets, EJB, JNDI, JDBC, XML, XSLT, and WML to Create Dynamic and Customizable Web Content*, Wrox, May 2000

5. Bayram, Zeki, *Business Object-Oriented Analysis and Design (BOOAD) Methodology*, Journal of Object-Oriented Programming (JOOP), March–April 1999, pp. 59–67

6. *The Business Benefits of EJB and J2EE Technologies Over COM+ and Windows DNA. A white paper by the Middleware Company, http://java.sun.com/products/ejb/ejbvscom.html*

7. *CORBA 2.2 Specification,* http://www.omg.org/corba/cichpter.html#idls&s, February 1998

8. *The Developer's Guide to Understanding Enterprise JavaBeans Applications*, Nova Laboratories, http://www.nova-labs.com/ejbguide/EJB_Guide_1_1aweb.pdf

9. Douglas, B., *Components: Logical, Physical Models*, Software Development Online, http://www.sdmagazine.com/uml/beyondobjects/s9912bo1.shtml, December 1999

10. Englander, Robert, *Developing Java Beans*, O'Reilly, June 1997

11. *Enterprise JavaBeans 1.0 Documentation*, http://java.sun.com/products/ejb/docs10.html

12. *Enterprise JavaBeans 1.1 Documentation*, http://java.sun.com/products/ejb/docs.html

13. The Esperanto Group, *MTS vs. EJB? Really?*, http://java.sun.com/products/ejb/pdf/zona.pdf

14. Gosling, James, Joy, Bill, and Steele, Guy, *The Java Language Specification*, Addison-Wesley Publishing Co., September 1996

15. Horton, Ivor, *Beginning Java 2*, Wrox Press, April 1999.

16. Horstmann, Cay S. and Cornell, Gary, *Core Java 2, Volume 2: Advanced Features*, Prentice Hall, December 1999

17. Hunter, Jason and Crawford, William, *Java Servlet Programming*, O'Reilly, November 1998

18. *Java Naming and Directory Interface Application Programming (JNDI API)*, Sun Microsystems, Inc., July 1999, http://java.sun.com/products/jndi/

19. Java Transaction API (JTA), Sun Microsystems, http://java.sun.com/products/jta/index.html

20. Java Transaction Service API (JTS), Sun Microsystems, http://java.sun.com:/products/jts/index.html

21. Jörelid, Lennart, *Use JDBC for Industrial-Strength Performance, Part 1*, January 2000, http://www-4.ibm.com/software/developer/library/jw-jdbc1/index.html

22. Jörelid, Lennart, *JDBC Usage for Industrial-Strength Performance, Part 2*, February 2000, http://www-4.ibm.com/software/developer/library/jw-jdbc2/index.html

23. JSP FAQ, http://java.sun.com/products/jsp/faq.html

24. JSP FAQ, http://www.esperanto.org.nz/jsp/jspfaq.html

25. JSP FAQ, http://www.jguru.com/jguru/faq/faqpage.jsp?name=JSP

26. JSP FAQ, http://www.jguru.com/jguru/faq/faqpage.jsp?name=Servlets

27. Kim, Won, et al, *Component-Based Knowledge Engineering Architecture*, Journal of Object-Oriented Programming (JOOP), October 1999, pp. 40–48

28. Ladd, Eric and O'Donnel, Jim, *Platinum Edition Using HTML 4, XML, and Java 1.2*, Macmillan USA, December 1998

29. Laitkorpi, Markku and Jaaksi, Ari, *Extending the Object-Oriented Software Process with Component-Oriented Design*, Journal of Object-Oriented Programming (JOOP), March–April 1999, pp. 41–50

30. Lemay, Laura and Cadenhead, Rogers, *Sams Teach Yourself Java 2 in 21 Days*, Sams Publishing, 1999

31. Lorentz, Diana and Denise Oertel, *Oracle8i SQL Reference, Release 8.1.5 and 8.1.6,* Oracle Corporation, 2000

32. Maring, Sheryl, *CORBA Developer's Guide, Release 2 (8.1.7),* Part No. A83755-01

33. Marshall, Chris, *Enterprise Modeling with UML*, Addison-Wesley Publishing Co., October 1999

34. Marshall, Martin, *EJB Flashpoint*, Informationweek Online, March 9, 1999, http://www.informationweek.com/732/32iuejb2.htm

35. MDE Enterprise Java APIs Team, *Deployathon*, HYPERLINK http://developer.java.sun.com/developer/ http://developer.java.sun.com/developer/ technicalArticles/Programming/deployathon/

36. Monson-Haefel, Richard, *Create forward-compatible beans in EJB, Part 1*, Java World, December 1999, http://www.javaworld.com/javaworld/jw-12-1999/jw-12-ssj-ejb1.html

37. Monson-Haefel, Richard, *Enterprise JavaBeans*, O'Reilly, June 1999

38. Monson-Haefel, Richard, *The Java Naming and Directory Interface (JNDI): A More Open and Flexible Model*, Java Report Online, 1998, http://www.javareport.com/html/features/archive/9802/haefel.shtml

39. Morgenthal, JP, *Understanding Enterprise Java APIs Why Corporate Java Developers Need to Know About JNDI, JTS, and JMS*, http://www.componentmag.com/html/from_pages/feature.shtml

40. Morisseau-Leroy, N., Solomon, M., and Momplaisir, G., *Oracle8i SQLJ Programming*, Osborne/McGraw-Hill, November 1999

41. Myers, Tom and Nakhimovsky, Alexander, *Professional Java XML Programming with Servlets and JSP*, Wrox Press, December 1999

42. Patricia Seybold Group, *Enterprise JavaBeans Technology Server Component Model for the Java Platform*, December 1998, http://java.sun.com/products/ejb/white_paper.html

43. Patzer, Andrew, et al, *Professional Java Server Programming: with Servlets, JavaServer Pages (JSP), XML, Enterprise JavaBeans (EJB), JNDI, CORBA, Jini and Javaspaces*, Wrox, 1999

44. Pawlan, Monica, *Using Session and Entity Beans to Write a Multitiered Application*, http://java.sun.com/products/ejb/articles/multitier.html

45. Perrone, Paul J. and Chaganti, Krishna, *Java Naming and Directory Service Interfaces*, http://www.distributedcomputing.com/fullarticle.asp?ID=1119925700PM

46. Pfaeffle, Thomas, *Oracle8i JDBC Developer's Guide and Reference, Release 8.1.5 & 8.1.6*, Oracle Corporation, 1999–2000

47. Portfolio, Tom, *Oracle8i Java Stored Procedures and Developer's Guide, Release 8.1.5 & 8.1.6,* Oracle Corporation, 1999–2000

48. *The Remote Method Invocation Specification,* Sun Microsystems, http://java.sun.com/products/jdk/1.1/docs/guide/rmi/spec/rmiTOC.doc.html

49. Scallan, T., *Assuring Reliability of Enterprise JavaBean Applications,* Java Developer Journal, January 2000, p. 30

50. Schmid, H.A., *Business Entity Components and Business Process Components,* Journal of Object-Oriented Programming (JOOP), October 1999, pp. 6–15

51. Seshadri, Govind, *Understanding JavaServer Pages Model 2 Architecture,* December 1999, http://www.javaworld.com/javaworld/jw-12-1999/jw-12-ssj-jspmvc.html

52. Smith, Tim and Bill Courington, *Enterprise JavaBeans and CORBA Developer's Guide, Release 8.1.5 & 8.1.6,* Oracle Corporation, 1999–2000

53. Sundsted, Todd, *JNDI Overview, Part 1: Introduction to Naming Services,* JavaWorld, January 2000, http://www.javaworld.com/javaworld/jw-01-2000/jw-01-howto.html

54. Sundsted, Todd, *JNDI Overview, Part 2: Introduction to Directory Services,* JavaWorld, February 2000, http://www.javaworld.com/javaworld/jw-02-2000/jw-02-howto.html

55. Sundsted, Todd, *JNDI Overview, Part 3: Advanced JNDI,* JavaWorld, March 2000, http://www.javaworld.com/javaworld/jw-03-2000/jw-03-howto.html

56. Szyperski, Clemens, *Component Software Beyond Object-Oriented Programming,* Addison-Wesley Publishing Co., 1999

57. Tanrikorur, Tulu, *Concepts for Simpler Design,* Software Development Online, http://www.sdmagazine.com/breakrm/features/s996f2.shtml, June 1999

58. *The Technical Benefits of EJB and J2EE Technologies Over COM+ and Windows DNA,* A white paper by the Middleware Company, http://java.sun.com/products/ejb/ejbvscom.html

59. Thomas, Anne, *Comparing MTS and EJB,* Patricia Seybold Group, http://java.sun.com/products/ejb/ejbvscom.html

60. Thomas, Anne, *Enterprise JavaBeans Technology Server Component Model for the Java,* http://java.sun.com/products/ejb/white_paper.html#ejbcompmod

61. Valesky, Thomas C., *Enterprise Javabeans: Developing Component-Based Distributed Applications*, Addison-Wesley Publishing Co., May 1999

62. Vogel, Andreas and Duddy, Keith, *Java Programming with CORBA, Second Edition*, Wiley Computer Publishing, New York, NY, 1998

63. Wright, Brian, *Oracle8i JavaServer Pages Developer's Guide and Reference Release 8.1.7*, Oracle Corporation, August 2000

64. Wright, Brian, *Oracle 8i SQLJ Developer's Guide and Reference Release 8.1.5 & 8.1.6*, A64684-01, Oracle Corporation, 2000

Index

D

F

G

T

Knowledge is power. To which we say,

crank up the power.

Are you ready for a power surge?

Accelerate your career—become an **Oracle Certified Professional** (OCP). With Oracle's cutting-edge *Instructor-Led Training*, *Technology-Based Training*, and this *guide*, you can prepare for certification faster than ever. Set your own trajectory by logging your personal training plan with us. Go to **http://education.oracle.com/tpb**, where we'll help you pick a training path, select your courses, and track your progress. We'll even send you an email when your courses are offered in your area. If you don't have access to the Web, call us at 1-800-441-3541 (Outside the U.S. call +1-310-335-2403).

Power learning has never been easier.

Get Your FREE Subscription to *Oracle Magazine*

Oracle Magazine is essential gear for today's information technology professionals. Stay informed and increase your productivity with every issue of *Oracle Magazine*. Inside each **FREE,** bimonthly issue you'll get:

- Up-to-date information on Oracle Database Server, Oracle Applications, Internet Computing, and tools
- Third-party news and announcements
- Technical articles on Oracle products and operating environments
- Development and administration tips
- Real-world customer stories

Three easy ways to subscribe:

1. Web — **Visit our Web site at www.oracle.com/oramag/. You'll find a subscription form there, plus much more!**

2. Fax — Complete the questionnaire on the back of this card and fax the questionnaire side only to **+1.847.647.9735.**

3. Mail — Complete the questionnaire on the back of this card and mail it to P.O. Box 1263, Skokie, IL 60076-8263.

If there are other Oracle users at your location who would like to receive their own subscription to *Oracle Magazine*, please photocopy this form and pass it along.

☐ YES! Please send me a FREE subscription to *Oracle Magazine*. ☐ N

To receive a free bimonthly subscription to *Oracle Magazine*, you must fill out the entire card, sign it, and date it (incomplete cards cannot be processed or acknowledged). You can also fax your application to **+1.847.647.9735.** Or subscribe at our Web site at www.oracle.com/oramag/

SIGNATURE (REQUIRED)	X		DATE	

NAME _____ TITLE _____

COMPANY _____ TELEPHONE _____

ADDRESS _____ FAX NUMBER _____

CITY _____ STATE _____ POSTAL CODE/ZIP CODE _____

COUNTRY _____ E-MAIL ADDRESS _____

☐ From time to time, Oracle Publishing allows our partners exclusive access to our e-mail addresses for special promotions and announcements. To be included in this program, please check this box.

You must answer all eight questions below.

1 What is the primary business activity of your firm at this location? *(check only one)*
- ☐ 03 Communications
- ☐ 04 Consulting, Training
- ☐ 06 Data Processing
- ☐ 07 Education
- ☐ 08 Engineering
- ☐ 09 Financial Services
- ☐ 10 Government—Federal, Local, State, Other
- ☐ 11 Government—Military
- ☐ 12 Health Care
- ☐ 13 Manufacturing—Aerospace, Defense
- ☐ 14 Manufacturing—Computer Hardware
- ☐ 15 Manufacturing—Noncomputer Products
- ☐ 17 Research & Development
- ☐ 19 Retailing, Wholesaling, Distribution
- ☐ 20 Software Development
- ☐ 21 Systems Integration, VAR, VAD, OEM
- ☐ 22 Transportation
- ☐ 23 Utilities (Electric, Gas, Sanitation)
- ☐ 98 Other Business and Services

2 Which of the following best describes your job function? *(check only one)*

CORPORATE MANAGEMENT/STAFF
- ☐ 01 Executive Management (President, Chair, CEO, CFO, Owner, Partner, Principal)
- ☐ 02 Finance/Administrative Management (VP/Director/ Manager/Controller, Purchasing, Administration)
- ☐ 03 Sales/Marketing Management (VP/Director/Manager)
- ☐ 04 Computer Systems/Operations Management (CIO/VP/Director/ Manager MIS, Operations)

IS/IT STAFF
- ☐ 07 Systems Development/ Programming Management
- ☐ 08 Systems Development/ Programming Staff
- ☐ 09 Consulting
- ☐ 10 DBA/Systems Administrator
- ☐ 11 Education/Training
- ☐ 14 Technical Support Director/ Manager
- ☐ 16 Other Technical Management/Staff
- ☐ 98 Other _____

3 What is your current primary operating platform? *(check all that apply)*
- ☐ 01 DEC UNIX
- ☐ 02 DEC VAX VMS
- ☐ 03 Java
- ☐ 04 HP UNIX
- ☐ 05 IBM AIX
- ☐ 06 IBM UNIX
- ☐ 07 Macintosh
- ☐ 09 MS-DOS
- ☐ 10 MVS
- ☐ 11 NetWare
- ☐ 12 Network Computing
- ☐ 13 OpenVMS
- ☐ 14 SCO UNIX
- ☐ 24 Sequent DYNIX/ptx
- ☐ 15 Sun Solaris/SunOS
- ☐ 16 SVR4
- ☐ 18 UnixWare
- ☐ 20 Windows
- ☐ 21 Windows NT
- ☐ 23 Other UNIX _____
- ☐ 98 Other _____
- 99 ☐ **None of the above**

4 Do you evaluate, specify, recommend, or authorize the purchase of any of the following? *(check all that apply)*
- ☐ 01 Hardware
- ☐ 02 Software
- ☐ 03 Application Development Tools
- ☐ 04 Database Products
- ☐ 05 Internet or Intranet Products
- 99 ☐ **None of the above**

5 In your job, do you use or plan to purchase any of the following products or services? *(check all that apply)*

SOFTWARE
- ☐ 01 Business Graphics
- ☐ 02 CAD/CAE/CAM
- ☐ 03 CASE
- ☐ 05 Communications
- ☐ 06 Database Management
- ☐ 07 File Management
- ☐ 08 Finance
- ☐ 09 Java
- ☐ 10 Materials Resource Planning
- ☐ 11 Multimedia Authoring
- ☐ 12 Networking
- ☐ 13 Office Automation
- ☐ 14 Order Entry/Inventory Control
- ☐ 15 Programming
- ☐ 16 Project Management
- ☐ 17 Scientific and Engineering
- ☐ 18 Spreadsheets
- ☐ 19 Systems Management
- ☐ 20 Workflow

HARDWARE
- ☐ 21 Macintosh
- ☐ 22 Mainframe
- ☐ 23 Massively Parallel Processing
- ☐ 24 Minicomputer
- ☐ 25 PC
- ☐ 26 Network Computer
- ☐ 28 Symmetric Multiprocessing
- ☐ 29 Workstation

PERIPHERALS
- ☐ 30 Bridges/Routers/Hubs/Gateways
- ☐ 31 CD-ROM Drives
- ☐ 32 Disk Drives/Subsystems
- ☐ 33 Modems
- ☐ 34 Tape Drives/Subsystems
- ☐ 35 Video Boards/Multimedia

SERVICES
- ☐ 37 Consulting
- ☐ 38 Education/Training
- ☐ 39 Maintenance
- ☐ 40 Online Database Services
- ☐ 41 Support
- ☐ 36 Technology-Based Training
- ☐ 98 Other _____
- 99 ☐ **None of the above**

6 What Oracle products are in use at your site? *(check all that apply)*

SERVER/SOFTWARE
- ☐ 01 Oracle8
- ☐ 30 Oracle8*i*
- ☐ 31 Oracle8*i* Lite
- ☐ 02 Oracle7
- ☐ 03 Oracle Application Server
- ☐ 04 Oracle Data Mart Suites
- ☐ 05 Oracle Internet Commerce Server
- ☐ 32 Oracle *inter*Media
- ☐ 33 Oracle JServer
- ☐ 07 Oracle Lite
- ☐ 08 Oracle Payment Server
- ☐ 11 Oracle Video Server

TOOLS
- ☐ 13 Oracle Designer
- ☐ 14 Oracle Developer
- ☐ 54 Oracle Discoverer
- ☐ 53 Oracle Express
- ☐ 51 Oracle JDeveloper
- ☐ 52 Oracle Reports
- ☐ 50 Oracle WebDB
- ☐ 55 Oracle Workflow

ORACLE APPLICATIONS
- ☐ 17 Oracle Automotive

- ☐ 35 Oracle Business Intelligence System
- ☐ 19 Oracle Consumer Packaged Goods
- ☐ 39 Oracle E-Commerce
- ☐ 18 Oracle Energy
- ☐ 20 Oracle Financials
- ☐ 28 Oracle Front Office
- ☐ 21 Oracle Human Resources
- ☐ 37 Oracle Internet Procurement
- ☐ 22 Oracle Manufacturing
- ☐ 40 Oracle Process Manufacturing
- ☐ 23 Oracle Projects
- ☐ 34 Oracle Retail
- ☐ 29 Oracle Self-Service Web Application
- ☐ 38 Oracle Strategic Enterprise Management
- ☐ 25 Oracle Supply Chain Management
- ☐ 36 Oracle Tutor
- ☐ 41 Oracle Travel Management

ORACLE SERVICES
- ☐ 61 Oracle Consulting
- ☐ 62 Oracle Education
- ☐ 60 Oracle Support
- ☐ 98 Other _____
- 99 ☐ **None of the above**

7 What other database products are in use at your site? *(check all that apply)*
- ☐ 01 Access ☐ 10 PeopleSoft
- ☐ 02 Baan ☐ 11 Progress
- ☐ 03 dbase ☐ 12 SAP
- ☐ 04 Gupta ☐ 13 Sybase
- ☐ 05 IBM DB2 ☐ 14 VSAM
- ☐ 06 Informix
- ☐ 07 Ingres
- ☐ 08 Microsoft Access
- ☐ 09 Microsoft SQL Server
- ☐ 98 Other _____
- 99 ☐ **None of the above**

8 During the next 12 months, how much do you anticipate your organization will spend on computer hardware, software, peripherals, and services for your location? *(check only one)*
- ☐ 01 Less than $10,000
- ☐ 02 $10,000 to $49,999
- ☐ 03 $50,000 to $99,999
- ☐ 04 $100,000 to $499,999
- ☐ 05 $500,000 to $999,999
- ☐ 06 $1,000,000 and over

If there are other Oracle users at your location who would like to receive a free subscription to *Oracle Magazine*, please photocopy this form and pass it along, or contact Customer Service at +1.847.647.9630

Form 5

OPRES

About the CD-ROM

The CD included with *Oracle8i Java Component Programming with EJB, CORBA, and JSP* contains a number of resources that have been referred to in the book.

Book Code

Code from the book is included on the CD under the **BookCode.zip** directory. This includes code from the following chapters:

- Chapter 1: Introduction to Distributed Computing Systems
- Chapter 4: Developing EJB Session Beans
- Chapter 5: Developing Session Beans: Advanced Topics
- Chapter 6: Introduction to CORBA
- Chapter 7: CORBA Sessions
- Chapter 8: CORBA Transaction Management
- Chapter 9: Purchase Order Components
- Chapter 10: Introduction to Programming with JavaServer Pages

Book Appendices

For easy reference, electronic versions of the following book appendices are provided on the CD for servlets, EJB, CORBA, and JSP:

NOTE
You must view these files with Adobe Acrobat Reader version 3.0 or greater

- Appendix A: Servlet Quick Reference and API Summary
- Appendix B: Enterprise JavaBeans Quick Reference and API Summary
- Appendix C: Oracle8*i* CORBA Quick Reference Guide for Java
- Appendix E: Web Server Installation and Configuration for Oracle JSP
- Appendix F: Oracle8*i* EJB and CORBA Tools, and JSP Support in JDeveloper

JSP and Servlet Samples

Sample JSP and servlet programs can be found on the CD under the **jspsamples.zip** directory. See **README.txt** for setup steps to run the samples.

WARNING: BEFORE OPENING THE DISC PACKAGE, CAREFULLY READ THE TERMS AND CONDITIONS OF THE FOLLOWING COPYRIGHT STATEMENT AND LIMITED CD-ROM WARRANTY.

Copyright Statement

This software is protected by both United States copyright law and international copyright treaty provision. Except as noted in the contents of the CD-ROM, you must treat this software just like a book. However, you may copy it into a computer to be used and you may make archival copies of the software for the sole purpose of backing up the software and protecting your investment from loss. By saying, "just like a book," The McGraw-Hill Companies, Inc. ("Osborne/McGraw-Hill") means, for example, that this software may be used by any number of people and may be freely moved from one computer location to another, so long as there is no possibility of its being used at one location or on one computer while it is being used at another. Just as a book cannot be read by two different people in two different places at the same time, neither can the software be used by two different people in two different places at the same time.

Limited Warranty

Osborne/McGraw-Hill warrants the physical compact disc enclosed herein to be free of defects in materials and workmanship for a period of sixty days from the purchase date. If the CD included in your book has defects in materials or workmanship, please call McGraw-Hill at 1-800-217-0059, 9am to 5pm, Monday through Friday, Eastern Standard Time, and McGraw-Hill will replace the defective disc.

The entire and exclusive liability and remedy for breach of this Limited Warranty shall be limited to replacement of the defective disc, and shall not include or extend to any claim for or right to cover any other damages, including but not limited to, loss of profit, data, or use of the software, or special incidental, or consequential damages or other similar claims, even if Osborne/McGraw-Hill has been specifically advised of the possibility of such damages. In no event will Osborne/McGraw-Hill's liability for any damages to you or any other person ever exceed the lower of the suggested list price or actual price paid for the license to use the software, regardless of any form of the claim.

OSBORNE/McGRAW-HILL SPECIFICALLY DISCLAIMS ALL OTHER WARRANTIES, EXPRESS OR IMPLIED, INCLUDING BUT NOT LIMITED TO, ANY IMPLIED WARRANTY OF MERCHANTABILITY OR FITNESS FOR A PARTICULAR PURPOSE. Specifically, Osborne/McGraw-Hill makes no representation or warranty that the software is fit for any particular purpose, and any implied warranty of merchantability is limited to the sixty-day duration of the Limited Warranty covering the physical disc only (and not the software), and is otherwise expressly and specifically disclaimed.

This limited warranty gives you specific legal rights; you may have others which may vary from state to state. Some states do not allow the exclusion of incidental or consequential damages, or the limitation on how long an implied warranty lasts, so some of the above may not apply to you.

This agreement constitutes the entire agreement between the parties relating to use of the Product. The terms of any purchase order shall have no effect on the terms of this Agreement. Failure of Osborne/McGraw-Hill to insist at any time on strict compliance with this Agreement shall not constitute a waiver of any rights under this Agreement. This Agreement shall be construed and governed in accordance with the laws of New York. If any provision of this Agreement is held to be contrary to law, that provision will be enforced to the maximum extent permissible, and the remaining provisions will remain in force and effect.

NO TECHNICAL SUPPORT IS PROVIDED WITH THIS CD-ROM.